DATE DUE

DEMCO 38-296

GUIDE to the YIVO ARCHIVES

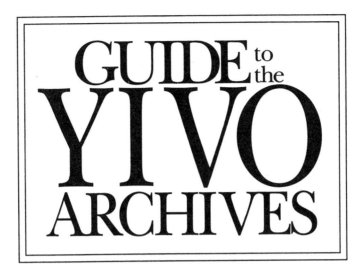

GUIDE to the YIVO ARCHIVES

Compiled and Edited by
Fruma Mohrer and Marek Web

YIVO INSTITUTE FOR JEWISH RESEARCH
New York

M.E. Sharpe
Armonk, New York
London, England

Library of Congress Cataloging-in-Publication Data

YIVO Archives.
Guide to the YIVO Archives / by YIVO Institute for Jewish Research;
compiled and edited by Fruma Mohrer and Marek Web.
p. cm.
Includes index.
ISBN 0-7656-0130-3 (alk. paper)
1. YIVO Archives—Catalogs. I. Mohrer, Fruma. 1950– .
II. Web, Marek. III. YIVO Institute for Jewish Research.
IV. Title.
Z6375.Y59   1997   97-34858
026.909´04924   dc21

CIP
Printed in the United States of America

The paper used in this publication meets the minimum requirements of
American National Standard for Information Sciences—
Permanence of Paper for Printed Library Materials,
ANSI Z 39.48-1984.

BM (c)   10   9   8   7   6   5   4   3   2   1

Contents

Preface

The publication of this guide marks the conclusion of a long and challenging project to create a comprehensive finding aid that will facilitate better access to the YIVO Archives. Much of the credit for making this undertaking possible goes to the generations of YIVO archivists who faithfully and painstakingly identified and cataloged hundreds of thousands of documents, giving shape and meaning to an inchoate mass of archival records. The present volume is intended to serve as a basic introduction to the YIVO Archives. It lists the collections in the archives and informs the reader in a concise manner about their contents. In addition, it makes it possible, with the help of the index, to do quick searches. While detailed reference is beyond the scope of this volume, the reader will find here enough clues to prepare him- or herself for a fruitful exploration of this vast repository of Jewish historical and cultural documentation.

Besides achieving the practical goal of producing a research tool for the user, the publication of the *Guide to the YIVO Archives* is meant to heighten awareness of YIVO's place in the Jewish community, of its potential as a resource center for the community in general and for Jewish scholarship in particular. The YIVO Archives, now in its seventy-second year, has played a prominent role in Jewish culture and scholarship over the entire span of its existence. Tangible traces of it can be found in a multitude of works that make use of documents preserved in the YIVO Archives and in countless acknowledgments and credits from those who have used its resources.

From its earliest years the YIVO Archives followed a policy of seeking out and gathering contemporaneous records as well as documents of the more distant past. The result of this policy was the accumulation of a vast and rich documentation that reflects the layers of time and bears witness to the unfolding of events in the general movement of Jewish history. On the one hand, readers will discover historical records that document broad and sweeping developments in the Jewish world. On the other hand, they will also find materials that in minute detail describe daily life, work, learning, culture, religious observance, changing traditions, politics and more.

This repository-level guide is the first such publication in the long history of the YIVO Archives. The completion of the guide coincides with a momentous event in the life of the YIVO Archives, the return of the pre-war YIVO collections that had been held in Vilnius, Lithuania, from the time of the destruction of the Vilna YIVO by the Nazis in 1942. Immediately after the war YIVO initiated a drive to reclaim the treasures from its library and archives looted by the Nazis. Over the years this effort bore fruit, resulting in the return of major portions of pre-war YIVO archival collections from France in 1946 and from Germany in 1947, and culminating most recently in the recovery of the collections discovered in Vilnius.

The publication of this volume coincides also with the final preparations of the YIVO Institute to move into its new home, the Center for Jewish History, whose premises will be shared jointly by three major Jewish archives and a museum (the YIVO Institute, the American Jewish Historical Society, the Leo Baeck Institute, and Yeshiva University Museum). As a result of this unprecedented joint venture the horizons and opportunities for research in Jewish history and culture will be greatly expanded. That the *Guide to the YIVO Archives* is coming off the press at this juncture will help to emphasize the Archives' research potential within the new partnership.

To all those who over the very long haul helped us make this project happen, we want to express our deepest gratitude. And to those who love to explore the Jewish past in the original, we offer this guide in the hope that it will be of value and assistance.

Fruma Mohrer and Marek Web
New York, April 1997

Acknowledgments

The YIVO Institute is deeply grateful to the J.M. Kaplan Fund and its president Joan K. Davidson and to the late Morris and Frieda Waletzky for generously funding the preparation of the *Guide to the YIVO Archives* for publication.

We wish to pay tribute to the late Hannah Fryshdorf, Assistant Director of the YIVO Institute, whose deep love for YIVO and its accomplishments was reflected in her firm and idealistic leadership and whose enduring influence is in no small measure responsible for the publication of this guide. We would like to thank the YIVO Board of Directors and its Chairman, Bruce Slovin, for their continuous support of this project. Our thanks to Samuel Norich, former Executive Director of the YIVO Institute, for his support and encouragement of the project from its inception, to Tom Freudenheim, Executive Director of YIVO, to Dr. Allan Nadler, YIVO Research Director and Dean of the Max Weinreich Center, and to Andrea Sherman, former YIVO Director of Publications.

For their daily collaboration and patient assistance with innumerable requests we are indebted to the entire YIVO staff, both past and present, as well as to all YIVO volunteers and, last but not least, to our friends and family members, for their support and participation.

In our work on the guide, we constantly relied on expert advice and generous help of many people. We wish to thank the following:

For assistance with bibliographical and published historical sources as well as standardization of foreign language words: Dina Abramowicz, Reference Librarian; Zachary Baker, Head Librarian; Elisheva Schwartz, Judaica Cataloger; Dr. Bella Hass Weinberg, Consulting Librarian; Beatrice Silverman Weinreich, Research Associate; Dr. Paul (Hershl) Glasser, Research Associate; Chana Mlotek, Music Archivist; Cathryn Krug, Senior Editor, University of Chicago Press; Pearl Lam; Chavie Mohrer; Herbert Lazarus; Nikolai Borodulin; Nina Warnke; Oscar and Sara Mohrer. For an in-depth review of the index and numerous valuable corrections and suggestions: Dr. Bella Hass Weinberg. For assistance with preparation of the manuscript and technical support: Yossi Weiss; Shaindel Fogelman; Sarah Levine; Jeffrey Salant; Jeffrey Shandler; Lorin Sklamberg; John Collis; Seth Kamil. For assistance with proofreading and reading the manuscript: Pearl Lam; Leo Greenbaum, Associate Archivist; Chana Mlotek; Nettie Krischer Plafker.

INTRODUCTION

The YIVO Institute and the YIVO Archives:
A Brief History

The YIVO Institute for Jewish Research (Yid. Yidisher Visnshaftlekher Institut) is a research, training, and resource center in Jewish studies specializing in the history and culture of Ashkenazic Jewry with emphasis on East European Jews and their descendants in the United States. The YIVO Institute maintains a library and archives, provides academic training at the Max Weinreich Center for Advanced Jewish Studies, conducts research projects, and issues scholarly publications. The YIVO Institute is a voluntary, independent, membership organization based in New York.

The YIVO Institute in Vilna

YIVO was founded in 1925 in the city of Vilna (Pol. Wilno; Lith. Vilnius). The idea of creating an academic institution dedicated to the study of Yiddish and East European Jewish culture was first expressed by the linguist Nahum Shtif in a memorandum *Organizatsye fun der yidisher visnshaft* (Organization of Jewish Scholarship, Berlin, 1924). His suggestion drew the attention of Jewish scholars in Berlin and also in Vilna, which was then an important center of Yiddish cultural activity in Poland.

On March 24, 1925, at a conference in Vilna of Jewish cultural organizations, Dr. Max Weinreich, a Yiddish linguist, was asked to prepare a statement of principles and an organizational outline for the future institute. At a second conference, which took place in Berlin on August 7–12, 1925, Weinreich's outline was accepted. A resolution was approved to begin preparations for the establishment of the new organization, to be called the Yidisher Visnshaftlekher Institut (known in English as the Yiddish Scientific Institute, and also by its Yiddish acronym, YIVO). The city of Vilna was spontaneously chosen by the organizers as the seat of the new institute, although no formal resolution was passed on this matter. In addition to Shtif and Weinreich, the organizing committee included Elias Tcherikower, Zalman Reisen, and Jacob Lestschinsky.

The new institute was organized in the following manner: A general membership convention approved the institutional by-laws, appointed a Central Board, and planned long-range programs. Two such conventions took place in Vilna, in 1929 and in 1935. The Central Board, whose first chairman was Zemach Shabad, carried out the executive functions and appointed the members of the Executive Office which managed the Institute's daily affairs. The Executive Office consisted of Max Weinreich, Zelig Kalmanovitch, and Zalman Reisen. The Honorary Board of Trustees (Curatorium) was chaired by Simon Dubnow, and its members were Albert Einstein, Sigmund Freud, Moses Gaster, Edward Sapir, and Chaim Zhitlowsky.

The work of the YIVO Institute was carried out by four sections: Philology, History, Economics and Statistics, Psychology and Education. The sections were chaired, respectively, by Max Weinreich, Elias Tcherikower, Jacob Lestschinsky, and Leibush Lehrer. In addition, several research commissions were organized, including the Ethnographic Commission, the Terminology Commission, and the Historical Commission on Poland. To support its research work YIVO established a library and archives, and also a Bibliographical Center for the purpose of creating a comprehensive bibliography of new Yiddish publications.

The aims of the YIVO Institute were formulated as follows: to serve as a center for organized research into all aspects of Jewish history and culture; to train Jewish scholars; to gather library and archival source materials relevant to YIVO's scholarly objectives; and to develop a broad base of support for the Institute in Jewish communities around the world.

The founders of YIVO espoused the Yiddishist philosophy which viewed Yiddish as a national Jewish language and considered the development of secular Jewish scholarship in this language as the future instrument of cultural and spiritual betterment of the Jewish people. The YIVO philosophy stood in contradistinction to the Wissenschaft des Judentums school of thought, which believed that Jewish culture had reached the end of its development due to the forces of emancipation and was henceforth to be studied intellectually and historically as a phenomenon of the past. YIVO, on the other hand, believed in the continuity and future of a national, creative Jewish culture and saw Jewish scholarship as a dynamic intellectual activity. Both the past and the present were to be studied from the perspective of a live and changing culture.

In the fifteen years between its establishment and destruction by the Nazis, YIVO experienced rapid growth and earned great respect as a leading center for the Jewish humanities. In Poland, YIVO became an authority in all matters concerning Yiddish culture. Association with YIVO was sought after not only by scholars but also by great numbers of people from all walks of life, who saw their work for YIVO as a fulfillment of their higher aspirations. In the 1920s and 1930s Societies of Friends of YIVO existed in Poland, the Baltics, Germany, France, England, North and South America, South Africa, and Palestine. The American branch of YIVO was organized as early as 1926.

YIVO involved its large numbers of societies and friends in collecting publications and documentation for its library and archives, participating in research surveys and field work, and organizing fundraising events. Especially effective were the YIVO volunteer *zamlers*, or collectors who engaged in searching for valuable documentation and sending it to YIVO. Some YIVO departments depended a great deal on these collectors, notably the Ethnographic Commission, the Terminology Commission, and most of all, the Archives.

A system was developed not only to keep in touch with collectors, but also to supervise their work effectively and channel their enthusiasm in the right direction. Collectors were instructed to carry out historical and economic surveys, to gather oral folklore and linguistic samples, and to conduct field work needed for various research projects. The main objective in these collecting activities was to create a solid documentary base for the study of contemporary Jewish life. Reflecting the spirit of *Zeitgeschichte*, YIVO focused its interest on the Jewish present, on the political and economic conditions of the Jewish populations of Eastern Europe during the critical inter-war period.

In 1935, a graduate training division, the Aspirantur, was added to existing YIVO departments. Named in honor of Zemach Shabad, the first YIVO Chairman, the Aspirantur's goal was to educate scholars who wished to work in Jewish studies.

YIVO strongly emphasized the need to publish works of its affiliate scholars. Each of YIVO's four sections published its own proceedings. YIVO's list of publications included the periodicals *Filologishe shriftn*, *Psikhologishe shriftn*, *Yidishe ekonomik*, *Yidish far ale*, *YIVO bleter* and numerous monographs, yearbooks, essays and articles. By 1941 the bibliography of YIVO publications included over 2,500 items.

After the outbreak of the Second World War, YIVO continued its work in Vilna, at first under Lithuanian and later under Soviet rule. Gradually, the Institute was merged into the Soviet cultural system and was forced to conduct its work in accordance with the new ideology. In August 1940 the Society of Friends of YIVO was liquidated. In October 1940 YIVO became part of the Institute of Lithuanian Studies and its name was changed to the Third Museum and Library of the Institute of Lithuanian Studies. In January 1941 YIVO was made part of the Academy of Sciences of the Soviet Socialist Republic of Lithuania and its name was changed to "Institute for Jewish Culture." During this time period, until January 1941, YIVO was headed by Moishe Lerer, a former YIVO archivist who was named the curator of the Institute by the Soviet authorities. Of the old leadership, Zalman Reisen was arrested and deported to Russia, where he perished, and Zelig Kalmanovitch was removed from his post. In January 1941, Noah Prylucki, a prominent linguist and member of the pre-war YIVO Executive Committee, was named the director of the reorganized institute. Prylucki, also the leader of the Jewish Folkist Party and a deputy to the Polish Diet, had fled from Warsaw to Vilna before the Nazi occupation.

Despite all these changes, the YIVO Library and Archives were left intact by the Soviet authorities. The library was even substantially enlarged by the addition of 20,000 new volumes.

With the outbreak of the Soviet-German war in June 1941, and the subsequent occupation of Vilna by the Nazis, the existence of the YIVO Institute in Vilna came to an end. Its collections were either dispersed or sent to Germany. The YIVO staff incarcerated in the Vilna Ghetto met their deaths prior to or during the final liquidation of the ghetto. Among the victims were: Zelig Kalmanovitch, who perished in the concentration camp in Klooga, Estonia; Uma Olkienicka, director of the YIVO Theater Museum; Noah Prylucki; and Moishe Lerer. Simon Dubnow was killed in

Riga, Latvia, on December 1, 1941. The historians Yitzhak Schipper and Emanual Ringelblum, the economist Menakhem Linder, and the folklorist Shmuel Lehman, all perished in Warsaw. Many other YIVO associates, collectors and friends, shared their fate.

The YIVO Institute in New York

Yet this was not to be the end of YIVO. The Institute was revived in New York by the members of the Central Board who had escaped from Nazi-occupied Europe, and by the leaders of the American branch of YIVO. The group included Max Weinreich, Elias Tcherikower, Jacob Lestschinsky, Leibush Lehrer, Shmuel Niger, Jacob Shatzky, and Naphtali Feinerman. In a statement issued in 1940, they declared the re-establishment of YIVO in New York, since "normal communications with the Institute in Vilna have been cut off."

The American branch, commonly called Amopteyl (an abbreviation of Amerikaner Opteyl), provided the initial organizational framework for the renewed Institute. Back in 1935 the Amopteyl had founded the Central Jewish Library and Archives (CJLA). In 1940 the Library had about 15,000 volumes and an undetermined number of archival collections. The CJLA became a part of YIVO when the Institute was inaugurated on American soil.

YIVO was initially located in the building of the Hebrew Immigrant Aid Society (HIAS) at 425 Lafayette Street. In 1942 the Institute acquired the former site of the Jewish Theological Seminary on West 123rd Street. In 1955 YIVO was moved to 1048 Fifth Avenue. As this volume is being prepared for publication, YIVO is awaiting completion of the construction of the Center for Jewish History on West 16th Street which will be its new home. YIVO will share these premises with the American Jewish Historical Society, the Leo Baeck Institute, and the Yeshiva University Museum.

In the United States, the YIVO Institute is governed by a Board of Directors. The first chairman of the Board was Shmuel Niger. The current Chairman, Bruce Slovin, assumed this post in 1990. From 1940 onward YIVO's Executive Directors were successively Naphtali Feinerman, Mark Uveeler, David Passow, Pinchas Schwarz, Shmuel Lapin, Joseph Berg, Morris Laub, Samuel Norich, Allan Nadler, Laurence Rubinstein, and Tom L. Freudenheim. During YIVO's American period Max Weinreich continued to play a central role in the Institute, holding the position of Research Director until his death in 1969.

YIVO did not succeed in re-establishing the four research sections of the pre-war period. In their place, less formal "circles" (*krayzn*), or study groups, were created— the Folklore Circle, the Historians' Circle, and so forth. The circles continued to be active until the 1960s, when they were dissolved.

From the beginning YIVO strove to maintain its teaching component, the Aspirantur (Research and Training Division), begun in Vilna. The New York Aspirantur got off to a start in the 1941–42 academic year but, because prospective students were being drafted for wartime military service, the program had to be discontinued after several semesters. The goal of establishing a permanent graduate studies department at YIVO was achieved in 1969 when the Max Weinreich Center for Advanced Jewish Studies was inaugurated. Adhering to its original principles, YIVO continues to occupy a prominent position in the study of the history and culture of East and Central European Jewry and in the collection and preservation of related documentary sources. It emphasizes research into the influence of the East European Jewish heritage on the development of the American Jewish community, and encourages general studies in Jewish Americana during the mass immigration and post-immigration periods. Finally, YIVO has emerged since the war as a resource and research center for the study of the Holocaust and its aftermath.

The Institute's aims have been pursued in a variety of ways: research projects, annual interdisciplinary conferences, colloquia, popular and academic educational programs, publications, exhibits, and media projects. Many of YIVO's endeavors are undertaken in cooperation with other academic and educational institutions in the United States and in other countries. For many years the Max Weinreich Center for Advanced Jewish Studies offered graduate courses in conjunction with Columbia University, City University of New York, New York University, Jewish Theological Seminary, Yeshiva University, Yale University, and Hebrew Union College. The Uriel Weinreich Yiddish Language Program, which has been in operation since 1968, is co-sponsored by YIVO and Columbia University. YIVO's annual research conferences—a tradition that goes back to the early days of the Amopteyl—bring together a representative group of scholars specializing in the Jewish humanities and social sciences. YIVO also co-sponsors international conferences, mainly in the field of Yiddish studies and East European Jewish history. YIVO continues to publish scholarly journals, anthologies, and monographs. Its periodic publications are: *YIVO Annual*, *YIVO bleter*, *Yidishe shprakh*, and the bilingual newsletter *Yedies fun YIVO/YIVO News*. The YIVO Library houses a comprehensive collection of books and periodicals relating primarily to East European Jewry, Yiddish language, Jewish literature and culture, the American-Jewish immigrant experience, and the Holocaust. At present, the Library holds over 320,000 volumes in Yiddish, Hebrew, English, Russian, Polish, French, and German. Some 40,000 of these volumes belonged to the YIVO Library in Vilna before the war and to the Strashun Collection of the Vilna Kehillah. These books were found in Germany after the war and were returned to the YIVO Library in New York.

The YIVO Archives in Vilna

The mission of the YIVO Archives is to locate, collect and preserve documentation pertinent to the history and culture of East European and American Jewry. The Archives was established at the same time as the other sections of the YIVO Institute in Vilna, that is, in 1926.

Reconstructing the holdings of the Archives during its Vilna period is a difficult task today. One reason for this is that no inventories—general or partial—of the Vilna archival collections survived. Moreover, it is reasonable to assume that a great part of the archival materials in Vilna remained uncataloged. Our knowledge of the organization and history of the pre-war YIVO Archives is based on several sketchy articles on the archives and the lists of new accessions published in the newsletter *Yedies fun yivo* and on reports of YIVO conferences in 1929 and 1935. In addition, the Central State Archives in Vilnius is in possession of several reports, compiled by the Jewish workers conscripted by the Einsatzstab Rosenberg in 1942, about the collections of pre-war YIVO and of other Jewish repositories in pre-war Vilna (Central State Archives, Vilnius, record group R633). But, most important, the contents of the YIVO archival collections rescued during and after the war provide a glimpse into the nature and organization of the pre-war YIVO Archives.

During the early period of YIVO in Vilna, the work of gathering, inventorying, and preserving archival records was done by the four YIVO sections. The sections conducted surveys in history, economics, and education and gathered oral folklore materials and terminology samples. The sections also received archival collections that were relevant to their fields of research. Thus, over the years, the section on Education and Psychology received a great number of records of various Jewish school systems in Poland. There was even a project, not realized in the end, to create a museum on Jewish education. The History Section took over the holdings of the vast Archives for the History of East European Jews, known in Yiddish as the Mizrakh Yidisher Historisher Arkhiv (assembled in the Ukraine in 1918–20 and relocated to Berlin in 1922), and eventually acquired a number of other collections pertaining to the history of Jews in Russia. The archival sources of the Terminology and Ethnography Commissions were built up mainly through the diligent work of their *zamlers*. The Esther Rachel Kaminska Theater Museum, established in 1928, became the recipient of many theatrical collections, including the personal papers of Esther Rachel Kaminska and the records of the Jewish Actors Union in Poland.

Soon after this system of departmental collecting was initiated, a variety of materials were received that did not belong to a particular section. Thus, the YIVO Central Archives was established in 1926. The Archives had two divisions: the Central Archives of the Jewish Press, which acquired and cataloged Jewish periodicals, and the Central Archives for documents and manuscripts. In 1937 a photographic archive was initiated.

During the Lithuanian/Soviet period (September 1939–June 1941) the archives was enlarged by additions of materials from the defunct Jewish schools and other educational institutions in Vilna, and from the Jewish Historical and Ethnographic Societies in Vilna and Kaunas (the Ansky Societies). Fragmentary records from all these institutions are found today in the Vilna section of the YIVO Archives.

Under the Nazi occupation the YIVO collections fell into the hands of the Einsatzstab Rosenberg, the Nazi unit created by Alfred Rosenberg, the Reich Minister for Occupied Eastern Territories. This group was charged with the looting and disposition of Jewish cultural treasures. The YIVO building in Vilna (which was located outside the ghetto) was converted into a processing center for ransacked Jewish libraries and archives from Vilna and the surrounding area. A group of twenty inmates from the Vilna Ghetto was taken each day to the YIVO building where selected collections were being prepared for shipment to the Institut der NSDAP zur Erforschung der Judenfrage in Frankfurt-am-Main. The group included, among others, Zelig Kalmanovitch, Uma Olkienicka, Abraham Sutzkever, Szmerke

Kaczerginski, Rokhl Pupko-Krynski, and Daniel Feinstein. The members of this group resolved to take the risk of hiding the more valuable YIVO documents from the Nazis. After the war this hidden collection of several thousand items was returned by Sutzkever and Kaczerginski to YIVO in New York.

The materials selected for the Einsatzstab Rosenberg were shipped to Frankfurt in 1942 and 1943; the remaining collections from the YIVO library and archives were to be either destroyed on the spot or sold to paper mills for recycling. To the best of our knowledge, not everything that was sent to Frankfurt reached its destination. Some crates ended up in Prague where their contents are presumed to be stored until the present day. Moreover, not all the materials that remained in Vilna were destroyed. After the war a Jewish Museum was established in Vilna which received large quantities of Jewish records found in the city. The museum was closed in 1949 and its collections were placed in several Vilna repositories. Meanwhile, the books and archival records from Vilna that were transferred to Frankfurt survived the final years of the war intact and were reclaimed by YIVO in New York in 1947. Finally, we should mention the archival collections of YIVO's Historical Section which remained in the personal possession of Elias Tcherikower, the Section's chairman. Tcherikower lived in Berlin from 1920 until 1933, and in Paris until 1940, and the collections "traveled" with him. Following the Nazi occupation of France, these records were placed in hiding in southern France. After the war they were returned to YIVO.

The odyssey of the Vilna YIVO collections continues still. In 1990, as the political rigors of the Soviet state began to give way to openness, and reforms and contacts with Vilna became possible again, YIVO was advised that parts of its pre-war library and archives had been found hidden among the Lithuanica collections of the State Bibliographic Center (commonly known as the Book Palace, since then merged with the Lithuanian National Library). The long and difficult negotiations with the Lithuanian authorities for the return of these collections to YIVO in New York, which were conducted over a period of five years against the background of momentous political upheavals in this region, finally yielded positive results. According to an agreement with the General Directorate of the Lithuanian Archives signed in December 1994, the YIVO archival collections are being sent in installments to YIVO in New York for processing, preservation, and photocopying. The originals are then returned to Vilnius and YIVO retains the photocopies. The agreement also calls for microfilming of the YIVO library materials in Vilna proper and for placing of the microfilms in the YIVO Library.

The YIVO Institute is committed to locating and arranging for the return of all of its collections from the pre-war period. It will therefore continue searching for the missing portions of its archives wherever they may be.

The YIVO Archives in New York

In 1938 the Central Jewish Library and Archives, the predecessor of the YIVO Library in New York, began accessioning literary manuscripts and institutional records. In 1940 Rebecca (Riva) Tcherikower was appointed the first YIVO Archivist.

The Archives, however, remained a part of the YIVO Library until about 1953 when these two departments became independent of each other.

Initially, the goal of the YIVO Archives in New York was to collect documents on Yiddish culture and on the Yiddish-speaking milieu in America. But soon its mission was significantly broadened. As the war progressed and the extent of the Jewish catastrophe in Europe became clear, the YIVO Archives widened its responsibilities to include documentation on the life and death of the destroyed communities of Europe. Efforts to rescue the remnants of Jewish archives in Europe gained prominence. With the passing of time, the YIVO Archives became a documentation center on both East European and American Jewry.

The growth of the YIVO Archives can be credited in great measure to the many outreach programs that were conducted over the years. Already in Vilna, YIVO was known as an "active" collector which organized special collecting campaigns around specific goals or topics. This method was adapted in New York and it proved most useful in enlarging the Archives in a purposeful way. The first two such initiatives were indicative of YIVO's new direction. An immigrant autobiography contest was organized in 1942 with the aim of establishing YIVO as a research center for the history of Jewish immigration to America. The purpose of a second initiative, the "Museum of the Homes of the Past" project, announced in 1943, was to encourage American Jews to deposit personal papers, iconographic records, and memorabilia that would document the vanished world of East European Jewry.

Between 1945 and 1954 YIVO was involved in a project to create the "Archives on Jewish Life Under the Nazis." For this purpose, a network of collectors was organized which included pre-war YIVO *zamlers* who had survived the war and were living in the DP (displaced persons) camps, Jewish chaplains and soldiers in the U.S. Army, and staff members of Jewish relief organizations assigned to the European theater. YIVO envoys were sent to Europe to coordinate collecting activities. YIVO collectors' groups were organized in 595 localities spanning a wide territorial area, from Bergen-Belsen to Shanghai. As a result of this campaign the archive on the Holocaust and its aftermath was assembled. The Archive included documents from ghettos, records of Nazi government agencies, records of wartime Jewish organizations, eyewitness accounts, records of the DP camps, and pictorial materials.

In 1950 YIVO initiated a collecting campaign which turned once again to the theme of contemporary Jewish life. The intention was to establish a central archives on the history of the Jews in the United States, with emphasis on the period of mass immigration, from the 1880s to 1924. In conceptualizing this goal, it was pointed out that American-Jewish historiography had hitherto been largely limited to studies of Jewish life in America prior to 1880. This excluded from consideration an important segment of American Jewry, that is, immigrant Jews from Eastern Europe. YIVO planned to locate available records of the American Jewish past, once again with the assistance of a collectors' network, and to secure these records for its Archives. This ambitious concept was realized in part, by acquiring the records of several American Jewish relief agencies dealing with Jewish immigration to the United States.

Although YIVO had correctly appraised the situation in Jewish scholarship and had drawn the right conclusion about the need for a national Jewish archival institution, it did not possess enough means to meet this great challenge. Still, the creation of a vast immigration archive marked a turning point in the history of the YIVO Archives. YIVO's readiness to accept and accommodate large institutional archives has met with a positive response from the organized Jewish community. From the 1950s to the present the YIVO Archives has received a steady stream of records from many leading American Jewish organizations such as the Hebrew Immigrant Aid Society (HIAS), the Joint Distribution Committee (JDC), the Workmen's Circle, the Educational Alliance, and the American Jewish Committee (AJC). In 1992 the Jewish Labor Bund in New York resolved to transfer the Bund Archives of the Jewish Labor Movement to the YIVO Archives. The Bund Archives had been gathering materials on Jewish socialist movements since its inception in Geneva in 1899, and its numerous collections add a new dimension to the YIVO Archives.

From 1979 to 1983 a Landsmanshaftn Project was conducted with highly successful results. During this period, YIVO located and placed in its Archives records of over 700 *landsmanshaftn*, which are now organized in 300 record groups. These records document the history of immigrant mutual aid societies in the New York area during the past hundred years.

Finally, mention should be made of several outreach programs to collect historical photographs. Two of these projects, one focusing on Polish Jewry (conducted 1970–75) and the other on Russian and Soviet Jewry (conducted 1985–88), succeeded in greatly enriching the territorial photographic collections on Poland and Russia. These collection projects also resulted in the staging of major traveling exhibitions, the publication of historical photographic albums, and the production of a documentary film (*Image Before My Eyes*).

In addition to its outreach collecting projects, the YIVO Archives regularly acquires papers, records, and memorabilia offered by numerous donors on a broad range of topics relating to the history and culture of East European and American Jewry. Over the years the YIVO Archives has become an established repository of primary sources in the Jewish humanities, preserving and providing access to a collection that is central to studying the past and the present of the Jewish people.

Organization of the YIVO Archives:
A Brief Overview

From the 1950s through the present several arrangement and description projects have been carried out that have resulted in the present organization of the YIVO Archives.

The YIVO–Yad Vashem Documentary Project, carried out primarily in the 1950s, saw the organization, arrangement, and description of collections that bore testimony to the Holocaust. This included, on one hand, the Vilna Archives, which in its entirety was viewed as a remnant of the destroyed Jewish communities of Eastern Europe, and on the other hand, the collections that documented the Holocaust.

In 1947 a portion of the YIVO Archives in Vilna which had been discovered by the

United States Army in Frankfurt, Germany, was returned to YIVO in New York. Documents in this group were identified and traced back to the original collections to which they had belonged in pre-war YIVO. To carry out this task, the original collections had to be researched and re-established under their proper titles. This work resulted in the creation of an archival division designated as the Vilna Archives. Included under this designation were the institutional records of the YIVO Institute in Vilna, as well as fifty other collections from the pre-war YIVO Vilna Archives.

The second major effort relating to the organization of the YIVO Archives was the Record Group Registration Project, supported by a grant from the National Endowment for the Humanities. It was conducted in the 1970s and its aim was to take complete inventory of all collections in the YIVO Archives. The need for this project and the manner in which it was carried out stemmed from the fact that the existing classification system in the YIVO Archives did not always follow the principles of provenance. Documents were often separated from their original collections and classified by subject or research category. Thus, early cataloging procedures in the YIVO Archives resulted in the dispersion of many record groups. In order to restore historical meaning both to the removed materials and to their original collections, a repository-wide restructuring of collections was required.

During the Record Group Registration Project, documents were reclassified and rearranged, as much as possible, according to their origin. During the course of this project the entire YIVO Archives was reorganized and separate descriptions were compiled for each record group. Each description included basic donor information, a biographical or historical note, inclusive dates, a scope and content note, and the main subject headings. Finally, each record group was assigned an inventory (RG) number which was based on the date of accession into the Archives. That is, record groups accessioned earlier received lower numbers and those accessioned later received higher ones. The following record group registration scheme was established:

RG numbers 1 to 99 were reserved for collections acquired by YIVO in Vilna. Number 100 was assigned to the institutional records of the YIVO Institute in New York. Numbers 101 to 199 were given to subject collections generated in the YIVO Archives. Beginning with Record Group 200, collections were assigned numbers consecutively in the order of their accession.

At the end of the project, record group (RG) numbers had been assigned to 750 collections. Several hundred record groups have been accessioned since that time and classified in accordance with the new system.

The YIVO Archives currently houses a total of about 1,400 collections, occupying over 10,000 linear feet. The Archives' holdings consist of manuscripts, correspondence, and printed materials as well as photographs, films, videotapes, sound recordings, art works, and artifacts.

The primary languages of the documents are Yiddish, English, Hebrew, Russian, Polish, French, and German. The holdings, while covering a wide range of topics relating to Jewish history and culture around the world, concentrate on four main areas, reflecting the history of YIVO collecting activities and the scholarly interests of the YIVO Institute. These areas are: Yiddish language, literature, and culture, including significant collections on the Yiddish theater and Yiddish press; East European history; history of the Jews in the United States; and the Holocaust.

Guide to the YIVO Archives:
Purpose, Organization, and Format

The reorganization of its archival holdings enabled the YIVO Archives to proceed to the next phase, that of the compilation of a *Guide to the YIVO Archives* and an index based on the text of the guide.

The purpose of this guide is to make accessible in a single volume information about the scope and content of the collections in the YIVO Archives and to highlight the subjects reflected in the documents. We are optimistic that the *Guide to the YIVO Archives* will provide a much needed and useful introduction to the Archives' holdings.

The descriptions of collections are selective and are not meant to be exhaustive. Moreover, both the guide and the index reflect those disparities which are inherent in a repository-level finding aid of limited length, in which vast differences in size between small and large collections cannot be adequately represented. Thus, large collections are only partially described, whereas small collections have entries with more complete descriptions.

Format of the Guide and the Index

This guide is arranged alphabetically by name of collection. Each collection entry has the following elements of description: collection title; dates of the author; inclusive dates of the collection; biographical/historical note; scope and content note; information on finding aids.

Each collection has an entry number and the entries are numbered consecutively. The index numbers refer to the entry numbers in the guide. Some large collections were subdivided into several entries, each one corresponding to a separate subgroup. The range of entry numbers associated with a single large collection that has been subdivided appears on the same line as the main title of the collection.

The headings in the index provide access to the titles of the collections and to the subjects listed in the scope and content note of each entry. The index headings do not, as a rule, refer to words or subjects listed in the biographical/historical part of the entry. Terms in the biographical/historical segment are indexed only if these terms are directly related to actual archival documents deposited in the collection.

Index headings include personal names; names of corporate bodies such as organizations; geographic names; conferences or meetings; titles of newspapers, periodicals, plays, and other works; and topical headings.

The index also may serve as a quick reference for acronyms.

Note on Standardization of Names

The compilers of the guide were faced, among other things, with the daunting yet all-important task of establishing uniform names, titles, and subject headings. The linguistic complexities reflected in documents of the YIVO Archives mirror the numerous historical and political changes in the East European Jewish past.

Not until all the collections were compiled into a single volume did the range of contradictory spellings become apparent. For example, an unusually large number of people were commonly known by several names, in Polish, Yiddish, Hebrew, and English. In addition, each of them had lived in cities that also were commonly known by different names depending on what country they belonged to at the time.

In order to resolve these and other problems, several sources were chosen for standardization purposes. Library of Congress (LC) spellings were followed for names of published authors. In the event that an LC spelling for a Yiddish or Hebrew writer was completely outdated and would not be recognized by historians or readers, a variety of published sources were used as alternatives. For Jewish writers and historical figures: the *Encyclopedia Judaica*. For musicians and composers: *Bibliography of Jewish Music* by Alfred Sendrey (New York, 1951). For figures in world history: *Encyclopedia Britannica*.

For contemporary spelling of place names we used the *Columbia-Lippincott Gazetteer of the World* (New York, 1961, not updated at the time of compilation of this guide). The *Gazetteer* was particularly appropriate for YIVO Archives documents because it included even very small population centers and provided rich historical background for each place name. For places not listed in the *Gazetteer*, or for spellings or versions used popularly in Jewish communities, we consulted *Where Once We Walked*, by Gary Mokotoff and Sallyann Amdur-Sack. For place names in France during World War II, including names of internment camps, we used the *Analytical Franco-Jewish Gazetteer, 1939–1945* by Zosa Szajkowski (New York, 1966). Finally, Yiddish versions of towns and cities were written in transliterated form using the YIVO rules for romanization. Russian place names are not presented in transliterated form but appear as in the *Columbia-Lippincott Gazetteer*.

For names not listed in any published sources, the most frequent version appearing in the archival documents was adopted as a standard.

Note on Transliteration and Capitalization of Foreign Language Words

This guide follows the main principles of the *Chicago Manual of Style* regarding foreign language words. Yiddish words have been written according to the YIVO rules of transliteration. For names of corporate entities in Yiddish, the first letter of each word is capitalized as for any English proper noun. Foreign language words are generally italicized if they are not commonly used in the English language. Words like *landsmanshaftn*, although appearing in the latest American language dictionaries, are italicized because they are not frequently used in English. For Hebrew language words and Hebrew names of organizations a variety of published sources were used, the *Encyclopedia Judaica* being the most frequent. Russian words, with the exception of place names, are spelled according to modified Library of Congress romanization rules. As stated above, Russian place names appear as in the *Columbia-Lippincott Gazetteer*.

The YIVO Archives:
Services and Policies

Archival Services

Reference Services

Researchers who wish to obtain information about the YIVO Archives are invited to send their inquiries in writing to the YIVO Archives, 555 West 57th Street, Suite 1100, New York, NY, 10019. The YIVO fax number is (212) 292–1892. Telephone inquiries can be made at (212) 246–6080.

In 1998 the YIVO Institute will move into the Center for Jewish History at 15 West 16th Street, New York, NY, 10011. The Center will house four institutions: the American Jewish Historical Society, the Leo Baeck Institute, the Yeshiva University Museum, and the YIVO Institute for Jewish Research. Researchers who wish to use the facilities of the YIVO Archives in 1998 are advised to obtain updated information on visiting hours as well as the new phone and fax numbers.

Information about archival holdings obtained on-line via RLIN (Research Libraries Information Network), of which the YIVO Institute is a member, should be transmitted to the YIVO Reference Archivist for confirmation as to the availability of the collection, languages of the documents, and accuracy of the information.

Reading Room Services

The YIVO Archives Reading Room is open to interested researchers Monday through Thursday, 9:30 A.M. to 5:30 P.M., with the exception of civil and Jewish holidays. An appointment should be arranged with an Archivist. Collections that are in the process of being arranged, preserved in the conservation shop, or microfilmed are usually closed to the public for the duration of the projects.

Access to Collections

Collections in the YIVO Archives are open to the public unless access was restricted by the donor at the time of collection transfer. In addition, access to records containing case files of living persons is generally denied unless: (1) there are no privacy issues; (2) the researcher is the subject of the case file; (3) there are no additional restrictions on access by the institution whose records are in question. The policy followed for case files of individuals who are no longer alive but whose children or grandchildren may be alive is consistent with privacy laws and with policies followed by other archival repositories in the United States with similar records of case files.

Researchers granted access to case files may read them only for the purpose of obtaining general historical data and may not record specific information about individuals. Researchers given access to such materials must sign a Confidentiality Form in which they agree to abide by all YIVO Archives requirements.

Reproduction Services

Permission to reproduce documents, photographs, films, and sound recordings, in whole or in part, is granted on a case-by-case basis depending on the condition of the original and the provisions of United States copyright law. Photocopy requests are carried out by YIVO staff members. Copies of microfilm reels can be ordered. Fees for all reproduction services are listed in the YIVO Reproduction Price List, available upon request.

Special Collections: Access and Reference

Music Collections

Written music, both published and unpublished, is currently deposited in the general YIVO Archives. Published music is also separately available in the YIVO Library and is accessible through the YIVO Library catalog.

All specific reference inquiries regarding music holdings in the YIVO Archives should be addressed to the Music Archivist.

For general information on music holdings, please consult the index to this guide under **Music: art, folk, popular; Music: choral; Music: Holocaust; Music: liturgical; Music: theater**.

Photographic and Film Archives

A sizable proportion of the photographic collections in the YIVO Archives is housed in the Photographic and Film Archives. The photographic collections comprise about 150,000 items, a large percentage of which are cataloged. For general information about the photographic holdings of the YIVO Archives the reader is referred to the index of this guide under the headings **Photographs** and **Photographers.**

The photographs of the Holocaust period are cataloged on a computer database. A major selection of photographs of the Yiddish theater are cataloged on a computer database, titled STAGEPIX. Photographs of Poland before the Holocaust and of Russia are accessible on the YIVO videodisc titled "People of a Thousand Towns." The videodisc stores about 15,000 photographs. To view photographs either on the videodisc or in the original, an appointment must be arranged with the Photo and Film Curator.

The Film Collection is open to the public by appointment with the Photo and Film Curator. For general information on the scope and content of the Film Collections the reader is referred to the index entry in this guide under the heading **Films.**

The **YIVO Slide Bank** is a division of the Photographic and Film Archives. The Slide Bank consists of slide reproductions of images from books and original photographs from the YIVO Library and Archives. The Slide Bank Card Catalog is available by appointment with the Photo and Film Curator. Up to fifty slides may be rented at a time at a fee of $25.00. Slides may be rented for four weeks.

Sound Archives

The Max and Frieda Weinstein Archives of Recorded Sound houses collections of recordings which include 78 rpm recordings, 33 rpm recordings, audiotapes, and compact discs. Some information on the general scope and content of the sound recordings holdings can be retrieved by consulting the index to this guide under the heading **Sound Recordings**. Researchers who wish to use sound listening facilities must make an appointment in advance with the Sound Archivist.

The Collection of 78 rpm Recordings is cataloged on a computer database. The Collection of Radio Programs is also cataloged on a computer database. These computer databases are currently housed in the Sound Recordings Room.

Art Collection

The **Art and Artifacts Collection** includes paintings, drawings, rare prints, and traditional and ceremonial art. There are about 3,000 original cataloged art objects. About 300 items consist of costumes, props, and set designs of the Yiddish theater. In addition to the Art and Artifacts Collection, the YIVO Archives holds papers of a number of artists, including cartoonists and theater designers. For information on art materials in the Archives, please consult the index to this guide under **Art and Artifacts** and under **Artists**. Reference questions regarding art holdings should be directed to the YIVO Archives Reference Archivist.

Statement on Copyright Ownership of Documents in the YIVO Archives

As a rule, the YIVO Archives does not own the copyright to papers that have been transferred to it unless the donor of the papers was the copyright owner and assigned her/his rights to the YIVO Institute.

In the case of private letters, the original writer of the letter, or her/his heirs or assignees, is the copyright owner. Permission to publish long quotations or entire texts which may surpass the "fair use" standard, as defined in Section 107 of the U.S. Copyright Act, must be sought from the original copyright owner or from her/his heirs or assignees.

Collection Policy of the YIVO Archives

The YIVO Archives accepts paper documents, photographs, films, artifacts and art works relating to all aspects of Jewish history and culture around the world. Of particular interest are materials relating to the history of East European Jews and their descendants in the United States. Prospective donors can contact the YIVO Archives to discuss pertinent issues such as conditions of transfer and literary property rights.

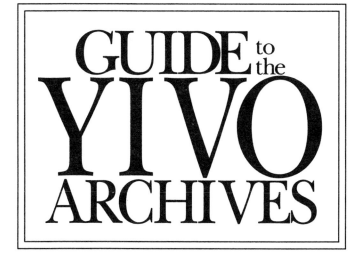

The Collections

THE COLLECTIONS

1. ABRAHAM COHEN BENEVOLENT SOCIETY.
  Records, 1919, 1954–1973. 1 in. (RG 1008)

Incorporated in 1919. Held annual memorial meetings for deceased members. Dissolved in 1973.
  Certificate of incorporation, 1919. Minutes, 1954–1972. Materials pertaining to dissolution, 1973.

2. ABRAHAM GOLDFADEN THEATRE (TEL AVIV).
  Records, 1951–1952. 5 in. (RG 293)

A Yiddish theater troupe, active in Tel Aviv, Israel.
  Minutes of meetings, payroll lists and financial reports, scripts, clippings and posters.

3. ABRAMOVITCH, RAPHAEL (1880–1963).
  Collection, 1920s–1930s. 6 in. (RG 390)

Jewish socialist leader, writer. Lived in Russia and the United States.
  These photographs were collected by Abramovitch in preparation for the book *Di farshvundene velt* (*A Vanished World*), published by the Forward Association, 1947.
  Photographs relating to Jewish life in Czechoslovakia, England, Estonia, France, Germany, Hungary, Israel, Italy, Latvia, Lithuania, Netherlands, Rumania, Russia and Spain.
  Card inventory, English.

4. ABRAMOWICZ, HIRSZ (1881–1960).
  Papers, 1920s–1960. ca. 1 ft. 5 in. (RG 446)

Yiddish educator, writer, journalist. Director for 24 years of the vocational school Hilf Durkh Arbet (Help Through Work) in Vilna. Born in Tomaszewo, Vilna province, Lithuania. Settled in New York after World War II.
  Correspondence with Yiddish literary figures. Letters to Dina Abramowicz, his daughter. Manuscripts of Abramowicz's articles about personalities and about literary and social questions. Clippings of articles by and about Abramowicz. Personal documents.

5. ADEL, BESSIE.
  Papers, 1947–1948, 1967. 7 1/2 in. (RG 1169)

Bessie Adel maintained contact with a few thousand families in displaced persons (DP) camps in the period 1947–1948. She corresponded with them and sent them packages of food. Lives in Los Angeles, California.

The collection consists mostly of letters, mainly in Yiddish, sent to Adel from the camps.

6. ADELEBSEN, JEWISH COMMUNITY.
Records, 1830–1917. 1 ft. 8 in. (RG 244)

The town of Adelebsen, Germany, was part of the Kingdom of Hanover until 1866 when it was incorporated into the Kingdom of Prussia. In 1871 Adelebsen became part of the German Empire.

The collection consists of financial, tax, synagogue and charity records. Administrative correspondence with the government. Minutes of Jewish communal election meetings. Financial materials include tax records, budgets. Regulations concerning baking of *matzos*, taxation matters, religious services. Synagogue documents include records of dues for synagogue seats and records of *aufrufs* (the honor, bestowed upon congregants, of being called up before the congregation to recite a blessing during the Torah reading). School records include materials about tuition, hiring of teachers and maintenance of the school. Records of the local charity society.

Inventory, English.

7. ADLER, CELIA (1889–1979).
Papers, 1911–1959. 1 ft. 3 in. (RG 399)

Yiddish actress, daughter of Jacob P. Adler. Performed with various American Yiddish theater companies. Born in the United States.

Correspondence, clippings, contracts, playbills and photographs relating to Celia Adler's career.

Photographs are cataloged in STAGEPIX.

8. ADLER, JACOB (1873–1974).
Papers, 1890s–1970. 10 ft. 5 in. (RG 473)

Yiddish humorist. Used many pen names, among them B. Kovner. Contributed to *Jewish Daily Forward* (NY), *Morgn zhurnal* (NY), *Freie Arbeiter Stimme* (NY), *Zukunft* (NY), *Kundes* (NY), *Kibitzer* (NY). Creator of fictional characters *Yente telebende* and *Moishe kapoyer*. Born in Dynów, Galicia. Immigrated to the United States in 1890.

Correspondence with individuals including: A. Almi, Shalom Asch, Nahum Baruch Minkoff, Abraham Cahan, Daniel Charney, Aaron Glanz-Leieles, Jacob Glatstein, Ephim Jeshurin, Zavel Kwartin, Herman (Chaim) Lieberman, Leibush Lehrer, Mani Leib, Kalman Marmor, Kadia Molodowsky, Moshe Nadir, Chaim Pett, Melech Ravitch, Yosele Rosenblatt, Sholom Secunda, Shea Tenenbaum, Baruch Vladeck, Berish Weinstein, M. Winograd, Zalmen Zylbercweig. Correspondence with organizations. Clippings of articles about Adler, including reviews of his memoirs and of the play *Yente telebende*. Clippings of articles by Adler including stories, jokes, poems. Manuscripts by Adler: plays, humorous sketches, skits, poems, articles, jokes, stories. Photographs of Adler, family and friends.

Inventory, Yiddish.

9. ADLER, JACOB P. (1855–1926).
Papers, ca. 1900–1926. 2 ft. 6 in. (RG 1177)

Major Yiddish actor who attained great popularity at the turn of the century. Adler's career began ca. 1879 in one of Abraham Goldfaden's theater companies. He subsequently performed in London, Chicago, Warsaw, Łódź, Lemberg (Lvov) and New York. Adler specialized in the dramatic and heroic roles of the plays of Jacob Gordin. Born in Odessa. Left for London, ca. 1883. Settled in New York ca. 1890.

Manuscripts and some printed copies of Yiddish plays. Photographs.
Photographs cataloged on STAGEPIX.

10. AIN, ABRAHAM.
Papers, 1940s–1950s. 2 ft. 6 in. (RG 336)

Abraham Ain was the secretary of the Friends of Swisłocz, a society of former residents of Swisłocz (Sislovich, Svisloch), Poland. Ain collected these materials for his articles on the Jews of Swisłocz, among them "Portrait of a Jewish Community in Eastern Europe," *YIVO Annual*, vol. 4 (1949).

Questionnaires filled out by 512 former residents of Swisłocz. Correspondence between displaced persons from Swisłocz and Ain.

11. ALGEMEYNE ENTSIKLOPEDYE.
Records, 1930s–1960s. 6 ft. 3 in. (RG 1149)

The *Algemeyne entsiklopedye* was originally planned as an encyclopedia of general Jewish knowledge in the Yiddish language. The managing editor was Abraham Kin. From the 1930s to the 1950s, 12 volumes were published by CYCO (Central Yiddish Culture Organization), New York. The first five volumes covered entries under the first two letters of the Yiddish alphabet. The next seven volumes were titled *Yidn*. In the 1950s *Yidn* was translated into English and published in four volumes under the title *Jewish People: Past and Present*.

Materials for *Jewish People: Past and Present*. Articles prepared for an unpublished Yiddish volume. Photographs. Correspondence. Financial reports. Minutes.

12. ALKON, JOSHUA (PINCHAS LEIB) (1896–1960).
Papers, 1929–1960. 1 ft. 3 in. (RG 503)

Yiddish writer, playwright. Contributed skits, stories, one-act plays to *Der tog* (NY), *Forverts* (NY), *Kundes* (NY). Used pen names J. Alkon, Joshua Alkon. Born in Sielce, Poland. Immigrated to the United States in 1912 and settled in Los Angeles.

Correspondence with Yiddish literary figures including Jacob Adler, Jacob Ben-Ami, H. Leivick, Shmuel Niger, H. Rosenblatt. Manuscripts of Alkon's novels and plays. Playbills, program notes.

13. ALKWIT, B. (1886–1963).
Papers, 1920s–1950s. 1 ft. 3 in. (RG 698)

Pen name of Eliezer Blum. Yiddish writer, poet. Contributed to *In zikh, Zukunft, Yidisher kemfer, Di feder, Freie Arbeiter Stimme, Undzer bukh, Kinder zhurnal, Der tog, Morgn zhurnal*. Born in Chełm, Poland. Immigrated to the United States in 1914.

The papers consist of manuscripts, correspondence, news clippings and photographs relating to Alkwit's career and personal life. Correspondents include Ephraim Auerbach, Shlomo Bickel, Jacob Glatstein, Moses (Moyshe) Leib Halpern, Leibush Lehrer, H. Leivick, Nahum Baruch Minkoff, Alexander Mukdoni, Shmuel Niger, Melech Ravitch, Lamed Shapiro, Moshe Starkman, Abraham Sutzkever, Tolush, Isaiah Trunk.

Inventory, Yiddish.

14. ALLIANCE ISRAELITE UNIVERSELLE.
Records, 1868–1930s. 4 ft. (RG 406)

Jewish organization founded in France in 1860 for the purpose of providing help to Jews suffering from religious discrimination. Headquarters in Paris. The Alliance intervened on behalf of Jews in Serbia, Rumania, Belgium, Russia, Switzerland, Morocco, Poland, Hungary, and other countries. It also provided assistance to large groups of Jewish refugee immigrants from Russia. Lastly, the Alliance established schools in many countries, especially in the Balkans and the Middle East.

Correspondence, reports, minutes, printed matter dealing primarily with Jewish immigration from Russia to the United States, Canada, Latin America, from the 1860s through 1930s. The bulk of the materials, however, relates to the heavy wave of immigration of the 1881–1885 period sparked by the May Laws and the pogroms which erupted in Russia in 1882.

The records reflect the relief work carried out on behalf of the refugees by Jewish organizations in Western Europe, of which the most notable was the Alliance Israélite. Others include the Mansion House Fund (London), the German Central Committee for Russian Jews (Germany), the Israelitische Allianz (Austria), similar committees in Königsberg, Brussels, and Geneva, the Hebrew Emigrant Aid Society (HEAS, a precursor of the Hebrew Immigrant Aid Society, HIAS), and HIAS in New York. The committees organized protest meetings against the pogroms, arranged transportation, and gave financial aid to immigrants. Many of the documents pertain to Brody, a border city between Russia and Austrian Galicia, which became a major transit point for immigrants on their way to the United States and to other countries.

Materials relating to the reaction of Jewish communities in France, England, Germany and the United States to the persecution of Russian Jews. Documents about immigration to the United States including: passenger lists; correspondence and prospectuses from shipping companies regarding transportation; statistics from the transit center at Brody; lists of pogrom victims (1905); HIAS reports on shelters and on vocational training in the United States; documents about agricultural colonization in the United States including reports from the Jewish Colonization Association, Woodbine Agricultural School, colonies in Louisiana and Colorado; statistical reports by HIAS on settlement possibilities in small American towns.

In addition, the collection contains reports on persecutions of Jews in Rumania; material on the Kishinev pogrom of 1903; reports from Casablanca, Morocco, 1918–1932; reports on the Tiszaeszlár blood libel case.

Inventory, English.

15. ALPERT, JACK (1903–1976).
Papers, 1950s. 1 ft. 8 in. (RG 1277)

Worker in millinery and knitting industries, occasional contributor to Yiddish press. Contributor to the Kurenets memorial book. Lived in Kurenets (Kurenits, Kurzeniec), Byelorussia. Came to the United States in 1921.

Manuscript of the Yiddish translation of the memorial book *Megilat kurenits*, published in Tel Aviv, 1956. Memoirs of life in Kurenets.

16. AMERICAN COUNCIL FOR WARSAW JEWS.
Records, 1943–1947. 1 in. (RG 1041)

Established in 1942 to "aid Jews in Warsaw and outlying cities; to give immediate aid to Warsaw Jews wherever they can be reached; to help the post-war reconstruction of the Warsaw Jewish community; to aid and centralize activities of Warsaw Jews in America." Sent envoys to Warsaw. Dissolved in the 1950s.

Membership records. Organizational records, including some minutes, 1943. Memoir by Samuel Wohl, 1947 (Yiddish). Press releases, correspondence, resolutions.

17. AMERICAN FEDERATION FOR POLISH JEWS.
Records, 1926, 1938, 1941–1963. 1 ft. 8 in. (RG 1015)

Formerly known as the Federation of Polish Jews in America. Founded in 1908 as the Federation of Russian-Polish Hebrews, primarily to "help Polish *landslayt* in New York in any possible way" and to strengthen the activities of *landsmanshaftn* in the city. Established the Beth David Hospital to aid members and newly arrived immigrants, ca. 1912. Contributed to the People's Relief Committee, 1919. Sent a delegate to the Versailles Peace Conference, 1919. In 1920, dropped "Russian" from name of organization. In 1926, changed "Hebrews" to "Jews." Established the World Federation of Polish Jews in 1935 for relief and economic assistance for Jews in Poland. The women's division, Ezra, was organized in 1931. Cooperated with the Association of Jewish Refugees and Immigrants from Poland in publishing *The Black Book of Polish Jewry*, 1943. In the mid-1940s, coordinated relief activities of New York Polish *landsmanshaftn* on behalf of their home towns and *landslayt*. In the 1950s campaigned actively against antisemitism and racial discrimination. Leaders included Dr. Joseph Tenenbaum, Zelig Tygel, Benjamin Winter.

Constitution. Minutes of committee meetings, 1940s–1950s. Financial and relief records, 1945–1947. Records of the Women's Division, 1942–1943. Organizational reports, 1940s. Material pertaining to membership. Correspondence, 1942–1963. Materials pertaining to conferences, mass protest meetings, commemorations, 1945–1954. Materials pertaining to the fourth World Conference of Polish Jews, 1945. Testimonies given in Palestine regarding Nazi brutality and accounts of escape from Nazi persecution. Reports pertaining to Jewish life in Poland. Publications. Yearbook, 1938. Bulletins, newsletters. Typescripts of chapters of *The Black Book of Polish Jewry*. Publicity materials. Photographs.

18–28 AMERICAN JEWISH COMMITTEE.
Records, 1918–1970s (bulk ca. 1930–1970s). 765 ft. (RG 347)

Organization founded in 1906 in New York by 34 prominent American Jews to defend Jewish civil and religious rights throughout the world. The original founders included Louis Marshall, Judge Mayer Sulzberger, Jacob Schiff, and Cyrus Adler. Judge Sulzberger was elected first president of the committee and served in that capacity until 1912. Among those who succeeded him were Louis Marshall, 1912–1929; Cyrus Adler, 1929–1940; Joseph Proskauer, 1943–1949; Jacob Blaustein, 1949–1954; Morris B. Abram, 1964–1968; Arthur J.

Goldberg, 1968–1969. The chief executive officer of the AJC was the Secretary, later re-named the Executive Vice President. Among those who occupied this position were: Herbert Friedenwald, 1906–1912; Herman Bernstein, 1913–1914; Morris D. Waldman, 1926–1943; John Slawson, 1943–1967. The American Jewish Committee (AJC) is governed by the National Executive Council and administered by the AJC Executive Committee. Headquar-ters are in New York with regional offices throughout the United States. There is also an office in Jerusalem. Current membership is estimated at 50,000.

At the outset, the AJC consisted of a small select group who interceded on behalf of Jews, privately and discreetly, in the traditional style of personal diplomacy. In 1907 and 1913 the AJC lobbied for a liberal American immigration policy and fought against the literacy test requirement for immigrants. In 1911 it campaigned successfully for the abrogation of the Russo-American Treaty of 1832 because of violations of Jewish rights in Tsarist Russia. At the Paris Peace Conference of 1919 the work of Julian Mack, Louis Marshall and Cyrus Adler was influential in securing minority rights for Jews. In the 1920s the AJC conducted a public relations campaign against Henry Ford's publication of the *Protocols of the Elders of Zion* in the *Dearborn Independent*.

In the 1930s the AJC began to widen its membership. By the 1940s the structure and approach of the AJC had undergone a fundamental change. The private diplomacy approach was supported more and more by organized educational and public relations programs, including an increasing number of scholarly studies and publications on antisemitism, civil and religious rights, interracial and intercultural relations.

With the rise of pro-Nazi and antisemitic groups in the United States the AJC campaigned against these movements, carrying out studies on Nazi activities and publicizing some of their findings in newspapers and magazines. In addition, the AJC studied conditions in various countries for their potential as havens for Jewish refugees from Europe.

During subsequent decades, the AJC continued its lobbying activities and public relations and educational programs, strengthening its research staff and promoting studies about big-otry, cultural diversity, intergroup cooperation and intercultural education. The AJC was particularly active in the civil and human rights areas, supporting legislation and court decisions addressing racial and religious discrimination in employment, higher education and housing. In 1951, the AJC published the five-volume *Studies In Prejudice*. The Committee also publishes the monthly magazine *Commentary* and co-sponsors the annual publication of the *American Jewish Year Book*.

The records deposited in the YIVO Archives include select series from the Records of the American Jewish Committee. The records consist of correspondence, minutes, and reports of executive offices, departments, local offices and chapters of the Committee. Series not de-posited at YIVO are at the Jacob Blaustein Library of the American Jewish Committee in New York.

An *Inventory of Records of the American Jewish Committee, 1906–1980*, by Seymour J. Pomrenze, was published by the AJC. The *Inventory* describes the entire AJC records includ-ing the records currently at the Blaustein Library and those at the YIVO Institute. In addition, there are unpublished finding aids to the portions of the AJC records deposited at YIVO.

The YIVO Archives has the following:

18–19 AJC EXECUTIVE OFFICE (EXO).
   24 ft. (RG 347.1)

YIVO has files of Morris Waldman (EXO-29), and files of the AJC Washington Representa-tive (EXO-30).

18. Morris Waldman Files.
    1918–1947 (bulk dates: 1930s–1947). 22 ft. (RG 347.1.29)

Morris Waldman was the AJC Secretary, 1928–1943 and its Executive Vice-President, 1943–1944.

Correspondence, reports, studies, statements, minutes of meetings, memoranda, speeches, and other papers. Portions of the Waldman files deal with Jewish affairs in foreign countries, especially Germany, Latin America, Poland, and Rumania. These include: petitions to the League of Nations on behalf of Jews; AJC relations with the British Joint Foreign Committee and Neville Laski; problems of Jewish reconstruction after World War II; the San Francisco Conference of 1945, and creation of the United Nations; Jewish immigration and efforts to rescue Jewish refugees; AJC involvement in Zionist affairs, Palestine as a Jewish homeland, the partition of Palestine, the Jewish Agency, and related matters.

Still other segments of the Waldman files pertain to AJC domestic programs and contain papers on Nazism and Nazi propaganda in the United States. Materials on AJC efforts to combat antisemitism, including AJC actions in denouncing the *Protocols of the Elders of Zion*, Father Charles E. Coughlin's activities, and Jewish-communist relationships. Materials on AJC interreligious activities, including Catholic-Jewish relations.

Additionally, there are minutes of meetings, reports, statements, and other papers on the work of AJC with the General Jewish Council. Reports, minutes of meetings, correspondence, and other papers relating to the AJC Survey Committee. Correspondence and other papers pertaining to AJC relations with the American Jewish Congress, World Jewish Congress, American Jewish Conference, Anti-Defamation League, B'nai B'rith, Council of Jewish Federations and Welfare Funds, Service Bureau for Jewish Education, U.S. governmental agencies. Correspondence, plans, studies, reports, and other papers on AJC administrative matters, such as AJC organization, programs and policies (including AJC historical data), fundraising, field offices, and staffing.

Shelf list, English.

19. AJC Washington Representative.
    1967–1968. 2 ft. (RG 347.1.30)

Correspondence, memoranda, and other papers concerning a variety of matters considered to be of national importance for the AJC by its Washington representative or other AJC officials. There are papers on discrimination by Arab countries against Jews and domestic issues such as executive suite discrimination, equal education, employment, and housing opportunity actions, fair campaign practices, hospital desegregation guidelines, interreligious activities, and other matters.

Shelf list, English.

20. AJC COMMUNITY SERVICES AND MEMBERSHIP DEPARTMENT (CSD).
    1944–1971. ca. 60 ft. (RG 347.4)

This department is responsible for implementing AJC policies and programs in local communities, chapters and field offices. The departmental files are arranged by local office. YIVO has files from the following offices: Atlanta, 1953–1968; Boston, 1947–1968; Chicago and Milwaukee, 1944–1971; Cleveland, 1950–1970; Newark, 1947–1964; San Francisco, 1946–1966; White Plains (for Westchester, Upstate New York), 1955–1968.

The files consist of administrative correspondence, activity reports, correspondence with national AJC, with national and local organizations and individuals. The papers pertain to subjects of local and national interest such as antisemitic incidents and personalities, segregation/desegregation, Catholic–Jewish relations, civil rights, communism, ecumenical activities, religion and education, social discrimination, urban renewal, women and the AJC, executive suite, extremism, housing, race relations, school prayers, Jewish attitudes (surveys of).

Shelf list, English.

21–24 AJC FOREIGN AFFAIRS DEPARTMENT (FAD).
    1930–1978. 187 ft. (RG 347.7)

This department was established in 1946 as a successor to the AJC Overseas Affairs Department. Its task is to monitor the condition of Jewish communities around the world; to aid Jewish communities in resisting antisemitic propaganda; to work for restitution and indemnification for Jewish victims of Nazism; to work for the development of Israel and for peace in the Middle East; to seek the liberalization of immigration policies. The department supervises the activities of the AJC foreign offices.

The records in this sub-group are divided into the following series:

21. Foreign Countries (FAD-1).
    1930–1973. 100 ft. (RG 347.7.1)

Reports, studies, memoranda, minutes, statements, briefs, correspondence, surveys, printed materials which relate to Jewish communities in over 75 countries. The foreign countries records are arranged by country. The following countries have files greater than 1 ft.: Argentina, Austria, Brazil, Egypt, France, Germany, Great Britain, Hungary, Iraq, Israel, Italy, Mexico, Morocco, Poland, Rumania, Soviet Union, Syria.

Significant topics covered in selected country files are:

Argentina. 1938–1973. 5 ft.: activities of the AJC Buenos Aires office; anti-Catholicism; antisemitism; Christian-Jewish relations; AJC delegations to Argentina; Israel and Argentina; Jewish organizations and leaders; emigration; general political situation.

Austria. 1946–1973. 1 ft. 8 in.: displaced persons and refugees; Christian-Jewish relations; Austrian government officials; the Jewish Community Council in Vienna; neo-Nazism; restitution; Simon Wiesenthal Documentation Center. Reports of AJC correspondents on condition of Jews.

Brazil. 1939–1973. 3 ft.: activities of AJC offices in Rio de Janeiro and São Paulo; antisemitism; Jewish studies centers; interfaith relations; political conditions and human rights; Sephardic community.

Egypt. 1948–1972. 1 ft. 10 in.: American Council of Voluntary Agencies for Foreign Service; Central Registry of Jewish Losses in Egypt; emigration of Jews from Egypt; ex-Nazi groups; German scientists; legislation involving Jews; Nasser's anti-Jewish activities; United Nations and anti-Jewish persecutions.

France. 1941–1973. 1 ft. 10 in.: relationship between the AJC and the Alliance Israélite; antisemitism; Centre de Documentation Juive Contemporaine; Conseil Représentatif des Juifs; Jewish agencies and communities; Libyan-French deals; North African refugees; French politics; Zionist activities.

Germany. 1930–1973. 12 ft. 11 in.: activities of advisors on Jewish affairs to the Governor of the U.S. Military Zone; Nazism and neo-Nazism; the AJC program on reeducation; AJC relations with German officials including Konrad Adenauer, Willy Brandt, Ernst

Reuther; German politics; Germany and Israel; the Oberammergau Passion Play; publication of *Mein Kampf*; radical right; reparations.

Great Britain. 1947–1973. 1 ft. 5 in.: activities of the AJC London office; Anglo-Jewish Association and Joint Foreign Committee; the Council of Christians and Jews; extremism and antisemitism; the Institute of Contemporary History (Wiener Library); Zionism.

Hungary. 1944–1973. 1 ft. 5 in.: Hungarian Nazis; refugees. There are also materials on antisemitism among Hungarian Catholic groups in the United States; Nazi activity in the United States.

Iraq. 1945–1972. 1 ft. 6 in.: condition of Iraqi Jews; Iraqi government and the press; relations of Iraq and Syria; U.S. government and Iraq.

Israel. 1945–1973. 26 ft.: activities of AJC officials and of the AJC office in Tel Aviv and Jerusalem; reports of AJC correspondents and of AJC missions to Israel; American public opinion on Israel; Arab–Jewish cooperative ventures; attitudes of Catholics and other Christians toward Israel; diaspora–Israel relations; AJC relations with the Israeli government; immigration; the status of Jerusalem; Sephardim; the Arab–Israeli wars.

Italy. 1947–1973. 4 ft.: conditions of Jews in Italy; antisemitic propaganda; Christian–Jewish relations.

Mexico. 1945–1972. 3 ft.: reports of AJC correspondents; programs of the AJC Mexico City office; antisemitism; Arab propaganda; Christian–Jewish relations; Jewish communal organizations; political situation in Mexico.

Morocco. 1945–73. 1 ft. 9 in.: conditions of Moroccan Jews; emigration; relations between AJC and the Moroccan Government.

Poland. 1944–1972. 1 ft. 3 in.: activities of American Jewish Joint Distribution Committee; antisemitism; Warsaw ghetto.

Rumania. 1948–1973. 1 ft. 1 in.: emigration; human rights violations.

Soviet Union. 1949–73. 16 ft.: antisemitism; visits of Soviet officials to the United States; anti-Zionism; dissent; emigration; human rights; the Jewish community in the Soviet Union; Jews and Birobidzhan; Polish Jews in the Soviet Union; Yiddish culture in the Soviet Union.

Syria. 1948–1973. 1 ft. 1 in.: condition of the Jews in Syria including materials on the Committee for the Rescue of Syrian Jews; Committee of Concern for Syrian Jews; trade agreements between the United States and Syria.

Shelf list, English.

22. Foreign Areas Files (FAD-2).
1935–1973. 18 ft. (RG 347.7.2)

These files include materials relating to matters of AJC concern in Africa, Asia, Europe, Latin America and the Middle East. Topics include: antisemitism; emigration and refugees; racial discrimination and segregation; extremism; Arab propaganda; communism; Jewish communities; AJC missions and delegations. The sub-series on Europe includes materials on the joint "Communauté" program of the AJC, the Anglo-Jewish Association, and the Alliance Israélite Universelle; Nazism and neo-Nazism; Institute of Eastern-European Affairs. The sub-series on Latin America includes materials on the United Nations; United States and Latin America; missions of Jewish organizations to Latin America (American Jewish Joint Distribution Committee, B'nai Brith, Hebrew Immigrant Aid Society, Jewish Agency); Jewish libraries and Jewish study programs; Latin American press and other media. The sub-series on the Middle East includes materials on Arab terrorism; Palestinians; British, French and German policies in the Middle East; energy crisis; U.S. Middle

Eastern defense bases; the Palestine Liberation Organization; the Arab–Israeli wars.
  Shelf list, English.

23. AJC Office in Israel (FAD-27–FAD-35).
  1952–1978. 40 ft. (RG 347.7.27–RG 347.7.35)

The office was established in 1961 in Tel Aviv. In 1967 it was moved to Jerusalem. The bulk of the series consists of subject files which are in turn divided into chronological sub-series: 1962–1969, 1970, 1971–1972, 1973 through 1978. Topics include AJC role in Middle East initiatives; tours of Israel sponsored by AJC; aspects of Christian involvement in Israel; Arab–Jewish relations; the Israeli government; the administration of the occupied territories; civil rights; United States and Israel. The series also includes editorial files of the AJC publications *Ammot* and *Tefutsot Israel*.
  Shelf list, English.

24. AJC Paris Office (FAD-41).
  1932–68. 34 ft. (RG 347.7.41)

Established in 1947 as the regional office for Europe and North Africa.
  The series consists of gegraphic files, subject files and international organizations files.
  The geographic files include materials on 40 countries in Europe, North Africa and the Middle East.
  The subject files cover the following topics:
  National AJC staff and lay committees in Germany; the national AJC Committee on Near Eastern Affairs; Augustin Cardinal Bea and the Pro Deo Project; AJC delegations to Europe, Israel, and North Africa; antisemitism, fascism, and neo-Nazism; Christian–Jewish relations and the Ecumenical Council; the Columbus Project (David Astor and psychopathology); denazification trials; the Eichmann case; freedom of information; the Gauting Conference; genocide; group libel; human rights; immigration; Jewish communal services conference; Jewish war orphans; racial discrimination; European restitution programs and operations; visas to enter the United States.
  The international organizations files consist of correspondence, reports, and other papers involving relationships between the AJC Paris Office and various organizations and groups such as: American Jewish Joint Distribution Committee, 1947–1952; Centre d'Information Israélite, 1947; Conference on Jewish Material Claims Against Germany, 1952–1962; Consultative Council of Jewish Organizations, 1946–1963; Council of Europe, 1951–1953; émigré organizations, 1942–1959; International Center, St. Paul the Apostle (Rome), 1964–1966; International Council of Christians and Jews, 1947–1949; International League, 1963–1966; International Refugee Organization, 1946–1949; London Conference, 1945–1946; Memorial Foundation for Jewish Culture, 1965–1967; PEN Club, 1953; United Jewish Educational and Cultural Organization, 1946–1951; United Nations and its various bodies, 1947–1967; World Brotherhood Organization; World Council of Churches; and World Jewish Congress.
  Shelf list, English.

25. AJC INFORMATION AND RESEARCH SERVICES DEPARTMENT (IRS).
  1930s–1940s. 21 ft. 3 in. (RG 347.8)

This department supervises the work of the library, performing statistical functions, doing research and collecting clippings.

The YIVO Archives has press clippings on Jewish affairs and a study on Nazi collaborators.

The clippings cover the time period of the 1930s–1940s and relate mainly to antisemitism in North America, England and Europe. There are materials on Father Charles E. Coughlin; Henry Ford; Amin al Husayni; Oswald Mosley; Julius Streicher. Topics include the anti-Nazi boycott, the *Protocols of the Elders of Zion*.

The "Nazi Collaborators Study" was compiled by Dr. Samuel Gringhaus in 1949. It includes documents about individuals from East European countries who were involved with the Nazi regime.

Inventory of the clippings.

26–28. AJC GENERAL RECORDS (GEN).
(RG 347.17)

Until 1964, the records retention at the AJC was based on maintaining centralized files to accommodate and group together materials from various departments in a pre-arranged sequence. These Central Files—now called General Records—were closed in 1962 when the AJC reverted to a system of departmental record groups.

YIVO has the following series from the General Records:

26. AJC Subject Files (GEN-10).
1930–1962. 140 ft. (RG 347.17.10)

This series consists of materials filed in alphabetical topical files. Main subjects include: agriculture, antisemitism, bigotry and prejudice, business and industry, executive employment, censorship, children and youth, church-state, civil liberties and rights, community relations, discrimination, education, employment, extremism, genocide, hate and violence, housing, human rights, immigration, integration, inter-group relations, international affairs, interreligious affairs, Jewish communal affairs, Jews and Judaism, labor, mass media, political philosophies, race relations, religion, restitution, social discrimination, the South, statelessness, veterans, war and peace, women, Zionism. These and other main subjects are further subdivided into secondary subjects.

Shelf list, English.

27. AJC Alphabetical Files (GEN-12).
1933–62. 60 ft. (RG 347.17.12)

This series consists of materials from various AJC departments concerning the AJC's relationship with individuals and organizations. The records are arranged alphabetically by name. Largest files include: American Council for Judaism, 1942–1962; American Jewish Conference, 1943–1948; Anti-Defamation League, 1945–1961; Jacob Blaustein, 1944–1962; Consultative Council of Jewish Organizations, 1946–1963; Council of Jewish Federations and Welfare Funds, 1945–1963; Eichmann Trial, 1960–1962; Irving M. Engel, 1946–1962; National Association of Intergroup Relations Officials, 1946–1962; National Council of Churches of Christ, 1950–1962; National Social Welfare Assembly, 1947–1962; Judge Joseph M. Proskauer, 1941–1962; John Slawson; United Nations.

Shelf list, English.

28. AJC Domestic Geographic Files (GEN-13).
1940–62. 60 ft. (RG 347.17.13)

Correspondence, reports, and other papers on a variety of subjects, arranged by state and localities thereunder.

The following select topics are included:

Admission to colleges and universities, adoption laws, antisemitism, the arts. Baccalaureate services, bible distribution/reading, bigotry and prejudice, business practices. Capital punishment, children/youth, church/state, civil liberties, civil rights, colleges and universities, communism, community relations. Discussion groups. Education, elections, emergency defense, employment and fair employment opportunities practices. Foreign affairs, fraternities/sororities. Hate groups/literature, higher education, holiday observances, hospitals, human rights. Insurance policies, integration, intergroup relations, interreligious affairs. Jewish community councils, Jewish federation/welfare funds. Labor, loyalty/security. Mass media, medical/dental schools, minorities, moral and spiritual values, motion pictures. Passion plays, pledge of allegiance, police practices/training, politics, prayers, professional societies, program appraisal/planning, public accomodations, public schools. Race relations, radio/television, refugees, relationship with organizations/groups, released time, religion and religious beliefs, religion and schools, resort advertising. Saturday school sessions, school-community relations, scientific evaluations, *shehitah* (ritual slaughter), social discrimination, Sunday closing, surveys of communities/programs. Tax exemption. Universities. Veterans programs, violence, visits by AJC representatives and other persons. Youth activities.

Noteworthy are: reports of visits by AJC representatives to specific communities, describing local conditions and covering other matters of AJC interest; reports relating to Joint Defense Appeal fundraising efforts; correspondence, reports, and other papers on the origin and development of AJC field offices; correspondence, legal briefs, and other papers on "cases" in which AJC was involved as amicus curiae or otherwise, pertaining to such matters as civil liberties/civil rights, education, employment, housing, and public accommodations, and background materials on specific cases; correspondence and other papers on relationships between local AJC officials and those of kindred local Jewish and other organizations; and other papers of significance to local Jewish communities.

Shelf list, English.

29–37 AMERICAN JEWISH JOINT DISTRIBUTION COMMITTEE.
Records, 1919–1950. 30 ft. 8 in. and 160 microfilm reels. (RG 335)

An organization, with headquarters in New York, active since 1914 in relief programs for Jewish communities around the world. Founded during World War I to help Jews suffering from the ravages of war, the AJDC represented the concerted efforts of three separate Jewish organizations. These were: the American Jewish Relief Committee, founded by prominent Jews of German background; the Central Relief, founded by Orthodox leaders; and the People's Relief, representing labor. In the post–World War I period the JDC, as it was commonly called, provided financial support, distributed food, set up health-care institutions and schools, created interest-free loan societies, and supported Jewish local and international service organizations in Europe and Palestine.

Following the revolution and the civil war in Russia, 1917–1920, the JDC joined the American Relief Administration in 1920 to improve living conditions for impoverished Jewish masses inside the Soviet Union. In 1924 the JDC formed a separate organization, called the American-Jewish Joint Agricultural Corporation (also known as the Agro-Joint), to continue its work in the Soviet Union. The Agro-Joint carried out its activities in the USSR until 1939.

In 1924, the JDC, together with the Jewish Colonization Association, founded the American Joint Reconstruction Foundation (AJRF) to help rebuild the economy in Eastern Europe through the establishment of cooperative credit institutions and savings banks. By 1931, over 700 loan cooperatives were being supported by the AJRF.

From 1933 until the end of World War II, the JDC was involved in helping refugees from Nazi persecution. In addition, the JDC financed the relief activities of the immigration organization HICEM and was also involved in wartime rescue activities.

Between 1945 and 1952, the JDC concentrated its efforts on aiding displaced persons in the camps in Germany, Austria and Italy, as well as providing transportation costs for Jews immigrating to Israel. From the 1950s through the 1970s, the JDC maintained programs in North Africa, Israel, Europe and Latin America.

Officers of the JDC included Felix Warburg, Paul Baerwald, Herbert Lehman, James Rosenberg, Julius Rosenwald, Joseph C. Hyman, Bernard Kahn.

The YIVO Archives has received several series of JDC records from the JDC Archives in New York:

29. AJDC REPORTS, 1916–1960.
4 ft. (RG 335.1)

Reports of JDC executive offices, 1930–1960. Materials on negotiations between the British government and the Jewish Agency headed by Chaim Weizmann, 1930. Reports on relief work done in Poland, 1916–1939.

30. AMERICAN JOINT RECONSTRUCTION FOUNDATION.
Records, 1920–1939. 11 ft. 8 in. (RG 335.2)

A corporation formed under the English Companies Act in 1924 by the AJDC and the Jewish Colonization Association (JCA). The American Joint Reconstruction Foundation (AJRF) engaged in economic rehabilitation by rebuilding Jewish-owned structures destroyed during World War I and by encouraging productive economic activity primarily among the Jews of Eastern Europe. Its most significant accomplishment was the establishment of hundreds of credit cooperative societies which provided credit and banking services for small business-men, farmers and artisans. The Foundation operated in several countries, including Bulgaria, Czechoslovakia, Estonia, Greece, Latvia, Lithuania, Poland, Rumania, Turkey, and briefly, Germany. The governing board included Herbert H. Lehman, Felix M. Warburg, Joseph C. Hyman, Sir Osmond d'Avigdor Goldsmid, Dr. Leon Bramson, Dr. Bernard Kahn, Dr. Louis Oungre.

AJRF General Records, 1921–1928. Lists of AJRF directors in Eastern Europe. Reports from Eastern Europe, Russia and Palestine. Correspondence of JCA, 1921–1923. Announcements and reports relating to cooperative work of JCA, AJRF, and ORT. Reports of AJRF activities in Europe, 1924–1928.

Reports, surveys, correspondence, minutes, clippings relating to: situation in Ukraine, 1920; situation in Poland, 1920–1938; situation in Lithuania, Latvia, Estonia, Rumania, Bessarabia, Czechoslovakia, Hungary, Austria, Turkey, Greece, Yugoslavia. Reports of 121 loan societies in Poland. List of 97 Jewish communities rebuilt after World War I. Financial reports of banks and loan societies. Reports on educational facilities in Hungary. Reports of ORT activities in various European countries. Minutes and reports dealing with HICEM. Press clippings from: Poland, 1921–1934; Lithuania, 1921–1938; Greece, 1933–1934.

Inventory, Yiddish, English.

31. AJDC WAR ORPHANS BUREAU.
   Records, 1919–1923. 14 microfilm reels. (RG 335.3)

Organized by the AJDC in 1919, to provide relief for Jewish war orphans mainly in Eastern Europe. Activities included finding foster families, building orphanages, exploring possibilities of adoption in the United States, Canada, South Africa and Palestine.

   These are adoption records of some 1,500 Jewish orphans from Soviet Russia for whom foster families were found abroad.
   Inventory, English.

32. AJDC SEARCH DEPARTMENT.
   Records, 1921. 2 microfilm reels. (RG 335.4)

Established in 1921 to help refugees and World War I survivors from Eastern Europe locate relatives in the United States and other countries.

   The records consist of questionnaires filled out by people wishing to locate relatives in the United States.

33. AJDC OFFICE IN LISBON.
   Records, 1939–1951. 32 microfilm reels. (RG 335.5)

The AJDC established an office in Lisbon which existed during and after World War II. It aided refugees from Nazi-occupied countries and supplied relief to survivors in DP camps after the war.

   Copies of outgoing correspondence as well as individual case files of the AJDC in Lisbon, 1941–1950. Correspondents include: American Friends Service Committee, 1942–1947; AJDC in Paris, 1945–1949; Intergovernmental Committee on Refugees, 1944–1947; HICEM, 1940s; Council for Refugee Settlement in Johannesburg, 1942–1947; National Refugee Service, 1942–1945. Correspondence with foreign embassies of England, Yugoslavia, Holland. Records of transportation and lists of refugees, 1940–1946. Reports, bulletins of the European AJDC.
   Inventory, Yiddish.

34. AJDC PERSONAL SERVICE DEPARTMENT.
   Records, 1946–1954. 97 microfilm reels. (RG 335.6)

This department was established during World War II, initially under the name Transmigration Bureau, to deal with individual cases of immigrants who applied to AJDC for help. After the war the Transmigration Bureau's accounting section was merged with the AJDC Accounting Department, while the Personal Service Department took over general migration matters. The department was headed by Reta L. Stein. In 1954, following the merger of HIAS and USNA into the United HIAS Service (UHS), the AJDC Personal Service Department was incorporated into the UHS and all its files were transferred to the new organization.

   Individual case files: correspondence with individuals and their relatives, and organizations such as USNA and HIAS. Migration materials arranged by countries: Argentina, Australia, Germany, Israel. General migration material. Files of the American Council of Voluntary Agencies for Foreign Service. Files on the following topics: immigration under the DP Act; relations with the HIAS; McCarran Immigration Act; President's Escape Program.
   Inventory, English.

35. AJDC LANDSMANSHAFTN DEPARTMENT.
Records, 1937–1940, 1945–1950. 15 ft. (RG 335.7)

Created in New York in 1919 to solicit aid from *landsmanshaftn* for their hometowns in Eastern Europe. Discontinued in 1924. Revived in 1937 in connection with the JDC reconstruction program. After World War II the Landsmanshaftn Department continued its relief work for survivors in Eastern Europe. Activities included immigrant aid and location of survivors.

Records of the Landsmanshaftn Fraternal Division, 1937–1940. Correspondence with *landsmanshaftn* of several hundred towns and cities in Poland. The correspondence includes reports about *gmilas khesed* (interest-free loan) societies in Poland supported by the AJDC, as well as documents reflecting local social and economic conditions. Correspondence, inter-office memoranda of Henrietta Buchman, JDC Assistant Executive Secretary, and Norman V. Gilmovsky, Landsmanshaftn Department head. Communications from local organizations and officials in Poland and other European countries.

Post-World War II records, 1945–1950. Includes general correspondence and inter-office memoranda of Louis H. Sobel, JDC Assistant Executive Secretary, and Solomon Tarshansky, Landsmanshaftn Department head. Correspondence with *landsmanshaftn*. Reports from survivor groups in Europe. Lists of survivors.

Inventory, English.

36. AJDC CLIPPINGS. 1950–1969.
15 microfilm reels. (RG 335.8)

Clippings of interest to AJDC from English, Yiddish and German newspapers in the United States. Included are clippings about: Austria, Czechoslovakia, Germany, Hungary, Arab countries, Russia. Organizations: AJDC, International Emergency Children's Fund, United Nations, United Jewish Appeal. Groups: Arab refugees, displaced persons. Topics: economic recovery of Europe, immigration, Black–Jewish relations, reparations.

Inventory, English.

37. AJDC PHOTOGRAPHS.
Records. ca. 1 ft. 8 in. (RG 335.9)

This subgroup consists of photographs depicting AJDC activities worldwide. The photographs are alphabetically arranged by country. Included are photographs of Algeria, Austria (DP period), Belgium, Bulgaria, China, Cyprus, Czechoslovakia, France, Germany (1930s and DP period), Greece, Holland, Hungary (DP period), Iran, Israel, Italy (DP period), Libya, Morocco, Norway, Poland (post-World War II period), Rumania, Switzerland, Tangier, Tunisia, United States, Yugoslavia.

Card Inventory, English.

38. AMERICAN JEWISH TERCENTENARY COMMITTEE.
Records, 1952–1954. ca. 24 ft. (RG 329)

Founded in 1952 to organize observance of the 300th anniversary of the American Jewish community which was celebrated in 1954.

Internal records of the Tercentenary Committee. Materials of the Board of Directors. Budget Committee records. By-laws. Minutes of the Steering Committee. Minutes of Plan-

ning Conferences. Correspondence with organizations and individuals: American Jewish
Congress; American Jewish Committee; B'nai Brith; Jewish Publication Society; Jewish
Theological Seminary. Individuals include: David Bernstein, Albert Greenfeld, Bernice
Koor, Milton Krents, Benjamin Lazarus, Henry Moses, William Rosenwald, Harold Shapiro.
Materials relating to celebration activities.

39. AMERICAN MEMORIAL TO SIX MILLION JEWS OF EUROPE.
Records, 1944–1986. 2 1/2 in. (RG 1206)

Committee formed in New York in late 1940s to erect a monument in New York to Jewish
victims of Nazism.

Correspondence, brochures, photographs, clippings, speeches, proclamations and other
materials concerning efforts of the Committee to erect a monument in Riverside Park, 1947–
1953. Photograph of Fiorello La Guardia, Rabbi Isaac Rubinstein, Julian Tuwim, Shalom
Asch and others at Warsaw ghetto memorial, New York, 1944. Collection also includes
clippings, manuscript articles by S.L. Schneiderman and other materials concerning later
efforts to build a monument, 1964–1986.

40. AMERICAN ORT FEDERATION.
Records, 1922–1960. 30 ft. 1 in. (RG 380)

Established in 1922 by Leon Bramson and Aron Syngalowski as the national organization of
the ORT in the United States. ORT, which was established in Russia in 1880, is an interna-
tional Jewish organization for vocational training. In the United States, ORT stands for
Organization for Rehabilitation through Training. The American ORT Federation established
a number of vocational schools in the United States, of which a notable example is the
Bramson School in New York. The Federation conducts fundraising activities in support of
ORT work worldwide. The American ORT Federation's headquarters are located in New
York City.

The records consist of correspondence, minutes, reports, financial and statistical records,
printed materials relating to the activity of the AOF and to ORT work worldwide, 1922–
1960.

General files, consisting of minutes of AOF Board of Directors, Executive Committee and
other committees, 1937–1951. Minutes and other materials of AOF conventions, 1949–
1960. Minutes and other records on budget negotiations between AOF and the AJDC, 1936–
1960. Correspondence of the American and international ORT leaders including Leon
Bramson, Aron Syngalowski, Israel Efroykin, Florence R. Dolowitz, William Haber, Paul
Bernick. Reports, including some by Syngalowski on situation in Poland, 1938. Reports of
others on ORT in the Soviet-occupied territories of Poland and Lithuania, 1940. Speeches
by William Haber, AOF president, 1950–1977.

Country files: correspondence, reports, press releases on ORT work in Argentina, Aus-
tralia, Austria, Bulgaria, Chile, China, Cuba, England, France, Germany, Hungary, Iraq,
Israel, Latvia, Lithuania, Mexico, Morocco, Poland, Rumania, South Africa, South America,
Switzerland, USSR. Extensive files on ORT in Poland, Israel, and on the DP camps in
Europe, 1945–1950. Additionally, there are statistics and reports on various countries com-
piled by the Statistical Analysis Section, 1947–1949.

Publicity files including press releases, press clippings, brochures, 1939–1950s. Editorial
materials for the *ORT Yearbook, 1963–1972*. ORT published reports.

Photographs of ORT vocational programs in Europe (Austria, Belgium, Canada, Chile,

China, England, France, Germany, Hungary, Italy, Poland, Rumania) United States, Canada, Middle East (Iran, Israel, Morocco, Tunisia) and Latin America (Cuba, Argentina, Uruguay). Films of ORT activities worldwide.

Inventory, English.

Inventory of the photographs, English.

41. AMERICAN OSE COMMITTEE.
Records, 1941–1955. 22 ft. 6 in. (RG 494)

OSE (Oeuvre de Secours aux Enfants—Society for the Aid of Children) is a health care organization based in Paris. It was founded in 1912 in St. Petersburg, Russia, and the name OSE was originally an acronym for Obshchestvo Zdravookhraneniia Evreev (Society for the Protection of the Health of the Jews). The OSE maintained branches in Russia, Poland, Rumania, and Central and Western Europe. The Polish name was Towarzystwo Ochrony Zdrowia (TOZ—Society for the Protection of Health). By 1939 OSE maintained hundreds of institutions which included hospitals, sanatoriums, nurseries, and camps. The institutions of OSE in Europe were destroyed during World War II. In the post-war period, OSE focused its attention on Africa, Israel, Latin America, and North America. Its work includes control of epidemic diseases, dissemination of public health information, and medical research.

The collection consists of records of the American OSE Committee in New York. General correspondence, 1941–1955, with Jewish organizations. Correspondence with OSE in France during World War II. Reports from Cracow, Poland, sent to Geneva, Switzerland, and from there to New York, 1940s. Files on North America, Europe, South America, Middle East. Files relating to immigration of children to the United States. Reports, minutes of meetings of the OSE Executive Committee, and Board of Directors. Financial reports. Lists of survivors of World War II. Photographs of OSE activities.

Inventory, English.

42. ANIK, HARRY AND BLOCH-ANIK, EVELYN.
Papers. 10 in. (RG 741)

Harry Anik was a pianist and composer. Born in New York.

The collection consists of musical works of Harry Anik, as well as works by other Jewish composers. Compositions for voice, piano and choir. Liturgical pieces. Yiddish folksongs. An oratorio, *I Hear Israel Singing*, by Harry Anik. Included also are papers of Anik's wife, Evelyn Bloch-Anik.

43. ANIKSTER BENEVOLENT PISCHEï TSHUVO ASSOCIATION.
Records, 1931–1976. 10 in. (RG 937)

Established in New York in 1939 by immigrants from Ankyščiai, Lithuania upon the consolidation of the Congregation Bnai Pischei Tshuvo Anshei Aniksty and the Anikster Benevolent Association. The congregation was established in 1887 for the purposes of religious study. In addition, it provided cemetery plots and free loans to members and supported the rabbi and talmud torah in Ankyščiai. The congregation maintained a synagogue at 135 Henry Street, New York. The Anikster Benevolent Association was organized in 1898. Following consolidation, the Anikster Benevolent Pischei Tshuvo Association maintained the synagogue until 1965 when the building was sold. Dissolved in 1976.

Legal documents, 1930s–1940s. Minutes, 1936–1939. Financial records, 1940s–1970s.

Meeting announcements. Correspondence. Materials pertaining to sale of synagogue and to the dissolution of the association. Seal.

44. ANTEPOLER YOUNG MEN'S BENEVOLENT ASSOCIATION.
   Records, 1923–1979. 15 in. (RG 883)

Organized in New York in 1906 by immigrants from Antopol, Byelorussia. Activities included establishing a loan fund for its members. A ladies auxiliary was organized in 1913, later disbanded and reorganized in 1929 as the Antepoler Young Ladies Auxiliary. After World War I, engaged in relief activities for *landslayt* in Antopol, sending funds to the Antopol *talmud torah* (religious school), Tarbut Hebrew schools, and to the local interest-free loan fund.

   Constitution of the Antepoler Y.M.B.A. Constitution of the Antepoler Ladies Auxiliary. Financial records, 1950s–1970s. Correspondence, 1960s–1970s. Anniversary journal. Announcements.

45. APENSZLAK, JAKOB (1894–1950).
   Papers, 1939–1945. 4 ft. 7 in. (RG 732)

Polish-Jewish journalist. Editor-in-Chief of *Nasz Przegląd* (Our Review), Warsaw, 1920s–1939, and *Nasza Trybuna* (Our Tribune), New York, through 1950. Born in Poland. Immigrated to the United States in 1939.

   The papers relate to Apenszlak's association with *Nasza Trybuna* and with Polish-Jewish organizations, and to his work on behalf of Polish-Jewish refugees during and after World War II.

   Correspondence. Manuscripts of Apenszlak and of others. Records of *Nasza Trybuna*. Photographs.

   Correspondents include the Polish National Council (in exile), London. There is also correspondence with organizations of Polish Jews in the United States, Germany, France and Canada, such as: Association of Refugees and Immigrants from Poland; Central Committee of Jews in Poland; Federation of Jews from Poland in the U.S. Occupation Zone in Germany; American Federation of Polish Jews; Canadian Federation of Polish Jews. Materials on topics relating to the Holocaust, including lists of Jewish survivors and refugees. Materials on the history of Polish Jews. Personal documents.

46. ARKIN, LEON (1888–1953).
   Papers, 1905–1947. 1 ft. 3 in. (RG 230)

Manager of the *Jewish Daily Forward*, Boston office. President of the Workmen's Circle. Member, YIVO Board of Directors.

   Correspondence with literary figures, organizations, including Yiddish school organizations, cultural groups and mutual aid societies. Includes letters from Baruch Vladeck to Arkin. Family correspondence, 1905–1941, from Lunna, Grodno, Kiev, Konotop, Białystok, Warsaw.

47. ARONSON, MICHAEL (1879–1963).
   Papers, 1950s. 1 ft. 3 in. (RG 580)

Yiddish journalist, novelist. Used pen names M. Rechtman and Y. Man. Wrote for or edited the *Keneder odler*, *Yiddishes Tageblatt*, *Morgn zhurnal*. Born in Zhitomir, Russia. Immigrated to the United States in 1894.

   The collection includes manuscripts of Aronson's works and clippings.

48. ARPIN, GOLDA SCHLOSBERG.
Papers, 1940s–1960s. 2 in. (RG 550)

Yiddish writer. Los Angeles.

The collection consists of manuscripts, typescripts, and clippings of her stories and essays.

49. ART AND ARTIFACTS.
Collection, 18th c.–1980s. ca. 3,000 items. (RG 101)

The collection consists of original art works, reproductions, and historical artifacts. Included are woodcuts, engravings, linoleum cuts, etchings, silkscreens, lithographs, drawings, paintings, watercolors and mixed media.

In addition to fine art works, there are also functional art works, such as theater drawings, costume and stage designs; political cartoons; and Jewish ceremonial art such as *mizrahs*, *ketubot*, Torah curtain designs, *megilot*.

Themes include: landscapes and shtetl scenes in Eastern Europe; Jewish holidays; Jewish types; portraits of individuals; Holocaust; Yiddish theater. A number of works were produced by Jewish artists incarcerated in ghettos and concentration camps during the Holocaust. There is also art produced by children in DP camps.

Artists include: Max (Moyshe) Band, Stanisław Bender, Benn, Henryk Berlewi, Joseph Budko, Yosl Cutler, Yonia Fain, J. Foshko, Isaac Friedlander, Todros Geller, Enrico Glicenstein, William Gropper, Chaim Gross, Moses (Moyshe) Leib Halpern, Hirschfang, Ephraim Kaganowski, Mané-Katz, Arthur Kolnik, Isaak Il'itch Levitan, Abraham Manievitch, Zuni Maud, Abbo Ostrowsky, Abel Pann, Saul Raskin, Diego Rivera, Emanuel Romano, Hermann Struck, Marek Szwarc, Yehuda Jennings Tofel, Abraham Walkowitz, Alfred Wolmark, Shloyme Yudovin.

Artists of the Holocaust period include: Aussenberg (Terezín); Alfred Kantor (Auschwitz-Birkenau); Kate Munzer (Paris); V.E. Bloch (Shanghai ghetto); Arnold Dagani (Transnistria); Bedrich Fritta (Fritz Taussig) (Terezín); Leo Haas (Terezín); Louis Heller (Łódź ghetto).

Card catalog, English.

50. ARTEF THEATER, NEW YORK.
Records, 1925–1940. 1 ft. 6 in. (RG 531)

Acronym for Arbeter Teater Farband (Workers' Theater Association). Organized ca. 1929 by the Young Workers' League, the ARTEF was influenced by communist groups. Its repertoire included many plays of strong ideological content. At its founding Kalman Marmor was president, Y. Adler, G. Sandler and David Abrams were secretaries; and Jacob Mestel was the director. The ARTEF was dissolved in 1940.

Playscripts, musical scores, programs, posters, photographs of actors and stage scenes. Clippings, programs and miscellaneous materials about the ARTEF.

51. ASCH, SHALOM (1880–1957).
Papers. ca. 2 ft. (RG 602)

Major novelist and dramatist, influenced early in his career by Isaac Leib Peretz. Honorary President of the Yiddish PEN Club. Author of novels and plays depicting the Eastern European Jewish "shtetl." His christological novels caused much controversy. Born in Kutno,

Poland. Lived in France. After 1938 settled in the United States. Died in London.

Manuscript of Asch's novel, *Moses*. A copy of *Motke ganef*, with handwritten notes and corrections by Asch. Photostats of letters by Asch. Correspondents include Baal Makhshoves, David Ben-Gurion, Hayyim Nahman Bialik, Moses Broderson, Jacob Dinesohn, Meir Dizengoff, Itsik Feffer, Pesakh Liebman Hersh, Peretz Hirschbein, Mark Jarblum, B. Kletzkin, H. Leivick, Herman (Chaim) Lieberman, Abraham Liessin, Peretz Markish, Solomon Mikhoels, Shmuel Niger, Hersh David Nomberg, Joseph Opatoshu, Israel Rabon, Maurice Samuel, Jacob Schiff, Zalman Shneur, Abraham Sutzkever, Edward Warburg, Max Weinreich.

52. ASEN, ABRAHAM (1886–1958).
Papers, 1930s–1950s. 2 ft. 1 in. (RG 510)

Translator, Yiddish poet, journalist, dentist. Contributed to *Kundes* (NY), *Zukunft* (NY), *Jewish Daily Forward* (NY), *Literarishe bleter* (NY), *Vokhnblat* (NY). Translated numerous English poetical works into Yiddish. Born in Brest-Litovsk. Immigrated to America in 1903. Died in Toronto.

Manuscripts, typescripts and clippings of Asen's translations. Included are translations of works by Byron, John Milton, Walt Whitman, as well as translations of Psalms, Ecclesiastes, Proverbs, Isaiah, Jeremiah and Job.

53. ASRO, ALEXANDER (1894–1962) and ALOMIS, SONIA (born 1896)
Papers, 1916–1961. 3 ft. 8 in. (RG 729)

Jewish actors, husband and wife, co-founders of the Vilna Troupe. Lived in Vilna, Poland, and the United States.

The papers relate to the careers of Asro and Alomis in the Yiddish theater and to their work with the Vilna Troupe. Correspondence and other documents relating to the establishment of the Vilna Troupe. Playscripts, programs, photographs, reviews, memorabilia. Reproductions and original art works by Asro, consisting of drawings, prints, paintings, sketches, theater designs.

Art works removed to and cataloged in Art and Artifacts, RG 101.

Photographs cataloged in STAGEPIX.

54. ASSOCIATED BENEVOLENT YOUNG MEN.
Records, 1937–1974. 7 1/2 in. (RG 930)

Established in New York in 1907 by immigrants from Włocławek, Poland, as the Independent Wlotzlawker Young Men's Benevolent Society. Associated with Congregation Ahavas Achim Włocławek, established in 1881. Affiliated with the Federation of Polish Jews in America. Changed name to Associated Benevolent Young Men in 1945.

Certificate of name change, 1945. Constitution. Minutes, 1949–1973. Financial records, 1963–1976. Materials pertaining to burial. Materials pertaining to membership. Correspondence. Meeting notices. Seal. Materials of Wloclawker Chebra Ahabath Achim.

55. ASSOCIATED LODZER LADIES AID SOCIETY.
Records, 1937–1973. 7 1/2 in. (RG 966)

Founded in New York in 1929 by immigrants from Łódź, Poland. Paid funeral expenses.

Members received burial through their husbands' membership in other Lodzer societies. Affiliated with the United Lodzer Relief Committee (est. 1914).

Minutes, 1937–1973. Financial report, 1948. Photograph. Correspondence. Minutes, United Lodzer Relief Committee, 1961–1967. Materials of the United Emergency Committee for the City of Łódź.

56. ASSOCIATION FOR JEWISH FARM SETTLEMENTS.
Records, 1932–1935. 2 ft. 11 in. (RG 419)

An organization in New York formed to create a Jewish agricultural colony for unemployed workers. Chaim Zhitlowsky was its honorary chairman.

Circulars and correspondence relating to organizational activities. Materials relating to the convention of 1933. Financial materials. Lists of candidates for colony membership, resolutions, by-laws, minutes of meetings.

57. ASSOCIATION FOR THE CARE OF THE AGED AND INFIRM (NEW YORK).
Records, 1935–1947. 10 in. (RG 385)

Minutes of Association meetings, 1936–1938, 1939, 1943. Minutes of the Superintendent's Committee, 1935–1938, 1939–1941. Reports, cases and circulars of the Social Workers' Committee. General correspondence of the Association, 1937–1943.

58. ASSOCIATION OF JEWISH COMMUNITY RELATIONS WORKERS.
Records, 1940s–1970s. 5 ft. 5 in. (RG 629)

A professional organization whose membership consisted of professional workers employed in Jewish centers and other community relations institutions. Based in New York, the Association of Jewish Community Relations Workers (AJCRW) was established in 1950 as a successor to the Community Relations Conference.

Correspondence, financial records, minutes, reports and printed material relating to the organization and activities of the AJCRW. Materials relating to the creation of the AJCRW, annual meetings, conferences. Materials on membership, constitution, Executive Committee. Budget and financial reports. President's reports. Correspondence and reports from Boston and Philadelphia offices. Publicity materials and materials relating to publications of AJCRW.

59. AUERBACH, EPHRAIM (1892–1973).
Papers, 1924–1969. 10 in. (RG 609)

Yiddish poet, short-story writer, teacher. Contributed to *Yiddishes Tageblatt, Di varhayt, Dos yidishe folk, Haynt, Literatur un lebn, Di yunge, Zukunft, Fun mentsh tsu mentsh, Di vokh, Yidish, Yidisher kemfer, Morgn zhurnal.* Taught in the Sholem Aleichem schools. Cofounder of CYCO (Tsentrale Yidishe Kultur Organizatsye—Central Yiddish Culture Organization). President, Yiddish PEN Club. Born in Beltsy, Bessarabia. From 1912 to 1915 lived in Palestine and Egypt. Immigrated to the United States in 1915.

The collection consists of correspondence between Auerbach and literary figures. Correspondents include: Shlomo Bickel, Menahem Boraisha, Daniel Charney, Aaron Glanz-Leieles, Jacob Glatstein, Ben Zion Goldberg, Abraham Golomb, Chaim Grade, Leibush Lehrer, H. Leivick, Itzik Manger, Mani Leib, Kadia Molodowsky, Shmuel

Niger, Melech Ravitch, Dov Sadan, Abraham Sutzkever, Michael Weichert.

60. AUSLANDER, JACOB.
Collection, 1935–1936. 2 in. (RG 656)

Collector for YIVO, New York.

The collection consists of underground anti-Nazi literature in German. Included are printed copies and film negatives of newspapers, flyers, materials in miniature form.

61. AUTOBIOGRAPHIES, AMERICAN-JEWISH.
Collection, 1942–1970s. 17 ft. 6 in. (RG 102)

In 1942 the YIVO Institute organized an autobiography contest on the theme "Why I Left Europe and What I Have Accomplished in America." There were 250 entries and 25 prizes were awarded. Since 1942 about 100 autobiographies on the same topic have been added to the collection.

The collection relates primarily to the immigrant experiences of Jews who left Europe between 1900 and the 1930s and settled in the United States. Included are autobiographies entered in the contest as well as autobiographies received after the contest. Correspondence with contestants, lists of contestants, notes, planning and publicity materials.

Card inventory, English.

62. AUTOBIOGRAPHIES OF JEWISH YOUTH IN POLAND.
Collection, 1932–1939. 7 ft. 11 in. (RG 4)

These autobiographies were submitted to YIVO in Vilna as entries to three contests (1932, 1934, 1939) sponsored by YIVO's Youth Research Division (*Yugntforshung*). Originally, there were over 600 autobiographies of which about 350 were recovered after World War II.

The collection consists of autobiographies and supplementary biographical materials, such as correspondence, diaries, documents, as well as records of the contest, including lists of the contestants, correspondence with them, reports and clippings.

The autobiographies relate primarily to the authors' childhood years during the World War I period and to their experiences as Jews growing up in inter-war Poland.

Inventory, Yiddish, English.

63. BACHELIS, BARUCH (BARNEY) (1886–1952).
Papers. 1 ft. 5 in. (RG 548)

Yiddish poet. Contributed to the *Kalifornyer yidishe shtime* (San Francisco), *Di tsayt* (Los Angeles). Born in Kiev province, Ukraine. Immigrated to the United States in 1901.

Manuscripts of Bachelis's poetry, correspondence, and clippings of his articles.

64. BACHELIS-SHOMER, ROSE (1882–1966).
Papers, 1911–1956. 1 ft. 1/2in. (RG 519)

Yiddish writer and playwright. Contributed to *Der tog, Yidishe kultur, Kalifornyer yom tov bleter*. Daughter of the Yiddish playwright, Nahum Meir Shaikewitz-Shomer. Wife of the Yiddish poet, Baruch (Barney) Bachelis (1886–1952). Born in Russia. Settled in New York in 1891.

Manuscripts by Rose Bachelis-Shomer relating to Nahum Meir Shaikewitz's life. Type-script of her book *Vi ikh hob zey gekent* (How I Knew Them) consisting of biographical sketches about literary personalities. Correspondence with literary personalities, notably Daniel Charney, Jacob Glatstein, Abba Gordin, Miriam Karpilow, Kalman Marmor, Joseph Rumshinsky, Nahum Meir Shaikewitz-Shomer, Abraham Shomer, Yehoash.

65. BADER, GERSHOM (1868–1953).
Papers, 1884–1953. 3 ft. 10 in. (RG 323)

Journalist, teacher, playwright. Pioneer of Yiddish press in Galicia, in the early 1900s. Contributor to *Yiddishes Tageblatt* (NY) and *Morgn zhurnal* (NY). Born in Cracow, Poland. Emigrated to the United States in 1912.

Source materials for his Hebrew lexicon of Jewish writers in Galicia. Includes short biographies of or letters from the writers Shmuel Yosef Agnon, Majer Bałaban, Judah L. Landau, Emil Sommerstein, Osias Thon, Israel Zeller. Works relating to Jewish life in Galicia.

66. BAMBERGER, BERNARD JACOB (1904–1980).
Papers, 1942–1945. 5 in. (RG 568)

Reform rabbi. Rabbi of Temple Beth Emeth, Albany, from 1929 to 1944. In 1944 he became rabbi of Temple Shaarey Tefila (New York).

The collection consists of correspondence between Bamberger and U.S. soldiers during World War II. Most of the correspondents were members of Bamberger's congregation.

67. BARATZ, LEON (born 1896).
Papers, 1920s–1954. 5 in. (RG 309)

Lawyer, teacher, publicist. Lived in Russia, Germany, France.

Manuscripts of Baratz's writings on Jewish conditions in Soviet Russia, Zionism, World Jewish Congress. Clippings of Baratz's articles. Baratz's autobiography.

68. BARKAN, CHAIM (born 1896).
Papers, ca. 1927–1966. 10 in. (RG 489)

Yiddish writer. Teacher in the Workmen's Circle schools, Philadelphia. Contributed sketches, stories, articles to *Di yidishe velt* (Philadelphia), *Frayhayt* (NY), *Jewish Daily Forward* (NY), *Freie Arbeiter Stimme* (NY), *Yidish*, *Kinder zhurnal* (NY). Born in Ungen (Ungheni), Bessarabia. Immigrated to the United States in 1920 and settled in Philadelphia.

Correspondence with Yiddish literary figures, including A. Almi, Menahem Boraisha, Abraham Cahan, Aaron Glanz-Leieles, Jacob Glatstein, Solomon Grayzel, Lippa Lehrer, Yudel Mark, Rose Nevodovska, Shmuel Niger, Melech Ravitch, Abraham Reisen, Isaac Nachman Steinberg.

69. BARON, AARON LOEB (1886–1954).
Papers. 5 in. (RG 1189)

Yiddish writer, poet. Contributed to *Yidish vort* (Cracow), *Zukunft* (NY). Wrote humorous sketches for the *Jewish Daily Forward*. Born in Lithuania. Immigrated to the United States in 1906.

Fragmentary manuscripts of skits, novels, stories. Clippings by and about Baron. Three song sheets and lyrics by Baron.

70. BARYSZER YOUNG MEN'S BENEVOLENT ASSOCIATION.
Records, 1934–1973. 5 in. (RG 887)

Organized in New York in 1905 by immigrants from Barysh (Pol. Barysz), Ukraine. Incorporated in 1948. Supported Jewish philanthropies. Dissolved 1974.
Membership book, 1934–1969. Financial records, 1948–1973. Correspondence.

71. BEHAR, NISSIM (1848–1931).
Papers, 1913–1927. 2 1/2 in. (RG 597)

Educator, philanthropist, communal leader. Headed the Alliance Israélite school in Constantinople from 1873–1882 and in 1882 helped found the Alliance school in Jerusalem. In 1901 Behar was sent to represent the Alliance in the United States. In 1906 he founded the National Liberal Immigration League which tried to prevent exclusion of immigration to the United States by opposing restrictive bills such as the Literacy Test Bill. The League presented its position at Congressional hearings. It worked on behalf of all ethnic groups. Behar was also one of the founders of the Federation of Jewish Organizations, an editor of the *Federation Review*, and a founder of the Jewish Big Brothers League. He was also active in the Histadrut Ivrit in the United States. Born in Jerusalem. Lived in France, Syria, Bulgaria, the United States.
The collection consists for the most part of correspondence of the National Liberal Immigration League and correspondence between Nissim Behar and his son, Manoel Behar, who was active in the league, 1914. Some reports and clippings.

72. BELARSKY, SIDOR (1900–1975).
Papers, 1920s–1970s. 3 ft. 6 in. (RG 721)

Singer of classical and folk music. Known for his performances, recordings and arrangements of Russian and Yiddish folksongs as well as for his appearances as a bass baritone soloist with orchestras and opera companies. Teacher of vocal music at Brigham Young University, Provo, Utah, 1930–1933, and at the University of Utah. Professor of Music at the Jewish Teachers Seminary–Herzliah Institute in New York City. Belarsky's original name was Israel Lifschitz. Born near Odessa, Ukraine. Came to the United States in 1930 on a concert tour and remained in this country.
The papers relate to Belarsky's career and consist of playbills, posters and programs, song books, sheet music, tapes, recordings, production plates, plaques, clippings, correspondence.

73. BELLARINA, BELLA (1896–1969).
Papers, 1910s–1960s. 2 ft. 6 in. (RG 574)

Yiddish actress. Played with the Vilna Troupe and the Yiddish Art Theater. Lived in Poland and the United States.
Correspondence with family, friends, writers, organizations. Personal documents. Manuscripts of plays, some with directors' annotations. Reviews of performances of the Vilna Troupe. Memoirs entitled *Zikhroynes vegn der vilner trupe* by Chaim Shneur, Bellarina's husband.

74. BELTON, ALBERT (?–1987).
> Papers, 1940s–1977. 2 1/2 in. (RG 733)

Adopted name of Béla Berend. Chief Rabbi of the Budapest ghetto during World War II.

The collection consists of documents relating mainly to Belton's libel suit against the World Federation of Hungarian Jews. Included are court documents, correspondence relating to Belton's activities in the rabbinate, and clippings relating to the case.

75. BEN-ADIR (1878–1942).
> Papers, ca. 1934–1942. 10 in. (RG 394)

Pseudonym of Abraham Rosin. Yiddish writer and socialist leader. Founder of Freeland League. Founder and editor of the monthly *Oyfn shvel* (On the Threshold). Lived in Byelorussia and the United States.

Correspondence with literary figures including Menahem Boraisha, Abraham Golomb, Vladimir Grossman, Louis Lamed, H. Leivick, Jacob Lestschinsky, Shmuel Niger, Melech Ravitch, Isaac Nachman Steinberg, Chaim Zhitlowsky. Manuscripts of Ben-Adir's works. List of printed articles by Ben Adir. Condolence telegrams. Scrapbook of clippings.

76. BEN-AMI, JACOB (1890–1977).
> Papers, 1902–1977. 5 ft. 2 in. (RG 755)

Stage name of Jacob Shchirin. Actor, director, producer. Travelled with Yiddish acting companies throughout Eastern Europe. Performed on the Yiddish and English stage in the United States and toured in South America, South Africa, and other countries. In 1918, together with Maurice Schwartz, he founded the Yiddish Art Theater in New York. Born in Minsk. Settled in the United States in 1912.

The papers relate to Ben-Ami's theatrical career and include playscripts, programs and playbills, posters and clippings, personal documents, photographs.

Inventory, Yiddish.

77. BEN-EZRA, AKIVA (born 1897).
> Papers. 2 1/2 in. (RG 841)

Yiddish writer. Pen name of Akiva Kostrometzky. Contributed to *Der tog, Morgn zhurnal, Der amerikaner, Undzer folk, Yidish vokhnblat, Zukunft, Hadoar*. Editor of the Hebrew bi-monthly *Hadoar l'noar*. Born in Horodec, near Kobrin, Poland. Immigrated to New York in 1914. Settled in Israel in the 1970s.

Correspondence with Yiddish literary figures.

78. BEN-ISRAEL, SHLOMO (1908–1989).
> Papers, 1910–1989. 3 in. (RG 1274)

Pen name of Shlomo Gelfer. Yiddish journalist, staff writer at the *Jewish Daily Forward* and commentator for the WEVD radio station. Also wrote mysteries (in Yiddish and Hebrew) and plays. Active in the Labor Zionist movement. Born in Brest-Litovsk, Russia. Settled in the United States in 1939.

Photographs, letters, manuscripts and programs of plays. Tapes of interviews with political, communal and literary figures, including Ben-Gurion, Amram Blau, Golda Meir, Hillel Rogoff, Pinchas Sapir, Isaac Bashevis Singer, Eli Wiesel.

79. BEN-YEHUDA, JACOB.
Papers, 1960s. 13 in. (RG 1267)

Manuscripts of a Hebrew-Yiddish word and phrase dictionary in eleven notebooks. Yiddish translation of Max Diamond's *Jews, God and History*.

80. BENJAMIN, MOSES.
Papers, 1918–1960s. 5 in. (RG 661)

Active member of the Workmen's Circle in Cleveland, Ohio. Materials relating to Benjamin's activities in the Workmen's Circle of Cleveland, including correspondence, lecture notes, speeches. Photograph, annual convention, Toronto, 1922.

81. BEREZER, DAVID.
Papers, 1935–1954. 2 ft. 10 in. (RG 371)

Teacher in Workmen's Circle School 2, Bronx, New York. Member of Board of Directors, YIVO.

School materials including class notes and workbooks on various subjects reflecting Berezer's career as a teacher. Miscellaneous correspondence of the United Rescue Committee for Łódź for the period 1935–1954. Photographs of students and teachers of the Workmen's Circle Schools.

82. BERKOVITCH, SHLOYME (1888–1954).
Papers, ca. 1930s–1953. 1 ft. 3 in. (RG 331)

Yiddish writer, teacher. Co-founder of the Sholem Aleichem Folk Institute in New York. Active in Yiddish educational and cultural organizations. Born in Pereyaslav, Ukraine. Immigrated to Canada in 1903. Moved to New York in 1923.

Correspondence with literary figures. Correspondence and materials relating to the Yiddish Culture Society, Sholem Aleichem Folk Institute, Congress for Jewish Culture, YIVO.

83. BERLIN COLLECTION.
Records, 1931–1945. 24 ft. (RG 215)

These are fragmentary records of agencies of the Nazi government. They pertain to: the propaganda apparatus in Nazi-occupied Eastern Europe and its role in the "Final Solution of the Jewish Question"; to the work with collaborationist groups in the occupied countries; and to efforts against the underground resistance movements. The records originated primarily in the Reich Ministry for Propaganda and in the Reich Civil Administration for Occupied Eastern Territories (Reichskommisariat für das Ostland).

The records are organized in two main sub-groups: Materials relating to Germany and materials relating to the occupied countries. The latter is divided geographically and pertains to the following territories: Generalgouvernement, Occupied Eastern Territories (Lithuania, Latvia, Estonia, Byelorussia, Ukraine), Austria, Czechoslovakia, Rumania, Hungary, Yugoslavia, the Netherlands.

The collection consists of correspondence, memoranda, reports, minutes of meetings, clippings, posters, pamphlets, photographs, transcripts, organizational charts of various Nazi propaganda offices. The following topics are included: Nazi racial policy; racial evaluations and definitions; genealogical investigations; Nazi policy on religion, ethnicity and the Church; Church position on the Jewish question; anti-Jewish legislation and decrees in Germany before 1939 and in the occupied territories after 1939; aryanization of Jewish-owned businesses; confiscation of Jewish property; criminality among Jews.

Topics referred to in the official reports: anti-Nazi underground activities; partisan movements; Jewish resistance; Soviet espionage; the morale of the Red Army; attitudes of the local population toward Jews; Fascist organizations around the world; conditions in German POW camps; forced labor. Noteworthy reports are: confidential situation reports by local Nazi administrations, schedules of transports to death camps and numbers of deportees. Monthly reports of the Hauptabteilung Propaganda of the Generalgouvernement in Cracow, comprised of the weekly propaganda reports of the five districts—Warsaw, Radom, Lublin, Galicia, Cracow, 1942–1943—and pertaining to police actions, activities of resistance groups, economic conditions, food situation, black market, recruitment of Polish labor to Germany, epidemics, mortality statistics. Reports of the Governor of the District of Warsaw relating to the typhoid epidemic, slave labor, industrial production, and situation in the Warsaw ghetto. Police report of the assassination of Reinhard Heydrich, 1942.

Inventory, English.

84. BERMAN, LEVI (born 1895).
Papers, 1912–1978. 7 in. (RG 1249)

Yiddish poet. Contributed to *Shriftn, Zukunft, Freie Arbeiter Stimme*. Born in Pikeliai, Lithuania. Came to the United States in 1915.

Correspondence relating to Berman's literary work. Family correspondence. Manuscripts of poems, diaries.

85. BERNFELD, SIEGFRIED (1892–1953).
Papers, 1910–1922. 3 ft. 9 in. (RG 6)

Writer, educator, psychoanalyst. Organizer of the Zionist youth movement in Austria during and after World War I. Founder of several Jewish educational institutions in Austria including the Hebrew Pedagogium in Vienna. Lived in Austria, Germany, France, and from 1937 in the United States.

Correspondence, by-laws, minutes, programs, financial records of Jewish educational institutions in Austria and Germany: Jüdisches Institut für Jugendforschung und Erziehung (Jewish Institute for Youth Research and Education), 1920–1922; Arbeitskreis für Jüdische Erziehung (Study Group for Jewish Education), 1918–1919; Baumgarten Jewish Children's Home; other institutions.

Records of Jewish youth organizations in Austria and Germany including student organizations, sport and tourism associations such as Blau-Weiss (Blue-White). Clippings about youth organizations, 1915–1919. Typescript by Ernst Zwicker entitled "Problems of the Jewish Youth Movement."

Records relating to Jewish youth publications which Siegfried Bernfeld edited: *Anfang*, 1910–1922; *Jerubaal*, 1918–1919; *Jugendblätter*, 1918–1919.

Manuscripts by Bernfeld on topics related to education and Zionism.

Inventory, Yiddish, English.

86. BERNSTEIN, ABRAHAM MOSHE (1866–1932).
Papers, 1878–1933. 3 ft. 4 in. (RG 36)

Cantor, choir master, composer of Jewish liturgical and popular music, music teacher, musicologist and writer. Born in Byelorussia. Lived in Vilna.

The collection relates to Bernstein's career and consists of the following:

Printed musical works by Bernstein. Musical manuscripts by Bernstein. Liturgical works: Friday evening prayer service; Sabbath morning service; High Holiday prayers; Psalms; *zemirot*; secular works; children's songs, 12 notebooks. Ethnomusicological works and transcriptions. Arrangements by Bernstein. Works attributed to Bernstein.

Manuscripts of articles and essays by Bernstein relating to Gershon Sirota, Solomon Sulzer, Abraham Baer Birnbaum. Partial Yiddish translation of Ecclesiastes. Choral volumes and individual part books in manuscript, used by A.M. Bernstein and his choir at Taharot Hakodesh Synagogue, Vilna. Printed music by others: Samuel Alman, Mattiah Bensman, Eduard Birnbaum, D. Deutscher, Aron Friedman, Sh. Greentsayg, Erno Hoffman, Louis Lewandowski, Arno Nadel, David Nowakowski, Aron Marko Rothmuller, Nakhum Sternheim, Joshua Samuel Weisser, Eliakum Zunser. Musical manuscripts by others.

Manuscript of A.M. Bernstein's autobiography, *Gilgulim*. Obituaries of Bernstein. A chart of photographs of famous cantors. Family photos of the Bernstein and Punski families.

Inventory, English.

87. BERNSTEIN, HERMAN (1876–1935).
Papers, 1897–1935. 29 ft. 2 in. (RG 713)

Author, journalist, translator, playwright. Active in Jewish communal organizations. Secretary of the American Jewish Committee. Founder in 1914 and editor of *Der tog*, editor of the *Jewish Daily Bulletin*. Correspondent for the *New York Herald* in Russia, 1917–1920, and at the Paris Peace Conference, 1919. Instituted a libel suit in the 1920s against Henry Ford and the *Dearborn Independent* for publishing the *Protocols of the Elders of Zion*. U.S. envoy to Albania, 1931–1933. Born in Vladislavov (Kudirkos Naumiesti), Lithuania. Lived in Russia and the United States.

Correspondence, clippings, manuscripts, notes, reports, relating to Bernstein's journalistic, literary and diplomatic careers. Correspondence with well-known literary, political, communal, and society personalities, 1908–1935. Includes Cyrus Adler, Viscount Edmund H. Allenby, Joseph Barondess, Bernard Baruch, Henri Bergson, Hayyim Nahman Bialik, Jacob Billikopf, Vladimir Bourtzeff, Louis Brandeis, Robert Cecil, Fyodor Chaliapin, Jacob de Haas, Albert Einstein, Henry Ford, Felix Frankfurter, Herbert Hoover, Vladimir Jabotinsky, Horace M. Kallen, Peretz Hirschbein, Peter Kropotkin, Herbert Lehman, Louis Lipsky, Judah L. Magnes, Louis Marshall, Henry Morgenthau, Max Nordau, Adolph Simon Ochs, David de Sola Pool, Bernard G. Richards, Theodore Roosevelt, Julius Rosenwald, Jacob Schiff, Harry Schneiderman, Maurice Schwartz, George Bernard Shaw, Sholem Aleichem, Nathan Straus, Henrietta Szold, Chaim Tchernowitz, Leo Tolstoy, Samuel Untermyer, Henry Van Dyke, Lillian Wald, Felix Warburg, Chaim Weizmann, Jefferson Williams, Stephen Wise, Israel Zangwill.

Correspondence and other materials relating to Bernstein's post as U.S. ambassador to Albania. Materials pertaining to Bernstein's editorial work at *The Day, Jewish Tribune, New York Herald, Jewish Daily Bulletin*. Materials pertaining to Bernstein's involvement with the American Jewish Committee.

Correspondence with organizations and institutions including American Jewish Congress, *American Hebrew*, HIAS, *Jewish Chronicle* (London), Jewish Community of New York, *Menorah Journal, New York American, New York Times*, ORT, U.S. Department of State, Yiddish Art Theater, Zionist Organization of America.

Articles, clippings, correspondence and court materials relating to the Ford libel suit.

Miscellaneous documents and reports relating to the Paris Peace Conference, the Jewish situation in Russia, 1917–1920, Russian revolutionary events of 1917. News dispatches from Russia, 1917–1920s.

Translations by Bernstein of Russian writings by Leonid Andreyev, Anton Chekhov, Maksim Gorkii, Leo Tolstoy, Ivan Turgenev. Plays adapted by Bernstein from various languages. Interviews with celebrities including Ahad Ha'am, Henri Barbusse, Pope Benedict XV, I.V. Chicherin, Henry Ford, Amin al Husayni, Ignacy Paderewski, Marshal Józef Piłsudski, Walther Rathenau, Edmond de Rothschild, Hjalmar Schacht, Leo Tolstoy, Menahem Ussishkin, Chaim Weizmann, Count Sergey Iulyevich Witte.

Articles by Bernstein about Russian history, Jewish contemporary problems. Manuscripts, notes, outlines of books relating to the *Protocols of the Elders of Zion*. Biographies of American Jews. Clippings: articles and translations by Bernstein and articles about Bernstein. Personal papers of Bernstein.

Inventory, English.

Index, English.

88. BERNSTEIN, MORDECHAI (1905–1966).
Papers. 1 ft. 8 in. (RG 285)

YIVO representative in Germany, 1946–1950.

The collection consists of guides to Jewish documents in German archives, compiled by Bernstein. Holdings of state, municipal, ducal and ecclesiastical archives are listed.

89. BERSHADER BENEVOLENT SOCIETY.
Records, 1937–1949. 5 in. (RG 816)

Founded in 1912 in Brooklyn by immigrants from Bershad, Ukraine. Affiliated with the Erste Bershader K.U.V. (established in 1906) and the Bershader Progressive Association (established in 1934). Organized the Bershader Relief after World War I. The Relief was reactivated during World War II.

Constitution. Minutes of Bershader Book Committee, 1944, 1946. Memorial booklet on Bershad. Correspondence, anniversary journals. Miscellaneous materials collected on the history of the Jews in the Ukraine, and on Lomazer, Shumsker, and Soroker *landsmanshaftn.*

90. BESSARABIAN FEDERATION OF AMERICAN JEWS.
Records, 1940–1950. 5 in. (RG 1028)

Originally organized in 1940 as the United Bessarabian Federation. Incorporated in 1942 as the Federation of Bessarabian Societies of America, Inc. In 1944 changed name to Bessarabian Federation of American Jews, Inc. The federation's objective was to coordinate relief efforts of independent Bessarabian *landsmanshaftn* in America for residents of Bessarabia and Bessarabian refugees to the United States. Special projects included supporting Bessarabian orphans in France and building a housing project in Israel. Affiliated with a women's division. Dissolved in the early 1950s.

Materials pertaining to the United Bessarabian Federation, including resolutions, bulletins. Materials pertaining to the Federation of Bessarabian Societies of America: certificate of incorporation, 1942; constitution; financial records; records of relief work; membership and mailing lists; correspondence; lists and materials of affiliated organizations; photographs.

91. BESSARABIER PODOLIER BENEVOLENT SOCIETY.
   Records, 1933–1974. 5 in. (RG 1024)

Founded in 1954 by former members of the Jewish People's Fraternal Order (JPFO) of the International Workers' Order (IWO) when the latter order was dissolved during the McCarthy era. In 1930, a group of members of the Zwanitz-Podolier Branch 277 Workmen's Circle broke away to join the IWO as its Branch 277. This branch merged with another Workmen's Circle branch to form the Podolier Branch 277 IWO, later affiliated with yet another branch, renaming itself the Baltic Podolier Branch 277 IWO. Was affiliated with the Emma Lazarus Club #277 IWO. Some of the members of Branch 277 supported the Zwanitz-Podolier Relief Committee. In 1954, members of Branch 277 formed the East Bronx Cultural Society. This later merged with the former Bessarabier Branch 302 IWO, to form the Bessarabier Podolier B.S., Inc.

   Records of the Bessarabier Podolier B.S., Inc.. Minutes, 1958–1960. Financial papers. Anniversary journals. Photographs. Materials of the East Bronx Cultural Society (photocopies): certificate of incorporation, 1955; constitution; minutes. Materials of the Baltic Podolier Branch 277 IWO: speeches, meeting announcements; anniversary journal; photographs. Materials of the Podolier Branch 277 IWO, including "wall newspapers," 1932–1940s. Materials of the Bessarabier Branch 302 IWO, including: minutes, 1943–1947; personal papers of the donor; miscellaneous; photograph.

92. BETH HAMEDRASH HAGODOL (NEW YORK).
   Records, 1878–1949. 3 ft. (RG 365)

Oldest orthodox Eastern European synagogue in New York, founded in 1852.

   Record book of the synagogue for the period 1852–1880s compiled by the vice-president J.D. Eisenstein. Lists of members, 1852–1872. List of deceased members. History of the synagogue in Yiddish, English and Hebrew. List of officers elected, 1873–1888. Constitution. Financial report, 1887. Report of the Maos Hittim Committee, 1888. Constitution of the Burial Society. Minutes of meetings and financial records, 1878–1945. Records of synagogue seats and of the *hevrah kadisha*, 1890–1894. Sale of cemetery plots. Membership ledgers, 1889–1925.

93. BIALLY, ANNA SAFRAN (born 1902).
   Papers, 1914–1916. 5 in. (RG 680)

Yiddish writer, poet. Contributed to periodicals such as *Nay lebn, Morgn frayhayt, Yidishe kultur, Yidish amerike, Naye prese*. Born in Siedlce, Poland.

   The papers consist of a photostatic copy of a five-volume diary, handwritten in Yiddish. The diary describes Bially's trip to the United States and the first few years of her life as an immigrant.

94. BIALOSTOTZKY, BENJAMIN JACOB (1892–1962).
   Papers, ca. 1929–1963. 5 ft. 10 in. (RG 479)

Yiddish journalist, poet, teacher. Active in the organization of early Yiddish schools in the United States. Teacher in the National Radical and Workmen's Circle schools. Member of the Pedagogical Council of the Workmen's Circle. Active in various Jewish cultural organizations. Contributed poems and essays to many Yiddish periodicals, including the *Jewish Daily Forward* (NY). Co-editor of *Yunge yidishe kemfer, Di kinder velt*. On editorial staff of

Yidisher kemfer and *Di tsayt*. Born in Pumpian, district of Kaunas. Immigrated to the United States in 1911.

Typescripts of Bialostotzky's works, essays, letters, speeches. Typescripts of works by others. Clippings of articles by and about Bialostotzky's writings. Clippings about other authors. Bialostotzky's notes about various Yiddish writers. Correspondence with Yiddish literary figures including Shlomo Bickel, Menahem Boraisha, Daniel Charney, David Einhorn, Ben Zion Goldberg, Abba Gordin, Chaim Shloyme Kazdan, Leon Kobrin, Malka Lee, Leibush Lehrer, H. Leivick, Raphael Mahler, Kalman Marmor, Shmuel Niger, Joseph Opatoshu, David Pinsky, Melech Ravitch, Abraham Reisen, A.A. Roback, Israel Jacob Schwartz, Mark Schweid, Zalman Shneur, Nahum Shtif, Abraham Sutzkever, Jennings (Yehudah) Tofel, Lazar Weiner, Max Weinreich, Berish Weinstein.

Inventory, English.

95. BIBERSTEIN, HANS and STEIN, ERNA .
Papers, 1884–1960. 1 ft. 3 in. (RG 1256)

Physicians from Breslau, Germany. Settled in New York.

Family papers of the Bibersteins. Correspondence, beginning with their courtship until 1931. Photographs of the same period including several photographs from military service in the German army during World War I. About 200 illustrated postcards.

96. BICKEL, SHLOMO (1896–1969).
Papers, 1920s–1969. 15 ft. 6 in. (RG 569)

Lawyer, essayist, literary critic, journalist. Active in the Zionist movement. Contributed to *Literarishe bleter* (Warsaw), *Der tog* (NY), *Zukunft* (NY), *Yidisher Kemfer* (NY), *Freie Arbeiter Stimme* (NY), *In zikh* (NY). Editor of *Frayhayt*, a Labor-Zionist weekly in Czernowitz, Rumania. Secretary of the Poalei Zion party in Czernowitz, 1919–1922. Chairman of the Kultur Lige in Bucharest. Executive Council member of the Alveltlekher Yidisher Kultur Kongres (World Congress for Jewish Culture) in New York. Member of YIVO Executive Board. Vice-chairman of the Yiddish PEN Club, New York. Born in Uścieszko (Ustechko), East Galicia, Poland. Lived in Bucharest, Rumania, until 1939 when he emigrated to the United States.

Manuscripts by S. Bickel including *Mishpokhe Hartshik*. Manuscripts by others including S. Bloch, Jacob Botoshansky, Dr. Eliezer Bickel, Rabbi Abraham Hertzberg. Correspondence with individuals: Salo W. Baron, Dr. Joseph Bernfeld, Marc Chagall, Daniel Charney, Abraham Golomb, Abba Gordin, Raphael Mahler, Itzik Manger, Shmuel Niger, Shlomo Noble, David Opatoshu, Mendel Osherowitch, David Pinsky, Melech Ravitch, Mordkhe Schaechter, Jacob Shatzky, Abraham Sutzkever, Joseph Tenenbaum, Jonas Turkow, Menashe Unger, Max Weinreich, Uriel Weinreich, Aaron Zeitlin, Chaim Zhitlowsky.

Correspondence with organizations. Clippings of articles by Bickel from various periodicals. Obituaries on Bickel's death. Correspondence and manuscripts relating to articles written by S. Bickel for the *Encyclopedia Judaica*. Lectures, radio talks, diaries. Personal documents. Some papers of Yetta Bickel, wife of S. Bickel.

Inventory, Yiddish.

97. BIELINKY, JACQUES (1881–ca. 1943).
Papers, 1926–1942. 1 ft. 8 in. (RG 239)

Publicist, writer. Died in the Majdanek death camp. Lived in Russia, France.

Correspondence with artists, journalists, periodicals, 1926–1940. Clippings of Bielinky's articles, 1926–1939, including articles from *L'Avenir Illustré, Le Judaïsme Séphardi*. Manuscripts of Bielinky's articles. Bielinky's diary of life in Paris under the Nazis, 1941–1942.

98. BIELSKER BRUDERLICHER UNTERSHTITZUNGS VEREIN.
Records, 1924–1949, 1975. 3 in. (RG 1046)

Founded in New York in 1888 by immigrants from Bielsk Podlaski, Poland. Established a loan fund in 1902 and an old age and disability relief fund in 1921. Affiliated with the United Bielsker Relief which aided *landslayt* in Israel. Associated with a ladies auxiliary.

Anniversary souvenir journals, 1924, 1928, 1938, 1948. Membership directory, 1949. Correspondence. Memorial book, 1975.

99. BIENSTOCK, VICTOR M.
Papers, 1941–1945. 5 in. (RG 693)

Journalist, war correspondent to U.S. press agencies during World War II. Reported from Portugal, Italy and France.

Bienstock's dispatches as well as other materials such as bulletins, mimeographed underground newspapers, pamphlets, leaflets. The materials relate to: war events in Western Europe, 1941, and in Italy and France, 1944; situation of Jews in Western Europe; concentration camps Gurs and Rivesaltes; partisans; underground publications in France such as *Undzer vort* and *Undzer kamf*.

100. BILMES, ISIDORE M. (1900–1962).
Papers. 5 in. (RG 694)

Yiddish writer. Born in the Ukraine. Settled in United States in 1920.

Manuscripts of works by Bilmes including playscripts and short stories.

101. BIOGRAPHICAL MATERIALS.
Collection. 23 ft. (RG 103)

This subject collection was assembled in the YIVO Archives from miscellaneous sources.

The collection consists primarily of clippings relating to Jewish literary and communal figures. The materials are arranged alphabetically by name of person.

102. BIRCZER YOUNG MEN'S BENEVOLENT SOCIETY.
Records, 1926–1954. 5 in. (RG 1003)

Founded in New York in 1897 by immigrants from Bircza, Poland. Established old-age and loan funds for members.

Constitution. Minutes, 1925–1954 (Yiddish/German written in Roman alphabet). Miscellaneous materials, including letter from artisans union in Bircza, 1926.

103. BIRMAN, MEIR (1891–1955).
Papers, 1918–1955. 5 microfilm reels. (RG 352)

Director of the HIAS office in Harbin, and later of the HIAS office in Shanghai.

The collection consists of materials relating primarily to Jewish immigration in the Far East.

Records of the Central Information Bureau for Jewish War Sufferers in the Far East, 1918–1947: minutes of meetings; correspondence with JDC, HIAS, HICEM, Jewish Community of Harbin; reports of activities, newspaper clippings; financial materials. Records of HIAS and HICEM in Shanghai, 1940s–1950s: financial reports, monthly activities reports; correspondence with HIAS, New York, and other organizations. Association of Immigrants from China, Tel Aviv: list of immigrants to Israel from Harbin and Tientsin. Correspondence with Jewish organizations in Shanghai. Correspondence with Jewish organizations and individuals, 1940s–1950s, various countries. Manuscripts and clippings of articles by M. Birman on the history of the Jewish community in the Far East. Personal papers of M. Birman including personal documents, correspondence with relatives and friends, New Year's greetings.

Inventory, English.

104. BIZONER CHEBRA B'NAI SHAUL.
Records, 1908–1976. 5 in. (RG 934)

Founded in New York in 1872 by immigrants from Bieżuń (Bizun), Poland, and dissolved in 1978. Also known as Bizoner Chebra Beis Shaul. The society provided burial grounds and had its own synagogue. A related group is the Independent Bizoner Congregation (founded 1907) which continued to function into the 1980s.

Minutes (Yiddish), 1908–1919. Minutes (English), 1919–1933, 1934–1947. Dues ledger. Membership records. Correspondence.

105. BLANK, JACOB (?–1989).
Papers, 1980–1986. 10 ft. (RG 1292)

Yiddish teacher and lecturer. Worked in Workmen's Circle schools and in Camp Boiberik (Rhinebeck, New York). Born in Międzyrzec. Settled in New York in 1930.

Manuscripts of lectures and speeches, primarily about Yiddish writers, and about the town of Międzyrzec.

106. BLANKSTEIN, LAZAR (1884–1973).
Papers, 1940s–1973. 6 ft. 3 in. (RG 1255)

Collector for YIVO. Specialized in gathering Yiddish and Hebrew proverbs. Born in Cracow, Poland. Came to the United States in 1941.

Alphabetized collection of proverbs in Yiddish, Hebrew and other languages. Photocopies of parts of old Yiddish and Hebrew books pertaining to folklore. Collection of biblical citations with comments. Notebooks with notations and proverbs. Correspondence, including letters from Dov Sadan.

107. BLINKIN, MEIR (1879–1915).
Papers. 5 in. (RG 1152)

Yiddish writer. Contributed to *Zukunft, Yidisher kemfer, Dos yidishe folk, Folksblat, Yidishe arbeter velt, Dos naye lebn.* Born in Pereyaslav, Ukraine. Immigrated to the United States in 1904.

The papers consist of correspondence, copies of Yiddish stories, translations from English into Yiddish, and photographs.

108. BLOCH, CHAIM (born 1881).
  Papers, 1920s–1960s. 3 ft. 4 in. (RG 513)

Biblical and Talmudic scholar. Born in Hungary, brought up in Delatyn, Galicia, lived in Vienna from 1914 until 1938. Emigrated to the United States in 1939. Died in New York.

Correspondence with rabbis, scholars, including: Rabbi Morris Adler, Rabbi Abraham Ben Yona Aitingen (Dukla), Rabbi Dr. Joseph Breuer, Rabbi Joel Fink, Rabbi Gershon Hager, Rabbi Menashe Klein, Rabbi Eliezer Z. Portugal, Rabbi Abraham Schischa, Rabbi Ephraim E. Yolles (Philadelphia).

Scholars and writers include: Gershom Bader, Shlomo Bickel, Eric Fisher, Nathan Michael Gelber, Ezriel Guenzig, Karpel Lippe, Yochanan Twersky. Rabbinic correspondence includes responsa. Correspondence with organizations. Correspondence from well known rabbinical and yeshiva personalities to Abraham Meyers. Manuscripts by Bloch including typescripts of his book *Sefer heikhal l'divrei hazal u pitgameihem.*

Inventory, Yiddish.

109. BLOWSTEIN, SIMON DAVID (ca. 1862–1932).
  Papers, 1919–1920. 2 1/2 in. (RG 675)

Lawyer, writer. Published a series of articles in the *Jewish Daily Forward* about the pogroms in the Ukraine in 1919–1920. Born in Szarogród (Shargorod), Podolia, Ukraine.

Manuscripts on pogroms against Ukrainian Jews. History of the Jewish community in Szarogród from the sixteenth century to 1920. Biographies of the rabbis of Szarogród.

110. BLUM, ABRAHAM (1893–1960).
  Papers. 3 ft. 4 in. (RG 426)

Jewish playwright and translator. Technical advisor to Abe Stark, president of the New York City Council. Lived in Russia, the United States.

Manuscripts of plays written or translated by Blum.

111. BLUM, BORUKH (1888–1965).
  Papers, 1930s–1960s. 8 in. (RG 1275)

Yiddish writer. Contributed to *Morgn frayhayt* and *Jewish Daily Forward.* Born in the Ukraine. Settled in New York in 1910.

Manuscript and typescripts of short stories.

112. BLUMENFELD, DIANA (1903–1961) and TURKOW, JONAS (1898–1988).
  Papers. 1 ft. 3 in. (RG 355)

Diana Blumenfeld-Turkow, wife of Jonas Turkow. Yiddish actress. Born in Warsaw. Prominent in the Yiddish theater in Poland and other countries. Settled in the United States in 1947.

Jonas Turkow, eminent theater personality, writer, civic leader. Born in Warsaw, Poland. Performed with a number of Yiddish ensembles in Poland. Performed in and directed Yiddish and Polish films. Active in the underground movement in the Warsaw ghetto. Left Poland in 1946 for a tour of the DP camps in Western Europe. Came to the United States in 1947. Settled in Israel in 1966.

Playbills, posters, clippings, tapes, financial materials, relating to Blumenfeld's and Turkow's theatrical careers in Poland and the United States. Materials relating to tours in Europe, the United States, Canada, Israel, South America, 1940s–1950s. Materials on pre-World War II performances in Poland.

113. BNAI ELEAZAR.
Records, 1926–1981. 5 in. (RG 1113)

Founded in 1925, organized in 1926 and incorporated in 1927 as a fraternal organization for descendants of Eleazar Friedman. The family originated in Wołkowysk, Byelorussia. Provides burial benefits. There is a branch in California known as B'nai Eleazar West.

Minute books, 1926–1939, 1940–1944, 1944–1951, 1951–1953. Three photographs, including one of Eleazar Friedman. Constitution, 1944, and constitutional amendments. Banquet programs. Miscellaneous materials including genealogical and historical information about the family.

114. BNAI PEARL FAMILY CIRCLE.
Records, 1923–1967. 2 1/2 in. (RG 1214)

Founded 1922 in New York by descendants of Pearl Gorlin.

Minutes, 1923–1967. Constitution. History of organization. Photograph of family members at Bar Mitzvah of David Levy, 1933.

115. BNAI REZITZA ASSOCIATION.
Records, 1936, 1956–1974. 8 in. (RG 918)

Founded in 1893 by immigrants from Rezekne (Rus. Rezhitsa), Latvia. Incorporated in 1927. Originally organized to establish a synagogue, located on Forsyth Street, New York. Affiliated with a ladies auxiliary.

Constitution. Minutes, 1956–1970. Financial records. Correspondence. Cemetery map.

116. BNEIS RACHEL LADIES CHARITY SOCIETY OF BROWNSVILLE.
Records, 1931–1957. 10 in. (RG 608)

Charity society based in Brownsville, a section of Brooklyn, New York.

Minute book, 1946–1957. Ledgers, journals, 1931–1956. List of members. Accounts of dues, 1931–1937, 1946–1953.

117. BOGIN, ANNA (born 1899).
Papers, 1950s–1960s. 5 in. (RG 565)

Yiddish poet and writer. Contributed to *Freie Arbeiter Stimme* (NY), *Zukunft* (NY), *Feder*, *Der shpigl* (Argentina). Born in Postawa, Byelorussia. Immigrated to the United States in 1911.

The collection consists of manuscripts of Bogin's poems and short stories, and some correspondence.

118. BOGOPOLER UNTERSTUTZUNGS VEREIN.
   Records, 1917–1975. 5 in. (RG 895)

Founded in New York in 1893 by immigrants from Bogopol, Ukraine. Established a *gmilas khesed* (interest-free loan) fund to aid needy members. Sent relief to Bogopol during World War I and World War II.
   Constitution. Minutes, 1943–1963. Financial records, 1930s–1960s. Membership records. Materials pertaining to burial, including three cemetery maps, 1925–1973. Materials pertaining to anniversary celebrations, including souvenir journals. Meeting announcements, 1940s–1970s.

119. BONUS, BEN (1920–1984) and BERN, MINA (born 1917).
   Papers, ca. 1940–1983. 1 ft. 8 in. (RG 1168)

Yiddish actors, husband and wife team.
   Ben Bonus performed with various companies in the United States. He excelled in the revue and was also prominent in dramatic roles. Born in Horodenka, Poland. Came to the United States in 1929.
   Mina Bern was born in Bielsk Podlaski, Poland. Performed on the Yiddish stage in Poland, and, during the war, in the Soviet Union. After the war, played in Hebrew theaters in Israel. Came to the United States in 1949.
   The collection relates to the theatrical careers of Bonus and Bern and consists primarily of printed and manuscript music and lyrics, and scripts of plays. Also includes photographs, flyers, programs, posters, and clippings.
   Photographs cataloged in STAGEPIX.

120. BOOKSTEIN, ABRAHAM (born 1877).
   Papers. 10 in. (RG 386)

Yiddish writer. Wrote for *Der tog, Freie Arbeiter Stimme, Morgn zhurnal*. Born in the Ukraine, settled in the United States.
   Manuscripts of A. Bookstein.

121. BORAISHA, MENAHEM (1888–1949).
   Papers, 1915–1957. 2 ft. 6 in. (RG 641)

Yiddish writer, poet. Born Menachem Goldberg. Contributed to *Haynt* (Warsaw), *Yidishe vokhnblat* (Warsaw), *Der tog* (NY), *Freie Arbeiter Stimme* (NY), *Frayhayt* (NY), *Di vokh* (NY). Born in Brest-Litovsk. In 1914, traveled to Switzerland and from there to the United States where he settled.
   The papers relate to Boraisha's literary career and consist of correspondence with Yiddish literary figures and organizations, clippings, manuscripts, photographs, and personal documents. Correspondents include Mendl Elkin, Aaron Glanz-Leieles, Peretz Hirschbein, Reuben Iceland, David Ignatoff, Berl Lapin, H. Leivick, Kadia Molodowsky, Shmuel Niger, Joseph Opatoshu, Abraham Sutzkever, Aaron Zeitlin, Chaim Zhitlowsky. Family correspondence.
   Inventory, Yiddish.

122. BORENSTEIN, JULIUS (1889–1975).
   Papers, 1960s–1972. 5 in. (RG 658)

Chairman, YIVO Executive Board. Vice-president and treasurer of the Workmen's Circle. Vice-president, Jewish Labor Committee. Lived in the United States.

YIVO correspondence, 1965–1972. Letters from Leibush Lehrer, H. Leivick, Abraham Sutzkever, Max Weinreich, and others. Correspondence with institutions.

123. BORNSTEIN, ABRAHAM.
Collection, 17th–19th century. 148 items or ca. 1 ft. (RG 224)

Collector.

A collection of textual fragments and prints. The fragments consist of 148 illustrated title and text pages of *mahzorim* (festival prayer books), *sidurim* (standard prayer books), the Pentateuch, scriptures, Hebrew grammar books and secular works. The prints consist of thirteen items by Ben Shahn (Dreyfus trial), Bezalel Schatz, Louis Lozowick, and six prints by Mané-Katz, based on the novel *Stempenyu* by Sholem Aleichem.

Inventory, English.

124. BOROUGH OF BROOKLYN LODGE.
Records, 1933–1965. 3 in. (RG 947)

Founded in 1898. Benefits included loans for members. Dissolved in 1965.

Rules and by-laws. Financial records. Loan fund materials. Cemetery records. Correspondence. Seal.

125. BRAINSKER BROTHERS AID SOCIETY.
Records, 1924–1971. 2 1/2 in. (RG 980)

Founded in New York in 1894 by immigrants from Bransk (Rus. Bryansk), Poland. Provided members with a loan fund. Active until 1979.

Minutes, 1963–1971. Materials pertaining to burial. Anniversary journal.

126. BRESLOVER AID SOCIETY.
Records, 1937–1984. 10 in. (RG 1213)

Founded in 1913 in Brooklyn, New York, by *landslayt* from Bratslav, Ukraine.

Correspondence, especially concerning benefits and cemetery matters. Financial records. Copy of poem describing society's history and listing names of several members.

127. BREZINER SICK AND BENEVOLENT SOCIETY.
Records, 1908–1976. 10 in. (RG 809)

Founded in New York in 1896 by immigrants from Brzeziny, Poland, and chartered in 1899. Established the Breziner Ladies Auxiliary in 1932 and the Breziner Relief Committee in 1945. Maintains ties and conducts joint activities with the Breziner *landsmanshaft* in Israel.

Constitution. Minutes, 1953–1970. Financial records pertaining to relief activities in Poland, Germany, Israel. Correspondence pertaining to World War II relief activities, 1941–1976. Untitled manuscript of Jacob Fogel's memoirs of Brzeziny. Anniversary journals, newspaper clippings, photographs, miscellaneous membership records, materials pertaining to the Breziner memorial book.

128. BRIESEN JEWISH COMMUNITY COUNCIL.
Records, 1871–1926. 3 ft. 5 in. (RG 15)

Town in Northern Poland, part of the German Empire until 1918. Known in Polish as Wąbrzeźno.

The bulk of the records cover the period when Briesen was in the German Empire and a small number of documents relate to the period following the town's return to Poland in 1918.

General records. Minute book. Materials relating to the election of municipal officers. Materials concerning the building of a *mikveh* (ritual bath house). Correspondence between the community and the Deutsch-Israelitischer Gemeindebund (German-Jewish Community Board) and the Verband der Deutschen Juden (Union of German Jews). Financial records, bill receipts.

Records of the communal board. Announcements of meetings. Correspondence, minutes of meetings, election materials, lists of officials, correspondence with the government.

Records relating to religious activities. Lists, correspondence, circulars relating to synagogue activities, including documents about the sale of the synagogue. Records relating to the hiring of a rabbi, cantor, ritual slaughterer, teacher.

Records relating to social welfare: Appeals for aid. List of contributions for cholera victims in Dobrzyń. Conference about wandering beggars. Correspondence and circulars from orphans' homes, 1903–1921. Correspondence with the Central Welfare Board of German Jews (Zentralwohlfahrtsstelle der Deutschen Juden).

Records of the Jüdischer Leseverein (Jewish Reading Society), 1901–1908, including agendas, lists of members.

Inventory, English.

129. BROMBERG, AARON (1891–1958).
Papers, ca. 1915–1950. 1 ft. 8 in. (RG 458)

Pioneer in the Yiddish school movement. Began his teaching career in Toronto, 1909. Lived in Toronto, Canada.

The collection consists primarily of educational materials and reflects Bromberg's work in Yiddish schools and organizations in Toronto. Children's publications and playscripts. Educational materials relating to the Bible and Jewish holidays. Notes for courses in Jewish history, Yiddish grammar. Curricula. Minutes of the Workmen's Circle, Branch 293.

130. BROWNSTEIN, R. Y.
Collection, 1911–1960s. ca. 4 ft. (RG 342)

Collector for YIVO, Philadelphia.

The bulk of the collection consist of scrapbooks containing information on the Jewish community of Philadelphia and other subjects.

131. BROWNSTONE, EZEKIEL A. M. (1897–1968).
Papers, ca. 1928–1965. 3 ft. 9 in. (RG 344)

Yiddish writer, poet. Contributed to *Kanader yid* (Winnipeg), *Der kamf* (Toronto), *Indzl* (Bucharest), *Di vokh* (Brussels), *Di goldene keyt* (Tel Aviv), *Freie Arbeiter Stimme*, *Zukunft*. Born in Novoselitsa, Bessarabia. Immigrated to Canada in 1913. Settled in Los Angeles.

Correspondence with writers including Shalom Asch, Peretz Hirschbein, H. Leivick, Shmuel Niger, Joseph Opatoshu, Israel Joshua Singer. Correspondence with family members and organizations. Poems and articles by Brownstone. Press clippings, 1921–1932. Manuscripts of other writers. Photographs of writers.

132. BRUSILOW, NATHAN (1892–1977).
Papers. 1 ft. 3 in. (RG 692)

Physician, writer. Born in Ovruch, Ukraine. Settled in the United States in 1924.
Manuscripts of Brusilow's writings, most of them unpublished.

133. BRYKS, RACHMIL (1912–1974).
Papers, 1945–1974. 11 ft. (RG 268)

Yiddish author, survivor of the Łódź ghetto. Lived in Poland, Sweden and the United States.
Correspondence with writers, publishers, editors, family and friends. Personal documents. Manuscripts of Bryks's books about the Łódź ghetto. Clippings about Bryks and about his works.

134. BUCHWALD, NATHANIEL (1890–1956).
Papers, 1938–1964. 3 in. (RG 1260)

Theater critic. Wrote for the Yiddish daily *Morgn frayhayt* from 1922 until 1956. Born in Labun, Ukraine. Came to the United States in 1910.
Typed translation of Buchwald's book *Teatr*. Photographs, pamphlets, clippings.

135. BUCZACZ-AMERICAN BENEVOLENT SICK AND AID SOCIETY.
Records, 1921–1960. 5 in. (RG 844)

Founded in New York in 1905 by immigrants from Buchach (Pol. Buczacz; Yid. Betshutsh, Bechuch), Ukraine. Affiliated with the United Buczaczer Ladies Auxiliary, First Buczaczer Society and the Circle of Buczaczer Friends. The Circle of Buczaczer Friends was organized in 1942. It grew out of the Betshutsher Literarisher Fareyn (Buczaczer Literary Society) which was founded in 1916 and reorganized in 1921 as the Betshutsher Literarisher Klub. It provided social, educational, and cultural activities for members and published a humorous newspaper read aloud at meetings. The Circle dissolved in 1970.
Constitution. Minutes, 1937–1948 (German, English). Financial records, 1942–1958. *Betshutsher nudnik*, handwritten Yiddish newspaper, three issues, 1921–1922. Materials pertaining to the Circle of Buczaczer Friends. Photographs.

136. BUGATCH, SAMUEL (1898–1984).
Papers, 1924–1973. 1 ft. 6 in. (RG 712)

Jewish composer, conductor of choral groups and synagogue choirs, lecturer, writer. Music director, Beth Tefiloh Synagogue, Baltimore, and Temple Adath Israel, Bronx. Composed and arranged liturgical and secular works. Compiled an anthology of Yiddish and Hebrew songs. Born in Rogachev, Byelorussia. Immigrated to the United States in 1913 and settled in Baltimore.
The collection consists of music manuscripts of Bugatch's original works, arrangements

of works by other composers. Included are arrangements of works by Osias Abrass, Joel Engel, Samuel Naumbourg, David Nowakowski, Josef (Yosele) Rosenblatt, Zeidel Rovner. Manuscripts by other composers. Included are liturgical works, Yiddish and Hebrew folk and art songs.

Inventory, Yiddish, English.

137. BULOFF, JOSEPH (1899–1985) and KADISON, LUBA.
Papers, 1920s–1970s. 8 ft. 4 in. (RG 1146)

Yiddish actors, husband and wife.

Joseph Buloff was a leading actor of the Yiddish and American stages. Appeared with the Vilna Troupe from 1918 to 1927. Came to the United States in 1928 on an invitation from Maurice Schwartz, and joined the Yiddish Art Theater. Performed in Yiddish in the Americas, Europe, South Africa, Israel. Directed and acted in nearly 200 plays in Russian, Polish and Rumanian. Began performing in English in 1936. Had a long and distinguished career on Broadway. Appeared in films from 1940. Frequently performed on television.

Luba Kadison is the daughter of Leib Kadison, the founder of the Vilna Troupe, and began her career as a member of this ensemble. In the United States she played leading female roles in the Yiddish Art Theater.

The collection relates to the theatrical careers of Joseph Buloff and Luba Kadison.

Manuscripts and printed versions of about 80 plays in Yiddish, English, German and Russian. Original drawings by Leib Kadison. Photographs of the Vilna Troupe, Joseph Buloff, Luba and Leib Kadison. Leib Kadison's ink drawings of Yiddish theater advertisements. Theater programs, 1920s–1970s. Clippings of reviews of productions. Musical scores to five Yiddish plays. Typescript of Joseph Buloff's memoirs. Seven audio cassettes of J. Buloff interviews and recitations conducted by Irving Genn, 1976–1978. Flyers, programs, posters and clippings for performances by Buloff and Kadison in the United States, Israel, Argentina and elsewhere. Correspondence of J. Buloff, 1960s–1970s. Publicity photographs of Buloff and Kadison. Press notices of Luba Kadison.

Inventory, English.
Photographs cataloged in STAGEPIX.

138. BUND ARCHIVES.
Collection, ca. 1870–1992. 720 ft. (RG 1400)

The Bund Archives was established in 1899 in Geneva by the Bund, a Jewish political party espousing socialist democratic ideology as well as cultural Yiddishism and Jewish national autonomism. Colloquially known as the Bund during the entire span of its existence, the full name of the party was changed several times following geographic dislocations of the party's center. These names were, in chronological progression, as follows: Algemeyner Yidisher Arbeter Bund in Lite, Poyln un Rusland (General Jewish Workers' Bund in Lithuania, Poland and Russia), 1897–1921; Algemeyner Yidisher Arbeter Bund in Poyln, 1919–1948; Jewish Labor Bund, and International Jewish Labor Bund, post-World War II until present. Other changes of names occurred intermittently during the course of the Bund's history in connection with factional splits or mergers. Finally, smaller Bund groups operating in various countries have adopted their own local names.

The Bund was founded as a clandestine revolutionary organization in Vilna on October 7, 1897, dedicated to the overthrow of the Tsarist system in Russia and to the defense of the Jewish working masses. In March 1898 its delegates participated in the founding of the

Russian Social Democratic Labor Party (RSDRP). The Bund joined the RSDRP as an autonomous group. In 1903 the Bund split with the RSDRP over the question of autonomy, but rejoined the Russian party again in 1906. After the final split in the RSDRP between the Bolsheviks and the Mensheviks in 1912, the Bund sided with the Mensheviks remaining in alliance with the Menshevik party until the dissolution of both the Bund and the Mensheviks in Soviet Russia in the years 1921–1923.

During its Russian period, the Bund adopted an ideological and political platform proclaiming Marxism of the social-democratic persuasion, as opposed to Leninism, and Jewish national and cultural autonomism, as opposed to nationalism and Zionism. After the failure of the 1905 revolution, the Bund's political tactics evolved from revolutionary violence to political action by legal means.

The party's ideological tenets as well as political decisions were adopted at the general conferences which were the Bund's highest authority. The Bund in the Russian empire was led by a Central Committee. Outside Russia the party was represented by its Foreign Committee which was based in Geneva, Switzerland. During the period of the Bund's illegal and semi-legal status in Russia, the Foreign Committee assumed many important organizational functions of the party apparatus. The Bund in Russia was partly legalized in 1906 but it did not dissolve its underground network. In 1912 the Bund took part for the first time in parliamentary elections to the Duma. After October 1917 an ideological dispute within the party divided its ranks and eventually resulted in the breakup of the Bund in Russia. In March 1919 a Communist group within the Bund in the Ukraine left the party and formed the Kombund (*Komunistisher bund*, Communist Bund). In 1921 the Communist faction of the Bund in Russia resolved to join the Russian Communist party (Bolsheviks). A minority established the short-lived Social Democratic Bund. By 1923 the last holdout groups of the Bund in Russia were eliminated from political life.

In the aftermath of World War I and the October Revolution, the center of the Bund was moved to Poland. In December 1917 an independent central committee for Poland was elected. At the first convention of the Polish Bund in April 1920 the Bund merged with the Jewish Social Democratic Party of Galicia. A sharp conflict of opinion developed in the party in 1920 over the question of joining the Comintern, but, despite a majority resolution in favor of such a step, it did not come to pass. However, this gave the Polish government a cause to severely persecute the party in the years 1920–1924, almost to the point of extinction. Nevertheless the Bund continued to be active in interwar Poland, becoming the largest and most influential Jewish labor party. In addition to its own network, the Bund controlled entirely or in large part other groups: the youth organizations SKIF (Sotsyalistisher Kinder Farband—Socialist Children's Union) and Zukunft (the Future), the sports federation Morgnshtern (Morning Star), the publishing house Kultur Lige, the Yiddish school network TSYSHO (Tsentrale Yidishe Shul Organizatsye—Central Yiddish School Organization), and more. An important power base for the Bund were artisan associations and trade unions. Through participation in elections, representatives of the Bund won many seats in Jewish communal institutions and in municipal councils across the country. In 1930 the Bund joined the Socialist International. During the Nazi occupation of Poland, the Bund was active in the Jewish resistance movement and was represented in the Polish National Council in-exile in London. After the war the Bund was re-established among the Jewish survivors in Poland, only to be dissolved in 1948 along with the other non-communist parties in the country.

Apart from having close ties with socialist groups in the United States, the Bund did not establish its presence in this country until after the outbreak of World War II. American representation of the Bund was established in New York in 1941. In 1947 the World Coordinating Committee of Bundist and Affiliated Jewish Socialist Organizations was formed at the

Bund world conference in Brussels. New York became the headquarters of the reconstituted Bund, also known as the International Jewish Labor Bund. This group is comprised of the Bund organizations in the United States and Israel, and of the older Bund groups which already existed in various countries before World War II.

The Bund Archives was founded in 1899 in Geneva to facilitate gathering and preserving vital organizational records and printed matter. The choice of place was necessitated by harsh political conditions in Russia where, due to police repressions, the Bund remained underground. In 1919 the Bund Archives was transferred to Berlin where it found quarters in the German Social-Democratic Party (SPD) building. Once again, unfavorable political conditions prevented moving the archives to Poland which by then had become the center of the Bund movement. In 1933 the Archives was smuggled over the border into France and relocated to Paris. In 1944 the Archives was captured by the Germans, but was abandoned when the German army was forced into a hasty retreat from Paris. In 1951 the Bund Archives was brought to New York where it continued its operations as part of the World Cooordinating Committee of the Bund. In 1992 the Bund Archives was transferred to the YIVO Institute and placed in the custody of the YIVO Archives. Bund archivists, in chronological order, included: Franz Kursky, David Meyer, Hillel Kempinski, Benjamin Nadel.

The Bund Archives was formed as a topical collection on the history of the Bund and on related topics such as Jewish and general socialist groups, other political movements, Yiddish culture, and the Holocaust. In addition, a large number of organizations and individuals donated their records and papers to the Bund Archives.

Among papers of individuals deposited in the Bund Archives, the following should be mentioned: Raphael Abramovitch; Israel Abramson; Boris Aisurovich; Aleksandrowicz (Max) family; Meir David Alter; Berl Ambaras; Grigori Aronson; David Berkingoff; Leib Berman; Lucjan Blit; Dina Blond; Abraham Cahan; Jacob Celemenski; Joseph Cohen; Lazar Epstein; Rafal Federman; Leo Finkelstein; Jerzy Gliksman; Bernard Goldstein; Aaron Goodleman; Liebman Hersch; Jacob Hertz; Morris Hillquit; Herschel Himelfarb; Ludwik Honigwill; Arcadius Kahan; Chaim Shloyme Kazdan; Joseph Kissman; Vladimir Kosovsky; Franz Kursky; Jacob Levin; Isaac Luden; Abraham Manievich; Shlomo Mendelson; Meir Mendelson; John Mill; Shmuel Milman; Emanuel Nowogrodsky; Leon Oler; Rose Pesotta; Noah Portnoy; Emanuel Scherer; Elias Schulman; Pinchas Schwartz; Boruch Shefner; Isaac Nachman Steinberg; Mendl Sudarski; Szaje Szechatow; Ahrne Thorne; Tsivyon (Ben-Zion Hofman); Charles Zimmerman; William Zuckerman; Arthur Shmuel Zygelboim. Records of organizations include United Hebrew Trades, various locals of the International Ladies Garment Workers Union, and the Amalgamated Clothing and Textile Workers Union.

The collection is noted for its vast quantities of printed matter ranging from leaflets and pamphlets to complete runs of periodicals. Included are illegal propaganda pamphlets and periodicals of the Bund's earliest period which were published abroad and smuggled into Russia, and proclamations and brochures printed in clandestine printing shops inside Russia. Printed materials are richly represented in all other topical divisions of the Archives. The collection also includes photographs, posters, minutes, reports, correspondence, financial ledgers, manuscripts, biographical materials.

The collection is divided into the following subject areas:

Jewish Labor Bund: Jewish labor movement before the rise of the Bund. Bund in Russia, 1897–1923 (including records of the Bund Foreign Commitee in Geneva, 1898–1919; of the Central Bureau of Bundist Groups Abroad; and of Bund cells in the Tsarist army). Bund in Galicia and Bukovina under Austrian rule. Bund in Poland, 1915–1948 (including records of the Bund Central Committee and of the local branches, records of the Zukunft, the SKIF, the TSYSHO, and materials about the Polish Bundists in the Soviet Union during World War II).

Bund in Latvia, 1919–1939. Bund in Rumania, 1919–1939. Bund in the United States (including records of the American Representation of the Bund, records of the World Coordinating Committee of Bundist Organizations). Bund in Canada, Mexico, South America, Australia, Israel. Bund in Central and Western Europe after World War II (including materials about the Bund in the DP camps). Bundist publications. Biography materials and filled-in questionnaires about Bund activists, arranged alphabetically by name.

Jewish political movements: Zionism; Poale-Zion; Zionist-Socialists; Territorialists; Folkists; religious groups; biographies.

International socialist movement: Socialist International; Free Trade Unions (ICFTU); socialist parties in Germany, Great Britain, France, and other European countries; biographies.

Russian revolutionary parties from 1873: Narodnaya Volya (populists); Rossiiskaia Sotsial'no-Demokraticheskaia Rabochaia Partiia (RSDRP, Russian Social-Democratic Workers Party); the Mensheviks; the Bolsheviks; the Socialist Revolutionary Party (S-R); Revolutions of 1905 and 1917; Jews in Russian revolutionary parties; biographies.

Polish revolutionary movements from 1880: the Proletaryat; Polish Socialist Party (PPS); Socjaldemokracja Królestwa Polskiego i Litwy (SDKPiL, the Social Democratic Party of the Kingdom of Poland and of Lithuania); trade unions in Poland; Jewish sections in the Socialist parties in Eastern Europe; biographies.

Anarchism: anarchism in Europe; anarchism in the United States; Jewish anarchists in the United States; biographies.

Communism, from 1918: The Comintern and aspects of Marxism-Leninism; Soviet Union; Poland; other countries; United States; Jewish Communists in Soviet Union, Poland, Israel, United States, Canada; biographies of communist leaders, of Jewish communists, and of Trotskyites.

World War II period and the Holocaust: Auschwitz, Prisoners' Registration Book, Block 8, 1943–1945; ghettos in Poland including diaries and photographs of the Łódź ghetto; underground publications of the Bund in Poland and France; materials on Drancy, France; records of the Bund's participation in the Polish government-in-exile in London; other aspects of the Holocaust and its aftermath; Erlich-Alter affair.

The Jewish labor movement and Jewish socialists in North America: United Hebrew Trades; Workmen's Circle; Jewish Labor Committee; International Ladies Garment Workers' Union; The Amalgamated Clothing Workers of America; Jewish labor cooperatives and leagues; Jewish socialist groups; biographies.

Yiddish culture: schools; cultural institutions; publications and press; personalities.

Photographs. Includes the following: Bund activities in Poland, Tsarist Russia and the United States; Częstochowa and the surrounding area in the immediate post–World War II period; Łódź ghetto; Yiddish writers; trade unions in the United States; Yiddish schools in Poland and the United States.

Topical guide, English

Shelf lists, English.

139. BURSTEIN, PAUL (PESACH) (1896–1986) and LUX, LILLIAN.
Papers, 1930s–1970s. 8 ft. 9 in. (RG 706)

Yiddish comedians, husband and wife.

Paul (Pesach) Burstein performed in the United States, Argentina, Israel, as well as in other countries. Born in Pułtusk, Poland. Moved to the United States in 1924. Lived for periods of time in Argentina and Israel.

Lillian Lux began her theatrical career at Maurice Schwartz's Yiddish Art Theater. Performed with P. Burstein in the United States, Argentina, and in other countries. Born in the United States.

Play scripts, clippings, sheet music, correspondence, photographs, personal documents. Autobiography of P. Burstein. Radio programs of the Lillian Lux show.

140. BUSKER BNAI BRITH SICK AND BENEVOLENT ASSOCIATION.
   Records, 1947–1967. 5 1/2 in. (RG 810)

Founded in New York in 1911 by immigrants from Busko, Poland. Activities included the establishment of a *shtibl* (small prayer house), 1911–1935; a *gmilas khesed* (interest-free loan fund). Sent relief to Busko. Organized an interest-free loan society there before World War II. Aided *landslayt* in Poland and Israel after World War II. Maintained contact with the Busker *landsmanshaft* in Israel.

Constitution. Minutes, 1947–1962. Correspondence. *Yortsayt* (commemoration of the dead) book. Photographs. Memorial book, 1965. Anniversary journals, including those of the New York–Boston Busker Relief Association and the Busker Orphan Asylum Foundation. Materials pertaining to the *landsmanshaft* in Israel, including statutes, 1957.

141. CAHAN, ABRAHAM (1860–1951).
   Papers, 1906–1952. 2 ft. 6 in. (RG 1139)

Yiddish and English writer, editor, socialist leader, prominent figure in Jewish public life. Founder of the *Jewish Daily Forward* and its editor-in-chief from 1901 until his death. Co-founder of the first Jewish trade union in the United States, the Progressive Tailors' Union. Other newspapers and periodicals Cahan contributed to: *Di arbeter tsaytung* (editor, 1894–1895); *Zukunft* (editor, 1893–97); *New York Sun, New York Press, North American Review, Short Story, Atlantic Monthly.* Cahan published several works of fiction in English, the best known being *The Rise of David Levinsky.* Born in Podberezha (Paberze), near Vilna. Immigrated to the United States in 1882.

Correspondence with Raphael Abramovitch, Shalom Asch, Mendel Beilis, David Bergelson, Eduard Bernstein, Jacob Dinesohn, Theodore Dreiser, Simon Dubnow, Felix Frankfurter, Julius Gerber, Saul Ginsburg, Baruch (Boris) Glassman, Rabbi Chaim Oyzer Grodzienski, Hutchins Hapgood, Morris Hillquit, William Dean Howells, Vladimir Jabotinsky, Alter Kacyzne, Karl Kautsky, Menahem Kipnis, Fiorello La Guardia, Algernon Lee, Jacob Lestschinsky, Herman (Chaim) Lieberman, Jean Longuet, Judah L. Magnes, H. L. Mencken, Melech Ravitch, Abraham Reisen, Zalman Reisen, Franklin D. Roosevelt, Yona Rosenfeld, Gustavo Sacerdote, Ludwig Satz, Zemach Shabad, Zalman Shneur, Upton Sinclair, Israel Joshua Singer, Norman Thomas, Boris Thomashefsky, Max Weinreich, Chaim Weizmann, Morris Winchevsky, Chaim Zhitlowsky, Zalmen Zylbercweig. Included also are several letters from Leo Frank to Cahan, while the former was imprisoned in Atlanta, Georgia.

Manuscripts by various authors sent to the *Jewish Daily Forward.* Authors include Alter Kacyzne, Ephraim Kaganowski, Karl Kautsky, Maurycy Orzech, Joseph Rumshinsky, Zalman Shneur, Mark Wischnitzer.

Notes and handwritten drafts by Cahan of stories, articles, essays, speeches. Personal documents, birthday greetings to Cahan. Letters from readers relating to the dispute between Shalom Asch and Cahan, 1941–1942. Correspondence between Shalom Asch and Jacob Dinesohn.

Inventory, English.

142. CAHAN, JUDAH LOEB (YEHUDE LEYB) (1881–1937).
Papers, 1920s–1930s, 1950s. 2 ft. 6 in. (RG 202)

Jewish ethnographer. Founding member of YIVO in Vilna and of the American branch of YIVO in New York. Secretary of the YIVO Folklore Section and member of the YIVO Executive Board. Born in Vilna. Immigrated to England in 1901. Settled in New York in 1904.

Manuscripts, correspondence and clippings relating primarily to Cahan's work in Yiddish folklore. Correspondence with Max Weinreich, Shmuel Zanvil Pipe, Zalman Reisen, Nechama Epstein and Nahum Shtif relating to the organization of YIVO, Vilna. Folklore materials such as proverbs, anecdotes, folksongs and folktales, including items used in *Shtudyes vegn yidisher folksshafung* (Studies on Jewish Folk Creativity), ed. Max Weinreich, New York, 1952. Materials of the J.L. Cahan Folklore Club of YIVO, 1949.

Inventory, English, Yiddish.

143. CAHN, DAVID (1853–1915).
Papers, 1879–1949. 2 in. (RG 1211)

Cantor. Served in the congregations Aheb Zedek, Adath Israel, Temple Shar Hashomayim, and Temple Rodeph Sholem, all in New York. Born in Cracow, Poland. Came to the United States ca. 1872.

Collection relates primarily to the career of David Cahn and also includes some material about other members of the Cahn family.

Scrapbook containing clippings, programs, invitations, contracts and correspondence. Photographs of Cahn with Cantor Pinchas Minkowsky of Odessa.

144. CAMINSKY, WILLIAM.
Papers, 1920s–1948. 5 in. (RG 699)

Member, Yiddish cultural organizations in Argentina, Brazil and the United States.

Materials of the Jewish cultural center and the Bergelson Library in Campinas, Brazil. Mimeographed newsletters and circulars of Jewish organizations in Argentina and New York. Yearbooks of the Borochow Workmen's Circle School #6, 1939–1948.

145. CAREY, DAVID (?–1984).
Papers. 5 in. (RG 1175)

Yiddish actor. Lived in New York.

The papers consist of Yiddish plays, skits.

146. CARL SCHURZ FOUNDATION-OBERLANDER TRUST FUND.
Records, ca. 1933–ca. 1945. 6 microfilm reels (RG 447)

Established in 1930 by Ferdinand Thun. Assisted refugee scholars from Germany and Austria by making grants to individuals and institutions. Based in Philadelphia.

The collection relates to the activities of the Foundation on behalf of German and Austrian refugee scholars during the Nazi period. Correspondence with organizations and about individual refugees seeking positions in American universities. Included are the American Committee for Christian Refugees, American Jewish Committee, National Coordinating

Committee, Emergency Committee in Aid of Displaced German Scholars (1940–1942), Joint Committee for the Readjustment of German Jews. Personal data forms filled out by individuals.

Inventory, English.

147. CASHER, ISIDORE (1886–1948).
Papers, 1922–1944. 6 in. (RG 413)

Yiddish actor. Associated with Maurice Schwartz's Yiddish Art Theater in New York.

Clippings of reviews of performances, photographs of stage scenes. Correspondence. Texts of theater roles.

Photographs are cataloged in STAGEPIX.

148. CAUCASIAN BENEVOLENT SOCIETY.
Records, 1932–1974. 8 in. (RG 890)

Founded in New York in 1924. Maintained a loan fund. Sent relief funds to the Caucasus, Birobidzhan and Israel. Affiliated with a ladies auxiliary.

Certificate of incorporation, 1924. Minutes, 1970–1972. Financial records, 1930s–1970s. Membership records, 1950s–1970s. Correspondence. Anniversary materials. Banner.

149. CENTRAL HUNGARIAN SICK BENEVOLENT AND LITERARY SOCIETY.
Records, 1941–1975. 5 in. (RG 989)

Established in 1904–1906. Contributed to Jewish charities. Supported institutions in Israel. Dissolved 1979.

Minutes, 1941–1972 (Hungarian, English). Financial records. Burial and monument permits.

150. CENTRAL YIDDISH CULTURE ORGANIZATION.
Records, 1938–1950s. 8 ft. 9 in. (RG 1153)

Yiddish title: Tsentrale Yidishe Kultur Organizatsye. Founded in New York, in 1938, as a national Yiddish cultural organization, CYCO functioned primarily as a Yiddish publishing house. Among others, it published the *Algemeyne entsiklopedye*.

Records consist of minutes, reports, administrative correspondence, correspondence with Yiddish writers, materials relating to publishing activities and conferences.

151. THE CERES UNION.
Records, 1858–1973. 8 ft. 7 in. (RG 919)

Founded in 1858 as the Ceres Lodge No. 5, United Order Sons of Moses. Organized largely by German-Jewish immigrants. After 1861 many members enlisted in the 6th Regiment of the National Guard of the State of New York. Three of them became officers. Established as an independent organization in 1863 and changed its name to the Ceres Union. Associated with the Yorkville Ceres Club, Ceres Frauen Verein, Ceres Sewing Club, Ceres Council. Began publication of monthly bulletin, *The Ceres Union*, in 1905. Affiliated with the Ceres Junior League in 1922 and with the Ceres Union Ladies Auxiliary, established 1931. Dissolved 1973.

Legal documents, 1926, 1973. Constitutions. Minutes, 1859–1864 (German), 1920–1972

(English). Financial records, 1920s–1970s. Materials related to membership, 1876–1894 (German), ca. 1900–1970s (English). Burial and endowments records, 1860–1973. Records relating to payment of sick benefits. Materials pertaining to anniversary celebrations, 1923–63, and to the *The Ceres Union* monthly bulletin, ca. 1900–1970s. Correspondence. Photographs. Seal.

152. CESHINSKY, MOSHE (1889–1967).
Papers, 1930s. 3 in. (RG 267)

Publisher and bookseller in Chicago.

The collection consists of clippings of book reviews published by the Ceshinsky Farlag in the 1930s.

153. CHAGY, BERELE (1892–1953).
Papers, 1921–1983. 3 in. (RG 1278)

Cantor. Began his cantorial career in Dvinsk (Latv. Daugavpils). Studied at the Boston Conservatory. Served as cantor in congregations in the United States and South Africa. Performed on the concert stage in the United States and in Great Britain. Recorded for the Columbia and HMV companies. Wrote for Yiddish newspapers and was the author of *Tefilot Khagy*. Born near Dvinsk, Latvia. Came to the United States in 1913. Settled in Johannesburg, South Africa, in 1922. Returned to the United States in 1937.

Scrapbook of clippings. Includes several photographs and letters.

154. CHAIM HERSCH WEISS FIRST JANOWER SICK AND BENEVOLENT ASSOCIATION.
Records, 1928–1972. 1 ft. 5 1/2 in. (RG 868)

Organized in New York in 1909 by immigrants from Janów, Poland. A group of Stanisławów *landslayt* joined ca. 1910. Established loan and relief funds and a Passover fund. Named after a rabbi from Janów. Dissolved 1973.

Constitutions. Minutes, 1948–1972. Financial records, 1931–1968. Membership records. Cemetery maps. Correspondence. Seal. Stamps.

155. CHAIT, N.
Papers, 1926–1945. 5 in. (RG 543)

Secretary of the Central School Board of the Workmen's Circle Schools in the New York area.

The papers consist of records of the Workmen's Circle Central School Board in New York which were in the possession of Mr. Chait.

Minutes of meetings of the Executive Committee of the Central School Board, 1937–1945. Annual reports of the Workmen's Circle Schools in New York, 1927, 1928, 1931, 1936. Reports of Workmen's Circle School Conferences, 1926, 1934–1939.

156. CHAMBERLAIN, JOSEPH P. (1873–1951).
Papers, 1933–1951. 2 ft. 3 1/2 in. (RG 278)

Lawyer, Professor of Public Law at Columbia University from 1923 to 1950. Active in the development of private, government, and international refugee agencies for European Jewish refugees, from 1933 to about 1950. Chairman of the National Coordinating Committee and its successor, the National Refugee Service. Co-founder of the German Jewish Children's Aid. American representative to the Intergovernmental High Commission for Refugees Coming from Germany, 1933. Member of the President's Advisory Committee on Political Refugees in the Franklin Delano Roosevelt administration.

Correspondence, memoranda, reports and printed matter relating to Chamberlain's work with the following organizations: American Christian Committee for Refugees; Fort Ontario Refugee Shelter, Oswego, NY; German Jewish Children's Aid; Intergovernmental Committee on Refugees; National Coordinating Committee; National Refugee Service; President's Advisory Committee on Political Refugees; War Refugee Board. Topics include Chamberlain's involvement with individual cases, visas, sponsorship, German-Jewish physicians and scholars, Intergovernmental Committee on Refugees at Evian, Bermuda Conference, Capital Transfer Plan for German-Austrian Refugees. Of particular interest are the minutes of the President's Advisory Committee, 1938–1943. Materials on settlement projects relating to Alaska, Argentina, Bolivia, Brazil, British Guiana, California, China, Colombia, Dominican Republic, Ecuador, Venezuela. Correspondents include Dean Acheson, Paul Baerwald, Joseph Beck, Francis K. Biddle, Bernard Dubin, Dwight D. Eisenhower, Felix Frankfurter, William Haber, Cordell Hull, James Houghteling, Joseph C. Hyman, Ruth Learned, James G. McDonald, Clarence E. Pickett, Leland Robinson, William Rosenwald, Joseph F. Rummel, E.J. Shaughnessy, Felix Warburg, George L. Warren.

Inventory, English.

157. CHANUKOFF, LEON (LEIVIK) (1892–1958).
Papers. 2 ft. 1 in. (RG 765)

Yiddish writer. Teacher at the Sholem Aleichem Folk Institute. Contributed to *Yidisher velt* (Philadelphia), *Der tog, Freie Arbeiter Stimme, Morgn zhurnal, Der amerikaner, Morgn frayhayt, Yidisher kurier, Keneder odler, In zikh,* and others. Born in Pskov district, Russia. Immigrated to the United States in 1914 and settled in Philadelphia.

The collection consists of correspondence, manuscripts of Chanukoff's prose and poetry, photographs, clippings of his articles.

158. CHARASCH, A.
Papers, 1912–1918. 1 ft. (RG 86)

Sociologist, author, member of the Zionist Socialist Labor Party (Sionistichesko-Sotsialisticheskaia Rabochaia Partiia, SSRP) in Russia. Active member of its various committees in Switzerland including the *Mariv Eropeyishe Lige* (Western European League) and the *Evakuatsiye Komitet* (Evacuation Committee), 1917–1918. Active in matters relating to Russian-Jewish émigré students.

The collection relates to Charasch's activities in the SSRP and to Russian-Jewish émigré students in the West during the years 1912–1918.

Correspondence with L. Abramson, Rafael Asch, Pinchas Dubinsky, Z. Gordin, Isaac Gorsky, Max Gratwal, M. Gutman, H. Manilevitsch, M. Michelis, Aron Syngalowski, M. Tinker, Y. Zakalnik.

Records of the Zionist Socialist Labor Party. Resolutions about émigrés returning to Russia through Switzerland and Germany, 1917–1918. Membership lists of the United Jewish Socialist Workers' Party, and of its Emigration Committee. Applications with photo-

graphs. Minutes of meetings and circulars of the party's Western European League, 1913.
Inventory, Yiddish.

159. CHARNEY, DANIEL (1888–1959).
Papers, 1920s–1959. 6 ft. 8 in. (RG 421)

Yiddish writer and journalist. Active in Jewish cultural, relief and immigration organizations in Eastern Europe and the United States, including: EKOPO (Evreiskii Komitet Pomoshchi Zhertvam Voiny—Jewish Relief Committee for War Sufferers), Berlin, 1926; HICEM, Paris, 1936; Jewish Writers' Union, New York, 1946; Louis Lamed Foundation, 1942–1956. Editor of Yiddish newspapers and periodicals in Soviet Russia, 1918–1922. Contributor to the Yiddish press around the world. Born in Dukor, Minsk province, Byelorussia. Brother of Shmuel Niger and Baruch Vladeck. Lived in Moscow, Vilna, Berlin and Paris. Settled in the United States in 1941.

Correspondence with individuals including Sidor Belarsky, Menahem Boraisha, Simon Dubnow, Aaron Glanz-Leieles, Jacob Glatstein, Chaim Grade, David Hofstein, H. Leivick, Jacob Lestschinsky, Abraham Liessin, S. Nepomniashchii, Shmuel Niger, Joseph Opatoshu, Melech Ravitch, Abraham Reisen, A.A. Roback, Abraham Sutzkever, Baruch Charney Vladeck, Max Weinreich, Aaron Zeitlin. Family correspondence. Clippings of articles by and about Charney. Manuscripts by Charney, photographs, personal documents. Diaries, 1935–1936.

Papers of Baruch Vladeck (1886–1938). Letters to B. Vladeck from Shalom Asch, Eduard Bernstein, Léon Blum, Marc Chagall, Albert Einstein, Karl Kautsky. Articles and obituaries about B. Vladeck.

Inventory, English and Yiddish.

160. CHASNICK-BIESHENKOWITZER SOCIETY.
Records, 1958–1975. 10 1/2 in. (RG 886)

Organized in New York in 1898 by immigrants from Chashniki, Byelorussia, as the Chasnek-Bieshinkovicher Verein. Dissolved in the 1970s. Activities included support for charitable institutions in the United States and Israel.

Minutes, 1966–1975. Financial records, 1958–1975. Membership records, 1958–1975. Seal.

161. CHAVER-PAVER (1901–1964).
Papers, 1938, undated. 4 in. (RG 1222)

Yiddish writer. Pseudonym of Gershon Einbinder. Born in Bershad, Ukraine. Came to America in 1923 and worked as a teacher in Yiddish progressive schools. Was a regular contributor to *Di frayhayt*.

Manuscripts by Chaver-Paver in Yiddish and English.

162. CHECHELNICKER BENEVOLENT ASSOCIATION OF GREATER NEW YORK.
Records, 1958–1971. 2 1/2 in. (RG 1054)

Founded in New York in 1928 by immigrants from Chechelnik, Ukraine. Built community center in Lydda, Israel, through the United Jewish Appeal.

Constitution, correspondence, receipts, photographs, certificate. Memoirs of Norman Hofferman, the donor of the collection.

163. CHERKASSER-SMELA BENEVOLENT ASSOCIATION.
Records, 1910–1963. 7 1/2 in. (RG 786)

Formed in New York in 1962 by immigrants from Smela, Ukraine, and Cherkassy, Ukraine, through the consolidation of the United Brothers of the Town of Smila (incorporated 1906) and the Cherkasser Benevolent Association (incorporated 1945). The United Brothers established the Relief Committee for the Smeler Political Convicts, 1913, and the Joint Smela Relief, Inc., 1928. Relief activities included establishing barrel woodwork factories in Smela, 1930.

Minutes, United Brothers of the Town of Smila, 1932–1943. Certificate of consolidation, 1962. Correspondence from Smela to the New York *landsmanshaft* and to the Smiller Benevolent Association in Philadelphia, 1910–1914, 1922, 1931–1932. Lists of relief packages received in the USSR, 1922, 1942–1948. Newspaper clippings. Notes in preparation of the Smeler memorial book. Souvenir journal of the Joint Smela Relief, Inc., 1938. Receipts from the Relief Committee for the Smeler Political Convicts.

164. CHERNIAK, J.A.
Papers, 1930–1962. 10 in. (RG 264)

Resident of Winnipeg, Canada. Active in Yiddish cultural organizations.

Correspondence relating to Cherniak's association with Yiddish cultural organizations. Letters from Freeland League, YKUF, YIVO, ORT, Canadian Jewish Congress, Yiddish schools, Jewish Labor Committee. Correspondence with individuals: Mendl Elkin, Peretz Hirschbein, Shmuel Niger, Chaim Zhitlowsky.

165. CHESTER, SAMUEL (1882–1941).
Papers, 1921–1936. 10 in. (RG 470)

Pseudonym of Osher Selig Khazanovich. Yiddish poet and writer. Published poems in the *Jewish Daily Forward, Freie Arbeiter Stimme, Tsayt gayst, Di feder, Frayhayt.* Also published short stories about life in America. Born in Kědainiai, Lithuania. Immigrated to the United States.

Manuscripts of Chester's novels and poems. Clippings. Correspondence, including letters from Moses (Moyshe) Leib Halpern, Moshe Nadir, Shmuel Niger, Abraham Reisen.

166. CHEVRA AHAVAS ACHIM ANSHEI KORSON.
Records, 1923–1946. 5 in. (RG 418)

Organized in New York in 1894 by former residents of Korsun (Ukraine). Established a synagogue. Supported charitable institutions in Korsun and the United States. Met at 98 Forsyth Street, New York.

Pinkas (record book), containing minutes and membership lists, 1923–1946.

167. CHEVRA AHAVATH ACHIM B'NAI KOLO.
Records, 1918, 1940–1979. 1 1/2 in. (RG 1057)

Established in New York in 1877 by immigrants from Koło, Poland, to maintain a synagogue and to help the needy in Koło. Originally located at 48 Avenue D, New York. Cooperated with the Koło *landsmanshaft* in Israel in assisting survivors there. Published a memorial book.

Constitutions. Minutes of a memorial meeting, 1975. Financial records. Souvenir journals, 1940, 1978. Correspondence. Bulletins, 1946–1979. Memorial book, 1958.

168. CHEVRA ANSHEI ANTEPOLER.
Records, 1909–1964. 3 in. (RG 1004)

Founded in New York in 1901 by immigrants from Antopol, Byelorussia. Incorporated in 1909. Maintained a synagogue located at 203 Henry Street, New York.

Certificate of incorporation, 1909. Minutes, 1929–1964. Constitution, Antepolier Untershtitsungs Verein. Charter, United Antipoler Association, 1909. Postcards, Antopol.

169. CHEVRA ANSHEY SZCZUCZYN-VE-ANSHEY GRAYEVE.
Records, 1936–1952. 2 in. (RG 1240)

Organized 1907 by *landslayt* from Szczuczyn and Grajewo, Poland. Provided members with benefits and maintained a synagogue and a cemetery.

Minutes book, 1936–1952.

170. CHEVRA BNEI ISRAEL ANSHEI ZUROW.
Records, 1934–1964. 2 in. (RG 1077)

Founded in New York in 1869 by immigrants from Żurów (Dzhuruv), Ukraine, to provide members with a place to pray. Also known as the Chevra Bnei Israel Anshei Zurow Galician.

Minutes, 1934–1964. Burial permits.

171. CHEVRA BNEI SHOMREI ISRAEL OF BROWNSVILLE.
Records, 1924–1970s. 15 in. (RG 1180)

Founded in 1924. Provided *gmilas khesed* (interest-free loans) and *hevrah kadisha* (burial) services.

Minutes, 1924–1950s. Ledgers, loan books, stamps, correspondence, photograph.

172. CHEVRA GOMLE CHESED ANSHE DROHOBYCH AND BORYSLAW.
Records, 1940–1975. 5 in. (RG 936)

Founded in New York in 1905 by immigrants from Drogobych (Pol. Drohobycz), Ukraine, as an Orthodox congregation. Established a synagogue and aided *landslayt* in Drohobycz.

Financial records, 1940s–1970s. Materials pertaining to burial. Seal.

173. CHEVRA KADISHA BETH ISRAEL.
Records, 1914–1967. 12 1/2 in. (RG 865)

A fraternal organization providing sick and death benefits for its members. The society was founded in 1858, closed to new members in 1948, and dissolved in 1967.

Minutes, 1943–1967. Financial records, 1943–1967. Membership records, 1920–1967. Burial permits, 1914–1966. Correspondence, 1950s–1960s. Announcements, cemetery map, seal.

174. CHEVRA KOL YISROEL OF BROWNSVILLE.
Records, ca. 1912–1945. 5 in. (RG 1027)

Synagogue founded in 1909 in Brownsville, Brooklyn, New York. Ceased its activities in the late 1950s.

Constitution, printed 1912, 1924. Correspondence, 1930s. Cemetery plot outlines. Membership records. Income and expenses ledgers, 1926–1937.

175. CHEVRA OIR LASHUMAIM ANSHEI STOPNITZ.
Records, 1925–1947. 2 1/2 in. (RG 916)

Founded in 1925 by immigrants from Stopnica, Poland. Met in a synagogue located at 81 Columbia Street, New York. Moved to 122 Columbia Street in 1935.

Minutes, 1925–1947.

176. CHMELNITZKY, MELECH (1885–1946).
Papers, 1899–1940s. 9 in. (RG 501)

Physician, Yiddish poet, writer and translator. Contributed to periodicals such as *Lemberger togblat* (Lwów), *Forverts* (NY), *Vilner tog* (Vilna), *Nayer folksblat*, *Lodzer tageblat* (Łódź), *Zukunft* (NY). Wrote articles on medical topics. Born in Konstantinovka, district of Kiev, Ukraine. Lived in Austria. Immigrated to the United States in 1939 and settled in New York.

Manuscripts of poems and articles. Correspondence with Yiddish literary figures and clippings.

177. CHMIELNIKER SICK AND BENEVOLENT SOCIETY.
Records, 1935–1978. 8 in. (RG 1081)

Organized in New York in 1929 by immigrants from Chmielnik, Poland, as the Chmielniker Sick and Benevolent Society of Poland, Inc. Conducted relief activities during World War II. After the war, sent financial aid to *landslayt* in Israel. The Chmielniker Young Ladies Auxiliary was established in 1931 to aid needy *landslayt* and to support charitable institutions.

Souvenir journal, 1935. Journal of the United Chmielniker Relief Committee, 1938. Meeting notices. Journal of the Association of Former Residents of Chmielniker in Israel, 1963, 1967–1976, 1978. Photographic plate, stamp, banners, cemetery map. Memorial book, 1960.

178. CHOJREW (VILNA).
Records, 1924–1930s. 1 ft. 3 in. (RG 49)

Central Committee for Religious Education. An educational organization, founded in 1924 at an Agudas Israel conference, with the support of the Chofetz Chaim (Rabbi Israel Meir Hakohen Kagan) and Rabbi Chaim Oyzer Grodzienski of Vilna. Based in Warsaw, it maintained a network of Orthodox Jewish schools for boys of all ages. The schools included *yeshivot ketanot* (junior yeshivot), *yeshivot gedolot* (higher yeshivot) and *hadorim* (elementary schools). In 1937 Chojrew maintained a total of 580 institutions with 73,311 students. Chojrew did not include the higher yeshivot of the Eastern provinces of Poland which had been organized in Vilna in 1924 into a separate organization, the Vaad Hayeshivot. An organizational newspaper, *Dos vort*, was published weekly in Vilna from 1924–1939 and represented both Chojrew and the Vaad Hayeshivot. Chojrew was active until the outbreak of World War II. This collection consists primarily of the records of the Vilna office of Chojrew.

Correspondence with teachers and applicants. Correspondence with schools and organizations. Miscellaneous materials: lists of students; financial materials; printed materials and circulars.

Inventory, English.

179. CHOTINER-BESSARABIER EMERGENCY CLUB.
Records, 1971–1980. 1 1/2 in. (RG 1052)

Established in New York in 1930 by immigrants from Khotin, Bessarabia, to provide emergency funds for needy members who could not pay rent, utility bills, etc. However, provided no sick, death or burial benefits. Club members received these benefits through membership in other societies.

Minutes, 1972–1980. Photograph.

180. CHOTINER YUGEND BRANCH 271 WORKMEN'S CIRCLE—
CHOTINER BESSARABIER BRANCH 200.
Records, 1934–1959. 10 in. (RG 1120)

Founded in 1909 in New York by immigrants from Khotin, Bessarabia, as a branch of the Workmen's Circle. Participated in relief efforts for the Khotin Jewish community through the United Chotiner Relief. Supported the Chotiner Hospital and the Moshev Z'kenim Relief.

Anniversary journals. Financial records. Pamphlets of various Bessarabian and Chotiner groups. Correspondence and other material pertaining to the publication of the memorial books. Photographs.

181. CHUDI, SIMON.
Papers, 1915–1949. 5 in. (RG 254)

Family papers. Poland, Sweden.

Family correspondence from Poland, Germany and Western Europe prior to and during World War II. Letters from DP camps in Germany and from Cyprus and Israel. Simon Chudi's diary, 1915–1920. Family photographs.

182. COGAN, EDNA.
Papers, 1920s–1950s. 7 in. (RG 549)

Yiddish teacher in Sholem Aleichem School #15, New York.

The collection relates to Cogan's teaching career and includes such teaching materials as school plays, Purim plays, Yiddish songs and poems. Personal correspondence, clippings, autobiographical notes.

183. COHEN, ISRAEL (1879–1961).
 Papers, 1905–1950s. 1 ft. 3 in. (RG 448)

Jewish writer and journalist. Active in the Zionist movement and secretary of the Zionist Organization in London. After World War I he toured Europe and reported on the pogroms of 1918–1919 in the Ukraine and on the Jewish situation throughout Europe. His books relate to Zionism and topics in Jewish history.

 Notes, correspondence, clippings, manuscripts of books, articles and reports on Jewish life in Austria, England, France, Germany, Hungary, Lithuania, Poland, Rumania, Russia, Spain, the Balkans, North Africa, ca. 1910–1930s. Includes materials on the pogroms in Poland, 1918–1919, and materials relating to the situation of Jews during the Nazi period. Manuscripts of works on Jewish history including biographies of Jewish personalities and a report on the Yiddish Language Conference in Czernowitz. Materials on the Minorities Treaties.

 Inventory, English.

184. COHEN, MICHAEL A. (1867–1939).
 Papers, 1921–1939. 5 in. (RG 313)

Physician, writer, anarchist. Contributed articles to *Freie Arbeiter Stimme* and other radical Yiddish newspapers in the United States. Born in Maków Mazowiecki, Poland. Emigrated to the United States in 1886.

 The papers relate to Cohen's association with the anarchist movement. Correspondents include Alexander Berkman, Emma Goldman, Peter Kropotkin, Rudolf Rocker. Correspondence, articles, appeals relating to the Sacco-Vanzetti case, 1925. Manuscripts by Cohen, autobiographical notes. Ledger of an unknown anarchist relief organization, 1920s.

185. COHEN, NESSA.
 Papers, 1931–1963. 2 1/2 in. (RG 1205)

Sculptor, United States.

 The papers relate primarily to Cohen's travels in France and Italy, and include correspondence, postcards, reproductions of artworks, other materials. Correspondents include Tullio Levi-Civita, David Tishman.

186. COMITE NATIONAL DE SECOURS AUX REFUGIES
 ALLEMANDS VICTIMES DE L'ANTISEMITISME.
 Records, 1933–1934. 2 microfilm reels (RG 334)

National Relief Committee For German Refugee Victims of Antisemitism. Organized in 1933 to deal with the problem of German-Jewish refugees in France. The Comité National eventually coordinated all immigration and relief work in France. Its activities included provision of food and lodging, and medical and job placement services.

 Materials on the founding and organizational structure of the Comité. Lists of board members, reports, minutes of meetings. Correspondence and other materials from HIAS-JCA-EMIGDIRECT (HICEM), government of France. List of German-Jewish students at Lucien de Hirsch school in Paris. List of German-Jewish refugees.

 Inventory, English.

187. COMMITTEE FOR THE REUBEN BRAININ CHILDREN'S
 CLINIC IN ISRAEL.
 Records, 1956–1987. 1 ft. 5 in. (RG 1231)

The committee was formed in 1954 by left-wing American-Jewish circles to support the establishment of a children's clinic in Israel. The clinic was opened in 1958 in the Tel Aviv area.

Minutes, 1956–1987. Correspondence, circulars, donor lists, certificates, clippings and other materials. Publications, including anniversary journals, 1958–1969, and bulletins, 1960–1987. Photographs of the clinic and of committee activities.

188. COMMITTEE FOR THE STUDY OF RECENT IMMIGRATION FROM EUROPE.
Records, 1943–1947. 22 microfilm reels. (RG 595)

The CSRIE was set up ca. 1943 by the American-Christian Committee for Refugees, the American Friends Service Committee, the Catholic Committee for Refugees, the National Refugee Service, and the U.S. Committee for the Care of European Children. Its purpose was to conduct a study on recent immigration from Europe. The results were published in *Refugees in America: Report of Recent Immigration from Europe*, by Maurice R. Davie, with the collaboration of Sarah W. Cohn, Betty Drury, et al., New York–London, 1947.

The collection relates to the study and includes the following:

General correspondence, 1944–1947. Materials on various refugee organizations, both Christian and Jewish, such as correspondence, printed material, reports. Interviews with refugee scientists, physicians and artists, including Nobel Prize recipients who made outstanding contributions to American life.

Inventory, English.

189. COMMITTEE OF JEWISH NAZI SURVIVORS' ORGANIZATIONS IN USA.
Records, 1965–1966. 1 in. (RG 1234)

Organized to centralize activities of Holocaust survivors organizations. Established 1965.

Meeting notices, circulars, minutes, correspondence, lists, and bulletins.

190. CONDELL, HEINZ (1905–1951) and LUBA B. (1912–1979).
Papers, 1928–1970s. 2 ft. 6 in. (RG 504)

Heinz Condell was an artist and a stage and costume designer. One of the founders of the Jewish Kulturbund-Theater in Berlin. Designer for the New York City Opera, Maurice Schwartz's Yiddish Art Theater and ARTEF (Arbeter Teater Farband) Company in New York. Lived in Germany and the United States.

Luba B. Condell, his wife, was an actress in New York. She performed with the Folksbiene Theater.

The papers relate to H. Condell's theatrical career in Germany and in the United States. Correspondence relating to work in the theater. Personal documents. Clippings of reviews and notices relating to productions of the Kulturbund-Theater in Berlin, 1930s. Clippings include reproductions of art work. Photographs of stage sets and designs. Original designs, including ink and paint on boards, for *Bronx Express* by Ossip Dymow and *Nathan the Wise* by Gotthold Ephraim Lessing. Materials relating to L. Condell's theatrical career: correspondence, clippings, photos, reviews, programs, scripts and personal documents.

Inventory, English.

191. CONGREGATION ACHEI GRODNO VASAPOTKIN AND CHEVRA MISHNAYOS.
Records, 1938–1959. 2 1/2 in. (RG 995)

The Chevra Mishnayos was established for the daily study of the six tractates of the Mishnah. Affiliated with Congregation Achei Grodno Vasapotkin which was established by the merger of Congregation Achei Grodno (founded 1893) and Congregation Achei Sapotkin (founded 1913).

Constitution, Chevra Mishnayos. Minutes, Chevra Mishnayos, 1938–1959. Souvenir journal.

192. CONGREGATION ADATH WOLKOWISK OF BROWNSVILLE.
Records, 1911–1933. 5 in. (RG 981)

Organized in Brooklyn in 1911 to provide members with free loans, cemetery plots, and a synagogue for study and prayer. From 1911 to 1938 the synagogue was relocated from Stone Avenue to Christopher Street, and then to Osborn Street and to Sachman Street, Brooklyn.

Materials pertaining to congregational regulations. Minutes, 1911–1913, 1919–1931. Financial records, 1920s–1930s. Membership records. Materials pertaining to synagogue activities.

193. CONGREGATION AGUDAS ACHIM ANSHEI TREMBOWLA KRANKEN UNTERSHTITZUNGS VEREIN.
Records, 1908, 1925–1948. 5 1/2 in. (RG 1070)

Founded in New York in 1901 by immigrants from Terebovlya (Pol. Trembowla), Ukraine. Provided aid to institutions in the home towns. After World War I, sent a delegate to Trembowla with relief funds. Maintained a synagogue on Houston Street, New York.

Constitution, 1908. Minutes, 1931–1948. Financial ledger, 1925–1934.

194. CONGREGATION AHAVATH ACHIM ANSHEI MOHILEV ON DNIEPER.
Records, 1913, 1961–1974. 1 1/2 in. (RG 1061)

Incorporated in New York in 1913 by immigrants from Mogilev, Byelorussia, as Congregation Ahavath Achim Anshe Mohilev al Nahar Dnieper, a religious corporation. Dissolved in the 1970s.

Certificate of incorporation, 1913. Financial materials. Burial permits. Correspondence.

195. CONGREGATION AHAVATH ZEDEK ANSHEI TIMKOWITZ.
Records, 1906–1965. 8 in. (RG 840)

Incorporated in 1892 by immigrants from Timkovichi, Byelorussia. Had its own synagogue on Henry Street, New York. At one time worked with an affiliated ladies auxiliary.

Minutes, 1906–1919. Financial records, 1930s–1960s. *Gmilas khesed* (interest-free loan fund) certificates, 1944–1964. Receipts, 1954–1965.

196. CONGREGATION ANSHEI KRASHNIK.
Records, 1905–1976. 5 in. (RG 815)

Founded in New York in 1897 by immigrants from Kraśnik, Poland. Established a relief committee after World War I. Sent financial assistance to a Kraśnik *landsmanshaft* in Israel.

Minutes, 1929–1972. Financial records, including cemetery deeds, 1906–1954. Jubilee journals. Memorial book, 1973. Miscellaneous, including materials pertaining to society in Israel.

197. CONGREGATION BIKUR CHOLIM OF
EAST NEW YORK (ANSHE SHEPETOVKA).
Records, 1940–1975. 5 in. (RG 862)

Founded in 1926 by immigrants from Shepetovka, Ukraine. Dissolved 1975.

Financial records, including minutes of several meetings, 1937–1960. Membership records, 1940s–1960s. Correspondence, 1950s–1975. Seal.

198. CONGREGATION BNEI ABRAHAM (HARLEM, NY).
Records, 1936–1952. 2 in. (RG 1237)

Orthodox synagogue founded by Jewish immigrants from the Austrian Empire. Burial Society founded in 1920.

Record book (*pinkas*) of the Burial Society, 1920–1944. Certificate of gift of a Torah scroll, 1921. Circular letters, 1927, 1944.

199. CONGREGATION BNEI JACOB ANSHEI BRZEZAN.
Records, 1903–1975. 21 in. (RG 885)

Organized in New York in 1894 by immigrants from Berezhany (Pol. Brzeżany), Ukraine, and incorporated in 1952 to establish a synagogue. Provided relief for *landslayt* after World War I, which included sending a delegate to Berezhany.

Financial records, 1930s–1960s. Membership records, 1903–1947. *Golden Book of Memories* (record of deaths of members). Wooden gavel.

200. CONGREGATION EZRAS ACHIM BNEI PINSK.
Records, 1904–1976. 4 in. (RG 780)

Organized in New York in 1866 by immigrants from Pinsk, Byelorussia, for the purpose of establishing a synagogue. Incorporated in 1904.

Constitutions. Minutes, 1909, 1934–1964. Financial records, 1908–1916, 1931. Cemetery maps. Correspondence, 1941–1976. Publication, 1954. Souvenir journal of Congregation Dorshei Tov Anshei Pinsk, 1941.

201. CONGREGATION MAHAZIKE HADAS (LONDON).
Records, 1891–1950s. 5 in. (RG 614)

Beit Hakneset Mahazike Hadas Ve-shomre Shabbos. Also known as Spitalfields Great Synagogue.

Copies of minutes of the synagogue meetings for the years 1891–1925. The minutes deal with matters of kashrut, the rabbinate, synagogue finances. Printed materials such as invitations, public announcements and circulars concerning religious matters.

202. CONGREGATION OHAV SHOLOM.
Records, 1917–1922. 1 1/2 in. (RG 1215)

Founded in 1894 in Brooklyn, New York.

Minutes, 1917–1922.

203. CONGREGATION RODEF SHOLEM INDEPENDENT PODHAJCER KRANKEN UNTERSHTITZUNGS VEREIN.
Records, 1973–1979. 2 1/2 in. (RG 1074)

Organized in New York in 1900 by immigrants from Podgaitsy (Pol. Podhajce), Ukraine. Owned a synagogue. In later years, met in the Podhajcer synagogue, 108 First Street, New York, owned by another Podhajcer society.

Constitution. Minutes, 1977–1979. Receipts, correspondence.

204. CONGREGATION SHEARITH ISRAEL (NEW YORK).
18th–20th century. 1 microfilm reel. (RG 370)

Popularly known as the Spanish and Portuguese Synagogue. It follows the Sephardic tradition and was the first synagogue in North America. Organized ca. 1706.

Contracts with rabbis, readers and cantors, sextons, and ritual slaughterers. Materials on Rabbi H. Pereira Mendes. Constitutions and by-laws of the synagogue. Some vital statistics, including births and marriages.

205. CONGREGATION TIFERES BETH JACOB—EZRAS ISRAEL ANSHEI BRONX.
Records, 1923–1950s. 3 in. (RG 1164)

Leather-bound, calligraphic *pinkas* of the *hevrah kadisha*, including minutes and lists of members. Record of plots, Kletzker Bruderlicher Unterstitzungs Ferein, 1923–1943.

206. CONGREGATION TIFERETH JOSEPH ANSHEI PRZEMYSL.
Records, 1917–1967. 7 1/2 in. (RG 793)

Originally organized in New York in 1891 for the purpose of founding a synagogue. Chartered in 1892. Was affiliated with the United Przemysler Relief, organized in 1938 to help *landslayt* in Przemyśl, Poland.

Constitution (German). Certificate of incorporation, 1892. Minutes, 1945–1965. Correspondence, 1930s–1940s. Correspondence regarding Nazi war crimes testimony and material claims against Germany, 1960s. Personal materials relating to Przemyśl, 1930s–1940s. Announcements, anniversary journal, 1941. Photographs. Memorial book, 1964. Materials of the United Relief for Przemyśl, 1946.

207. CONGRESS FOR JEWISH CULTURE.
Records, 1948–1970s. 3 ft. 6 in. (RG 1148)

Yiddish name: Alveltlekher Yidisher Kultur Kongres. Organization founded to coordinate and initiate Yiddish cultural activities, including the publication of books. Based in New York, with a branch in Buenos Aires.

Materials on the founding conference of 1948, such as minutes and speeches. Press releases. Photographs. Correspondence. Minutes of meetings.

208. CORALNIK, ABRAHAM (1883–1937).
Papers, 1920s–1930. 4 ft. (RG 321)

Yiddish journalist and essayist. Active in the Zionist movement. Zionist representative to the Council of the Jewish Agency, 1929. Editor of the Zionist paper *Die welt*. Contributor to *Der tog* in New York and to the German and Russian press. Born in Uman, Ukraine. Immigrated to the United States in 1915.

Clippings of Coralnik's articles in *Der tog* and other publications. Correspondence, manuscripts and typescripts of Coralnik's works. Bibliographic notes. Records of the Koralnik Farlag (Coralnik Publishing).

209. DAMESEK, SOLOMON (1896–1962).
Papers, ca. 1944–1959. 10 in. (RG 471)

Hebrew and Yiddish writer. Hebrew teacher. Contributed to *Ha-ivri* (NY), *Der tog* (NY), *Zukunft* (NY), *Amerikaner* (NY), *Yidisher kemfer* (NY), *Hadoar* (NY). Born in Nesvizh (Pol. Nieśwież), district of Minsk, Byelorussia. Came to the United States in 1921.

Correspondence with Yiddish writers including B. Alkwit, Benjamin Jacob Bialostotzky, Nahum Bomze, Daniel Charney, Joseph Rolnick.

210. DANZIS, MORDECHAI (1885–1952).
Papers, 1901–1981 (bulk: 1945–1948). 10 in. (RG 1170)

Journalist. Active in the Revisionist-Zionist movement. Contributed to a variety of Yiddish newspapers in Galicia (Poland) and in the United States. Editor of the Yiddish daily *Der tog* (NY). Born in Podolia, Ukraine. Came to the United States in 1905.

Correspondence, 1945–1948, concerning Danzis's work as editor of *Der tog* and of *Bafrayung*, a Revisionist-Zionist publication. Manuscripts of speeches, articles and stories by Danzis and others. Bulletins, flyers and notices, 1935–1948, concerning Revisionist-Zionist activities, especially of Irgun Zva'i Le'ummi, and American League for a Free Palestine. United Nations press releases, 1946–1948.

Papers of Leah Danzis concerning publication of Hebrew translation of Mordechai Danzis's book *Eygn likht*, 1968–1975. Miscellaneous materials, such as records of Danzis's broadcast on WEVD, "News of the Week in Review," n.d.

211. DASHEVSKY, LOUIS (YEHUDA LEIB) (1890–1974).
Papers, 1920s–1960s. 5 in. (RG 695)

Yiddish writer and poet. Carpenter. Contributed to *Der groyser kundes*, *Freie Arbeiter Stimme*, *Der amerikaner*, *Yidisher arbeter*. Born in Kherson district, Ukraine. Moved to Argentina in 1907. Settled in the United States in 1910.

The collection consists of manuscripts of Dashevsky's writings and clippings of his works, and some correspondence.

212. DAVID KANTROWITZ FAMILY BENEVOLENT ASSOCIATION.
Records, 1921–1979. 1 in. (RG 1059)

Incorporated in 1909 by descendants of Russian born Mirke (Miriam) Becker to unite those descended from her by blood or marriage, to aid members and to commemorate the memory of departed members. Gave interest-free loans. Contributed to charities.

Constitution. DKFBA Golden Book and Family Register, 1979. Family magazine, 1925. Souvenir handkerchief of relative's funeral, 1921.

213. DAVIDOFF, LEO.
  Papers, 1946–1951. 1 ft. 3 in. (RG 1289)

Physician who served on missions on behalf of the World Health Organization.

  A diary of Davidoff's trip to Israel in 1951, English. Slides of his missions to Czechoslovakia, Poland, Israel, 1946–1950.

214. DAVIDSOHN, MICHL (1883–1941).
  Papers, 1901–1930s. 10 in. (RG 260)

Yiddish writer, poet, translator, teacher. Lived in the Ukraine and the United States.

  Manuscripts, typescripts of Davidson's plays, poems and other works. Materials from the school Mahzikei Talmud Torah d'Borough Park, 1901–1920s: exams, exercises, children's Hebrew compositions.

215. DAVIDSON, JACOB (1892–1987).
  Papers, 1930–1987. 2 ft. 1 in. (RG 1224)

Composer, conductor, teacher. Graduate of the Music and Cantorial School of Częstochowa, Poland, and the Vienna Conservatory of Music. Directed various choirs such as Hazomir and synagogue choirs in New York. Born in Warsaw. Came to the United States in 1913.

  The papers relate to Davidson's musical career. Mansucript and printed music, including songs, Yiddish and Hebrew choral music, liturgical music for cantors, ca. 1930–ca. 1984. Correspondence with cantors, musicians, Yiddish writers and others, ca. 1949–ca. 1984. Miscellaneous material, including a list of compositions by Davidson, biographical material, photographs, a tape of Annie Davidson singing Davidson's works.

216. DAY-MORNING JOURNAL.
  Records, 1922–1972. 34 ft. 2 in. (RG 639)

The *Day-Morning Journal* (*Der tog-morgn zhurnal*) was a Yiddish daily in New York formed through the merger of *The Day* (*Der tog*) and the *Jewish Morning Journal* (*Morgn zhurnal*). In 1970 circulation was estimated at 50,000. The newspaper ceased publication in 1971.

  The Day, a Yiddish daily, was founded in 1914 by a group of New York intellectuals and businessmen led by Judah Magnes and Morris Weinberg. *The Day* was established as a non-partisan liberal newspaper with high intellectual standards. Under the editorship of William Edlin, its staff included Shmuel Niger, David Pinsky, Aaron Glanz-Leieles, Peretz Hirschbein. *The Day* reached its peak circulation of 81,000 in 1916. In 1919 it absorbed *Di varhayt*. Its readership declined after World War I.

  The *Jewish Morning Journal*, a New York Yiddish daily, was founded in 1901 by the Orthodox publisher Jacob Saperstein. Peter (Peretz) Wiernik was its chief editorial writer and later became editor-in-chief. In 1916 its circulation reached 111,000 and in the same year Jacob Fishman was appointed editor, directing the paper from 1916 to 1938. Prominent journalists included Jacob Glatstein, Bernard Gorin, Alexander Mukdoni, Jacob Magidov, and Gedaliah Bublick. In 1928 the *Morning Journal* absorbed the *Yiddishes Tageblatt*. As was the case with most Yiddish newspapers, its readership declined after World War I.

  The collection consists of records of *The Day* and of the *Day-Morning Journal*.

  Records of *The Day*, 1914–1945. Consists of administrative files, correspondence and manuscripts of editors. The administrative materials include inter-office memoranda, minutes, payroll lists, materials relating to the strike at *The Day* in 1941. The correspondence includes files of the Managing Editor, Solomon Dingol, and of the editors Samuel Margoshes, 1926–1934, Ben Zion Goldberg, 1935–1937, and Abraham Bookstein. Materials on immigration and the immigration quota of 1924, including correspondence with Congressman Samuel Dickstein concerning problems faced by Jewish immigrants, 1924–1927. Correspondence with readers. Manuscripts by various authors submitted to *The Day*, many of them unpublished. Writers include Daniel Charney, Ossip Dymow, Peretz Hirshbein, Jacob Milch, Isaac Nachman Steinberg, Chaim Zhitlowsky.

Records of the Day-Morning Journal include administrative records, 1950–1971, inter-office correspondence and memoranda, minutes of Staff Committee. Correspondence with publishers Morris Weinberg and Arthur Jacobs, and editors Aaron Alperin, David Meckler, Samuel Margoshes, Aaron Glanz-Leieles. Materials and correspondence relating to specific columns such as Krumer shpigl, Tribune, Froyen un mener. Manuscripts by various authors. Photographs of Jewish personalities.

Inventory, Yiddish.

Card inventory of the photographs.

217. DEBORAH REBEKAH LODGE NO. 13, INDEPENDENT ORDER OF ODD FELLOWS.
Records, 1912–1926, 1971–1975. 11 in. (RG 958)

A lodge of the Rebekah Assembly of the Independent Order of Odd Fellows. Conducted social and charitable activities. Contributed to Jewish philanthropies.

Minutes, 1971–1975. Financial ledger, 1912–1926 (German). Certificates, banners, capes.

218. DEITCH, MATTES (1894–1966).
Papers, 1920s–1960s. 1 ft. 4 in. (RG 518)

Yiddish writer. Contributed to many dailies and periodicals, among them *In zikh* (NY), *Zukunft* (NY), *Freie Arbeiter Stimme* (NY), *Literarishe bleter* (Warsaw). Born in Rokitno, Ukraine. Settled in the United States in 1916.

Correspondence with Yiddish literary figures including Menahem Boraisha, Daniel Charney, Aaron Glanz-Leieles, Jacob Glatstein, Peretz Hirschbein, H. Leivick, Abraham Liessin, Itzik Manger, Shmuel Niger, Melech Ravitch, Abraham Sutzkever, Wolf Younin. Manuscripts of Deitch's writings. Clippings of his writings and reviews.

219. DELATIZER AID BENEVOLENT SOCIETY.
Records, 1932–1974. 5 in. (RG 889)

Established in New York in 1905 by the *landslayt* from Delatycze, Byelorussia. Maintained a *hevrah kadisha* (burial society). Established a society loan fund, 1914.

Constitution. Financial records, 1932–1971. Meeting announcements. Constitution of the Drisser Brothers Benevolent Society.

220. DEMBITZER LANDSLEIT.
Records, 1953–1974. 2 1/2 in. (RG 1047)

Established in 1950 and incorporated in New York in 1955 to unite all former residents of

Dębica, Poland, to "revive and uphold the traditions of our Dembitzer birthplace through social, cultural, non-political means." Assisted in the publication of a memorial book.

Certificate of incorporation, 1955. Constitution. Minutes, 1953–1970. Bulletins. Memorial book, 1960.

221. DIJOUR, ILYA (born 1896).
Papers, ca. 1910–1964. 3 microfilm reels. (RG 589)

Teacher, writer, administrator in Jewish immigration relief organizations. Dijour devoted a major part of his life to dealing with the problem of Jewish immigration. Member of the Jewish People's Party (Yidishe Folkspartei) in the Ukraine. General secretary of EMIGDIRECT in Berlin. Held major administrative positions in HIAS and HICEM in Berlin, Paris, Lisbon and New York from 1923 to the 1950s. Member of the Board of Directors of the YIVO Institute. Contributed to the Russian press and wrote books and articles in English, Yiddish and German on the problem of Jewish immigration, including articles in the *YIVO bleter*. Born in Zvenigorod, district of Kiev. Lived in Poland, Germany, France. In 1940 moved to Lisbon where the offices of HICEM were established after its evacuation from Nazi-occupied Paris. In 1942 immigrated to the United States.

The collection reflects for the most part Dijour's activities in HIAS. There are also some materials relating to his personal life. Correspondence, manuscripts, financial records, forms, reports, statistical surveys, printed material. Manuscripts of Dijour's memoirs. General HIAS correspondence, 1936–1964. Lectures, reports, correspondence and notes on migration problems. Personal documents including correspondence with Mrs. Dijour.

222. DIMONDSTEIN, BORIS (born 1892).
Papers, ca. 1929–1957. 1 ft. 3 in. (RG 400)

Born Berl Dworkin. Yiddish playwright, poet, editor of the periodical *Literarishe heftn*, Los Angeles.

Correspondence with Yiddish writers and Jewish cultural organizations. Included are Abba Gordin, Naftoli Gross, David Ignatoff, Kalman Marmor, Abraham Reisen, Joseph Rolnick. Manuscripts of Dimondstein. Manuscripts from the office of *Literarishe heftn*.

223. DISPLACED PERSONS CAMPS AND CENTERS IN AUSTRIA.
Records, 1945–1951. 16 ft. 8 in. (RG 294.4)

Displaced persons (DP) camps for Jewish Holocaust survivors were established in Austria in 1945 by UNRRA (United Nations Relief and Rehabilitation Agency). They were administered by the U.S. Army and UNRRA and later by the International Refugee Organization (IRO). The camps existed until 1952. The number of Jewish residents in the camps was highest in 1948 when it reached 25,000. The Jewish displaced persons were represented by the Central Committee of Liberated Jews. The DP population consisted mainly of refugees from Hungary, Rumania, Poland and Czechoslovakia. There were altogether 12 camps located in Salzburg, Linz, Ebelsberg, Saalfelden, Puch, Hallein, Wegscheid, Wels and Enns. With the establishment of the State of Israel in 1948 and the enactment of the Displaced Persons (DP) Act in 1948 in the United States, a gradual closing of the camps began. Most of the camps were closed by 1952.

The records of the DP camps and centers in Austria were received from various sources between 1946 and 1960. The records were gathered as a result of a wide collection project on the experience of Jewish displaced persons.

The record group is comprised of correspondence, circular letters, minutes, leaflets and posters, relating to the camp administration as well as to cultural, educational, political and religious life in the camp. There are lists of camp residents, search lists, individual case files. Materials on camp committees, political parties, international and Jewish relief agencies, and American military authorities. Included are materials from Bad Gastein, Bad Ischl, Bindermichel, Ebelsberg, Ebensee, Enns, Hallein, Ranshofen, Steyr, Wegscheid (Tyler 337), Wels.

Files of organizations include: Israelitische Kultusgemeinde, Central Committee of Liberated Jews in Upper Austria, International Committee for Jewish Concentration Camp Inmates, AJDC, Jewish Agency. Files of camps are arranged by camp name and include records of camp committees and of other institutions active in the camps. Files of supervising authorities include materials from the U.S. military, UNRRA and IRO.

Inventory, English.

224. DISPLACED PERSONS CAMPS AND CENTERS IN GERMANY.
Records, 1945–1952. 51 ft. (RG 294.2)

The DP Camps and Centers in the American Zone of Germany were established by UNRRA (United Nations Relief and Rehabilitation Agency) and the U.S. Army in order to provide care to thousands of former inmates of Nazi concentration camps and forced labor units. Camp residents included Holocaust survivors who did not wish to return to their country of origin, and refugees such as Polish Jews who fled Poland after the pogrom in Kielce in 1946. The camps, which existed from 1945 until 1953, provided temporary shelter; health, cultural, educational and financial programs; and immigration services.

Until 1947 the official administrator of the DP program was UNRRA. In 1947 the IRO (International Refugee Organization) took over this role. The internal administration of the camps as well as the assistance programs were handled by the Central Committee of Liberated Jews and its local branches. The American Jewish Joint Distribution Committee as well as other Jewish organizations such as the Jewish Agency and the World Jewish Congress provided substantial material support and immigration aid.

The DP camps in the British Zone were administered by the British army. The DP population in the British Zone was represented by the Central Jewish Committee which had its seat in the Bergen-Belsen DP camp.

By 1953 most of the camp residents had immigrated to Israel or the United States or to other countries. The flow of immigration was facilitated by the DP Act of 1948 and the establishment of the State of Israel.

Records relating to the camps in the American Zone of Germany:

Files of the Central Committee of Liberated Jews in the American Zone and of its departments. Files of the Central Court of Honor. Minutes and other materials of First through Third Congresses of Displaced Persons in the American Zone.

Files of local DP camps. These files are comprised of materials from centers, camp committees as well as local branches of DP organizations and relief agencies. By far the largest in this series are records of camps Feldafing and Föhrenwald. In addition, the following localities are represented: Amberg, Augsburg, Bad Reichenhall, Bamberg, Berchtesgaden, Deggendorf, Eggenfelden, Eschwege, Frankfurt am Main, Fritzlar, Fulda, Gauting, Giebelstadt, Gersfeld, Hasenecke, Heidelberg, Heidenheim, Hofgeismar, Kassel, Krailing-Planegg, Lampertheim, Landau, Landsberg, Munich, Neu-Freiman, Neu-Ulm, Plattling, Pocking-Waldstadt, Poppendorf, Regensburg, Rochelle, Schwabach, Schwäbisch Hall, Straubing, Stuttgart, Tirschenreuth, Vilseck, Wetzlar, Windsheim, Zeilsheim, Ziegenhain.

Files of camps vary in content. They include lists of displaced persons; materials on cultural, educational and religious activities. Materials on schools are fragmentary. Records of camps in the Stuttgart region, for example, contain materials on the Beit Bialik school, including children's drawings and exercise books.

Files of professional, social, cultural and political organizations. Included are: Union of Employees of the Central Committee, Union of Invalids, Union of Jewish Students, Jewish Actors Union, *landsmanshaftn*, political parties, ORT, AJDC.

Eyewitness accounts and other materials on the Holocaust collected by the Central Historical Commission.

Records of the DP camps in the British Zone. Includes materials of the Congresses of Survivors in the British Zone and files of the Central Committee in Bergen-Belsen. Announcements, files on religious affairs, lists of communities and committees. Records of the Central Court of Honor. Reports of the Central Historical Commission. Police and court documents relating to former kapos, blackmarketeers and thieves. Miscellaneous organizational files.

Materials of the French Zone and of Berlin, including reports, lists and statistics pertaining to the Berlin Jewish community and to Jewish displaced persons. Election leaflets, printed matter about religious affairs, cultural materials, newsletters, Yiddish radio announcements, JDC reports and correspondence.

Inventory, English.

225. DISPLACED PERSONS CAMPS AND CENTERS IN ITALY.
Records, 1945–1950. 13 ft. (RG 294.3)

Following the end of World War II, up to the time of the Displaced Persons Act, Italy was the principal transit country for Jewish displaced persons who wished to leave Europe and settle in Palestine. Their stay in Italy was prolonged by the British anti-immigration policy which until 1948 barred them from entering Palestine en masse. In 1945 there were about 12,000 Jewish displaced persons in Italy. The DP population rose at times to 30,000 as it was constantly replenished by newcomers who took the places of those who had succeeded in leaving for Palestine. The DP camps were set up in Italy and cared for by UNRRA (later IRO), with supplementary aid from AJDC, ORT and other voluntary organizations. ORT and the AJDC set up workshops and trade schools to teach employment skills. AJDC also played a major role providing educational facilities to residents, supported a yeshiva and helped maintain kosher kitchens. Both AJDC and ORT provided health facilities. The camp residents were governed by their own elected representation, the Central Committee of Liberated Jews (Merkaz Ha-pleitim; Organizzazione dei Profughi Ebrei), and by local camp committees. The Central Committee was headquartered in Rome. The closing of the camps began in 1948. In that year alone 20,000 displaced persons left for Israel. The Central Committee resolved to cease activity on October 1, 1950.

These records were gathered in Italy by individuals as well as by Friends of YIVO groups active in the DP camps. The majority of the records were transferred to YIVO from the offices of the Central Committee by David Kupferberg. Included are correspondence, circular letters, publications, broadcast texts, lists of displaced persons and search lists of relatives, Court of Honor files, posters, handicraft items by school children.

Files of the Central Committee of the Organization of Jewish Refugees in Italy. Materials relating to the founding conference. Reports and minutes of meetings. Correspondence with district committees and with camps. Reports of Central Committee departments.

Files of the Statistics Department: search inquiries from relatives and agencies abroad wishing to locate individuals in Italy. Some lists of survivors in Italy prepared by the World Jewish Congress and the AJDC.

Files of the Central Court of Honor: correspondence, minutes, reports and verdicts, including cases which involved Nazi collaborators.

Files of the Cultural and Educational Department: materials on the Cultural Conference, July 1948. Drawings and notebooks of children. Records of camp schools, the Jewish Students' Organization, theatrical ensembles. Photographs of cultural and educational activities in various camps.

Files of individual DP camps: minutes and correspondence of camp committees; election materials; radio broadcast announcements by camp administrations as well as by political groups. Included are materials from camps Adriatica, Barletta, Grugliasco, Trani, Cremona.

Files of political parties, cultural and professional organizations, *landsmanshaftn* and relief agencies. Included are materials from the Association of Lithuanian Jews, lists of Vilna refugees.

Posters and children's art works from various camps.

Inventory, English.

226. DISPLACED PERSONS CAMPS AND CENTERS: PHOTOGRAPHS.
(RG 294.5)

Photographs of about 70 DP camps and centers in Austria, Germany and Italy which depict daily life and major events in these places. There are images of living conditions; social, cultural and political activities; emigration.

Card inventory, English.

227. DISTRICT COURT OF JERUSALEM: EICHMANN TRIAL.
Records, 1961–1962. 12 ft. 1 in. (RG 674)

Adolf Otto Eichmann, Nazi official and SS officer during World War II, was chief of operations in the Nazi plan to annihilate European Jewry. He was abducted by the Israeli government in May 1960 from his hiding place in Argentina. Eichmann was tried by the Jerusalem District Court and was charged with "crimes against the Jewish people . . . crimes against humanity . . . war crimes, and membership in an 'enemy organization.'" The trial lasted from April to December 1961. He was found guilty and sentenced to death. Eichmann was hanged after his appeal was dismissed by the Israeli Supreme Court in May 1962 and after the president of Israel rejected his plea for clemency.

The collection consists of mimeographed, typewritten and photostated copies of documents published by Israeli authorities and covering the pre-trial and the trial period. There are also some non-official materials such as news clippings, pamphlet and news releases.

The following are included:

Materials prepared by the Israeli police. Inventory of police documents and eyewitness accounts. Pre-trial interrogation of Eichmann by Captain Less. Transcripts from tapes. Lists of documents mentioned during the interrogation. Analyses prepared by the police arranged by topic: Eastern Europe, Western Europe, gas killings, deportations, sterilization.

Records of the trial. Copies of the trial proceedings, summaries of defense and prosecution, indictment, testimonies.

Non-official material. Glossary of Nazi terms. Legislation regarding punishment of war criminals. Clippings from newspapers including the *Jerusalem Post*. Arab propaganda pamphlets.

Inventory, English.

228. DJINDJIKHASHVILI, NODAR (born 1939).
    Collection, 1978–1979. ca. 5,000 items. (RG 1218)

Born in Georgia, USSR. Received Ph.D. in Philology from the USSR Academy of Sciences, a degree in Fine Arts from the University of Moscow, a Master's Degree in Filmmaking from the Moscow Institute of Cinematography. Immigrated to the United States in 1980.

Slides of photographs of Jewish life and sites taken by Djindjikhashvili and artist Albert Ben-Zion (Tsitsiashvili) on a tour of the Soviet Union in 1978 and 1979. Localities represented in the collection include: Krasnaya Sloboda, Makhachkala, Tashkent, Derbent, Baku, Bukhara, Kiev, Novorossiisk, Kishinev, Chufut-Kale, Vilnius, Kaunas, Minsk, Berdichev, Vitebsk, Moscow (synagogues), Riga, Leningrad, Vinnitsa, Babi Yar, Zhitomir, Odessa, Samarkand, Sachkhere, Poti, Sukhumi, Vani, Kutaisi, Kareli, Gori, Tbilisi (Ashkenazic synagogue, Jewish Quarter, Central Synagogue).

229. DLUZNOWSKY, MOSHE (1906–1977).
    Papers, 1930s–1970s. 11 ft. 8 in. (RG 1193)

Yiddish writer, journalist. Contributed to a wide variety of periodicals including *Parizer vokhnblat* (Paris), *Moment* (Warsaw), *Morgn zhurnal* (NY), *Der tog* (NY), *Jewish Daily Forward* (NY), *Zukunft* (NY), *Yidisher kemfer* (NY), *Freie Arbeiter Stimme* (NY), *Kinder zhurnal* (NY), *Hadoar* (NY), *Hatsofe* (NY), *Nerot Shabat* (NY). Born in Tomaszów Mazowiecki, Poland. Immigrated to Paris, France, in 1930. Settled in the United States after World War II.

The collection relates to Dluznowsky's literary career and personal life, and consists of personal documents, memoirs, biographical materials, correspondence with individuals, correspondence with organizations, legal documents, manuscripts of stories, novels, dramas and articles, printed materials, clippings, notes, programs, photographs. Correspondents include Joseph Buloff, Marc Chagall, Chaim Grade, Chaim Kazdan, H. Leivick, David Licht, Sol Liptzin, Shmuel Niger, Joseph Opatoshu, Melech Ravitch, Abraham Reisen, A.A. Roback, Maurice Schwartz, Zvee Scooler, Zalman Shneur, Isaac Bashevis Singer, Jacob Waislitz, Max Weinreich. Photographs include some depicting Jewish life in Morocco.

Inventory, Yiddish.

230. DOBROSZYCKI, LUCJAN (1925–1995).
    Papers, 1939–1947. 5 in. (RG 634)

Historian. Research Associate at the YIVO Institute for Jewish Research, Professor of Holocaust Studies at Yeshiva University. Author of works on the history of Jews in Poland in the 20th century. Editor of the *Chronicle of the Lodz Ghetto* published in English by Yale University Press. Co-editor, together with Barbara Kirshenblatt-Gimblett, of *Image Before My Eyes*. Born in Poland. Settled in the United States.

The papers relate to Dobroszycki's research activities and consist primarily of photostatic copies of documents relating to the Warsaw ghetto. There is also a microfilm of some documents from the Emanuel Ringelblum Archive in the Jewish Historical Institute in Warsaw.

231. DOBRUSZKES, AZARIA.
    Collection, 1940s–1975. 10 in. (RG 387)

Collector for YIVO, Brussels, Belgium.

Circulars, clippings, printed materials, program notes, postcards, and correspondence relating to educational, cultural and political activities of the Jewish community in Belgium.

232. DOMBIER BENEVOLENT SOCIETY.
Records, 1880s, 1913–1939. 5 1/2 in. (RG 781)

Organized in New York in 1916 by immigrants from Dąbie, Poland. Merged with the Kladowa Society in 1970.

Constitution. Minutes, 1916–1922. Personal materials and photographs pertaining to the Kash family in Dąbie and in the United States, 1913–1939. Pall cloth.

233. DORA LIPKOWITZ VOLUNTARY AID AND SICK BENEFIT SOCIETY.
Records, 1970–1976. 2 1/2 in. (RG 953)

Founding date unknown. Provided cemetery benefits for members. Dissolved in 1976.

Minutes. Materials pertaining to burial and finances. Seal.

234. DOROSHKIN, JACOB.
Papers, 1955–1974. 12 1/2 in. (RG 746)

Yiddish cultural activist. Contributed articles to *Morgn frayhayt*. Lived in New York, Florida.

The papers consist of scrapbooks of Doroshkin's articles and clippings on Yiddish language, Yiddish cultural institutions, correspondence and manuscripts.

235. DROPKIN, CELIA (1888–1956).
Papers, ca. 1908–ca. 1950. 17 1/2 in. (RG 1294)

Yiddish poet and writer. Was among the first Yiddish Modernist poets. Published poems and short stories in *Di naye velt, In zikh, Shriftn, Tog, Zukunft*, and other Yiddish-language periodicals. The only book of her poems, *In heysn vint*, was published in New York in 1935. Also wrote in Russian and English. Took up painting in her later years. Born in Bobruisk, Byelorussia. Settled in New York in 1912. Died in New York.

Manuscripts and clippings of Dropkin's poems and short stories. List of Dropkin's writings and of articles about her. Personal documents and photographs. Letters from Joseph Hayyim Brenner, Helen Londinsky, Feygl Rolnick, Shea Tenenbaum.

236. DUBNOW, SIMON (1860–1941).
Papers, 1632–1938. 4 ft. (RG 87)

Historian, political thinker, educator, collector of historical and ethnographic documents. One of the founders and directors of the Jewish Historical and Ethnographic Society in St. Petersburg and editor of its quarterly *Evreiskaya Starina*. Co-founder of the YIVO Institute in Vilna and chairman of its Honorary Board of Trustees (Curatorium). After the Kishinev pogrom, Dubnow was among those who called for an active Jewish self-defense. He supported Jewish participation in the 1905 elections to the Duma. Active in the Society for Equal Rights of the Jewish People in Russia. Founder in 1906 of the Jewish People's or "Folkist" party which existed until 1930s in the Ukraine, Russia, Poland, and the Baltic countries.

Dubnow coined the term "autonomism," a theory of Jewish nationalism and cultural autonomy in the Diaspora in which Yiddish was considered one of the instruments of autonomy and the Jewish national language of the future. Dubnow authored a number of significant and pioneering works in Jewish history. Topics included general Jewish history, Polish and Russian Jewry, Jewish communities and Hasidism.

Dubnow was one of the first to encourage and initiate the collection and preservation of Jewish historical documents. He corresponded with communities throughout Russia and Poland, appealing for community registers, memorabilia, letters, manuscripts, folklore materials, rare books and Hasidic literature. Large numbers of rare documents were sent to Dubnow in response to this appeal.

Born in Mstislavl, Byelorussia. Lived in St. Petersburg, Odessa, Vilna. In 1922 left Russia and settled in Berlin. In 1933 settled in Riga, Latvia. In 1941, Dubnow was killed by a Gestapo officer during the deportation of the Jewish community of Riga to a death camp.

Correspondence with individuals, 1885–1936, including: Shmuel Alexandrovich, Isaak Antonovsky, Solomon Bernstein, Martin Buber, Simon Goldlust, Shmuel Silberstein, Abraham Taub, Maxim Vinawer, Max Weinreich, Yehuda Leib Weisman, Chaim Zhitlowsky, Chaim Zuskind.

Records of Jewish communities. Originals and copies of community registers (*pinkasim*), and other historical documents from Mstislavl, 1760–1895; Pińczów, 1632–1740; Piotrowice, 1726–1809; Stary Bykhow, 1686–1869; Tykocin, 1769–1777; Zabłudów, 1650–1783; Birzai, 1755–1796; Dubno, 1670–1671; Lublin, 18th century; Międzyrzec, 1816; Novaya Ushitsa, 1839–1840.

Historical documents relating to: restrictions and privileges issued by governments to Jewish populations; blood libel trials; *Gzerot Takh-Tat* (Chmielnicki massacres of 1648–49); documents from Russian Justice Ministry and Senate, 1799–1800.

Materials on pogroms in the Russian empire, 1880–1907. Includes pogroms in Kishinev (1903), Gomel (1903), Białystok (1906). Materials on Hasidism. Extracts of books, correspondence, documents by and about Hasidic rabbis and about Hasidism.

Family papers. Includes papers of Rabbi Benzion Dubnow, grandfather of Simon Dubnow. General family correspondence.

Inventory, Yiddish, Russian.

237. DUBOIER YOUNG MEN'S PROGRESSIVE ASSOCIATION.
Records, 1938–1979. 5 in. (RG 1022)

Founded in 1928 at the wedding of a *landsman* from Duboy, Byelorussia.

Minutes, 1939–1958. Anniversary journal. Meeting announcements, 1938–1979, including those of the Duboier Young Ladies Club, 1940s.

238. DUBOV, SARA and JACOB.
Papers, 1910–1950s. 5 in. (RG 1186)

The Dubovs were active in Yiddish cultural circles in Chicago. They were among the founders of the Sholem Aleichem Folk Institute in Chicago in 1925 and maintained contacts with many Yiddish writers.

Correspondence from Jacob Dubov to Sara. Correspondence from Yiddish writers including Chaim Grade, Moses (Moyshe) Leib Halpern, H. Leivick, Kadia Molodowsky, Abraham Sutzkever. Photographs of H. Leivick, Peretz Hirschbein and David Pinsky.

239. DUBOVSKY, BENJAMIN (born 1888).
    Papers. 5 ft. 5 in. (RG 468)

Physician, Yiddish journalist. Wrote a weekly column on medical questions in the *Morgn zhurnal* (NY). Contributed to the *Amerikaner* (NY), *New yorker vokhnblat* (NY), *Jewish Daily Forward* (NY), *Der tog* (NY), and the *Freie Arbeiter Stimme* (NY). Contributed to English language medical and scientific journals. Born in Talna, Ukraine. Immigrated to the United States in 1905.

    Manuscripts and clippings of Dubovsky's articles on medical topics as well as articles on the Bible, Eichmann trial.

240. DUKLAR RELIEF SOCIETY.
    Records, 1944–1968. 2 1/2 in. (RG 799)

Organized in New York in 1920 by immigrants from Dukla, Poland, for relief purposes. Incorporated in 1923. Aided *landslayt* in Europe and Israel after World War II. Dissolved in the 1970s.

    Minutes, 1948–1958. Financial records, 1955–58. Correspondence, 1951–1968. Membership lists. News clippings.

241. DUNTOW, JOSEPH.
    Papers, 1947–1950s. 3 ft. 9 in. (RG 545)

Secretary, Workmen's Circle Southern District, Miami, Florida.

    The collection relates to Duntow's activities in the Workmen's Circle, Southern District. Correspondence, reports and materials from Workmen's Circle publications.

242. DYMOW, OSSIP (1878–1959).
    Papers, ca. 1900–1958. 3 ft. 3 in. (RG 469)

Pseudonym of Joseph Perelman. Russian and Yiddish playwright and writer. Published stories, serials, sketches, and many plays. Most of the plays were written in Russian. Many were adapted to the Yiddish theater and some were translated into Polish, Hebrew and German. He contributed to *Der tog* (NY), *Kundes* (NY). His memoirs, *Vos ich gedenk*, New York, 1943–1944, were first published in serial form in the *Jewish Daily Forward* (NY).

    Manuscripts of plays, sketches, radio dramas, stories, articles and autobiographical writings in Russian, Yiddish, English and German. Family correspondence. Clippings by and about Dymow. Theater programs, contract.

    Inventory, Yiddish.

243. ECKSTADT, SHLOYME.
    Papers, 1918–1935. 10 in. (RG 1230)

Yiddish actor and director. Lived in Estonia, the United States.

    Manuscripts of plays in Yiddish and Russian, some adapted or translated by Eckstadt. Manuscripts of articles on the Yiddish theater. A Yiddish translation of an article by Leon Trotsky on class stratification in the Soviet Union. Telegrams of congratulations, Tallinn, Estonia, 1923. Programs from the Moscow Art Theater and of a Yiddish production of Ibsen's *Ghosts* performed in New York. Photographs of the Moscow Art Theater, clipped from a book.

244. EDELSTADT, DAVID (1866–1892).

Papers, 1880s. 5 in. (RG 517)

Prominent Yiddish poet of the Jewish socialist and anarchist movements. Born into an assimilated Jewish Russian family, Edelstadt began writing in Russian. After the pogrom in Kiev in 1881, he immigrated with his family to the United States. Edelstadt was influenced by the anarchist movement and in 1890 became the editor of the anarchist *Freie Arbeiter Stimme*, a position he held until shortly before his death. Edelstadt's poems, which reflected his involvement with the cause of the worker, attained worldwide popularity among the Jewish working class. He died of tuberculosis in Denver, Colorado, at the age of 26.

Manuscripts and typed copies of Edelstadt's poems, short stories and articles. Letters by Edelstadt to his sister Sonya Edelstadt-Telson.

245. EDLIN, WILLIAM (1878–1947).

Papers, 1900–1947. 7 ft. 1 in. (RG 251)

Journalist, editor of *The Day* (*Der tog*). Socialist leader, co-founder and president of the Workmen's Circle, secretary of the Keren Hayesod in the United States. Born in Priluki, Ukraine. Immigrated to the United States in 1891.

Correspondence and other materials pertaining to individuals: Jacob P. Adler, Joseph Barondess, Herman Bernstein, Abraham Cahan, Jacob de Haas, Ossip Dymow, Eugene Debs, Isadora Duncan, Samuel Gompers, Peretz Hirschbein, Harold Ickes, Vladimir Jabotinsky, Jacob Kalich, Herbert H. Lehman, Jack London, Joseph Margoshes, Molly Picon, Sholem Aleichem, Alfred E. Smith, Rabbi Chaim Soloveichik, Nathan Straus, Jr., Baruch Charney Vladeck, Felix Warburg, Chaim Weizmann, Rabbi Stephen Wise, Aaron Zeitlin, Dr. Chaim Zhitlowsky.

Correspondence and other materials relating to the Socialist Party and other organizations: ICOR, American Jewish Congress, American ORT Federation, *The Day*, Educational Alliance, *Morning Freiheit*, HIAS, Keren Hayesod, Zionist Organization of America, *Zukunft*. Manuscripts by Edlin: *Heroes in Chains*, *The Jew*. Manuscripts of Edlin's translations into Yiddish of literary works. Clippings of Edlin's column "What Is New in the Socialist World," 1935–1937. Clippings about Edlin, 1897–1945. Personal correspondence. Financial records. Autobiographical materials. Manuscripts of other writers.

Inventory, English.

246. EDUCATIONAL ALLIANCE.

Records, 1888–1968. 133 ft. 4 in. (RG 312)

Cultural and educational institution in New York's Lower East Side, established in 1889 to promote Americanization of Jewish immigrants. Since 1924 has been operating as a community center.

Minutes of Educational Alliance administrative and steering committees, correspondence of lay leaders and administration officials, general administration records. Correspondence, reports and other records of various Educational Alliance divisions, clubs, classes, summer camps. Materials relating to: Legal Aid Bureau, 1931–1939; Stuyvesant Neighborhood House, 1919–1950; Art School, 1920s–1950s; Youth Division; Young Adult Division; People's Synagogue; School of Religious Work; New York School of Social Work; New York University survey "The Lower East Side," 1950s.

A photograph series depicts: the Educational Alliance building; camps; groups and clubs; individuals, English classes, gym classes. Educational Alliance Art School.

Inventory, English.

Card inventory of the photographs.

247. EICHLER, BENJAMIN.
Collection, 1839–1972. 8 in. (RG 1097)

Jewish communal leader in Slovakia after World War II. Elected president of the Central Union of Jewish Religious Communities, Bratislava, 1955. Collected documents relating to Jewish Communities in Slovakia. Emigrated to Canada, 1972.

Materials on the history of the Jewish community of Slovakia, 1918–1972, pertaining mostly to the Holocaust and post-Holocaust period.

Materials relating to non-Jews who aided Jews; partisans and resistance fighters; people active in Jewish community affairs after World War II; the Sered labor camp, including testimony about the camp, lists of Jewish prisoners and deportations; transports.

Annotated copies of photographs of: Slovakian labor camps (mostly Sered, some may be from Novaky); postwar Slovakian synagogues, monuments, memorial meetings, mass graves from Holocaust period.

Statutes of Jewish communities and charitable organizations in Czechoslovakia before 1938, including the following communities: Košice, Nádaše, Smolenice, Stará Turá, Bratislava, Svätý. Materials relating to: Jewish cemeteries in Slovakia after World War II; graves in the old Jewish cemetery in Bratislava; mass graves in Petrzalka.

248. EIGER, HERMAN (CHONEN) (1897–1971).
Papers. 10 in. (RG 619)

Yiddish writer, agronomist. Wrote children's stories, poems. Co-editor of *Der yidisher farmer*, contributed to the *Jewish Daily Forward*, *Morgn zhurnal*, *Der tog*, *Der groyser kundes*. Born in Ostrowiec near Kleck, Byelorussia. Immigrated to the United States in 1909.

The collection consists of manuscripts and clippings of Eiger's humorous stories.

249. EINHORN, DAVID (1886–1973).
Papers, 1914–1940s. 1 ft. 8 in. (RG 277)

Yiddish poet. Long-time member of the Jewish Labor Bund. Lived in Russia, Switzerland, Poland, Germany, France and the United States.

Correspondence with Einhorn's wife. Correspondence with Jewish and international socialist leaders: Victor Alter, Angelica Balabanoff, Abraham Cahan, Henryk Erlich, Vladimir Medem, Baruch Vladeck.

Correspondence with writers and journalists: Shalom Asch, Isaac Babel, Martin Buber, Simon Horontchik, Abraham Liessin, Shmuel Niger, Joseph Opatoshu, Zalman Shneur, I.J. Singer, Yehoash. Correspondence with Yiddish publications.

250. EINSATZGRUPPEN.
Records, 1941–1942. 2 ft. 3 in. (RG 557)

The Einsatzgruppen were special mobile killing units established by the Reichssicherheitshauptamt (RSHA—Reich Security Main Office). Positioned in the rear of the German army, they functioned mainly in German-occupied territories of the USSR where they murdered between 500,000 and 1,000,000 Jews. After the combat period was at an end in a particular area, the Einsatzgruppen became local branches of the RSHA. There were four Einsatzgruppen operating in the invaded areas of the USSR designated with the letters A, B, C and D. They were subordinated administratively to the respective army command and functionally to the RSHA.

Selected Einsatzgruppen records:

RSHA reports on the activities of Einsatzgruppen in the USSR, 1941–1942. These reports were based on the reports sent by the four Einsatzgruppen to Berlin. Between June 1941 and April 1942, 195 reports were issued. Reports Nos. 1 to 30 are missing in this collection.

Reports from the Occupied Eastern Territories. These were issued by the commanders of the Einsatzgruppen after the units had become stationary local branches of the RSHA. The reports relate to topics such as "actions" (i.e. extermination raids), executions, forced labor, camps, ghettos, Judenrat, Jewish badges, pogroms by local populations, final solution, partisans.

Card inventory.

251. EISNER, GUSTAVE (1886–1939).
Papers, 1905–1938. 10 in. and 5 microfilm reels (RG 316)

Journalist in Łódź, Poland. Active in the socialist movement. Member of the Executive Board of the American branch of YIVO. Owner, Gustave Eisner Travel Bureau, New.York City.

Family and general correspondence. Manuscripts by Eisner. Personal documents. Materials relating to the Polska Partia Socjalistyczna (Polish Socialist Party), 1905–1912. Records of court cases against party members active in the 1905–1907 revolution in Poland. Party proclamations. Materials pertaining to various Łódź *landsmanshaftn* in the United States. Records of the Gustave Eisner Travel Bureau which specialized in travel arrangements to Eastern Europe and Palestine. Films relating to the trips to Eastern Europe and Palestine as well as some about American Jewish life.

The films were placed and cataloged in the Film Collection, RG 105.

252. ELFENBEIN, ISRAEL (1890–1964).
Papers, 1915–1964. 5 ft. 5 in. (RG 773)

Rabbi, Hebrew scholar, author and editor. Director, Educational Department of the Mizrachi Organization in the United States. Editor, *Or Hamizrach* and contributor to *Sinai, Talpiot, Jewish Quarterly Review, Jewish Forum*. Born in Buchach (Pol. Buczacz) Ukraine. Immigrated to the United States in 1906.

Correspondence with and relating to congregations in Nashville, Chicago, New York City, Seagate (Brooklyn). Correspondence with periodicals, organizations. Correspondence relating to the *Elfenbein Jubilee Volume*. Correspondence relating to *Rashi Responsa*. Correspondence and other materials relating to activities of the Mizrachi movement including correspondence relating to *Or Hamizrach*. Personal and family correspondence. Personal documents. Financial papers. Correspondence with scholars, rabbis, writers and communal figures including Cyrus Adler, Shmuel Yosef Agnon, Salo Baron, Chaim Bloch, Yosef Burg, Louis Finkelstein, Solomon Freehoff, I. Goldfarb, Leo Jung, Mordechai Kossover, Joseph Lookstein, A. R. Malachi, Jacob Mann,

Louis Marshall, Alexander Marx, David de Sola Pool, Eliezer Silver, Chaim Tchernowitz, Dr. Ephraim Urbach. Sermons, addresses, talks. Clippings from *Jewish Forum*. Manuscripts by Elfenbein and others relating to Jewish personalities, Jewish history and liturgy, and Elfenbein's book *Rashi Responsa*.

Inventory, English.

253. ELINITZER KRANKEN UNTERSTITZUNGS VEREIN.
Records, 1945–1976. 5 in. (RG 891)

Founded in New York in 1895 by immigrants from Ilintsy, Ukraine. At one time owned a synagogue on Clinton Street, New York. Maintained a loan fund for members.

Constitution. Minutes, 1946–1975. Financial records, 1945–1959. Loan fund materials. Correspondence pertaining to burials. Membership records, 1930s–1950s.

254. ELKIN, MENDL (1874–1962).
Papers, 1913–1961. 5 ft. (RG 453)

Actor, theater director, journalist, writer and first Chief Librarian of the YIVO Library and Archives in New York. Elkin's main interest was Yiddish theater. He translated plays into Yiddish, acted on stage, directed productions, founded new theater groups, contributed to drama journals and was involved in theater organizations. Together with Alexander Granowsky he established the Yiddish Chamber Theater in Russia in 1917, and later founded an experimental theater in New York known as Undzer Teater. He contributed extensively to Yiddish publications, co-edited the theater journals *Tealit* (NY) and *Yiddish Theater* (NY), and published works by Peretz Hirschbein. In 1921 he was elected president of the Yidisher Artistn Fareyn (Jewish Actors Union) in Warsaw. In 1936 Elkin was active in the establishment of the Central Jewish Library in New York. In 1940 this library became the YIVO Library and Archives. Elkin was the Chief Librarian until his death in 1962. Born in Brozha, near Bobruisk, in Byelorussia. Immigrated to the United States in 1923.

Correspondence with Yiddish literary figures and Jewish institutions. Included are Shalom Asch, David Bergelson, Menahem Boraisha, Daniel Charney, Solomon Dingol, Ossip Dymow, Jacob Glatstein, Moses (Moyshe) Leib Halpern, Abraham Joshua Heschel, Peretz Hirschbein, David Ignatoff, Judah A. Joffe, Alter Kacyzne, Leon Kobrin, Leibush Lehrer, H. Leivick, Raphael Mahler, Kalman Marmor, Jacob Mestel, Shmuel Niger, Joseph Opatoshu, David Pinsky, Zalman Reisen, Isaac Bashevis Singer, Elias Tcherikower, Max Weinreich, Chaim Zhitlowsky, Zalmen Zylbercweig.

Manuscripts of Elkin's memoirs, plays and adaptations. Manuscripts of plays by others. Elkin's articles about the theater. Photographs of Elkin and friends. Drawings of characters in *Amnon and Tamar* produced by the Vilna Troupe.

Photographs are cataloged in STAGEPIX.

255. ELLSTEIN, ABRAHAM (1907–1963).
Papers, 1940s–1964. 5 in. (RG 522)

Jewish composer, conductor and pianist. Composed extensively for the Yiddish musical theater and also wrote the scores for several Yiddish films. Composed liturgical works for the synagogue as well as several hundred Yiddish songs. Born in New York.

Programs, news clippings and other materials relating to Ellstein's career.

256. ELLSTEIN, HERSCHEL.
    Papers. 10 in. (RG 521)

Jewish composer and choir conductor. United States.
    Handwritten scores of musical works for synagogue services.

**257. EMPIRE STATE LODGE NO. 460, INDEPENDENT ORDER
    OF ODD FELLOWS.**
    Records, 1936–1977. 7 1/2 in. (RG 873)

A fraternal lodge of the Independent Order of Odd Fellows. Shares common cemetery
grounds with the Empire Fellowship Association, Sochrochiner Lodge, Independent
Sochrochiner B.A., Shevas Israel Anshe Raigod in the Washington Cemetery, Brooklyn.
    By-laws of the lodge. Minutes, 1950–1953, 1959–1977. Membership records, 1930s,
1940s, 1960s, 1970s.

258. ENTIN, JOEL (ca. 1875–1959).
    Papers, ca. 1896–ca. 1959. 2 in. (RG 1235)

Writer, theater critic, active in the Labor Zionist movement. Teacher of Yiddish language,
Yiddish drama. Born in Pohost, Russia. Settled in the United States in 1891.
    Manuscripts of school essays. Poetry in English. Notes on the theater. Correspondence
with family. General correspondence. Texts of eulogies and other material concerning
Entin's death. Photographs of Entin, family, friends. Photograph of the graduating class of
the Jewish Teachers Seminary in New York, 1922. Articles by and about Entin.

259. EPHROS, GERSHON.
    Papers, 1954–1977. 7 in. (RG 1242)

Cantor of congregations in Virginia, New York and New Jersey. Taught music in Hebrew
schools. Composer of religious and secular works. Published his own compositions and also
compiled cantorial anthologies. Born in Serock, Poland. Came to the United States in
1911. Died in New York.
    Photocopies of religious and secular music. Included are Sabbath and wedding services,
psalms, poems set to music, and arrangements for cantor, chorus and organ/piano.

260. EPPELBAUM, MENAHEM BAERUSH (BERISH) (1887–1945).
    Papers, ca. 1913–1930s. 1 ft. (RG 449)

Yiddish writer. Born and educated in Poland. Immigrated to the United States in 1922 and
lived in New York and later in Philadelphia.
    Manuscripts of Eppelbaum's literary works. Correspondence, clippings and photographs.
Translation of Yehuda Steinberg's *Hassidic Tales* and memoirs.

261. EPSTEIN, SHIFRA.
    Collection, 1970s. 1 ft. (RG 220)

This collection originated as a YIVO project to collect materials on the Bobover *purim shpil*
(a play performed traditionally on Purim day) in Borough Park, Brooklyn. The project
director was Shifra Epstein.

The collection consists of video and audio tapes as well as scripts and photographs of the Bobover *purim shpil* of 1977.

262. ERLICH, RACHEL (SHOSHKE) (1909–1991).
Papers, 1934–1984. 2 ft. 4 in. (RG 1300)

Research Associate of the YIVO Institute for nearly half a century, specializing in Yiddish language and literature. Member of the Bund party in Poland prior to World War II and of the Jewish Labor Bund in the United States. Born Rachel Fligel in Białystok, Poland. Settled in the United States in 1941. Died in New York.

Notes for courses in Yiddish literature given at the Max Weinreich Center for Advanced Jewish Studies. Lexicographic materials prepared for the *Groyser verterbukh fun der yidisher shprakh* (Great Dictionary of the Yiddish Language). Letters from Isaiah Berlin, Jacob Glatstein, Leopold Haimson, Roman Jakobson, Yudel Mark, Leon Oler, Leo Rosten, Lionel Trilling, Mordecai Tsanin, Max Weinreich. Photostatic copy of a manuscript on the early Jewish labor movement in the United States, German, 256 pages. Photographs of the Erlich family including Henryk Erlich, the leader of the Bund party in Poland.

263. ERSHTE BOLSHOWCER SICK BENEVOLENT SOCIETY AND LODGE NO. 517, INDEPENDENT ORDER BRITH ABRAHAM.
Records, 1909–1930. 5 in. (RG 872)

Lodge No. 517 was founded in New York by immigrants from Bolshovtsy (Pol. Bolszowce), Ukraine, as the Ershte Bolszowcer Arbeter Lodge No. 517 Independent Order Brith Abraham. The Ershte Bolshowcer Sick Benevolent Society was founded ca. 1909 as a mutual aid society. The two became affiliated with each other ca. 1924.

Minutes of the Lodge No. 517, 1909–1923. Minutes of the Sick Benevolent Society and Lodge, 1925–1930. Miscellaneous materials including bulletin of the Chevra Rodfey Tsedek Anshei Bolszowce, 1930s.

264. ERSTE BUDZANOWER KRANKEN UNTERSHTITSUNG VEREIN.
Records, 1929–1946, 1971. 2 1/2 in. (RG 997)

Established in New York in 1895 by immigrants from Budanov (Pol. Budzanów), Ukraine. Activities included establishment of a synagogue. Supported a talmud torah (religious school) in Budanov.

Minutes, 1929–1940, 1971. Golden book (record of deaths of members). Record book of interest-free loans. Souvenir journal. Memoirs about Budanov.

265. ERSTE SADAGORER KRANKEN UNTERSHTITZUNG VEREIN.
Records, 1903–1973. 2 1/2 in. (RG 917)

Organized in New York in 1903 by immigrants from Sadgora, Ukraine. Provided burial plots for members. Dissolved in the 1970s.

Correspondence and financial records, 1926–1973. Cemetery records, 1903–1959. Seal.

266. ERSTE SANDOWA WISHNIER KRANKEN UNTERSHTITZUNG VEREIN.
Records, 1949–1980. 2 1/2 in. (RG 1151)

Founded in New York in 1919 by immigrants from Sudovaya Vishnya (Pol. Sadowa Wisznia), Ukraine. Supported a small synagogue from 1919 to 1941. Arranged dances, dinners, weekends in Lakewood and the Catskills for a membership of 75 families. Provided burial and other benefits. Dissolved.

Minutes. Financial records (two books). Constitution.

267. ERSTE TAUSTER UNTERSTUTZUNG VEREIN.
Records, 1899–1974. 4 in. (RG 1089)

Established in New York in 1898 by immigrants from Touste (Tolstoye), Ukraine, and incorporated in 1899 to promote "the benevolent instincts of the members and to engage in religious worship according to the Hebrew faith." Contributed to Jewish philanthropies.

Certificate of incorporation, 1899. Constitution. Financial records. Cemetery materials. Correspondence. Agreement between society and meeting hall, 1903 (German).

268. ERSTE TREMBOWLER KRANKEN UNTERSTITZUNG VEREIN.
Records, 1957–1968. 1 in. (RG 1073)

Founded in New York in 1897 by immigrants from Terebovlya (Pol. Trembowla), Ukraine. Dissolved 1968.

Minutes, 1957–1968. Seal.

269. ERSTER KNIHININ STANISLAUER KRANKEN UNTERSHTITZUNG VEREIN.
Records, 1937–1977. 7 1/2 in. (RG 1090)

Organized in New York in 1907 by immigrants from Knihinin, Ukraine. Maintained a loan fund. Dissolved in 1977.

Minutes, 1953–1968 (German, English). Financial records, 1937–1977. Membership list, 1968. Seal.

270. ERSTER KRZYWCZA ON SAN BENEVOLENT SOCIETY.
Records, 1908, 1946–1966. 1 in. (RG 1013)

Founded in 1920 by former residents of Krzywcza, Poland. Established a relief committee after World War I to aid institutions in home town. Affiliated with a Krzywczer society in Israel that provides relief for indigent members.

Minutes, 1946–1966. *Ketubah* (marriage contract) of the secretary of the society, 1908.

271. ERSTER SAMBORER KRANKEN UNTERSTITZUNG VEREIN.
Records, 1930–1975. 10 1/2 in. (RG 960)

Founded in New York in 1884 by immigrants from Sambor, Ukraine. Dissolved in 1975.

Certificate of incorporation. Minutes, 1930–1974 (German). Financial records, 1957–1966. Cemetery records. Correspondence. Meeting notices. Dissolution ballots.

272. ESTHER-RACHEL KAMINSKA THEATER MUSEUM.
Collection, ca. 1900–1939. 59 ft. 2 in. (RG 8)

In 1927, Ida Kaminska and Zygmunt Turkow donated the papers of Esther Rachel Kaminska, known as the "mother" of Yiddish theater, to the YIVO Institute in Vilna. With the gift, the Esther-Rachel Kaminska Yiddish Theater Museum was established as part of YIVO. The present collection consists of what remains of the museum's original holdings.

The collection includes handwritten manuscripts, playbills, posters, correspondence, clippings and photographs relating to Jewish theater in Poland and other countries before World War II. The following materials are included:

Original manuscripts and handwritten copies of plays in Yiddish by S. Ansky, Leon Kobrin, Joseph Lateiner, N. Rakow, Isidore Zolatarevsky and others. Playbills of theater productions, concerts, recitals, shows, films, amateur performances. Posters of theater performances. Photographs of individual actors arranged alphabetically. Materials on amateur drama circles in Poland. Clippings of critical reviews. Biographical materials about actors, directors, producers, musicians, composers.

The following theater groups are among those represented in the collection: Vilna Troupe; Ararat, Łódź; VIKT (Varshever Yidisher Kunst Teater—Warsaw Yiddish Art Theater); Yung-Teater, Warsaw; GOSET (Gossudarstvennyi Evreiskii Teatr—State Jewish Theater), Moscow; Yiddish Art Theater, New York; Habimah, Moscow–Tel-Aviv.

Materials on theater personalities are comprised of fragments of individual collections which were in the possession of YIVO in Vilna. There are extensive files on Herz Grossbard, David Herman, Ida Kaminska, Esther Rachel Kaminska, Nahum Lipovski, Zygmunt Turkow, Yosef Vinogradov, Rudolf Zaslavsky.

Card catalog for playbills, posters, photographs, Yiddish.

Inventory of plays, Yiddish.

273. ETTINGER, MOISHE (born 1908).
Papers, 1950s–1970s. 2 1/2 in. (RG 1191)

Yiddish poet. Contributed to periodicals such as *Literarishe heftn* (NY), *New yorker vokhnblat* (NY), *Yiddisher kemfer* (NY), *Zukunft* (NY). Born in Kalush, Ukraine. Immigrated to the United States in 1938.

Correspondence with Yiddish writers, periodicals, 1950s–1970s.

274. EYEWITNESS ACCOUNTS OF THE HOLOCAUST PERIOD.
Collection, 1939–1945. 18 ft. 4 in. (RG 104)

The YIVO Institute was involved in several projects to collect written testimonies by survivors of the Holocaust. The first organized effort took place during the years 1945–1948. Informants were sought out mainly in the DP camps in Germany, Austria and Italy, but also in Poland and other countries of Eastern Europe. YIVO also received a substantial number of eyewitness accounts from other Jewish organizations which were involved in similar projects, in particular from the Jewish Historical Commission in Poland and the World Jewish Congress, Hungarian Section. The second project was conducted in 1954 as part of the YIVO–Yad Vashem Documentary Projects. Several hundred respondents were interviewed and their recollections were recorded by YIVO interviewers. Finally, the YIVO Archives has been acquiring Holocaust testimonies continuously since the 1960s.

The testimonies document the Jewish experience in all countries under Nazi occupation between September 1939 and May 1945. Included are: accounts relating to ghettos and death, labor and internment camps; testimonies of Jews on the Aryan side and in hiding;

memoirs of Jewish partisans and underground fighters. The collection is organized into three series, each series corresponding to a different collection project.

Series I includes the earliest testimonies and consists of 1,143 items. A large proportion of this series relates to Poland; a smaller but significant group of materials pertains to Hungary. There are a few accounts from Austria, Belgium, France and Holland. Large number of accounts pertain to the following places: Auschwitz, Warsaw, Vilna, Łódź, Radom, Paris, Lvov, Skarżysko-Kamienna.

Series II includes 500 interviews with survivors collected in 1954. Series III includes most testimonies received from the 1960s to the present. Series III also includes a series of accounts written by partisans. Presently there are over 300 accounts in this series.

Inventories and indexes to each of the three series, English, Yiddish.

275. EZRAS TORAH FUND.
Records, 1926–1936, 1958–1968. 2 ft. 11 in. (RG 237)

An organization founded in New York in 1915 by the Union of Orthodox Rabbis of America to provide financial assistance to rabbis and Torah scholars in Europe. Rabbi Joseph Elijah Henkin was its director for many years.

The collection consists of correspondence with rabbis and Torah scholars mostly in Poland, Rumania, Hungary, Russia, Palestine and the United States. There are also some printed reports, as well as materials relating to Rabbi Henkin. The bulk of the records cover the 1926–1936 period.

Inventory, Yiddish.

276. FALLER, JAMES (1885–1951).
Papers, ca. 1900–ca. 1960s. 2 ft. 1 in. (RG 643)

Adopted name of Jacob Felhendler. Used pen name Ben-Dovid and Y. Berson. Yiddish and English playwright and journalist. Wrote poems, stories, articles for *Lemberger tsaytung, Morgn zhurnal, Yiddishes Tageblatt, Der tog, Freie Arbeiter Stimme, Keneder odler* (Montreal). Born in Łuków, near Siedlce, Poland. In 1906 immigrated to London and from there to New York.

Plays by Faller in Yiddish and English. Clippings of his articles. Correspondence, including photocopies of several hundred letters from Sholem Aleichem to James Faller (the originals are in Beth Sholem Aleichem, Tel Aviv).

277. FAMILY LODGE NO. 189, INDEPENDENT ORDER BRITH ABRAHAM.
Records, 1935–1955. 2 1/2 in. (RG 830)

Founding date unknown. A lodge in the Independent Order Brith Abraham fraternal order.

Financial records. Correspondence, 1953–1955.

278. FARBAND FUN YIDISHE STUDENTN FAREYNEN (BERLIN).
Records, 1918–1926. 2 ft. 1 in. (RG 18)

Union of Jewish Student Associations. Organized in 1924 for the purpose of developing collaboration between local associations of Jewish students. The membership of these associations was comprised mainly of students from Eastern Europe, many of whom went to study in the universities of Germany and other Western countries.

Correspondence, reports, minutes of meetings, and posters relating to the activities of the

Union and of other, smaller student groups. Correspondence with: student groups in Germany, Poland, Latvia, Russia and Hungary; the Jewish Socialist Student Organization, Berlin; the Marxist section of the Jewish Student Organization; Jewish organizations, such as ORT, Zionist groups. Minutes from a Poalei Zion student group, 1922–1926. The collection also includes records of the Association of Jewish Students in Germany.

279. FARBER, ROBERT (YERAKHMIEL) (1894–1978).
Papers, 1966–1976. 10 in. (RG 779)

Yiddish writer. Wrote for *Di naye velt* (NY), *Frayhayt, Morgn frayhayt, Yidishe kultur, Zamlungen, Kamf, Di naye prese* (Paris). Born in Brześć, Poland. Lived in Łódź (Poland), Odessa (Russia). Immigrated to the United States in 1914.

The papers consist of typescripts, clippings and miscellaneous correspondence.

280. FAUST, JACK.
Papers, 1927–1942. 2 in. (RG 737)

Journalist. Correspondent of the Jewish-Polish daily *Chwila* in Lwów, Poland.

The collection consists of Faust's correspondence and clippings of Faust's articles in *Chwila*.

281. FEDER, MORRIS (1891–1958) and ZHELAZO, ELIEZER and ZHELAZO, ROSE.
Papers. 1 ft. 10 in. (RG 803)

Yiddish actors. Members of the Vilna Troupe. Lived in Poland, the United States.

Manuscripts and printed copies of Yiddish plays by various playwrights including Peretz Hirschbein and Abraham Goldfaden. Theater programs. Sheet music of the Yiddish theater. Clippings. Photographs of stage productions including some of the Vilna Troupe. Correspondence and personal documents.

Photographs cataloged in STAGEPIX.

282. FEDERMAN, RAFAL (born 1892).
Papers, 1942–1960. 1 ft. 8 in. (RG 299)

Yiddish writer and journalist. Vice-chairman of the American section of the World Federation of Polish Jews. President of the United Czenstochower Relief Committee. Lived in Poland and the United States.

Bulletins, circulars, correspondence relating to the World Federation of Polish Jews. Manuscripts and clippings of Federman's articles. Manuscript and review of Federman's book *On the Shores of the Warta and East River*. Materials pertaining to the Częstochowa *Yizkor* books.

283. FEINBERG, LEON (1897–1969).
Papers, 1920s–1968. 14 ft. 7 in. (RG 601)

Yiddish journalist, poet, novelist, translator. Editor of *Frayhayt* and *Der tog*. President of the Yiddish PEN Club in New York and the I.L. Peretz Yiddish Writers Union. Contributed to many Yiddish periodicals such as *Freie Arbeiter Stimme, Yiddishes Tageblatt, Morgn zhur-*

nal, Jewish Daily Forward, Zukunft, Der groyser kundes, Yidisher kemfer, Literarishe bleter (Warsaw), *Di goldene keyt, Epokhe* (editor). Born in Kodyma, Ukraine. Joined the Red Guard during the Russian revolution of 1917. Left Russia and arrived in Palestine in 1919. Immigrated to the United States in 1921.

Correspondence with Yiddish literary figures and with organizations. Correspondents include A. Almi, Ephraim Auerbach, Shlomo Bickel, Menahem Boraisha, Ossip Dymow, Jacob Glanz, Aaron Glanz-Leieles, Jacob Glatstein, Abraham Golomb, Chaim Grade, Peretz Hirschbein, David Ignatoff, Rachel Korn, H. Leivick, Itzik Manger, Mani Leib, Moshe Nadir, Shmuel Niger, Joseph Opatoshu, Abbo Ostrowsky, Melech Ravitch, A.A. Roback, Isaac Bashevis Singer, Abraham Sutzkever, Malka Heifetz Tussman, Zishe Weinper. Family correspondence.

Correspondence of the Yiddish PEN Club and the I.L. Peretz Yiddish Writers Union. Clippings, circulars and correspondence about the World Conference of Yiddish Writers, 1964. Lists of Yiddish PEN Club members. Clippings: articles about writers, about Leon Feinberg and his works. Clippings about various topics collected by Feinberg for reference. Topics include Yiddish language, Yiddish writers, Yiddish literature, Jews in the Soviet Union, Russian-Jewish writers.

Manuscripts of Feinberg's works: poems, translations, plays, fragments of novels. Manuscripts of other writers: Ossip Dymow, Mani Leib, A. Mukdoni, Moshe Nadir, Boruch Rivkin. Speeches and lectures. Personal documents. Photographs.

Inventory, Yiddish.

284. FEINSTONE, SOL.
Collection, 1482–1939. 7 in. (RG 320)

Chemist, farmer, collector of rare documents.

Rare documents relating to the following: Inquisition in Salamanca, Spain, 1482. Jewish community of Prague, 1752. Business records of a German-Jewish merchant, 1849. Correspondence from American Jews including Mordecai Manuel Noah, the Gratz family, Henry Solomon, Samuel Hays and Simon Etting, 1784–1838. Records of benevolent societies affiliated with the New York Uptown Talmud Torah, 1928–1935. Records of the Hirsch family hotel in Prague, 1926–1939.

285. FELSHIN, URI.
Papers, 1910s–1920s. 2 1/2 in. (RG 710)

Mohel (ritual circumciser) and wine merchant in Harlem, New York City.

The collection consists of a scrapbook of memorabilia relating to his activities as *mohel* and wine merchant. Included are advertisements, invitations, receipts, photographs, clippings.

286. FIBICH, FELIX and JUDITH.
Papers, 1946–1963. 5 in. (RG 534)

Jewish dancers, husband and wife. Lived in Poland, USSR, France. Settled in the United States in 1950.

Clippings, invitations, programs and other publicity materials pertaining to the Fibich's performances in Poland, France, Israel and the United States.

287. FILMS.
  Collection, 1930s–1950s. 75 items. (RG 105)

The collection is of mixed provenance and consists mostly of 16 mm films and some 8 mm and 35 mm films. There is also a group of VHS and 3/4-inch tapes. Many of the films are registered as part of other record groups in the YIVO Archives and were physically separated from these record groups, placed in the Film Collection, and cataloged for preservation purposes and for improved access to researchers. The collection includes the following series:
  Amateur Films. ca. 75 items, 1920s–1930s. Amateur home movies made by American Jews on trips to Eastern Europe, mainly Poland. One segment of this series consists of films produced by Gustave Eisner who owned the Gustave Eisner Travel Bureau in the inter-war period and arranged trips back to Poland and to Palestine. The Eisner films include some of Palestine and of American-Jewish life. Amateur films made by Abraham Twersky of the Sholem Aleichem Houses in the Bronx which include images of a number of notable cultural figures in the Yiddish secular world.
  Films of towns and cities commissioned by *landsmanshaftn*. 2 items. 1920s–1930s. *A Pictorial Review of Kolbuszowa*, 1929. A film about Sędziszów, Poland, 1935.
  Post-war films made by social welfare organizations. 1940s–1960s. About 40 items. Films produced by social welfare organizations such as the HIAS and the AJDC describing the situation of Jewish refugees and displaced persons and organizational work carried out on their behalf. Included are films about HIAS's involvement with Hungarian refugees in 1956.
  Miscellaneous films. A film about Jewish refugees in Shanghai in the late 1940s. 8 mm footage of the Warsaw ghetto and the Cracow ghetto during World War II. Yiddish language newsreel made of a memorial ceremony held in Skierniewice, Poland, in 1947 for Holocaust victims. A film produced by Moisey Ghitzis about Yiddish writers. *A Scientific Expedition to Birobizhan* (1929), a silent film by the faculty of Brigham Young University, Utah.
  Catalog and index, English.

288. FIRST AUSTILER AID SOCIETY.
  Records, 1940s–1971. 2 in. (RG 1005)

Chartered as The First Austiler Aid Society in New York, 1911. Was affiliated with the United Austiler Relief Committee which raised money for *landslayt* from Ustilug (Pol. Uściług), Ukraine, after World War II.
  Constitution. Minutes, 1968–1971. Memorial journal, United Austiler Relief Committee, 1948. Theater programs from Ustilug, pre-World War II.

289. FIRST BACAUER SICK AND BENEVOLENT ASSOCIATION.
  Records, 1905–1976. 10 in. (RG 938)

Established in New York in 1903 by immigrants from Bacău, Rumania. Also known as the Erster Bacauer Romanischer Kranken Untershtitsung Fareyn or First Bacauer Rumanian American Kranken Untershtitzung Verein. Dissolved 1976.
  Constitutions. Financial records, 1922–1975 (German, English). Materials pertaining to burial. Correspondence. Materials pertaining to 60th anniversary celebration and to dissolution. Seal. Stamps.

290. FIRST BEITCHER SICK BENEVOLENT SOCIETY.
  Records, 1929–1979. 17 1/2 in. (RG 772)

Organized in New York in 1903 by immigrants from Biecz, Poland, to send relief to Biecz after a fire. Chartered later that year. Affiliated with the Beitcher Sisterhood and Young Beitcher Social League. Aided *landslayt* in Biecz after World War I and World War II. Established a free loan society for *landslayt* in Israel.

Constitution. Minutes, 1929–1942. Financial records, 1969–1972, 1977. Relief work records, 1940–1962. Membership applications. Bulletins, 1949–1979. Correspondence. Memorial book, 1960. Photographs.

291. FIRST BELZER BESSARABIER SICK BENEVOLENT ASSOCIATION.
Records, 1925–1960. 5 in. (RG 1002)

Founded in New York in 1900 by 28 immigrants from Belz (Beltsy), Moldavia. Affiliated with the Ladies Auxiliary of the First Belzer Bessarabier Sick Benevolent Association (organized 1930) and with the Federation of Bessarabian Societies of America, Inc. Dissolved ca. 1974.

Souvenir journals, 1925, 1937. Film of last banquet, 1960. Photograph.

292. FIRST BRATSLOW PODOLIER SICK BENEFIT SOCIETY.
Records, 1915–1944. 15 in. (RG 836)

Founded in New York in 1914 by immigrants from Bratslav (Pol. Bracław), Ukraine. Established a relief committee during World War I.

Constitution. Minutes, 1915–1920. Minutes of relief fund, 1944. Membership dues records, 1925–1942. Membership loan information, 1927–1944. Financial materials. Gavel.

293. FIRST BRATSLOWER LADIES AUXILIARY.
Records, 1934–1961. 5 in. (RG 835)

Founded by immigrants from Bratslav (Pol. Bracław), Ukraine.

The First Bratslower Ladies Auxiliary was affiliated with the First Bratslow Podolier Sick Benevolent Association. Participated with the latter in a relief fund for *landslayt* from Bratslav.

Minutes, 1933–1936, 1938–1944. Financial and membership records, 1930s–1950s. Gavel.

294. FIRST BRITCHANER BENEVOLENT ASSOCIATION.
Records, 1932–1977. 1 ft. 10 in. (RG 973)

Established in New York in 1895 by immigrants from Brichany (Briceni), Moldavia. Organized an interest-free loan fund in 1925 and an old-age fund in 1935. Affiliated with the Brichaner Bessarabier Relief Association. Dissolved 1977.

By-laws. Minutes, 1932–1977. Financial records, 1936–1970s. Materials pertaining to old-age and loan funds. Golden book (record of deaths of members). Membership records. Materials pertaining to cemetery and burial. Seal, stamp.

295. FIRST BROOKLYN ROUMANIAN-AMERICAN CONGREGATION.
Records, 1901–1907. 1/2 in. (RG 1216)

Founded in 1894 in Brooklyn, New York.

Minutes, 1901–1907.

296. FIRST BUCECER INDEPENDENT BENEVOLENT ASSOCIATION.
   Records, 1925, 1961–1972. 2 in. (RG 909)

Founded in New York in 1925 by *landslayt* from Buchach (Buczacz, Betshutsh, Bechuch), Ukraine, to provide cemetery, sick and death benefits. Activities included support of institutions in America and in Buchach.
   Cemetery deed. Constitution (Yiddish). Minutes (English), 1961–1972. Financial records. Correspondence, 1966–1970.

**297. FIRST CONGREGATION OF KENSINGTON TIFERET ISRAEL
   (BROOKLYN, NY).**
   Records, 1910–1925. 2 in. (RG 302)

A synagogue located in Brooklyn, NY.
   Minute-book for the years 1910–1925.

298. FIRST DIMERER PROGRESSIVE SOCIETY.
   Records, 1925–1950. 1 1/2 in. (RG 1007)

Organized in New York in 1919 by immigrants from Dymer, Ukraine. Maintained a loan association. Helped members serving in the U.S. armed forces during World War II.
   Amendments to constitution, 1950. Minutes, 1939–1943. Dues records, 1925–1932.

299. FIRST DJOURINER PODOLIER ALLIANCE.
   Records, 1915–1979. 5 in. (RG 892)

Founded in New York in 1915 by immigrants from Dzhurin, Ukraine. The constitution states that the question of affiliation with a synagogue is never to be raised. The society provided a loan fund for membership. The Ladies Committee of the society sponsored relief activities during World War II.
   Constitution. Minutes, 1915–1925. Financial records, 1950s–1970s. Anniversary journal. Meeting announcements. Photograph. Gavel.

300. FIRST INDEPENDENT LOPOSHNER SOCIETY.
   Records, 1930. 5 in. (RG 876)

Organized in New York in 1915 by immigrants from Lapuszna (Lapushna), Moldavia. Activities included establishment of an interest-free loan fund for its members.
   Constitution. Membership record book, and oversize bound volume presented to the society by the Dzuriner Sick Benevolent Association, 1930. Grave-plot reservation receipts.

**301. FIRST INDEPENDENT MIKULINCER SICK AND
   BENEVOLENT ASSOCIATION.**
   Records, 1910–1956. 1 ft. 3 1/2 in. (RG 828)

Founded in New York in 1899 by immigrants from Mikulintsy (Pol. Mikulińce), Ukraine. Was joined by the First Mikulinzer Lodge No. 556, Independent Order Brith Abraham (established 1909). The two apparently merged in the 1940s.

Minutes, 1918–1950s (German, Yiddish). Minutes of the First Mikulinzer Lodge, 1910–1928 (German). Record book of the burial committee, 1920s. Financial records, 1940s–1950s, including membership dues book, 1924–1931. Correspondence.

302. FIRST INDEPENDENT ODESSER LADIES SICK BENEVOLENT ASSOCIATION.
Records, 1961–1972. 5 in. (RG 859)

Founding date unknown. Contributed to the Odessa Center League. Supported activities in Israel. Dissolved 1972.
Minutes, 1964–1972. Financial records, 1961–1972.

303. FIRST INDEPENDENT STOROZNETZER BUKOWINER SICK AND BENEVOLENT ASSOCIATION.
Records, 1904–1977. 7 1/2 in. (RG 901)

Organized in New York by immigrants from Storozhinets, Ukraine. Incorporated in 1904. Established a war relief committee during World War I. Also maintained a relief committee and a Ladies of the War Relief during World War II. Sent relief funds and packages to *landslayt* in Europe and Israel.
Certificate of incorporation, 1904. Constitution. Minutes, 1911, 1946–1953. Financial records, 1948–1976. Materials pertaining to burial, 1904–1977. Souvenir journals. Meeting announcements. Photographs.

304. FIRST INDEPENDENT ZINKOWER SOCIETY.
Records, 1952–1975. 3 in. (RG 962)

Organized in New York by *landslayt* from Zinkov, Ukraine. Founding date unknown. Provided burial and funeral expenses. Dissolved 1976.
Minutes, 1973–1976. Financial records, 1952–1974. Cemetery map.

305. FIRST KLEVANER SICK AND BENEVOLENT SOCIETY.
Records, 1944–1973. 1 ft. 3 in. (RG 881)

Founded in New York in 1902 by immigrants from Klevan (Pol. Klewan), Ukraine. Original purpose included establishment of a synagogue. Also known as the Klevaner-Voliner Benevolent Association. Activities included the establishment in the 1930s of a *gemilas khesed* (interest-free loan fund) for its poor members. It also conducted relief work for *landslayt* in Klevan after World War I and World War II.
Constitution. Minutes, 1944–1966. Financial records, 1940s–1970s. Correspondence, 1960s–1970s. Banner.

306. FIRST KLIMONTOVER SICK BENEVOLENT SOCIETY.
Records, 1915–1921. 3 in. (RG 969)

Founded in New York in 1905 by immigrants from Klimontów, Poland. Organized a relief committee in the 1940s to aid survivors of the Holocaust. Assisted rabbi from home town to come to New York and head a congregation.
Minutes, 1917–1921. Financial records, 1915–1921.

307. FIRST KOPYCZYNZER SICK AND BENEVOLENT SOCIETY.
Records, 1943–1975. 2 1/2 in. (RG 970)

Founded in New York in 1895 by immigrants from Kopychintsy (Pol. Kopyczynce), Ukraine. Also known as the Erste Kopyczyncer Kranken Untershtitsung Verein. Dissolved in the 1970s.
Cemetery records. Correspondence. Seal.

308. FIRST KOROPIECER BENEVOLENT ASSOCIATION.
Records, 1967–1975. 2 1/2 in. (RG 946)

Organized in New York in 1909 by immigrants from Koropets, Ukraine. In 1938 there were 83 members. Dissolved in 1976.
Financial records. Seal.

309. FIRST KRASNER SICK AND BENEVOLENT SOCIETY.
Records, 1931, 1950–1980. 11 in. (RG 910)

Founded in Brooklyn in 1905 by immigrants from Raigorodok (Krasny Gorodok), Ukraine. First meeting was held on Powell Street in East New York. Society members ran an independent credit union.
Constitution. Minutes, 1950s–1970s. Membership roster, 1973. Correspondence. Photographs. Tape recording of banquet, 1980.

310. FIRST KRASNOBRODER AID SOCIETY.
Records, 1922–1934. 1 in. (RG 1012)

Founded and incorporated in New York in 1912 by immigrants from Krasnobród, Poland. Established a *maos hittim* (Passover fund for the poor) committee to aid *landslayt* in Krasnobród and a *gmilas khesed* fund (interest-free loan fund) to aid members in New York.
Minutes, 1922–1929. Materials pertaining to political activities in Krasnobród, 1929–1934. Photographs.

311. FIRST KRASNYSTAUER YOUNG MEN'S BENEVOLENT SOCIETY.
Records, 1940–1955. 2 1/2 in. (RG 1051)

Founded in New York in 1915 by immigrants from Krasnystaw, Poland. Maintained an emergency fund for members in need. Conducted extensive relief work during World War II.
Constitution. Minutes, 1940–1954.

312. FIRST KRYSTONOPOLER SICK AND BENEVOLENT SOCIETY.
Records, 1947–1974. 2 1/2 in. (RG 971)

Founded in New York in 1895 by immigrants from Krystynopol, Ukraine. Originally owned a synagogue. In early years sent *maos hittim* (Passover fund for the poor) to *landslayt* in home town. Organized a relief committee between World War I and World War II. In recent years has sent *maos hittim* contributions to Russian immigrants in the United States.
Constitution. Financial records, 1947–1959.

313. FIRST KULACZKOWITZER KRANKEN UNTERSHTITSUNG VEREIN.
Records, 1913–1952, 1965. 7 1/2 in. (RG 783)

Organized in New York in 1911 by immigrants from Kulachkovtsy (Pol. Kułaczkowce), Ukraine. Chartered in 1913. Associated with a ladies auxiliary.
Minutes, 1913–1955. Financial records, 1928–1946. Funeral parlor receipt books, 1913–1952, 1965.

314. FIRST LESZNOWER SICK AND BENEVOLENT SOCIETY, SONS OF JACOB SOLOMON.
Records, 1910–1977. 5 in. (RG 926)

Established in 1903 by immigrants from Leshnev (Pol. Leszniów), Ukraine. Originally a religious society which rented a loft on the Lower East Side where members could pray on weekends.
Minutes, 1964–1975. Financial records, 1962–1977. Records pertaining to sick benefits and burial. Membership lists. Correspondence. Seal.

315. FIRST LUBERER BENEVOLENT ASSOCIATION.
Records, 1937–1976. 2 1/2 in. (RG 998)

Established in New York in 1895 by immigrants from Lyubar (Yid. Luber), Ukraine. Provided interest-free loans for members. After World War II, maintained a Luberer Relief Organization together with other *landsmanshaftn* to aid survivors in Israel and South America.
Constitution. Minutes, 1969–1976. Financial reports. Anniversary journals.

316. FIRST OTTYNIER YOUNG MEN'S BENEVOLENT ASSOCIATION.
Records, 1946–1967, 1970s. 5 in. (RG 1036)

Founded in 1900 by immigrants from Otynya (Ottynia), Ukraine. Organized the United Ottynier Relief in 1914 which was active until 1950. Incorporated members of the Ottynier Young Ladies and Young Men's Progressive Association into the society in 1929. Organized first Ottynier Ladies Aid Society in 1939.
Minutes, 1946–1967. Correspondence. Bulletins, including a short history of the society.

317. FIRST POGREBISHT BENEVOLENT SOCIETY.
Records, 1964–1972. 2 1/2 in. (RG 1093)

Founded in Brooklyn in 1911 by immigrants from Pogrebishchenski (until 1945, Pogrebishche), Ukraine. Maintained an emergency fund for needy members as well as an old-age fund. Dissolved in the 1970s.
Constitution. Financial records, 1964–1972. Seal.

318. FIRST POVOLOTCHER SICK BENEVOLENT ASSOCIATION.
Records, 1942–1977. 2 1/2 in. (RG 1088)

Organized in New York ca. 1907 by immigrants from Pavoloch (Povoloch), Ukraine. Maintained a loan fund. Supported Israel Bonds. Was associated with a ladies auxiliary. Dissolved 1977.
Minutes, 1942–1975. Financial records, 1961–1977.

319. FIRST PRAGER INDEPENDENT ASSOCIATION.
Records, 1930–1978. 2 1/2 in. (RG 1034)

Organized in New York in 1913 by immigrants from Praga, a borough of Warsaw, Poland. Supported the Haym Solomon Warshauer Home for the Aged. Was affiliated with the Warshauer Relief, 1920s, and the American Council for Warsaw Jews, 1940s. Also worked with its ladies auxiliary.

Constitutions. Minutes, 1974–1975. Financial statements, 1943–1938. Membership booklets, 1960s. Materials pertaining to anniversaries. Meeting announcements. Correspondence of the secretary.

320. FIRST PRESSBURGER SICK AND BENEVOLENT SOCIETY.
Records, 1906–1974. 10 in. (RG 854)

Founded in New York by immigrants from Bratislava (Pressburg, Pozsony), Slovakia. Dissolved in the 1970s.

Financial records, 1948–1974. Membership application book, 1906–1951 (German, English). Burial permits, 1914–1973. Correspondence, 1950s–1970s.

321. FIRST PROBUZNA SICK AND BENEVOLENT SOCIETY.
Records, 1942–1975. 2 1/2 in. (RG 1017)

Organized and incorporated in New York in 1904 by immigrants from Probezhna (Pol. Probużna), Ukraine.

Certificate of incorporation, 1904. Constitution. Minutes, 1947–1975.

322. FIRST PROGRESSIVE LADIES OF DINEWITZ.
Records, 1945–1967. 2 1/2 in. (RG 870)

Founded in New York by immigrants from Dinovitz (Dunayevtsy), Ukraine. A women's mutual aid society providing sick and death benefits to members. Dissolved 1967.

Minutes, 1945–1966. Financial records, 1950s–1960s. Correspondence, 1950s–1960s.

323. FIRST PRZEMYSLER SICK BENEFIT SOCIETY.
Records, 1906–1965. 3 ft. 10 in. (RG 932)

Founded in New York in 1889 by immigrants from Przemyśl, Poland, to "create a spirit of good fellowship." Maintained a loan fund. Supported the Lemberger Home for the Aged, New York.

Constitutions. Legal documents, including certificate of incorporation of the Przemysler Central Relief Society, Inc., 1919. Minutes, 1947–1957. Cemetery materials. Membership records, 1908–1964. Financial records, 1920–1960. Photograph. Memorial book, 1964.

324. FIRST RADOMER CONGREGATION, CHEBRA AGUDAS ACHIM ANSHEI RADOM.
Records, 1909–1927. 2 1/2 in. (RG 1038)

Founded in New York in 1903 by immigrants from Radom, Poland. Maintained a synagogue. Supported the United Radomer Relief for United States and Canada.

Membership applications, ca. 1910–1927.

325. FIRST RASHKOWER BENEVOLENT SOCIETY.
Records, 1926–1974. 7 1/2 in. (RG 825)

Founded in New York in 1914 by immigrants from Raszków (Ger. Raschkow), Poland. Dissolved in 1979.

Constitution. Minutes, 1926–1934, 1942–1950. Financial records, 1958–1974. Burial records. Gavels. Banner.

326. FIRST ROZISHTCHER BENEVOLENT ASSOCIATION.
Records, 1925–1976. 2 1/2 in. (RG 1091)

Founded in New York ca. 1912 by immigrants from Rozhishche (Pol. Rozyszcze), Ukraine. Maintained a loan fund for members. Dissolved 1976.

Minutes, 1927–1935, 1969–1976. Membership records, 1960s–1970s.

327. FIRST SOKORONER DR. BRAUNSTEIN PROGRESSIVE SOCIETY.
Records, 1931–1975. 3 in. (RG 961)

Organized in New York in 1919 by immigrants from Sekiryany (Yid. Sokorone, Rum. Secureni), Ukraine. Provided lectures and entertainment for members. Benefits included burial. Dissolved in the 1970s.

Minutes, 1951–1905. Financial records, 1958–1975. Burial permits, 1931–1975. Meeting notices. Golden book (record of deaths of members). Seal, stamp.

328. FIRST SOROKER BESSARABIER MUTUAL AID SOCIETY.
Records, 1910–1950s. 1 ft. 1 in. (RG 832)

Founded in New York in 1897 by immigrants from Soroki (Rum. Soroca), Moldavia. Activities included extensive relief work for the home town in the 1920s and 1930s and for *landslayt* in Israel in the 1950s. Worked with the Soroker Relief in the United States, a central organization composed of First Soroker Mutual Aid, Soroker Young Friends B.E.L., First Soroker Bessarabier Ladies. Merged in the 1930s with the Seltzer Lodge. Supported the Bessarabian Federation of American Jews after World War II.

Pinkas (record book) of the *hevrah kadisha* (burial society), 1910–1953, including minutes, rules, names of officers and deceased society members. Golden book (record of deaths of members). Materials from Soroki relating to relief activities of American *landslayt*, 1920s–1930s. Memorial book of the Jewish hospital in Soroki, 1922. Materials pertaining to trip of Morris Seltzer to Soroki for distribution of relief funds, 1925. Personal materials, book of memoirs about Soroki by David Seltzer. Correspondence. Anniversary journals. Endowment fund report. Photographs of Soroki, 1920s–1930s. Constitution, First Soroker Bessarabian Ladies Aid Society. Materials pertaining to the Bessarabian Federation of American Jews. Address list of the First Soroker Ladies Aid Society.

329. FIRST STRYJER SISTERS BENEVOLENT SOCIETY.
Records, 1950–1968. 5 in. (RG 863)

Founded in New York in 1904 by immigrants from Stry (Pol. Stryj), Ukraine. Organized to provide burial for women from Stryj. Dissolved 1968.

Minutes, 1953–1968. Financial records, 1950s–1960s. Membership records, 1952–1968.

330. FIRST TLUMACZER BENEVOLENT SOCIETY.
Records, 1916–1973. 7 1/2 in. (RG 1172)

Organized in New York by immigrants from Tłumacz, Ukraine.
Minute book, 1916–1973. 3 ledgers.

331. FIRST USCIE ZIELONE SICK AND BENEVOLENT ASSOCIATION.
Records, 1911, 1930–1964. 5 in. (RG 845)

Established in New York by immigrants from Ustse Zelene (Pol. Uście Zielone), Ukraine, and incorporated in 1911. Maintained a synagogue on Ridge Street, New York. The society split in 1926, leading to the establishment of a second association, the First American Uscie Zielone Sick Support Society.
Certificate of incorporation, 1911. Minutes, 1930–1948. Financial records, 1940–1963.

332. FIRST USHITZER PODOLER BENEVOLENT ASSOCIATION.
Records, 1913–1971. 3 in. (RG 1084)

Organized in New York in 1911 by immigrants from Staraya Ushitsa, Ukraine. Incorporated to aid *landslayt* in New York and in the home town.
Certificate of incorporation, mounted on decorative panel, 1913. Golden book (record of deaths of members). Banner.

333. FIRST WARSHAUER I.M. BAUMGOLD LODGE 338, ORDER BRITH SHOLOM.
Records, 1933–1940. 1 in. (RG 1220)

Organized in New York by *landslayt* from Warsaw, Poland.
Minutes, 1933–1940.

334. FIRST WASHKOUTZ BUCOWINAER SICK AND BENEVOLENT SOCIETY.
Records, 1926, 1950s. 5 in. (RG 993)

Founded in New York in 1903 by immigrants from Vashkovtsy (Rum. Văşcăuţi), Ukraine. Contributed to Jewish philanthropies. Conducted extensive relief work for *landslayt* in Israel in the 1950s.
Constitution. Financial records, 1954–1956. Relief work records including correspondence with *landslayt* and records of packages sent. Membership lists. Correspondence.

335. FIRST WIZNITZ BUKAWINAER LADIES SOCIETY.
Records, 1938–1966. 10 in. (RG 852)

Organized in New York in 1921 by immigrants from Vizhnitsa (Vijnita), Ukraine, as the First Wiznitz Bucowiner Ladies Benevolent Association. Name legally changed in 1923. Society now dissolved.
Minutes, 1956–1966. Seal.

336. FIRST WOJNILOWER SICK BENEVOLENT SOCIETY.
Records, 1913–1977. 1 ft. 5 1/2 in. (RG 834)

Founded in New York in 1905 by immigrants from Voinilov (Pol. Wojniłów), Ukraine. Was joined by the First Wojnilower Lodge No. 674, Independent Order Brith Abraham (established in 1913).

Constitution. Minutes and financial records of the First Wojnilower Lodge, 1913–1917. Minutes and financial records of the First Wojnilower S.B.S., 1917–1977. Minutes of the Gate Committee, 1956–1971. Correspondence, 1940s–1960s. Newspaper clippings.

337. FIRST YEZIERNA SICK AND BENEVOLENT SOCIETY.
Records, 1900–1973. 1 ft. 5 1/2 in. (RG 950)

Founded in New York in 1899 by immigrants from Jeziorany, Poland, "to help the members in the event of sickness and distress." Also known as the First Jezierna Chevra. Dissolved in the 1970s.

Constitution. Minutes, 1938–1972. Financial records, 1953–1973. Materials pertaining to burial. Correspondence. Seal.

338. FIRST ZAWICHOSTER YOUNG MEN'S BENEVOLENT ASSOCIATION.
Records, 1914–1953. 2 1/2 in. (RG 964)

Founded in New York in 1913 by immigrants from Zawichost, Poland, to provide *landslayt* with "spiritual and material benefits." Conducted relief work for home town after World War II.

Minutes, 1941–1953. Anniversary journal, 1931. Photographs.

339. FIRST ZBARAZER RELIEF SOCIETY.
Records, 1943–1977. 5 in. (RG 982)

Founded in New York in 1925 by immigrants from Zbarazh (Pol. Zbaraż), Ukraine. Between the two world wars, aided communal institutions in Zbaraż. After World War II, aided survivors in relocating to the United States.

Minutes, 1943–1977 (German, English). Financial records. Membership records, 1946–1973.

340. FIRST ZBOROWER SICK AND BENEVOLENT ASSOCIATION.
Records, 1934–1978. 11 in. (RG 798)

Founded in New York in 1896 by immigrants from Zborov (Pol. Zborów), Ukraine, to establish a synagogue and provide mutual aid.

Constitutions; financial reports; membership ledgers; souvenir journal, 1934; meeting announcements; newspaper clippings.

341. FIRST ZDUNSKA WOLA BENEVOLENT SOCIETY.
Records, 1902, 1915–1977. 6 in. (RG 808)

Founded in New York in 1902 by immigrants from Zduńska Wola, Poland. Activities included relief work during World War I and after World War II, the establishment of a credit union in Israel, the erection of Holocaust monuments in Israel and Zduńska Wola. The society was affiliated with the American Federation for Aid to Polish Jews and supported the Reuben Brainin Children's Clinic, Tel Aviv, Israel.

Incorporation charter, 1902. Minutes, 1928–1937. Financial records, 1951–1955. Anniversary journal, 1952. Correspondence. Miscellaneous materials relating to the Committee for the Reuben Brainin Clinic in Israel, the American Federation for Aid to Polish Jews. Photographs.

342. FIRST ZELECHOVER PROGRESSIVE SOCIETY.
Records, 1944–1974. 5 in. (RG 1025)

Founded in New York ca. 1900 by immigrants from Żelechów, Poland. Original purpose included establishment of a synagogue. Split over political differences in the 1920s. Was reestablished by World War II survivors, 1951. The Chicago *landsmanshaft* published monthly bulletins to unite scattered Zelechover *landslayt*, as well as an autobiographical volume by Y.M. Weissenberg and a memorial book.

Minutes. Expense book for the Weissenberg book fund. Publications, 1940s–1960s. Membership list of the New York society. Photographs.

343. FISCHER, LEO (born 1883).
Papers, 1918–1950s. 3 ft. 6 in. (RG 559)

Vice-president of United Rumanian Jews of America. Owner of Fischer Press, New York. Lived in Rumania and the United States.

The collection relates primarily to Rumanian-Jewish affairs and to Fischer's efforts to defend Jewish minority rights in Rumania and to provide economic assistance to the Jewish community. Correspondence with Jewish personalities from Rumania, including Wilhelm Filderman and with leaders of the Free Rumanian Movement (1940–1950). Correspondence with Rumanian-Jewish philanthropic and cultural organizations especially United Rumanian Jews of America. Correspondence with the royal family and with high ranking members of the Rumanian government, including King Carol II, King Ferdinand I, Vintilă Brătianu, Ion Gheorghe Duca, Nicolae Titulescu, Gheorghe Tătărescu, Ion Inculeţ, in the period following World War I.

Correspondence of Fischer Press and Fischer Apartments. Personal documents. Financial papers. Reports and clippings relating to Jewish life in Rumania, 1918–1940. Memoirs of Leo Fischer.

344. FISHMAN, AARON.
Papers, 1953–1965. 10 in. (RG 377)

Secretary of the Yiddish Culture Society in Philadelphia.

The papers relate to Fishman's activities in Jewish cultural organizations in Philadelphia. Minutes of meetings and correspondence of the Yiddish Culture Society. Letters from Noah Goldberg, Israel Jacob Schwartz, Israel Chaim Pomerantz. Correspondence with Yiddish schools and organizations.

345. FISHZON, MISHA (born 1880) and ZASLAVSKA, VERA (1881–1939).
Papers, 1890s–1930s. 2 ft. 6 in. (RG 203)

Jewish actors, husband and wife. Lived in Russia, Rumania and the United States.

Manuscript of memoirs of Vera Zaslavska. Manuscript of memoirs of Misha Fishzon, titled *Untern forhang fun yidishn teater* (Behind the Curtain of the Yiddish Theater). Playscripts. Photographs of Vera Zaslavska; Misha Fishzon; Jewish actors in Russia and Rumania; the Lyric Theater in New York. Clippings, including obituaries.

Photographs are cataloged in STAGEPIX.

346. FOLKLORE, JEWISH.
Collection. 1 ft. 3 in. (RG 125)

The collection consists of miscellaneous materials pertaining to Jewish folklore and includes the following:

Materials relating to YIVO projects. Entries for the contest about the symbolic meaning of the number "7" according to Jewish tradition, 1953. Collections of proverbs and sayings. Replies to a questionnaire from the *Jewish Daily Forward* about Jewish customs, 1945. Folk poetry, mainly in the style of *badkhones* (rhymes performed by a *badkhn*—wedding entertainer). Samples of *ketubot* (marriage contracts), *t'noyim* (engagement contracts), divorce letters, amulets, etc.

347. FOLKSBIENE THEATER.
Records, 1930s–1960s. 1 ft. 6 in. (RG 512)

A Yiddish theater group in New York City established in 1915 under the auspices of the Workmen's Circle.

The collection includes manuscripts of plays by Abraham Goldfaden, Sholem Aleichem, Isaac Bashevis Singer, Friedrich Hebbel. Photographs of Folksbiene productions.. Scrapbooks containing ads, reviews and articles about the Folksbiene. 13 tapes of Folksbiene performances in the 1950s–1960s.

348. FORWARD ASSOCIATION.
Records, 1913–1972. ca. 8 ft. (RG 685)

Incorporated in 1901 in New York, the Forward Association was the publisher of the *Jewish Daily Forward* until 1983, when the paper became a weekly. From 1912 to 1940 it also published the monthly *Zukunft*. Adolph Held was general manager for a number of years.

The collection consists of financial records, correspondence, reports, minutes of meetings, documents, news clippings and other materials relating to the activities of the general manager. Included are: reports on the circulation of the *Forward*; reports of the advertising department to the Board of Directors; correspondence from the *Forward* offices in Chicago, Detroit, Boston, Los Angeles, Philadelphia; correspondence relating to the Liberal Party, 1944–1951.

Inventory, English.

349. FOX, CHAIM LEIB (1897–1984).
Papers, 1940s–1960s. 2 ft. 1 in. (RG 502)

Yiddish writer. On the editorial staff of the *Leksikon fun der nayer yidisher literatur* (Biographical Dictionary of Modern Yiddish Literature), New York, 1956. Contributed poems, articles, essays and stories to *Indzl, Lodzer veker, Literarishe bleter, Folkstsaytung, Vilner tog, Keneder odler* (Montreal), *Zukunft* (NY), *Forverts* (NY), *Morgn zhurnal* (NY), *Freie Arbeter Stimme* (NY). Born in Łódź, Poland. Lived in Palestine in the 1930s, in France, 1948–1953. Immigrated to the United States in 1953.

Correspondence relating primarily to work on the *Leksikon*. The letters contain biographical information on Yiddish writers. A manuscript of the anthology *Dos yidishe literarishe lodzh* (The Jewish Literary Łódź).

350. FOX, LOUIS.
Papers, mid-19th century–1955. 5 in. (RG 1132)

Louis Fox was born Louis Fuchs in Elizavetgrad, Ukraine. Settled in Providence, Rhode Island, United States.

The collection consists of family photographs and tapes of folk songs, liturgical chants and original compositions sung by Fox.

351. FRANK, HELENA.
Papers. 5 in. (RG 337)

Translator of Yiddish and Hebrew writers.

Manuscripts of English translations by H. Frank, mostly of works by the Sephardic Hebrew novelist Yehuda Burla (1886–1969).

352. FRANKEL, GODFREY.
Collection, 1946–1947. 14 items. (RG 1238)

Photographer, social worker, writer. His work has appeared at the Museum of Modern Art in New York, the George Eastman House in Rochester, the Smithsonian Institution, the Museum of the City of New York, the Cleveland Museum of Art. His photographs have been reproduced in *Life*, *The New York Times*, *Ladies Home Journal* and other publications.

14 photographs of Manhattan, 1946–1947, part of Frankel's New York series. Included are images of: the Lower East Side; shop windows; Yiddish store signs; children playing; pushcart on Orchard Street; Third Avenue elevated train; Times Square restaurant; May Day Parade; Canal Street subway stop; view from Brooklyn Bridge.

353. FRATERNAL ORDER OF BENDIN SOSNOWICZER.
Records, 1960–1983. 2 1/2 in. (RG 1198)

Founded in New York in 1928 by *landslayt* from Będzin and Sosnowiec, Upper Silesia, Poland.

Minutes, 1960–1983. Constitution, 1962.

354. FREIE ARBEITER STIMME.
Records, 1946–1977. 1 ft. 4 1/2 in. (RG 763)

Yiddish anarchist publication founded in New York in 1890. Its first editor was the Jewish socialist poet David Edelstadt. The publication was discontinued in 1977.

The records consist of correspondence, minutes of staff meetings, financial records, lists of contributors, articles, circulars, materials about the Yiddish PEN Club.

355. FREUND, MICHAEL (?–1962).
Papers, 1920s–1960s. 5 in. (RG 511)

Social worker. Member of the research staff of the Council of Jewish Federations and Welfare Funds, 1930–1945. European representative of the JDC, 1919–1925. Secretary, Conference of Jewish Social Service, 1933–1936. Contributor to many periodicals including *Jewish Social Service Quarterly, American Jewish Year Book.*

Manuscripts and typescripts of articles dealing with Jewish social welfare. Newsclippings from Polish-Jewish press relating to the work of the JDC in Poland, 1920s.

356. FRIEDLAND, ISAAC (1884–1965).
   Papers, 1948–1964. 10 in. (RG 440)

Yiddish writer and journalist, editor of the periodical *Kheshbn* in Los Angeles. Born in Zhitomir, Ukraine. Came to the United States in 1906.
   Correspondence with Yiddish writers.

357. FRIEDMAN, PHILIP (1901–1960).
   Papers, 1930s–1959. 20 ft. 5 in. (RG 1258)

Historian. Earned his doctoral degree at the University of Vienna in 1925. His dissertation was entitled "The Jews of Galicia in Their Struggle for Political Emancipation." In the inter-war period Friedman published studies on the Jews of Galicia and Łódź. Lecturer at the Institute of Judaic Studies in Warsaw. After World War II Friedman collected documentation on the Holocaust and wrote extensively on the subject. First director of the Central Jewish Historical Commission in Poland in the post-war period. Consultant to the Nuremberg International Military Tribunal. Lecturer at Columbia University. Director of YIVO-Yad Vashem bibliographical series on the Holocaust. Born in Lwów, Poland. After the war settled in the United States.

The collection relates primarily to Friedman's post-war research on the history of the Holocaust as well as to his administrative activities in various organizations. The bulk of the collection consists of secondary sources collected by Friedman.

Correspondents include: H. G. Adler, Hannah Arendt, Rachel Auerbach, Salo Baron, Ben Zion Dinur, Nathan M. Gelber, Rudolf Glanz, Jacob Glatstein, Israel Halpern, Arthur Hertzberg, Raul Hilberg, Joseph Kermish, Israel Klausner, A. M. Klein, Leibush Lehrer, H. Leivick, Jacob Lestschinsky, Raphael Mahler, Nahum Baruch Minkoff, Shmuel Niger, Joseph Opatoshu, Koppel Pinson, Leon Poliakov, Gerald Reitlinger, A.A. Roback, Isaac Schwarzbard, Hillel Seidman, Genia Silkes, Anna Simaite, Isaac Nachman Steinberg, Michael Weichert, Mark Wischnitzer.

Materials on the Holocaust are primarily arranged by ghetto or concentration camp. Included are: eyewitness accounts collected by the Central Jewish Historical Commission in Poland; depositions relating to the trial of Michael Weichert; materials on Nazi war criminals.

Papers relating to Friedman's organizational activities include: records of the Historian's Circle of the YIVO Institute; records of the YIVO–Yad Vashem joint projects; records of the Central Jewish Historical Commission in Poland.

The collection also includes Friedman's personal papers and a bibliography of his writings.
   Inventory, Yiddish.

358. FRIEDMAN, TUVIAH.
   Papers, 1932–1986. 3 ft. 4 in. (RG 1196)

Investigator of Nazi war criminals. Founder and director of Institute of Documentation of the Holocaust Era, Haifa–New York.

Files concerning Friedman's investigations of Nazi war crimes and criminals, including primarily photocopies of original German personal records, as well as correspondence, clippings, reports, U.S. government documents and other materials. Files on: Kurt Waldheim; Josef Mengele. Materials on Gestapo and SS officers: Rudolf Batz; Herbert Becker; Adolf von Bomhard; Lothar Beutel; Herbert Bottscher; Hans Bothmann; Theodor Dannecker; Erich Ehrlinger; Theodor Eicke; Werner Fromm; Wilhelm Fuchs; Hans Geschke; Max Grosskopf; Amon Leopold Goeth; Hans Grunewald; Herbert Hagen; Franz Heim; Kurt Hintze; Konrad Hitschler; Rudolf Höss; Walter Huppenkothen; Heinz Jost; Herbert Kappler; Georg Keppler; Wilhelm Keppler; Kurt Knoblauch; Karl Koch; Wilhelm Koppe; Martin Sandberger; Leopold Spann; Bruno Streckenbach; Friedrich Warzok; Gustav Willhaus; Josef Witiska; Karl Zech. Materials on German officials in Warsaw and in the Warsaw ghetto including SS and police commanders Paul Moder, Arpad Wigand, Ferdinand von Sammern-Frankenegg, Jürgen Stroop, Franz Kutschera, Paul Otto Geibel, Ludwig Wilhelm Hahn, Hermann Höfle, Franz Konrad and Josef Meisinger. Files on Jewish property looted by Nazis.

359. FRIENDS OF ALEXANDROVSK BENEVOLENT ASSOCIATION.
Records, 1922, 1926–1979. 10 in. (RG 843)

Established in New York by immigrants from Aleksandrovsk, Ukraine, and incorporated in 1926. Affiliated with the Alexandrowsker Relief, Inc. Activities included maintaining a loan fund and support for Israel. Dissolved June 1979.

Certificates of incorporation. Constitution. Minutes, 1926, 1955–1979. Financial records, 1930s–1970s. Anniversary journals. Materials relating to burial services, including a calligraphic *pinkas* (record book).

360. FRISCH, DANIEL (1897–1950).
Papers, 1939–1950. 5 in. (RG 354)

President of the Zionist Organization of America. Born in Palestine. Lived in Rumania. Came to the United States in 1921.

Correspondence with Zionist organizations and American-Jewish leaders: Stephen Wise, Abba Hillel Silver, Henry Ellenbogen. Personal and family letters.

361. FRYSHDORF, HANNAH (1920–1989).
Papers, 1945–1988. 10 in. (RG 1243)

Assistant Director of the YIVO Institute. Was active in Yugnt-Bund Tsukunft in Poland, the youth organization of the Jewish Labor Bund. Participated in the Warsaw ghetto uprising. Born in Warsaw, Poland. Came to the United States in 1949. Died in New York.

Typescripts of articles by Jonathan Frankel, Arcadius Kahan, Irena Klepfisz, Dan Miron and others. Reports and articles relating to YIVO. Photographs of H. Fryshdorf, family and friends in Poland, Sweden, the United States. Miscellaneous materials, including a talk by Fryshdorf about the Warsaw ghetto.

362. GARVIN, PAUL.
Collection, 1958. 10 in. (RG 391)

Linguist, School of Languages and Linguistics, Georgetown University, Washington, D.C.

The collection consists of taped interviews in Yiddish with two Hungarian-Jewish survivors, natives of villages in south-western Hungary. The interviews were conducted by Paul Garvin in New York in the summer of 1958.

363. GASTER, MOSES (1856–1939).
Papers, ca. 1900–1920s. 5 in. (RG 375)

Rabbi, scholar and Zionist leader. Haham of the English Sephardic community. Member, honorary Curatorium (Board of Trustees) of YIVO.

Circular letters and printed appeals for charitable aid from institutions in Palestine.

364. GASTWIRTH, HENRY (born 1869).
Papers, ca. 1907–1953. 10 in. (RG 1096)

Yiddish playwright and translator. Active in the Yiddish theater in New York during the early decades of the twentieth century. Born in Kolbuszowa, Poland. Settled in the United States ca. 1900.

The papers include: autobiographical materials by Gastwirth; playscripts by Gastwirth; a handwritten play by Jacob Gordin, *On a heim* (Homeless), 1907.

365. GEBIRTIG, MORDECAI (1877–1942).
Papers, 1920s–1942. 2 1/2 in. (RG 740)

Yiddish folk poet and carpenter whose songs are among the best known in Yiddish folk literature. His most famous song "Undzer shtetl brent" (Our Town Is On Fire) was composed after the pogrom in Przytyk, Poland, in 1938. Gebirtig was killed by the Nazis during the deportations from the Cracow ghetto. Born in Cracow, Poland.

The collection consists of manuscripts of Gebirtig's songs, including "Kinderyorn," "Hulyet, hulyet, kinderlakh," "Reyzele," "Undzer shtetl brent." There are also some musical arrangements of his songs.

366. GEISEL, EIKE.
Papers, ca. 1910–ca. 1930. 3 in. (RG 1287)

Author of book on the Jewish quarter of Berlin, *Im Scheunenviertel*, Berlin, 1981.

Photographs (104 prints and 101 negatives) of Jews in Berlin and of Jewish life in Eastern Europe.

367. GELBART, MICHL (1889–1962).
Papers, 1940s–1960s. 6 1/2 in. (RG 467)

Jewish composer, music critic, music teacher in the Workmen's Circle schools. As a child sang cantorial music in synagogues and at the age of 16 was synagogue choir director in Łódź, Poland. Music critic for *Der tog* (NY). Contributed to various Yiddish periodicals. Wrote music to Yiddish poems and to six children's operettas. Compiled songbooks for Yiddish secular schools. Born in Ozorków, near Łódź. In 1912 immigrated to the United States.

Manuscripts of Gelbart's musical compositions. Clippings by and about Gelbart. Several plays for children. A children's operetta. Compositions for solo piano and for full orchestra. Arrangements of liturgical music for solo and choir. Lectures given by Gelbart.

368. GELERNT, HENOCH (1892–1960).
Papers, 1930s–1950s. 1 in. (RG 332)

YIVO collector. France, the United States.

Correspondence with individuals and organizations: James Bernstein, Daniel Charney, Bernard Kahn, H. Leivick, Elias Tcherikower, AJDC, HIAS-HICEM.

Reports about child welfare in the Ukraine, 1920s. Handbills from Jewish communal elections in Germany, 1927.

369. GELLERMAN, JILL (born 1948).
Papers, 1975–1976. 5 in. (RG 1126)

Dancer, dancing teacher, folklorist. Specialized in Jewish and American dance. Author of several published studies relating to dance. Conducted projects on Hasidic dance and other topics in Jewish folklore. Lives in New York.

Video tapes of Hasidic dance relating to the Satmar, Bobov, Lubavitch and Stolin groups. Events include weddings, bar mitzvas, *farbrengens* (special religious gatherings conducted by Lubavitcher Hasidim), religious holiday celebrations.

370. GENEALOGY AND FAMILY HISTORY.
Collection, ca. 1870–1987. 15 ft. (RG 126)

The collection is comprised of papers of individuals and families and of compilations of genealogical charts and family histories. About 370 family names are indexed. These papers relate mainly to personal and family affairs. The bulk of the papers relate to the Russian Empire, and more specifically, to the territory of the former Pale of Settlement. Other papers originated in Germany, Austria, Palestine, inter-war Poland, and the United States.

The papers are arranged by name of family and include the following: birth, marriage and death certificates; military service passes; education diplomas; permissions to engage in business; "international" travel passports for use inside the Russian empire; foreign passports; immigration documents; family correspondence; memoirs, diaries; recorded interviews; family trees; family histories.

Card inventory and index, English.

371. GENEALOGY AND FAMILY HISTORY (VILNA ARCHIVES).
Collection, 1811–1939. 1 ft. 3 in. (RG 44)

The collection consists of family documents including family trees, correspondence, financial papers, relating to the following families: Pollak, of Prossnitz, Moravia, 1828–1938; Schimerling, of Göding, Moravia, 1920s; Rothschild, 1811–1917; Fischbein; Rabbi Eleasar Low; Lenneberg; Mayer-Coma.

372. GERMAN JEWISH CHILDREN'S AID.
Records, 1933–1953. 34 microfilm reels and 128 ft. (RG 249)

The German Jewish Children's Aid was established in the United States in 1934 to receive and place Jewish refugee children from Nazi Germany. The GJCA negotiated with the U.S. government for the admission of a limited number of children within the quota law. It guaranteed financial support, worked with local community agencies to find foster homes, met the children at the port of entry and transferred them to their new places of residence. The Board of Directors included: Joseph Proskauer, Solomon Lowenstein, Max Kohler, Joseph Hyman, Paul Felix Warburg, Jacob Billikopf. The Executive Director was Cecilia Razovsky. Lotte Marcuse was Director of Placements.

The GJCA was affiliated with the National Coordinating Committee, National Refugee Service and USNA. It received financial support from the National Council of Jewish Women. In 1942 the GJCA became the European Jewish Children's Aid.

The records of the GJCA relate to the entire range of activities involved in receiving and placing refugee children from 1933 through the 1950s. The later materials are records of the European Jewish Children's Aid. Activities included: maintaining the reception center in New Jersey; transportation arrangements; placement in homes; issuing affidavits and passports; granting scholarships; naturalization of children; setting of GJCA policy.

By-laws, minutes, reports, correspondence and certificate of incorporation. Correspondence of executive officers, mainly Cecilia Razovsky, 1930s. Correspondence between William Haber and Lotte Marcuse, 1939–40. File of Dr. Solomon Lowenstein. Minutes of meetings of the Finance Committee. Field reports, inter-office memoranda, financial and statistical reports. Correspondence with organizations and governmental agencies: Society of Friends (Quakers) in Vienna; Israelitische Kultusgemeinde of Vienna; Zentralwohlfahrtsstelle division of the Reichsvertretung (later Reichsvereinigung) der Juden in Deutschland; Federation for the Support of Jewish Philanthropic Societies; Department of Justice; New York State Department of Social Welfare; U.S. Immigration and Naturalization Service; American Friends Service Committee; American Jewish Congress; B'nai Brith; National Council of Jewish Women.

Correspondence with individuals: Max S. Perlman, William Rosenwald, Paul Felix Warburg.

In addition to the general administrative records, there are thousands of case files.

Inventory, English.

373. GERMANY (VILNA ARCHIVES).
Collection, 1567–1940. 4 ft. 7 in. (RG 31)

A collection of miscellaneous documents pertaining to Jewish life in Germany. These documents were part of the archives of YIVO in Vilna before World War II.

The documents are of varied provenance and include the following:

Older documents, 17th and 18th centuries. Official documents issued by various German rulers to their Jewish subjects. Included are: *Schutzbriefe*; permissions to conduct a trade; litigation between the Jews of Frankfurt and the city municipality, 1732–1738; a *mohel* book.

Personal and family papers. These are papers of 59 German-Jewish individuals and families, including communal figures and rabbis, 19th and 20th centuries, that consist of family correspondence, personal documents, business and financial records. Of special interest are: papers of Lina Morgenstern, a writer and social worker, 1860s–1900; Julius Rodenberg, publisher of *Deutsche Rundschau*, 1853–1913; Bondi family of Frankfurt and Mainz, 1814–1938; Ernst Rabel, professor of international law and member of the International Court of Justice, 1925–1936; Rabbi Joseph Jonah Horovitz, Frankfurt am Main.

Fragmentary records of German-Jewish communities, mostly from the Polish territories under German domination (the Grand Duchy of Posen), including minutes of meetings, by-laws, communal registers, financial records, correspondence, printed matter. The following communities are represented: Berlin, Bromberg (Pol. Bydgoszcz), Filehne (Pol. Wieleń), Frankfurt am Main, Hamburg, Mannheim, Neisse (Pol. Nysa), Raschkow (Pol. Raszków), Rybnik.

Inventory, English.

374. GERSHEVITCH, LEO.
Papers, 1904, 1921–1948. 2 ft. 6 in. (RG 273)

Resident of Tientsin, China for over 20 years. President of the Tientsin Jewish Hebrew Association, The Tientsin Zionist Organization. Representative of the Jewish Agency.

Records of the Tientsin Hebrew Association. Correspondence with other Jewish communities in the Far East, especially Harbin, 1922–1934. Records of the local benevolent society in Tientsin. Materials on: Jewish schools, 1922–1940; Jewish Club "Kunst," 1923–1948; Jewish community of Harbin, 1921–1938. Clippings on the history of the Jews in China.

375. GEYER, MEYER (1875–1947).
Papers, 1937–1946. 7 in. (RG 240)

Journalist, prominent Jewish communal leader in Lwów, Poland. Emigrated to the United States in 1937.

Documents concerning Geyer's immigration to the United States. Correspondence, fragments of manuscripts.

376. GHITZIS, MOISEY (1894–1968).
Papers, 1927–1968. 5 in. (RG 598)

Yiddish novelist, playwright, journalist, contributed to the *Freie Arbeiter Stimme*, *Shikage*, *Shikager kurier*, *Yidishe velt* (Philadelphia), *Meksikaner shtime*, *Havaner lebn* (Cuba), *Literarishe bleter* (Warsaw), *In zikh*, *Zukunft*. Editor of *Literarishe zamlungen* (Chicago). Produced a film on Yiddish poets and writers in America. Born in Chotin, Bessarabia. Emigrated to the United States in 1922 and settled in Chicago.

Correspondence with Yiddish writers, including Aaron Glanz-Leieles, Jacob Glatstein, David Hofstein, H. Leivick, Itzik Manger, Shmuel Niger, Joseph Opatoshu. Reviews of Ghitzis's works. Copy of a 16 mm film on Yiddish writers produced by Ghitzis.

The film was removed to and is cataloged in the Collection of Films, RG 105.

377. GINSBURG, ISIDOR (ISSER) (1872–1947).
Papers, 1894–1947. 5 in. (RG 456)

Physician, Yiddish journalist and writer. Contributed to *Der folks advokat*, *Nayer gayst*, *Fraye gezelshaft*, *Freie Arbeiter Stimme* (NY), *Zukunft* (NY), *Hadoar*. Was a regular columnist for the *Jewish Daily Forward*. Wrote about Jewish history, political matters, Hebrew literature. Born in the province of Kaunas, Lithuania. Immigrated to the United States in 1893.

Correspondence with Jewish literary figures including Shalom Asch, Abraham Cahan, Alexander Harkavy, Abraham Liessin, Judah L. Magnes, Abraham Reisen, Zalman Shneur. Clippings of articles by or about Ginsburg. Personal documents.

378. GINSBURG, SAUL (1866–1940).
Papers. 15 in. (RG 1121)

Historian of Russian Jewry. Russian and Yiddish writer. Contributed to many Russian, Yiddish and Hebrew periodicals and also edited or published a number of them. These included: *Hamagid*; *Voskhod* (St. Petersburg), whose editorial board he joined in 1899; *Der fraynd*, the first Yiddish daily in Russia, founded by Ginsburg in 1903; the historical periodical *Perezhitoe*; *He-avar*, a Hebrew periodical, which he edited in 1918; *Evreiskaia mysl* (Jewish Thought) and *Evreiskii vestnik* (Jewish Herald), which he edited during the Soviet period from 1922 to 1928. Ginsburg's historical essays also appeared in *Zukunft* (New York) and on a regular basis in the *Jewish Daily Forward* (New York). In 1901, Ginsburg, together with Pesakh Marek, compiled an early anthology of Yiddish folksongs, *Evreiskie narodnye pesni* (Jewish Folk Songs). From 1897 to 1903 Ginsburg was secretary of the Hevrah Mefitsei Haskalah in Petersburg. He was co-founder of the short-lived Jewish Literary and Scientific Society which was closed down by the Tsarist government in 1910. Born in Minsk, Byelorussia. Left the Soviet Union in 1930, lived briefly in Paris, and moved to New York in 1933.

Correspondence with individuals. Family correspondence. Manuscripts, notes, relating to members of the Jewish intelligentsia in 19th century Russia, including Alexander Braudo, Judah Leib Katzenelson, Mikhail Kulisher. Manuscripts relating to Ginsburg's family history. Typescript of biography of Ginsburg written by his son Michael, titled *My Parents in Their Time*. Newspaper clippings and notebook of Ginsburg's memoirs *From the Past*, in Russian. Personal documents. Obituary notice. Photographs.

379. GINSBURGER, MOSHE (born 1865).
   Papers, 18th century-1930s. 5 in. (RG 276)

Rabbi. Jewish historian and scholar. Lived in France.

The collection relates to biblical scholarship, Jewish history and the history of the Jews in Alsace.

Older manuscripts: biblical commentary in Aramaic. Marriage contract, 1788. Synagogue seating arrangement in a French town, 1846.

Ginsburger's notes on the history of the Jews in Alsace. Photographs of Jewish synagogues and religious art objects.

380. GINZBURG, JOSEPH.
   Papers, ca. 1945–1950s. 5 in. (RG 544)

Lecturer on Yiddish literature. Venice, California.

About 70 notebooks containing lectures on topics in Yiddish literature by Ginzburg.

381. GINZBURG, MORDECAI (1894–1970).
   Papers, 1930–1966. 5 in. (RG 617)

Yiddish and Hebrew journalist. For many years worked for the *Keneder odler* (Montreal). Contributed to *Jewish Daily Forward* (NY), *Der amerikaner*, *Lodzer vokhnblat*, *Hatsofe*, *Haboker*. His pen names included Karliner Khosid, Onkl Borukh, Reb Mordkhele, Slonimski. Born in Slonim, Grodno district. In 1930 immigrated to Canada.

Correspondence with individuals and Jewish cultural institutions.

382. GLANZ, RUDOLF (1892–1978).
   Papers, 1930s–1970s. 18 ft. 9 in. (RG 1133)

Historian, philologist, lecturer, archivist, lawyer. Obtained a doctoral degree in law from the University of Vienna in 1918. Founded the YIVO Circle of Western Jewish Scholars in Vienna and was a visiting lecturer in YIVO's training division in Vilna. From 1938 to 1954

Glanz was a research associate at the YIVO Institute. Author of books on Jewish history. Published monographs on folklore and Jewish history in YIVO publications such as the *YIVO bleter*. Also published articles in the *Yidisher kemfer* (New York) and *Filologishe shriftn fun YIVO* (Vilna). Specialized in the period of Jewish emigration from Germany and from Eastern European countries. Glanz's topics included: the Jewish lower classes and their slang; group relations between Jews and other ethnic groups; and the history of the Jews in the Far West. Long-standing member of the Poalei-Zion (Labor Zionist) movement and archivist at the Labor Zionist Archives.

Correspondence with individuals including Salo Baron, Shlomo Bickel, Oscar Handlin, Abraham Joshua Heschel, Judah A. Joffe, Guido Kisch, Moses Rischin, Emanuel Ringelblum, Max Weinreich.

Manuscripts. Studies of the Jewish lower classes in Germany, and of their slang, including "Sozialgeschichte des niederen jüdischen Volkes in Deutschland" (Social History of the Jewish Lower Class in Germany), German and English versions. Studies of: Jewish immigration to the United States; German Jews in the United States; Jews in California, Alaska, and other states; Jews and the Irish; Jews and Chinese; Jews and Mormons; philosemitism. Bibliographic and source materials on American-Jewish history. Clippings and bibliography about Glanz. Personal documents. Copy of dissertation titled "The Jews of Montana" by Benjamin Kelson.

Correspondence with organizations: American Jewish Historical Society; Emergency Committee in Aid of Displaced Foreign Scholars; Farband (Labor Zionist Order); Jewish Publication Society of America; Jewish Teachers' Seminary; Jewish Theological Seminary; Leo Baeck Institute; Library of Congress; YIVO.

Inventory, English.

383. GLANZ-LEIELES, AARON (1889–1966).
Papers, 1914–1966. 9 ft. 3 in. (RG 556)

Yiddish poet, writer, teacher, speaker, lecturer, editor. His prose appeared under the name A. Glanz and his poetry under the pseudonym A. Leieles. Founder and long-standing member of many Yiddish educational and cultural institutions in the United States and Canada including the Jewish Writers' Union, Workmen's Circle Schools, Yiddish Culture Society, Congress for Jewish Culture, American branch of YIVO. Together with Jacob Glatstein and Nahum Baruch Minkoff, Glanz-Leieles published the journal *In zikh* which appeared from 1920 to 1940. Periodicals Glanz-Leieles either wrote for, edited or co-edited: *Dos naye lebn* (NY), *In zikh* (NY), *Undzer vort*, *Dos naye land*, *Zukunft*, *Yidisher kemfer*, *Freie Arbeiter Stimme* (NY), *Folks shtime* (NY), *Yiddishes Tageblatt* (NY), *Der tog* (NY), *Der groyser kundes*, *Der hamer*, *Der veker*, *Literarishe bleter*, *Di goldene keyt* (Tel Aviv). Born in Włocławek, Poland. Moved to London in 1905. Immigrated to the United States in 1909 and settled in New York.

The collection consists of correspondence with individuals and organizations, manuscripts, news clippings and personal documents relating to the life and career of Glanz-Leieles.

Correspondents include B. Alkwit, Shlomo Bickel, Marc Chagall, Daniel Charney, Jacob Glatstein, Abba Gordin, Chaim Grade, Szmerke Kaczerginski, Leibush Lehrer, Mani Leib, H. Leivick, Shmuel Niger, David Pinsky, Maurice Schwartz, Abraham Sutzkever, Elias Tcherikower, Menashe Unger, Max Weinreich, Aaron Zeitlin, Chaim Zhitlowsky.

Manuscripts by Glanz-Leieles including poems, diaries (1939–1940), plays, lectures, speeches, articles about various topics. Manuscripts by other writers including poems by

Moses (Moyshe) Leib Halpern, Mani Leib, Peretz Markish, Leon (Leib) Feinberg, Melech Ravitch. Materials relating to *In zikh* such as manuscripts about the periodical, clippings, correspondence, notes. Personal papers.

Inventory, Yiddish.

384. GLASER, MICHAEL.
Papers, 1937–1940s. 2 1/2 in. (RG 771)

Author of projects to evacuate Jews from Poland, 1930s–1940s. Married the daughter of Maurice Waldman, Secretary General of the American Jewish Committee. Born in Poland. Immigrated to the United States ca. 1940.

The collection consists of mimeographed and typed memoranda as well as correspondence relating to Glaser's ideas about solving the Jewish problem in Poland. The memoranda are titled: "The Jewish Problem and British Policy," "The Jewish Problem in the United States," "Remarks on the Necessity for a Change in Jewish Tactics," "Project for Financing of Jewish Emigration from Poland."

385. GLASSMAN, BARUCH (BORIS) (1893–1945).
Papers, ca. 1925–1945. 1 ft. 3 in. (RG 374)

Yiddish writer of short stories and novels. Also wrote in English. Contributed to English periodicals such as *Menorah*, *Jewish Spectator* (New York), *Jewish Sentinel* (Chicago) and to the Yiddish press in New York, London, Montreal, Warsaw, Moscow, and Minsk, including *Zukunft*, *Freie Arbeiter Stimme*, *Yidisher kempfer*, *Literarishe bleter*, *Epokhe*. Born in Mozyr, Byelorussia. Immigrated to the United States in 1911. Returned to Poland for a few years in the 1920s.

The collection consists for the most part of Yiddish manuscripts of Glassman's short stories, novels and essays. There are also some English manuscripts. Some correspondence from individuals and publishers. Personal documents, clippings.

386. GLATSTEIN, JACOB (1896–1971).
Papers, 1920s–1960s. 8 ft. (RG 353)

Yiddish poet, essayist and literary critic. Co-founder of the *In zikh* literary group in the 1920s. Columnist for the *Day Morning Journal*. Born in Lublin, Poland. Emigrated to the United States in 1914.

Correspondence with writers and literary figures including: Jacob Ben-Ami, Benjamin Bialostotzky, Menahem Boraisha, Daniel Charney, Solomon Dingol, Aaron Glanz-Leieles, Ben Zion Goldberg, Chaim Grade, Peretz Hirschbein, Ephim Jeshurin, A.M. Klein, Louis Lamed, Leibush Lehrer, H. Leivick, Jacob Lestschinsky, Herman Lieberman, Itzik Manger, Joseph Margoshes, Berl Mark, Alexander Mukdoni, Moshe Nadir, Shmuel Niger, Melech Ravitch, Maurice Schwartz, Jacob Isaac Segal, Hillel Seidman, Lamed Shapiro, Zalman Shazar, Abraham Sutzkever, Jonas Turkow, Jacob Waislitz, Simon Weber, Zishe Weinper, Max Weinreich, Aaron Zeitlin.

Manuscripts of Glatstein's poetry. Materials relating to the *In zikh* group, 1920s. Clippings of Glatstein's writings and about Glatstein.

Inventory, Yiddish.

387. GLENN FAMILY.
   Papers, 1908–1978. 1 ft. 6 in. (RG 1282)

These are the papers of Menachem Gershon Glenn, a writer; Jacob Glenn, a physician; and Ida Glenn, a Yiddish actress and singer. The two brothers and sister come from the Glembocki family which has its roots in Kaunas province, Lithuania.

Menachem Gershon Glenn (1898–1978) settled in the United States in 1914. Received a Ph.D. in Jewish studies. Authored books in English and Yiddish and was a frequent contributor to Yiddish, Hebrew and English periodicals.

Jacob Glenn (1905–1974) came to the United States in 1923 and was a practicing physician and a writer on health in the Yiddish, Hebrew and English press. Wrote several books in Yiddish and English. Was a columnist on health topics for the *Jewish Daily Forward* and the *Jewish Press*, and a regular contributor to the *Nyu yorker vokhnblat*. Also wrote a column on Jewish names.

Ida Glenn had a short career as a Yiddish actress and singer with the Vardi-Yoelit Theater Studio in the late 1920s.

Papers of Dr. Jacob Glenn: manuscripts, photographs, diplomas, other personal documents, letters and clippings. Papers of Dr. Menachem Glenn: personal documents, photographs, clippings and correspondence, including letters from Ben Zion Goldberg, Hirsch Leib Gordon, Ari Ibn-Sahav, Yehuda Karni, Leibush Lehrer, Dov Sadan, Yitshak Shmulevitsh. Papers of Ida Glenn: personal documents, photographs, letters. An unpublished recording of Yiddish songs by Ida Glenn is located in the YIVO Sound Archives (Sound Recordings, RG 115).

388. GLICKMAN, JONAH JOSEPH.
   Papers. 2 1/2 in. (RG 667)

Hebrew teacher, Mesifta Torah Vadaat, Brooklyn, New York.

The collection, which relates to Glickman's teaching career, consists of several notebooks containing stories, Hebrew grammatical exercises, vocabulary lists in Hebrew, Yiddish and Russian.

389. GLUBOKER BENEVOLENT ASSOCIATION.
   Records, 1893–1969. 13 in. (RG 1111)

Organized in New York in 1893 by immigrants from Glubokoye, Byelorussia.

Constitution, in Yiddish, 1911, 1926. Membership application book, Yiddish, 1908–1926. Minute books, Yiddish, 1893–1969. Three books of financial statements, 1912–1913, 1928–1930, 1932–1937. Wooden voting box with marble balls.

390. GOLDBERG, ISAAC LEIB (1860–1935).
   Papers, 1901–1919. 5 in. (RG 17)

Philanthropist, communal worker, Zionist leader. One of the first members of the Hibbat Zion movement (1882), he founded the Ohavei Zion society in Vilna. Delegate to the First Zionist Congress. In 1900 was appointed representative of the Zionist Organization in the Vilna district. Active in various industrial ventures in Palestine, including the establishment of the Geulah Company for the purchase of land in Palestine and the Carmel Wine Company. Founder of two Hebrew newspapers, *Ha'am* and *Ha-aretz*.

Reports, memoranda, printed materials and correspondence relating to Goldberg's Zionist activities during the years 1901–1919. Organizations include: Palestine Land Development; Jewish Colonial Trust, 1901–1913; Anglo-Palestine Company, 1910–1915; JCA (Jewish Colonization Association), 1909–1912; Jewish National Fund; Palestine Industry Syndicate, 1907–1913; Carmel Company; Geulah Company. Documents also pertain to Zionist cultural activities, industrial projects in Palestine, Zionist organizations in England, Austria, Germany, Poland. Reports and documents of Russian Zionist groups, 1902–1905.

391. GOLDBERG, NOAH (1902–1968).
Papers, 1930–1968. 1 ft. 3 in. (RG 599)

Yiddish short-story writer, poet. Contributed to the *Amerikaner, Frayhayt, Hamer, Zukunft, Jewish Daily Forward, Yidisher kemfer, Der tog.* Co-editor of the monthly *Yidish lebn*; on the editorial board of the quarterly *Kheshbn.* Born near Bobruisk, Byelorussia. Came to the United States in 1924.

The papers consist of correspondence with Yiddish literary figures, 1945–1968, manuscripts of Goldberg's works, clippings of his stories and literary critiques. Correspondents include A. Almi, Shlomo Bickel, Menahem Boraisha, Daniel Charney, Jacob Glatstein, David Ignatoff, H. Leivick, Abraham Liessin, Kalman Marmor, Shmuel Niger, Jacob Pat, Isaac Bashevis Singer, Abraham Sutzkever.

392. GOLDFADEN, ABRAHAM (1840–1908).
Collection, 1879–1930s. 3 ft. (RG 219)

Playwright, poet, composer, producer and director. Founder of the Yiddish theater. Staged first Yiddish theater production in Jassy, Rumania, 1876. Born in Starokonstantinov, Ukraine. Lived in Russia, Rumania, Poland, Germany, England. Settled in the United States in 1903.

The collection was assembled by Jacob Shatzky for Shatzky's work on the history of Yiddish theater and includes both Goldfaden's papers and materials about him. Manuscripts of 24 plays, 1881–1906. Manuscripts of Goldfaden's poems and articles. Letters of Goldfaden, some copied by Shatzky in notebooks. News clippings about Goldfaden. Playbills, front pages of published plays.

Inventory, English.

393. GOLDFADEN CAMP NO. 9, ORDER BNAI ZION.
Records, 1906–1951. 10 in. (RG 1065)

Founded in 1908 as the Abraham Goldfaden Zion Camp No. 9, a branch of the Order Sons of Zion (Bnai Zion). Provided members with insurance, death benefits, social and cultural activities. Camp No. 9 was associated with a ladies auxiliary.

Constitution. Minutes, 1914–1932. Financial records, 1929–1936. Membership materials, 1939. Correspondence. Materials pertaining to Bnai Zion and other chapters, including the Bistritz & Vicinity Chapter 33.

394. GOLDMAN, ABRAHAM LEIB (1885–1970).
Papers, 1940s–1960s. 4 ft. 7 in. (RG 632)

Yiddish teacher. Active in the organization of the Yiddish secular school systems in Canada and the United States including Sholem Aleichem and Workmen's Circle Schools. Formulated and taught a new system of Yiddish stenography. Born in Szreńsk, Poland. Immigrated to Canada in 1907 and settled in the United States in 1912.

The papers relate to A.L. Goldman's educational activities in various Yiddish schools. Records of Yiddish schools: correspondence, circulars, teaching materials, student materials. News clippings relating to: I.L. Peretz School, Toronto; Camp Heymshul; Ahad Ha'am School, Brooklyn; Workmen's Circle Schools in Crown Heights, Williamsburg (Brooklyn, NY); Sholem Aleichem Folk Schools in the Bronx, Flatbush, Perth Amboy. Miscellaneous educational materials.

Inventory, Yiddish.

395. GOLDOVSKY, H. (1893–1948).
Papers, 1920s–1940s. 1 in. (RG 296)

Yiddish poet. Lived in Byelorussia, United States.

Letters to Goldovsky by Yiddish literary and cultural figures, including Jacob Glatstein, H. Leivick, Mani Leib, Lamed Shapiro, Chaim Zhitlowsky.

396. GOLDSMITH, MORRIS (MOISHE) (born 1902).
Papers, 1923–1946. 3 in. (RG 1291)

Member of a Kobrin *landsmanshaft*, active in the Labor Zionist movement. Born in Kobrin, Byelorussia. Lived in Palestine, 1920–1923. Settled in New York in 1923.

Records of the Kobriner Young Folks Center in New York including correspondence with the Tel Chai school and other Jewish institutions in Kobrin. 3 issues of the journal *Naye vintelakh* published by the students of the Tel Chai school. Records of the Kobriner Branch #250 of the National Jewish Workers Alliance. Documents relating to Zionist activities in the Bronx. Delegate card to the 22nd Zionist Congress, 1946.

397. GOLOMB, ABRAHAM (1888–1982).
Papers, 1945–1958. 10 in. (RG 455)

Jewish educator, writer. Director of the Jewish Teachers' Seminary in Vilna, 1920s. Published articles and books on education. Contributed to *Shul un lebn* (Warsaw), *Bikher velt* (Warsaw), *Di naye shul* (Warsaw), *Oyfn shvel* (NY), *Frayland* (NY). Member of various school organizations including the Tsentraler Bildungs Komitet (Central Education Committee) in Vilna.

Correspondence with Yiddish writers and scholars including Menahem Boraisha, H. Leivick, Jacob Lestschinsky, Joseph Opatoshu, Max Weinreich. Correspondence with Yiddish schools and cultural organizations.

398. GOMBINER YOUNG MEN'S BENEVOLENT ASSOCIATION.
Records, 1926, 1952–1979. 10 in. (RG 842)

Established in New York in 1923 to help bring *landslayt* from Gąbin, Poland, to the United States. Affiliated with the Gombiner Relief Committee, Gombiner Lending Society, Gombiner Ladies Auxiliary. American Gombiner societies joined to build the Gombiner House in Israel, to establish a loan fund for *landslayt* there and to publish a memorial book.

Constitution; minutes, 1952–1977; financial records, 1967–1979; photographs; memorial book, 1951.

399. GOODMAN, SAUL (born 1901).
Papers, 1920s–1980s. 5 in. (RG 1179)

Teacher, writer, active in Yiddish cultural groups. Taught in the Workmen's Circle Schools. Executive Secretary of the Sholem Aleichem Folk Institute and Executive Secretary of the Freeland League. Editor, *Oyfn shvel*. Co-editor, *Bleter far yidisher dertsiung*. Wrote for *YIVO bleter*, *Yidish*, *Dos fraye vort* (London), *Kultur un dertsiung*, *Pedagogisher buletin*, *Yidisher kemfer*. Born near Płock, Poland. Settled in the United States in 1921.

Correspondence with family members, Yiddish cultural figures and writers. Photographs, speeches, personal documents.

400. GORDIN, ABBA (1887–1964).
Papers, 1930s–1950s. 2 1/2 in. (RG 271)

Yiddish, Hebrew, and Russian writer. Lived in Russia, the United States and Israel.
Correspondence with literary and cultural figures.

401. GORDIN, JACOB (1853–1909).
Papers, ca. 1893–1910. 4 ft. 2 in. (RG 530)

Prominent Yiddish playwright and journalist who played an important role in the development of the Yiddish theater. Author of more than a hundred plays. For many of his works, Gordin borrowed and adapted plots from playwrights such as Hugo, Gogol, Ibsen and Shakespeare. Gordin enjoyed great popular success and his works were performed by the leading Yiddish actors of the day. Born in Mirgorod, Ukraine. Emigrated to the United States in 1891.

Manuscripts of about 100 plays. Correspondence with literary and theatrical personalities including Jacob P. Adler, Julius Adler, David Ignatoff, David Kessler, Kalman Marmor, Abraham Reisen, Lillian Wald. Telegrams and greeting cards to Gordin. Programs, notices, tickets. Newspaper clippings of articles about Gordin's plays. Contracts, financial records. Bibliographical materials. Biographical information relating to members of the Gordin family.

Inventory, Yiddish.

402. GORDON, HIRSCH LOEB (LEIB) (1896–1969).
Papers, 1909–1964. 4 ft. (RG 505)

Physician. Scholar in Semitic languages. Yiddish and Hebrew playwright, poet and journalist. Soldier in the Jewish Legion during World War I. Held doctoral degrees in philosophy, Semitic languages, literature, and Egyptology, and master's degrees in diplomacy, psychology, pedagogy and art history. Wrote scholarly works on Semitic and ancient Egyptian archeology, medicine, history. Published translations of Egyptian hieroglyphics. Prepared an anthology of short stories. Contributed articles to *Hatsefira* (Warsaw), *Moment* (Warsaw), *Der tog* (New York), *Jewish Daily Forward* (New York), *Yiddishes Tageblatt* (New York), *Morgn zhurnal* (New York), *Zukunft* (New York), *Der kundes* (New York), *Hadoar* (New York), *Harofe*, *Ha-ivri* (New York). Born in Daugeliszki, district of Vilna. Lived in Berlin, Rome, Palestine. Settled in the United States ca. 1920.

Manuscripts by Gordon relating to the Bible, kabbalah, semitica, medicine. Manuscripts of literary works such as songs and plays, articles for the Yiddish press. Personal documents: diplomas, membership cards, family correspondence and genealogical tree.

403. GORN, SOLOMON (1879–1975).
    Papers, 1910–1970. 5 in. (RG 705)

Yiddish writer. Born in Russia. Came to the United States at the turn of the century. Lived in New York and later in Portland, Oregon.
   The papers consist of manuscripts of Gorn's plays and stories, and some letters, mainly from Abba Gordin.

404. GOTTSCHALK, MAX (born 1889).
    Papers, 1939–1945. 1 microfilm reel. (RG 330)

Belgian sociologist, educator, author, lawyer, authority on social and economic problems. President of HICEM, 1939–40. Director of the Research Institute in Peace and Post-War Problems of the American Jewish Committee.
   Correspondents include: U.S. Office of War Information, 1943; Governor of New York State; New School for Social Research; Conference on Jewish Relations; Jewish Agricultural Society. Press releases, statistical surveys, printed matter, lectures. Personal papers.

405. GRACKIN, MAX and LIBBY.
    Papers, 1917–1920s. 5 in. (RG 1163)

Max and Libby Grackin were active members of the Jewish People's Relief Committee for Jewish War Sufferers, Bronx District. Libby Grackin was active in Sholem Aleichem School No. 1.
   The collection relates to the Jewish People's Relief Committee and includes badges, buttons, armbands, convention journals, correspondence, flyers, invitations, photographs. There are also some materials of the Sholem Aleichem Folk School.

406. GRADE, CHAIM (1910–1982).
    Papers, 1952–1968. 4 ft. (RG 566)

Major Yiddish poet, novelist, essayist. Contributed to various periodicals including *Der tog* (Vilna), *Morgn zhurnal* (New York), *Goldene keyt* (Tel Aviv). Important member of the Yiddish literary group "Yung vilne" in Poland before World War II. Recipient of many literary awards as well as honorary degrees from several Jewish universities in the United States. Born in Vilna. Settled in New York in 1948.
   The collection consists of several thousand letters to Chaim Grade, mostly from his readers, but also from Yiddish writers and cultural organizations.

407. GRAUBARD, BENJAMIN (1894–1957).
    Papers, 1930s–1950s. 2 1/2 in. (RG 665)

Yiddish literary critic. Teacher in Workmen's Circle schools in Chicago and Philadelphia.
   The papers consist of correspondence, manuscripts of articles and talks, criticisms of his book *A fertl yorhundert*. Correspondents include Jacob Glatstein, Joseph Opatoshu, H. Leivick.

408. GREENBERG, ELIEZER (1896–1977).
    Papers, 1949–1977. 1 ft. (RG 752)

Yiddish poet, translator, teacher. Contributed to *Der groyser kundes, Studio Signal, Frayhayt, Der hamer, Freie Arbeiter Stimme, Oyfkum, Dos vort, Hemshekh, Zukunft, Kinder zhurnal, Shoybn, Yidisher kemfer, In zikh, Literarishe bleter*. Vice-president of the Yiddish PEN Club. Born in Lipkan, Bessarabia. Immigrated to the United States in 1913.

Correspondence. Typescripts of Greenberg's poems. Articles and essays on Yiddish literature. Manuscripts of other Yiddish writers: Moshe Dluznowsky, Noah Goldberg, Josef Okrutny, Leib Olitzky, David Opalov. Reviews of the anthology *A Treasury of Yiddish Poetry*, compiled by Irving Howe and Greenberg. Materials relating to the Yiddish PEN Club. Photographs. Clippings of Greenberg's articles.

409. GREENBERG, NAHUM.
Collection, 1933–1953. 4 ft. 2 in. (RG 486)

Collector of antisemitica, attorney. Brooklyn, New York.

A collection of newspaper clippings from the American press on antisemitism and Nazism in the United States and Germany, 1930s–1940s. Topics include: Father Coughlin, 1938–1942; America First Committee, 1941–1942; antisemitism in England, Oswald Mosley; Jews in Germany, 1938; report of the Anglo-American Palestine Commission, 1946; Nuremberg trial. There is also a series of clippings arranged chronologically, 1933–38.

410. GREENBLAT, ALISA (1888–1975).
Papers, ca. 1900. 5 in. (RG 538)

Yiddish poet and writer. Contributed to *Amerikaner* (NY), *Di yidishe velt* (Philadelphia), *Yidisher kemfer* (NY), *Freie Arbeiter Stimme* (NY), *New Yorker vokhnblat* (NY), *Der Tog* (NY), *Jewish Daily Forward* (NY), *Kinder zhurnal* (NY), *Morgn zhurnal* (NY), *Letste nayes* (Israel), *Davar* (Israel). Born in Ozarinet near Kamenets-Podolski, Ukraine. Emigrated to the United States in 1910.

Photographs of A. Greenblat and her family, mainly in Philadelphia, ca. 1900–1920.

411. GRIS, NOAH (1902–1985).
Papers, 1912–1976. 1 ft. 3 in. (RG 762)

Journalist, teacher, writer, essayist. Librarian at the Bibliothèque Nationale in Paris. Born in Galicia, Poland. Settled in France in 1953.

The papers consist of correspondence with Yiddish literary and communal figures as well as a manuscript by Moishe Bielinki, Moscow.

412. GROBER, CHAYELE (1898–1978).
Papers, 1930s–1950s. 9 in. (RG 590)

Yiddish actress, singer and writer. Member of the Habimah Theater in Moscow. Her writings appeared in *Di yidishe tsaytung* (Buenos Aires), *Keneder odler* (Montreal). Born in Białystok, Poland. Lived in the United States and Israel.

The collection consists of scrapbooks containing programs, clippings, photographs, posters and reviews relating to Grober's career as a singer and actress.

Photographs cataloged in STAGEPIX.

413. GRODNER-LIPKANER BRANCH 74, WORKMEN'S CIRCLE.
Records, 1919–1964. 20 in. (RG 782)

Established through a merger of the Grodner and Lipkaner branches of the Workmen's Circle, 1973. The Grodner branch was originally established as the Grodno Revolutionary Untershtitsung Fareyn. Chartered and joined Workmen's Circle in 1906. Activities included the formation of the United Grodner Relief in 1915.

Minutes, including dues and expense records, 1930s–1960s. Financial records, including records from Grodno, 1919–60s. Correspondence, bulletins, notices, ballots, newsletters, anniversary journals, 1926, 1947, 1950, 1956. Photographs.

414. GRODZISKER MUTUAL AID SOCIETY.
Records, 1926–1963. 2 1/2 in. (RG 1010)

First established in New York in 1911 by immigrants from Grodzisk Mazowiecki, Poland. Reestablished, 1913. Was affiliated with the Junior Grodzisker Mutual Aid Society and the Grodzisker Ladies Auxiliary. Formed a relief committee, 1938.

Anniversary journals, 1920s–1960s. Meeting announcements. Photograph.

415. GROPPER, WILLIAM (1897–1977).
Papers, ca. 1930–ca. 1940. 3 ft. (RG 1290)

Painter, muralist, book illustrator and cartoonist. Created political cartoons for several leading periodicals in the United States including the radical *New Masses* and the Communist Yiddish daily *Morgn frayhayt*. After the Holocaust, Jewish themes dominated Gropper's art. Born and died in New York.

The collection consists of several hundred political cartoons which Gropper drew for the *Morgn frayhayt*.

416. GROSS, LOUIS (born 1900).
Papers, 1937–1958. 2 ft. 11 in. (RG 429)

Yiddish journalist, radio commentator. Producer of Yiddish programs in Philadelphia and Miami, 1952–1958.

Scripts of Gross's radio talks, commentaries and other appearances. Clippings. Sound recordings of Jewish folk, theater and cantorial music. Correspondence pertaining to the radio programs. Correspondence relating to the visit of the Soviet-Jewish writers Solomon Mikhoels and Itsik Feffer to the United States in 1943.

417. GROSS, NAFTOLI (1896–1956).
Papers, 1929–1950s. 3 ft. (RG 450)

Yiddish poet, folklorist and translator. Staff member of the *Jewish Daily Forward*. His poetic works include *Psalmen* (Psalms), *Der vayser rayter* (The White Horseman) and *Yidn* (Jews). Translated *Psalms*, the five scrolls (*megillot*) and, together with Abraham Reisen, the poetry of Solomon ibn Gabirol. Born in Kołomyja, Poland, he immigrated to the United States in 1913 and settled in New York.

Manuscripts of Gross's literary works including Yiddish translation of *Psalms*, stories, poems. Biographies of Vladimir Medem and Eugene Debs.

418. GROSSINGER'S COUNTRY CLUB.
    Records, ca. 1920–1983. 6 ft. (RG 1195)

A popular resort in the Catskill Mountain region, located near Liberty, New York.

    Photographs, correspondence and other materials concerning Grossinger's Country Club and the Grossinger family. Correspondence of Jennie Grossinger, 1954–1962, concerning social and philanthropic activities. Includes correspondence with prominent politicians, entertainers, and others. Copies of *The Grossinger News*, 1947, 1954. Fiftieth anniversary program, 1964. Photo albums, 1951–1959, include photographs of: prominent politicians, entertainers and athletes; wedding of Debbie Reynolds and Eddie Fisher; foreign military trainees, 1968; New York State Beauty Pageant, 1961; testimonial for Jennie Grossinger, 1954; U.S. Air Force award ceremony, 1958; Grossinger family travel pictures, 1966–1969. Photographs of Grossinger's Country Club, including family, guests, staff, facilities and grounds. Certificates, diplomas and awards of Paul and Bunny Grossinger, 1955–1983. Original cartoon drawings by Hy Rosen and others. Sound recordings of: radio show with Eddie Fisher; radio advertisement for Grossinger's rye bread; interview with Jennie Grossinger.

    Correspondence index, English.

    Card inventory of the photographs, English.

    Sound recordings placed in the Sound Archive.

419. GROSSMAN, ABRAHAM.
    Papers, 1935–1948. 2 ft. 1 in. (RG 286)

Chairman of the United Non-Sectarian Boycott Council of the Bronx. Member, Bronx League for the American and World Jewish Congresses.

    Newspaper clippings, correspondence, typed copies of newspaper articles dealing mainly with the American boycott of Nazi goods in the 1930s, and with the activities of the Boycott Council.

420. GROSSMAN, IRVING (born 1900) and GOLDBERG, DIANA (born 1908).
    Papers, 1897–1918, 1940s–1950s. 3 ft. 9 in. (RG 411)

Yiddish actors, husband and wife, United States.

    Manuscripts of about 50 Yiddish theater songs and parts of operettas. Photographs, clippings and programs relating to the careers of I. Grossman and D. Goldberg.

    Inventory, English.

421. GROSSMAN, KURT RICHARD (1897–1972).
    Papers, 1938–1945. 2 microfilm reels. (RG 591)

German journalist. General Secretary of the Deutsche Liga für Menschenrechte (German League for Human Rights) in Berlin in 1926. Established and directed the Demokratische Flüchtlingsfürsorge Prag (Democratic Refugee Relief). After World War II Grossman became a recognized spokesman on problems concerning Jewish refugees including German restitution and compensation. Wrote a number of works relating to the Jewish refugee problem. In 1938 moved from Germany to Paris and in 1939 settled in New York.

    The collection relates to Grossman's activities during the years, 1938–1945. Correspondence, press releases, memoranda, reports, bulletins, relating to: Demokratische Flüchtlingsfürsorge Prag and its successor Secours Démocratique aux Réfugiés (Paris); Zentral-vereinigung der Deutschen Emigration, Paris, 1936; Liga für Menschenrechte, 1938; OSE, 1939–1941; Joint Anti-Fascist Refugee Committee, 1942; Hapoel Hamizrachi of America, 1942; Jewish Agency, 1944; American Committee for the Rehabilitation of European Jewish Children; International Red Cross.

Inventory, English.

422. GROSSMAN, SAMUEL S.
Papers, 1922–928. 5 in. (RG 524)

Member of the Jewish Art Theater, 1920s. Playwright, translator. Educational director of the Brooklyn Jewish Center.

English translations of H. Leivick's *Shmates* (Rags) and Peretz Hirschbein's *Grine Felder* (Green Fields) and other plays. A few letters relating to royalty payments in connection with the production of these plays.

423. GROSSMAN, VLADIMIR (1884–1976).
Papers, 1950s–1960s. 2 ft. 11 in. (RG 1279)

Jewish journalist and social worker. Studied in Russian universities. Worked for the Jewish Colonization Association and for ORT, 1924–1976. Wrote articles in Yiddish, Russian, and also in Danish. Edited a number of periodicals, including *Der yidisher emigrant, Parizer haynt, Zibn teg.* Was correspondent for *Der tog* (New York) and *Haynt* (Warsaw). Wrote several books on Jewish topics. Born in the Caucasus. Lived in Paris and Geneva. Died in Geneva.

Correspondence with A. Almi, Grigori Aronson, Noah Gris, Adolph Held, Efim Jeshurin, Israel Knox, Joseph Leftwich, Leon Leneman, Israel London, Yehudah Minkin, Melech Ravitch, Israel Silberberg-Cholewa, Aryeh Tartakower, Ilya Trotsky, Mordecai Tsanin, Tsivyon (Ben-Zion Hofman), Marc Yarblum. Manuscripts, clippings, miscellaneous materials.

424. GRUNER ZWEIG KRANKER UNTERSHTITSUNGS VEREIN.
Records, 1935–1973. 2 in. (RG 1119)

Founded in Brooklyn, New York, in 1879. Provided sick, death and burial benefits.

Constitution, 1935. Correspondence. Minutes, 1879–1964. Financial records, 1963–1973.

425. GÜNZBURG, BARON HORACE DE (NAFTALI HERZ) (1833–1909).
Papers, 1850–1895. 5 in. (RG 89)

Member of a distinguished Jewish family in Russia which was known for its efforts on behalf of Russian Jewry with the Tsarist authorities. Banker, philanthropist, communal leader. Patron of scientific, cultural, and social institutions and of writers, artists and musicians. Günzburg fought to prevent the passing of anti-Jewish decrees and participated in the Pahlen Commission (1883–1888) which was established to review the laws pertaining to Jews. Headed the Hevrah Mefitsei Haskalah (Society for the Promotion of Culture). As Chairman of the Jewish Colonization Association (JCA), Günzburg encouraged the development of agriculture and crafts among Jews. Born in Zvenigorodok, Kiev province.

The collection relates to Günzburg's philanthropic and communal activities as well as to

Jewish life in Russia. Correspondence between Günzburg and Russian authorities about the unjust conscription of Jews into the Russian army and about improving the political and legal status of Russian Jews. Correspondence between the Hevrah Mefitsei Haskalah and Jewish journalists about the Jewish press in Russia, in particular about the newspapers *Hamelitz* and *Kol Mevasser*. Correspondence with rabbis of Russia and Poland about establishing a rabbinical seminary in Russia. Minutes of meetings of the Hevrah Mefitsei Haskalah. Petitions to the government about the political and legal situation of Jews in Russia. Records of the Vilna Committee for Improvement of the Situation of Russian Jews, 1869. Materials relating to anti-Jewish propaganda in Russia.

Inventory, Russian.

426. GUREVITCH, GRIGORI (1852–1929).
Papers, 1880–1929. 5 in. (RG 88)

Pseudonym of Gershon Badanes. One of the first Russian-Jewish revolutionaries. Studied in Austria, Germany and Belgium. Became disillusioned with socialism after the pogroms of 1880. After the 1917 revolution immigrated to France. Died in Paris.

Correspondence with Pavel Axelrod, 1925; Jacob Lestschinsky, 1929; N. Grinberg, 1924–1928; Nachman Meisel, 1922. Reports and accounts about pogroms in the Ukraine, 1917–1919. Various manuscripts and notes. Gurevitch's published Yiddish translation of M. Aldanov's *St. Helena*.

Inventory, Yiddish.

427. GUTERMAN, PINCHAS (born 1906).
Papers. 2 in. (RG 748)

Hebrew and Yiddish writer. Contributed to *Letste nayes, Dos vort, Di yidishe tsaytung*. Born in Miechów, Lublin province, Poland. Settled in Palestine.

The papers consist of manuscripts of Guterman's works, including the autobiographical novel *Mayn shtetl* (My Town), and some clippings.

428. GUTMAN, CHAIM (1887–1961).
Papers, 1913–1960. ca. 5 ft. (RG 439)

Yiddish humorist, satirist, and theater critic. Used pen name *Der lebediker*. Wrote columns for New York Yiddish dailies and periodicals such as *Der kibetser* and *Der kundes*. Grew up near Minsk, Byelorussia and emigrated to the United States in 1905.

Letters to Gutman from Yiddish literary figures such as Reuben Brainin, Daniel Charney, Mendl Elkin, Aaron Glanz-Leieles, Chaim Grade, Mani Leib, Kalman Marmor, Melech Ravitch, Zalman Reisen, Maurice Schwartz, Israel Joshua Singer, Abraham Sutzkever. Clippings of articles by and about Gutman. Manuscripts of Gutman's writings. Autobiographical notes. Photographs of Gutman, family and friends.

429. GUTTMACHER, ELIYAHU (1796–1874).
Papers, 1840s–1874. 4 ft. 7 in. (RG 27)

Rabbi, talmudic scholar, mystic, communal leader. Early Zionist. A disciple of Rabbi Akiva Eiger of Posen. In 1822 Rabbi Guttmacher was appointed the rabbi of Pleschen. In 1841 he became the rabbi of Grätz. During his lifetime he was known as the Tsadik of Grätz and thousands of Jews flocked to him for blessings and advice. Guttmacher was also known for his support of Rabbi Zvi Hirsch Kalischer, an early Zionist, and for his extensive collection of funds for institutions in Palestine. Born in Borek (Poznań province, Western Poland). Lived in Grätz (Grodzisk Wielkopolski, Poznań province).

The bulk of the collection consists of several thousand *kvitlekh* (written requests to a rabbi asking for a blessing or advice) arranged in alphabetical order by name of town or city. The *kvitlekh* were received from Jews residing in Poland and other, mostly European, countries. They reflect the social history of European Jews in the mid-19th century and relate to financial, medical and family problems.

In addition, the collection includes the following:

General correspondence, including inquiries relating to religious matters. Family correspondence, legal documents such as court and government papers, bills. Certifications by unidentified authors. Discussions on Jewish law by unknown authors. Amulet. Business documents. Receipts for contributions to charitable institutions in Palestine.

Inventory, English.

430. HAFFKINE, WALDEMAR MORDECAI (1860–1930).
Papers, 1895–1938. 13 ft. 8 in. (RG 1296)

Scientist, philanthropist. Received his doctoral degree in natural sciences in 1884. Was a student of E. Metchnikoff. Joined the staff of the Pasteur Institute in 1889. In 1892 and 1893, he discovered vaccines against cholera and the bubonic plague. From 1893–1895 and from 1896–1915, he lived in India where he established laboratories and carried out mass inoculation programs. In 1915 he moved to Paris. Thereafter, Haffkine became active in Jewish affairs, including minority rights in Eastern Europe, agricultural settlements in Palestine, and colonization in the USSR. He established a foundation to aid yeshivot, called the Haffkine Foundation, and wrote in defense of traditional Judaism.

The bulk of the papers consists of a photostat of Haffkine's diary. There is also a typed transcript thereof prepared by Edythe Lutzker, as well as a guide to the diary and annual indices. The diary is fragmentary for the period 1895–1908, but is complete for the period May 1915 to October 1930. The original manuscript is at the Hebrew University in Jerusalem.

The remainder of the papers consist of copies of Haffkine's letters; documents relating to his activities in India; biographical materials on Haffkine. There are photographs of Haffkine and of his activities in India.

Biographical materials on Edythe Lutzker.

431. HALPERN, MOSES (MOYSHE) LEIB (1886–1932).
Papers, ca. 1910–1930s. 10 in. (RG 464)

Yiddish poet, painter. Member of the literary group *Di yunge* during the World War I period. Published collections of poems *In nyu york* (1919) and *Di goldene pave* (1924). Born in Złoczów, East Galicia, and immigrated to the United States in 1908.

Manuscripts, typescripts and clippings of his published and unpublished poems. A self-portrait drawn by Halpern. Part of the collection consists of corrected proofs submitted to the publisher Farlag Matones, which were included in the book *Moshe Leib Halpern*, New York, 1934.

432. HAMPEL, MORDECHAI (1905–1982).
Papers, 1960s–1970s. 5 in. (RG 714)

Yiddish journalist, writer, editor of memorial books. Born in Będzin, Poland. Settled in Palestine in 1932.

The collection consists primarily of newspaper clippings of articles by Hampel and by his wife Tzipora. Included are articles about Jews from the province of Zagłębie in Poland and miscellaneous photographs of memorial events for Holocaust victims from Zagłębie.

433. HARENDORF, SAMUEL JACOB (1900–1970).
Papers, 1930s–1960s. 1 ft. 3 in. (RG 616)

Yiddish writer, playwright, also known as S.I. Dorfson. Contributed articles and short stories to the *Moment* (Warsaw), *Yudisher morgnpost* (Vienna), *Di naye tsayt* (Vienna), *Dos yudishe folksblat* (Mukačevo, 1926), *Morgn zhurnal* (NY). Director of the London office of the *Morgn zhurnal*. Born in Chęciny, province of Kielce, Poland. Settled in Prague, Czechoslovakia, in 1931 and in London ca. 1939.

Correspondence with writers, organizations, periodicals. Manuscripts and typescripts of plays in Yiddish and English, and of an unfinished novel. Photographs of Harendorf, photographs of stage scenes of Yiddish plays. Theater programs. Personal documents.

434. HARKAVY, ALEXANDER (1863–1939).
Papers. 1 ft. 1/2 in. (RG 761)

Lexicographer of Yiddish, journalist, teacher. HIAS representative at Ellis Island, 1904–1909. Lecturer for the Board of Education, New York, the Workmen's Circle, and the Jewish Teachers' Seminary. Member of the Linguistics Section of YIVO, 1928. Compiled Yiddish-Hebrew-English dictionaries. Contributed to *Israelitische presse*, *Yidishe gazetn*, *Nyu yorker ilustrirte tsaytung*, *Teater zhurnal*, *Fraye gezelshaft*, *Freie Arbeiter Stimme*, *Yiddishes Tageblatt*, *Jewish Daily Forward*, *Zukunft*, *Morgn zhurnal*. Contributed to Hebrew publications such as *Hamagid*, *Hamelitz*, *Hayom*, *Hatsefira*, *Ha-pisga*, *Ner hamaaravi*, *Ha-leum*. Born in Nowogródek, Byelorussia. Immigrated to the United States in 1882.

The papers consist of entries, on index cards, for a Yiddish dictionary.

435. HASIDISM.
Collection, 1948–1949. 2 ft. 1 in. (RG 127)

A YIVO project headed by Professor Abraham Joshua Heschel.

Notes and descriptions related to Hasidic customs, legends, writings, gathered by Rabbi E. Abraham of New York, 1948–49, from interviews with Holocaust survivors. The project was not completed and the collection is fragmentary. Photocopies of manuscripts by Hasidic rabbis.

436. HATIKVO BENEFICIAL SOCIETY.
Records, 1917, 1930–1975. 5 in. (RG 986)

Incorporated in New York in 1917. Took over the cemetery property of the Mordecai Lodge No. 24, Order Brith Abraham, in Washington Cemetery, Brooklyn, 1917. Dissolved in the 1970s.

Certificate of incorporation, 1917. Dissolution form. Minutes, 1952–1956. Financial records, 1950s. Materials pertaining to burial, including cemetery deed between the society and the Mordecai Lodge No. 24, O.B.A., 1917.

437. HAUPTAMT WISSENSCHAFT (BERLIN).
Records, 1939–1945. 9 ft. 2 in. (RG 216)

A division of the Dienststelle (Office) of the Nazi Party (NSDAP—Nationalsozialistische Deutsche Arbeiterpartei) under the direction of Alfred Rosenberg. It maintained files on scholars and scholarly institutions, checked and reported on their political reliability, and examined their political credentials before granting promotions, appointments or honors.

The records consist of individual files on German academic personalities, scientists and academic institutions. They include reports, newspaper clippings, summaries of lectures, petitions, applications and correspondence of various Nazi officials. The records are incomplete.

Inventory, English.

438. HAVANER LEBN.
Papers, 1932–1935. 5 in. (RG 1245)

Weekly Yiddish publication in Havana, Cuba. Founded in 1932. Editor was Oscar Pinis.

Two bound volumes of printed issues of *Havaner lebn*. Correspondence of the editor.

439. HAVRUSA.
Collection, 1956–1965. 1 in. (RG 1233)

Cultural organization dedicated to preserving and developing Hebrew language and culture. Founded in January 1936.

Notebook of Meyer Levine, secretary and treasurer of Havrusa, containing minutes, correspondence, clippings, financial records, and membership list.

440. HEBREW-AMERICAN TYPOGRAPHICAL UNION.
Records, 1888–1961. 7 ft. 6 in. (RG 445)

Local 83 of the International Typographical Union. Founded in New York in 1888, incorporated in 1891, it covered typographical work in the Yiddish, Hebrew and Slavic languages. In 1961 the Union merged with the New York Typographical Union, Local 6.

Certificate of incorporation, 1891. Manuscript of union by-laws, 1888. Minutes of regular and executive meetings, 1901–1959. Correspondence with unions, organizations and individuals. Financial records, 1948–1954. Membership register, 1898–1948. Scrapbooks, memorabilia, press clippings about the strike against *The Day*, 1941.

441–468 HEBREW IMMIGRANT AID SOCIETY—HIAS.
Records, ca. 1900–ca. 1970. 415 ft. and 851 microfilm reels. (RG 245)

An international Jewish immigrant and refugee service founded in 1909 in New York through the merger of the Hebrew Sheltering House and the Hebrew Immigrant Aid Society. HIAS activities included financial and legal aid, transportation arrangements, educational and vocational programs, location of missing relatives, lobbying in the United States and other governments on behalf of individual cases.

Until 1915, HIAS confined its activities to the United States. During World War I, HIAS helped refugees in Europe and the Far East. In the period 1920–1922, HIAS established offices in Europe to assist war and pogrom victims. In 1927, HIAS joined with the Jewish Colonization Association (JCA) of London and EMIGDIRECT of Berlin to form

HICEM, whose headquarters were in France and which dealt with European operations. HICEM was dissolved in 1945. At the end of 1953, HIAS had offices in 50 countries. In 1954, HIAS merged with the United Service for New Americans to form the United HIAS Service.

The records of HIAS reflect the activities of all of its administrative offices in the United States and abroad. The collection is comprised of the records of HIAS, HICEM and the United HIAS Service. This record group is divided into the following subgroups:

441. HIAS BOARD OF DIRECTORS AND STEERING COMMITTEES.
1913–1952. 6 microfilm reels. (RG 245.1)

Minutes of the Board of Directors and of the annual meetings. Minutes of meetings of permanent and ad hoc committees of HIAS, including the Executive Committee, Committee on Work in Foreign Countries, U.S. Immigration Stations (later Committee on Overseas Work), Budget, Membership, House and Shelter, Citizenship, Law and Work in Palestine. These records were loaned to the YIVO Archives for the purpose of photocopying and they were returned to HIAS thereafter.

442. HIAS ELLIS ISLAND BUREAU.
1905–1923. 26 microfilm reels. (RG 245.2)

Records of HIAS representatives at the U.S. Immigration Station at Ellis Island, New York, relating to intercessions on behalf of Jewish immigrants, mainly those who were detained or were awaiting deportation. The case files include correspondence of HIAS representatives Irving I. Lipsitch and Samuel Littman with relatives, sponsors, and with U.S. Government officials, including Secretary of Labor. Subjects files include: cases affected by illness, Jewish holidays, missionaries, clothing for immigrants, citizenship lectures, verifications of landing. Correspondence with organizations includes: United Hebrew Charities, National Desertion Bureau, Association for the Protection of Jewish Immigrants.
   Inventory, English.

443. HIAS FOREIGN RELATIONS DEPARTMENT.
1915–1973. 23 microfilm reels. (RG 245.3)

Records relating to HIAS's efforts to locate individuals overseas on behalf of relatives in the United States. Correspondence, search forms, affidavits, visas, financial and transportation records.

444–462 HIAS AND HICEM MAIN OFFICES, NEW YORK.
190 microfilm reels. (RG 245.4)

Records of the main HIAS administration from 1907 until the merger of HIAS and the United Service for New Americans in 1954 to form the United Hias Service. Records of the New York office of HICEM, 1940–1945. The following series are included:

444. Reports and Minutes of HIAS Meetings and Conventions.
1905–1955. 3 reels. (RG 245.4.1)

Minutes of the Board of Directors, 1909–1922. Minutes of the Executive Committee, 1915–1921. Minutes of the Committee on U.S. Immigration Stations and Foreign Relations, 1914–

28. Records of the Immigration Advisory Board, 1917. HIAS annual reports, 1911–1945. HIAS survey, 1940–1941.
Inventory, English.

445. Minutes and Reports of HICEM.
1927–45. 7 reels. (RG 245.4.2)

Reports of HICEM activities in Paris and New York, 1920s–1940s. Minutes of meetings of the HICEM Board of Directors, Paris, New York. Minutes of meetings of HICEM committees, New York. Correspondence between HICEM Paris and HIAS New York. Correspondence with Adolfo Benarus, Sir O.E. d'Avigdor Goldsmid, Sir Neill Malcolm, Dr. Bruno Weil, HICEM in Zagreb and Prague, Hilfsverein der Deutschen Juden. Correspondence of Ilya Dijour, Executive Secretary of HICEM, New York, 1942–1945. Statistical materials.
Inventory, English.

446. Correspondence Between HIAS and HICEM Offices.
1940–1945. 3 reels. (RG 245.4.3)

Correspondence between Isaac Asofsky, HIAS, New York and Ilya Dijour, HICEM, New York regarding visas, transportation, medical and other arrangements for Jewish war refugees. Correspondence of Max Gottschalk, HICEM. Correspondence of HICEM with Solomon Dingol. HIAS and HICEM inter-office memoranda.
Inventory, English.

447. International Migration Problems.
1914–1953. 2 reels. (RG 245.4.4)

Records relate primarily to international organizations and conferences established or convened in order to deal with the Jewish refugee crisis caused by Nazi persecution. Meetings and plenary sessions of the Intergovernmental Committee on Refugees, 1938–1944, including the Conference at Evian and the Ottawa Conference of British and American Members. Materials on the Bermuda Conference. Post-war immigration problems.
Inventory, English.

448. Migration Statistics and Studies.
1881–1943. 1 reel. (RG 245.4.5)

Statistics on Jewish and general immigration into the United States, 1881–1943. Statistics on immigrants from Germany, 1933–1936.
Inventory, English.

449. Correspondence of HIAS and HICEM with Organizations.
1909–1953, 10 reels. (RG 245.4.6 and RG 245.4.7)

Correspondence with Jewish Colonization Association, American Jewish Joint Distribution Committee, American Jewish Committee, Council of Jewish Federations and Welfare Funds, Jewish Telegraphic Agency, American Council of Voluntary Agencies for Foreign Service, American Friends Service Committee, National Refugee Service, War Refugee Board.
Inventory, English.

450. Correspondence of HIAS with Individuals.
   1910–1922, 1 reel. (RG 245.4.8)

Correspondence with Joseph Barondess, Herman Bernstein, Alfred Cohen, Abram I. Elkus, Louis S. Gottlieb, Max J. Kohler, Edward Lauterbach, Julian W. Mack, Louis Marshall, Max Meyerson, Adolph S. Ochs, Leon Sanders, Jacob Schiff, Ben Snelling, Lucius L. Solomons, Oscar S. Straus, Cyrus L. Sulzberger, Meyer Sulzberger, Samuel Untermeyer, Morris Weinberg, Stephen S. Wise, Simon Wolf.
   Inventory, English.

451. Correspondence of HICEM with Individuals.
   1941–44, 2 reels. (RG 245.4.9)

Correspondence with Alvin Johnson, Myron C. Taylor, Victor Frankl, Mme. Marguerite Fux, Bernard Mélamède.
   Inventory, English.

452. United States and Canada.
   1909–1970s. 6 reels. (RG 245.4.10)

Materials on immigration into the United States. Statistical reports about HIAS activities in the United States, 1936–1951. HIAS protest against the literacy test provision in the Burnett Immigration Act, 1914–1916. Materials relating to legislation on immigration, ca. 1919–1922. Materials of the U.S. Senate and House Committees on Immigration. Citizens Wives Organization: petition, correspondence, 1931. Materials about the HIAS Boston branch, 1915–1922; San Francisco branch, 1915–1921. HIAS efforts to prevent deportation of Jews to Russia via Arkhangelsk, 1914–1915. HIAS activities on Ellis Island, 1914–1918. HIAS appeals of deportation orders, 1916–1920. HIAS Educational Department: Lecture Series, list of lecturers, correspondence with lecturers.
   Materials on immigration into Canada. Correspondence of HIAS and HICEM with the Jewish Immigrant Aid Society-JIAS.
   Inventory, English.

453. Palestine.
   1916–1950. 2 reels. (RG 245.4.11)

Correspondence, memoranda, reports and statistical surveys relating to the activities of HIAS and HICEM in Palestine and to facilitating immigration to Palestine in the period 1916–1950. List of 567 emigrants from Spain to Palestine aboard the *SS Nyassa*, 1944.
   Inventory, English.

454. Europe.
   1917–1951. 17 reels. (RG 245.4.12)

Materials on immigration activity and relief work in Austria, the Baltic states, Belgium, Czechoslovakia, Danzig, France, Germany, Great Britain, Greece, Holland, Hungary, Italy, Luxembourg, Poland, Portugal, Rumania, Russia, Spain, Sweden, Switzerland, Turkey, Yugoslavia.
   Inventory, English.

455. Latin America, Central America, West Indies.
     1921–1949. 14 reels. (RG 245.4.13)

Materials on Argentina, Bolivia, Brazil, British Honduras, Chile, Colombia, Costa Rica, Cuba, Curaçao, Dominican Republic, Ecuador, El Salvador, Guatemala, Haiti, Honduras, Jamaica, Mexico, Nicaragua, Panama, Paraguay, Peru, Puerto Rico, Surinam (Dutch Guiana), Trinidad, Uruguay.
     Inventory, English.

456. Australia and New Zealand.
     1911–1951. 1 reel. (RG 245.4.14).

Inventory, English.

457. Far East.
     1916–1941. 8 reels. (RG 245.4.15)

China, Japan, Philippines, Siam, Siberia.
     Inventory, English.

458. Africa.
     1936–1945. 1 reel. (RG 245.4.16).

Inventory, English, Yiddish.

459. Transportation.
     1936–1943. 2 reels. (RG 245.4.20)

Correspondence, memoranda, reports and lists relating to transportation of refugees. Lists of passengers. Reports about ship voyages. Included are materials on the *SS Navemar* (1941); *SS Serpa Pinta* (1942–1943); *SS Guinea* (December 1941); *SS Alsina* (1941).
     Inventory, English.

460. Individual Cases and Lists of Immigrants.
     1940–1945. 15 reels. (RG 245.4.21)

Correspondence of HICEM relating to select individual cases, mainly of refugees stranded in Lisbon.
     Inventory, English.

461. HIAS Histories.
     1868–1954. 1 reel. (RG 245.4.26)

A History of HIAS by Dr. Aryeh Tartakower, 1939. Y. Parsky's notes on HIAS in Eastern Europe, 1950. Dr. Mark Wischnitzer's notes and manuscript of his book *Visas to Freedom: The History of the HIAS*. Research materials on aid to immigrants in San Francisco.
     Inventory, English.

462. HIAS Records of Arrival.
     1909–ca.1978. 122 reels. (RG 245.4.41)

Index cards providing information about all HIAS assisted immigrants who arrived in the United States from 1909 to ca. 1978. The cards, filed by name of individual and by port of arrival, usually give dates and places of birth, last place of residence, destination and some other details.

463. HICEM MAIN OFFICE IN EUROPE.
   1935–1953. 50 ft. (RG 245.5)

On the eve of World War II, this office was located in Paris. Closed on June 19, 1940, re-opened in October 1940 first in Bordeaux and finally in Marseilles. Incorporated in the UGIF (Union Générale des Israélites de France) in 1943. Re-established in Paris following liberation of France, September 10, 1944. Closed in November 1945.

The records are divided into the following series:

France I: Records of the Paris HICEM office from 1935 to the closing of the office in 1940. Minutes of meetings of HICEM, 1939–1940. Records of the HICEM Marseilles Bureau. Correspondence and memoranda of HICEM directors. Correspondence with organizations: ICA (also known as JCA), AJDC, Comité Central d'Assistance aux Emigrants Juifs, 1938–1940. Correspondence of Dr. James Bernstein, Edouard Oungre, Max Gottschalk.

Correspondence with HIAS and HICEM offices and with local Jewish organizations in 37 countries. Reports from and correspondence with: Magyar Izraeliták Pártfogo Irodája (Hungarian Jewish Aid Committee), 1935–1940; Aid Committee in Trieste, Italy; Kovno, Lithuania; Riga, Latvia; Amsterdam Committee for Jewish Refugees (Comite voor Joodsche Vluchtlingen); Central Council for German Jewry in London; Committee aiding refugees in Zagreb, Yugoslavia; aid committees for refugees in Portugal, Rumania, Switzerland, North Africa; SOPROTIMIS in Buenos Aires, Argentina, and Chile; organizations in Mexico, Ecuador, Paraguay, Colombia. Records of BELHICEM (Belgian HICEM), set up in Brussels in October 1939 to maintain contacts inside Germany and the Czech Protectorates.

Materials relating to internment camps in France, including: Argelès, Brens, Gurs, Rieucros, Récébédou. Correspondence with UGIF. Correspondence with government authorities in different localities, including Agde, Agen, Albi, Auch, Avignon, Béziers, Carcassonne, Clermont-Ferrand, Gap, Grenoble, Limoges, Marseilles, Nice, Périgueux, Perpignan, Oloron, Valence, Vichy, Montpellier, Annecy, Aulus-les-Bains, Pau. Correspondence with the Consistoire in Lyons. Correspondence with Rabbi Joseph Cohen, Chief Rabbi of Bordeaux.

Correspondence with HICEM in Lisbon. Correspondence with Casablanca, Morocco. Fragmentary passenger lists for a handful of steamship voyages carrying refugees, from various countries.

France II: Records of HICEM European office in Marseilles, 1940–1944. Correspondence and reports about internment camps for the Jews. Correspondence with the interned. Correspondence with the Vichy government; with HICEM in Lisbon, Bucharest, and New York; with the Jewish Agency in Istanbul and Jerusalem.

France III: Central files of individual cases processed by the office during the war years. Correspondence, memoranda, and reports relating to location of relatives and aid to refugees.

France IV: Records of HICEM, later of HIAS, after the war. Correspondence with the Provisional Intergovernmental Committee for the Movement of Migrants from Europe (PICME); with Jewish relief organizations; with HIAS offices. Reports on activities. Materials on emigration from Austria, Bulgaria, Czechoslovakia, Germany, Holland, Hungary, Poland, Rumania, and Italy. Documentation on post-war search for survivors, relatives. Records of offices in Bordeaux, Toulouse, Lyons, Marseilles, Nice.

Inventory, English.

464. HICEM AND HIAS OFFICE IN LISBON.
1940–1951. 171 microfilm reels. (RG 245.6)

This office was activated in Lisbon in June 1940 to handle wartime immigration overseas. It was closed in November 1945 and its records were taken over by HIAS.

Correspondence with and about refugees arranged by name, 1940–1947. Correspondence with organizations, foreign consulates, with HICEM offices in France. Country files. Monthly statistical and other reports of SOPROTIMIS (Sociedad de Proteccíon a los Inmigrantes Israelitas). Lists of refugees, passengers on ships, internees, displaced persons, 1941–1945. Central files of individual cases processed by the Lisbon office during the war. Central files of individual cases processed after the war.

Inventory, Yiddish.

465. HIAS EUROPEAN OFFICE IN PARIS.
1945–1958. 261 microfilm reels. (RG 245.7)

Established in Paris at the end of 1945 following the dissolution of HICEM.

Correspondence and related documents on about 6,000 individual cases, arranged by region: Europe, Latin America, Australia, Israel, North Africa, Africa, Asia. General correspondence, reports, publications, financial records, relating to world-wide Jewish immigration after the war, including correspondence with organizations: IRO, AJDC, USNA, yeshivot, *landsmanshaftn*, the Jewish Agency, organizations in DP camps.

Inventory, English.

466. UNITED HIAS SERVICE, MAIN OFFICE, NEW YORK.
1954–1967. 264 ft. (RG 245.8)

Established by a merger between HIAS and the United Service for New Americans in 1954 to consolidate immigration efforts.

Administrative records including: UHS organization chart; minutes of committee meetings; annual meetings; by-laws; annual reports, 1954–1964; inter-office correspondence. Correspondence of Ann S. Petluck, Director of U.S. operations. Reference and resource materials on immigration such as speeches, reports, statistical materials, bulletins, clippings. Reports relating to immigration to Israel. Correspondence of UHS European headquarters in Geneva and of UHS offices in Paris, Brussels, Vienna. Correspondence with UHS Latin American headquarters in Rio de Janeiro. Correspondence concerning China. Materials on Jewish Immigrant Aid Society, Canada.

Records of individual cases filed by year and by card number. There are over 17,000 individual files in this series covering the years 1955–1959.

Photographs relating to immigration, 1900–1960s, including: scenes of Ellis Island; HIAS offices in New York; displaced persons; immigrants; HIAS relief and immigration work in various countries, including China, France, Japan, Latvia, Poland. Films relating to HIAS activities.

Inventory, English.

Card inventory of the photographs.
Films placed in RG 105.

467. UNITED HIAS SERVICE, OFFICE IN CHILE.
   1945–1969. 30 ft. (RG 245.9)

Correspondence and financial records of the UHS office in Chile relating to the immigration of Jews from Chile to the United States after 1946. Includes individual cases, correspondence with HIAS offices in Brazil, France, United States and other countries.

468. HICEM OFFICE IN PRAGUE, 1934–1940s.
   9 microfilm reels. (RG 245.10)

Established in 1936 to facilitate relief for the growing mass of German-Jewish refugees in Czechoslovakia. Was successor to the National Committee for Refugees Coming from Germany which coordinated the relief work from 1934.

   These are files of Mrs. Marie Schmolka, a HICEM representative, who was also involved with the National Committee and with a number of German-Jewish immigrant groups.

   Minutes of the National Committee, 1934–1937. Correspondence of HICEM, Prague, with: Czech government agencies; American Consulate in Prague; HICEM, Paris; High Commissioner of the League of Nations for Refugees Coming from Germany; AJDC, Mukačevo; government of New Zealand; various refugee organizations. Correspondence of the National Committee. HICEM financial reports and bookkeeping records. Case files of HICEM in Prague, 1936–1939.

   Inventory, English.

469. HEBREW TECHNICAL INSTITUTE (NEW YORK).
   Records, 1884–1939. 7 ft. 6 in. (RG 754)

The Hebrew Technical Institute was founded in November 1883 by the United Hebrew Charities, the Hebrew Orphan Asylum and the Hebrew Free School. It functioned as a vocational school from 1884 to 1939 and provided training in mechanical drawing, woodwork, metal work, instrument making, electricity and auto mechanics for students between the ages of 14 and 17.

   The records consist of class-standing records, 1884–1939; roll books, 1896–1939; Graduate Center record books, 1886–1939; annual reports and catalogs, 1889–1939.

   Inventory, English.

470. HEIFETZ, VLADIMIR (1900–1970).
   Papers, 1920s–1970. 3 ft. 4 in. (RG 1259)

Composer, conductor, choral director and pianist. Graduated from the St. Petersburg Conservatory in 1917. Was the concert accompanist for Fyodor Chaliapin and Michel Fokine. Played in a trio with S. Bacewicz and Gregor Piatigorsky. In the United States he served as musical director of the Rudolf Schildkraut Theatre, the chorus of the Poale Zion (Farband), the Yiddish Culture Chorus, the Patterson Singing Society in New Jersey, Temple Anshe Chesed, the Jamaica Jewish Center. Heifetz wrote over 80 compositions and about 200 arrangements and orchestrations. He wrote music for the Yiddish Art Theater, Folksbiene Theater, and for several motion pictures. He also composed a symphony, an opera, an oratorio and a number of cantatas.

The papers consist of correspondence, manuscripts and published works of Heifetz and other composers, including Abraham W. Binder, Harry Coopersmith, Abraham S. Ellstein, Joel Engel, Michl Gelbart, Max Helfman, Reuven Kosakoff, Marc Lavry, Boris Levenson, Leo Low, Jacob Schaefer, Mordechai Zeira, Zavel Zilberts.

Inventory and index, English.

471. HEISLER, KALMAN (1899–1966).

Papers, 1930s–1960s. 2 ft. 1 in. (RG 514)

Yiddish poet. Contributed to periodicals such as *In zikh* (NY), *Freie Arbeiter Stimme* (NY), *Der tog* (NY), *Jewish Daily Forward* (NY), *Frayhayt* (NY), *Zukunft* (NY), *Literarishe bleter* (Warsaw). Born in Komarno, Eastern Galicia. Lived in Prague, Czechoslovakia. Immigrated to the United States in 1921.

Correspondence with literary figures and institutions. Typescripts and manuscripts of Heisler's poetry, plays and memoirs. Clippings of Heisler's works. Reviews and criticism of Heisler's works.

472. HELLER, ALTER CHAIM (born 1889).

Papers, 1910–1959. 5 in. (RG 430)

Yiddish journalist, writer, poet, translator. Lived in the Ukraine and the United States.

Correspondence with literary figures such as A. Almi, Jacob Glatstein, Ben Zion Goldberg, Abraham Reisen. Personal documents.

473. HELLER, SELIG (1894–1970).

Papers, ca. 1917–1966. 5 in. (RG 611)

Yiddish writer, poet. Contributed to *Di velt*, *Freie Arbeiter Stimme*, *Zukunft*, *Der tog*. Co-editor of the Chicago journal *Undzer veg*. Born in Wolpa, district of Grodno. Immigrated to the United States in 1906. Settled in Chicago.

Manuscripts and correspondence relating to Heller's literary career and personal life. The correspondents include Kalman Marmor, S. Niger, Tolush.

474. HENRY CLAY LODGE NO. 15, INDEPENDENT ORDER BRITH ABRAHAM.

Records, 1890–1947. 1 ft. (RG 784)

Founded in 1888 by immigrants from Płock, Poland, as a lodge of the Independent Order Brith Abraham. Incorporated the Boris Schatz Benevolent Society in 1932.

Minutes, 1915–1919 (German); financial documents, 1928–1947; membership registration book, 1890–1899; miscellaneous membership records, 1920–1947; correspondence, 1930s; calendar booklets; ballots; announcements; invitations; cemetery maps; history of the I.O.B.A., 1937; constitution, I.O.B.A., 1928; incorporation records of the Boris Schatz B.S., Inc., 1932; photograph; gavels.

475. HERBERT, LEON M. (1885–1965).

Papers, ca. 1930–1965. 1 ft. 6 in. (RG 603)

Physician, Yiddish and Hebrew writer, Yiddish literary critic, translator, classicist. Wrote articles relating to literature, music, theater, the classics, medicine and psychiatry. Contributed to Yiddish periodicals such as *Lemberger togblat* (Lwów, Poland), *New Yorker vokhnblat* (NY), *Der tog* (NY), *Di varhayt* (NY), *Yidisher kemfer* (NY), *Freie Arbeiter Stimme* (NY), *Dos naye lebn*. Hebrew periodicals included *Ha-doar, Ha-umah, Harefuah*. Editor of *Harofe Ha-ivri* (NY), and co-editor of *Dos yidishe folk* (NY). Used pen name L. Raytses. Born in Lwów. Immigrated to the United States in 1903.

Manuscripts and typescripts of plays, articles, poems and translations. Correspondence with individuals and institutions. Clippings. Correspondence and other materials relating to Alfred Nossig (1864–1943, writer, sculptor, musician and early Zionist). Personal documents.

476. HERMAN, DAVID (1876–1937).
Papers, ca. 1932–1946. 7 in. (RG 209)

Theater director, actor, teacher. Directed the Vilna Troupe. Born in Warsaw. Came to the United States in 1934.

Correspondence, manuscripts, posters, playbills, photographs. Manuscripts of plays. Correspondence with Shalom Asch, Peretz Hirschbein, Melech Ravitch. Photographs of Sara Herman. Obituaries.

Photographs are cataloged in STAGEPIX.

477. HERSCHBERG, ABRAHAM SAMUEL (1858–1943).
Papers, 1930s. 1 ft. 3 in. (RG 292)

Yiddish and Hebrew writer, scholar and historian. Early Zionist. Lived in Białystok and Palestine. Died in the Białystok ghetto.

Typescripts of Herschberg's *Pinkas byalistok*, a two-volume history of the Jews of Białystok, published posthumously in 1949–1950. Biographical sketch of Herschberg.

478. HERTZBERG, IRVING.
Collection, 1960s. 1 ft. (RG 600)

Photographer, Brooklyn, New York. His photographs of the Hasidic community of the Williamsburg section of Brooklyn served to illustrate George Kranzler's study *Williamsburg—U.S.A.: The Face of Faith. An American Hassidic Community*, Baltimore, 1972. The book depicts the community in the 1960s and won the 1967 Seltzer-Brodsky Prize given by the YIVO Institute.

The 8 × 10 black-and-white photographs are subdivided into the following topical series: street scenes of Jewish Williamsburg; the people of Williamsburg; Williamsburg weddings; making a living; holidays; Williamsburg in the Catskills. Essay and captions by George Kranzler accompany the photographs.

479. HERWALD, TANHUM BER (1872–1951).
Papers, 1893–1948. 1 ft. (RG 255)

Prominent journalist, member of the Jewish Territorialist Organization. Lived in England.

The collection relates primarily to Herwald's participation in the Jewish Territorialist movement and the Freeland League.

Materials on Freeland League, 1931–1946: colonization projects in British Guiana, New Zealand, British Honduras, South Africa. Materials on the Territorialist movement: correspondence, including Israel Zangwill; reports, pamphlets, clippings of Herwald's articles. Personal documents. Copies of *Der yidisher zhurnal*, 1905.

480. HEVRAH MEFITSEI HASKALAH SOCIETY (VILNA).
Records, 1909–1938. 1 ft. 8 in. (RG 22)

The Hevrah Mefitsei Haskalah Society (Society for the Promotion of Culture Among the Jews of Russia) was founded in St. Petersburg in 1863 with the financial support of wealthy Jews such as the Günzburgs and Leon Rosenthal. Its original purpose was to disseminate Russian language and culture among the Jews in order to encourage assimilation and to remove the cultural and religious barriers between Jews and Russians. The founders believed that this would hasten the granting of civic equality to Jews. The society's practical objectives were to teach Russian language and culture, to promote secular education, and to publish books and periodicals in Russian and Hebrew. Eventually, branches were opened in Moscow, Riga, Kiev, Grodno, Vilna, and other cities. The society was dissolved by the Soviet authorities in 1930. The Vilna branch was founded in 1909. It maintained schools, encouraged the formation of cultural centers, organized cultural activities such as lectures and conferences. The Vilna branch continued to exist until 1938.

The collection relates to the activities of the Vilna branch of the society. Administrative records: by-laws, 1909; membership lists, 1910–1913; financial reports and records, 1909–1913. Correspondence of the Hevrah Mefitsei Haskalah Information Bureau, 1914–1918. Correspondence of the Hevrah Mefitsei Haskalah Relief Committee for War Sufferers, 1915.

Records of the Hevrah Mefitsei Haskalah School 'Zemach Shabad,' Vilna: student lists; parent lists; financial records, 1935–1938; miscellaneous correspondence, 1919–1935.

Inventory, English.

481. HIRSCH, BARON MAURICE DE and LOEWENTHAL, WILHELM.
Papers, 1855–1900. 3 microfilm reels. (RG 318)

The Jewish Colonization Association (JCA) was founded in London in 1891 by Baron Maurice de Hirsch to aid economically deprived Jews in Russia. One of the JCA's first major projects was the development of an agricultural settlement in Argentina for Russian-Jewish émigrés. Dr. Wilhelm Loewenthal, a physicist and naturalist, was appointed by de Hirsch as the first director of the settlement project.

Papers of Baron Maurice de Hirsch, including personal documents, 1855–1899. Materials relating to Hirsch's contacts with the Russian government on the founding of Jewish schools in Russia, 1887–1889, including correspondence from the Russian Ministry of Education. Reports, correspondence and other materials relating to the JCA project in Argentina, including reports by de Hirsch and Loewenthal. Records of the founding of the JCA, including Hirsch's correspondence with his lawyers, 1894–1900.

Inventory, Yiddish, English.

482. HIRSCH, DAVID (born 1890).
Papers, 1892–1934. 13 ft. (RG 1225)

Composer of Jewish theater music. One of the earliest composers for the Yiddish theater in Rumania, he provided musical notation for the melodies of Abraham Goldfaden. Born in Khyrov (Pol. Chyrów), Ukraine. Lived in Austria. Settled in Chicago.

Instrumental and director's parts of about 300 operettas and musical plays. Liturgical compositions and songs. There is a large amount of Rumanian music in manuscript and print.

483. HIRSCHBEIN, PERETZ (1880–1948).
Papers, 1900–1957. 8 ft. 1 1/2 in. (RG 833)

Yiddish dramatist and novelist. Hirschbein's plays, such as *Grine felder* (Green Fields), became classics of the Yiddish theater and were translated into English, German and Hebrew. In 1908, while in Russia, Hirschbein organized a drama group in Odessa, which although short-lived, played an important role in the early development of Yiddish theater. The group produced plays by Shalom Asch, David Pinsky, Jacob Gordin and Sholem Aleichem. In the 1920s, Hirschbein travelled around the world for several years together with his wife Esther Shumiatcher-Hirschbein, and subsequently wrote many travelogues in Yiddish which were published and widely read. Throughout his literary career, Hirschbein regularly contributed articles, novels, stories to *The Day* (*Der tog*) in New York. Born in Kleszczele, Poland. In 1930 settled in New York. He died in Los Angeles.

Correspondence with Shalom Asch, Hayyim Nahman Bialik, Mendl Elkin, Ben Zion Goldberg, Szmerke Kaczerginski, H. Leivick, Kalman Marmor, Nachman Meisel, Paul Muni, Shmuel Niger, Joseph Opatoshu, David Pinsky, Melech Ravitch, Maurice Schwartz, Jacob Shatzky, Zalman Shneur. Correspondence with family members. Correspondence of Esther Shumiatcher-Hirschbein with Solomon Dingol, Mendl Elkin, Aaron Glanz-Leieles, Ben Zion Goldberg, H. Leivick, Nachman Meisel, Kadia Molodowsky, Joseph Opatoshu, David Pinsky, Melech Ravitch, Jacob Isaac Segal. Manuscripts of dramatic works. Manuscripts of articles on various topics such as travels in the Far East and the Soviet Union, and Yiddish theater. Manuscripts of short stories, novels and poems. Memoirs by Hirschbein. Clippings of articles by and about Hirschbein. Photographs, personal documents of Peretz Hirschbein, Esther Shumiatcher-Hirschbein and Omus Hirschbein, their son.

Inventory, Yiddish.

484. HIRSCHLER, RENE (1905–1944).
Papers, 1943. 1 ft. 3 in. (RG 221)

Rabbi, chaplain of French Foreign Legion (1939–1943). Chief Chaplain for foreign-born Jews in internment camps in the French free zone (1943). Performed relief work in concentration camps, detention and forced labor camps and was active in underground efforts for Jews in hiding. Died in Auschwitz.

Correspondence with individuals in camps concerning relief packages, supplies for Jewish holidays, location of relatives, efforts to secure funds. Includes letters to French government officials and Jewish leaders concerning Jewish situation.

485. HIRSZHAUT, JULIAN (YEHIEL) (1908–1983).
Papers, 1939–1945. 3 ft. 4 in. (RG 720)

Yiddish journalist. Contributed to *Naród* (Warsaw), *Der emes* (Warsaw), *Der nayer veg* (Paris), *Haynt* (Warsaw). Editor of *Di tsionistishe shtime* (Paris), *YIVO bleter* (New York). Hirszhaut wrote extensively on the Holocaust period in Poland. He also collected historical documents on this topic. Born in Drohobycz, Poland. Moved to France in 1946 and settled in the United States in 1951.

Eyewitness testimonies, newspaper clippings, printed material and photographs relating to Jews in Poland under Nazi occupation. The several hundred eyewitness testimonies were collected ca. 1945 by local Jewish historical commissions in Białystok, Katowice, Kraków, Lublin, Łódź, Warsaw. The testimonies are in Polish, Yiddish and German.

Materials relating to the Łódź ghetto: photographs; ghetto money; printed announcements by Mordechai Chaim Rumkowski; a handwritten Zionist newspaper from the ghetto edited by Dawid Joskowicz. Miscellaneous materials from Jewish organizations in post-war Poland, such as Ichud and the Central Jewish Historical Commission.

Inventory, Yiddish.

486. HOFFMAN, IDA (1876–ca. 1969).
Papers, ca. 1900–ca. 1966. 10 in. (RG 669)

Nurse, communal worker. Worked in Palestine in the years following World War I. Lived in Cuba and in the United States.

Correspondence, including letters from Henrietta Szold and Lillian Wald. Personal documents such as passports, citizenship papers, curriculum vitae. Photographs, memorabilia, autograph books, daily journals.

487. HOLZER, RACHEL.
Papers, 1930s–1960s. 10 in. (RG 535)

Jewish actress. Played in the Cracow Jewish Art Theater directed by Jonas Turkow, as well as in the Vilna Troupe. Born in Cracow, Poland. Settled in Australia.

Correspondence with writers and actors including Ida Kaminska, Rachel Korn, Melech Ravitch, Abraham Sutzkever, Jonas Turkow. Correspondence with organizations. Clippings, announcements, programs, posters. Photographs of R. Holzer.

Photographs cataloged in STAGEPIX.

488. HOLZMAN, MAX.
Papers, 1920s–1957. 5 in. (RG 368)

Collector for YIVO, Palm Springs, California.

Correspondence with Yiddish literary and cultural figures and organizations. Materials relating to the Yidisher Kultur Farband in the United States.

489. HORODISHTER KORSONER LODGE.
Records, 1930–1974. 10 in. (RG 855)

Founded in New York by immigrants from Gorodishche (Pol. Horodyszcze), Byelorussia. Dissolved in the 1970s.

Minutes, 1951–1959. Financial and membership records, 1930–1970. Correspondence, 1940s–1970s.

490. HORODOKER BENEVOLENT SOCIETY.
Records, 1907–1962. 2 1/2 in. (RG 1197)

Established in New York in 1903 by *landslayt* from Gorodok, Byelorussia.

Constitution. Minutes of the society, 1940–1953. Minutes of the *hevrah kadisha* (burial society), 1930–1962, and of the Horodoker Relief Association Banquet Committee, 1936. Invitation to the bar mitzvah of Joseph Berkman at the Horodoker Synagogue, 1936. Photograph of J. Berkman (taken in Smorgon).

491. HOROWITZ, ISRAEL and HAIM A.
Papers, 1940s–1961. 2 in. (RG 555)

Israel Horowitz was the author of an anthology of Yiddish and Hebrew proverbs.

His brother, Haim A. Horowitz, was a Yiddish writer whose pen name was Chaim Vital. Haim A. Horowitz wrote for *Literarishe bleter, Dos yidishe folk, Jewish Daily Forward.* Born in Smorgon, district of Vilna. Lived in Palestine, Bulgaria, Sweden, Poland. Immigrated to the United States in 1941.

The papers consist of letters to Israel and Haim Horowitz from Jewish scholars and writers including Marcus (Mordecai) Ehrenpreis, Abraham Reisen, Zalman Shneur, A.S. Yehudah. Also, five postcards sent from the Warsaw ghetto in 1941.

492. HOURWICH, ISAAC A. (1860–1924).
Papers, 1896–1924. 4 ft. 7 in. (RG 587)

Publicist, economist, lawyer and lecturer. Active in the Jewish labor movement in the United States and an authority on immigration matters. One of the founders of the Protocol movement in the garment industry. One of the organizers of the first American Jewish Congress in 1918. Author of *Immigration and Labor*.

Manuscripts, documents, printed material, reports, minutes of meetings, memoranda, clippings and correspondence relating primarily to Hourwich's intellectual and organizational involvement in the labor movement, including his extensive participation in arbitration proceedings. Materials relating to the labor movement in Russia. Materials on socialist theory, Jewish Labor Bund, labor laws in the Soviet Union. Materials on the Jewish labor movement in the United States. Documents of the Independent Jacket Makers Union of New York and Federated Hebrew Trade Unions of Greater New York. Minutes of meetings of the Board of Grievances of the Cloak, Suit and Skirt Industry. Minutes and reports of various arbitration proceedings.

Correspondence with: Abraham Cahan, Judah L. Magnes, Zalman Reisen, Isaac Sturner. Articles by Hourwich on socialism, capitalism, Jewish rights, Zionism. Hourwich's unfinished memoirs. Bibliography of Hourwich's works compiled by A.S. Kravetz. Documents on the organization of the American Jewish Congress.

Inventory, English.

493. HOWE, IRVING (1920–1993).
Papers, 1960s–1970s. 2 ft. 8 in. (RG 570)

Literary and social critic. Professor of English Literature at Brandeis University and at Hunter College, New York. Author of works relating to literature, political and social history, and the Jewish immigration experience in the United States. Co-editor, with Eliezer Greenberg, of *A Treasury of Yiddish Stories* (1954) and *A Treasury of Yiddish Poetry* (1969). Editor of the publication *Dissent*.

The collection consists of tapes and transcripts of interviews, source materials and manuscripts for Howe's book *World of Our Fathers* (1976). The interviews relate to the Jewish labor movement and the Lower East Side. The interviews are with Israel Breslow, Pearl Halpern, Adolph Held, Abraham Kazin, Paul Novick, Louis Painkin, Isidore Wisotsky, Charles Zimmerman, Abe Zwerlin.

494. HUSIATYNER-PODOLIER FRIENDSHIP CIRCLE.
Records, 1961–1977. 2 1/2 in. (RG 1055)

Founded in New York in 1950 by immigrants from Gusyatin (Pol. Husiatyń), Ukraine. Began with the establishment of a ladies auxiliary. Later, the Circle was formed by 100 *landslayt*. Built a kindergarten and a trade school in Israel. Supported charities.

Minutes, 1971, 1977. Correspondence. Photographs. Memorial book, 1968.

495. HYMAN, JOSEPH H.
Papers, 1920s–1930s. 2 in. (RG 1144)

American Jewish Joint Distribution Committee representative in Latvia, Lithuania and Estonia in the inter-war years.

The collection relates to Hyman's work for the AJDC and includes the following: photographs of a children's home in Riga, 1927; miscellaneous documents and clippings relating to the AJDC.

496. I.L. PERETZ YIDDISH WRITERS' UNION.
Records, 1903–1970s. ca. 16 ft. (RG 701)

Also called Jewish Writers' Union. Founded in New York in 1915 as a union of Yiddish journalists. Its first president was Hillel Rogoff and its first secretary was Joseph Margoshes. The union was a member of the United Hebrew Trades. It participated in strikes and labor disputes and fought for job security, severance pay benefits and a minimum wage. A relief fund was organized for Yiddish writers in Europe as well as for members in financial need. In 1929 the union had 200 members. Although the union continued to be active in labor disputes, its membership and role declined steadily. While still in existence in the 1980s, it had relinquished much of its role as a labor union and functioned primarily as a literary association.

Minutes of meetings. Accounting records. Financial reports and correspondence. Photographs of members. Materials on the Fund for Jewish Refugee Writers. General correspondence with individuals, organizations and publishers. Correspondence relates to the Works Progress Administration, contracts, labor disputes, strikes, labor conditions. Correspondents include: Baal Makhshoves (Isidor Eliashev), Shlomo Bickel, Menahem Boraisha, Reuben Brainin, Abraham Cahan, Simon Dubnow, Ossip Dymow, Alexander Harkavy, David Ignatoff, H. Leivick, Kalman Marmor, Alexander Mukdoni, Shmuel Niger, David Pinsky, Melech Ravitch, Abraham Reisen, Zalman Reisen, Kasriel Sarasohn, Zalman Shneur, Lamed Shapiro, Jacob Shatzky, Baruch Vladeck, Max Weinreich, Chaim Zhitlowsky. Organizations include: Jewish Labor Bund, Central Yiddish Culture Organization, *The Day* (*Der tog*), *Jewish Daily Forward*, *Freie Arbeiter Stimme*, HIAS, *Keneder odler*, Jewish Labor Committee, *Morgn zhurnal*, Jewish National Workers Alliance, *Di yidishe velt* (Philadelphia), Jewish Writers' Fund for Suffering Writers in Europe, *Kinder zhurnal*, *Morgn frayhayt*, ORT, Workmen's Circle, YIVO.

Photographs of Yiddish writers arranged in alphabetical order.

Inventory, English.

497. ICELAND, REUBEN (1884–1955).
Papers, 1906–1954. 1 ft. 3 in. (RG 753)

Yiddish poet and translator. One of the founders of the literary group *Di yunge*. Contributed to *Zukunft*, *Literarishe shriftn*, *Der firer*, *Der tog*. Editor of *Literatur un lebn* (1915). Co-editor with Mani Leib of *Der indzl* (1925–26). Translated works of German, English and

Chinese authors, notably the prose and poetry of Heinrich Heine. Born in Radomyśl Wielki, Poland. Immigrated to the United States in 1903.

Correspondence, manuscript of Iceland's poetry, photographs and miscellaneous materials. Correspondence with Menashe Unger, Shlomo Bickel, Ben Zion Goldberg, Moses (Moyshe) Leib Halpern, Rashel Weprinsky, Chaim Zhitlowsky, Daniel Charney, H. Leivick, Itzik Manger, Mani Leib, Shmuel Niger, Melech Ravitch, Zalman Reisen.

498. IGUMENER INDEPENDENT BENEVOLENT ASSOCIATION.
Records, 1913–1974. 5 in. (RG 893)

Founded in New York in 1899 by immigrants from Cherven (until 1920s, Igumen), Byelorussia, to promote "unity and brotherly friendship." Provided loans for its members and retained the services of a doctor. Attempted to send a delegate with funds to Igumen after the 1917 Russian Revolution. In 1978, the society's president visited Igumen and distributed funds there.

Constitution. Minutes, 1919–1939. Photographs.

499. INDEPENDENT BERLADER BENEVOLENT ASSOCIATION.
Records, 1958–1974. 2 1/2 in. (RG 949)

Established in New York in 1919 by immigrants from Bârlad (Berlad), Rumania. Active until 1975.

Dues ledger. Correspondence. Meeting notices.

500. INDEPENDENT BRODSKY BENEVOLENT ASSOCIATION.
Records, 1941–1974. 5 in. (RG 979)

Organized in 1900 as the Lazar I. Brodsky Lodge No. 258, Independent Order Brith Abraham. Later changed name to Independent Brodsky Benevolent Association, Inc., but maintained contact with Independent Order Brith Abraham. Dissolved 1975.

Minutes, 1941–1957. Financial records, 1950–1974.

501. INDEPENDENT BUKARESTER SICK AID ASSOCIATION.
Records, 1901–1976. 2 ft. 7 in. (RG 826)

Founded in New York in 1901 by immigrants from Bucharest, Rumania. Incorporated in 1910. Activities included establishment of a loan fund in 1914, a ladies auxiliary in 1931, a relief fund in 1932 and an old age fund in 1933. Merged with the Independent Young Men's Roumanian Benevolent Association, 1931. Supported HIAS in relief activities after World War II. Supports institutions in Israel.

Constitutions; minutes, 1949–1962, 1963–1966; financial records; membership records, including registration book, 1901–1925 (German, English); correspondence; souvenir journals; miscellaneous materials.

502. INDEPENDENT BURDUJENER SICK AND BENEVOLENT SOCIETY.
Records, 1938–1976. 10 in. (RG 853)

Organized in New York in 1906 by immigrants from Burdujeni, Rumania. Activities included establishment of a free loan fund for members. Supported institutions in Israel. Dissolved 1976.

Minutes, 1938–1940, 1947–1976; financial records, 1930s–1970s; burial permits; seal.

503. INDEPENDENT ELIZABETHGRAD LADIES BENEVOLENT ASSOCIATION.
Records, 1961–1975. 5 in. (RG 861)

Founded in New York in 1905 by immigrants from Elizavetgrad (Kirovograd), Ukraine. This women's society owned its own cemetery plots. Activities included support for institutions in Israel. Dissolved 1975.

Financial records, 1960s–1970s.

504. INDEPENDENT FRYMCIE RADYMNOER FRAUEN KRANKEN UNTERSTUTZUNGS VEREIN.
Records, 1914–1954. 2 1/2 in. (RG 1050)

Organized in New York in 1905 by immigrants from Radymno, Poland. Also known as the Independent Fremtsche Radimnauer Frauen K.U.V. Dissolved in the 1970s.

Cemetery agreements and permits, 1914–1926. Membership materials. Seal.

505. INDEPENDENT GREATER NEW YORK SICK AND BENEVOLENT ASSOCIATION.
Records, 1915–1947. 1 1/2 in. (RG 1060)

Established in 1897 by garment workers as a fraternal organization not limited to *landslayt*. Maintained loan and old-age funds and provided burial for members. Later merged with lodges which were part of the Knights of Pythias.

Constitution. Minutes, 1947. Souvenir journals, 1927–1947. Armband of burial committee.

506. INDEPENDENT JAWOROWER ASSOCIATION.
Records, 1932–1962. 8 in. (RG 967)

Founded in New York in 1913 by immigrants from Yavorov (Pol. Jaworów), Ukraine, to provide the younger members of the Jaworower society with an alternative to the older, more orthodox Erste Jaworower Kranken Unterstitzung Verein. The two societies merged in 1948.

Minutes, 1932–1949 (Yiddish, German). Minutes of the Erste Jaworower K.U.V., 1921–1938. Financial materials.

Memorial book, 1956.

507. INDEPENDENT JOKAI LODGE.
Records, 1929–1937. 2 in. (RG 1117)

Hungarian-Jewish mutual aid society founded in New York in 1912 as part of the Independent Order Brith Abraham. In 1925 the society withdrew from the IOBA.

Minutes, 1929–1936. Silver Jubilee book, 1937.

508. INDEPENDENT KINSKER AID ASSOCIATION.
Records, 1930–1980. 5 in. (RG 911)

Founded in New York in 1904 by immigrants from Końskie, Poland. Maintained a relief committee after World War II to aid survivors who came to the United States. Sent food packages to *landslayt* in Israel.

Financial records, 1930s–1950s. Correspondence. Journal.

509. INDEPENDENT LEMBERGER LADIES AID SOCIETY.
    Records, 1952–1972. 5 in. (RG 905)

Organized in New York in 1920 by the *landslayt* from Lwów (Lvov, Lemberg), Poland, to raise money for charity and provide sick benefits and burial for members. Incorporated in 1921. Affiliated with First United Lemberger Home for the Aged.
    Certification of original 1921 incorporation, 1952. Minutes, 1966–1972. Financial records: receipt books, 1954–1972. Donated receipts. Dues payment sheets. Materials related to burial: permits, map, correspondence. Membership address book. Meeting notices. Correspondence. Society stamps.

510. INDEPENDENT LUTZKER AID SOCIETY.
    Records, 1914–1976. 12 1/2 in. (RG 904)

Founded in Brooklyn in 1914 by immigrants from Lutsk (Pol. Łuck), Ukraine, and incorporated the same year. Associated with the Ladies Auxiliary, established 1927. Affiliated with the United Lutzker Relief Committee.
    Certificate of incorporation, 1914. Constitution. Minutes, 1935–1940, 1961–1976. Financial records, 1915–1966. Books of the Old Age Fund. Anniversary journals. Materials pertaining to other New York Lutsker societies: First Lutzker Benevolent Association; United Lutzker Young Men and Young Ladies Association; Lutzker Branch 538 of the Workmen's Circle; United Lutzker Relief Committee; banners of the Independent Lutzker Aid Society and of the Ladies Auxiliary of the Independent Lutzker Aid Society.

511. INDEPENDENT MESERITZER YOUNG MEN'S ASSOCIATION.
    Records, 1911–1977. 10 in. (RG 823)

Founded in New York in 1901 by immigrants from Międzyrzec Podlaski (Yid. Meserits, Mezritsh or Mezrich), Poland. Activities included the formation of a relief committee after World War I and sending delegates to the home town where the society established an orphanage, a loan society and a hospital. Instrumental in founding the United Meseritzer Relief, Inc., 1936, through which it aided *landslayt* before World War II and continued its activities in Israel after the war.
    Constitution. Minutes, 1911–1937, 1949–1968. Newsletter. Memorial book, 1978.

512. INDEPENDENT MOGELNITZER BENEVOLENT SOCIETY.
    Records, 1910–1929, 1945. 3 in. (RG 984)

Organized in New York in 1906 by immigrants from Mogielnica, Poland. Maintained a relief committee. Affiliated with a Mogelnitzer organization in Israel. Supported a loan fund there.
    Minutes, 1910–1929. Materials pertaining to relief activities.

513. INDEPENDENT NEMIROVER BENEVOLENT SOCIETY.
    Records, 1964–1975. 5 in. (RG 933)

Founded in New York in 1905 by immigrants from Nemirov, Ukraine. Incorporated 1906. Dissolved 1975.
    Minutes, 1964–1975. Financial records. Membership records. Correspondence. Seal.

514. INDEPENDENT OPOLER BENEVOLENT SOCIETY.
Records, 1929, 1941–1961. 2 1/2 in. (RG 1032)

Founded in New York in 1912 by immigrants from Opole, Poland. An Opoler Young Men's Society had been founded in 1906 and had failed. Worked with a ladies auxiliary.

Membership records, 1941–1961. Anniversary journal, 1929. Meeting announcements of the Independent Order of the Independent Opoler Ladies Auxiliary. Memorial book, 1977.

515. INDEPENDENT ORLER BENEVOLENT SOCIETY.
Records, 1890s–1984. 2 ft. 9 in. (RG 1023)

Founded in New York by immigrants from Orla (Poland) as a lodge affiliated with the Order Brith Abraham. Became independent in 1919. Was affiliated with a sisterhood. In 1970, brought a suit against the Polish government for using the old Orler synagogue as a warehouse, and won the case.

Constitution. Golden book (record of deaths of members), including minutes of the *hevrah kadisha* (burial society), 1890s–1957. Anniversary journal. Cemetery deed and map. Photographs, financial records, correspondence.

516. INDEPENDENT ROHATYNER YOUNG MEN'S BENEVOLENT ASSOCIATION.
Records, 1953–1977. 1 in. (RG 1082)

Organized in New York in 1903 by immigrants from Rogatin (Pol. Rohatyn), Ukraine. Held cultural activities. Aided home town. Associated with a ladies auxiliary established in 1934 to help needy *landslayt*.

Minutes, 1965–1977. Meeting announcements. Program.

517. INDEPENDENT SKIERNIEWICER BENEVOLENT ASSOCIATION.
Records, 1913–1963. 10 in. (RG 811)

Founded in New York in 1913 by immigrants from Skierniewice, Poland. Organized the Skierniewicer Relief Committee for aid to the home town during World War I. Established the Skierniewicer Patronat in the 1930s to free political prisoners in Skierniewice. In 1937, the Relief Committee and the Patronat joined to form the United Relief Committee for Skierniewice. Established a *gmilas khesed kase* (interest-free loan fund) in 1955 for *landslayt* in Israel.

Minutes, 1913–1958 ; anniversary journals; memorial book, 1955; photographs; newspaper clippings. Film of memorial service in Skierniewice, 1947.

Film removed to and cataloged in RG 105.

518. INDEPENDENT SLONIMER BENEVOLENT ASSOCIATION.
Records, 1924, 1948–1978. 1 ft. 8 in. (RG 1284)

Established in 1901 in New York by immigrants from Slonim, Byelorussia. Sponsored various forms of aid to members, including a loan fund, death benefits. Jointly with the Slonim *landsmanshaft* in Israel erected a monument in Kiryat Shaul to the Slonim Jewish community. Supported publication of the four-volume *Pinkas Slonim*.

Constitutions, 1924, 1943. Membership ledgers. Death-benefit ledgers. Printed announcements of gatherings. Commemorative brochure of the unveiling of the monument in Kiryat Shaul. Photographs.

519. INDEPENDENT TARNOWER KRANKEN UNTERSTUTZUNGS VEREIN.
Records, 1946–1973. 2 1/2 in. (RG 1069)

Organized in New York before 1917 by immigrants from Tarnów, Poland, to aid the sick and needy.
Constitution. Membership application book, 1946–1971 (older application forms in German).

520. INDEPENDENT ZETLER YOUNG MEN'S BENEVOLENT ASSOCIATION.
Records, 1920–1973. 1 ft. 9 in. (RG 824)

Founded in New York in 1904 by immigrants from Dyatlovo (Pol. Zdzięcioł; Yid. Zetl), Byelorussia. Established an old-age fund, a loan fund, and a *hevrah kadisha* (burial society) for members. Provided relief for *landslayt* after World War I, which included sending a delegate to Zetl. Aided survivors after World War II.
Constitution; minutes, 1920–1942, 1952–1957; financial records, 1949–1957, 1961–1973; golden book (record of deaths of members); photographs; miscellaneous.

521. INSTITUT DER NSDAP ZUR ERFORSCHUNG DER JUDENFRAGE (FRANKFURT AM MAIN).
Records, 1930–1945. ca. 23 ft. (RG 222)

Nazi institute which collected materials related to the Jewish question and participated in Nazi propaganda activities against the Jews. Was subordinate to Alfred Rosenberg.
Bulletins of Nazi news agencies and newsletters of various organizations. Photographs from Hungary, India, Palestine, Germany, Greece, Holland, England, Poland, the United States, France and Russia relating to Jewish life and antisemitism. Topics include: rabbis, ghetto life including the Jewish quarter of Salonika in 1941, the Rothschilds, rare Jewish book fragments and manuscripts, Jewish caricatures, religious customs, synagogues, costumes, personalities, art, theater, literature, finance, commerce, non-Jews. Clippings of anti-Jewish propaganda from various countries. Anti-Jewish legislation in Hungary, Italy, Bulgaria, Belgium, France, Rumania. Materials relating to Jews in Austria, Belgium, Bulgaria, Czechoslovakia, Denmark, France, Germany, Greece, Hungary, Italy, Latin America, Latvia, Estonia, Lithuania, North Africa, Norway, Poland, Rumania, Russia, Sweden, Switzerland, United States. Manuscripts of antisemitic works, statistics about Jewish communities. Police identification cards of German Jews, 1938–1942.
Inventory, Yiddish, English.

522. ISH-KISHOR, JUDITH.
Papers, 1920s–ca. 1940. 1 ft. 8 in. (RG 666)

Writer of juvenile and historical fiction. Lived in the United States.
Manuscripts of short stories and Jewish historical fiction. Correspondence with Ish-Kishor's father, the Zionist leader Ephraim Ish-Kishor, 1930s. Correspondence with individuals, organizations, publishers, editors.

523. ISRAEL CANTOR FAMILY SOCIETY.
Records, 1926–1988. 1 ft. 4 in. (RG 1257)

Established in 1913 by the descendants of Israel Cantor who came from Rudni, near Minsk, Byelorussia.
   Minute books, constitutions, genealogical tree, anniversary materials, memorabilia.

524. ISRAELITE FRATERNITY OF BROOKLYN.
Records, 1961–1973. 2 1/2 in. (RG 1006)

Established in Brooklyn, date unknown. Dissolved in the 1970s.
   Financial records. Address book. Seal.

525. JACKSON, MORDECHAI.
Papers, 1950s–1970s. 5 in. (RG 1108)

Jewish actor.
   Materials relate to the Yiddish theater. Manuscripts of two plays: *Hotsmakh shpil*, *Der farkishefter shnayderl*. Clippings relating to actors, photographs, miscellaneous programs, announcements.

526. JACOBSON, JACOB.
Papers, 1910s. 2 1/2 in. (RG 778)

Yiddish playwright. Lived in the United States.
   Manuscripts of plays. Materials relating to the Yiddish theater such as posters, announcements, clippings, reviews, contracts. Photographs of Jacob Jacobson and his wife.
   Photographs cataloged in STAGEPIX.

527. JAFFE, MORDECAI (1899–1961).
Papers, 1909–1960. 1 ft. 3 in. (RG 624)

Yiddish poet, literary critic, translator, teacher. Contributed to numerous periodicals including *Morgn zhurnal* (NY), *Jewish Daily Forward* (NY), *Der tog* (NY), *Zukunft* (NY), *Freie Arbeiter Stimme* (NY), *Letste nayes* (Tel Aviv), *Di goldene keyt* (Tel Aviv), *Literarishe bleter* (Warsaw). Born in Dusetos, Lithuania. Immigrated to Canada in 1927. Settled in the United States in 1937.
   Manuscripts of Jaffe's poems, short stories, translations. Personal documents. Correspondence with organizations. General correspondence including Shlomo Bickel, Daniel Charney, Aaron Glanz-Leieles, H. Leivick, Shmuel Niger, Joseph Opatoshu, Abraham Sutzkever, Malka Heifetz Tussman. Family correspondence. Materials for the anthology of Hebrew poetry in Yiddish (published). Materials on the theme of motherhood in world poetry.

528. JANUSZ KORCZAK MEDICAL SOCIETY.
Records, 1943–1987. 9 in. (RG 1200)

Organization of Polish-Jewish physicians in the United States. Founded in 1943 as American Polish Medical Alliance. Later called Medical Alliance–Association of Jewish Physicians from Poland.

Photocopies of minutes, 1959–1985. Correspondence, 1943–1986. Programs, announcements and invitations for meetings and conferences, 1955–1987. Photographs, 1951–1980. Membership lists.

529. JASPER, HARRY.
Papers, 1905–1949. 2 1/2 in. (RG 1202)

Active member of Poalei Zion and later Zionist-Socialist Workers Party (S.S.) in Pińsk, Poland. Came to United States in 1905.

The papers relate primarily to Jasper's continued contact with revolutionary groups in Pińsk. Correspondence concerning political activities in Pińsk and other matters, 1905–1912. Includes many letters from Khaytshe Kolodny, a political activist and friend of Jasper's. Photographs of friends and fellow members of the Zionist-Socialist Workers Party in Pińsk. Memoirs about Pińsk and about Zionist Socialists.

530. JEITELES, BERTHOLD (1872–1958).
Papers, 1942–1946. 2 1/2 in. (RG 717)

Chemist, talmudic scholar, rabbi. Inmate of Terezín who managed to save documents from the ghetto. Lived in Prague, Czechoslovakia. Immigrated to the United States after World War II.

The papers consist of documents relating to Dr. Jeiteles's life in Terezín, as well as a copy of the Jeiteles family tree.

531. JENOFSKY, ABRAHAM (1901–1976).
Papers, 1931–1976. 1 ft. 3 in. (RG 734)

Yiddish journalist. General secretary of YKUF (Yidisher Kultur Farband), New York.

The papers consist of correspondence, personal documents, reports, manuscripts, photographs and clippings relating to Jenofsky's literary career and to his organizational activities. Minutes of the Ambidjan conferences, March, October, 1949. Materials on the National Committee of ICOR. Manuscripts, articles, essays on Birobidzhan. Letters from Chaim Zhitlowsky and Maurice Schwartz. Manuscript by Marc Chagall.

532. JESHURIN, EPHIM H. (1885–1967).
Papers, ca. 1900–1960s. ca. 202 ft. (RG 451)

Yiddish bibliographer and journalist active in the Jewish labor movement. Held positions in the Workmen's Circle, Jewish Labor Committee, YIVO, the Forward Association. Born in Vilna, emigrated to the United States ca. 1907 and settled in New York.

The bulk of the collection consists of extensive card bibliographies relating to the personal lives and careers of hundreds of Jewish writers. There are an estimated 300,000 entries in this bibliography. Clippings of biographical articles about Yiddish writers and of literary reviews. Materials (mainly clippings) for a volume on Vilna which Jeshurin edited and published in 1935. Photographs of personalities active in the Workmen's Circle. Correspondence, including Simon Dubnow, Chaim Grade, Mani Leib, Melech Ravitch, Dov Sadan, Abraham Sutzkever, Uriel Weinreich.

Inventory, Yiddish, English.

533. JEWISH AGENCY, VIENNA OFFICE.
Records, 1947–1954. 1 ft. 3 in. (RG 301)

Vienna branch of the international, non-governmental body organized in 1922 and expanded in 1929, to assist in the development and settlement of Israel.

The records relate to Jewish Agency work with displaced persons following World War II, and include the following:

Correspondence with banks, vendors, Jewish National Fund, Keren Hayesod, and offices of the Jewish Agency in Geneva, Jerusalem and Paris. Circulars and flyers. Financial records, including journals and account books, auditors' reports, cash books, ledgers, and records of support payments to individuals. Reports of the Immigration and Purchasing Departments. Correspondence and lists concerning release funds.

534. JEWISH AGRICULTURAL SOCIETY—BARON DE HIRSCH FUND.
Records, 1890s–1960s. 1 ft. 3 in. (RG 651)

The Baron de Hirsch Fund, New York, was established in 1891 by Baron Maurice de Hirsch to assist and settle East European Jewish immigrants in the United States. Its objective was to promote the development of Jewish settlements as well as trade schools. The Jewish Agricultural Society was a subsidiary of the Fund and was chartered in New York in 1900 to provide agricultural training for East European immigrants. The JAS acquired land in New York, New Jersey, Pennsylvania and Connecticut. Among its many projects was the Baron de Hirsch Agricultural School, Woodbine, New Jersey. The JAS published *The Jewish Farmer*, an English and Yiddish monthly.

Several hundred photographs from the files of *The Jewish Farmer* depicting Jewish farm settlements in the United States. Included are photographs of the Baron de Hirsch Agricultural School in Woodbine, New Jersey. Documents relating to the Baron de Hirsch Fund and to the JAS: by-laws, reports, certificates of incorporation, list of applicants, awards. JAS news releases, 1937–1961.

535. JEWISH COLONIZATION ASSOCIATION (PARIS).
Records, 1898–1913. 4 microfilm reels. (RG 236)

Philanthropic association which assisted Jewish immigration and agricultural colonization throughout the world. Founded in 1891 by Baron Maurice de Hirsch. Headquarters maintained in Paris until relocated to London in 1949.

The collection consists of correspondence and reports relating to colonization projects in various countries, including Argentina, Austria, Belgium, Brazil, Canada, Chile, Cyprus, Germany, Palestine, Poland (Galicia), Russia, 1898–1913.

Inventory, Yiddish.

536. JEWISH CUSTOMS (VILNA ARCHIVES).
Collection, 1830s–1930s. 3 ft. 4 in. (RG 41)

The collection consists of materials relating to Jewish religious life in Europe between the 1830s–1930s.

Topics include: marriages, births, divorces, deaths, bar mitzvahs, holidays, the Sabbath, daily customs, ritual slaughter (*shehitah*), ritual baths, mezuzahs, prayers, *kvitlekh* (requests to a rabbi for a blessing).

Items include: marriage contracts, divorce deeds, wedding invitations, birth announcements, bar mitzvah speeches, New Year's cards, correspondence, photographs.

537. JEWISH DAILY FORWARD.
Records, 1954–1956. 10 in. (RG 686)

Yiddish newspaper based in New York, established in 1897. Abraham Cahan was the editor from 1903 to 1951. For much of its existence the newspaper espoused the cause of democratic socialism and supported the Jewish labor movement. One of its popular columns, the "Bintel Brief" [Bintl brif] offered advice on a variety of topics to several generations of Jewish immigrants. The paper reached a peak circulation of nearly 200,000 during World War I, after which its readership declined steadily. By 1970 circulation had fallen to 44,000. In the 1980s the *Jewish Daily Forward* changed from a daily to a weekly paper.

The collection contains records of the "Bintel Brief" department and consists of letters asking for personal advice.

538. JEWISH DRAMA SOCIETY (CAIRO, EGYPT).
Records, 1918–1946. 5 in. (RG 281)

Organized in 1905. Staged plays for Yiddish-speaking public in Cairo. During both world wars, special performances were given for Jewish soldiers.

Playbills, program notes, scripts, correspondence with Egyptian radio.

539. JEWISH EDUCATION COMMITTEE (NEW YORK).
Records, 1939–1967. 7 ft. 6 in. (RG 592)

The Jewish Education Committee was organized in 1939 in New York to coordinate a wide variety of administrative, educational and financial services to the various Jewish school systems in New York. Two predecessor organizations, the Jewish Education Association and the Bureau of Jewish Education, merged with the JEC. The schools that were served by the JEC included Orthodox, Reform, Conservative and Yiddish secular schools. Its departments offered financial aid to individual schools, helped to develop curricula, and maintained teacher services such as a teachers' group insurance. The JEC also maintained the Board of License for Hebrew Teachers, as well as teacher training institutions and the Hebrew Teachers Union. Its publications included *World Over*, as well as a Hebrew magazine, textbooks, song books, and arts and crafts guides. The JEC department of statistics published studies in the field of Jewish education. Executive directors for the period 1939–1967 included Alexander Dushkin, Israel Chipkin and Azriel Eisenberg.

The collection consists mostly of administrative records of the JEC. There are also materials from two affiliated organizations, the National Council of Jewish Education and the American Association for Jewish Education.

JEC administrative materials. Circulars, 1942–1967. Staff memoranda. Minutes of committee meetings. Minutes of consultant meetings. Materials on services to schools. Reports, tests and questionnaires, proceedings of pedagogical conferences. Minutes, lectures, circulars on in-service courses. Pedagogical materials on art, dance, music, drama. Awards and contests including Bible contests. Materials on services to teachers. Licensing of teachers, lists of licenses. Reports on teacher placement. Hebrew Teachers' Welfare Association. Minutes of Board of Review meetings. Materials relating to schools and organizations affiliated with the JEC: United Synagogue schools, New York Federation of Reform Religious Schools,

Associated Hebrew Schools of Westchester, East New York Talmud Torah Council, Bronx Council, Flatbush Council. Materials relating to JEC publications. Memos and reports on adult education. Public relations materials such as press releases. Research and experimentation: surveys, statistical materials relating to Jewish education. Circulars, minutes, reports, annual conference materials, publications relating to the National Council of Jewish Education and to the American Association for Jewish Education. Materials relating to National Organization of Jewish Education, World Union for Jewish Education, Jewish Agency, Alliance Israélite Universelle.

Inventory, English.

540. JEWISH EDUCATION SERVICE OF NORTH AMERICA (JESNA).
Records, 1940–1981. 62 ft. (RG 1184)

Coordinating, planning and service agency for Jewish education in the United States. Founded in New York in 1939 as the American Association for Jewish Education (AAJE), adopting its new name in 1981. Services Jewish educational institutions through a network of national organizations and bureaus of Jewish education. Sponsored the National Curriculum Research Institute, National Board of License and other projects. Conducts statistical and educational surveys, organizes conferences and provides placement services.

Correspondence, minutes, reports and memorabilia of the AAJE mainly of the period 1962–1981. Following series are included: files of Isaac Toubin, AAJE Executive Director, 1962–1979; community files; correspondence with Jewish communal organizations; files of the National Curriculum; files of the AAJE Governing Council, 1965–1974, and of the Executive Committee, 1968–1981; files of the Research Institute, 1974–1978, and of the Association for Multi-ethnic Programs; community service materials, 1965–1978.

541. JEWISH FAMILY AND CHILDREN'S SERVICE (DETROIT).
Records, ca. 1924–ca. 1963. 121 microfilm reels. (RG 364)

An affiliate agency of the Jewish Welfare Federation in Detroit formerly called the Jewish Social Service Bureau (JSSB).

This collection consists predominantly of records of the Jewish Social Service Bureau and, to a much lesser extent, of records of the Jewish Family and Children's Service. The bulk of the collection consists of records of individual cases which were processed by the JSSB. Additionally, there are administrative records which include the following: general correspondence, 1926–1963; minutes of staff and committee meetings, 1924–1955. Records of various institutions which at some point merged or were affiliated with the JSSB, such as the Resettlement Service, Jewish House of Shelter, Jewish Child Placement Bureau, Hebrew Orphan Home.

Inventory, English.

542. JEWISH MUSIC ALLIANCE.
Records, 1930s–1960s. 14 ft. (RG 1252)

Founded by Jacob Schaefer and Mendi Shein in 1925 for the purpose of fostering Yiddish choirs. Maintained choruses in New York, Chicago, Philadelphia, Detroit, Washington, Patterson, Newark, and Brighton. Was associated with the YKUF (Yidisher Kultur Farband). Published a number of Yiddish songbooks. Ceased its activities in the 1980s.

Manuscripts of instrumental works. Manuscripts of choral works by J. Schaefer and others. Orchestrations and scores. Publications and printed music. Papers of Jacob Schaefer. Programs of performances, clippings, photographs.

543. JEWISH MUSIC SOCIETIES.
Records, 1908–1931. 1 ft. 8 in. (RG 37)

These materials are of mixed provenance and they relate to various Jewish music societies in Eastern Europe.

Correspondence, minutes of meetings, memoranda, reports, financial records, playbills, posters, printed materials relating to the following music societies: Society for Jewish Folk Music, St. Petersburg, 1908–1920; Society for Jewish Music, Moscow, 1923–1928; Carmel-Jewish Musical, Dramatic and Literary Society, Riga, 1910–1920; Kultur Lige Music Section, Kiev, 1920–1926; Jewish Historical and Ethnographic Society, Music Section, Leningrad, 1927–1929; Jewish Folk Kapelye in the Name of Winchevsky, Vinnitsa, 1927–1931; Muzikalisher Kabinet, Institut fun Yidisher Proletarisher Kultur (Institute for Jewish Proletarian Culture, Department of Music), Kiev.

Inventory, English.

544. JEWISH OCCUPATIONAL COUNCIL.
Records, 1939–1965. 4 ft. (RG 460)

Established in 1939 in New York as a national advisory and coordinating agency for Jewish organizations and communities in the United States and Canada engaged in educational and vocational programs and job placement.

Correspondence and memoranda with local Jewish vocational service agencies. Reports on occupational trends among the Jewish population. Publications issued by the U.S. Department of Labor and by Jewish vocational and counseling centers.

545. JEWISH SOCIALIST VERBAND.
Records, 1954–1965. 1 ft. 3 in. (RG 688)

Jewish organization founded in 1921 and devoted to the cause of democratic socialism and the perpetuation of Yiddish secular culture. The Verband was closely identified with the Workmen's Circle and the *Jewish Daily Forward*. The official organ of the Verband was *Der veker*.

The collection consists of correspondence, circulars, press releases, clippings of announcements, speeches, relating to the Verband's activities in the 1950s and 1960s.

546. JEWISH STATE SCHOOLS IN THE VILNA SCHOOL DISTRICT.
Records, 1847–1910. 2 ft. 1 in. (RG 52)

The Jewish state schools in the Russian Empire were established in 1844 by a decree of Nicholas I. This network was intended to serve as a counterbalance to the traditional heder. The schools had a diverse teaching program ranging from two to four years of instruction. The supervisors of these schools were Christians. A percentage of the Jewish candle- and-meat tax was used for the financial support of the schools. The first schools were opened in Vilna and Zhitomir in 1847. Because of the schools' assimilationist character, they aroused strong opposition from the Jews. By 1861 only 5 schools remained.

Correspondence with the Vilna School District. Lists of teachers and students. Teaching materials. Reports relating to the financial support of the schools in Vilna, Disna, Święciany,

Molodechno, Oszmiana, Lida, Vileika, Radoshkovitse. Minutes of the meeting of the Vilna Provincial Commission for Jewish schools, 1853. Conversion of the Vilna elementary school into a high school. Applications to take teachers' exams. Report about conditions in the heders and the situation of teachers in private schools.

Inventory, Yiddish.

547. JEWISH TELEGRAPHIC AGENCY (NEW YORK).
Records, 1930s–1960s. 14 microfilm reels. (RG 562)

Agency for the gathering and dissemination of Jewish news, servicing the Jewish and non-Jewish press of various countries. Originally established in 1914 as the Jewish Correspondence Bureau by Jacob Landau in The Hague. In 1919 it was reestablished in London by Landau and Meir Grossman as the Jewish Telegraphic Agency. JTA headquarters were moved to New York in 1922. The JTA publishes the *Jewish Daily Bulletin* and in 1962 established a weekly bulletin, *Community News*. Boris Smolar was the JTA managing editor from 1924 to 1968.

The collection consists of JTA news dispatches and clippings arranged in the following topical series: geographical areas, countries, regions; subject headings; personalities.

548. JOACHIMOWICZ, ABRAHAM (1909–1982).
Papers, 1940s–1970s. 1 ft. 6 in. (RG 1266)

Yiddish writer. Survivor of the Łódź ghetto and Auschwitz concentration camp. Some of his poems were set to music in the Łódź ghetto by David Beigelman. Born in Łódź. Settled in the United States in 1949.

Manuscripts and typescripts of poems with music composed by David Beigelman, Samuel Bugatch, Michl Gelbart, Henech Kon, Sholom Secunda, and others. Included are songs written during the Holocaust period. 42 audiotapes including performances of Joachimowicz's songs set to music.

549. JOFFE, JUDAH ACHILLES (1873–1966).
Papers, 1893–1966. 16 ft. 3 in. (RG 546)

Yiddish linguist, teacher, lexicographer, writer. Specialist in early Yiddish literature. Translator of more than a dozen languages. Co-editor of the *Groyser verterbukh fun der yidisher shprakh* (Great Dictionary of the Yiddish Language). Co-founder of the American branch of YIVO. Active in the Linguistics Section of YIVO. Born in Bakhmut, Ukraine. Emigrated to the United States in 1891.

Correspondence with individuals including Salo Baron, Bernard Baruch, Sidor Belarsky, Ber Borochov, Judah Leob (Leib) Cahan, Mendl Elkin, Ben Zion Goldberg, Jacob de Haas, Alexander Harkavy, Ephim Jeshurin, Yudel Mark, Kalman Marmor, Henry Morgenthau, Melech Ravitch, Zalman Reisen, Edward Sapir, Max Weinreich, Uriel Weinreich, Yehoash. Correspondence with organizations. Family correspondence. Letters from former students. Biographical materials, such as curriculum vitae, autobiographical notes, I.D. cards, letters of recommendation. Financial records. Clippings of Joffe's publications, of articles about him. Reports, minutes, plans, memoranda and correspondence relating to the Great Dictionary of the Yiddish Language.

Materials relating to the YIVO Institute. Notes of Executive Committee meetings. Notes on Board of Directors meetings. Materials of the Research and Training Division. Materials on YIVO Annual Conferences. Materials on YIVO in Vilna. Materials relating to Joffe's courses and lectures: notes on Yiddish courses, Yiddish composition, phonetics, morphology, etymology. Materials relating to the following topics: dictionaries; Russian literature and linguistics; Old-Yiddish language and literature; the *Bovo-bukh* by Elias Levita (Elia Bachur). Materials including articles relating to music, musicians, Yiddish songs, music institutions, recordings. Folklore materials about folksongs, proverbs, anecdotes. Notes for a Yiddish–English dictionary. Notes for a Russian–English dictionary.

 Inventory, English, Yiddish.

550. JUDAICA.
 Collection, 16th–19th century. 1 ft. 10 in. (RG 106)

This collection is comprised of photostat or microfilm copies of rare books and manuscripts in Old Yiddish from various European libraries. These include the Bodleian Library in Oxford, Cambridge University Libraries, Bavarian State Library in Munich, British Museum in London, Hamburg Library. There is a subsidiary collection of Judeo-Arabic pamphlets on microfilm received from Robert Attal of Tunisia.

 The collection includes prayer books, glossaries, prescriptions, recipes, medical treatises, storybooks, scientific texts, poetry, folksongs, commentaries. The materials have been arranged by library of origin, with the Judeo-Arabic titles forming a separate group.

 Inventory, English.

551. JUDKOFF, SIMON (1889–1959).
 Collection. 10 in. (RG 488)

Portrait photographer, Yiddish writer. Contributed short stories to the *Freie Arbeiter Stimme* (NY). Also worked for *Di tsayt*. Born in Dziewieniszki, Vilna province, Lithuania. Immigrated to the United States in 1907.

 Glass negatives of photo portraits of Jewish personalities.

552. JUDSON, SOLOMON (1878–1970).
 Papers, 1911–1965. 1 ft. 3 in. (RG 579)

Yiddish and Hebrew writer. Wrote for *Hatsefira*, *Ha-Ivri*, *Hapisgah*, *Ha-Tehia*, *Ha-leum*, *Jewish Daily Forward*. From 1913 was a regular columnist for the *Morgn zhurnal* and from 1920 to 1951 was its co-editor. Editor of *Der amerikaner*, on editorial staff of *Tog morgn zhurnal*. Used the pen name Dr. Klorman. Born in Dereczyn, district of Grodno. Immigrated to the United States in 1898.

 The papers consist of general correspondence, letters from readers to "Dr. Klorman," some manuscripts, personal documents. Correspondents include Joseph Barondess, Mendel Beilis, Alexander Harkavy, A. Litwin, Abraham Reisen, Zalman Reisen, Menahem Ussishkin, Yehoash, Chaim Zhitlowsky.

553. KACYZNE, ALTER (1885–1941).
 Collection, 1917–1930s. 4 ft. 1 in. (RG 1270)

Yiddish writer and professional photographer. Prominent in Jewish literary and artistic circles in Warsaw before World War II. Wrote novels, poetry, plays, film scripts, journalistic articles. Disciple of Isaac Leib Peretz, and friend and confidant of S. Ansky (who appointed

Kacyzne as the executor of his literary estate). Kacyzne completed Ansky's unfinished play *Tog un Nakht*. Contributed to and edited a number of Yiddish newspapers and magazines in Poland, including *Literarishe bleter, Bikher velt, Folkstaytung, Vilner tog, Undzer ekspres.* In 1937–1939 published and edited his own literary magazine *Mayn redndiker film.* Born in Vilna. Lived in Ekaterinoslav (Ukraine) and Warsaw. After the Nazi onslaught on Poland, fled to Lwów. Killed in Tarnopol during a pogrom perpetrated by the Ukrainians in the first week of July 1941.

Kacyzne owned a photographic studio in Warsaw which he operated until 1939. In 1921 he was commissioned by the Hebrew Immigrant Aid Society in New York to do a series of photographs that would depict the Jewish immigration theme. He took these photographs at the HIAS office in Warsaw. In 1923 Kacyzne began his collaboration with the *Jewish Daily Forward* in New York. For the paper's weekly Art Section, Kacyzne took a series of photographs depicting Jewish life in scores of communities throughout Poland. Kacyzne also photographed Yiddish theater performances and made numerous photo portraits of Jewish personalities.

The collection consists of Kacyzne's photographic works.

Photographs of Jewish life in Poland taken in 70 communities. Topics include: Jewish types; family; work; trade; street scenes; marketplace; poverty; religious life; schools; summer camps; landscapes. Photographs of Jewish immigrants at the HIAS office in Warsaw.

Theater photographs. Stills of scenes from various performances. Portraits of actors and directors, notably of the Vilna Troupe. Photo album compiled in honor of the first anniversary of the Association of Jewish Drama Artists in Vilna, 1917 (includes photographs of actors in roles).

Articles published in the Yiddish press about Kacyzne after his death.

Card catalog, English.

554. KADISON, LEIB (1880–1947).
Papers, 1916–1947. 10 in. (RG 1100)

Set designer, actor, director in the Yiddish theater. Founder of the Vilna Troupe, 1915. Director of Dramatics, Workmen's Circle Summer Camp. Born in Kaunas, Lithuania. Settled in the United States ca. 1931.

The papers relate to Kadison's theatrical career and personal life. Art works: original stage designs for the Yiddish theater; drawings of stage characters; portraits of the Kadison family; miscellaneous drawings. Photographs of the Vilna Troupe, including scenes of performances. Individual and group photographs of troupe members, including photographs of Luba Kadison and Joseph Buloff. Photographs of Leib Kadison and family. Programs of Vilna Troupe productions. Clippings, theater posters.

Photographs cataloged in STAGEPIX.

555. KADISON, POLA (1901–1981).
Papers, 1920s–1981. 10 in. (RG 1098)

Pianist, arranger and composer. Daughter of Leib Kadison and the actress Khana Kadison. Graduated from the Vilna Conservatory of Music. Performed with Habimah and with the Vilna Troupe. Came to the United States ca. 1920. Accompanist to many performers. Pianist for Camp Boiberik, 1954–1974. Pianist for Old Age Home of the Workmen's Circle.

Manuscripts and printed sheet music, including original compositions and arrangements by Pola Kadison. Yiddish folk songs, music and lyrics. Concert programs, newspaper clippings, publicity material of performances by Pola Kadison. Materials related to Camp Boiberik. Photographs of Pola Kadison, the Kadison family and friends.

Photographs cataloged in STAGEPIX.

556. KAHAN, ARCADIUS (AVROM) (1920–1982).
Papers. 5 in. (RG 1156)

Economist. Specialized in general and Jewish economics and agriculture. Professor of Economics at University of Chicago. Collaborated with Salo W. Baron on an economic history of the Jews. Member, YIVO Executive Board. Born in Vilna. Immigrated to the United States in 1950.

Notes, photocopies of essays, statistics, index cards, on various subjects relating to Jewish history such as Jewish economy, Russian revolution, vocational training for Jews.

557. KAHAN, JACOB (1900–1973).
Papers, ca. 1945–1972. ca. 3 ft. (RG 691)

Yiddish writer. Contributed to *Haynt* (Warsaw), *Emes*, *Nayer veg* (Warsaw), *Dos naye lebn*, *Undzer lebn*, *Gut morgn*, *Zukunft*, *New yorker vokhnblat*, *Tsionistishe shtime*. Born in Biała Podlaska, Poland. In 1948 moved to Paris, France. Settled in the United States in 1954.

Correspondence, photographs, manuscripts, clippings, personal documents. Materials concerning Jews in Białystok.

558. KAHAN, LAZAR (1880–1976).
Papers, 1908–1940s. 2 1/2 in. (RG 422)

Yiddish writer, journalist, editor of the Warsaw Yiddish daily *Undzer ekspres*. Lived in Poland, Shanghai, the United States.

Correspondence with literary figures including Abraham Cahan, Hayyim Nahman Bialik, Shmuel Niger, Hersh David Nomberg, Moishe Taich, Joseph Tunkel, Zalman Wendroff, Aaron Zeitlin, Hillel Zeitlin.

Theater materials of Lazar Kahan's wife, the Yiddish actress Shoshana Rose: texts of plays, posters.

559. KAISER, SAMUEL (1891–1982).
Papers. 5 in. (RG 1127)

Yiddish writer. Active in the labor movement. Author of a book, *S'vilt zikh dertseyln*. Born in Turzysk, Volhynia. Immigrated to the United States in 1910.

Manuscripts of stories and novels, all incomplete.

560. KALISHER LANDSMANSHAFT AND VICINITY, WORKMEN'S CIRCLE BRANCH 361—KALISHER NON PARTISAN RELIEF COMMITTEE.
Records, 1950s–1970s. 5 in. (RG 1161)

Founded in the early 1950s as a *landsmanshaft* of immigrants from Kalisz, Poland. Became affiliated with the Workmen's Circle in 1961.

Souvenir journals. Polish articles on Kalisz. Minutes, 1960s–1970s. Correspondence. Invitations. Flyers. Photographs of: Hashomer Hatzair in Kalisz, 1934; the Kalisher tailors' cooperative in Łódź, 1946; the cemetery in Kalisz, 1979. Kalisz memorial book.

561. KALISHER SOCIAL VEREIN.
Records, 1962–1977. 1 in. (RG 1049)

Founded in New York in 1929 by immigrants from Kalisz, Poland. Worked with the Kalisher book committee to publish a memorial book.
Constitution, 1962. Minutes, 1972–1977. Bulletins.

562. KALLEN, HORACE MEYER (1882–1974).
Papers, 1922–1952. 21 ft. 8 in. (RG 317)

Philosopher, writer, educator. Co-founder of the New School for Social Research, New York, in 1919 and dean of its Graduate Faculty of Political and Social Science, 1944–1946. An early advocate of consumer rights and environmental controls. Active in liberal, educational and Jewish groups. Served on government committees: Presidential Commission on Higher Education, New York City Commission on Inter-group Relations. Born in Bernstadt, Germany. Came to the United States in 1887.
 The papers relate to Kallen's interests in the fields of education, philosophy, Zionism, Jewish affairs, consumerism, co-operative movement, political activism. Correspondence with over 1,000 organizations including American Jewish Congress, World Jewish Congress, American Association for Jewish Education, Federal Council of Churches of Christ in America, Julian W. Mack School, Menorah Association, New School for Social Research, President's Commission on Higher Education. About 4,000 individual correspondents including Max Ascoli, Roger Baldwin, Salo W. Baron, Jacob Billikopf, Louis D. Brandeis, Israel S. Chipkin, John Dewey, Felix Frankfurter, Philip R. Goldstein, Sidney Hook, Alvin Johnson, Julian W. Mack, Jerome Nathanson, Edmond de Rothschild, George Santayana, Hans Simon, Louis Sturz, Stephen S. Wise.
 Inventory, English.
 Index, English.

563. KALUSZER LADIES SOCIETY.
Records, 1958–1974. 1 1/2 in. (RG 959)

Organized in New York in 1919 by immigrants from Kalush (Pol. Kałusz), Ukraine. Also known as the Kalusher Ladies Society, Inc. Dissolved 1974.
 Minutes, 1958–1974 (German). Seal.

564. KAMAIKO, SOLOMON (ZALMAN) BARUKH (1879–1957).
Papers, 1920–1941. 5 in. (RG 381)

Yiddish journalist. Contributed to *Yidisher herold*, *Folks advokat*, *Yiddishes Tageblatt*, *Yidisher kurier* (Chicago). Born in Anykščiai, Lithuania. Came to the United States in 1889.
 Albums of Yiddish newspaper clippings, mostly from Chicago. Includes Kamaiko's articles as well as clippings of his memoirs.

565. KAMENETZ-PODOLER RELIEF ORGANIZATION.
Records, 1945–1974. 2 1/2 in. (RG 972)

Founded in 1944 to furnish "aid and assistance for the relief of human suffering in the city of Kamenets-Podolski, USSR and to the residents and former residents . . . who suffered from the war, nazism and fascism. . . ." Rehabilitated refugees. Built a children's village in Israel.

Certificate of incorporation, 1945. By-laws. Anniversary journals. Correspondence. Meeting notices. Photographs. Memorial book, 1965.

566. KAMENETZER LITOVSKER MEMORIAL COMMITTEE.
Records, 1928–1970. 5 in. (RG 968)

Founded in New York in 1961 by *landslayt* from Kamenets (Pol. Kamieniec Litewski), Byelorussia, to publish a memorial book and to coordinate annual memorial meetings of Kamenetzer societies. Affiliated organizations are: Kamenetz-Litovsker Women's Malbish Arumim (organization to provide clothing for the poor) League; Congregation Kochob Jacob Anshei Kamenetz Lite; Ladies Auxiliary of the Kamenetzer Shul; Kamenetz-Litovsker Young Friends Workmen's Circle Branch 309; Lopates Family Circle; Rudnitzky Cousins Club; Bonchik Family Circle; Kamenetz Litovsker U.V.

Minutes, financial records, Women's Malbish Arumim League, 1950s–1960s. Correspondence. Meeting notices. Anniversary journals of the Lopates Family Circle and Kamenetz Litovsker U.V. Memorial book, 1970. Publication materials pertaining to the memorial book.

567. KAMINSKA, IDA (1899–1980) and MELMAN, MEIR (1900–1978).
Papers, 1960s–1980. 12 1/2 in. (RG 994)

Ida Kaminska: Leading Yiddish actress in theater and film. Daughter of Esther Rachel Kaminska. Together with her first husband Zygmunt Turkow, Kaminska established the Warsaw Jewish Art Theater in the inter-war period. Artistic director of the Jewish State Theater in Poland after World War II. Toured Israel, Europe, North and South America with this company. Nominated for an Oscar for her role in the film *The Shop on Main Street*, 1967.

Meir Melman: Husband of Ida Kaminska. Yiddish stage actor. Member of the Vilna Troupe and the Warsaw Art Theater, before 1939. Managing director of the Jewish State Theater of Warsaw.

At the outbreak of World War II, Ida Kaminska and Meir Melman fled Warsaw for the Soviet Union. They returned to Poland after the war and immigrated to the United States in 1969.

The papers pertain predominantly to Ida Kaminska's theatrical career in the United States until her death. A smaller proportion of materials pertains to the pre-1969 period when Mrs. Kaminska and Mr. Melman lived in Warsaw and led the Esther Rachel Kaminska Jewish State Theater in Poland.

The collection consists of photographs, letters, telegrams, clippings, awards, notes, personal documents and includes materials pertaining to: the stage production of *Mother Courage* by Bertold Brecht; *Sore-Sheyndel from Yehupetz* by Joseph Lateiner; *Mirele Efros* by Jacob Gordin; materials about the film *The Shop on Main Street* and the TV production *Mandelstam's Witness* (CBC, 1975). Correspondence of Mr. Melman as director of the Jewish State Theater in Warsaw. Photographs taken at the 50th anniversary memorial service for Esther Rachel Kaminska in Warsaw, 1975. Obituaries and condolences on Meir Melman's death in November 1978.

568. KANIEVSKY, AARON (1890–1960).
Papers, 1920s–1950s. 1 ft. 3 in. (RG 1110)

Yiddish literary and theater critic. Wrote extensively for *Der tog*. Also wrote for *Der amerikaner*, *Di yidishe velt*, *Yom tov bleter*. Born in Rzhishchev, Kiev province. Settled in Philadelphia in 1908.

The papers consist of manuscripts, correspondence (1920s–1950s), clippings, programs, invitations. Also included are some papers, such as correspondence and manuscripts, of the poet Alter (Arthur) Esselin (1889–1974). Esselin, whose real name was Ore Serebrenik, was born in Chernigov, Ukraine, and settled in the United States in 1908.

569. KAPLAN, ABRAHAM (FAMILY).
Papers, 1902–1985. 5 ft. (RG 1288)

Abraham Halevi Kaplan, a businessman, active in modern Hebrew education, the Zionist movement, and Yiddish culture, was born in 1885 in the Ukraine. Lived in Palestine in 1907–1910, 1924–1939. Lived in the United States in 1912–1924, 1939–1963. Died in Israel in 1979.

Family papers of Abraham Kaplan, and of his relatives and descendants, including the compiler of this collection, Judge Jair Kaplan of Boston. Manuscripts of Abraham Kaplan including lectures in Yiddish on the Bible and on Jewish holidays.

570. KAPLAN, SIMA.
Papers, 1915–1971. 2 1/2 in. (RG 1208)

Yiddish writer and cultural activist. Lived in the United States.

Correspondence from Kaplan's family in Białystok, 1915, 1921–1941, 1945. Material concerning Kaplan's involvement in Yiddish cultural activities, 1925–1971, including correspondence, drafts of letters by Kaplan, manuscript articles and speeches. Photographs.

571. KARAITES.
Collection. 10 in. (RG 40)

Jewish sect originating in the 8th century which recognized the Scriptures but did not accept the Oral Law. The Karaite movement flourished in the Middle East and later spread to Europe. The Karaites developed their own liturgy, rituals and laws. In the 1930s there were about 12,000 Karaites in the world. The Nazi regime did not consider the Karaites to be Jews and gave orders to spare them and give them favorable treatment. Karaite groups settled in Israel after World War II and were encouraged by the government to establish their own institutions.

The collection consists of manuscripts relating to Karaites. Included are studies by Raphael Mahler, Reuben Fahn, G. Levi-Badanitch, Ananiasz Zajączkowski, A. Kahan, Majer Bałaban. Topics include: Karaites in Poland; Karaites and the Tartars in Crimea; Karaites in Galicia.

572. KARPILOW, MIRIAM (1888–1956).
Papers, ca. 1900–1950s. 1 ft. 3 in. (RG 383)

Yiddish writer. Born in Minsk, Byelorussia. Came to the United States in 1905.

Manuscripts, clippings, correspondence and photographs relating to M. Karpilow's career and personal life.

573. KARTUZ-BEREZER BENEVOLENT ASSOCIATION.
Records, 1944–1970, 1982. 2 in. (RG 1118)

Organized in New York by immigrants from Bereza Kartuska, Poland.

Minutes, 1944–1970, in Yiddish. Pamphlet, *Der khurbn fun kartuz bereze* (The Destruction of Kartuz Bereza), New York, 1982.

574. KASTOFF, MEIR (1886–1958).
Papers, 1901–1959. 1 ft. 8 in. (RG 414)

President, Hebrew-American Typographical Union (HATU), which was Local 83 of the International Typographical Union.

The collection relates primarily to HATU, Local 83. Correspondence with organizations such as Israeli typographical unions, typographical unions in Poland, Hebrew-American Typographical Union, Local 83. Correspondence with individuals: Daniel Charney, David Pinsky. Kastoff's memoirs, *Mit fuftsik yor tsurik: A kapitl zikhroynes* (Fifty Years: A Chapter of Memoirs); Kastoff's diaries, 1944–1955. Materials relating to the strike at the *Jewish Daily Forward*, 1908, and at the *Abend blat*, 1898. HATU's 45th anniversary yearbook.

575. KATZ, ALEPH (1898–1969).
Papers, 1920s–1969. 8 ft. 4 in. (RG 650)

Yiddish poet and journalist. Pen name of Morris (Moshe) Abraham Katz. Contributed to periodicals such as *In zikh, Oyfkum, Freie Arbeiter Stimme, Di vokh, Dos yidishe folk, Zukunft, Yidisher kemfer, Kinder zhurnal*. Born in Młynów, Volhynia. Immigrated to the United States in 1913.

The papers consist of correspondence, articles, clippings of reviews and translations, printed material and financial records relating to the literary activities of Aleph Katz. Correspondents include Ephraim Auerbach, B. Alkwit, Menahem Boraisha, Aaron Glanz-Leieles, Chaim Grade, Mani Leib, Lipa Lehrer, Itzik Manger, Alexander Mukdoni, Moshe Nadir, Melech Ravitch, Zalman Reisen, Max Weinreich. Manuscripts include draft for a textbook *Lebedike verter*. Materials for the *Groyser verterbukh fun der yidisher shprakh* (Great Dictionary of the Yiddish Language). Autobiography of Chaim Yeruchem ben Reb Yaakov Hakohen Katz, the father of Aleph Katz.

576. KATZ, JACOB (1907–1974).
Papers, 1930s–1970s. 2 1/2 in. (RG 1157)

Yiddish writer, teacher. Contributed to American and Israeli newspapers. Took part in the Warsaw ghetto uprising. Deported to several concentration camps, among them, Treblinka, Majdanek, and Budzyń. After the war Katz was active in the administration of the DP camp in Feldafing. Born in Żółkiewka, near Lublin, Poland. Immigrated to the United States in 1949.

Manuscript of a play by Katz titled *In blut un fayer*. Correspondence, 1946–1971. Photographs of J. Katz in Poland in the 1930s; of DP camps. Documents from DP camps. Clippings from DP camp newspapers.

577. KATZ, MORRIS (born 1901).
Papers, 1935–1952. 5 in. (RG 704)

Dentist, Yiddish writer. Contributed to publications such as *Belgishe bleter, Di yidishe prese, Dos vort*. Born in Łódź, Poland. Lived for some years in Czechoslovakia and Belgium. Fled to London in 1940. Settled in the United States in 1950.

The collection consists of clippings, correspondence and personal documents relating to Katz's literary activities and personal life.

578. KATZ, MOSES (1864–1941).
Papers. 5 in. (RG 229)

Jewish anarchist leader in the United States. Editor, publicist, lecturer, playwright. Editor of *Freie Arbeiter Stimme*.

Manuscripts, mostly of Katz's Yiddish plays.

579. KAZDAN, CHAIM SHLOYME (1883–1979).
Papers, 1942–1975. 1 ft. 3 in. (RG 672)

Teacher, Yiddish writer and literary critic. Chairman, Tsentrale Yidishe Shul Organizatsye (Central Organization of Yiddish Schools), Poland, 1920s–1939. Member of the Central Committee of the Bund in Poland. Lecturer in Yiddish Literature and Methods of Teaching at the Jewish Teachers' Seminary, New York. Contributed to many periodicals including *Hofenung* (Vilna), *Di yidishe velt, Bikher velt* (Kiev), *Folkstsaytung, Arbayter luakh, Di vokh, Literarishe bleter, Undzer tsayt, Di naye shul, Shul un lebn* (Warsaw).

The papers consist of correspondence, memoirs, manuscripts, articles, songs, clippings and photographs relating to Kazdan's career. Correspondents include Shalom Asch.

580. KEHILLAT HAHAREDIM (FRANCE).
Records, 1939–1947. 14 ft. 7 in. (RG 340)

French name: Association des Israélites Pratiquants. Association of Orthodox Jews organized in 1936 by Rabbi Schneur Zalmen Schneersohn (Chnéerson), to conduct religious and educational activities throughout France. During the German occupation, the organization engaged in underground activities, rescuing and supporting Jews, especially children. Originally centered in Paris, its headquarters were moved to Marseilles in 1940, to Dému in 1942, and to St. Etienne-de-Crossey in 1943. After the war, the organization concerned itself chiefly with searching for children hidden in Christian homes throughout the French countryside and with working for their return to a Jewish environment. A questionnaire was distributed by the Kehillat Haharedim to numerous municipalities in France, inquiring about the existence of Jewish children and expressing the organization's willingness to take custody of such children and to provide for them.

The records reflect the Kehillat Haharedim's activities during and after World War II.

World War II Period. Correspondence with children's homes and youth homes in Seignebon-Dému, St. Etienne-de-Crossey, Brout-Vernet, St.-Gervais-les-Bains. Correspondence relating to the provision of food for children's homes. Letters from children. Correspondence with internees of camps in Verny, Gurs, Rivesaltes, Les Milles, Barcarès, Récébédou, Aubagne, Rieucros, Argelès-sur-Mer. Correspondence regarding relief work in the camps, including the sending of provisions, clothes and religious articles. Lists of refugees and internees. Correspondence with rabbis, including Rabbi Elie Munk, Rabbi David Chaim Met, Rabbi Shlomo Kunstlinger, Rabbi Shlomo Fuchs.

Correspondence with the UGIF, HICEM. Bulletin of the Kehillat Haharedim. Materials on yeshivot in Marseilles, St. Etienne-de-Crossey, and in Heide, Belgium, including lists of students. Materials on vocational courses offered by the Kehillat Haharedim, such as tailoring. Financial records.

Post War Records. Circulars sent to municipalities in France inquiring about the fate of Jewish children. Responses of the municipalities, written on the returned questionnaires.

Correspondence with the OSE. Correspondence with organizations in England and Poland relating to the fate of rescued Jewish children. Correspondence regarding the return of children sheltered in Catholic institutions. Correspondence with the Commission on the Status of Jewish War Orphans, with the Fédération de Sociétés Juives de France, Centre de Documentation Juive Contemporaine, AJDC, HICEM.

Letters from children in children's homes. Lists of children, reports on their condition, on the fate of their parents. Statistical reports on children's homes. Lists of students, programs of studies and financial records from educational institutions in Eragny, Boissy-St. Léger, Tragny.

Materials relating to the Kehillat Haharedim school in Paris. Reports on students in the Talmud Torah, lists of students. Materials from schools and Talmud Torahs, such as "Chaim L'Yisrael," Talmud Torah in Mulhouse, Metz, Grenoble, Brussels, Limoges. Requests to government schools to free children from writing on the Sabbath.

Materials relating to religious activities. Correspondence, minutes of the Coordinating Committee of the Synagogues of Paris, 1945. Correspondence of the Vaad Harabonim, 1944–1945. Materials on *kashrut*, Passover, 1941. Materials of the synagogue of the Kehillat Haharedim. Correspondence of the Rashi Synagogue, Ezras Yisroel Synagogue, Beit Yisrael Synagogue, Adath Israel Synagogue.

Materials relating to kashrut, burials, provision of matzot. Reports on *shehitah*, kosher wine. Lists and correspondence relating to relief packages of kosher food. Correspondence relating to the *mikveh*.

Materials relating to Nazi victims. Materials on project to found an Association of Victims of Nazism. Correspondence with Comité d'Aide Immédiate aux Déportés et Victimes de la Guerre. List of deportees.

Correspondence with branches of Kehillat Haharedim in Moirans, Toulouse, Marseilles. Lists of members of Kehillat Haharedim in Paris.

Inventory, Yiddish, English.

581. KEIDANER ASSOCIATION.
Records, 1930–1949. 1 1/2 in. (RG 1048)

Established in New York in 1900 by immigrants from Kědainiai (Rus. Keidany), Lithuania. Associated with the Keidaner Ladies Aid Society of the Keidaner Orphan Asylum. Sponsored loans, relief activities and Passover funds to aid needy *landslayt* in Kědainiai.

Anniversary journals, 1930, 1940. Monthly bulletin of the association and the Keidaner Ladies Aid Society, 1936–1949.

582. KESSLER, ISRAEL.
Papers, 1880–ca. 1900. 10 in. (RG 266)

Wedding entertainer (*badkhn*) in Radziechów, Kowel and Tarnopol, Galicia (Eastern Poland).

Badkhones materials used by Kessler. Includes rhymed wedding songs, bar mitzvah speeches, rhymed tombstone epitaphs, etc. A notebook recording Kessler's activities as a matchmaker. Letters from fellow *badkhonim*.

583. KESSLER, JOSEPH (1891–1979).
Papers, 1935–1979. 10 in. (RG 1001)

Born in Brichany. Emigrated to the United States in 1910. Served as president of the Britchaner Bessarabian Relief Association. Honorary president, Britchaner Relief in Israel. Chairman, Workmen's Circle Histadrut Division. Died in the Bronx, New York.

Financial papers. Correspondence with Britchaner Relief in Israel, 1950s–1960s. Souvenir journals of the Britchaner Bessarabian Relief, 1937–1941, 1946. Publications: Workmen's Circle Division of the National Committee for Labor Israel; United Organizations for Israel Histadrut. Photographs.

584. KHEVRE KOL AHAVAS KHAYIM.
Records, 1949–1970. 2 1/2 in. (RG 978)

Owned synagogue at 592 Marcy Street, Brooklyn, where the society met in the 1940s and 1950s. Provided members with funeral expenses. Contributed to charitable institutions.

Minutes, 1949–1960. Financial records, 1959–1970.

585. KHINOY, MARK (1884–1968).
Papers, ca. 1908–ca. 1962. 2 ft. 6 in. (RG 644)

Russian and Yiddish journalist. Russian revolutionary, member of the Menshevik Party. Contributed to the Russian socialist newspaper *Novyi Mir*, the Menshevik paper *Narodnaia Gazeta* (NY), *Svobodnaia Rossiia, Jewish Daily Forward, Veker, Zukunft, Sotsialicheskii vestnik* (NY). Born in the province of Chernigov, Ukraine. Emigrated to the United States in 1913.

Correspondence with individuals, ca.1908–ca.1962. Materials about individuals involved in the Russian revolutionary movement. Materials about Russian émigrés, the Menshevik party, *Narodnaia Gazeta*, Socialist Party (USA), Jewish Socialist Verband, *Jewish Daily Forward, Zukunft*, the Rand School. Personal materials.

586. KIELTZER SICK AND BENEVOLENT SOCIETY OF NEW YORK.
Records, 1927–1980. 2 1/2 in. (RG 1056)

Organized in New York in 1905 by immigrants from Kielce, Poland, as the Kieltzer Sick and Benevolent Society of Russian Poland, Inc. Maintained a loan fund for members. Provided housing for new arrivals. Associated with a ladies auxiliary, founded 1923, for charitable activity. Affiliated with the Kieltzer and Chenchiner Relief to aid *landslayt.* Changed to present name in 1954.

Constitution. Souvenir journals, 1927, 1980. Souvenir journals of the Kieltzer and Chenchiner Relief Committee, 1937, 1941. Publication by the Committee for the Resettlement of Kielcer Jews, 1946.

587. KILBERT, LEON.
Collection, ca. 1941–1945. 2 1/2 in. (RG 1204)

Historian of the Jewish community of Płock, Poland. Lives in New York.

Photocopies and some originals of documents from the Emanuel Ringelblum archives and other collections at the Jewish Historical Institute in Warsaw.

Manuscript by Icchok Bernstein on conditions in Warsaw ghetto, 1941–1943 (with English summary). Account by Symcha Guterman about the occupation of Płock by Nazis (Polish translation), 1981. Other materials concerning Płock and the Warsaw ghetto.

588. KIN, ABRAHAM (1883–1967).
Papers, 1940–1955. 2 ft. 5 in. (RG 554)

Yiddish writer, editor. Published the *Folks shtime* in Berditchev in 1913. Managing editor of the *Algemeyne entsiklopedye* (General Encyclopedia of Jewish Knowledge, in Yiddish), Paris, New York, 1934–1966. Co-editor of *Vitebsk amol* and editor of *Oyfn shvel*, the organ of the Freeland League. Born in Berditchev. Immigrated to the United States and lived in New York.

Materials on the Freeland League, on colonization projects in Australia, British Guiana: manuscripts, correspondence, reports, clippings. There are also materials on the *Algemeyne entsiklopedye*, 1942–1955, including correspondence and lists of contributors. Personal documents.

589. KINDER ZHURNAL and FARLAG MATONES.
Records, 1920s–1960s. 9 ft. 7 in. (RG 465)

Kinder zhurnal and Farlag Matones were both founded by the Sholem Aleichem Folk Institute, an organization established in New York in 1918 to coordinate a secular Yiddish school system. *Kinder zhurnal*, a children's magazine, was in existence from 1920 to 1981. Its first editor, Shmuel Niger, served from 1922 to 1948. The magazine published works by writers such as Mani Leib, Aleph Katz, Jacob Glatstein, Kadia Molodowsky. Farlag Matones was established in 1925 as a publisher of children's books but became a leading publisher of Yiddish literature and of such well-known authors as Menahem Boraisha, Jacob Glatstein, Chaim Grade, Moses (Moyshe) Leib Halpern, Leibush Lehrer, Isaac Bashevis Singer, Hillel Zeitlin, Aaron Zeitlin. Lippa Lehrer was the manager and leading figure of both organizations, and was editor of *Kinder zhurnal* for a number of years. The records of *Kinder zhurnal* and Farlag Matones were combined by Lippa Lehrer, and reflect primarily the years of his involvement.

Administrative reports, 1939–1960. Correspondence, minutes, clippings, bills, posters relating to the Anniversary Committee, 1932–1960. Correspondence, 1920s–1960s, with individuals and organizations, including Shalom Asch, Shlomo Bickel, Aaron Glanz-Leieles, Jacob Glatstein, Chaim Grade, H. Leivick, Shmuel Niger, Joseph Opatoshu, Lamed Shapiro, I.J. Singer, Isaac Bashevis Singer, Malka Heifetz Tussman, Max Weinreich, Aaron Zeitlin, Chaim Zhitlowsky.

Kinder zhurnal records: manuscripts of poems, plays, stories, songs and drawings. Authors include David Bridger, Bella Gottesman, Itzik Kipnis, Rivke Kope, Kadia Molodowsky, Mates Olitsky, Malka Heifetz Tussman.

Financial documents. An unpublished bibliography of Hillel Zeitlin's Yiddish articles. Inventory, English, Yiddish.

590. KIPILER YOUNG MEN'S BENEVOLENT ASSOCIATION.
Records, 1958–1972. 2 1/2 in. (RG 1044)

Organized in New York in 1925 by immigrants from Kopyl, Byelorussia. Supported institutions in the home town. Provided free loans for members.
Minutes, 1958–1972. Banner.

591. KIRSHENBLATT-GIMBLETT, BARBARA.
Collection, ca. 1900–1970s. 2 ft. 1 in. (RG 683)

Associate Professor of Folklore and Folklife, University of Pennsylvania. Chairman, Department of Performing Arts, New York University. Anthropologist, ethnographer. Member, teaching staff of Max Weinreich Center for Advanced Jewish Studies. Collector for YIVO. Editor, *Jewish Folklore and Ethnography* (NY). Grew up in Toronto, Canada. Settled in the United States.

The collection consists primarily of published folk and popular Jewish and Yiddish sheet music. Included are choral and orchestral arrangements, theater music, and some manuscripts of Jewish liturgical music. Miscellaneous music catalogs. Slides and text of a Bobover Purim play. Slides of the wedding of the daughter of Rabbi Ben-Zion Halberstam in Bobowa, Poland, in 1931. Manuscripts of papers submitted for courses in Jewish folkore, especially relating to Orthodox and Hasidic communities in Brooklyn.

Inventory, English

592. KLÁR, ZOLTAN.
Papers, 1944–1945. 10 in. (RG 346)

Hungarian Jew, physician, inmate of the Mauthausen concentration camp. Was in charge of Block 6 of the camp, designated as the "Jewish Hospital."

The collection consists of photostatic copies and carbon copies of documents relating to Dr. Klár's medical work in the Jewish hospital in Mauthausen. It includes medical records kept by Dr. Klár, and an affidavit and signed statements by Dr. Klár confirming authenticity of these records.

593. KLEIN, HENRY H. (ca. 1879–1955).
Papers, ca. 1910s–1950s. 2 ft. 11 in. (RG 856)

Lawyer, writer, distributor of antisemitic literature. Investigator for the City of New York in the 1920s. Published books, newspapers, and brochures on corruption and graft. Sought impeachment of Franklin D. Roosevelt and other political figures. Wrote anti-Zionist and antisemitic works about the threat of international Jewish influence.

Books, manuscripts, pamphlets, legal documents, correspondence, photographs, relating to Klein's life and career. Materials relate mainly to Klein's antisemitic and anti-Zionist activity and include: lawsuits against individuals and reprints of antisemitic articles from the *Dearborn Independent*, 1920s; reprints of the *Protocols of the Elders of Zion*; copies of H.H. Klein's *Weekly News*.

594. KLIGSBERG, MOSES (MOYSHE) (1902–1975).
Papers, 1930s–1974. 16 ft. (RG 719)

Author, sociologist, journalist. YIVO staff member. Active in the Bund party in Poland. Wrote for *Yugnt veker*, *Naye kultur*, *Foroys* (Warsaw), *Zukunft*, *YIVO bleter*. Editor, *YIVO News*. Conducted YIVO radio programs on WEVD. Secretary, United Jewish Survivors of Nazi Persecutions. Born in Warsaw. Came to the United States in 1941.

The papers relate to Kligsberg's scholarly interests and to his work at YIVO. Included are: Manuscripts relating to topics in Jewish sociology, psychology. Kligsberg's survey of the autobiographies of Jewish youth in Poland gathered by YIVO in the 1930s for a contest. Materials relating to the *YIVO News*, YIVO radio programs, YIVO contests. Materials relating to the collection of archival materials for the YIVO Archives. Materials on the Bund. Papers of Herman Kruk, librarian, archivist and diarist in the Vilna ghetto. Records of the United Jewish Survivors of Nazi Persecutions, 1946–1957.

595. KLING, BERTHA (1886–1978).
Papers, 1907–1978. 1 ft. 3 in. (RG 1171)

Yiddish poet. Contributed to periodicals including *Literarishe heftn*. Born in Nowogródek, Byelorussia. Came to the United States in 1899 and settled in New York.

Correspondence: Jacob Ben-Ami, Yitzhak Dov Berkowitz, Daniel Charney, Ben Zion Goldberg, Peretz Hirschbein, David Ignatoff, Szmerke Kaczerginski, Mani Leib, H. Leivick, Abraham Liessin, Itzik Manger, Ida Maze, Kadia Molodowsky, David Pinsky, Olga Rabinowitz (wife of Sholem Aleichem), Melech Ravitch, Maurice Samuel. Photographs of the Kling family, Sholem Aleichem family, and of Yiddish writers, such as Peretz Hirschbein, David Ignatoff, Itzik Manger, Mani Leib, Moshe Nadir. Woodcuts by Arthur Kolnik. Manuscripts of poems by Bertha Kling and Moses (Moyshe) Leib Halpern.

596. KLUB ZYRARDOW.
Records, 1909, 1920–1977. 2 1/2 in. (RG 801)

Organized in New York in 1963 by immigrants from Żyrardów, Poland, for the purpose of publishing a memorial book on Żyrardów. Activities included erecting a monument for Holocaust victims, and reconstruction and maintenance of the Jewish cemetery in Żyrardów.

Correspondence pertaining to *landslayt*, 1920s, 1952–1958; a *pinkas* (record book), 1963–1972; speeches; autobiographical materials; miscellaneous materials relating to the Żyrardów Branch 301, Workmen's Circle, and to the Żyrardów *landsmanshaft* in Israel.

597. KOBRIN, LEON (1872–1946).
Papers, 1898–1950. 7 ft. 1 in. (RG 376)

Yiddish playwright, novelist. Pioneer of Yiddish literature in America. Born in Vitebsk, Byelorussia. Came to the United States in 1892.

Manuscripts of Kobrin's plays, stories, memoirs and fragments of novels. Clippings of Kobrin's articles and about Kobrin, 1920s–1940s. Correspondence with individuals including Jacob P. Adler, S. Ansky, Shalom Asch, Abraham Cahan, Ossip Dymow, Ben Zion Goldberg, Jacob Gordin, Alexander Harkavy, Isaac A. Hourwich, Abraham Liessin, Kalman Marmor, Shmuel Niger, Maurice Schwartz, Boris Thomashefsky, Baruch Vladeck, Yehoash, Chaim Zhitlowsky.

Inventory, Yiddish, English.

598. KODIMA BENEVOLENT SOCIETY.
Records, 1935–1973. 10 in. (RG 864)

Incorporated in New York in 1929 and dissolved in 1973. Activities included the establishment of a ladies auxiliary.

Minutes, 1959–1973. Financial records, 1940s–1970s. Membership records, 1966–1970. Correspondence, 1950s–1970s. Burial permits, 1935–1971. Seal, stamp.

599. KOLBUSZOWA RELIEF ASSOCIATION.
Records, 1919–1967. 8 in. (RG 888)

Organized in New York after World War I by members of the Kolbuszower Young Men's Benevolent Society to aid inhabitants of Kolbuszowa, Poland. Was active in the 1930s. Incorporated in 1942. Erected a monument to Holocaust victims. Sent packages to *landslayt* in Poland and Israel. Affiliated organizations included: Kolbuszower Y.M.B.S.; Kolbuszower Chevrah Bnei Chaim Machnei Reuben, Kolbushover Teitelbaum Wallach Lodge No. 93, Independent Order Brith Abraham.

Certificate of incorporation, 1942. Constitution. Minutes, 1946–1948. Financial records, 1940s, 1960s. Publications and journals, 1930s–1940s. Materials from Kolbuszowa. Photographs. Memorial book, 1971. Materials of the Kolbuszower Teitelbaum Ferbriderungs Ferayn Congregation, 1913, and the Kolbushover Teitelbaum Wallach Lodge No. 98, I.O.B.A.

600. KOLBUSZOWER YOUNG MEN'S BENEVOLENT SOCIETY.
Records, 1919–1974. 8 in. (RG 957)

Organized in New York in 1899 by immigrants from Kolbuszowa, Poland. Members organized the Kolbuszowa Relief Association after World War I. Aided Kolbuszowa and Jewish charities in America.

Constitution. Minutes, 1953–1974. Anniversary journals, 1919–1949.

601. KOLOMEAR FRIENDS ASSOCIATION.
Records, 1906–1973. 1 ft. 8 in. (RG 792)

Originally organized in New York in 1904 by immigrants from Kolomyya (Pol. Kołomyja), Ukraine, for the purpose of founding a synagogue. Also called Tsvishn (Among) Kolomear Young Friends. Formed the United Kolomear Relief during World War I and the Refugee Committee during World War II.

Constitutions. Minutes, 1939–1954. Financial documents, 1953–1972. Membership ledger. Application forms, 1907–1956. Membership books pertaining to illness, sick and death benefits, 1933–1967. Journal, 1929. Memorial book, 1957. Photographs.

602. KON, HENECH (1890–1972).
Papers, 1956–1968. 2 in. (RG 1102)

Composer for the Yiddish theater, journalist. Composed music for theatrical works by H. Leivick, S. Ansky, as well as for poems by Isaac Leib Peretz. Arranged Yiddish songs and edited albums of songbooks. Contributed articles on music in periodicals such as *Literarishe bleter*, *Jewish Daily Forward*, *Yung-yidish*. Born in Łódź, Poland. Immigrated to the United States in 1940.

Letters, clippings, poems, programs, and sheet music.

603. KOPE, RIVKA (1910–1995).
Papers, 1960s–1980s. 5 in. (RG 1176)

Yiddish poet, short-story writer. Pen name of Rivka Kopelovitch. Contributed to *Naye prese*

(Paris), *Undzer vort* (Paris), *Freie Arbeiter Stimme, Zukunft*. Born in Warsaw. Immigrated to Paris, France, in 1931.

The collection consists of correspondence with Yiddish writers and cultural figures. Included are Shlomo Bickel, Malka Lee, Melech Ravitch, Malka Heifetz Tussman, Rashel Weprinsky, Hinde (Anna) Zaretski.

604. KOPISTER BENEVOLENT ASSOCIATION.
Records, 1951–1976. 2 1/2 in. (RG 943)

Organized in New York in 1905 by immigrants from Kopisty, Czechoslovakia. Benefits included wedding and *shiva* (seven-day mourning period) funds. Also held lectures. Aided home town in early years. Dissolved 1976.

Minutes, 1951–1976. Financial records.

605. KORENCHANDLER, YEKHEZKEL (1899–).
Papers, 1929–1975. 10 in. (RG 444)

Yiddish writer. Lived in Poland. Settled in Paris, France.

Correspondence with Yiddish literary figures. Miscellaneous materials on Jewish cultural life in France.

606. KORMAN, EZRA (born 1888).
Papers, 1926–1959. 5 in. (RG 457)

Yiddish writer. Active in Yiddish cultural life in Detroit. Born in Kiev, Russia. Immigrated to the United States in the 1920s and settled in Detroit.

Correspondence with Yiddish literary figures including Shlomo Bickel, Menahem Boraisha, Daniel Charney, Rachel Korn, Malka Lee, H. Leivick, Kadia Molodowsky, Joseph Opatoshu, Melech Ravitch, Joseph Rolnick, Isaac Nachman Steinberg.

607. KORMAN, NATHAN DAVID (1901–1981).
Papers, 1953–1972. 7 1/2 in. (RG 673)

Yiddish writer, poet. Contributed to many periodicals including *Radomer vokhnblat, Morgn frayhayt, Der hamer, Yidishe kultur*. Born in Radom, Poland. Immigrated to the United States in 1927, settling in Philadelphia.

The collection of letters includes correspondence with Chaim Barkan, Symcha Lev, Louis Miller, Paul Novick, Isaac Rontch, Moses Schulstein.

608. KOROSTISHEVER AID SOCIETY.
Records, 1920–1953. 2 1/2 in. (RG 791)

Founded in Detroit, Michigan, in 1920 after a conference held there to unite American Korostishever *landslayt* to aid residents of their home town, Korostyshev, Ukraine. Affiliated with the Relief Committee for War and Pogrom Sufferers of Korostishev (United Korostitchev Relief). Established a ladies auxiliary, ca. 1930.

Anniversary journal, 1950, including membership directories for New York, Chicago, Detroit, and Los Angeles *landsmanshaftn*.

609. KOSICE AND VICINITY CHAPTER 59, BNAI ZION.
    Records, 1966–1978. 1 in. (RG 790)

Founded in New York in 1952 by immigrants from Košice, Czechoslovakia, for philanthropic purposes and to locate survivors from Košice. Affiliate of the Zionist fraternal organization Bnai Zion.
    Correspondence, 1976–1978. Bulletins, invitations, 1966–1977. Personal documents. Photographs.

610. KOSSUTH ASSOCIATION OF NEW YORK.
    Records, 1930–1971. 6 in. (RG 906)

Founded in 1904 by Hungarian-Jewish immigrants. Society originally called Kossuth Ferencz Literary Sick and Benevolent Association and was named after the son of Lajos Kossuth, president of the Hungarian Party of Independence. Incorporated in 1934.
    Financial records, 1947–1971. Anniversary journals, 1930, 1939, 1954 (Hungarian, English).

611. KOVENSKY, MAXIM.
    Papers, 1906–1913. 10 in. (RG 774)

Member of the Socialist Revolutionary Party (S-R), Russia.
    Materials on the Socialist Revolutionary Party in Russia including flyers, appeals, clippings from the Russian and Yiddish press.

612. KRAJEWSKA, MONIKA (1948–).
    Papers, 1976–1980s. 7 1/2 in. (RG 1137)

Folklorist, photographer. Specialist in Jewish funerary art in Poland. Together with husband Stanislaw Krajewski, conducted many expeditions throughout Poland and discovered old Jewish cemeteries and tombstones, most of them in disuse. Studied and photographed engravings on tombstones. Krajewska's photographs were shown in an exhibition in Poland titled *A Time of Stones*. She authored a book by the same title. In 1984, an exhibit of her photographs titled *Traces in the Landscape* was organized by the YIVO Institute in New York. Lives in Warsaw, Poland.
    The collection consists of photographs by Monika Krajewska of Jewish cemeteries and synagogues in Poland. An article by Krajewska on the subject of Jewish funerary art is included.

613. KREIN, MARY (1891–1980).
    Papers, 1959–1973. 4 in. (RG 1104)

Poet. Active in the Workmen's Circle and other Yiddish cultural groups. Born in Russia. Immigrated to the United States.
    The papers include a record book of Workmen's Circle Branch 968, 1959–1973. School programs of Workmen's Circle schools in the 1960s. A record book of the Yiddish Culture Club in Brooklyn. Correspondence. Manuscripts of poems. Photograph of Mary Krein.

614. KREINER, MORRIS LEIB (1908–1990).
      Papers, 1925–1984. 4 ft. 7 in. (RG 1283)

A native of Sighet, Rumania, active in Sighet fraternal associations in New York, including the Sighet-Maramaros Young Men's Society, Sighet-Maramaros Federation, Congregation Anshe Sfard (Queens). Shop chairman of Local 35 of the ILGWU. Came to the United States in 1933. Lived in New York.

Ledgers, minutes, photographs, circulars, speeches, printed materials from Sighet *landsmanshaftn* in the United States and in Israel. Included are records pertaining to special projects such as the memorial book, a memorial building in Tel Aviv, a loan fund. Minutes, sermons, photographs, and other materials relating to the Congregation Anshe Sfard in Queens, and to the Congregation Anshe Maramaros on the Lower East Side. Minutes and other materials of Local 35 of the ILGWU. Personal papers: photographs of the Kreiner family, the city of Sighet; letters from Shimon Orenstein, Eli Wiesel, S. Gross (member of the Israeli Knesset); manuscripts of philosophical essays and talks. Poems, in Yiddish, by Bella Jacobowitz, Kreiner's cousin. Bulletins of the Sun and Surf Senior Citizens' Club in Coney Island.

615. KREITMAN, ESTHER (1891–1954).
      Papers, 1930s–1940s. 2 in. (RG 341)

Short-story writer, novelist. Sister of Israel Joshua Singer and of Isaac Bashevis Singer. Contributed to *Dos fraye vort* (London), *Whitechapel lebt, Loshn un lebn*. Born in Biłgoraj. Lived in Warsaw, Antwerp, Paris, London.

The collection consists of correspondence with individuals, including Joseph Opatoshu, Isaac Bashevis Singer, Baruch Vladeck, Stephen Wise.

616. KREITZBERG, YASHA.
      Papers. 5 ft. (RG 878)

Jewish composer.

The papers consist, for the most part, of sheet music, including theater music, both printed and manuscript. There are also some personal documents.

617. KREITZBURGER JACOBSTADTER BENEVOLENT ASSOCIATION.
      Records, 1921–1977. 7 1/2 in. (RG 944)

Founded in New York in 1918 by immigrants from Krustpils, Latvia. Dissolved 1977.

Minutes, 1942–1976. Financial records, 1951–1977. Membership records. Sick-benefit and cemetery materials. Correspondence.

618. KREMENITZER WOLYNER BENEVOLENT ASSOCIATION.
      Records, 1935–1977. 8 in. (RG 788)

Founded in New York in 1915 by immigrants from Kremenets (Pol. Krzemieniec), Ukraine. Formed a relief committee during World War I. Built a library in Israel after World War II.

Constitution. Minutes, 1967–1974. Financial records, 1946–1958. Correspondence. Anniversary journals. Periodical published by Kremenitzer *landslayt* in Israel. Memorial books, 1954, 1965.

619. KREMENTCHUGER LADIES BENEVOLENT ASSOCIATION.
Records, 1914, 1939–1977. 10 in. (RG 1087)

Established in New York in 1900 by immigrants from Kremenchug, Ukraine, and incorporated in 1914 as the Ladies Krementchuger Benevolent Association (also known as the First Ladies Krementschuger Benevolent Association). Provided burial services. Supported philanthropic institutions.

Certificate of incorporation, 1914. Minutes, 1960–1976. Financial records, 1940s–1970s. Membership directory. Correspondence. Cemetery map.

620. KRIVOZER FRATERNAL SOCIETY OF GREATER NEW YORK.
Records, 1927–1961. 5 in. (RG 912)

Formed in New York in 1918 by immigrants from Krivoye Ozero, Ukraine, to send a *landsman* to California for tuberculosis treatment. Later expanded activities to include mutual aid for members. Between the two world wars conducted extensive relief and refugee relocation work. In addition, the society supported a farm established by Krivozer Jews on land alloted by the Soviet government. Recent activities include aid to institutions in Israel. Affiliated groups were: Krivozer Beneficial Association of Philadelphia; Independent Krivozer Ladies Auxiliary (established 1927); committees in Chicago, Boston, Lawrence (Massachusetts), St. Paul (Minnesota), Canada.

Minutes, 1933–1947. Financial records, 1950s–1960s. Anniversary journal.

621. KROKER BENEVOLENT ASSOCIATION.
Records, 1899, 1910–1977. 5 in. (RG 789)

Founded in New York in 1908 by immigrants from Krakės (Yid. Krok), Lithuania. Formed a relief committee during World War I.

Minutes, 1910, 1916, 1938. Financial records. Membership records. Chart of members' cemetery plots, 1931–1968. Announcements, speeches, invitations, some in rhyme form, 1910–1977. Photographs. Miscellaneous documents from Krakės and the United States.

622. KROTOSZYN JEWISH COMMUNITY COUNCIL.
Records, 1828–1919. 2 ft. 6 in. (RG 14)

The Polish town of Krotoszyn (province of Poznań, Western Poland) was annexed by Prussia following the partition of Poland in 1793. The Jewish community of Krotoszyn had been in existence since the 14th century and was known for its participation in Jewish affairs in Poland, notably its representation in the Council of the Four Lands. Under Prussian domination the community became Germanized. Toward the end of the 19th century there was a decline in the Jewish population and by 1918, when Krotoszyn was returned to Poland, the Jewish community had ceased to exist.

YIVO holds only part of the Krotoszyn communal archives. Another portion was sent ca. 1910 to the Gesamtarchiv der Deutschen Juden in Berlin. The fate of this group of documents is unknown.

These are primarily records of the Jewish communal administration. Correspondence, minutes, reports, financial records and other documents relating to community life under Prussian rule. Correspondence with the government mainly about taxation and communal administration. Correspondence with regimental commanders of the Prussian army regarding

Jewish soldiers from the Krotoszyn area. Correspondence, statutes, lists of members, financial records of charity societies. Materials on the distribution of goods among the poor. Documents relating to appointment of religious functionaries. Records of sale of synagogue seats. Reports and other materials from the religious school. Records of marriages and deaths.

Inventory, English.

623. KRULL, CHAIM (1892–1946).
Papers, 1922–1940s. 5 in. (RG 382)

Yiddish poet. Born in Łódź, Poland. Immigrated to the United States in 1922.

Correspondence with Yiddish cultural and literary figures, including David Bergelson, David Ignatoff, Mani Leib, H. Leivick, Abraham Liessin, Kalman Marmor, Shmuel Niger, Baruch Vladeck.

624. KUDRYNCER BENEVOLENT SOCIETY.
Records, 1940–1978. 7 1/2 in. (RG 787)

Organized in New York in 1900 by immigrants from Kudrintsy (Kudryńce), Ukraine, as the Independent First Kudryncer Congregation Sick and Aid Society. Maintained a loan fund and a synagogue on Houston Street, New York.

Constitution. Minutes, 1943–1969. Souvenir journal, 1955. Correspondence, 1978. Newspaper clippings. Wooden ballot box.

625. KUPERSTEIN, ISAIAH (1950–).
Papers, 1940–1974. 5 in. (RG 697)

Historian. Director of the Education Department of the Holocaust Memorial Museum, Washington, D.C.

The papers pertain to the experiences of David Gertler, a functionary of the Jewish administration in the Łódź ghetto. Gertler was head of the *Sonderabteilung* (Special Unit) which performed the function of secret police in the ghetto. He was deported to the Auschwitz concentration camp in 1944.

Recorded interview with Gertler by I. Kuperstein. Kuperstein's observations and evaluation of the interview, 1974. Proceedings of the Court of Honor of the Jewish Rehabilitation Commission against Gertler, 1948, including reports of witnesses. Correspondence of Gertler. Summary report of the trial of the former Gestapo officials in Łódź, Fuchs and Bradfisch, at which Gertler was a witness.

626. KUPINER-PODOLIER MEMORIAL COMMITTEE.
Records, 1939–1979. 1 in. (RG 1058)

Since 1960 the Committee has held annual memorial meetings for inhabitants of Kupin, Ukraine, who were killed during World War II.

Minutes, 1960–1977, of the Monish Kupersmith Kupiner Circle, 1939–1947. Minutes of the Kupiner Podolier Branch 329 Workmen's Circle, 1945. Short history of Kupin.

627. KURSKY, FRANZ (1876–1950).
Papers, 1939–1942. 5 in. (RG 226)

Historian. Leader of the Jewish Labor Bund, founder and director of the Bund Archives. Lived in Russia, Switzerland.

Correspondence, materials relating to the Victor Alter–Henryk Erlich affair (leaders of the Bund party in Poland, executed in the Soviet Union in 1941).

628. KURTZ, AARON SAMUEL (1891–1964).
Papers, 1920–1964. 4 ft. 7 in. (RG 523)

Yiddish poet, editor and lecturer. Published in *Di yidishe velt* (Philadelphia), *In zikh* (NY), *Naye lebn* (NY), *Der tsvayg* (Philadelphia), *Hayntike lider* (NY) and in communist periodicals such as *Der hamer*, *Morgn frayhayt* (NY), *Sovetish heymland* (Moscow). Born in Vitebsk district, Byelorussia. Immigrated to the United States in 1911 and lived in Philadelphia and New York.

Correspondence with Jewish writers. Clippings from Yiddish newspapers. Manuscripts by Kurtz. Photographs of Solomon Mikhoels and Itsik Feffer during their trip to the United States during World War II on behalf of the Jewish Anti-Fascist Committee in the Soviet Union.

629. KUSSMAN, LEON (1884–1974).
Papers, 1906–1973. 1 ft. 10 in. (RG 745)

Poet, short-story writer, playwright, teacher. Contributed to *Yiddishes Tageblatt*, *Varhayt*, *Dos naye land*, *Freie Arbeiter Stimme*, *Der groyser kundes*, *Der amerikaner*. For many years was on the staff of *Morgn zhurnal*. Born near Mitava, Latvia. Moved to London in 1911 and immigrated to the United States in 1913.

The collection includes correspondence, manuscripts, published essays and articles, clippings and photographs relating to L. Kussman's literary career.

630. KUTNO SOCIETY BNAI JACOB.
Records, 1884–1974. 10 in. (RG 857)

Organized in New York in 1872 by immigrants from Kutno, Poland. Activities included support of Hebrew Immigrant Aid Society (HIAS) and institutions in Israel. Dissolved 1974.

Minutes, 1953–1974; financial records, 1946–74; burial permits, 1884–1974; cemetery map; seals.

631. LABOR ZIONIST ALLIANCE.
Records, 1963–1988. 16 ft. 4 in. (RG 1254)

Established in 1912 under the name Farband—Labor Zionist Order (Yidisher Natsyonaler Arbeter Farband) as an educational and mutual benefit fraternal organization. Its leaders included Issachar Bontchek, Boruch Zukerman, David Pinsky, Hayyim Greenberg, Joseph Schlossberg, Jacob Katzman. Maintained a network of secular Yiddish and Hebrew schools, cultural centers, summer camps. Published periodicals *Yidisher kemfer* and *Jewish Frontier*. Also known as the Jewish National Workers Alliance.

Correspondence, minutes, publicity materials, photographs relating to activities of the Alliance and of its parent organization, the Labor Zionist Organization of America.

632. LABOR ZIONIST ORGANIZATION OF AMERICA.
Records, 1904–1967. 126 microfilm reels and 66 ft. 3 in. (RG 606)

U.S. branch of the Socialist Zionist Party, Poalei Zion, founded in 1905 at a convention in Baltimore. In 1907 the LZOA joined Poalei Zion parties from other countries to form IHUD—World Confederation Poalei Zion. In 1912 the LZOA founded a fraternal order, the Jewish National Workers Alliance (known also as Farband-Labor Zionist Order). In the 1920s the LZOA organized the Histadrut campaign and the women's socialist Zionist organization Pioneer Women. In 1935 Habonim was organized as the youth division of LZOA. LZOA is a member of the World Zionist Organization. It publishes *Yidisher kemfer* (from 1906) and *Jewish Frontier* (from 1934).

Correspondence, reports, minutes, proceedings and other materials of the LZOA National Conventions, Executive Committee, other lay committees and administrative departments relating to all LZOA organizational activities and to the political and ideological issues of the Labor Zionist movement. The records consist of the following series: general correspondence arranged in chronological or name/subject files; correspondence with LZOA branches and members (geographic files); Pioneer Women files, 1913–1952; Farband Yiddish schools files, 1911–1947; Habonim and Young Poalei-Zion files, 1914–1954. Included is correspondence with Zionist organizations, Israeli political parties, United Jewish Appeal, Jewish Education Committee, Jewish Welfare Board, Jewish National Fund, Jewish Agency, American Jewish Committee.

633. LADIES AND MEN'S SOCIETY OF KONIN.
Records, 1959–1985. 1 in. (RG 1221)

Established by immigrants from Konin, Poland, in New York in 1923.

Correspondence. Various flyers and circulars concerning fundraising drives and memorial meetings. Lists of members and addresses.

634. LADY McKINLEY BENEVOLENT SOCIETY.
Records, 1907, 1936–1972. 2 1/2 in. (RG 952)

Organized in 1901. Also known as Lady McKinley Lodge. Dissolved 1972.

Financial records. Cemetery permits. Correspondence.

635. LAHISHINER LADIES AUXILIARY.
Records, 1942–1980. 5 in. (RG 896)

Founded in New York in 1935 by immigrants from Logishin (Pol. Lohiszyn), Byelorussia, for social and charitable purposes by thirteen women at a meeting of the Lahishin Social Benevolent Society, the brother group. Since 1945 supported children in an orphanage in Israel. Dissolved 1980.

Minutes, 1965–1977. Financial records, 1950s–1970s. Materials pertaining to relief and charitable work. Meeting announcements, 1948–1980. Gavels. Stamp. Materials of the Lahishin Social Benevolent Society.

636. LAIKIN, BENJAMIN.
Papers, 1940s–1978. 2 ft. 1 in. (RG 605)

Collector for YIVO. Detroit, Michigan.

The collection consists of correspondence, circulars, invitations, newsletters, relating to the Jewish community of Detroit. Organizations include the Jewish Community Council of Detroit, Jewish Teachers Seminary and Jewish Welfare Federation of Detroit. Correspondence of B.M. Laikin with Jewish writers: B.I. Bialostotzky, Menahem Boraisha, David Ignatoff, N.B. Minkoff, I.J. Schwartz, Abraham Twersky.

637. LAKE, GOLDIE.
Papers, 1980–1982. 5 in. (RG 1124)

Jewish playwright, teacher, film producer, community worker. Cleveland, Ohio.

Interviews conducted by Goldie Lake and Carole Kantor about Jewish immigrant family life. Mimeographed copy of Goldie Lake's play *Many Small Worlds*, as well as reviews, programs and clippings pertaining to the play.

638. LAMPEL, LOUIS (1904–1965).
Papers. 5 in. (RG 821)

Yiddish writer. Contributed to periodicals such as *Frayhayt* (NY), *Kalifornyer yidishe shtime* (Los Angeles), *Hamer, Spartak, Feder*. Born in Kańczuga, near Przemyśl, Poland. Immigrated to the United States in 1920.

Typescripts of novels, short stories and poetry. Biographical material. Photograph of Lampel.

639. LAMPORT, ARTHUR.
Papers, 1939–1940. 2 1/2 in. (RG 687)

Banker, philanthropist. Active in plans to arrange resettlement of European Jewish refugees in the Dominican Republic, 1939–1940.

The collection relates to Lamport's efforts to resettle Jewish refugees. Minutes of meetings and memoranda. Plans for resettlement of refugees. Statistics on the Dominican Republic. Correspondence with: James N. Rosenberg; the government of the Dominican Republic; the Dominican Republic Settlement Association (DORSA). Agreement between the Dominican Republic and DORSA, January 1940.

640. LANDAU, REYZL (born 1892).
Papers, 1911–1950s. 2 in. (RG 588)

Yiddish poet. Contributed to *Kinder zhurnal* (NY), *Yidisher kemfer* (NY), *Keneder odler* (Montreal). Wife of the poet Zishe Landau. Born in Mozyr, Byelorussia. Moved to the United States in 1906.

The collection includes: correspondence with the actor Menashe Oppenheim, 1950s; letters from R. Landau's husband, Zishe Landau, 1911; typescripts of Zishe Landau's poems.

641. LANDSMANSHAFTN.
Collection, 1905–1980. 15 ft. (RG 123)

This subject collection has been formed to house fragmentary records of Jewish benevolent societies and federations known under the name of *landsmanshaftn*. These mutual aid societies were established by immigrants usually, but not exclusively, from the same villages, towns and cities in Eastern Europe.

The collection contains materials pertaining to over 500 *landsmanshaftn*. Included are charters, certificates of incorporation, constitutions, minutes, financial records, membership records, burial records, publications, clippings.

This collection is cataloged in Appendix II to *A Guide to YIVO's Landsmanshaftn Archive* by Rosaline Schwartz and Susan Milamed, YIVO, New York, 1986.

642. LANG, HARRY and ROBBINS, LUCY .
Papers, 1921–1968. 15 in. (RG 1250)

Harry Lang (1888–1970), Yiddish writer and journalist, was active in the labor and socialist movements. Contributed to the *Zukunft*, *Yidisher kemfer*, *Der veker*, *Jewish Daily Forward*. In the 1920s and 1930s traveled to Eastern Europe, the Soviet Union and Palestine, and published a series of articles about the Jewish communities there. Wrote plays for the Yiddish stage. Born in Skuodas, Lithuania. Immigrated to the United States in 1904.

Lucy Robbins Lang was Harry Lang's wife. She wrote an extensive autobiography and co-authored several Yiddish plays with her husband. Was active in labor and socialist organizations.

Typescripts of Lucy Robbins Lang's autobiography (over 2,000 pages), particularly emphasizing her involvement in the radical movements. Typescripts of Yiddish plays by the Langs. Scrapbook of articles from the *Jewish Daily Forward* by and about Eliahu Tenenholtz, a Yiddish actor and writer.

643. LAPIN, BERL (1889–1952).
Papers, 1909–1954. 1 ft. 3 in. (RG 423)

Yiddish poet, translator, journalist. Born near Wołkowysk, Poland. Lived in Poland, Argentina, the United States.

Correspondence with writers including Menahem Boraisha, Aaron Glanz-Leieles,. Jacob Glatstein, Chaim Grade, Peretz Hirschbein, David Ignatoff, H. Leivick, Kalman Marmor, Isaac Leib Peretz, David Pinsky, Melech Ravitch, Abraham Reisen, Isaac Nachman Steinberg, Chaim Zhitlowsky. Family correspondence. Clippings of articles by and about Lapin. Manuscripts of Lapin's Yiddish translations of Shakespeare's sonnets.

644. LATICHEVER PROGRESSIVE SOCIETY.
Records, 1939–1975. 7 1/2 in. (RG 897)

Incorporated in New York in 1924 by immigrants from Letichev, Ukraine. Acquired title to cemetery lot in Montefiore Cemetery from the surviving trustees of the First Latichever Lodge No. 224, Independent Order Brith Sholom, 1926. Maintained a loan fund. Dissolved 1979.

Financial records, 1950s–1970s. Membership lists. Correspondence, 1939–1976. Materials pertaining to burial.

645. LEAH BENEVOLENT SOCIETY.
Records, 1924–1967. 7 1/2 in. (RG 929)

A women's society established in the 1880s to provide sick benefits, death benefits, burial for members. Dissolved after 1967.

Financial records, 1920s–1950s. Cemetery permits.

646. LEAVITT, EZEKIEL (1878–1945).
Papers, 1890–1945. ca. 3 ft. (RG 218)

Conservative rabbi, teacher, principal, newspaper editor, author and lecturer. New York City.

Correspondence from individuals: Cyrus Adler, Joseph Barondess, Hayyim Nahman Bialik, Louis D. Brandeis, Alexander Harkavy, Mordecai Kaplan, Judah L. Magnes, Max Nordau, David de Sola Pool, Solomon Schechter, Abba Hillel Silver, Upton Sinclair, Israel Joshua Singer, Henrietta Szold, Stephen S. Wise. Correspondence from organizations. Personal documents. Manuscripts of Leavitt's writings. Photographs of friends and relatives.

Inventory, English.

647. LECHOWITZER LADIES AUXILIARY.
Records, 1946–1961. 3 in. (RG 990)

Founded in New York in 1934 by immigrants from Lyakhovichi (Pol. Lachowicze), Byelorussia, to raise funds to support the home town as well as charities in New York and to arrange social functions. Affiliated with the Congregation Bnai Isaac Anshei Lechowitz, established 1889. Met in the congregation's building at 217 Henry Street, New York.

Minutes, 1952–1960. Financial records, 1947–1956. Meeting announcements, including notices of Congregation Anshei Lechowitz.

648. LEE, MALKA (1904–1977).
Papers, 1916–1964. 6 ft. 8 in. (RG 367)

Pseudonym of Malka Leopold-Rappaport. Yiddish poet. Born in Poland. Emigrated to the United States in 1921.

Several hundred letters from Yiddish literary, artistic and cultural figures including Menahem Boraisha, Marc Chagall, Daniel Charney, Solomon Dingol, Aaron Glanz-Leieles, David Ignatoff, Leon Kobrin, H. Leivick, Itzik Manger, Kalman Marmor, Jacob Mestel, Kadia Molodowsky, Shmuel Niger, Joseph Opatoshu, Melech Ravitch, Abraham Reisen, Maurice Schwartz, Zalman Shneur, Abraham Sutzkever.

Manuscripts of Malka Lee's works. Clippings. Family photograph. Yiddish manuscripts of Malka Lee's husband, Aaron B. Rappaport.

649. LEHRER, DAVID (1898–1973).
Papers, 1940–1970. 5 in. (RG 664)

Yiddish journalist. Contributed to *Folkstsaytung* (Warsaw), *Literarishe bleter, Belgishe bleter, Parizer haynt, Der tog, Zukunft.* A staff member of the YIVO–Yad Vashem Documentary Projects in the 1950s. Born in Warsaw. In 1921 left Poland for Berlin, settling in Belgium in 1922. Came to the United States in 1941.

The papers consist of notes and clippings relating to antisemitism, Nazism, Jewish situation in Europe before and during World War II.

650. LEHRER, LEIBUSH (1887–1964).
Papers, ca. 1908–1968. 8 ft. 9 in. (RG 507)

Yiddish educator, scholar, writer. Co-founder of the Sholem Aleichem Folk Institute and the

American branch of the YIVO Institute. Founder and director of Camp Boiberik, Rhinebeck, NY. Secretary of the Psychological-Pedagogical section of YIVO. Contributed to numerous Yiddish and English publications including *Der Yidisher kemfer*, *Freie Arbeiter Stimme* (NY), *Kultur un dertsiung* (NY), *Literarishe bleter* (NY), *Jewish Frontier* (NY), *Jewish Social Studies* (NY).

Correspondence with brothers David and Lippa and other family members, 1907–1964. Correspondence with individuals including Ephraim Auerbach, Menahem Boraisha, Joshua Fishman, Jacob Glatstein, Aaron Glanz-Leieles, Abraham Golomb, Oscar Handlin, David Ignatoff, Zelig Kalmanovitch, Mordechai Kaplan, H. Leivick, Shmuel Niger, Melech Ravitch, A.A. Roback, Jacob Shatzky, Israel Steinbaum, Salomon Suskovich, Abraham Sutzkever, Yokhanan Twersky, Max Weinreich, Aaron Zeitlin.

Correspondence with organizations, including the YIVO Institute. Materials relating to YIVO–Yad Vashem Documentary Projects. Manuscripts of poetry, drama, fiction, essays. Translations, speeches and lectures. Miscellaneous pedagogical materials. Materials relating to Camp Boiberik. Research materials such as questionnaires, statistics, correspondence and reports on various topics including reactions to the Eichmann trial. Personal materials. Clippings of articles by and about Lehrer.

Inventory, English, Yiddish.

651. LEHRER, LIPPA (1890–1963).
Papers, 1920s–1960s. 10 in. (RG 459)

Founder of Farlag Matones and editor of *Kinder zhurnal*. Active in the Sholem Aleichem Folk Institute in New York. Born in Warsaw, Poland. Emigrated to the United States in 1913 and settled in New York.

Correspondence with Yiddish literary figures such as Jacob Adler, Chaim Grade, Moses (Moyshe) Leib Halpern, Mani Leib, H. Leivick, Itzik Manger, Noach Nachbush, Shmuel Niger, Maurice Schwartz, Abraham Sutzkever, Aaron Zeitlin.

652. LEIBOWITZ, ESTHER (?–1988).
Papers, ca. 1942–ca. 1983. 3 ft. 9 in. (RG 1246)

Fundraiser, radio personality. Founder and president of the Zion Dov Ber Torah Fund. Hosted a radio program on WEVD in New York to raise funds for a yeshiva in Mea Shearim. Born in Jerusalem. Immigrated to the United States ca. 1916.

The papers relate to Leibowitz's fund raising activities on behalf of the Zion Dov Ber Torah Fund and to her radio show on WEVD. Included are radio scripts, correspondence from listeners, manuscripts of articles and speeches by Leibowitz.

Recordings of radio programs were removed to the Sound Archives and cataloged in the Collection of Recorded Radio Programs.

653. LEIVICK, H. (HALPER) (1888–1962).
Papers, ca. 1914–1959. ca. 29 ft. (RG 315)

Pen name of Leivick Halpern. Major Yiddish writer, poet, playwright. Active in the Bund in Russia, he was arrested twice, the second time in 1906. Exiled to Siberia for life, Leivick succeeded in escaping and arrived in the United States in 1913. His numerous dramas and lyrical poems deal primarily with the theme of human suffering. Editor of *Zamlbikher* and *Zukunft*. Member of the first YIVO Executive Board in the United States, 1941. Born in Igumen, Byelorussia. Settled in the United States in 1913.

Manuscripts of Leivick's plays including *Der golem* (The Golem), *Der nes fun geto* (The Miracle of the Ghetto). Manuscripts of poems, articles and speeches. Manuscripts of other writers collected by Leivick as editor of *Zamelbikher* and *Zukunft*. Correspondence and other materials from schools, libraries, cultural and political organizations and theaters. Correspondence with about 2,000 individuals, among them: B. Alkwit, Ben-Adir, Jacob Ben-Ami, David Bergelson, Samuel Bugatch, Joseph Buloff, Ossip Dymow, Michl Gelbart, Baruch (Boris) Glassman, Ben Zion Goldberg, Abraham Golomb, Abba Gordin, Chaim Grade, Moses (Moyshe) Leib Halpern, Peretz Hirschbein, Reuben Iceland, David Ignatoff, Franz Kursky, Joseph Opatoshu, David Pinsky, Jacob Shatzky, Max Weinreich, Stephen Wise. Family correspondence. Clippings: reviews of plays. Photographs of Leivick's family, of performances of Leivick's plays.

Inventory, Yiddish.

654. LEKSIKON FUN DER NAYER YIDISHER LITERATUR.
Records, 1920s–1960s. 10 in. (RG 1150)

English title: *Biographical Dictionary of Modern Yiddish Literature*, New York, 1956–1981, 8 volumes, published by the Congress for Jewish Culture. Editors included Shmuel Niger, Jacob Shatzky, Berl Kagan, Elias Schulman, Israel Knox, Ephraim Auerbach, Moshe Starkman. The lexicon consists of biographical entries on Yiddish writers in print.

The records include correspondence with writers and autobiographies submitted to the lexicon. Included are autobiographies which were not accepted for publication.

655. LENSKY, LEIB (1909–1991).
Papers, ca. 1930–1991. 5 ft. (RG 1297)

Yiddish actor and lexicographer. From 1930 until 1946 lived in France where he performed in the Yiddish theaters in Paris. Also performed in Jean Renoir's film *La Grande Illusion*. In the United States he acted mostly for English-language theaters, film, television, advertising. Performed on the Hebrew stage in the United States and in Israel. Staff member of the *Groyser verterbukh fun der yidisher shprakh* (Great Dictionary of the Yiddish Language). Born in Poland. Died in New York.

Programs, photographs, film stills, clippings, relating to Lensky's career. Materials about the Yiddish theater in Paris. Film and stage scripts including adaptations from Yiddish literature made by Lensky.

656. LERER, SHIFRA and WITLER, BEN-ZION (1905–1961).
Papers, 1930s–1961. 5 ft. (RG 671)

Shifra Lerer: Yiddish actress and singer, wife of Ben-Zion Witler.

Ben-Zion Witler: Yiddish actor. Was a member of various theater companies and performed in England, France, the United States, North Africa, Austria, Latvia, Israel, Argentina, Uruguay. Appeared on stage together with Shifra Lerer. Born in Belz, Poland. Died in the United States.

The papers relate to the theatrical careers of Witler and Lerer. The bulk of the collection is comprised of playscripts including scripts with musical scores. In addition, there are photographs of B.Z. Witler and a scrapbook of his obituaries.

Photographs cataloged in STAGEPIX.

657. LESTSCHINSKY, JACOB (1876–1966).
   Papers, 1900–1958. 2 ft. 1 in. (RG 339)

Economist, sociologist, demographer, author of publications on Jewish economics. Founding member of the YIVO Institute in Vilna, Poland, and Secretary of its Section for Economics and Statistics, 1925–1939. Member of the YIVO Executive Board. Contributor to the *Jewish Daily Forward*. Lived in Poland and in the United States.

   Lestchinsky's correspondence with individuals and institutions. About 1,800 letters to and from prominent figures, including David Bergelson, Abraham Cahan, Simon Dubnow, Henryk Erlich, David Hofstein, Zelig Kalmanovitch, Leib Kvitko, Abraham Liessin, Hersh David Nomberg, Helena Peretz, Zemach Shabad, Werner Sombart, Baruch Vladeck, Chaim Zhitlowsky. Family correspondence and personal documents.

   Inventory, English, Yiddish.

658. LETTERS.
   Collection, 1800–1970s. 6 ft. 3 in. (RG 107)

This collection is of mixed provenance and was assembled in the YIVO Archives. Accessions consisting of a few letters are included in this collection and are arranged by the name of the writer.

   Letters to and from several hundred Jewish personalities, mainly writers, political thinkers, community leaders and rabbinical figures. Correspondents include Jacob P. Adler, S. Ansky, Shalom Asch, Mendel Beilis, David Bergelson, Hayyim Nahman Bialik, Nathan Birnbaum, Ber Borochow, Reuben Brainin, Adolphe Crémieux, Albert Einstein, Zechariah Frankel, Sigmund Freud, Maksim Gorkii, Rabbi Chaim Oyzer Grodzienski, Alexander Harkavy, Rabbi Isaac Herzog, Samuel David Luzzatto, Golda Meir, Mendele Moykher Sforim, Emanuel Ringelblum, Sholem Aleichem, Nahum Sokolow, Judah Steinberg, Henrietta Szold, Boris Thomashefsky, Leon Trotsky, Chaim Weizmann, Morris Winchevsky, Leopold Zunz.

659. LEVIATIN, DAVID.
   Papers, 1980. 10 in. (RG 1122)

David Leviatin worked as an interviewer for the Reynolds Hills Project of Photography and Oral Histories, 1980. The interviews dealt with the life experiences of the Jewish inhabitants of a colony in Reynolds Hills, Peekskill, New York, and included discussions of their political views. The colony was established in 1929 by East European Jewish needle-trade workers.

   The papers consist of 40 interviews and other materials relating to the project.

660. LEVIN, DOV (born 1925).
   Papers, 1934–1982. 3 in. (RG 1269)

Historian of Lithuanian Jewry. On the faculty of the Hebrew University in Jerusalem. Born in Kaunas, Lithuania. Was in the Kaunas ghetto. Settled in Israel in 1945.

   Letters and documents relating to Levin's refugee experiences, including copies and originals of a diary, September–December 1944. Papers relating to Levin's academic activities.

661. LEVIN, ELIYAHU.
   Papers, 1921–1955. 2 in. (RG 325)

Yiddish writer and teacher, Memphis, Tennessee, and New York. Born in Bragin, Byelorussia.

The collection consists of correspondence with Yiddish cultural figures and institutions. Included are letters to Levin's wife, Esther Levin.

662. LEVIN, LEIZER.
Papers, 1945–1953. 2 in. (RG 516)

Member of the Pińsk *landsmanshaft* in New York.

The papers relate to aid provided by the Pińsk *landsmanshaft* in the United States to Holocaust survivors from Pińsk, Poland. Correspondence. Reports to the JDC from the association of Pińsk survivors in Warsaw, 1946. Receipts.

663. LEVIN, MAX.
Papers, 1940s–1960s. 5 in. (RG 593)

Yiddish poet. Philadelphia.

The collection consists of correspondence, personal papers, clippings and manuscripts relating to Max Levin's literary career and to his personal life.

Inventory, English.

664. LEVIN-SHATSKES, YIZHAK (1892–1963).
Papers, 1920s–1960s. 2 1/2 in. (RG 1130)

Yiddish writer. Active in the Bund party in Latvia as well as in municipal politics in Daugavpils (Dvinsk) after 1920. Contributed to and edited Russian and Yiddish periodicals such as *Dvinskoe ekho* (Dvinsk), *Dos folk* (Riga), *Frimorgn* (Riga), *Undzer vort* (Riga), *Naye tsayt* (Riga), *Folkstsaytung* (Warsaw), *Der veker* (New York), *Zukunft* (New York), *Gerekhtikeit* (New York), *Der fraynd* (New York), *Kultur un dertsiung* (New York). Secretary (from 1938) of the Jewish Socialist Verband in America. Was on the executive boards of the Forward Association, the Jewish Labor Committee and the Congress for Jewish Culture.

Clippings of articles from Riga, Dvinsk. Passport, membership cards, notebook.

665. LEVITATS, ISAAC (1907–).
Papers, 1940s–1960s. 9 ft. 7 in. (RG 663)

Teacher, educator. Director of the Board of Jewish Education in Akron, Ohio; Syracuse, New York; and Milwaukee, Wisconsin, among others. Published articles and works on Jewish education and history in publications such as *YIVO bleter*, *Ha-doar*, *Dortn*. Born in Zagare, Lithuania. Immigrated to the United States in 1926. Lived in Palestine from 1935 to 1940.

The papers relate to Levitats's work in the field of education in the United States, Israel and Canada. Reports, correspondence, clippings, memos, surveys, pamphlets, minutes of meetings and curricula relating to the Boards of Jewish Education in Akron (Ohio), Syracuse (NY), Milwaukee (Wisconsin), North Bellmore (NY) and numerous other cities in the United States. Curriculum materials: teaching guides and manuals on teaching Hebrew, Bible, Jewish holidays, music, drama. Materials relating to schools in Haifa and to various high schools in New York City. Levitats's doctoral dissertation. Memoirs.

Card inventory, English.

666. LEVITT, LEMUEL (ca. 1881–1939).
   Papers, 1890–1920s. 5 in. (RG 1109)

Jewish community figure in Winnipeg, Canada. Educator, journalist. Worked for HIAS in Galați (Galatz), Rumania, and was active in assistance programs to pogrom survivors. School principal of the Winnipeg Talmud Torah in the 1920s. Born in Olgopol, Ukraine. Immigrated to Canada in 1924.

   Photographs from Galatz, Rumania, and Olgopol, Ukraine, including photographs of pogrom survivors ca. 1918 in Olgopol and a family photograph, 1890, in Olgopol. Clippings from Rumanian, Yiddish, Hebrew newspapers from Galatz, Kishinev, Winnipeg, 1910s–1930s. Materials relating to HIAS work in Rumania. Correspondence.

667. LEVITZ, JACOB (born 1914).
   Papers, 1924–1950s. 2 in. (RG 769)

Adopted name of Jacob Danilevitch. Educator, writer, teacher and principal in Hebrew and Yiddish schools in the United States and Mexico. Consultant for the Jewish Education Bureau, Boston. Professor of Yiddish at the New School for Social Research. Contributed to: *Freie Arbeiter Stimme, Literarishe bleter, Zukunft, Kinder velt, Meksikaner lebn.* Born in Kolno, Poland. Immigrated to the United States in 1931.

   Miscellaneous correspondence with individuals and institutions in Mexico, Poland, the United States. Manuscripts by others including Hebrew responsa by Rabbi Chaim Rabinovitch from the Yeshiva Beis Yitschok in Slobodka.

668. LEVY, JOSEPH HILLEL (1891–1955).
   Papers, 1930s–1950s. 1 ft. 3 in. (RG 478)

Yiddish poet. Contributed to numerous periodicals such as *Literarishe bleter* (Warsaw), *In zikh* (NY), *Freie Arbeiter Stimme* (NY). Included in *Antologye fun galitsishe dikhter* (Anthology of Galician Poets) by M. Neugrochel, New York. Born in Cracow, Poland. Lived in Germany from 1914 to 1939. Settled in London, England.

   Manuscripts mostly of Levy's poetry. Correspondence with Yiddish literary figures such as Gershom Bader, Jacob Glatstein, David Ignatoff, Esther Kreitman, A.A. Roback.

669. LEWIN, LOUIS (1868–1941).
   Papers. 2 1/2 in. (RG 760)

Rabbi, historian. Published books and studies on the history of the Jews of Germany and Poland. Born in Żnin, province of Posen (Poznań), Poland. In 1937 he settled in Palestine.

   Notes on the history of the Jews of Cracow. Photographs of cemeteries and synagogues in Polish towns.

670. LEWITAN, JOSEPH D.
   Papers. 6 ft. (RG 735)

Official at the United Nations. Relative of Isaac Ilitch Levitan (1861–1900), the Russian landscape painter.

   The collection includes: A landscape painting entitled *Etude* by I. I. Levitan. A drawing signed "Michaelson." Three paintings by an unidentified artist. 60 albums of photographs and postcards.

   Landscape painting by I.I. Levitan is cataloged in the Art Collection, RG 101.

671. LIBIN, SOLOMON (1872–1955).

Papers, 1914–1952. 1 ft. 8 in. (RG 1201)

Pen name of Israel Zalman Hurwitz. Yiddish writer and playwright. Long-time contributor to the *Jewish Daily Forward* in which he published short stories for over half a century. His plays attained great popularity on the Yiddish stage in the United States and in Europe, and some were made into films. Born in Gorki, Byelorussia. Emigrated from Russia to London in 1891 and to New York in 1892.

Correspondence, 1914–1952, including letters from Libin's readers in the *Forward*, and correspondence concerning productions of his plays. Manuscripts of plays and stories. Clippings of Libin's published works. Programs for plays and events. Box-office statements, 1919.

672. LICHT, DAVID (1904–1978).

Papers, 1920s–1960s. 3 ft. 4 in. (RG 797)

Actor, director, playwright, writer. Member of the Vilna Troupe. Director, Folksbiene Theater in New York. Born in Lvov (Lemberg, Lwów), Poland. Lived in Argentina and the United States.

The papers consist of manuscripts, typescripts, photographs, clippings, correspondence, programs, posters, personal documents and sheet music relating to David Licht's theatrical career.

673. LICHT, MICHL (1893–1953).

Papers, ca. 1928–1954. 1 ft. 8 in. (RG 373)

Yiddish poet. Born in the Ukraine. Settled in the United States in 1913.

Typescripts, manuscripts, correspondence, clippings, printed material and photos relating to Licht's career. Included are manuscripts of his books *Velvel Got* and *Letste Lider*. Licht's translations of works by Emily Dickinson, T.S. Eliot and Ezra Pound. Drawings and paintings by his wife, Evelyn Licht, were placed in the Art Collection (RG 101).

674. LIEBERMAN, HERMAN (CHAIM) (1890–1963).

Papers, 1920s–1950s. 5 ft. 10 in. (RG 435)

Yiddish essayist and literary critic. Wrote for the daily *Yiddishes Tageblatt*. As a Labor Zionist was active in the founding of the Jewish National Workers Alliance (Farband) Yiddish secular schools. In the 1930s Lieberman became an orthodox Jew and joined the religious Zionist movement. In his writings Lieberman attacked left-wing Yiddish writers. His book *The Christianity of Shalom Asch* is an attack against Shalom Asch's christological novels. Lived in the Ukraine and in the United States (New York).

The bulk of the collection consists of letters from readers. There are also letters from rabbis, notably Rabbis Berl Baumgarten, S.I. Bick, Zvi Yehuda Hacohen Kook, Ezekiel Landau, Chaim E. Moseson, Chaim Porille, Samuel Ephraim Tiktin. Correspondence includes letters from writers A. Almi, Shlomo Bickel, Abba Gordin, Solomon Grayzel, Ida Maze, Hillel Seidman, Joseph Tunkel. Many of the letters in the collection relate to Lieberman's book on Shalom Asch.

675. LIEBERT, SARAH (1892–1955).

Papers, 1920s–1950s. 2 1/2 in. (RG 427)

President, Sholem Aleichem Women's Organization. Member, National Council of Jewish Women. Lived in Poland, the United States.

Correspondence with Yiddish literary figures and Jewish community leaders.

676. LIEBMAN, ISAAC (1900–1959).
Papers, 1940s–1950s. 5 in. (RG 480)

Yiddish journalist. Founder of the *Nyu yorker vokhnblat* and its editor from 1935 until his death. Contributed articles, poems to *Di tsayt* (NY), *Freie Arbeiter Stimme* (NY), *Groyser kundes* (NY). Born in Petrikov, district of Minsk, Byelorussia. Immigrated to the United States in 1918.

The papers relate to the activities of the *Nyu yorker vokhnblat*. Correspondence with literary figures, 1936–1948, including Jacob Adler, A. Almi, Michl Licht, Saul Raskin, Zalman Shneur. Photographs, including staff of the *Nyu yorker vokhnblat*. Manuscripts submitted to the *Nyu yorker vokhnblat* by writers.

677. LIEBMAN, SEYMOUR.
Papers, 1950s–1970s. 10 in. (RG 1143)

Historian, specialist on Latin-American Jewry. Representative of the American Jewish Committee in Mexico. President, Southeast Region, Zionist Organization of America.

Printed materials, correspondence, notes, manuscripts relating to Jewish life in Mexico, Central America, South America, Rumania. The materials reflect Liebman's career in Jewish organizations as well as his work as a historian.

678. LIESSIN, ABRAHAM (1872–1938).
Papers, 1906–1944. 14 ft. 7 in. (RG 201)

Pen name of Abraham Walt. Yiddish poet, journalist. Prominent in the Jewish Labor Bund party. Editor of *Zukunft* (NY). Lived in Russia and the United States.

The collection relates primarily to Liessin's work as editor of *Zukunft*. Correspondence with over 1000 individuals including Richard Beer-Hofman, Eduard Bernstein, Hayyim Nahman Bialik, Boris Dov Brutzkus, Marc Chagall, Eugene Debs, Simon Dubnow, David Einhorn, Saul Ginsburg, Jacob Glatstein, David Hofstein, Itzhak Katzenelson, Moshe Kulbak, Leib Kvitko, H. Leivick, Jacob Lestschinsky, Judah Magnes, Itzik Manger, Mani Leib, Louis Marshall, Moshe Nadir, Der Nister (Pinchas Kahanovitch), Shmuel Niger, Hersh David Nomberg, Isaac Leib Peretz, David Pinsky, Abraham Reisen, Zalman Reisen, Zalman Shneur, Nahum Shtif, Elias Tcherikower, Baruch Charney Vladeck, Max Weinreich, Morris Winchevsky, Hillel Zeitlin, Chaim Zhitlowsky. Manuscripts of Liessin's own articles, poems. Manuscripts submitted by about 620 authors to Liessin as editor. Clippings of poems and articles in the *Jewish Daily Forward* and *Zukunft*. Clippings about Liessin. Personal papers relating to jubilee celebrations, family matters, Liessin's death. Materials on the Bund, 1905.

Inventory, Yiddish.

679. LIFSCHITZ, SAMUEL (1883–1961).
Papers, 1906–1950s. 3 microfilm reels. (RG 402)

Staff member of the Hilfsverein der Deutschen Juden, Berlin, 1907–1938. Lived in Poland, Germany and the United States.

Materials relating to Lifschitz's work for the Hilfsverein. Correspondence relating to German-Jewish emigration in the 1930s. Individual immigrant cases. Personal documents. Photographs of personalities.

Inventory of photographs.

680. LIFSCHUTZ, EZEKIEL (1902–).
Papers, 1960s–1970s. 15 in. (RG 676)

Historian, teacher, archivist. Taught in the Sholem Aleichem Folk Schools and the Jewish Teachers' Seminary in New York. YIVO Archivist, 1954–1973. Contributed to *Radomer vokhnblat, Oyfkum, Literarishe bleter, YIVO bleter, Zukunft, Freie Arbeiter Stimme, Kultur un dertsiung, Di goldene keyt, American Jewish Historical Quarterly, American Jewish Archives.* Born in Radom, Poland. Immigrated to the United States in 1923 and settled in New York.

Correspondence with individuals: Mordechai Altshuler, Yosef Gutman, Nathan David Korman, Chone Shmeruk, Abraham Sutzkever, Ruth Wisse. Notes and source materials for various works. Family correspondence.

681. LIGHTFOOT, VIRGINIA DORSEY.
Papers, 1939–1941. 2 1/2 in. (RG 715)

In 1939, Virginia Dorsey Lightfoot of Takoma Park, Maryland, became involved in an effort to rescue a group of about 328 Jews from Breslau, Germany, and settle them in Alaska. Lightfoot was married to James Herndon Lightfoot.

Correspondence with individuals active in rescue work on behalf of German Jews. Correspondents include: James G. McDonald; Cecilia Razovsky (National Refugee Service); Marjorie Page Schauffler (American Friends Service Committee). An album containing biographical notes and photographs.

682. LINDER, SOLOMON (1886–1960).
Papers, 1912–1960. 2 ft. 6 in. (RG 443)

Yiddish journalist, member of anarchist groups. On the staff of *Arbeter fraynd* in London. Editor of *Freie Arbeiter Stimme.* Born in Złoczów, Poland. Lived in England and the United States.

Correspondence with the *Freie Arbeiter Stimme* relating to anarchism, 1917–1960, including letters from Emma Goldman and other leading anarchists. Correspondence with Yiddish literary figures. Typescripts by various authors. Clippings from the anarchist press. Copies of a few English-language anarchist newspapers, ca. 1912. Materials relating to Rudolf Rocker including correspondence between Linder and the Rocker publications committee. Typescripts in German by Rocker.

683. LINDY, DAVID.
Papers, 1870s–ca. 1900. 2 1/2 in. (RG 272)

Badkhn (wedding entertainer). Kėdainiai, Kaunas province, Lithuania.

A bound volume dated 1870, of songs, rhymes, and poems, handwritten by Lindy. Topics include marriage, politics, social and religious matters. A letter by A. Lindy, Lindy's son, about David Lindy. A recording by A. Lindy of his father's tunes.

684. LIPSONIAN KINSMEN.
Records, 1922–1981. 15 in. (RG 1112)

Fraternal organization based on family membership. Founded in 1921, incorporated in 1922 by Samuel Lipson and other descendants of Sholem and Rose Lipshitz and Israel and Rebecca Nishinewitz, originally from the province of Minsk, Byelorussia. Provided burial benefits, loans, support for charities. Sent gifts to servicemen during World War II.

Golden Book documenting family relationships. Constitution of 1938 with certificate of incorporation, 1922. Constitution of 1961. Minute books, 1921–1922 (Yiddish), 1922–1927 (English), 1961–1972 (English). Newsletter, 1942–1981. 16 reels of film. Financial statement for 1926.

Films removed to and cataloged in RG 105.

685. LIPTZIN, SAMUEL (1893–1980).
Papers, 1950s–1970s. 1 ft. 3 in. (RG 879)

Yiddish writer, humorist. Long-standing contributor to the *Morgn frayhayt*. Also contributed to *Folks shtime* (Warsaw), *Der groyser kundes*, *Di varhayt*, *Der humorist*. Born in Lipsk, Suwałki province, Poland. Immigrated to the United States in 1909.

Correspondence with publishers and editors of Yiddish newspapers and periodicals. Correspondence with friends and family. Liptzin's works in English translation.

686. LITHUANIAN CONSISTORY OF THE RUSSIAN ORTHODOX CHURCH.
Records, 1807–1911. (RG 46)

Office of the Russian Orthodox Church dealing with religious conversions.

Files of about 390 cases of conversions to the Russian Orthodox faith by Jews residing in the former Pale of Settlement, 1819–1911. The majority of the converts were women. The files consist of applications to the Consistory, reports regarding the conversions, affidavits by priests and correspondence.

Inventory, Yiddish.

687. LITHUANIAN JEWISH COMMUNITIES.
Records, 1844–1940 (bulk dates 1919–1926). 40 ft. (RG 2)

The collection relates to Jewish communities situated in the part of Lithuania that formed the independent Republic of Lithuania from 1919 to 1940. The bulk of the materials relates to the period of Jewish national autonomy in Lithuania, 1919–1923, and to its subsequent demise, 1923–1926. These records originated in the Ministry for Jewish Affairs of the Lithuanian government and in local Jewish communities.

The smaller part of the collection, which covers the years 1844–1918 and 1926–1940, consists of miscellaneous communal and private records which were acquired at various times by YIVO in Vilna and by the Kaunas branch of the S. Ansky Historical and Ethnographic Society.

General records of the Ministry for Jewish Affairs, the Jewish National Council, and the Jewish parliamentary group in the Lithuanian Diet. Minutes of meetings, reports, statistics. Decrees relating to Jewish minority rights. Records regarding municipal elections. Records of the Conference of Jewish Communities, 1920. Files of several departments of the Ministry.

Records of Jewish communities in the period of Jewish national autonomy, 1919–1926. Correspondence, vital statistics, minutes of meetings of the community councils. Local election materials. Included are about 110 communities, with extensive files for the following: Anykščiai (Anikst), Biržai (Birzhe), Vilkaviškis (Vilkavishki), Ukmergė (Wilkomir), Jonava (Yaneve), Marijampolė, Panevėžys (Ponevezh), Prienai (Pren), Kėdainiai (Kaidan), Kretinga, Radviliškis (Radvilishok), Raseiniai (Rasayn), Šiauliai (Shavl).

Miscellaneous communal records, 1844–1940, including *pinkasim* (registers) of the communities, charitable societies and burial societies. For the most part, the materials are from Kaunas (Kovno).

Miscellaneous materials on Jewish political parties, including Zionist groups, Jewish aid societies, commercial and trade associations, mainly 1920s and 1930s.

Records of the S. Ansky Historical and Ethnographic Society in Kaunas, 1922–1940, including minutes, correspondence with members, appeals for support, financial files. Materials on Jewish life in Lithuania, mainly about education and theater. Photographs of: the Ministry for Jewish Affairs; the first Zionist Congress in Lithuania; personalities, including rabbis; Jewish towns and landmarks.

Inventory, Yiddish, English.

688. LITVINOVSKY, ARYEH (1860–1937).

Papers, 1924–1937. 3 in. (RG 1210)

Yiddish writer. Born in Novaya Praga near Elizavetgrad, Ukraine. Immigrated to United States in 1924 and kept a dry goods store in New Haven, Connecticut.

Seven volumes of notes, poems, memoirs, stories and other material by Litvinovsky, ca. 1924–1937. Published book by Litvinovsky, From *Times Gone By*, in Yiddish and English, 1985.

689. LITWIN, A. (1862–1943).

Papers, 1907–1940s. 7 ft. 1 in. (RG 206)

Pen name of Samuel Hurwitz. Yiddish journalist, editor, ethnographer, poet. Co-founder of the first Poale Zion group in Minsk. Active in the Poale Zion movement in the United States. Born in Minsk, Byelorussia. Immigrated to the United States in 1901, but returned to Poland in 1904. Settled permanently in New York in 1912.

Yiddish folkore materials, including notebooks of songs, folk plays, folktales, folk humor, anecdotes, proverbs. Clippings of Litwin's articles relating to various topics, including: Russia, 1917–1930; Palestine and Zionism; towns and cities in Europe; *landsmanshaftn*; Poale Zion activities, 1915–1928; Jewish occupations; colonization and farming; Jewish holidays; Yiddish theater; education. Poems by Litwin. Photographs of personalities, towns in Europe. Correspondence with Abraham Cahan, Saul Ginsburg, Abraham Liessin, Baal Makhshoves (Isidor Eliashev), Shmuel Niger, Zalman Reisen, Sholem Aleichem, Israel Zinberg. Family correspondence.

Inventory, English, Yiddish.

690. LODZER YOUNG LADIES AID SOCIETY.

Records, 1954–1975. 2 1/2 in. (RG 1095)

Founded in New York in 1919 by immigrants from Łódź, Poland, at a wedding reception of a member of their brother society, the Lodzer Young Men's Benevolent Society. Supported charities and Lodzer relief activities. Dissolved 1975.

Minutes, 1954–1972. Souvenir journal. Meeting announcements.

691. LODZER YOUNG MEN'S BENEVOLENT SOCIETY.
Records, 1927–1943. 7 1/2 in. (RG 1045)

Founded in New York in 1902 by immigrants from Łódź, Poland. Affiliated in 1915 with the General Relief Committee for Jewish War Sufferers in Łódź. Sent two delegates to Łódź in 1920 to bring relief funds. Affiliated in 1935 with the United Emergency Committee for the City of Łódź. Associated with the Lodzer Young Ladies Aid Society.

Anniversary journals, 1927–1977. Memorial book, 1943. Correspondence, 1930s. Newspaper clippings.

692. LOKSHIN, HELEN (?–1981).
Papers, 1945–ca. 1950. 2 1/2 in. (RG 1125)

AJDC field representative in the Wetzlar camp for displaced persons in post-war Germany.

The papers consist of correspondence with AJDC relating to the Wetzlar camp. Notes, pamphlets, photographs.

693. LOMAZER YOUNG MEN'S AND WOMEN'S BENEVOLENT ASSOCIATION.
Records, 1956–1976. 2 in. (RG 817)

Founded in New York in 1916 by immigrants from Łomazy, Poland. Active in relief work after World War I. Sent a delegate to Łomazy and provided funds to rebuild the synagogue, destroyed by fire. Relief work after World War II included financial and material assistance for *landslayt* in DP camps.

Constitution. Jubilee journals, 1956, 1961, 1971, 1976.

694. LOMZER AID SOCIETY.
Records, 1914–1917. 13 in. (RG 851)

Established in New York in 1898 by immigrants from Łomża, Poland, to help needy *landslayt*. In 1937 the society joined with four other Lomzer organizations to form the United Lomzer Relief Committee to aid the town of Łomża. Sponsored a loan fund, mutual dues fund and a *maos hittim* fund (Passover campaign for the poor).

Minutes, 1914–1939. Financial reports, 1957–1966. Meeting announcements: *The Lomzer Bulletin*, 1946–1956. Materials relating to anniversary celebrations. Materials pertaining to the Lomzer memorial book. Golden book (record of deaths of members) of the *hevrah kadisha* (burial society) of the Lomzer Aid Society. Materials pertaining to other Łomża organizations: Lomzer Shul–Anshe Łomża V'Gatch, Lomzer Ladies Relief Society, United Lomzer Relief Committee.

695. LONDINSKY, SHMUEL (1889–1956) and HELEN (born 1896).
Papers, 1920s–1970s. 10 in. (RG 403)

Husband and wife. Yiddish writers. Shmuel Londinsky was a poet, journalist and editor of

Ilustrirte yom-tov bleter. Lived in Lithuania and the United States. Helen Tobenblat-Londinsky published articles in the *Zukunft* and the *Nyu yorker vokhenblat*. Lived in Poland and the United States.

Correspondence with literary figures including Mani Leib, Alexander Mukdoni, Shmuel Niger. Manuscripts by the Londinskys. Clippings and reviews. Personal documents.

696. LONDON, ISRAEL (born 1898).
Papers, ca. 1947–1964. 10 in. (RG 485)

Yiddish journalist, publisher. Co-founder of the publishing house Der Kval. Worked for *Wiener morgnpost* (Vienna), *Parizer bleter* (Paris), *Parizer haynt* (Paris), *Der tog* (Vilna), *Havaner lebn* (Havana), *Havaner lebn almanakh* (Havana), *Morgn zhurnal* (NY). Born in Hrubieszów, Poland. Lived in Argentina, Austria, Germany, France and Cuba before immigrating to the United States in 1943.

Correspondence, manuscripts and typescripts, relating to London's publishing activities. Letters from Daniel Charney, Aaron Glanz-Leieles, Jacob Glatstein, Abraham Golomb, H. Leivick, Leib Olitzky, Melech Ravitch, Zalman Shneur, Abraham Sutzkever. Manuscripts and typescripts by H. Leivick, Reuveni, Isaac Bashevis Singer, Abraham Sutzkever. Typescript of a Yiddish translation of a work by Shmuel Yosef Agnon.

697. LOUIS LAMED FOUNDATION FOR THE ADVANCEMENT OF HEBREW AND YIDDISH LITERATURE.
Records, 1940–1960. 4 ft. 7 in. (RG 526)

The Louis Lamed Foundation was established by the Detroit Jewish communal leader, Louis Lamed, in 1940. The Foundation, which was active until 1960, awarded annual prizes to the authors of outstanding works in Hebrew and Yiddish. It also supported publications dealing with the bilingual character of Jewish literature. Shmuel Niger was chairman from 1941 to 1953, and jury members included Joseph Opatoshu, Abraham J. Heschel, Isaac N. Steinberg. Winners included Jacob Glatstein, Israel Efros, Menahem Boraisha, I.J. Schwartz, H. Ayalti, Aaron Zeitlin, Jacob Isaac Segal, Zalman Shneur, Chaim Tchernowitz, H. Leivick and Aaron Glanz-Leieles. Lamed also established a chair for Jewish Studies at Wayne State University.

Records of the Board of Directors relating to the establishment of the fund, including minutes, announcements. Correspondence of the Board of Directors with Louis Lamed. Correspondence with Louis Lamed from writers including Shalom Asch, Shlomo Bickel, Menahem Boraisha, Aaron Glanz-Leieles, Jacob Glatstein, Abraham Golomb, Chaim Grade, Leibush Lehrer, Itzik Manger, Joseph Opatoshu, Melech Ravitch, Zalman Shneur, Yechiel Yeshaia Trunk, Stephen Wise, and Aaron Zeitlin. Correspondence with organizations. Materials on the Chair for Jewish Studies at Wayne State University, 1954–1959. Clippings about the Foundation. Clippings on Jewish writers including articles and biographical information about prize winners.

Inventory, English, Yiddish.

698. LOW, LEO (1876–1960).
Papers, 1895–1971. 5 ft. 3 in. (RG 1140)

Jewish composer, arranger, choral conductor, teacher, lecturer. One of the first to collect, arrange and popularize Yiddish and Hebrew folk and art songs. Choir conductor at the Great Synagogue in Vilna, Bucharest Reform Temple, Tłomackie Synagogue in Warsaw, Hazomir and Grosser Club choruses in Warsaw, choruses of the Jewish National Workers Alliance and Workmen's Circle in New York. Born in Wołkowysk, Grodno province. Immigrated to the United States in 1920. Lived in Palestine from 1934–1938 and returned to reside in the United States.

Correspondence, original musical works and arrangements by Leo Low, printed sheet music of compositions by Leo Low, personal documents. Correspondents include Samuel Alman, Israel Alter, Abraham M. Bernstein, Abraham W. Binder, Gershon Ephros, Michl Gelbart, Mordechai Herschman, Meyer Posner, Jacob Rapoport, Josef (Yosele) Rosenblatt, Salomon Rosowsky, Jacob Weinberg, Lazar Weiner, Chemjo Vinaver, Julius Wolfsohn, Stefan Wolpe. Compositions by Leo Low include liturgical works, Jewish holiday songs, folk songs. Arrangements and rearrangements include works by Samuel Alman, Platon Brounoff, Julius Chajes, Isaac Dunayevsky, Michl Gelbart, Solomon Golub, Moses Beer Korotiansky, Zavel Kwartin, Marc Lavry, Louis Lewandowski, Shalom Postolsky, Baruch Leib Rosowsky, Zeidel Rovner, M. Schneyer, Mark Warschawski, Leib Yampolsky, Mordechai Zeira. Poets whose works were set to music by Low include Hayyim Nahman Bialik, David Edelstadt, Szmerke Kaczerginski, Isaac Leib Peretz, Abraham Reisen, Morris Rosenfeld, Zalman Shneur.

Inventory, English.

699. LÖWENTHAL, KARL (?–1975).
Papers, 1939–1945. 2 1/2 in. (RG 718)

Löwenthal resided in Amsterdam in the period 1939–1945. He corresponded with inmates of concentration camps in Vught, Westerbork and Terezin.

The collection relates to Löwenthal's contacts with concentration camp inmates. Correspondence, receipts for packages sent to Terezin and Vught, certificates for food packages sent through Joodsche Raad, Amsterdam.

700. LOYAL AMERICAN LODGE NO. 402, INDEPENDENT ORDER OF ODD FELLOWS.
Records, 1925–1970. 8 in. (RG 871)

Founded in 1925 as a fraternal lodge of the Independent Order of Odd Fellows. Provided mutual aid and social benefits for members. Established cemetery, distress and sick benefits committees. Supported various philanthropies.

By-laws. Minutes, 1925–1928, 1940–1944. Financial records, 1946–1948, 1953–1970. Correspondence, 1930s–1940s.

701. LOYAL BENEVOLENT SOCIETY.
Records, 1886–1969. 1 ft. 3 in. (RG 900)

Established in New York in 1886 as the Hirsch Liska Lodge No. 66, Order Brith Abraham. Also known as the Hirsch Liska Sick and Benevolent Society. Subsequently incorporated as an independent mutual aid association.

By-laws. Minutes of the Hirsch Liska Lodge, 1920–1923 (German). Minutes of the Loyal Benevolent Society, 1923–1949. Financial records, 1940s–1960s. Materials pertaining to membership, 1886–1944 (German, English). Correspondence. Cemetery map. Voting box.

702. LUBANER AND VICINITY BENEVOLENT SOCIETY.
Records, 1941–1976. 7 1/2 in. (RG 945)

Founded in New York in 1923 by immigrants from Lubań, Poland. Supported Jewish causes and charitable organizations. Dissolved in the 1970s.

Minutes, 1965–1976. Financial records, 1964–1976. Cemetery records. Correspondence. Meeting notices. Dissolution ballots.

703. LUKOWER and MEZRICHER SOCIETY (LOS ANGELES).
Records, 1935–1982. 2 in. (RG 1129)

Formed in 1970 through a merger of the Lukower (Łuków, Poland) Club, organized in 1953, and a Mezricher (Międzyrzec, Poland) society in Los Angeles. Conducted fund-raising drives for Israel.

Minutes, 1953–1955 (Yiddish), 1969–1982 (English). Jubilee book, 1935. Certificates of award.

704. LUTOWISKER YOUNG MEN'S BENEVOLENT SOCIETY.
Records, 1922–1978. 1 ft. 8 in. (RG 827)

Founded in New York in 1911 by immigrants from Lutowiska, Ukraine. Established a loan fund for its members. Activities included sending relief to *landslayt* in Israel after World War II.

Constitutions; minutes, 1922–48, 1953–72; financial records, 1941–65, 1978; membership applications, 1936–65, and other records; sick benefit applications, 1930–58; anniversary journals; cemetery maps; gavel; stamp; banner.

705. LUTZKY, AARON (1894–1957).
Papers, 1909–1957. 2 ft. (RG 613)

Pen name of Aaron Zucker. Yiddish poet. Contributed to *Yiddishes Tageblatt*, *Der tog*, *Jewish Daily Forward*, *Di feder*, *Der groyser kundes*, *In zikh*, *Nay yidish*, *Kinder zhurnal*, *Freie Arbeiter Stimme*, *Frayhayt*, *Der amerikaner*, *Di goldene keyt*. Born in Demidovka, District of Lutsk, Vohlynia.

Manuscripts of Lutzky's poems. Clippings of his printed poems and articles. Notebooks of rhymes and notes.

706. MAITLIS, JACOB (1900–1984).
Papers, 1937–1940. 5 in. (RG 571)

Yiddish journalist and essayist. Secretary of the Friends of YIVO Society in London. Contributed to German language periodicals: *Jüdische Rundschau* (Berlin); *Israelitisches Wochenblatt* (Hamburg); *Jüdische Pressezentrale* (Prague); *Der Israelit* (Zurich); *Selbstwehr* (Frankfurt a/M). Contributed to Yiddish periodicals: *Lodzer folksblat*; *Di yidishe velt* (Berlin); *Di tsayt* (London); *Loshn un lebn* (London); *Yidisher kemfer*; *Zukunft* (NY); *Di goldene keyt* (Tel Aviv); *Keneder odler* (Montreal); *YIVO bleter*. Contributed to English periodicals: *Jewish Chronicle*; *Zionist Review*; *Polish Jewish Observer*. Born in Miedzechów, near Sosnowiec, Poland. Settled in London, England.

Materials relating to the YIVO Society in London. Minutes of the YIVO Society, 1937–1940. Correspondence of Maitlis with YIVO, 1930–1941; on behalf of YIVO, 1937–1939. Copies of YIVO circulars, 1937–1939. Materials relating to Polish-Jewish refugees in England, 1939–1940. Materials relating to Yiddish journalists' and writers' organizations in London.

707. MAKOVER UNTERSTITZUNGS VEREIN.
Records, 1952–1976. 5 in. (RG 942)

Founded in New York ca. 1925 by immigrants from Maków Mazowiecki, Poland. Dissolved 1976.
   Minutes, 1952–1976. Financial records, 1952–1977. Materials pertaining to burial.

708. MAKOWER YOUNG MEN'S AID SOCIETY.
Records, 1915–1969. 3 in. (RG 1043)

Founded in 1907 by immigrants from Maków Mazowiecki, Poland. Affiliated with the United Makower Relief which was established after World War I to aid *landslayt* and reestablished in 1945 to aid war survivors.
   Correspondence. Photographs from Maków, 1915–1940s. Memorial book, 1969.

709. MALACHOVSKY, HILLEL (1860–1943).
Papers. 5 in. (RG 305)

Yiddish and Hebrew writer, teacher. Contributed to *Hamelitz, Voskhod, Ha-ivri, Ha-leumi, Yiddishes Tageblatt* (NY), *Yidisher herald, Morgn zhurnal*. Born in Minsk region, Byelorussia. Settled in the United States at the turn of the century.
   The papers consist of newspaper clippings of Malachovsky's writings.

710. MALEK, EUGENE (?–1979).
Papers. 15 ft. (RG 806)

Musician, choral director. Lived in the United States.
   Printed and manuscript music including folksongs, oratorios, cantatas, liturgical music, choral works, dance music. Programs, clippings and photographs of Eugene Malek.

711. MALTZ, SAUL (1906–1985).
Papers, 1928–1986. 10 ft. 3 in. (RG 1229)

Yiddish poet, teacher. Taught in Workmen's Circle schools in Detroit and New York and served as secretary of the Central School Board of the Workmen's Circle. Born in Grójec, Poland. Came to the United States in 1921.
   School materials, especially relating to the Yiddish schools in Detroit and New York, including curricula and syllabi, administrative records, students' works, scripts for pageants and plays, yearbooks, newsletters, song sheets, and other materials, 1939–1985. Song books, playscripts, newsletters and other materials from Camp Boiberik and Kinder Ring. Materials from Circle Lodge, the Workmen's Circle adult summer camp, where Maltz served as cultural director, 1928–1970. Miscellaneous correspondence and other materials concerning Maltz's activities in the Workmen's Circle, the Yiddish PEN Club and other cultural organizations, 1954–1986. Correspondence with Yiddish cultural figures, friends and family, 1941–1986. Photographs of school and camp activities, Yiddish cultural events, friends and family. Manuscripts and clippings of poetry and articles by Maltz.

712. MANI LEIB (1883–1953).
Papers, 1915–1953. 1 ft. 8 in. (RG 491)

Pen name of Mani Leib Brahinsky. Prominent Yiddish poet. Published poems in the *Jewish Daily Forward* (NY), *Freie Arbeiter Stimme* (NY), *Yidisher kemfer* (NY), *Di varhayt* (NY), *Dos naye lebn* (NY), *Zukunft* (NY). Leading member of the American Yiddish literary group, *Di Yunge*, which believed in art for art's sake and sought to replace the traditional moral and political themes in Yiddish literature by free artistic expression and new forms. Co-editor of the anthology *Indzl*, 1925. Wrote ballads and tales for children. Born in Nezhin, Ukraine. Immigrated to the United States in 1905.

Correspondence with Yiddish literary figures including Reuben Iceland, David Ignatoff, Aleph Katz, H. Leivick, Itzik Manger, David Pinsky, Melech Ravitch, Abraham Reisen, Abraham Sutzkever. Galley proofs of poetry. Lists of titles of poems and translations. Photographs of Mani Leib, family and friends. Manuscripts and printed copies of several hundred poems by Mani Leib. Poems translated by Mani Leib from English, Russian and other languages into Yiddish. Mani Leib's poems translated into Hebrew, English, Spanish. Articles about Mani Leib.

Inventory, Yiddish.

713. MANUSCRIPTS.
Collection. 44 ft. 7 in. (RG 108)

These manuscripts are of mixed provenance. A sizeable portion of the manuscripts was originially submitted to the periodical *Zukunft*, New York.

The collection consists of manuscripts of published and unpublished works in Yiddish, Hebrew and English. Authors include: Hirsz Abramowicz, Ephraim Auerbach, Y.D. Berkowitz, Menahem Boraisha, Reuben Brainin, Marc Chagall, Simon Dubnow, Abraham Duker, Ossip Dymow, Saul Ginsburg, Rudolf Glanz, Aaron Glanz-Leieles, Jacob Glatstein, Ben Zion Goldberg, Nachum Goldmann, Chaim Grade, Peretz Hirschbein, Reuben Iceland, Naftali Herz Imber, Malka Lee, Leibush Lehrer, Jacob Lestschinsky, Mani Leib, Shmuel Niger, Mendel Osherowitch, Emanuel Ringelblum, Maurice Schwartz, Isaac Bashevis Singer, Israel Joshua Singer, Nahum Sokolow, Yehiel Yeshaia Trunk, Max Weinreich, Mark Wischnitzer, Yehoash, Wolf Younin, Chaim Zhitlowsky.

Inventory, Yiddish.

714. MAPPING AND SURVEY OFFICE OF THE GERMAN ARMY HIGH COMMAND.
Records, 1940–1943. 5 ft. (RG 379)

German name: Oberkommando der Wehrmacht: Abteilung für Kriegskarten u. Vermessungswesen.

Bound volumes of published maps, plans, and geographical information about localities in Europe, North Africa, the Middle East, prepared by the German General Staff (Generalstab des Heeres) for military use during World War II. Includes country, city, highway and naval maps, lists of towns, statistical information on Jews and Jewish populations in various cities. Countries and regions include Great Britain, Greece, Iceland, Iraq, Italy, Libya, Luxembourg, Malta, Morocco, Near East, Netherlands, Northeast Africa, Norway, Poland, Portugal, Rumania, Russia, Sardinia, Sicily, Spain, Sweden, Switzerland, Tunisia, Ukraine.

715. MAPS.
Collection, 20th century. 3 ft. 4 in. (RG 109)

This subject collection was assembled in the YIVO Archives and is of mixed provenance.

The collection consists of printed and hand-drawn maps of countries, regions, cities and towns around the world. The maps are grouped into two series, General and Holocaust. Both series are arranged alphabetically by geographical place name.

The General series includes: political maps; topographic maps; city and street maps; maps showing Jewish populations of various countries. The collection focuses on Europe and Israel. Included are maps of Austria, Germany, England, Israel, Lithuania, Palestine, Poland, Russia.

The Holocaust series includes: maps and plans of concentration camps, extermination centers; maps of ghettos; maps of deportation routes from various countries to concentration camp points; maps showing centers of resistance and underground activity; maps of Europe showing locations of concentration camps; maps of POW camps in Germany. Countries include Austria, Czechoslovakia, Hungary, Germany, Russia and the Soviet Union. The greatest number of maps relate to Poland.

716. MARCUS, ISAIAH (1934–).
   Papers, 1900–1932. 2 1/2 in. (RG 384)

Rabbi, Massachusetts.
   Correspondence with rabbis in the United States and in Eastern Europe. Correspondents include Rabbi Isaac Blaser and Rabbi Moses Mordechai Epstein.

717. MARGOLIN, ANNA (1887–1952).
   Papers. 10 in. (RG 1166)

Pen name of Rosa Lebensbaum. Yiddish poet, journalist. Contributed to *Der tog*, *Naye velt*, *Freie Arbeiter Stimme*, *In zikh*, *Zukunft*, *Dos naye lebn*, *Literarishe bleter*. Born in Brest-Litovsk. Visited United States in 1906. Lived in London, Palestine, Warsaw. Immigrated to the United States in 1914.
   Letters from Yiddish writers including S. Dingol, H. L. Gordon, R. Iceland and family members. Letters from Margolin to others. Manuscripts by Margolin.

718. MARGOSHES, JOSEPH (1866–1955).
   Papers, 1911–1949. 2 ft. 7 in. (RG 324)

Yiddish journalist. Wrote for *Der tog* and *Morgn zhurnal*. Born in Lwów, Galicia. Immigrated to the United States in 1903.
   Clippings of Margoshes's articles on Hasidism. Manuscripts of Hasidic tales, articles about Hasidism and Hasidic leaders. Correspondence, mainly with rabbis, 1925–53.

719. MARGULIES, B.
   Papers, 1942–1954. 1 in. (RG 1217)

Chairman of the Federation of Polish Jews in Great Britain and Ireland. Member of the Itzik Manger Jubilee Committee.
   Papers relate to Margulies's efforts to provide financial support for the Yiddish poet Itzik Manger: correspondence, particularly with Melech Ravitch, concerning funds for Manger's support. Several letters from Manger, 1942–1954. Manuscripts and typescripts by Manger. Clippings.

720. MARGULIES, ISAAC (1855–1919).
Papers, 1894–1955. 5 in. (RG 1099)

Yiddish and Hebrew writer, journalist. Used the pseudonym "Y-M" or "Y-M Hatzioni." Contributed to the Yiddish, Hebrew, and German-Jewish press, including *Der Israelit* (Vienna), *Hatsefira, Togblat* (Lwów), *Der tog* (Cracow), *Folksshtime* (Sanok), *Machzikei Hadas*. Taught at the Baron de Hirsch School in Sasów, 1892–1914. Son of the musician and singer Berl Broder. Born in Podkamen (Pol. Podkamień), Ukraine. Died in Złoczów.

Typescripts of articles by Margulies, written in Złoczów, and Sasów, 1894–1919. Collection of articles by Margulies presented by the youth of Złoczów and Sasów in honor of his sixtieth birthday. Biographical essay. Yiddish play and poems by Ber Margulies, son of Isaac Margulies.

721. MARK, MENDEL (1900–1974).
Papers, 1921–1951. 1 in. (RG 623)

Yiddish teacher, active in the Yiddish secular school movement in Latvia. Wrote for *Der shtrom* (Libau), *Yidishe shprakh* (NY), *Naye vegn*. Worked on the *Groyser verterbukh fun der yidisher shprakh* (Great Dictionary of the Yiddish Language). Active in YIVO. Born in Polonga, Latvia. Immigrated to Canada in 1938 and to the United States in 1945.

Correspondence with literary figures such as Shmuel Niger, Max Weinreich, and Leibush Lehrer. YIVO materials from Vilna, Riga, 1925–1933. Miscellaneous materials such as election flyers from Latvia, 1930s; Yiddish newspaper from Riga, 1925.

722. MARK, YUDEL (1897–1975).
Papers, 1930s–1975. 12 ft. 1 in. (RG 540)

Yiddish linguist, educator, writer. Secretary and Vice-President of the Folkspartei (People's Party) in Lithuania, 1920s. Secretary-General of the Jewish National Council, Lithuania, 1923. Founder and principal of the Jewish Real Gymnasium (secondary school) in Wilkomir (Lith. Ukmergė, 1920. Co-founder of the YIVO Institute in Vilna. Consultant, Jewish Education Committee, New York. Vice-president, Council for Jewish Education. Contributed articles to *Vilner tog* (Vilna), *Di naye shul* (Vilna), *Shul vegn* (Warsaw), *Zukunft* (NY), *Jewish Daily Forward* (NY), *Undzer shul* (NY), *Kultur un dertsiung* (NY), *Oyfn shvel* (NY), *Yidisher kemfer, Yidishe dertsiung, Kinder tsaytung, YIVO bleter* (Vilna, NY). Co-editor of *Yidishe shprakh* and editor of *Pedagogisher byuletin* (NY). Co-editor together with Judah Joffe of the *Groyser verterbukh fun der yidisher shprakh* (Great Dictionary of the Yiddish Language). Wrote Yiddish textbooks and workbooks for Yiddish schools. Born in Polonga, Lithuania. Immigrated to the United States in 1936. Settled in Israel in 1970.

The papers relate to Mark's position as consultant at the Jewish Education Committee, to his activities in the field of education and to his literary career.

Correspondence with Yiddish literary and educational figures, such as Ephraim Auerbach, Aaron Glanz-Leieles, Jacob Glatstein, Abraham Golomb, Chaim Grade, David Ignatoff, Chaim Kazdan, Leibush Lehrer, Joseph Mlotek, Shmuel Niger, Chaim Ormian, Abraham Reisen, Mordkhe Schaechter, Isaac Bashevis Singer, Isaac Nachman Steinberg, Abraham Sutzkever, Max Weinreich, Uriel Weinreich. Correspondence with organizations. Materials relating to the Commission for Yiddish Schools of the Jewish Education Committee: minutes, circulars, reports, surveys, curricula, examinations, Yiddish for adults, visits to schools. Circulars, correspondence with the Teacher's Association, 1943–1963. Circulars and reports of the Sholem Aleichem Folk Institute. Essay contests of the Yiddish PEN Club: list of topics, winners. Congress for Jewish Culture: correspondence, circulars, reports, 1940–1963. Correspondence with YIVO. Manuscripts by Yudel Mark: articles on Yiddish, Jewish education, Yiddish literature. Manuscripts by other writers on educational topics. Surveys on the use of Yiddish conducted in various states.

Inventory, English, Yiddish.

723. MARMOR, KALMAN (1879–1956).
Papers, 1880s–1950s. 37 ft. (RG 205)

Yiddish writer, literary critic, editor, lecturer, political activist. Founding member of the World Union of Poalei Zion and editor of the party's weekly, *Der yidisher kemfer*. In 1906 joined the Socialist Party (USA) and in 1919, the American communist movement. From 1922 was a contributor to the *Morning Freiheit*. Was a lecturer at the Institute for Jewish Proletarian Culture in Kiev, 1933–1936. Born in Lithuania. Lived in Russia, Switzerland, England, the Soviet Union, the United States.

Autobiographical materials including the manuscript and clippings of Marmor's *Lebens–geshikhte* (Autobiography) and of his diaries, 1896–1954. Family correspondence. Personal documents. General correspondence consisting of several thousand letters, 1900–1950s. Correspondents include: Shalom Asch, Baal Makhshoves (Isidor Eliashev), Joseph Barondess, Israel Belkind, Izhak Ben-Zvi, David Bergelson, Yitzhak Dov Berkowitz, Ber Borochov, Reuben Brainin, Joseph Hayyim Brenner, Abraham Cahan, Solomon Dingol, Itsik Feffer, Moses Gaster, Zevi Hirsch Gershoni (pseudonym, Gersoni, Henry), Jacob Gordin, Yizhak Grunbaum, Alexander Harkavy, Theodor Herzl, Peretz Hirschbein, Reuben Iceland, David Ignatoff, Samuel Jacob Imber, Leon Kobrin, Philip Krantz, Zishe Landau, H. Leivick, Abraham Liessin, Judah L. Magnes, Raphael Mahler, Itzik Manger, Mani Leib, Samuel Margoshes, Jacob Milch, Shmuel Niger, Joseph Opatoshu, David Pinsky, Noah Prylucki, Abraham Reisen, Zalman Reisen, Maurice Schwartz, Nahum Shtif, Sholem Aleichem, Abraham Sutzkever, Henrietta Szold, Menahem Ussishkin, Chaim Weizmann, Yehoash. Biographical materials, letters and manuscripts of writers collected by Marmor as editor and author: Joseph Bovshover, David Edelstadt, Jacob Gordin, David Ignatoff, Isaac Leib Peretz, Zalman Reisen, Yehoash, Chaim Zhitlowsky.

Correspondence, circulars, invitations and other materials from political organizations: Ambidjan Committee, Communist Party of United States, *The Daily Worker*, Friends of Soviet Russia, Histadrut Haivrit, ICOR, YKUF, Manchester Zionist Organization, Poalei Zion, Zionist organizations in Basel, Edinburgh, Glasgow, Leeds. Materials on various Jewish organizations in Chicago. Correspondence, circulars from schools and cultural institutions: Institute for Jewish Proletarian Culture, Kiev; International Workers Order Schools, Children's Schools of the Jewish Peoples' Fraternal Order, Sholem Aleichem Schools (NY). Materials from Yiddish theater organizations: Yiddish Theater Museum; drama and music societies; ARTEF. Materials on the Jewish press including *Yidisher kemfer, Morgn frayhayt, Hadoar*, Jewish Telegraphic Agency, *Canadian Jewish Weekly, Freie Arbeiter Stimme, Zukunft, Jewish Daily Forward*. Photographs of individuals and groups.

The Marmor collection includes papers of David Edelstadt, Aaron Liebermann, Jacob Milch and Morris Winchevsky. Marmor utilized the papers in writing biographical essays about these personalities.

Inventory, Yiddish.

724. MARTIN, RUDOLF.
Papers, 1940s. 2 1/2 in. (RG 804)

Former inmate of concentration camps at Westerbork and Bergen-Belsen.

Typescript of Martin's memoirs, with sketches of camp layouts at Westerbork and Bergen-Belsen. Documents such as identification cards, postcards, printed materials relating to both camps. Clippings.

725. MASUR, JENNY.
Papers. 5 in. (RG 653)

Co-editor of the book *Jewish Grandmothers*, published in 1976 by Beacon Press, Boston.
Transcripts of interviews used in the book.

726. MAUD, ZUNI (1891–1956).
Papers. 4 ft. 8 in. (RG 1138)

Artist, cartoonist, puppeteer, playwright, writer and poet. Studied at the Cooper Union Art School, Baron de Hirsch Art School and National Academy of Art, New York. Did illustrations for *Der kibitser* and stage and costume design for productions by Maurice Schwartz in the Yiddish Art Theater. Contributed articles to *Der kundes* (NY), *Jewish Daily Forward* (NY), *Di tsayt* (NY), *Kinderland* (NY), *Kinder zhurnal* (NY), *Frayhayt* (NY). Illustrator of a number of books. In 1925, together with Yosel Cutler, founded the "Modicot" marionette theater. Wrote plays, children's stories and poems. Born in the district of Grodno, Byelorussia. Immigrated to the United States in 1905.

The collection consists primarily of original art works: paintings, drawings, woodcuts, wood carvings. Other materials incude cartoons, political illustrations, book illustrations, clippings of articles, correspondence, typed manuscripts, unpublished music, photographs, programs, personal documents.
Inventory, English.

727. MAX ROSH BENEFICIAL SOCIETY OF HARLEM.
Records, 1903–1910, 1954–1971. 7 1/2 in. (RG 927)

Established in 1903. Named after Max Rosh, a founding member who served as the society's first treasurer. Dissolved 1971.

Minutes, 1903–1910. Financial records, 1954–1970. Materials pertaining to burial. Correspondence.

728. MEISEL, MAX N.
Papers, 1916–1953. 2 ft. 4 in. (RG 257)

Jewish bookseller and publisher, New York. Editor of the *New York Tageblatt* (NY).

Records of Meisel's publishing house: ledgers and business correspondence. Letters to Meisel as editor of the *New York Tageblatt*, 1916–17. Bankruptcy papers of the Jewish Book Agency, 1921–22.

729. MEISELS, ABISH (1897–1959).
    Papers, 1920s–1950s. 5 in. (RG 428)

Yiddish playwright and theater producer in England. Owner of the New Yiddish Theater in London.
    Manuscripts of Meisels's plays. Clippings of Meisels's articles, reviews of his productions. Materials on the Yiddish theater in England.

730. MELAMED, MOSHE (1882–1954).
    Papers, 1930s–1950s. 2 1/2 in. (RG 322)

Yiddish writer. Member of the Jewish anarchist agricultural colony in Clarion, Utah, 1910–1917.
    Correspondence with literary and cultural figures, 1924–1953. Minutes of the executive board meetings and newspaper clippings about the Jewish anarchist agricultural colony in Clarion, Utah, 1910–1914.

731. MELNICK, NACHUM and ROSENBLUM, DEVORAH (born 1909).
    Papers, 1920s–1960s. 1 ft. 8 in. (RG 1147)

Yiddish actors, husband and wife team. Performed with the Vilna Troupe. Toured Europe and the Americas. Settled in Argentina.
    The collection pertains to the artistic careers of Nachum Melnick and Devorah Rosenblum and consists of scripts, publicity programs, sheet music, photographs, clippings, set designs, drawings.
    Photographs cataloged in STAGEPIX.

732. MELTZER, FAIVL (PHILIP) (born 1893).
    Papers, 1943–1950s. 1 ft. 8 in. (RG 1261)

Yiddish writer of children's poetry and stories. Contributed to *Morgn frayhayt*. Born in Bukovina, Rumania. Came to the United States in 1913.
    Manuscripts of poems for children.

733. MEMOIRS OF AMERICAN-JEWISH SOLDIERS.
    Collection, 1945–1946. 10 in. (RG 110)

The collection was assembled as a result of the YIVO essay contest held in 1945–1946, on the theme "My Experiences and Observations as a Jew and a Soldier in World War II."
    The collection consists of 52 essays submitted by the contestants. Related correspondence and photographs.

734. MENACHOVSKY, MOSHE (1893–1963).
    Papers, 1927–1964. 5 in. (RG 424)

Yiddish writer. Lived in Russia, Canada.
    Correspondence with Yiddish literary figures, organizations. Personal documents.

735. MENDELSON, SAMUEL.
    Papers, 1930s–1950s. 10 in. (RG 295)

YIVO collector.

Letters from Yiddish literary figures and communal leaders covering the 1930s to the 1950s.

736. MENORAH BENEVOLENT SOCIETY.
Records, 1919–1969. 5 in. (RG 902)

Organized in New York in 1905. Incorporated in 1919 to provide medical assistance and burial endowments. Arranged social activities for members. Dissolved in the 1970s.

Minutes, 1919–1960s. Financial statements. Membership applications.

737. MERESON, JACOB (1866–1941).
Papers, 1920s–1940. 10 in. (RG 262)

Physician, journalist, translator. His translations were published by the YIVO Institute in Vilna. Lived in Lithuania and the United States.

Manuscripts of Mereson's translations of scientific, philosophical and psychological works from English to Yiddish. Correspondence with Yiddish literary figures.

738. MESTEL, JACOB (1884–1958).
Papers, 1914–1958. 13 ft. 4 in. (RG 280)

Yiddish actor, director, theater critic, historian, poet, essayist and playwright. Director of the ARTEF Theater, New York, 1930s. Performed with Jacob Ben-Ami and Maurice Schwartz. Assistant editor of the *Leksikon fun yidishn teater* (Lexicon of the Yiddish Theater), Volumes 1–3. Lived in Poland, Austria and the United States.

Correspondence with individuals: Jacob Ben-Ami, Ossip Dymow, Ovsei Liubomirskii, Kalman Marmor, Nachman Meisel, Melech Ravitch, Dov Sadan, Michael Weichert and Zalman Zylbercweig.

Correspondence with organizations: Hebrew Actors' Union, IKUF, YIVO. Manuscripts of plays collected by Mestel as director, including adaptations by Mestel. Mestel's writings: manuscripts of poems, plays, essays, articles, notes, translations. Theater production materials: scripts with Mestel's direction notes, prop and set design notes. Miscellaneous theater materials, including theater programs. Clippings: Mestel's writings, biographical articles, reviews of performances. Family correspondence and personal papers including papers of Sara Kindman-Mestel. Photographs relating to Yiddish theater in New York, 1930s–1950s.

Inventory, English, Yiddish.

Photographs are cataloged in STAGEPIX.

739. METZKER, ISAAC (1901–1984).
Papers, 1930s–1970s. 10 in. (RG 1174)

Yiddish writer, journalist for the *Jewish Daily Forward*, 1930s–1970s. Editor of the English version of *A Bintel Brief* [Bintl brif] and numerous books in Yiddish. Born in the village of Łanowicze, Galicia. Immigrated to the United States in 1924.

The collection consists of correspondence with Yiddish writers, including: Rachel Auerbach, Abraham Cahan, Daniel Charney, Eliezer Greenberg, Rachel Korn, Abraham Liessin, Itzik Manger, Shmuel Niger, Lamed Shapiro. Notes and Yiddish manuscripts.

740. MEYERS, ABRAHAM.
Papers, 1931–1948. 5 in. (RG 233)

Philanthropist who supported yeshivot throughout the world. Lived in New York.

The papers relate to A. Meyers's philanthropic activities. Correspondence primarily with rabbinical figures affiliated with yeshivot in Lithuania, Palestine, Poland and the United States. Includes letters from Mendel Beilis, Rabbi Eliyahu Meir Bloch (Telz), the Chofetz Chaim, Rabbi Shmuel Ehrenfeld, Rabbi Eliezer Yehudah Finkel, Rabbi Yehiel Gordon, Rabbi Aaron Kotler, Rabbi Baruch Ber Leibovitz, Rabbi Isser Zalmen Meltzer, Rabbi Yechezkel Sarna, Rabbi Yosef Yitschok Schneerson, Rabbi Eliezer Silver, Rabbi Moshe Soloveitchik, Rabbi Elchonon Wasserman. Clippings relating to Meyers.

741. MICHALPOLIER PODOLIER BENEVOLENT ASSOCIATION.
Records, 1925–1967. 2 1/2 in. (RG 1009)

Established in New York in 1925 by immigrants from Mikhailovka (until 1946, Mikhalpol), Ukraine. Worked with a ladies auxiliary. Contributed to Jewish philanthropies.

Minutes, 1925–67.

742. MIDDLE VILLAGE BENEVOLENT ASSOCIATION.
Records, 1962–1974. 5 in. (RG 988)

Established in 1925. Met in Congregation Machzikei Harav, Queens. Dissolved 1975.

Financial records, 1971–1975. Materials pertaining to burial, 1962–1974. Seal.

743. MIDLO, CHARLES.
Papers. 2 1/2 in. (RG 750)

Physician, scholar. Commented on and annotated *Das Deutsche Gaunerthum*, Leipzig, 1858, by F.C.B. Avé-Lallement. Lallement (1809–1892) was a noted German criminologist and philologist who explored the influence of Yiddish and Hebrew on the language of the underworld.

Handwritten notes, comments and summaries of *Das Deutsche Gaunerthum* as well as a microfilm copy of the book. Manuscript fragment of an unpublished article on Avé-Lallement.

744. MIKULINCER INDEPENDENT LODGE.
Records, 1961–1974. 5 in. (RG 948)

Organized in New York by *landslayt* from Mikulintsy, Ukraine. Founding date unknown. Provided *shiva* (seven days of mourning) benefits for members. Active until 1975.

Financial records, 1960s–1970s.

745. MILBAUER, ISAAC.
Papers, 1930–1959. 1 in. (RG 319)

Active member of the Sholem Aleichem Folk Institute, New York.

The collection consists of correspondence with Yiddish literary figures. Included are letters from Benjamin Jacob Bialostotzky, Leibush Lehrer, Lippa Lehrer, Yudel Mark.

746. MILL, JOHN (JOSEPH SOLOMON) (1870–1952).
    Papers, 1907–1938. 2 1/2 ft. (RG 415)

Active in the Jewish socialist movement in Russia and Poland. Founding member of the Jewish Labor Bund. Lived in Ponevezh (Panevėžys), Vilna, Warsaw, Switzerland. Settled in the United States.
    Correspondence with leading figures in the Jewish Labor Bund, including Bronisław Grosser, Moshe Gurevitch, M. Kopelson, Beinish Mikhalevich, Anna Rosental, Baruch Vladeck.

747. MILLER, BARUCH (1892–1980).
    Papers, 1930s–1970s. 10 in. (RG 1264)

Yiddish writer. Worked in the garment industry as a presser. Most of his stories deal with the needle-trade workers. Born in Bessarabia. Immigrated to the United States in 1911.
    Manuscripts of short stories and a notebook of poetry.

748. MILLER, LOUIS (1889–1967).
    Papers, ca. 1921–1967. 3 ft. 5 in. (RG 573)

Adopted name of Eliezer Meller. Yiddish poet, playwright. Contributed to *Yidisher kemfer* (NY), *Di naye velt* (NY), *Di vokh* (NY), *Der groyser kundes* (NY), *Poezye* (NY), *Dos vort* (NY), *Morgn frayhayt* (NY), *Der hamer* (NY). Founded the periodical *Kultur* (Chicago), 1925. Born in Lanovtsy (Łanowce), Ukraine. Immigrated to the United States in 1906. Lived in the United States and France.
    This record group also includes papers of Tzvi Hirschkan and Rashel Hirschkan. Tzvi Hirschkan (Tzvi-Hirsch Kahn, 1886–1938), Yiddish writer, wrote for *Der tog*, *Di vokh*, *Bikher velt*, *Zukunft*, *Morgn frayhayt*. Born in Tsashnik, Byelorussia. Immigrated to United States in 1925. Rashel Hirschkan, a Yiddish writer, wrote for the *Morgn frayhayt*.
    Correspondence of Louis Miller with individuals and organizations. Reviews of Miller's works. Manuscripts of Miller. Correspondence and manuscripts of Tzvi Hirschkan. Diary written in the 1920s. Last will. Correspondence of Rashel Hirschkan with writers. Letters from the editors of *Morgn frayhayt*. Letters from Hirschkan and Miller.

749. MILLER, MORDECHAI (1895–1946).
    Papers, 1920s–1940s. 5 in. (RG 401)

Yiddish writer. Lived in Ukraine, Canada.
    Manuscripts and clippings of Miller's literary works.

750. MILLER, S. (ISAIAH) (1895–1958).
    Papers, 1940s–1950s. 5 in. (RG 388)

Yiddish novelist, essayist. Lived in Ukraine and the United States.
    Correspondence with literary figures including Joel Entin, Kalman Marmor, Nahum Baruch Minkoff, Alexander Mukdoni, Joseph Opatoshu, Joseph Rolnick, Jacob Isaac Segal, Lamed Shapiro. Manuscripts of Miller's writings. Clippings about Miller and of his writings.

751. MILLNER, JOSEPH (1887–1963).
    Papers, 1940s–1950s. 5 in. (RG 594)

Yiddish and French writer. Wrote primarily on the history of French Jewry. Contributed to *Moment* (Warsaw), *Undzer lebn* (Warsaw), *Parizer haynt*, *Undzer vort* (Paris), *Tsionistishe bleter* (Paris), *Le Monde* (Paris), *Journal de la Communauté* (Paris). Editor-in-chief of the weekly *La Tribune*. Born in Chełm, Poland. Settled in France, ca. 1909.

The papers relate to Millner's literary career and include clippings of Millner's articles relating to French-Jewish history, reviews by the French press of Millner's book *Yidn in frankraykh*. Correspondence.

752. MILWITZKY, WILLIAM.
Papers. 5 ft. 3 in. (RG 378)

Linguist and folklorist, teacher of foreign languages. Traveled through the Balkans in 1898–1899, collecting linguistic, literary and folkloric data relating to Judesmo.

Bibliographic information and clippings relating to the Sephardic Jews and to Judesmo. Roman-character transcriptions of Judesmo texts collected by Milwitzky, manuscripts by Milwitzky including autobiographical material. Original field notes gathered by Milwitzky in 1898–1899, containing proverbs, sayings, etc. Correspondence from scholars, including Sephardim from the Balkans. Ephemeral Sephardica from the Balkans and the United States.

753. MINKOFF, NAHUM BARUCH (1893–1958) and
COOPERMAN, HASYE (1907–1991).
Papers, 1930s–1980s. 16 ft. 8 in. (RG 398)

Nahum Baruch Minkoff was a Yiddish writer, poet, literary historian and critic, editor of the Yiddish literary monthly *Zukunft*. Was one of the founders of the *In zikh* group of Yiddish poets. Taught at the Jewish Teachers' Seminary and the New School for Social Research in New York. Born in Warsaw, immigrated to the United States in 1914. Married Hasye Cooperman in 1931.

Hasye Cooperman was an author, poet and educator. Dr. Cooperman taught American and Comparative Literature at the New School for Social Research. She received the American Poetry Magazine Award in 1957.

The papers reflect the careers of both Minkoff and Cooperman.

Minkoff papers: Correspondence with Yiddish writers, including Baal Makhshoves (Isidor Eliashev), Jacob Maitlis, David Opatoshu, H. Rosenblatt. Clippings about Yiddish writers. Various manuscripts, many of them submitted to the *Zukunft*. Materials on the Yiddish literary group *In zikh*. Cooperman papers: Correspondence with writers and organizations, including Milton R. Konvitz. Manuscripts of poems, short stories. Lecture notes. Doctoral dissertation.

Inventory, English, Yiddish.

754. MINSK JEWISH COMMUNITY COUNCIL.
Records, 1825–1921. 3 ft. (RG 12)

The Jewish community of Minsk, Byelorussia, was represented by the community council (*kehillah*) from the 16th century through 1920. Under the Tsarist regime, the *kehillah* was in charge of internal Jewish affairs and was empowered to collect taxes. The *kehillah* was dissolved after 1920 when Minsk became a Soviet possession.

Fragmentary records include registers of births, marriages and deaths. Statistics of the Jewish population. Tax rolls and reports to various authorities regarding tax collection.

Correspondence regarding Jewish recruits for military service, applications from individuals to avoid army service. Miscellaneous correspondence with the municipality, the police and the governor's office. Membership lists and contribution lists to major synagogues in Minsk.
Inventory, Yiddish.

755. MINSKER LADIES BENEVOLENT SOCIETY.
Records, 1948, 1957–1974. 5 in. (RG 907)

Organized in New York in 1895 by immigrants from Minsk, Byelorussia. Provided sick and death benefits and burial services for its members. Dissolved 1974.
Minutes, 1970–1971. Financial records, 1957–1970. Materials pertaining to burial. Correspondence.

756. MINTZ, MENACHEM MENDEL.
Papers, 1928–1933. 2 1/2 in. (RG 724)

Contributor to the *Tog morgn zhurnal*.
The papers consist of a notebook of Hebrew riddles relating to biblical themes, many of which were published in the *Morgn zhurnal*.

757. MIROSHNIK, KONSTANTIN.
Collection, 1900–1980. 1 ft. 2 in. (RG 1194)

Konstantin Miroshnik emigrated from the Soviet Union and settled in Israel. He was commissioned by the YIVO Institute in 1980 to collect photographs of Jewish life in Russia and the Soviet Union.
Copies of photographs acquired from Soviet émigrés in Israel and from institutions, including Yad Vashem and the Central Zionist Archives. Subjects include: family life; landmarks; Zionism; World War II and the Holocaust; Jews in the Soviet Army; Jewish dissidents in the 1960s and 1970s.

758. MIZRAKH YIDISHER HISTORISHER ARKHIV (BERLIN).
Records, 1802–1924. 35 ft. (RG 80)

German name: Ostjüdisches Historisches Archiv (Archives for the History of East European Jews). In 1919 a group of Jewish activists and representatives of Jewish organizations established a committee in Kiev to collect and publish historical and documentary materials relating to the anti-Jewish pogroms in the Ukraine, 1918–1920. The committee was called the Redaktsyons Kolegye Oyf Zamlen Un Oysforshn Di Materyaln Vegn Di Pogromen In Ukrayne (Editorial Committee for the Collection and Investigation of Materials Relating to the Pogroms in the Ukraine). The founding organizations were the Jewish National Secretariat, the Central Committee of Kiev to Aid Pogrom Victims, and the Folksfarlag (People's Press). The head of the Editorial Committee was Nahum Shtif and its secretary was Elias Tcherikower.
A great deal of original material was collected. These included testimonies, photographs, clippings, and original documents. In 1921 the collection was transferred to Berlin where a new organization, the Mizrakh Yidisher Historisher Arkhiv (Ostjüdisches Historisches Archiv), was founded to assume custody of these records. In 1925 the MYHA merged with the YIVO Institute in Vilna. The MYHA records which are now at the YIVO Archives are

only a fraction of the original archive. The larger part was sent from Berlin to Vilna and was destroyed in Vilna during the Holocaust period.

The record group is comprised of: administrative records of the MYHA and of its predecessor organization, the Editorial Committee, in Kiev; documents relating primarily to the pogroms in the Ukraine; documents on the period of Jewish autonomy in the Ukraine, 1918–1920; miscellaneous historical documents on Russian Jewry.

Pogrom materials include files on the effects of the pogroms on the Jewish communities. Eyewitness accounts arranged by locality. Lists of pogrom victims. Statistics on relief work in the Ukraine. Elias Tcherikower's notes about the pogroms. Photographs of victims, destruction. JDC materials about Ukrainian pogroms.

Minutes of meetings of the Jewish National Council, Kiev, 1917–1918. Minutes of meetings of the Jewish National Assembly in the Ukraine, 1918. Material relating to various departments of the Jewish Ministry.

Records of Jewish organizations. Minutes, memoranda, bulletins and other materials of the following: United Zionist Labor Movement in Russia; Relief Commission for Jewish Writers and Artists in Carlsbad; Committee of Jewish Delegations in Paris; Bund; Poalei Zion.

Petitions to the Tsar about Jewish matters, 1860–1892. Jewish protests against antisemitic theatrical performances by Russian groups, 1864. Correspondence between the Prime Minister Stolypin and Nicholas II, ca. 1910. Material about the Kishinev pogroms and the Beilis trial. Secret police report from Cherkassy District about a conference of the Zionist-Socialist Party, 1911. Clippings regarding the Jewish Legion, 1915. Materials about the trial of the Zeirei Zion (Zionist Youth) in Kiev, 1922. Materials relating to the Schwarzbard trial. Clippings relating to the following topics: nationalist and political groups in the Ukraine, 1919–1920; professional organizations, 1919; international political situation, 1919; Red Cross and government relief programs in the period following the pogroms; Jews in Galicia, Lithuania, Germany, Amsterdam, Palestine, Poland, 1918–1919.

Diary of the Editorial Committee regarding investigations of the pogroms (kept daily by Tcherikower), 1919. Minute-books of the Editorial Committee. Accounting records. Correspondence of the Editorial Committee and the MYHA, 1919–1924, with individuals, organizations, publishing houses, including: Shalom Asch, G.E. Gurevitch, Pinchas Dubinsky, Simon Dubnow, David Mowshowitch, OSE (Berlin), JDC.

Inventory, Yiddish, English.

759. MLOTEK, JOSEPH (born 1918) and CHANA (born 1924).
Papers, 1950–1990. 5 in. (RG 1142)

Joseph Mlotek: Education Director of the Workmen's Circle from 1966 to 1990. From 1991, managing editor of the *Forverts*. Teacher in the Yiddish school system. Active in Yiddish cultural and educational organizations such as the Workmen's Circle, Congress for Jewish Culture, Forward Association, WEVD. Hosted radio programs of the Workmen's Circle on WEVD. Producer and narrator of several Yiddish text and music recordings. Editor, *Kultur un Lebn*, and *Kinder-tsaytung*. Co-editor of weekly, later bi-weekly, column *In der velt fun yidish* in the *Forverts*. On the editorial board of *Zukunft*. Together with his wife, Eleanor (Chana) Mlotek, edited *Perl fun der yidisher poezye* (Tel Aviv, 1974) and compiled *Pearls of Yiddish Song*. Author of Yiddish textbook, *Yidishe kinder, Alef* (1971). Journalist for the Warsaw Yiddish newspaper *Di Folkstsaytung*. Born in Proszowice, Poland. Lived in Warsaw. From 1941–1947 lived in Shanghai. Settled in the United States.

Chana Mlotek (Eleanor Gordon Mlotek): Folklorist, ethnomusicologist. Music Archivist at the YIVO Institute in New York. Active in the Y.L. Cahan Folklore Club at YIVO. Contributed articles on folklore to *YIVO bleter*, *Yugntruf*, *The Field of Yiddish*, and *Studies in Yiddish Language, Folklore and Literature*. On the editorial board of *Yidisher folklor*. In addition to the works produced jointly with her husband listed above, Mlotek also compiled the musical anthologies *Mir trogn a gezang* and *We Are Here* (*Songs of the Holocaust*), the latter jointly authored with Malke Gottlieb.

The papers relate primarily to J. Mlotek's activities as the Workmen's Circle Education Director. Correspondents include Shlomo Bickel, Chaim Grade, Yudel Mark, Dov Noy, Melech Ravitch, Dov Sadan, Abraham Sutzkever, Aaron Zeitlin. Materials include cassettes and correspondence of the *Forverts* column *Perl fun der yidisher poezye* jointly authored by Joseph and Chana Mlotek. Materials on the Moscow Book Fair, 1979. Materials relating to J. Mlotek's personal education.

760. MOLODETZNER YOUNG MEN'S BENEVOLENT ASSOCIATION.
Records, 1913–1965. 3 in. (RG 1199)

Founded in New York by the *landslayt* from Molodechno, Byelorussia.

Minutes, 1920–1936. Ledgers, 1913–1954. Dues book. Miscellaneous bills, correspondence, permits, and other materials concerning burials at Montefiore Cemetery, ca. 1914–ca. 1915.

761. MOLODOWSKY, KADIA (1894–1975).
Papers, 1950s–1960s. 5 ft. 10 in. (RG 703)

Yiddish poet, writer, playwright, teacher. Editor of the journal *Svive* and *Di heym* (Israel). Received several prizes for her literary work. Born in Bereza Kartuska, Poland. Immigrated to the United States in 1935. Lived in Israel from 1950–1952. Died in New York.

Correspondence with family members and literary figures such as Shalom Asch, Abraham Asen, David Bergelson, Shlomo Bickel, Joseph Buloff, Aaron Glanz-Leieles, Jacob Glatstein, Chaim Grade, David Ignatoff, Ephim Jeshurin, Rachel Korn, Leibush Lehrer, H. Leivick, Ida Maze, Joseph Opatoshu, I.J. Schwartz, Isaac Bashevis Singer, Moshe Starkman, Abraham Sutzkever, Malka Heifeitz Tussman, Max Weinreich, Berish Weinstein, Aaron Zeitlin. Manuscripts and clippings of poems, novels, plays, short stories, reviews, translations, and articles on a variety of political, historical and social topics. Included is a series of articles on famous women, written under the pen name Rifka Silberg. The women include: Amalia Freud, Queen Esther, Esther Rachel Kaminska, Baroness Clara de Hirsch, Bruriah (wife of Rav Meir), Golda Meir, Glückel of Hameln, Greta Garbo, George Eliot, Henrietta Szold, and the mother of the Vilna Gaon. Personal documents, including legal documents such as contracts, identification cards. Financial records. Family photographs.

Papers of Simcha Lev (1896–1974), historian and Yiddish writer, husband of Kadia Molodowsky. The papers are comprised of notes on various topics in Jewish history.

Inventory, Yiddish.

762. MONDRY, ADELA.
Papers, 1938–1942. 2 1/2 in. (RG 261)

Singer. Active member of Jewish organizations in Detroit, Michigan.

The collection consists of correspondence with Yiddish literary figures, family members and organizations. Correspondents include family members from Mława, Poland (1940) and individuals such as Benjamin Jacob Bialostotzky, Fishl Bimko, Abraham Golomb.

763. MONIAK, MORDECHAI (1895–1938).
   Papers, 1883–1913. 1 ft. 3 in. (RG 412)

Cantor, composer. Born in Kishinev. Died in New York.

The papers consist of manuscripts of liturgical music as well as Yiddish songs, Russian translations of operatic arias, and notes on music theory.

Composers include A. Dunayevsky, Gedaliah Grossman, Borukh Konstantiner, Louis Lewandowski, Pinchas Minkowsky, Samuel Naumbourg, Zeidel Rovner, Wolf Shestapol, Nissan Spivak, Salomon Sulzer.

Inventory, English.

764. MORRISON, BERYL.
   Papers, 1950s–1960s. 1 ft. 3 in. (RG 1141)

Chairman of the YIVO Committee in Miami, Florida.

Correspondence with Yiddish writers. Minutes and financial ledgers of YIVO Committee meetings. Notes and lectures. Text of Morrison's speeches. Essays by Morrison on Yiddish literary figures.

765. MOSES FAMILY SOCIETY.
   Records, 1918–1979. 1 ft. 3 in. (RG 839)

Established in 1910 by seven children of Moses Cohen, a Jewish immigrant from Srednik (Seredžius), Kovno province, Lithuania. The society's original purposes included organizing family get-togethers, establishing a loan fund and providing benefits to members. Current activities include charitable work, social functions, burial services.

Constitution; minutes, 1961–77; financial records, 1950s–1960s; membership records; correspondence; bulletins, 1938–1976; anniversary journals; invitations; family trees; photographs; tape recording of reminiscences of society's history, 1979.

766. MOTIUK, KALMAN.
   Collection, 1923–1960. 1 ft. 3 in. (RG 307)

Collector for YIVO.

Miscellaneous printed matter relating to Jewish life in New Brunswick, New Jersey.

767. MOUNT SINAI HEBREW MUTUAL BENEFIT SOCIETY.
   Records, 1935–1976. 7 1/2 in. (RG 956)

Founded and chartered in 1870 for the "promotion of friendship and sociability among its members." Provided sick and death benefits. Dissolved 1976.

Constitution. Minutes, 1953–1967. Financial records, 1935–1966. Bulletins. Materials pertaining to burial.

768. MRACHNY, MARK (1892–1975).
   Papers, 1930s–1950s. 5 in. (RG 520)

Yiddish journalist, active in the anarchist movement. Editor of the *Freie Arbeiter Stimme* (NY). Born in Kaunas, Lithuania. Came to the United States in 1928.

Correspondence with literary figures including Leibush Lehrer, H. Leivick, Jacob Lestschinsky, Mani Leib, Shmuel Niger, Abraham Reisen, Lamed Shapiro, Chaim Zhitlowsky.

Manuscripts and holographs by H. Leivick, Mani Leib, Abraham Reisen, Chaim Zhitlowsky.

769. MUKDONI, ALEXANDER (1878–1958).
Papers, 1918–1958. 2 ft. 11 in. (RG 227)

Pen name of Alexander Kappel. Yiddish essayist, columnist, theater critic, translator. Wrote for the Yiddish periodicals *Morgn zhurnal*, *Zukunft*, *Yidisher kemfer*, *Der groyser kundes*, and *Teater un kunst*. Lived in Russia, Poland and the United States.

Correspondence with individuals and organizations: Ben Adir, Shlomo Bickel, Marc Chagall, Baruch (Boris) Glassman, Jacob Glatstein, H. Leivick, Mendele Moykher Sforim, Paul Muni, Shmuel Niger, Melech Ravitch, Zalman Reisen, Ignacy Schipper, Nahum Shtif, Isaac Nachman Steinberg, Abraham Sutzkever. Manuscripts of articles by Mukdoni including fragments of his memoirs.

Inventory, Yiddish, English.

770. MULLER, ERNST.
Papers, 1960s. 4 ft. (RG 636)

Physician, internist. Lived in the United States.

The collection consists of *Gutachten* (medical reports) on behalf of Dr. Muller's patients, who had been victims of Nazi persecution and were submitting restitution claims to the German government.

771. MUSEUM OF THE HOMES OF THE PAST.
Records. 4 ft. (RG 111)

In the years 1943–1945 YIVO conducted a project to gather materials on Jewish life in Europe. The project was conceived in 1943 when it became clear that the European Jewish community faced total destruction. The Museum of the Homes of the Past was to house artifacts and documents commemorating Jewish life as it existed before the Holocaust. The collecting campaign produced large quantities of letters, documents, photographs, artifacts and memorabilia.

The collection consists mainly of correspondence between Jews in the United States and their relatives in Europe. There is also correspondence of YIVO with the donors of the letters.

772. MUSIC.
Collection. 1846–1973. ca. 18 ft. (RG 112)

This collection was assembled in the YIVO Archives and is of mixed provenance. It consists of published and unpublished works of Yiddish and Hebrew; art; folk, popular, and theater music; Holocaust songs; liturgical and Hasidic music; choral music; and instrumental compositions. The collection is divided into the following series:

Sheet music. 1897–1969. 6 ft. 3 in.

Published popular, folk, art and theater music, mainly of the United States. Composers and

arrangers include: Joseph Brody, Abraham Ellstein, Louis Friedsell, Abraham Goldfaden, Solomon Golub, Pinchas Jassinowski, Jack Kammen, Henry Lefkowitch, David Meyerowicz, Sigmund Mogulesko, Alexander Olshanetzky, Arnold Perlmutter, Joseph Rumshinsky, H.A. Russotto, Peretz Sandler, Sholom Secunda, Solomon Shmulewitz-Small, Herman Wohl.
   Inventory, English.

Choral music. 1909–1973. 10 in.

Yiddish and Hebrew folk and art songs, classical compositions. Composers and arrangers include: Samuel Alman, Abraham Wolf Binder, Samuel Bugatch, Julius Chajes, Harry Coopersmith, Abraham Ellstein, Charles Davidson, Maurice Goldman, Vladimir Heifetz, Max Helfman, Pinchas Jassinowski, Mark Lavry, Henry Lefkowitch, Boris Levenson, Leo Low, Meyer Posner, Jacob Schaefer, Ephraim Shkliar, Lazar Weiner, Zavel Zilberts.
   Inventory, English.

Composers and compilers. 1846–1972. 6 ft.

Yiddish and Hebrew folk, popular and art songs. Theater, liturgical and Hasidic music. Music of the Holocaust. Composers, arrangers, and compilers include: Joseph Achron, Ilya Aisberg, Paul Ben Haim, Israel Brandmann, Samuel Bugatch, Mario Castelnuovo-Tedesco, Julius Chajes, Joel (Julius) Engel, Michl Gelbart, Mikhail Gnessin, Abraham Goldfaden, Solomon Golub, Vladimir Heifetz, I. Kaplan, Menahem Kipnis, S. Kisselgof, Henech Kon, H. Kopit, Alexander Krein, Paul Lamkoff, Boris Levenson, Pesach Lvov, Moses Milner, O. Potoker, Salomon Rosowsky, Aron Marko Rothmuller, Anton Rubinstein, Nathan Samaroff, Lazare Saminsky, Mordecai Sandberg, J. Schuman, Moshe Shalit, Harold Shapero, Ephraim Shkliar, Ljubow Streicher, Joachim Stutschewsky, A. Veprik, Jacob Weinberg, Lazar Weiner, Leo Zeitlin, Alexander M. Zhitomirsky. Compilations of music of the Holocaust include works by Zami Feder, Szmerke Kaczerginski, Henech Kon, Johanna Spector.
   Inventory, English.

Miscellaneous.

Manuscripts and published musical works.
   Materials about Jewish music organizations and choruses, cantors, programs, newspaper clippings, photographs, postcards. Composers include Ben Yomen, Meir Bogdanski, Max Helfman.

773. MUSIC (VILNA ARCHIVES).
   1882–1940. 27 ft. (RG 7)

Materials in this collection were originally part of the Esther Rachel Kaminska Theater Museum at the YIVO Institute in Vilna.
   Manuscripts of musical works for the Yiddish theater, including music for about 300 operas, operettas and vaudeville skits. There are also manuscripts and printed sheets of art, popular, dance and liturgical music. Composers, arrangers and musicians include: David Beigelman, Joseph Brody, Adolf Gimpel, Sigmund Mogulesko, Isaac Nozik, Arnold Perlmutter, Joseph Rumshinsky, Peretz Sandler, Sholom Secunda, Herman Wohl. Playwrights include: Abraham Goldfaden, Jacob Gordin, Moishe Hurwitz, Joseph Lateiner, Solomon Libin, Nahum Meir Shaikewitz (Shomer), Boris Thomashefsky, Isidore Zolatarevsky.
   Inventory, English.

774. NAREVKER UNTERSHTITSUNGS VEREIN.
   Records, 1960–1974. 5 in. (RG 1092)

Organized in New York in 1890 by immigrants from Narew, Poland. Associated with a ladies auxiliary.
   Minutes, 1968–1974. Financial records, including sick-benefits payment book, 1940s–1950s. Records of the Narevker Ladies Auxiliary, 1960–1973. Stamp.

775. NATHAN MARCUS BENEVOLENT SOCIETY.
   Records, 1931–1973. 1 folder. (RG 1053)

A mutual aid society. Founding date unknown. Dissolved in the 1970s.
   Correspondence, 1954–1973. Cemetery agreements.

776. NATIONAL CONFERENCE OF JEWISH COMMUNAL SERVICE.
   Records, 1927–1969. 10 ft. (RG 338)

Organized in 1899 as the Conference of Jewish Charities, to represent professional groups active in Jewish communal work. In the 1970s its membership included 300 groups and 2,000 professionals in all fields of communal service. The Conference holds annual meetings and publishes the *Journal of Jewish Communal Service*.
   By-laws. Constitutions. Lists of officers. Membership lists. Lists of organizational members. Reports to the Executive Committee, 1950s–1960s. General correspondence. Correspondence of the president, Philip Bernstein, 1952–1954. Correspondence relating to membership dues, elections. Financial records, budgets, taxes, payroll records. Financial records of the National Conference of Jewish Social Service. Files of NCJCS committees including Executive Committee, Budget Committee, Committee on International Jewish Social Welfare, Committee on Training in Jewish Communal Service, Committee on Professional Education. Files relating to organizations and individuals: Federation of Welfare Funds and Community Councils, National Jewish Welfare Board, National Conference of Social Work, Jewish Agency for Palestine, Association of Jewish Community Relations Workers. Correspondents include Bertram H. Gold, Maurice Bernstein, Sylvia Horowitz, Solomon Gold, Sidney Z. Vincent, Saul Schwartz.
   Materials relating to conventions and conferences. Conference proceedings, nominations, annual meetings. Clippings about conferences.
   Inventory, English.

777. NATIONAL COORDINATING COMMITTEE FOR AID TO REFUGEES COMING FROM GERMANY.
   Records, 1932–1940. 6 microfilm reels. (RG 247)

The National Coordinating Committee was established in 1934 by the AJDC at the suggestion of the State Department. The NCC was to maintain close links with the Intergovernmental High Commission for Refugees established at the League of Nations in 1933 to deal with the problem of Jewish refugees from Nazi Germany. The NCC's main function was to coordinate the relief work of affiliated private refugee agencies in the United States. The financial support of the NCC came mainly from the American Jewish Joint Distribution Committee. The NCC was succeeded in 1939 by the National Refugee Service which was formed to deal with the great increase in immigration from all countries of Central and Eastern Europe. NCC officers included: Joseph P. Chamberlain, chairman, who was at the same time the American member of the Intergovernmental High Commission for Refugees; Paul Felix Warburg, treasurer; Cecilia Razovsky, executive director and secretary. There were about 15 affiliated organizations which dealt with the different categories of refugees. These included the American Christian Committee for German Refugees, American Friends Service Committee, American Jewish Committee, American Jewish Congress, American Joint Distribution Committee, Emergency Committee in Aid of Displaced German Scholars, German Jewish Children's Aid, Hebrew Immigrant Aid Society, National Council of Jewish Women.

Most of the NCC records cover the period 1937–1939, with a smaller proportion of the materials covering the earlier period, 1933–1936.

Files of Cecilia Razovsky. Correspondence between Razovsky and NCC board members, members of affiliated agencies, and other individuals, such as Joseph P. Chamberlain, Albert Einstein, M. Feinberg, Myron Falk, Jr. Correspondence between the NCC and organizations and government agencies, such as Family Welfare Association, Emergency Committee on Displaced Foreign Psychologists, Emergency Committee in Aid of Displaced German Scholars, National Council of Jewish Women, General Committee of Immigrant Aid at Ellis Island and New York Harbor, State Department. Statistics of activities of the NCC and its constituent agencies. Periodic statistical reports from local agencies in Baltimore, Boston, Buffalo, Chicago, Cincinnati, Cleveland, Hartford (CT), Rochester (NY), San Francisco and other cities. Reports by the Jewish Family Welfare Society. Reports by the Brooklyn Section of the National Council of Jewish Women, 1937–1939. Periodic statistical reports of arrivals from Germany and their destination by cities, 1938. NCC Manual on Immigration, 1939: immigration regulations, visas, affidavits. Manual of Mental Examination of Aliens. *SS St. Louis*, 1939: passenger permits and names, names of relatives. Cash journals, clippings.

Inventory, English.

778. NATIONAL COUNCIL FOR BESSARABIAN JEWS.
Records, 1950–1972. 2 in. (RG 1029)

Organized in 1950 as a division of the Histadrut campaign in America. Was affiliated with Histadrut Ha-ovdim and the National Committee for Labor Israel. Many members were formerly associated with the Bessarabian Federation of American Jews, Inc.

Minutes, 1950–1951. Bulletins, 1950s–1960s. Publications including those of the World Federation of Bessarabian Jews, 1960s–1970s. Photograph album of the First World Conference of Bessarabian Jews, 1958. List of World War II survivors from Bessarabia.

779. NATIONAL COUNCIL OF JEWISH WOMEN, SEARCH DEPARTMENT.
Records, 1946–1950s. 4 microfilm reels. (RG 618)

National U.S. organization, founded in 1893 by Hannah Greenbaum Solomon. It ran a variety of social services which included programs for needy families, vocational guidance, services for immigrants. After World War II, the National Council of Jewish Women ran a Search Department for Jewish survivors and tried to locate American relatives.

Correspondence, reports and forms relating to the search activities of the NCJW during the years 1946–1950s.

780. NATIONAL DESERTION BUREAU, NEW YORK.
Records, 1905–1950s. ca. 808 ft. (RG 297)

Agency organized in 1905 which provided assistance to Jewish immigrant women who had been deserted by their husbands. The name was later changed to Family Location Service. Was active until 1966 when it merged with the Jewish Family Service.

About 20,000 files on individual cases of desertion of families by husbands. Index-card file of clients, alphabetically arranged.

781. NATIONAL JEWISH UKRAINIAN COMMITTEE OF THE JEWISH COUNCIL FOR RUSSIAN WAR RELIEF.
Records, 1943–1946. 1 in. (RG 1079)

Organized in the mid-1940s to mobilize Jewish Ukrainian *landsmanshaftn* in the United States to raise relief and rehabilitation funds for *landslayt*, to be distributed through the Jewish Council for Russian War Relief. Led by Rabbi Abraham Bick, president.

Minutes, 1945. Correspondence, relief reports, contribution lists, 1943–1946.

782. NATIONAL REFUGEE SERVICE.
Records, 1938–1946. 69 microfilm reels. (RG 248)

Established in 1939 in New York in order to help refugees from Europe fleeing Nazi persecution, many of them from Germany and Austria. The NRS was the successor agency to the National Coordinating Committee, which had been formed in 1934 as an umbrella organization to coordinate the work of affiliated agencies engaged in immigrant relief work.

The NRS program included: a migration service which dealt with affidavits, sponsorship, visas and other legal aspects of the immigration process; financial aid; a placement service; vocational and retraining programs; a capital loan service; resettlement to smaller communities; and an Americanization program. The NRS also communicated with the U.S. government on matters relating to immigration legislation and special cases. Officers of the NRS included Joseph P. Chamberlain, Chairman of the Board; William Rosenwald, President; Paul Felix Warburg, Secretary; Albert Abramson; Arthur D. Greenleigh. The Executive Committee included Harry Greenstein, William Haber, Joseph C. Hyman. In 1946 the NRS became the United Service for New Americans.

Records of NRS Executive Offices: Data on officers and members of the Board of Directors. Directory of NRS professional staff. Minutes, agendas and reports of Board meetings. NRS by-laws, charter. Minutes of Executive Committee meetings. Monthly reports and memoranda of Executive Directors.

Files of executive officers: William Haber, Ann S. Petluck, Cecilia Razovsky. Includes correspondence, memoranda, reports, case files. Files of Albert Abramson, Stella Baruch, Milton Feinberg, Arthur Greenleigh, Augusta Meyerson, Ephraim R. Gomberg.

Records of NRS departments and committees: Social and Cultural Department, Publicity Department, Division for Social Adjustment, Steering Committee–Joint Supervisory Group, Community Relations Department, Employment Department, Department of Research and Information, Migration and Alien Status Committee, Retraining Committee, Technical Advisory Committee, Employment and Retraining Division, Migration Department, Resettlement Division, Relief and Case Work Department, Family Service Committee, Central Reception and Information Service, Department of Economic Adjustment, Subcommittee on Reclassification, Speakers Bureau.

Correspondence and materials relating to organizations affiliated with the NRS: American Committee for Christian German Refugees, American Friends Service Committee, American Jewish Committee, American Jewish Congress, AJDC, Independent Order of B'nai Brith,

Federal Council of Churches of Christ in America, Emergency Committee in Aid of Displaced Foreign Scholars, Emergency Committee in Aid of Displaced Foreign Physicians (also Psychologists, Social Workers, Scientists), German Jewish Children's Aid, National Council of Jewish Federations and Welfare Funds, Musicians Emergency Aid Bureau, National Council of Jewish Women.

Correspondence and materials from unaffiliated independent organizations: Jewish Family Welfare Society, Hebrew Free Loan Society, Jewish Social Services Association, Jewish Telegraphic Agency, Jewish Theological Seminary, Jewish War Veterans, Jewish Welfare Board, Refugee Economic Corporation, Federation for the Support of Jewish Philanthropic Societies, National Conference of Social Work, United Jewish Appeal, United Palestine Appeal, Council of Service to Foreign Born, War Refugee Board, Jewish Refugee Committee in England, Refugee Children's Movement.

Correspondence with and materials from: U.S. immigration authorities and government offices including U.S. Departments of Justice, Labor, Agriculture, Interior, State.

Financial records: budgets, payrolls, grants, loans, accounting records. Correspondence with Milton Feinberg on financial matters. Topics related to administrative activities, the immigration settlement and resettlement process, financial and fundraising activities and publicity.

Administrative activities: formation of the NRS, its structure and organization, as well as the final months of National Coordinating Committee activities. Division of responsibility between NRS and National Council of Jewish Women.

Publicity activities: materials of the Speakers Bureau, bulletins, newsletters. Fund-raising projects.

Immigration process: immigration laws and regulations, alien registration, visas, temporary visas, affidavits, deportations, illegal entrants, ship arrivals and departures, statistical studies; refugees from Hungary, Italy, Czechoslovakia, Spain, Danzig; Camp Kitchener in England.

Resettlement process: resettlement projects throughout the United States by city and by state; placement, vocational training and special programs for refugees, especially foreign physicians, scholars, scientists, social workers, psychologists, musicians. Social and cultural adjustment activities. Materials on special refugee camps in the United States such as Fort Ontario, Oswego, New York; internment camps in Texas, Tennessee, Oklahoma and other states.

Correspondents include: Shalom Asch, Paul Baerwald, Jacob Billikopf, Jacob Blaustein, Joseph P. Chamberlain, Daniel Charney, Milton Feinberg, Joseph C. Hyman, Alvin S. Johnson, James G. McDonald, William Rosenwald.

Inventory, English.

783. NEMENZINER BENEVOLENT ASSOCIATION.
Records, 1958–1976. 5 in. (RG 941)

Founding date unknown. Organized by immigrants from Nemenčinė (Pol. Niemenczyn), Lithuania. Dissolved in 1976.

Minutes, 1958–1976. Financial records, 1960s–1970s.

784. NEUMAN, WOLF.
Papers, 1935–1966. 10 in. (RG 572)

Yiddish writer. Lived in Philadelphia.

The papers consist of Neuman's manuscripts, clippings of his articles and correspondence. Included are some personal papers of Samuel S. Grossman, a Yiddish writer in Philadelphia, who passed away in the 1930s.

785. NEVODOVSKA, ROSE (1899–1971).
Papers, 1890s–1960s. 2 ft. 1 in. (RG 657)

Yiddish writer, poet. Contributed poems and essays to *Zukunft, Keneder odler, Freie Arbeiter Stimme, Der tog, Morgn zhurnal, Kinder zhurnal*. Born in Białystok, Poland. Settled in the United States in 1928.

Manuscripts of poems, articles and translations by R. Nevodovska. Correspondence, personal documents, clippings of Nevodovska's poems and articles. Manuscripts by Mordecai Jaffe.

786. THE NEW YORK SOCIAL CLUB.
Records, 1885, 1953–1954. 7 1/2 in. (RG 955)

Organized in 1883 and incorporated in 1885 for benevolent, literary, dramatic, and musical purposes. Met in Chelsea Hall, New York, in the 1960s.

Certificate of incorporation, 1885. Financial records. Gavels, seal, pennant.

787. NICKOLAYEVER UNTERSTITZUNGS VEREIN OF CHICAGO.
Records, 1939–1970. 3 in. (RG 1063)

Organized in Chicago in 1927 by immigrants from Nikolayev, Ukraine. Conducted relief activities during World War I and World War II. Did charitable work together with the Ladies Auxiliary of the Nickolayever U.V.

Souvenir journals, 1938–1954. Bulletins.

788. NIEDERLAND, WILLIAM G. (ca. 1905–1993).
Papers. 10 in. (RG 757)

Professor of clinical psychiatry, State University of New York.

The papers consist of transcripts, articles, lectures relating to Niederland's psychiatric research conducted among survivors of the Holocaust and his involvement in German restitution claims. Included are 32 *Gutachten* or psychiatric studies concerning survivors, and unpublished articles and lectures relating to the "Survivor Syndrome" (a clinical term coined by Niederland). Materials on the proposed neo-Nazi march on the Jewish community of Skokie, Illinois, in 1977.

789. NIGER, SHMUEL (1883–1955).
Papers, 1907–1950s. 42 ft. (RG 360)

Pen name of Samuel Charney. Prominent Yiddish literary critic and historian. Active in Yiddish cultural and community organizations. Contributed to numerous newspapers and periodicals, among them *Di yidishe velt* (Vilna), *Der tog* (NY), and the *Jewish Daily Forward* (NY). Edited or co-edited periodicals and books, including: the first volume of the *Leksikon fun der nayer yidisher literatur un prese*, edited by Zalmen Reisen, Vilna, 1914; *Zukunft*, (NY); *Kinder zhurnal*, (NY); *Dos naye lebn*, (NY); *Zhitlovski-zamlbukh*, (NY); *Ale verk fun I.L. Peretz*; first volume of the *Leksikon fun der nayer yidisher literatur*, New York, 1956. Niger held important positions in many Jewish organizations, among them, the following: president, Sholem Aleichem Folk Institute; chairman of the Executive Board of the YIVO Institute; founder and president of the Louis Lamed Fund for Jewish Literature in Yiddish and Hebrew; co-founder of the World Congress for Jewish Culture; chairman of the *Groyser verterbukh fun der yidisher shprakh* (Great Dictionary of the Yiddish Language). Teacher of Yiddish literature at the Jewish Teacher's Seminary, New York. Niger was also active in CYCO (Central Yiddish Culture Organization), Jewish Writers Union, Yiddish Pen Club, Jewish Publication Society of America. Born in Dukor, District of Minsk, Byelorussia. Immigrated to the United States in 1919 and settled in New York.

Correspondence with several thousand individuals, 1907–1961, including S. Ansky, Shalom Asch, David Bergelson, Nathan Birnbaum, Menahem Boraisha, Ber Borochov, Marc Chagall, Jacob Dinesohn, Simon Dubnow, Aaron Glanz-Leieles, Jacob Glatstein, Chaim Grade, Reuben Iceland, Leon Kobrin, Louis Lamed, Leibush Lehrer, H. Leivick, Jacob Lestschinsky, Abraham Liessin, Joseph Opatoshu, Isaac Leib Peretz, David Pinsky, Alexander Pomerantz, Moshe Starkman, Isaac Nachman Steinberg, Abraham Sutzkever, Max Weinreich, Chaim Zhitlowsky.

Family correspondence, 1909–1960, with Niger's mother, wife, children, brothers Daniel Charney and Baruch Vladeck, other relatives. Letters from readers of Niger's columns. Correspondence with hundreds of organizations including Yiddish periodicals, publishing houses, educational and cultural institutions, professional associations, especially institutions he was closely involved with such as YIVO, Congress for Jewish Culture, Louis Lamed Fund, *The Day*, I. L. Peretz Yiddish Writers' Union, *Zukunft*.

Manuscripts and typescripts of major works by Niger on Isaac Leib Peretz, Shalom Asch, H. Leivick, Isaac Meir Dick. Bibliographical materials on various topics in Yiddish literature. Speeches and lectures. Manuscripts of other writers, including Salo Baron, Daniel Charney, Philip Friedman, Szmerke Kaczerginski, Yona Rosenfeld, Abraham Reisen.

Clippings of Niger's regular columns published in *The Day* (*Der tog*), *Day-Morning Journal* (*Der tog-morgn zhurnal*), *Di yidishe velt*. Niger's articles pertaining to other writers, or on topics of Jewish interest, such as Jewish education, Yiddish literature, Zionism, religious issues, the Holocaust, Niger's travels. Clippings by other writers about Niger. Biographical materials about Niger, 1907–1957. Manuscripts and notebooks of Niger's diary. Materials on Niger's activities in Russia during World War I and his immigration to the United States. Personal documents such as passports, invitations, including invitation to the Czernowitz Conference on Yiddish, 1908. Materials relating to copyright. Obituaries.

Inventory, Yiddish, English.

790. NISSENSON, AARON (1898–1964).
Papers. 10 in. (RG 628)

Yiddish poet and writer. Contributed to many periodicals such as *Morgn zhurnal, Yiddishes Tageblatt, Dos yidishe folk, Freie Arbeiter Stimme, Zukunft, Yidisher kemfer*. Born in the district of Minsk, Byelorussia. Immigrated to the United States in 1911.

Manuscripts, correspondence and photographs relating to Nissenson's literary career.

791. NOBLE, SHLOMO (1905–1986).
Papers, 1920s–1970s. 1 ft. 3 in. (RG 747)

Teacher, historian, linguist. Staff member of YIVO from 1944. Taught at the Jewish Teachers' Seminary, New York, and at the YIVO Institute. Editor, *YIVO bleter* and *YIVO Annual*. Born in Sanok, Poland. Immigrated to the United States in 1919.

The collection relates primarily to Noble's scholarly and editorial work at the YIVO Institute as well as to his personal life. Papers submitted to the *YIVO Annual* and *YIVO bleter*. Manuscripts titled *Yidn in England* submitted to the YIVO Society in London. A bibliography of the American Yiddish press compiled by YIVO in Vilna together with the Yiddish Culture Society in New York in 1932. Correspondence with Max Weinreich, Hans Sperber, Abraham Aharoni.

792. NOCOMA CLUB.
Records, 1952–1975. 5 in. (RG 977)

Incorporated in 1905. Instituted a benevolent fund in 1965. Dissolved 1974.

Constitutional amendments and resolutions. Minutes, 1967–1974. Financial records, 1967–1974. Burial records. Meeting notices. Correspondence. Seal.

793. NOVECK, IRVING.
Papers, 1923–1980. 1 ft. 5 in. (RG 1248)

Cantor. Active in *landsmanshaftn* from Krynki, Poland, and in the Hapoel Hamizrachi movement.

The papers primarily relate to Noveck's work with the Krinker Relief Committee, Krinker Memorial Committee and Krinker Yugnt Krayz.

Correspondence with groups from Krynki in the United States, Poland, Brazil and Israel. Records of contributions and packages sent to Poland and Israel. Materials concerning war damage claims, and a suit by the Krinker Relief Committee against the American Federation of Polish Jews. Personal materials, photographs. Hand-drawn map of Krynki.

794. NOVICK, HANNAH.
Papers, ca. 1910–1950s. 1 ft. 8 in. (RG 474)

Teacher, Workmen's Circle Schools and Farband Labor Zionist Order Schools.

The papers relate to H. Novick's activities as an educator. Educational materials such as curricula, games, exams, clippings, plays, materials on holidays and other topics studied in Workmen's Circle Schools, Farband Labor Zionist Order Schools and Camp Kindervelt. Photographs of Camp Kindervelt and of the Jewish Teacher's Seminary in New York.

795. NOVICK, PAUL (PESAKH) (1891–1989).
Papers, 1900–1988. 18 ft. 4 in. (RG 1247)

Journalist, political activist. Active for many years in the Communist Party. Editor in chief of the Yiddish daily *Morning Freiheit*, New York, from 1939 until it closed in 1988. Born in Brest-Litovsk, Russia. Lived in Zurich (1910–1912), New York (1912–1917), Petrograd, Moscow, Minsk and Vilna (1917–1919). Settled permanently in New York in 1920.

The papers pertain to Novick's work as the editor in chief of the *Morning Freiheit*, and to his activities in the Communist Party, United States.

Correspondence, manuscripts of articles and speeches, memoranda, flyers, press releases, pamphlets, photographs and clippings. Manuscripts of other authors. Materials relating to Novick's expulsion from the Communist Party, United States, in 1973. Correspondents include: Herbert Aptheker, David Bergelson, Alexander Bittleman, Reuben Brainin, Marc Chagall, Peggy Dennis, Howard Fast, Lion Feuchtwanger, Joshua Gershman, Ben Gold, Mike Gold,

Itche Goldberg, Ber Green, William Gropper, Abraham Jenofsky, Leon Kobrin, Malka Lee, Ber Mark, Kalman Marmor, Gina Medem, Jacob Milch, Michał Mirski, Melech Ravitch, Isaac Raboy, Sid Resnick, Morris Schappes, Upton Sinclair, Hersh Smolar, Aaron Vergelis, Chaim Zhitlowsky.

796. NOWINSKI, IRA (born 1942).
Papers, 1970s–1980s. 3 in. (RG 1181)

Photographer. Graduate of San Francisco Art Institute. His photographs are housed in several public collections including the Library of Congress and the Museum of Modern Art in New York. His photographs have also appeared in several publications including *In Fitting Memory: The Art and Politics of the Holocaust* (1991). Photographed scenes of Jewish life in San Francisco. Born in New York. Lives in San Francisco, California.

The collection consists of: 95 black-and-white photographs of Soviet Jews in San Francisco, 1970s–1980s; photographs of Holocaust monuments around the world.

797. ODESS, SAUL.
Papers, ca. 1919–1961. 5 in. (RG 527)

Collector for YIVO. The United States.
Correspondence to Odess from Jewish organizations and Yiddish literary figures.

798. ODESSA YOUNG MEN OF HARLEM SICK BENEVOLENT ASSOCIATION.
Records, 1898–1974. 5 in. (RG 975)

Established in New York in 1912 by immigrants from Odessa, Ukraine. Soon after, founded a ladies auxiliary which existed until 1925. Held joint functions with the "downtown" Odessa society. Organized the Odessa Home for the Aged. Dissolved 1973.

Certificate of incorporation, 1912. Constitutions. Minutes. Financial records, 1952–1970. Materials pertaining to burial. Anniversary journal. Photograph. Personal documents of Samuel Dix, charter member. Banner.

799. ODESSAR YOUNG MEN'S BENEVOLENT ASSOCIATION.
Records, 1950s–1968. 10 in. (RG 858)

Incorporated in New York in 1901. Established a loan fund for members. Paid dues to the Odessa Center League. Supported institutions in Israel. Dissolved 1968.

Certificate of incorporation, 1901; minutes, 1961–1967; financial records, 1950s–1960s; burial permits, 1958–1968; seal; stamps.

800. OKUN, ISRAEL (1877–1941).
Papers, ca. 1920–1941. 5 in. (RG 263)

Engineer, director of the ORT Vocational School in Vilna, Poland, 1920s.
Mimeographed notes and manuscript relating to courses on electricity given at the ORT Vocational School in Vilna. Essays on Jewish life in Argentina. Clippings of articles on Jewish life in Argentina and Vilna. Personal documents. Obituaries.

801. OLITZKY, LEIB (1894–1975).
Papers, 1940s–1960s. 1 ft. 3 in. (RG 610)

Yiddish poet, teacher. Taught in the TSYSHO schools in Poland before World War II. Co-editor of Yiddish Bukh publishing house in Warsaw. Contributed to *Varshever almanakh* (Warsaw), *Literarishe bleter* (Warsaw), *Naye folkstsaytung* (Warsaw), *YIVO bleter* (Vilna), *Zukunft, Yidishe kultur* (NY), *Yidishe shriftn, Dos naye lebn, Folksshtime* (Warsaw), *Sovetish heymland* (Moscow). Born in Turzysk, Poland. During World War II Olitzky lived in the Soviet Union. Returned to Poland after the war and remained there until 1958 when he emigrated to Israel.

The collection consists primarily of correspondence with writers and includes some manuscripts. Correspondents include Yitzhak Dov Berkowitz, Benjamin Jacob Bialostotzky, Abba Gordin, Chaim Grade, Ber Mark, Jacob Mestel, Kadia Molodowsky, Melech Ravitch, A.A. Roback, Dov Sadan, Dawid Sfard, Abraham Shlonsky, Chone Shmeruk, Zalman Shneur, Leopold Staff, Abraham Sutzkever, Michael Weichert, Aaron Zeitlin. Personal documents. Correspondence and other materials relating to Olitzky's 60th birthday.

802. ONWARD SOCIETY.
Records, 1913–1983. 1 ft. 10 in. (RG 1159)

Club organized in 1912 by American-born young men to help cure a local boy suffering from tuberculosis. Reorganized in 1925 as part of the I.O.B.A. Established as an independent society in 1927. At its peak the society had close to 800 members and 10 committees. Provided sick and hospital benefits, social activities and burial. Active in World War II relief. Published the journal *Onward Spirit*, 1913–1983.

Minutes, 1940–1983. Album of clippings from *Onward Spirit*, 1913–1948. Issues of *Onward Spirit*, 1934–1983. Printed matter. Photographs. Reports. Publications. Banner, trophy, altar cloth, plaque.

803. OPATOSHU, JOSEPH (1886–1954).
Papers, 1901–1960. 9 ft. 2 in. (RG 436)

Pen name of Joseph Meir Opatowsky. Yiddish novelist and short-story writer. His best known work is *In poylishe velder* (In the Polish Woods), written in 1921 as the first volume of a trilogy. Was on the staff of *The Day* for 40 years. Born near Mława, Poland. Immigrated to the United States in 1907.

Correspondence with literary, artistic and communal figures: Shalom Asch, Baal Makhshoves (Isidore Eliashev), David Bergelson, Martin Buber, Marc Chagall (including some sketches), Simon Dubnow, Itsik Feffer, Lion Feuchtwanger, Aaron Glanz-Leieles, Jacob Glatstein, Shmuel Halkin, Itzik Kipnis, Leib Kvitko, H. Leivick, Itzik Manger, Peretz Markish, Shmuel Niger, David Pinsky, Noah Prylucki, Melech Ravitch, Abraham Reisen, Zalman Reisen, Zalman Shneur, Sholem Aleichem, Nahum Shtif, Israel Joshua Singer, Isaac Nachman Steinberg, Abraham Sutzkever, Baruch Vladeck, Max Weinreich, Yehoash, Israel Zangwill, Aaron Zeitlin, Hillel Zeitlin, Chaim Zhitlowsky.

Correspondence with organizations. Family correspondence. Personal documents.

Lectures, 1921–1951, by Opatoshu on the works of I.L. Peretz, H. Leivick, H.D. Nomberg and various other topics. Manuscripts of stories, fragments of novels, dramatizations. Press clippings of Opatoshu's stories in Yiddish and Hebrew, reviews of his works, reports of his travels to Soviet Russia. Manuscripts of other authors, including Jacob Shatzky, Shmuel Niger, Yechiel Yeshaia Trunk. Materials on Mława including statistical data, maps, memorabilia, memoirs. Photographs of Opatoshu, his family and friends. Reproductions of drawings.

Inventory, Yiddish, English.

804. OPPENHEIM, MENASHE.
Papers, 1935–1960s. 1 ft. 3 in. (RG 684)

Yiddish actor. Performed in Poland. In 1939 Oppenheim came to the United States on an invitation from Maurice Schwartz. He remained in the United States after the outbreak of World War II.

The papers relate primarily to Oppenheim's acting career and include correspondence, personal documents, scripts of plays, sheet music and photographs.

Photographs cataloged in STAGEPIX.

805. OPPENHEIMER, ERIC (?–1960).
Papers. 10 in. (RG 437)

American doctoral student at a German university. At the time of his death he was working on a thesis about German political parties after World War I.

Notes on German political parties after World War I. Term papers for political science courses. Clippings.

806. OPPER, RINA (born 1896).
Papers, 1921–1969. 5 in. (RG 274)

Pen name of Rayne Opoczynski. Yiddish writer. Lived in Poland and the United States.

Correspondence from Opper's relatives in Poland and the United States. General correspondence, 1936–1969. Manuscripts including typescript of Opper's biography of her brother, Perec Opoczyński, a Jewish journalist who perished in the Warsaw ghetto. Articles by Opper.

807. ORAL HISTORY COLLECTION ON THE LABOR MOVEMENT.
Collection, 1964–1968. 6 ft. 10 in. (RG 113)

In 1963 the YIVO Institute sponsored an oral history project on the history of the Jewish community in America. Its objective was to carry out interviews on various themes with leaders and participants in the development of the American Jewish community and its institutions. The project's first theme was the American Jewish labor movement from the turn of the century to the period of the New Deal. The project director was Moses Kligsberg, sociologist and YIVO staff member. Forty-three persons were interviewed. The project continued until 1968 but was not completed.

Correspondence, reports, and printed materials relating to the progress of the project. Tapes of 43 interviews. Typed transcripts of the interviews.

Card catalog, Yiddish.

808. ORMIAN, CHAIM (1901–1982).
Papers, 1920s–1963. 1 in. (RG 728)

Pedagogue, scholar in the field of Jewish education. From 1925 to 1936, taught in the Hebrew Gymnasium (secondary school) in Łódź. Author of several books on pedagogy and psychology. Contributed to *Lodzer tageblat*, *Dos kind* (Warsaw), *YIVO bleter* (Vilna). Born in Tarnów, Galicia. Settled in Israel in 1936.

The papers consist of correspondence and printed materials relating to Ormian's activities in the field of education. Correspondents include A.A. Roback and Leibush Lehrer. Materials from YIVO in Vilna relating to its Section on Education and Psychology.

809. ORT SOCIETY, VILNA.

Records, 1898, 1920–1940. 2 ft. 11 in. (RG 47)

Initials of the Russian Obshchestvo Rasprostraneniia Truda Sredi Evreev (Society for the Spreading of Vocational Work Among Jews). Founded in 1880 in Russia, as a society for the promotion of vocational training and for the development of agriculture, ORT operated vocational and agricultural schools, as well as agricultural colonies and factories. At first ORT functioned only in Russia, but later extended its activities to Poland, Lithuania, Latvia, Bessarabia, Germany, France, Bulgaria, Hungary and Rumania. Extensive assistance programs were also set up in Africa, Asia, South America and Israel.

The ORT Society in Vilna was established after World War I. It provided vocational, agricultural and handicraft training courses and supported Jewish agricultural cooperatives in and near Vilna.

The collection consists of minutes of meetings, correspondence, reports, circulars, financial records, miscellaneous teaching materials, lists, relating to the administration and activities of the ORT Society in Vilna, 1920–1940.

Administration records. Minutes of meetings of the executive committee, 1922–1939. Financial reports, 1922–1937. Contracts, reports, memoranda to Soviet authorities in Vilna, 1940. Correspondence: Central Committee of the ORT Society in Poland; District School Board in Vilna; Jewish Teachers' Union, Vilna; Jewish Community Council, Vilna; ORT Union, Berlin, Paris; ORT offices in Białystok, Łódź, Rovno, Kaunas, Riga, London, New York.

Records relating to schools and courses of the ORT Society in Vilna. Curricula, class schedules, financial records, correspondence, minutes of meetings, and other papers of the Trade School and Vocational School, as well as other schools.

Records relating to agricultural colonies and loan societies: loan applications, statistical questionnaires about Jewish families working on farms in various localities.

Inventory, Yiddish.

810. ORT VOCATIONAL SCHOOL (VILNA).

Records, 1921–1939. 4 ft. 7 in. (RG 21)

The ORT Vocational School in Vilna, also called the Technicum, was founded in 1921 to train young people in the fields of mechanics and electrical maintenance. The school was subsidized by ORT, the Vilna Kehillah and the Vilna municipality. For the first three years the director was Israel Okun. From 1924 until the closing of the school in 1934, the directorship was assumed by Matityahu Schreiber. The school had a technical library and published its own textbooks in Yiddish.

Correspondence, memoranda, reports, financial records, lists, relating to the activities of the school. Budgets, 1922, 1924–1940. Lists of members of the administration and executive board. Articles and leaflets on the history, organization and goals of the Technicum. General reports, 1926, 1928, 1930, 1932–1933.

Correspondence with: ORT Central Committee in Warsaw, 1920s–1930s; ORT Vilna, 1923, 1928–1930, 1937–1939; Ministry of Education, Warsaw, 1922, 1923, 1928–1939; Board of Education, Vilna District, 1920s–1930s; Executive Board of TSYSHO (Central Yiddish School Organization), Warsaw.

Materials on teachers, students and curricula. Teachers' applications, teachers' registration cards. Classroom roll-books, teachers' personal documents, student registration cards, student health records, students' personal documents. Lists of students, graduation diplomas, curricula for general and vocational subjects, teacher assignments, student papers, materials on exams.

Inventory, Yiddish.

811. OSHEROWITCH, HIRSH (born 1908).
Papers, 1960s–1980s. 5 in. (RG 991)

Yiddish poet. Contributed to *Dos vort, Di yidishe shtime, Folksblat, Der emes* (Moscow). In 1948 Osherowitch was arrested by Soviet authorities and sentenced to 10 years in a labor camp of which he served seven years. Born in Panevėžys, Lithuania. Lived in the Soviet Union. Settled in Israel.

Correspondence with writers. Posters relating to literary evenings. Photographs of Osherowitch and other writers. Clippings of reviews and poems.

812. OSHEROWITCH, MENDEL (1887–1965).
Papers, 1920s–1967. 10 ft. (RG 725)

Yiddish journalist, novelist, historian. From 1914 he was a staff member of the *Jewish Daily Forward* and was on its editorial board for many years. Contributed to periodicals including *Yidisher kemfer, Zukunft, Freie Arbeiter Stimme*. Editor, *Yidn in ukrayne*. President, I.L. Peretz Yiddish Writers' Union, New York. Organizer, Federation of Ukrainian Jews. Born in Trostyanets, Ukraine. Immigrated to the United States in 1909 after a short stay in Palestine.

The collection consists of correspondence, manuscripts, printed matter, clippings, photographs and other materials relating to the activities of Mendel Osherowitch. There is also some posthumous material.

Correspondence with individuals and organizations including Shalom Asch, Salo Baron, David Ben-Gurion, Abraham Cahan, Albert Einstein, Aaron Glanz-Leieles, Emma Goldman, Sol Hurok, Jacob Lestschinsky, Zalman Reisen, Jacob Shatzky, Abraham Sutzkever, Max Weinreich.

Manuscripts and typescripts by Osherowitch including his memoirs and his first novel, *Entangled* (unpublished). Articles and other works relating to Abraham Cahan, *Jewish Daily Forward*, topics in Jewish history. Radio scripts. Manuscripts by other authors including Abraham Cahan, Pierre Dreyfus, Hillel Rogoff, Dov Sadan, Moshe Starkman. Clippings relating to various topics and individuals. Photographs of individuals including Theodor Herzl, Hillel Rogoff, Abraham Cahan. Miscellaneous materials, including an antisemitic pamphlet published in the United States by the Headquarters of the Russian Fascists, 1932. Personal papers.

Inventory, English.

813. OSMAN, ISRAEL (1887–1951).
Papers, 1915–1938. ca. 1 in. (RG 607)

Yiddish writer. Contributed to *Der groyser kundes, Der tog, Zukunft, Ha-ivri, Ha-doar.* Born in Wyszków, Warsaw district, Poland. Came to the United States in 1913.

The collection consists of correspondence with literary figures, including Peretz Hirschbein, Mordechai Judenson, Abraham Liessin, H. Rosenblatt, Yehoash.

814. OSOFSKY, DOROTHY (?-1979).
Papers, 1939–1979. 3 ft. (RG 1178)

Jewish musicologist. Created the Jewish Family Music Bank at the American Jewish Congress, 1978–1979. The JFMB recorded Jewish professional musicians such as the folksinger Masha Benya and the composer Samuel Bugatch, as well as amateur singers in Brooklyn, New York.

The collection relates to Osofsky's field work for the JFMB and consists of approximately 100 cassettes of interviews and recorded songs, as well as slides, photographs, songsheets, scholarly papers, and administrative records.

815. OSTREICHER GALIZIANER LODGE NO. 288, INDEPENDENT ORDER BRITH ABRAHAM.
Records, 1907–1976. 12 in. (RG 899)

Founded in New York in 1904 as a lodge of the Jewish fraternal order, Independent Order Brith Abraham (IOBA). The IOBA's original aims were to aid members in times of need, supply medical help, visit the sick, provide burial and endowments, and help the new immigrant with the Americanization process. Lodge No. 288 purchased cemetery plots in Mt. Zion and Beth David cemeteries. The IOBA has merged with the fraternal order Bnai Zion.

Minutes (Yiddish and English), 1945–1963, including minutes of cemetery committee. Financial records, including membership dues book, 1935–1958. Correspondence and documents pertaining primarily to burial, 1907–1976. Materials related to membership. Cemetery maps.

816. OSTROLENKER FRIENDSHIP SOCIETY.
Records, 1918–1973. 10 in. (RG 860)

Organized in New York by immigrants from Ostrołęka, Poland, as the Ostrolenker Lodge No. 607, Independent Order Brith Abraham, 1911. Filed for incorporation of the Ostrolenker Friendship Society in 1950 and transferred cemetery property to the new membership corporation. Contributed to the Al Tidom Association to aid Soviet Jews and to the United States Grand Lodge of the Independent Order Brith Abraham. Dissolved in 1973. Funds were distributed to various Jewish charities.

Financial records of the Ostrolenker Lodge, 1945–1972. Financial records of the Friendship Society, 1950–1973. Correspondence, 1950s–1960s, including correspondence pertaining to the Lodge. Burial permits pertaining to the Ostrolenker Lodge. Seal of the Ostrolenker Friendship Society.

817. OSTROLENKER PROGRESSIVE YOUNG FRIENDS.
Records, 1920s, 1937–1970. 2 1/2 in. (RG 1040)

Founded in New York in 1912 by a group of *landslayt* from Ostrołęka, Poland, who felt a need to form their own society rather than belong to the existing Independent Ostrolenker Young Men. Joined the Ostrolenker Relief during World War I. Society's ladies auxiliary established in 1932.

Constitution. Minutes, 1939–1970. Journal, 1937. Membership directory. Photograph.

818. OSTROWO JEWISH COMMUNITY COUNCIL.
Records, 1824–1919. 10 ft. (RG 13)

The town of Ostrowo (Ostrów Wielkopolski, Poznań province, Western Poland) was under German domination from 1793 to 1918. The Jewish community which had existed there since 1724 became thoroughly Germanized in time. The community declined in size after 1918 when the province of Poznań became part of independent Poland.

The records of the Ostrowo Jewish community cover the German period. Records of communal officers include: materials on the elections of communal officers, rabbis, cantors, slaughterers and sextons; synagogue seat contracts; marriage registers; lists of the poor and petitions for aid; school and vocational apprenticeship records; tax rolls and other financial documents; government regulations and decrees; vital statistics, birth records. Records of the Community Council include minutes of election meetings, correspondence with the government, communal decisions and protests, rolls of community members listing profession and citizenship status.

Inventory, English.

819. OSTROWSKY, ABBO (1885–1975).
Papers, ca. 1900–1975. 4 ft. 8 in (RG 681)

Painter, graphic artist, educator. Founded the Educational Alliance Art School and served as director and instructor. His works were exhibited in galleries across the United States and in England and France. Born in Elizavetgrad, Russia. Settled in New York in 1908.

The papers consist of correspondence, exhibition catalogs, reports, newspaper clippings, publicity releases, photographs and art work relating to the artistic career of Ostrowsky as well as to his involvement with the Educational Alliance.

Correspondence with museums such as the Baltimore Museum of Art, the U.S. National Museum, Library of Congress, Metropolitan Museum of Art, Bezalel Museum in Jerusalem, Tel Aviv Museum, pertaining to sales and exhibitions of Ostrowsky's works.

Correspondence with Stanley M. Isaacs, president of the Educational Alliance, and Edith Isaacs. Materials on Stanley Isaac's political career, 1937–1961.

Correspondence with the alumni of the Art School including the Soyer brothers, Leonard Baskin, Elias Newman, Chaim Gross, Peter Blume and Jacob Epstein.

Correspondence of the Educational Alliance Art School. Reports on the Art School's activities, lecture announcements, exhibitions. Ostrowsky's lectures on Elementary Drawing. Materials relating to exhibitions and art sales held at the Educational Alliance. Correspondence with Maurice Glickman, Jacob Epstein. Materials on the student organization of the Art School, The Palette Club.

Correspondence with the American Federation of Arts, with various art councils and neighborhood settlement schools. Materials on the National Federation of Settlements. Materials on the various art programs of organizations affiliated with the United Neighborhood House.

Exhibition catalogs. Original drawings by Ostrowsky in pencil as well as in pen and ink. Works include prints and etchings of Maine and France and of the excavations for New

York's Second Avenue Subway, as well as a portrait painting of Abraham Liessin. Photographs of the Educational Alliance and University Settlement: students' art works; students and faculty including Abbo Ostrowsky, Chaim Gross, Jacob Epstein, Peter Blume. Clippings pertaining to Ostrowsky's career, the school, well-known alumni. Manuscript of autobiographical works by Ostrowsky. Diary entries, 1924.

Inventory, English.

Art works have been placed and cataloged in the Art Collection, RG 101.

820. OSTROWSKY, WILLIAM.
Papers, 1936–1945. 1 ft. 8 in. (RG 287)

Collector for YIVO, Los Angeles.

Clippings of political cartoons relating to World War II from various English and Yiddish newspapers. Included are works by William Gropper and Zuni Maud and clippings of art from the Holocaust period by Arthur Szyk.

821. OVED, MOSHE (1883–1958).
Papers, ca. 1915–1958. 2 ft. 3 in. (RG 396)

Yiddish writer, poet, sculptor, jeweller, owner of the Cameo Corner antique shop, London, England.

Correspondence with Yiddish literary figures including Shalom Asch, Jacob Glatstein, Chaim Grade, Peretz Hirschbein, Shmuel Niger, Joseph Opatoshu, David Pinsky, Melech Ravitch, Maurice Schwartz, Zalman Shneur, Nahum Sokolow, Abraham Sutzkever, Aaron Zeitlin, Hillel Zeitlin.

Manuscripts of Oved's autobiography, poetry and prose. Clippings about Oved. Photographs of sculpture and sculpture exhibitions. Sketches for Oved's sculptures. Personal documents.

822. OZAROWER YOUNG MEN'S SOCIETY.
Records, 1927–1977. 3 in. (RG 903)

Founded in New York in 1927 by immigrants from Ożarów, Poland, as an offshoot of the already existing Ozarower society. Aimed to help the needy in Ożarów. Later, joined with Ozarower societies in Detroit, Toronto, Montreal, to raise relief funds.

Minutes, 1927–1959. Financial records, 1940s–1970s. Materials related to anniversary celebrations.

823. PACKER, VICTOR (1897–1958).
Papers, 1920–ca. 1950. 8 ft. 11 in. (RG 1295)

Yiddish actor. Performed with Yiddish theater groups in Poland, Lithuania and the United States, including the Kompaneyets troupe in Poland, the Folks Teater in Kaunas, and the Yiddish Art Theater in New York. Organized cultural events in Jewish summer camps. Hosted radio programs in Yiddish on WLHT radio station in Brooklyn. Was also an accomplished silversmith and furniture designer. Born in Białystok, Poland. Immigrated to the United States in 1924.

The papers pertain to Packer's stage and broadcasting career. Skits, lyrics and poems written or adapted by Packer. Manuscripts of plays. Jokes and anecdotes. Texts of broadcasts, including serialized dramatizations of works by Abraham Bookstein. Programs, posters and photographs, reflecting Packer's career, including a scrapbook from Kaunas. Financial and legal documents. Correspondence, including letters from Joseph Rumshinsky and Wolf Younin. Manuscripts of musical compositions and sheet music.

824. PANNONIA LODGE NO. 185, INDEPENDENT ORDER OF ODD FELLOWS.
Records, 1920–1963. 2 ft. 2 in. (RG 869)

Founded in 1916 as a chapter of the Grand Lodge of the State of New York, Independent Order of Odd Fellows. Members were Hungarian-speaking Jews who conducted their business in that language until 1939. Established a relief committee, a cemetery committee, a loan fund, an old-age and disability fund. Affiliated with the Pannonia Rebekah Lodge No. 130, I.O.O.F.

Minutes of regular meetings, 1920–1939 (Hungarian), 1939–1942, 1952–1963 (English). Minutes of the Burial Committee, 1920–1936 (Hungarian). Minutes of the Old Age Pension and Disability Committee, 1934–1942 (Hungarian), 1944–1962 (English). Minutes of the Silver Jubilee Committee, 1940–1941. Financial records, 1921–1937 (Hungarian), 1950s–1970s (English). Correspondence, Disability Committee, 1940s–1950s. Miscellaneous materials, including materials pertaining to the Pannonia Rebekah Lodge.

825. PARGMAN, BEZALEL.
Papers. 10 in. (RG 736)

Diarist. Poland, the United States.

The papers relate to Pargman's personal life and to the history of the town of Jadów, Poland. Manuscript of Pargman's diary. A manuscript entitled *Yadover yizkor bukh* prepared by several former residents of Jadów. Family photographs.

826. PASINSKY, MOTL (1903–1924).
Papers, 1923–1925. 2 in. (RG 475)

Yiddish poet. Born in Białystok. Immigrated to the United States.

Correspondence and manuscripts of poems and stories.

827. PAT, JACOB (1890–1966).
Papers, 1910s–1966. 2 ft. 1 in. (RG 541)

Jewish labor leader, teacher, Yiddish writer. Active in the Bund party and in the TSYSHO Yiddish secular school system in Poland before World War II. Leading member of the Jewish Labor Committee, Congress for Jewish Culture, the Workmen's Circle Schools. Wrote and edited works for the Workmen's Circle Schools. Contributed novels, stories, articles, dramas, children's plays, literary criticism to periodicals such as *Hazefira* (Warsaw), *Haynt* (Warsaw), *Shul vegn* (Warsaw), *Literarishe bleter, Vilner tog, Grininke beymelekh, Morgn frayhayt* (NY), *Jewish Daily Forward* (NY), *Zukunft* (NY), *Di goldene keyt* (Israel). Born in Białystok, Poland. Came to the United States on a visit in 1938 and remained due to the outbreak of World War II.

Notebooks, speeches and articles by Pat. Clippings of his writings. Correspondence from his son in the United States army during World War II. Bibliography of his writings.

828. PATT, EMANUEL (1912–1971).
   Papers. 1 ft. 8 in. (RG 452)

Physician and journalist. Active in Jewish socialist and cultural organizations. Contributed to various Yiddish newspapers, including *Der tog* (The Day) and the *Tog morgn zhurnal* (*The Day Morning Journal*), where he published a regular column on medical matters. Born in Białystok. Immigrated to the United States in 1940.

   Clippings of his column *Fragn fun gezunt*, which appeared in the *Tog morgn zhurnal*.

829. PAUL REVERE LODGE NO. 464, INDEPENDENT ORDER BRITH ABRAHAM.
   Records, 1936–1968. 5 in. (RG 829)

Founded in New York in 1908 by immigrants from Snyatyn (Pol. Śniatyń), Ukraine. In the 1930s was called the Sniatyner Lodge 464 and later changed its name to the Paul Revere Lodge No. 464, IOBA Founded a loan fund (1912) and a sick-benefits fund (1915). Minutes, 1936–1968. Minutes of the Sniatyner American Lodge, Inc., 1941–1951. Anniversary journal, 1958.

830. PERKOFF, ISAAC (born 1870).
   Papers, ca. 1900–1930s. 1 in. (RG 326)

Yiddish journalist and theater critic. Ukraine, London.

   The papers consist of correspondence, including letters from organizations, individuals, family members, and letters from the YIVO office in Vilna, 1928–1931.

831. PERLMAN, LOUIS (1886–1972).
   Papers, 1950–1971. 1 ft. (RG 1298)

Writer. Occasional contributor to the Yiddish dailies *Der amerikaner*, *Der tog*, and *Forverts*. Owner of a laundry in Brooklyn. Born in Byelorussia. Died in Miami Beach, Florida.

   Yiddish manuscripts and clippings of writings by Louis Perlman.

832. PERLMUTTER, SHOLEM (1884–1954).
   Papers, 1880s–1950s. ca. 114 ft. (RG 289)

Writer, playwright, professional prompter in the Yiddish theater. Founder and secretary of the League of Yiddish Playwrights. Founder of the Society of Jewish Composers, Lyricists and Publishers. Served on the Executive Committee of the *Leksikon fun yidishn teater* (Lexicon of the Yiddish Theater).

   The collection consists of a wide variety of Yiddish theater materials gathered by Perlmutter, and includes Perlmutter's personal papers.

   About 1,300 manuscripts of Yiddish plays from the United States and Europe. Letters to Perlmutter from actors and playwrights as well as other theater personalities. Correspondents include Jacob Adler, Sigmund Feinman, Jacob Gordin, Jacob Kalich, David Kessler, Paul Muni, Noah Nachbush, Alexander Olshanetsky, Molly Picon, Zalman Reisen, Joseph Rumshinsky, Ludwig Satz, Maurice Schwartz.

   Music of the early Yiddish theater in Europe and the United States. Four hundred eighty-three operettas and plays with music. Directors' copies with texts and instrumental parts. Liturgical music, songs, compositions and printed sheet music. Manuscripts by Joseph

Brody, G. Finkelstein, Louis Friedsell, Abraham Goldfaden, J. Gropper, Alexander Olshanetzky, Arnold Perlmutter, Joseph Rumshinsky, Sholem Secunda, Herman Wohl, Khone Wolfsthal.

Notes, biographical materials, and clippings of articles about actors, playwrights, musicians. Includes some personal papers of Abraham Goldfaden, Samuel Goldenburg, Joseph Rumshinsky and Ludwig Satz.

Records of the Society of Jewish Composers, Publishers and Songwriters. Records of the Society of Yiddish Playwrights. Records of the Hebrew Actors' Union.

Clippings of articles about cantors. Manuscript of a biography of Zavel Kwartin by Perlmutter.

Photographs. Perlmutter's family photographs. Ludwig Satz's collection of photographs. Photographs of actors and performances.

Art works. Photographs and drawings of set designs and costume designs. Drawings in ink, crayon, pencil, watercolors, of general subjects.

Theater posters from various countries, including Argentina, Brazil, Germany, Rumania, the United States. Programs and playbills.

Inventory of the Theater Collection, Yiddish.

Inventory of the Music Collection, English.

Photographs cataloged in STAGEPIX.

833. PERLOV, JOSEPH.
Papers, 1941–1962. 2 1/2 in. (RG 700)

Active in Yiddish cultural institutions, including Sholem Aleichem Folk Institute.

The papers consist of correspondence with Farlag Matones, Workmen's Circle, YIVO, Camp Boiberik and other organizations.

834. PERSKY, ABRAHAM.
Papers. 5 in. (RG 645)

Yiddish journalist, poet. Used pseudonym Avishag. Lived in the United States.

The papers consist of manuscripts of plays and poems as well as clippings of Persky's works.

835. PERSONENSTANDARCHIV KOBLENZ.
Records, 1677–1938. 3 ft. 4 in. (RG 242)

The Personenstandarchiv (Vital Records Archive) in Koblenz, Germany, was a branch of the Reichssippenamt (Reich Racial Office), which was in charge of determining racial pedigrees of individuals. The archive contained documents confiscated by the Nazis in the 1930s and 1940s from various Jewish communities. Prior to 1914, all these communities had been within the German Empire. Today they are part of Germany or Poland.

This collection consists of photostatic copies of original documents in the Personenstandarchiv made in 1950–1951 for YIVO by Gregor Raskin, a YIVO representative in Germany. The materials consist of birth, death, marriage and cemetery records, community registers, communal tax lists, manuscripts of community histories, communal by-laws. Extensive material is to be found on the following communities: Berlin, Coswig, Dessau, Ellrich, Erfurt, Frankfurt an der Oder, Fraustadt (Wschowa, Pol.), Jauer (Jawor, Pol.), Konstadt (Wolczyn, Pol.), Langendorf (Satulung, Rumania), Magdeburg, Neisse (Nysa, Pol.), Mecklenburg-Schwerin, Trabbin, Zerbst.

Inventory, English.

836. PETRUSHKA, MOISHE.
Papers, 1920s–1980s. 5 in. (RG 1192)

Secretary of the Jewish Socialist Verband. On the board of the World Federation of Polish Jews. Active in the Jewish Labor Committee. Lived in Poland and the United States.

Materials relating to the Jewish Labor Committee, the World Federation of Polish Jews, Jewish Socialist Verband. Materials on Simkha Petrushka, a Yiddish writer and translator. General correspondence. Photographs. Clippings.

837. PETT, CHAIM (1900–1959).
Papers, 1930s–1959. 1 ft. 8 in. (RG 438)

Yiddish poet, writer. Born in Wolpa, in the district of Grodno, Poland. Immigrated to the United States in 1922.

Correspondence with writers, including Abraham Cahan, Ben Zion Goldberg, Abba Gordin, David Ignatoff, Kalman Marmor. Correspondence with family. Manuscripts of Pett.

838. PHILIP BERNSTEIN SICK BENEFIT ASSOCIATION.
Records, 1894, 1965, 1971–1975. 2 1/2 in. (RG 925)

Organized in 1893 by ten men attending the burial of Philip Bernstein, a Rumanian immigrant, in Washington Cemetery, Brooklyn. Incorporated in 1894. Established an old-age fund to assist older members in paying dues, 1940. Dissolved 1975.

Certificate of incorporation, leather-bound, 1894. Constitution. Minutes, 1971–1975. Membership records. Seal.

839. PHOTOGRAPHS (VILNA ARCHIVES).
Collection, 1910s–1930s. 8 ft. 4 in. (RG 9)

This diverse collection was assembled in the YIVO Archives in Vilna.

The collection includes photographs or negatives of the following: Jewish life in various countries including Palestine and Argentina; books, manuscripts; YIVO exhibits; photographs of personalities; blood-libel trials; pogroms.

Card inventory of the photographs of personalities.

840. PHOTOGRAPHS OF PERSONALITIES.
Collection, 1880s–1970s. 25 ft. (RG 121)

Photographs of mixed provenance collected from various sources.

The collection consists of photographs of individuals noted for their contributions to Jewish life: writers, scholars, historians, scientists, philosophers, community leaders, rabbinical figures, political figures, musicians, cantors. Included are photographic portaits, family photographs, group photographs.

Card inventory, English, Yiddish.

841. PIATERER PROGRESSIVE BENEVOLENT SOCIETY.
Records, 1926, 1939–1970s. 3 in. (RG 1085)

Established in New York in 1925 by immigrants from Piategorsk (Pyatigorsk), Ukraine. Incorporated in 1926. Conducted relief work for home town after World War I. Worked through the Russian War Relief to aid *landslayt* during World War II. Built a youth center in Israel.

Certificate of incorporation, 1926. Minutes, 1939–1967. Dues ledger, correspondence, photographs.

842. PICON, MOLLY (1898–1992).
Papers, ca. 1900–1972. 2 ft. 1 in. (RG 738)

Popular U.S. actress. Performed in Yiddish and English. Played in Kessler's Theater as well as in many other groups. In 1935, toured in a vaudeville show together with her husband, Jacob Kalich. From 1942 managed the Molly Picon Theater in New York. After World War II, visited DP camps and toured Australia, South Africa, and Europe. In the 1960s she performed on stage and in television and film productions.

Photographs, scripts, playbills, musical scores, correspondence, recordings, plaques and art objects relating to Picon's theatrical career. Personal photographs of Picon and her husband. Photographs of Picon in various stage and film productions including the films *Fiddler on the Roof*, *East and West*, *Mamele*, *Yidl mitn fidl*, *Milk and Honey*, and the plays, *Kuni Leml*, *Motel Peysi*. Manuscripts of plays including *Shmendrik* and *Yankele*. Music by Abe Ellstein, Mordecai Gebirtig, Abraham Goldfaden, Molly Picon, Joseph Rumshinsky. Playbills and programs from films and theater. Scrapbook of correspondence, theater tickets. Recordings of songs performed by Picon. Plaques, citations, awards. Original art items including portraits, illustrations and cartoons on various topics, many of them studies of Picon.

Inventory, English.

Photographs cataloged in STAGEPIX.

Recordings placed in Sound Archive: Collection of 78 rpm recordings.

843. PILCH, JUDAH (born 1903).
Papers, 1900–1930s. 2 1/2 in. (RG 1145)

Jewish educator, lecturer, communal figure. Director, National Curriculum Research Institute, American Association for Jewish Education. Held executive positions in other Jewish educational organizations and was active in various Jewish communal organizations. Author of articles and monographs on Jewish education. Born in Russia. Immigrated to the United States in 1923.

The collection includes: Photograph of a Zeirei Zion conference. Articles by Pilch on the 19th Zionist Congress in Prague. Photograph of American-Jewish educational leaders, 1910. Materials relating to the League of Jewish Youth of America. Copies of the youth publication *Hed-Ha-Galil*.

844. PILIVER PODOLIER SOCIETY.
Records, 1930–1975. 2 1/2 in. (RG 1068)

Organized in New York in 1915 by immigrants from Pylyava, Ukraine. Maintained a loan fund and an old-age fund.

Minutes, 1971–1975. Financial records. Souvenir journals, 1930, 1950, 1955.

845. PILOWSKY, JACOB (1898–1969).
Papers, 1935–1963. 1 ft. 8 in. (RG 466)

Yiddish writer. Contributed articles and stories to *Vilner tog* (Vilna), *Letste nayes* (Kaunas), *Morgn frayhayt* (New York), *Yidishe kultur* (NY), *Dos yidishe vort* (Chile), *Di goldene keyt* (Israel). Born near Vilna. Moved to South America in 1924 and settled in Chile. Immigrated to Israel in 1963.

Correspondence from individuals and organizations. Includes reports on Jewish education in Chile written by Pilowsky.

846. PINCUS, AARON.
Papers, 1929–1966. 10 in. (RG 528)

Graduate of the Woodbine Agricultural School, Woodbine, New Jersey. Founder and president of the Toms River Community of Jewish Farmers, Toms River, New Jersey. Pincus led the Community from 1925 to 1948. The Community, established shortly after World War I with the encouragement of the Jewish Agricultural Society, was primarily a poultry center. It was comprised of independent farmers united through economic cooperation such as cooperative purchasing. The community reached a peak membership of 360 farmers, but by 1960 more than half of the homesteads had been abandoned.

The papers reflect Pincus' activities as president of the Toms River Community and include: official communal records; minutes of meetings, 1929–1953; greetings on the occasion of the 25th anniversary of the Community; circulars, newspaper clippings.

847. PINE, HARRIS.
Papers, 1920s–1980s. 1 ft. 2 in. (RG 1293)

Collector, writer on Jewish music. Lived in Syracuse, New York.

The collection consists of published music. Included are liturgical, popular, theater, klezmer and Hebrew works.

848. PINSKY, DAVID (1872–1959).
Papers, 1893–1949. 12 ft. (RG 204)

Yiddish writer, playwright, essayist, translator, editor. An associate of Isaac Leib Peretz at the outset of his literary career. Together with Peretz edited the popular magazine *Yom-tov bletlekh*, Warsaw, 1890s. Editor of socialist and Zionist-Socialist periodicals and newspapers in the United States, including *Dos abend blatt*, *Der arbayter*, *Yidisher kemfer*, *Di tsayt*, *Zukunft*. Active in Jewish political life, first as a Zionist, then as a member of the Socialist Bund, and from 1916 a prominent member of the Poalei Zion (Labor Zionist) movement. President of the Jewish National Workers Alliance (Farband). First president of the Yiddish PEN Club. Co-founder of other Yiddish cultural institutions. Born in Mogilev, Byelorussia. Lived in Moscow, Warsaw, Berlin, New York, Tel Aviv.

Correspondence with approximately 1,350 individuals and organizations. Family correspondence. Letters from individuals including S. Ansky, Baal Makhshoves, Hayyim Nahman Bialik, Nathan Birnbaum, Ber Borochov, Jacob Dinesohn, Saul Ginsburg, Jacob Glatstein, Peretz Hirschbein, David Ignatoff, Joseph Jaffe, David Kessler, Judah L. Magnes, Golda Meirson (Meir), Nahum Baruch Minkoff, Shmuel Niger, Moshe Olgin, Joseph Opatoshu,

Isaac Leib Peretz, Abraham Reisen, Joseph Schlossberg, Sholem Aleichem, Mordecai Spector, Nachman Syrkin, Baruch Vladeck, Chaim Weizmann, Hillel Zeitlin, Zerubavel, Chaim Zhitlowsky. Correspondence with Yiddish organizations.

Correspondence with the Jewish National Workers Alliance, 1916–1942, including the main office and branches in the United States and Canada as well as its affiliated Yiddish schools. Correspondence with the Poalei Zion party in the United States and Canada, 1914–1947; Palestine, 1924–1937; Poland, 1936. Correspondence of the party's press organs, *Der yidisher arbeiter*, 1923–1926; *Yidisher kemfer*, 1931–1933; *Di tsayt*, 1921–1922. Letters from affiliated organizations such as Hehalutz, Pioneer Women, League for Labor Palestine.

Manuscripts of novels, plays, poems, essays, and articles. Personal documents and photographs.

Inventory, Yiddish.

849. PINSON, KOPPEL (1904–1961).
Papers, 1930s–1940s. 5 in. (RG 462)

Historian. Professor of History at Queens College. Author of works relating to modern European history, with emphasis on nationalism, contemporary Germany and modern Jewish history. History editor of the *Encyclopedia of the Social Sciences* (1929–1935) and an editor of *Jewish Social Studies* (1938–61). UNRRA Director of Education and Culture for Displaced Persons in Germany and Austria. Member of the Research Commission and of the Board of Directors of the YIVO Institute. Born near Vilna. Immigrated to the United States in 1907.

Notes on the Bund, Nathan Birnbaum, Simon Dubnow. Clippings on the Soviet Union and nationalism, 1930s–1940s.

850. PLAFKIN, REUBEN.
Papers, 1916–1920s. 2 1/2 in. (RG 1158)

Secretary, Jewish Peoples' Relief Committee, Detroit, 1916–1920s.

The papers relate to the Jewish People's Relief work in Detroit and consists of: correspondence with Boruch Zukerman; financial records; receipts for donations; clippings; certificates.

851. PLAYS.
Collection. 12 ft. 1 in. (RG 114)

This collection was assembled in the YIVO Archives and is of mixed provenance.

The collection consists of manuscripts and copies of manuscripts of Yiddish plays and translations or adaptations from plays in other languages. Playwrights include: Ossip Dymow, Sigmund Feinman, Abraham Goldfaden, Jacob Gordin, Jacob Jacobson, Harry Kalmanovitch, Leon Kobrin, Zisl Kornblith, Joseph Lateiner, Solomon Libin, N. Rakow, Moishe Richter, Nahum Meir Shaikewitz, Sholem Aleichem, William Siegel, Boris Thomashefsky, Isidore Zolatarevsky, Miriam Shomer Zunser. There are translations into Yiddish of works by the following authors: Leonid Andreyev, Maksim Gorkii, Leo Tolstoy, William Shakespeare, Paddy Chayefsky.

Inventory, Yiddish.

852. PLOTZKER YOUNG MEN'S INDEPENDENT ASSOCIATION.
Records, 1859, 1918–1973. 12 1/2 in. (RG 785)

Organized in New York in 1893 by immigrants from Płock, Poland. Contributed to building a hospital in Płock after World War I. Established a loan fund for *landslayt* in Israel after World War II.

Constitutions. Financial documents, 1928–1948. Membership ledger, 1928–1942. Cemetery records. Speeches, meeting announcements, souvenir journals. Calendar booklets, 1920–1968. Photographs. Miscellaneous, 1859, 1920.

853. PODOLSKY, W.E. (1888–1961).
Papers, ca. 1914–1962. 10 in. (RG 461)

Jeweller. Active in Jewish communal organizations in London, England. Treasurer, YIVO Committee in London. Represented the Trades Advisory Council at the Jewish Defence Committee of the Board of Deputies of British Jews. Active in the Jewish Socialist Organisation, Friends of Yiddish, *Freie Arbeiter Stimme*, and the Workers' Circle Friendly Society.

Correspondence with Yiddish literary figures and Jewish organizations such as the Freeland League, Workmen's Circle and YIVO. Podolsky's diary. Personal documents.

854. POKSHIVNITZER RELIEF COMMITTEE.
Records, 1934–1971. 12 1/2 in. (RG 908)

Founded in New York ca. 1930 by immigrants from Koprzywnica, Poland, for purposes of overseas relief. Burial plots were secured through an affiliated group, the Chevra Divre Chaim. Close relations have been maintained with the Pokshivnitzer *landsmanshaft* in Israel.

Minutes, 1944–58. Financial records. Correspondence with the Pokshivnitzer society in Israel. Photographs. Records of Chevra Divre Chaim, a congregation in Brooklyn led by Rabbi Menachem Binyomin Ben-Zion Rottenberg-Halberstam.

855. POLAND (VILNA ARCHIVES).
Collection, ca. 1850–1939. 8 ft. 4 in. (RG 28)

The collection consists of ephemeral and fragmentary materials relating to Jewish communities in over 200 Polish cities and towns. Included are printed materials, announcements, invitations, circulars, notes, minutes, correspondence and posters. The following topics are included: Political organizations such as Agudas Israel, Bund, He-haluz, Mizrachi, Poalei Agudas Yisrael, Poale Zion. Community elections, elections to the Sejm (Polish Diet). Business and economics: banks, credit unions, taxes. Labor: trade unions, strikes. Cultural activities and groups: Yiddish cultural organizations, publishing houses. Religious matters: synagogues, ritual slaughter (*shehitah*), rabbinical figures. Sports clubs, games. Historical events: pogroms, German occupation of Poland during World War I.

Card inventory, Yiddish.

Card inventory of the posters, English.

856. POLISHUK, ISIDORE S. (YITSHAK) (1882–1964).
Papers, 1942–1964. 1 ft. 3 in. (RG 1286)

Yiddish writer. Active in the Labor Zionist movement. Published books and articles on topics in philosophy. Born in the Ukraine. Came to the United States and settled in Chicago in 1904.

Typescripts of Polishuk's unpublished works. Letters from Jacob Glatstein, Chaim Grade,

Simon Halkin, B. Idelson, David Ignatoff, Aryeh Leon Kubovy (Kubowitzki), H. Leivick, Chaim Lieberman, H. Rosenblatt.

857. POLOTZKER WORKINGMEN'S BENEVOLENT SOCIETY.
Records, 1960–1971. 15 in. (RG 867)

Organized in New York in 1905 by immigrants from Polotsk, Byelorussia. Activities included support of Jewish philanthropies and State of Israel. Dissolved in the 1970s.

Minutes, 1966–1969. Financial records, 1960s–1970s. Membership records. Correspondence, 1971. Stamp.

858. POMERANTZ, ALEXANDER (1901–1965).
Papers, 1920s–1960s. 2 ft. 6 in. (RG 500)

Yiddish writer, bibliographer. Contributed to *Morgn frayhayt* (NY), *Der tog* (NY), ICOR (NY), *Naye lebn* (NY), *Zukunft* (NY). Member of the faculty of the Institute for Jewish Proletarian Culture at the Ukrainian Academy of Science, Kiev, 1933–1935. Compiled a bibliography of Yiddish literature in the Soviet Union. Author of *Sovetishe harugey malkhus* (Martyrs of the Soviet Regime), YIVO, Buenos Aires, 1962. Used pen names Yehoshua Grodner and P. Aleksander. Born in Grodno, Byelorussia. Immigrated to the United States in 1921. Lived in the Soviet Union from 1933–1935.

Correspondence with Yiddish literary figures, including Abraham Cahan, Daniel Charney, Chaver-Paver, Max Erik, Itsik Feffer, H. Leivick, Kalman Marmor, Shmuel Niger, Melech Ravitch, Abraham Reisen. Correspondence with Yiddish cultural and political organizations in the United States. Material on the Institute for Jewish Proletarian Culture in Kiev: Pomerantz's lecture notes, diplomas, clippings. Biographical notes on Max Erik. Manuscripts of published and unpublished articles by Pomerantz. Manuscripts and notes on executed Jewish writers in the Soviet Union. Materials relating to Grodno and Grodno *landsmanshaftn*. Articles about Pomerantz.

859. POMERANTZ, ISRAEL CHAIM (1901–1962).
Papers, ca. 1925–1960s. 10 in. (RG 238)

Yiddish editor, educator. Director of the Sholem Aleichem Folk Institute, Chicago. Member of the Bureau of Jewish Education, Chicago. Lived in the Ukraine, the United States.

The collection consists of correspondence with organizations such as Workmen's Circle, Jewish Education Committee, Jewish Teachers' Seminary, YIVO. Correspondence with individuals including Menahem Boraisha, Daniel Charney, Mendl Elkin, Abraham Golomb, Peretz Hirschbein, David Ignatoff, H. Leivick, David Pinsky.

860. PORATH, JONATHAN.
Collection, 1965–1974. 5 in. (RG 1114)

Rabbi of Temple Beth Or in Clark, New Jersey. Between 1965 and 1974 led several group visits to the Soviet Union, where he took photographs of Jewish religious life.

Over 600 color slides and 3 films (8 mm) of synagogue scenes in Moscow, Leningrad, and Odessa.

861. POSNER, MEYER (1890–1931).
Papers, ca. 1918–1931. 1 ft. 6 in. (RG 217)

The collection consists of bound notebooks of liturgical music for cantor and choir, compiled or composed by Meyer Posner. There are also bound notebooks of Yiddish and other choral songs and notebooks of musical illustrations for his book on harmony.

Liturgical music: excerpts of works by about 50 composers, including Nissan Blumenthal, A. Dunayevsky, Eliezer Gorowitch, Louis Lewandowski, Pinchas Minkowsky, Samuel Naumbourg, David Nowakowski, Zeidel Rovner, Wolf Shestapol, Solomon Sulzer. Choral works in Yiddish include music by Platon Brounoff, Leo Low, Jacob Beimel.

Inventory, English.

862. POSTCARDS AND GREETING CARDS.
Collection, 1910s–1960s. 5 ft. (RG 122)

The collection consists of several thousand illustrated postcards and greeting cards. Included are rare postcards bearing artistic illustrations, photographic images and poetic texts, and cards depicting folklore and religious themes, such as the Jewish New Year and other holidays. The greeting cards relate primarily to the New Year. Included are invitations to weddings and bar mitzvahs.

Postcards are cataloged in a computer database.

Index of subject headings.

863. POSY, ARNOLD (born 1893).
Papers, 1938–1978. 10 in. (RG 1219)

Yiddish writer, editor. Pen name of Arie Pozikov. Was editor of and contributed to *Yidisher ekspres* (London), *Milvoker yidishe shtime, The Jewish Home, American Jewish Life, Kosher Butcher Shtime*. Born in Byelorussia. Moved to London in 1914 and to the United States in 1920.

The papers consist primarily of manuscripts of essays and other works by Posy. Correspondence with Yiddish cultural figures and writers, including Aleph Katz, Solomon Simon, Aaron Zeitlin and others. Copies of a pamphlet by Posy, *Hitler's* Mein Kampf *and the Present War*. Issues of *Oyfkum* and *Der khaver* with articles by Posy.

864. PRAGER-WARSCHAUER BRANCH 386, WORKMEN'S CIRCLE.
Records, 1930–1970. 2 1/2 in. (RG 1033)

Established in 1915 as a branch of the Workmen's Circle by *landslayt* from Praga (a suburb of Warsaw) who immigrated to the United States after the 1905 Russian Revolution. Supported the Haym Solomon Warschauer Home for the Aged. Conducted relief work for Warsaw *landslayt*. Merged with the Nashelsker Branch 622 Workmen's Circle, ca. 1970.

Minutes, 1968–1969. Anniversary journals, 1930–1965.

865. PREISS, MICHAEL (1904–1979).
Papers, 1920s–1960s. 5 in. (RG 506)

Actor in the Yiddish and German theater. Performed in the Free Yiddish Theater in Vienna, 1920s, and the Yiddish Art Theater in New York. Lived in Austria and the United States

Correspondence, personal documents, reviews, clippings, playscripts, programs, posters, and photographs relating to Preiss's career.

Photographs cataloged in STAGEPIX.

866. PRICE, GEORGE M. (1864–1942).
   Papers, 1880s–1940s. 5 in. (RG 213)

Founder and director of the Health Center of the International Ladies Garment Workers Union. Editor of the *Buffalo Workers News* (German). Lived in Russia and the United States.

   The papers relate to Price's work in social medicine and hygiene and include the following: an autobiography of Price; manuscripts by Price in English and Russian relating to social medicine and hygiene; report on a trip to Soviet Russia; clippings from the *Buffalo Workers News*, 1880s.

867. PROGRESS MUTUAL AID SOCIETY.
   Records, 1905–1964. 2 ft. 3 1/2 in. (RG 1021)

Established in 1905. Was associated with a ladies auxiliary. Dissolved in 1964.

   Minutes, 1905–1964. Financial records, 1940s–1960s. Membership records, 1912–1940s, 1951–1956. Burial records. Correspondence. Materials pertaining to dissolution.

868. PROGRESSIVE HORODENKER BENEVOLENT SOCIETY.
   Records, 1914–1979. 20 in. (RG 820)

Founded in New York in 1914 by immigrants from Gorodenka (Pol. Horodenka), Ukraine, as the Progressive Horodenker Young Men's and Ladies Sick Benevolent Society, Inc. Formed a joint relief organization after World War I with the First Horodenker Society and the Horodenker Lodge, Independent Order Brith Abraham. Organized a ladies auxiliary in 1940 and its own relief committee in 1944. Also organized a junior league for children of members in 1935. Name changed to Progressive Horodenker Benevolent Society, Inc. in 1961. Collaborated with *landsmanshaft* in Israel to publish memorial book. Affiliated with Horodenka Friendship Club of Toronto, founded 1972.

   Certificate of change of name, 1961. Constitution. Minutes, 1914–1953. Financial reports, 1975–1977. Anniversary journals, including those of the United Horodenker Relief Committee, 1948, and the First Horodenker S.B.S., 1965, 1970. Correspondence. Newsletter, 1941–1964, 1966. Meeting announcements. Memoirs and history of the society. Photographs, memorial book (1963), miscellaneous.

869. PROGRESSIVE KOVLER YOUNG FRIENDS BRANCH 475, WORKMEN'S CIRCLE.
   Records, 1908–1948. 10 in. (RG 866)

Founded in 1908 by immigrants from Kovel, Ukraine, and became affiliated with the Workmen's Circle in 1910. Established a relief committee during World War I. Sent a delegate to Kovel to distribute aid to *landslayt*. After World War II, cooperated with other Kovler institutions in providing assistance to institutions in Israel.

   Minutes, regular and executive meetings, 1917–1948. Membership records, 1908–1910. Materials pertaining to the Workmen's Circle, 1917–1922.

870. PROGRESSIVE MISHNITZER YOUNG MEN'S SOCIETY.
   Records, 1936, 1948–1975. 5 in. (RG 913)

Founded in New York in 1911 by immigrants from Myszyniec, Poland. Provided members with cultural events such as lectures on labor issues. Supported institutions in Myszyniec. Minutes, 1948–1975. Anniversary journal. Photograph.

871. PROGRESSIVE SAMBORER YOUNG MEN'S BENEVOLENT ASSOCIATION.
Records, 1910–1977. 5 in. (RG 796)

Founded in New York in 1910 by immigrants from Sambor, Ukraine. Incorporated in 1915. Formed a *hevrah kadisha* (burial committee) to perform traditional burial rites. Affiliated with the Federation of Polish Jews and with the Erster Samborer K.U.V. Established the United Samborer Relief Society, Inc., 1937.

Constitutions. Minutes, 1937, 1945–1946 (German). Minutes of the United Samborer Relief Society, 1956. Financial documents, 1910, 1930s–1960s. Legal documents from Sambor. Correspondence from Europe, including Sambor, 1912–1975. Lists of Holocaust survivors from Sambor. Journals, bulletins, invitations, newspaper clippings, photographs. Draft of a history of the First Samborer K.U.V., 1889–1975. Materials pertaining to the United Samborer Relief Society, United Samborer Orphans Organization, Erster Samborer K.U.V., United Samborer Ladies Relief Society, a Samborer *landsmanshaft* in Israel. Memorial book, 1980.

872. PROSKUROVER ZION CONGREGATION.
Records, 1945–1978. 5 in. (RG 1228)

Established in New York by *landslayt* from Proskurov, Ukraine.

Memorial book of deceased members. By-laws of the *hevrah kadisha* (burial society). Scroll containing names of deceased members.

873. PRUDENTIAL BENEVOLENT ASSOCIATION.
Records, 1936–1952. 2 1/2 in. (RG 974)

Organized in New York in 1899 by immigrants from Priluki, Ukraine, as the Erster Priluker Society. Adopted constitution in 1918. Later changed name to Prudential Benevolent Association, Inc. Lent money to members at low interest rates. Provided cemetery grounds. Contributed to charities.

Constitution. Minutes, 1936–1952. Financial statements.

874. RABBINICAL AND HISTORICAL MANUSCRIPTS.
Collection, 1567–1930s. 9 ft. 7 in. (RG 128)

The collection is of mixed provenance. Part of it was deposited in the YIVO Archives in Vilna before World War II. The second part of the collection was gathered in France and Germany after World War II by Gershon Epstein, a YIVO collector.

The collection consists of letters, loose manuscripts as well as bound manuscript volumes, notes, notebooks, legal documents, rabbinical certificates. Included are: letters to and from rabbinical (including Hasidic) and scholarly figures; rabbinical responsa, novellae and commentaries on the Bible, the Talmud and liturgical texts; prayers; kabbalistic and ethical works; sermons; Hebrew dictionaries and other grammatical works; communal documents, such as registers and minute books; folklore material, such as cookbooks; miscellaneous historical documents.

The larger part of the collection is arranged by country. Included are materials from Austria, Czechoslovakia, France, Germany, Holland, Hungary, Italy, Lithuania, Tunisia, Palestine, Poland, Rumania, the United States, Russia, the USSR, Yugoslavia. The authors are for the most part rabbinical figures: Ezekiel ben Yehudah (Nodah B'yehudah) Landau, Abraham Tiktin, Gedaliah Tiktin, Israel Joshua Trunk, Abraham Abusch Lissa of Leszno, Meir Loeb ben Jehiel Michael Malbim, Meir Simhah Ha-Kohen of Dvinsk, and others

Communal documents include: proceedings of the rabbinical court of Metz (France) for 1771–1790; responsa and records of the rabbinical court, Frankfurt am Main, 1564–65, c. 1763–1830; register of the Jewish community of Oberndorf (Württemberg), 19th century; album of the Sephardic community in Yugoslavia, 1930s.

Inventory, English.

875. RABBINICAL SCHOOL AND TEACHERS' SEMINARY, VILNA.
Records, 1847–1914. 20 ft. 5 in. (RG 24)

The Rabbinical School in Vilna was one of several Jewish state schools established in the Russian Empire in 1847. The purpose of these schools was to undermine and replace the traditional *heder* system of education.

The school in Vilna consisted of two divisions: a pedagogical division, which trained teachers for Jewish state elementary schools, and a rabbinical division, which prepared state-appointed rabbis. Rabbinical students enjoyed certain benefits such as exemption from military service and from some taxes. The financial upkeep of the school was derived from a share of the Jewish communal candle-and-meat tax. The state schools were unpopular because of their assimilationist policies. The Rabbinical School was closed in 1873, but the Teachers' Seminary remained in existence until 1914.

Records of the Rabbinical School, 1847–1873. Administrative records. Correspondents include: Ministry of Education for the Province of Byelorussia; Curator of the Vilna School District; Governor-General of Vilna. Correspondence relates to the following topics: courses; appointment of teachers; school finances; teachers' affairs. Financial reports. Minutes of the Pedagogical Council. Lists of students, teachers, officials. Lists of textbooks. Diplomas of teachers and students. Examination lists. Materials relating to payment of salaries to school officials. Lists of towns and firms paying taxes for the support of the school, 1854–1855. Materials relating to the closing of the Rabbinical School.

Records of the Teachers' Seminary. Correspondence from the Ministry of Education. Correspondence and circulars from the Vilna School District. Materials relating to the candle taxes, 1874. Financial records. Hiring of teachers and officials. Teachers' record books. Student affairs. Graduation certificates. Curricula, reports. List of students. Book of student grades. Reports on school work. Lists of permitted and prohibited books. Examination lists.

Inventory, Yiddish, English.

876. RABINOVITCH, BARUCH MORDECHAI (1896–1980).
Papers, 1930–1939, 1960s. 3 in. (RG 1071)

Baruch Mordechai Rabinovitch was born in Ostre-Volin (Ostrog), Ukraine, 1866. Died in New York, 1939. Upon his departure for the United States in 1930, the community officials of Ostre appointed Rabinovitch delegate to the New York Ostre *landsmanshaft.*

The papers reflect Rabinovitch's communal activities. Handwritten certificates honoring B.M. Rabinovitch's work on behalf of communal institutions in Ostre, 1930 (Hebrew). Handwritten certificate (Yiddish) appointing him community representative to the New York *landsmanshaft*. Photographs. Correspondence of his son, Hersh Rabinovitch. Memorial book of great rabbis and scholars, Ostre, 1907.

877. RABINOWITZ, HYMAN (1873–1926).
Papers, ca. 1900. 9 in. (RG 1281)

Cantor, *badkhn* (wedding entertainer), actor, composer and arranger of liturgical music and incidental music to Yiddish plays. Performed under the name Khayim Bass. A founder of the First United Warschawer Sick Benevolent Society. Born in Warsaw. Lived in London for a short while. Settled in the United States.

Music manuscripts, notebooks containing lyrics for Rabinowitz's repertoire as a *badkhn*, and photographs.

878. RABOY, ISAAC (1882–1944).
Papers, 1926–1952. 1 ft. 3 in. (RG 372)

Yiddish writer. One of the novelists of "Di yunge," Raboy introduced the theme of the Jewish farmer into Yiddish literature. Born in the Ukraine, grew up in Bessarabia, immigrated to the United States in 1904.

Correspondence of Raboy with Itsik Feffer, David Ignatoff, Leib Kvitko, Mani Leib, Joseph Rolnick. Clippings of Raboy's works. Manuscripts of Raboy's memoirs and other works.

879. RADIO PROGRAMS.
Collection. (RG 130)

Recordings of radio broadcasts. There are over 200 16-inch recordings of music, comedy, soap operas, news, commercials, poetry and drama spanning the years 1936–1955. The majority represent programming from New York-based stations such as WEVD, WBBS, WHN, and WMCA. Recordings of WEVD radio programs include those separated from the papers of Zvee Scooler such as " The Forward Hour." Represented in these recordings are the Barry Sisters, Jan Bart, Moishe Oysher, Nohum Stutchkoff, Dave Tarras.

Catalog of Recorded Radio Programs, English.

880. RADOMYSLER BENEVOLENT SOCIETY.
Records, 1930–1979. 15 in. (RG 814)

Founded in New York in 1904 by immigrants from Radomyshl (Pol. Radomyśl), Ukraine, as the Radomysler Unterstitzung Verein. Changed name to present title and incorporated in 1910. Activities included relief work after World War I and World War II.

Constitution. Minutes, 1930–1949. Financial records, 1930–1979. Correspondence. Anniversary materials. Scrapbook, diary, travel accounts of Samuel Kipnis, 1922–1963. Publication of the Radomysler Ladies Auxiliary of Chicago. Photograph.

881. RADOSHITZKY, HARRY (YITZHAK HERSH) (1883–1962).
Papers, 1909–1955. 1 ft. 3 in. (RG 558)

Yiddish poet, writer, author of children's books. Contributed to *Di yidishe vokh* (Warsaw), *Lodzer tageblat* (Łódź), *Lodzer folksblat* (Łódź), *Groyser kundes* (NY), *Zukunft* (NY), *Freie*

Arbeiter Stimme (NY), *Frayhayt* (NY), *Morgn zhurnal* (NY), *Kinder zhurnal* (NY). Born in Radoszyce, Poland. Immigrated to the United States in 1920 and settled in New York.

The collection consists of manuscripts and correspondence. The manuscripts include an autobiography, poems, articles, notes. Correspondents include Daniel Charney, Philip Friedman, Abba Gordin, David Ignatoff, H. Leivick, Shmuel Niger, Melech Ravitch, Abraham Reisen, Zalman Reisen, A.A. Roback, Isaiah (Jeshajahu) Spiegel, Moshe Starkman, Abraham Sutzkever, Shea Tenenbaum, Tolush, Zalmen Zylbercweig.

882. RADZINER PROGRESSIVE SOCIETY.
Records, 1924–1977. 5 in. (RG 880)

Founded in New York in 1924 by immigrants from Radzyń Podlaski, Poland. Activities included financial support of the Radziner *landsmanshaft* in Israel.

Minutes, 1924–1967, 1973–1977. Annual reports of Radziner society in Israel, 1968–1971, 1974. Materials pertaining to the Radziner society in Israel.

883. RADZIVILLER-WOLINER BENEVOLENT ASSOCIATION.
Records, 1929–1962. 3 in. (RG 951)

Organized in New York in 1916 by immigrants from Radzivilov (Pol. Radziwiłłów; from 1940 Chervonoarmeisk), Ukraine. Provided a loan fund for members. Between and during the two world wars organized a relief committee which aided Radzivilov and refugees.

Correspondence. Souvenir journals. Visual materials pertaining to the *Linas Hazedek* (hostel or hospice committee) in Radzivilov, including photographs and hand-painted cards.

884. RAM, PHILLIP.
Papers. 2 1/2 in. (RG 1190)

Yiddish journalist, playwright. New York.

Manuscripts of a Yiddish play and short story. English translation of David Bergelson's *The Witness*. Manuscripts of poems by Menke Katz in English. Clippings from the Yiddish press.

885. RAN, LEIZER.
Collection, 1926–1953. ca. 12 ft. 6 in. (RG 327)

Leizer Ran was an archivist in the YIVO Archives in Vilna, 1930s. From 1947 to 1953 he lived in Havana, Cuba, where he collected materials on the local Jewish community.

Predominantly printed matter relating to the economic, political, cultural and religious life of Jews in Cuba. Materials from organizations: Zionist groups, youth groups, cultural institutions, communal welfare organizations, groups for World War II refugees, *landsmanshaftn*, ORT. Records of an archive-museum of Jewish life in Cuba, organized by the JDC in Havana. Photographs of Jewish life in Cuba.

Card inventory, Yiddish.

886. RANDALL, MERCEDES M.
Papers, 1944. 2 1/2 in. (RG 612)

Author of a pamphlet, *The Voice of Thy Brother's Blood*, published in 1944 by the Women's International League for Peace and Freedom.

The collection relates to the preparation of the pamphlet *The Voice of Thy Brother's Blood*. Included are: a printed copy of the pamphlet; a report; copies of letters sent to various individuals including people active in Jewish relief organizations, radio commentators, clergymen, and well-known Americans; a press release, 1944.

887. RAPPAPORT FAMILY CIRCLE.
Records, 1952–1961. 1 1/2 in. (RG 1076)

Organized in 1939 to promote closer relations between descendants of Gershon Leib and Bella Rappaport and to provide assistance including burial services. Sponsored many social events.
Constitution. Financial materials, 1954–1961. Correspondence, banner.

888. RASKIN, GREGOR.
Collection, 1355–1950. 1 ft. 3 in. (RG 265)

Gregor Raskin was a YIVO correspondent in Germany, 1949–1950.
The collection consists of photostatic copies of documents relating to Jewish life in various parts of Germany, 1355–1950. Materials from the Weissenburg Municipal Archives: letters, petitions, 15th–16th centuries. Weissenburg Bezirksamt (county) archives: government orders, petitions, antisemitic pamphlets, materials relating to the Nazi period. Municipal Archives of Nuremberg: governmental and financial documents. Documents from miscellaneous sources: correspondence, reports related to the Nazi period.
Inventory, English.

889. RASKIN, SAUL (1886–1966).
Papers, 1940, n.d. 3 in. (RG 1239)

Artist. Studied lithography in Odessa. Continued studies in art schools in Germany, France, Switzerland, and Italy. Worked for Yiddish newspapers as a cartoonist, especially for *Der groyser kundes* (NY). Wrote articles on art and theater in *Tsayt-gayst, Freie Arbeiter Stimme, Zukunft, Dos Naye lebn* (NY). Published albums of his art works, including a series of engravings based on the tractate *Pirke avot* (Ethics of the Fathers), 1940. Born in Nogaisk, Russia. Immigrated to the United States in 1904. Died in New York.
The collection consists of 45 engravings for the *Pirke avot* album and 13 miscellaneous art works of Raskin.

890. RATCHEVER-VOLYNER AID ASSOCIATION.
Records, 1935–1963. 2 1/2 in. (RG 992)

Founded in New York in 1914 by immigrants from Rogachev (Yid. Ratchev), Byelorussia. Established a loan fund. Promoted cultural activites. Affiliated with the Ratchever Volyner Froyen Klub, established in 1943 to raise funds for homeless children.
Constitution. Minutes, 1935–1963. Speeches, correspondence, notices.

891. RATNER, MARC (1871–1917).
Papers, 1906–1913. 3 microfilm reels. (RG 83)

Lawyer, socialist leader in Russia. One of the founders of SERP (Sotsialisticheskaia

Evreiskaia Rabochaia Partiia—Jewish Socialist Workers' Party) which was based on a synthesis of nationalist and socialist ideas. Appeared as counsel for the defense in political trials and as civil prosecutor in the trials against pogrom instigators. Ratner initiated the campaign for recognition of a Jewish section of the Socialist International. Born in Kiev. In 1905 was compelled to leave Russia because of his activities. Lived in Switzerland, Austria (Vienna) and Rumania (Iaşi).

The collection relates primarily to the activities of the SERP. Materials relating to SERP conferences: minutes, lectures, resolutions on Jewish autonomy, territorialism, economy, emigration.

Correspondence with Abraham Appelbaum, Shimon Aronson, Ber Borochov, Pinchas Dubinsky, Misha Fabrikant, Z. Goldin, Michl Levitan, Yehuda Novakovski, Virgilia Verdaro, Chaim Zhitlowsky, Alexander Zuskind.

Materials of Poalei Zion, Socialist Revolutionaries, Zionist Socialists, International Committee for the Support of the Jobless in Russia, and office of the Socialist International.

Inventory, Yiddish.

892. RAY HEIT CHAPTER OF THE KITTEVER LADIES RELIEF AUXILIARY.
Records, 1947–1975, 1979–1980. 5 in. (RG 985)

Established in New York in 1947 as the Kittever Ladies Relief Auxiliary by immigrants from Kuty, Ukraine. Worked with the Kittever Sick and Benevolent Society to provide aid for surviving *landslayt* after World War II. Renamed for Ray Heit, the first auxiliary president. Disbanded 1980.

Minutes, 1947–1980. Financial records, 1948–1960. Meeting announcements. Photographs. Memorial book, 1958.

893. RECHTMAN, ABRAHAM (1890–1972).
Papers, 1920s–1960s. 10 in. (RG 677)

Folklorist, writer, printer. Member of the S. Ansky Ethnographic Expedition. Contributed to *Dos vort*, *Yivo bleter*, *Kinder zhurnal*, *Dos yidishe likht*. Wrote under pen name of Ish Yemini and Doktor Zamler. Born in Proskurov, Ukraine. Lived for two years in Palestine. Came to the United States in 1916.

Correspondence with individuals and family members. Manuscript of a translation of Itzhak Katzenelson's *Sheshet yemei bereshit*. Manuscripts of Yiddish and Hebrew poems. Photographs. Personal documents.

Inventory, Yiddish.

894. REFUAH VECHAIM SOCIETY, PHILADELPHIA.
Records, 1954–1967. 3 ft. 9 in. (RG 442)

Society founded by Mrs. Meta Wertheimer to aid sick people in Israel and Europe.

General correspondence including letters requesting aid from the society. Circulars from religious organizations in the United States and Israel. Contributions, receipts, appeals, reports.

895. REGENSBURG, JOSEPH (1879–1930).
Papers, 1900–1939. 1 ft. 3 in. (RG 20)

Doctor. Specialized in psychology and psychiatry. Received his doctorate and medical degree from the University of Berlin. Practiced medicine in Vilna. Active Zionist. Contributed to the Zionist newspaper *Undzer fraynd* and to *Di tsayt*, *Folks gezunt*. Co-editor of the *Yidishe tsaytung*, 1919–1920. Born in Friedrichstadt, Courland. Settled in Vilna in 1915.

The collection relates to Dr. Regensburg's activities in the fields of psychology and psychiatry. Material relating to psychological disorders. Papers from the Psychiatric University Clinic in Moscow, 1914. Regensburg's notes and papers on psychology and psychiatry. Printed leaflets and circulars relating to lectures and meetings.

896. REICHEL, BROCHO (born 1883).
Papers, ca. 1900–ca. 1953. 5 in. (RG 404)

Dentist, active in the Hadassah movement. Lived in Poland, the United States.

Correspondence with: Henrietta Szold; Joshua Heschel Farbstein and Yizhak Grunbaum, deputies to the Polish Diet; orphanages in Warsaw, 1920s; Jewish schools in Poland; Hadassah in the United States. Materials about Junior Hadassah, 1920s–1930s. Personal documents.

897. REIF, ABRAHAM ISAAC (1871–1946).
Papers, 1900–1934. 8 in. (RG 1272)

Cantor, composer of liturgical and operatic music. Born in Austria. Settled in New York at the turn of the century.

Manuscripts of liturgical compositions by Reif and by others. Yiddish theater music.

898. REISEN, ABRAHAM (1876–1953).
Papers, 1924–1948. 2 1/2 in. (RG 232)

Yiddish poet, short-story writer. Son of the Hebrew-Yiddish poet Kalman Reisen. His brother was the literary historian Zalman Reisen and his sister the poet and writer Sarah Reisen. Was a prolific author; many of his poems were set to music. Born in Minsk province. Lived in Warsaw. Moved to the United States in 1914, settling in New York.

Correspondence with Yiddish literary figures: Shalom Asch, Daniel Charney, Abraham Golomb, Alexander Mukdoni, Melech Ravitch. Clippings of Reisen's articles.

899. REISS, LIONEL S. (1894–1987).
Papers, 1920s. 6 in. (RG 1160)

Artist. Traveled abroad in the 1920s to study different Jewish communities. His works are included in collections at the Jewish Theological Seminary in New York, the Brooklyn Museum, and the YIVO Institute for Jewish Research. Born in Austria. Immigrated to the United States in 1899.

Over 100 drawings, sketches, charcoals and watercolors, depicting scenes of Jewish life in Europe, the Middle East and the United States in the 1920s. Themes include the Jewish quarters of Warsaw, Łódź, Radom, Vilna, Kovno, Lemberg, Minsk, Paris, Venice, Safed. The drawings also depict Jews in kibbutzim and Hasidic Jews.

900. REJMAN, BERL.
Papers, 1953–1971. 5 in. (RG 690)

Collector for YIVO. New York.

The papers consist mainly of notebooks containing B. Rejman's comments on newspaper articles. Included is correspondence with Aaron Zeitlin and clippings of articles by the latter.

901. RESSLER, BENJAMIN (1901–1983).
Papers. 2 ft. 1 in. (RG 1173)

Yiddish novelist, poet, playwright. Contributed to *Lemberger morgn*, *Literarishe bleter*, *Di yidishe prese* (Antwerp), *Zukunft*. From 1929 on the staff of *Der tog*. Also worked for *Tog morgn zhurnal*, *Algemeiner zhurnal* (NY). Born in Kopychintsy, Ukraine. Immigrated to the United States in 1928.

About 20 plays and novels in Yiddish, Hebrew, and English. Clippings of articles.

902. REUBEN GUSKIN BABROISKER BRANCH 206, WORKMEN'S CIRCLE.
Records, 1958–1977. 2 in. (RG 812)

Founded in 1908 as the Babroisker Branch of the Workmen's Circle by immigrants from Bobruysk, Russia. Renamed for Reuben Guskin, organizational leader and *landsman*, after his death in 1962. Activities included establishment of a relief committee after World War I and publication of a memorial book together with *landslayt* in Israel after World War II.

Minutes, 1958–1977.

903. RIAZANIFKER BENEVOLENT ASSOCIATION.
Records, 1928–1964. 7 1/2 in. (RG 882)

Organized in New York in 1913 by immigrants from Ryzhanovka, Ukraine. Activities included working with the ladies auxiliary.

Rules and regulations of the society. Minutes, 1941–1951. Financial records, 1930s–1960s. Correspondence, 1940s–1950s. Burial permits, 1928–1957.

904. RIEUR, JACQUES.
Papers, 1920s–1960s. 5 in. (RG 585)

Director, American Jewish Joint Distribution Committee, Warsaw office, in the 1920s.

The papers relate to Rieur's activities in the JDC and to his work as a translator in the U.S. War Department during World War II. Reports of the Joint Distribution Committee in Poland, 1920s, written by Rieur. Maps of Poland showing Joint Distribution Committee activities. Charts of JDC structure. Materials relating to Rieur's work as a translator for the War Department in the 1940s. Family documents.

905. RIVKIN, BORUCH (1883–1945).
Papers, 1930s–1960s. 7 ft. (RG 476)

Pen name of Baruch Abraham Weinrib. Yiddish literary critic and essayist. Co-editor of *Di literarishe velt* and of *Zukunft*. On the staff of *The Day*. Also used the pen name Mark Toleroze. Born in Latvia. Immigrated to the United States in 1911.

Correspondence with Yiddish literary figures such as Daniel Charney, Chaim Grade, David Ignatoff, H. Leivick, Kalman Marmor, Shmuel Niger, Joseph Opatoshu. Manuscripts by Rivkin, Abraham Liessin, H. Leivick, David Pinsky and Rivkin's wife, Mina Bordo Rivkin. Correspondence with readers. Clippings of Rivkin's articles.

906. ROBACK, ABRAHAM AARON (1890–1965).
Papers, ca. 1925–1960. 1 ft. 3 in. (RG 596)

Yiddish scholar, psychologist. Librarian at Harvard University. Contributed to *Keneder odler* (Montreal), *Dos naye lebn* (NY), *Literarishe velt* (NY), *Dos yidishe folk* (NY), *Yidisher kemfer* (NY), *Freie Arbeiter Stimme* (NY), *Filologishe shriftn* (Vilna). Born in Goniądz, district of Białystok. Immigrated to Canada in 1892.

The papers consist of correspondence with individuals and institutions. Correspondents include Abraham Golomb, Ephim Jeshurin, Melech Ravitch, Jacob Shatzky, Max Weinreich, Zalmen Zylbercweig.

907. ROBINSON, NEHEMIAH (1898–1964).
Papers, 1950s–1960s. 5 in. (RG 627)

Lawyer. Research Associate, Institute for Jewish Affairs of the World Jewish Congress. Participated in the Conference on Jewish Material Claims Against Germany. Published numerous articles relating to Jewish communities around the world and on topics of Jewish interest. Born in Lithuania. Immigrated to New York in 1940.

The collection consists of reports, bulletins and clippings by N. Robinson relating to: World Jewish Congress; German-Jewish relations, 1933–63; antisemitism; Nazi war criminals.

908. ROGOFF, HILLEL (1883–1971).
Papers, 1933–1968. 5 in. (RG 646)

Yiddish writer. Active in the socialist movement. Editor of the *Jewish Daily Forward*, 1951–1964. Contributed to *Zukunft* (NY), *Freie Arbeiter Stimme* (NY), *Di naye velt* (NY), *Der veker* (NY). Used pen names Yitzchak Elchonon, Ger Toyshev. Born in Berezin, province of Minsk, Byelorussia. Immigrated to the United States in 1890.

The collection consists of correspondence, typescripts and printed materials. Miscellaneous correspondence with individuals including readers of the *Forward*. Photographs of Rogoff. Clippings of Rogoff's articles. Bibliography of Rogoff's works.

909. ROGOW, DAVID (born 1915).
Papers, 1948–1980s. 5 in. (RG 759)

Yiddish actor. Staff member, YIVO Institute for Jewish Research. Staff member, *Groyser verterbukh fun der yidisher shprakh* (Great Dictionary of the Yiddish Language). Managing Editor, *YIVO News*. Performed in Europe and in the United States with a variety of theater companies including a puppet theater, Maydim (Vilna), Davke (Vilna), the Yiddish State Theater (Minsk, Byelorussia), MIT (Minchener Yidisher Kunstteater, Munich), Folksbiene (New York). Performed in productions by Maurice Schwartz, David Licht and Joseph Buloff. Member, Hebrew Actors Union. Born in Vilna. Immigrated to the United States in 1950.

The papers include correspondence, theater programs, photographs, clippings, personal documents.

910. ROHATYNER YOUNG MEN'S SOCIETY.
Records, 1928–1964. 5 in. (RG 1016)

Organized in New York in 1894 by immigrants from Rogatin (Pol. Rohatyn), Ukraine. Constitution. Minutes, 1928–1960. Memorial book, 1962. Photograph.

911. ROLNICK, JOSEPH (1879–1955).
Papers, ca. 1909–1955. 3 ft. 2 in. (RG 359)

Yiddish poet. Born in the village of Zhukhovich (Bolshiye Zukhovichi), Minsk province, Byelorussia. Settled in the United States in 1906.

Correspondence with literary figures, 1928–1955, including Aaron Glanz-Leieles, Jacob Glatstein, Chaim Grade, Reuben Iceland, H. Leivick, Mani Leib, Kalman Marmor, Nahum Baruch Minkoff, Isaac Bashevis Singer, Abraham Sutzkever, Baruch Vladeck. Manuscripts of poems, essays. Clippings of articles about Rolnick.

912. ROSEN, JOSEPH A. (1887–1949).
Papers, 1921–1938. 16 ft. (RG 358)

Agronomist, official of the American Jewish Joint Distribution Committee (JDC). JDC representative at the American Relief Administration in Soviet Russia, 1921–1923. Organizer of relief for impoverished and declassed Soviet Jews. Director of the American Jewish Joint Agricultural Corporation (Agro-Joint), 1924–1949. Born in Moscow. Came to the United States in 1903.

The Agro-Joint was established on J. Rosen's initiative for the purpose of developing Jewish agricultural settlements in the Soviet Union. In addition to the settlements, the Agro-Joint also subsidized Jewish factories, cooperatives, schools and health care facilities. The work was supported financially by the JDC and the American Society for Jewish Farm Settlements (ASJFS), a consortium of private subscribers. The official Soviet government agency which supervised colonization and countersigned all agreements with the Agro-Joint was KOMZET (Komitet po Zemleustroistvu Trudiashchikhsia Evreev—Committee for the Settlement of Toiling Jews on Land). The Agro-Joint projects in the Soviet Union were discontinued by the Soviet government in 1938. The Agro-Joint was dissolved in 1954.

Records of the Agro-Joint Director General. Agreements of the American Relief Administration (ARA) and the Joint Distribution Committee with the Soviet government, 1922–1923. Agreements between the Agro-Joint and the Soviet government, 1924, 1927, 1928. Agreements of the Agro-Joint and the American Society for Jewish Farm Settlements (ASJFS) with the Soviet government, 1929, 1930, 1933, 1938. Materials relating to relief work of the JDC within the framework of the American Relief Administration, 1922, including the appointment of J. Rosen as the JDC representative at the ARA. Statistics, reports, miscellaneous correspondence relating to JDC activities in Russia. Minutes, memos, reports, legal documents, certificate of incorporation, and general correspondence relating to the ASJFS, its formation, fund-raising activities, 1927–1939.

Records of the Agro-Joint Main Office, Moscow. Annual and periodic reports of the Agro-Joint including statistics, financial estimates, financial reports, analyses of expenditures, relating to Agro-Joint work, 1924–1937. General correspondence files: incoming and outgoing letters, reports, and memoranda. Materials relating to land surveys and allocations in the Crimea: statistics, surveys, memos, correspondence, relating to the Salsk district,

Chernomor district, Changar peninsula, Azov, Kuban, Odessa district, Samara district, Povolzhe, Krivoy Rog, Kherson, the Far East, Siberia.

Materials relating to contacts with KOMZET. Correspondence, minutes of KOMZET meetings, statistical information, reports. By-laws of the OZET (Obshchestvo po Zemleustroistvu Trudiashchikhsia Evreev—Association For the Settlement of Jews Toiling On Land) and AGRO-KUSTBANK (Evreiskii Agrarno-Kustarnyi Bank—Jewish Agricultural and Craftsmen Bank). Register of Agro-Joint assets transferred to KOMZET.

Records of the Agro-Joint Agricultural Department. Materials relating to agricultural activities in specific colonies. Reports by agronomists, summaries, statistics, financial reports, minutes of meetings, landscape plans, diagrams, drafts of projected constructions, field experiments, relating to various regions as well as to specific agro-sectors and collectives in the provinces of Crimea, Ekaterinoslav (Dnepropetrovsk), Kherson, Krivoy Rog, Odessa, Volhynia, Byelorussia.

Records of the Agro-Joint Relief and Industrialization Department. Materials relating to non-agricultural activities, mostly financial aid to mutual aid societies, savings and loan associations, health care organizations, factories, vocational schools.

Materials relating to colonization projects in Rhodesia, Alaska, Santo Domingo, British Guiana, 1937–1940.

Photographs of Jewish agricultural settlements, institutions, schools, factories, medical centers, supported by the JDC and Agro-Joint, arranged alphabetically by name of town or colony.

Inventory, English.

913. ROSENBLATT, H. (1878–1956).
   Papers, 1921–1956. 6 in. (RG 363)

Pseudonym of Hayyim Rosenblueth. Yiddish poet. Rosenblatt's poetry reflects the transitional stage between the Yiddish social lyricists and the later poets, those belonging to "Di yunge," who emphasised individual emotions. Lived in Russia. Came to the United States in 1892. On the first editorial board of *Kheshbn*, the Yiddish literary quarterly. Lived in New York, Detroit. Settled in Los Angeles in 1921, becoming an active member of the Yiddish cultural community there.

Correspondence with over 600 writers including Menahem Boraisha, Baruch (Boris) Glassman, Peretz Hirschbein, Szmerke Kaczerginski, Abraham Liessin, Mani Leib, Shmuel Niger, Zalman Reisen, Israel Joshua Singer, Yehoash.

914. ROSENFELD, MORRIS (1862–1923).
   Papers, 1894–1923. 5 ft. 5 in. (RG 431)

Noted Yiddish poet. His poetry dealt with the theme of social justice for Jewish workers. Staff writer of the *Jewish Daily Forward*, *Yiddishes Tageblatt*, *Arbeter fraynd* (London) and other newspapers and magazines. Rosenfeld's poems were widely popular among Jewish workers throughout the world. Born in the village of Boksze in the Suwałki district. Lived in London. Immigrated to the United States in 1886.

Correspondence with labor leaders, writers, editors, translators, including Friedrich Adler, Joseph Barondess, Reuben Brainin, Abraham Cahan, Solomon Golub, Alexander Harkavy, S. B. Kamaiko, Edwin Markham, Kalman Marmor, Louis Marshall, Zalman Reisen, Jacob Schiff, Abraham Shomer, Upton Sinclair, Rose Pastor Stokes, Anna Strunski Waling, Leo Wiener, Stephen S. Wise, Israel Zangwill.

Personal and family correspondence. Printed literary works. Manuscripts and drafts of planned publication. Translations of Rosenfeld's poems into English, German and other languages. Printed and manuscript sheet music. Drawings and illustrations to Rosenfeld's poems. Reviews and articles about Rosenfeld.

Inventory, English, Yiddish.

915. ROSENFELD, SAMUEL (1869–1943).
Papers, ca. 1900–1942. 10 in. (RG 211)

Journalist, author, Zionist. Editor of the Yiddish newspaper *Der fraynd* (St. Petersburg) and the Hebrew *Hazefira* (Warsaw). Was responsible for the Yiddish edition of Herzl's *Die Welt* (Vienna). Staff writer for *The Day* (NY). Lived in the Ukraine, the United States.

Correspondence with Yitzhak Dov Berkowitz, Alter Druyanov, Simon Dubnow, Jacob Glatstein, Yizhak Grunbaum, Vladimir Jabotinsky, Shmuel Niger, Joseph Opatoshu, Morris Winchevsky. Manuscripts of articles by Rosenfeld and of his doctoral dissertation: *Die Philosophie Krochmals als Hegelianer* (The Philosophy of Krochmal As Hegelian).

916. ROSENFELD, YONA (1880–1944).
Papers. 1 ft. 3 in. (RG 647)

Yiddish novelist, short-story writer, playwright. Contributed to *Literarishe bleter* (Warsaw), *Moment* (Warsaw), *Yidishe velt, Teater velt, Zukunft* (NY), *Veker, Jewish Daily Forward*, (NY). Born in Czartorysk, Volhynia. Immigrated to the United States in 1921.

The papers relate to Y. Rosenfeld's literary career. Typescripts and clippings of his works. Translations of his works. Clippings of criticisms, reviews, obituaries. Personal documents.

917. ROSENSTEIN, CHAIM (1898–1966).
Papers, 1930–1965. 5 in. (RG 542)

Yiddish writer, journalist, playwright, translator. Wrote for many periodicals including *Literarishe bleter, Di oystralishe yidishe nayes* (Australia), *Undzer tsayt* (NY). Husband of Rachel Holzer, the Yiddish actress. Born in Nowy Dwór, near Warsaw. Immigrated to Melbourne, Australia, in 1939.

Clippings of Rosenstein's published articles, 1930–1965. Chronological listing of these clippings with bibliographical data.

918. ROTH, JACOB.
Collection, 1945–1970s. 2 ft. (RG 328)

Lawyer, amateur photographer. Collector for YIVO. Lived in Poland, France.

Photographs of Jewish landmarks around the world, taken by Roth during his travels, including images of monuments and memorials to the Holocaust.

919. ROTHBART, JACOB M.
Papers, ca. 1918–1970s. 2 ft. 3 in. (RG 492)

Life insurance agent, author, chairman of the Friends of YIVO in Pittsburgh.

Correspondence with Yiddish literary figures, including H. Leivick, Yudel Mark, Jacob Milch, Kadia Molodowsky, David Pinsky, Melech Ravitch, Abraham Reisen, Jonas Turkow.

Correspondence with family. Typescripts and mimeographed copies of Rothbart's memoirs.

920. ROTHENBERG, ANNA SHOMER.
Papers, 1916–1951. 5 in. (RG 303)

Singer, United States.

The papers relate to Rothenberg's artistic career and include concert programs and clippings. There is also correspondence with Isaac A. Hourwich, Moshe Olgin, David W. Senator, Milton Steinberg, Rose Pastor Stokes, Henrietta Szold. Many of the letters pertain to the activities of Mailamm–American Palestine Music Association.

921. RUBACHA, SARAH BEYER.
Papers, 1925–1980. 5 in. (RG 1265)

Teacher at the Coralnik School, a Yiddish secular school, in Brooklyn, New York, which was affiliated with the Farband–Labor Zionist Order.

Minutes, souvenir journals and photographs relating to the Coralnik School. Personal letters. Manuscript of poetry by Hayim Rubacha.

922. RUBIN, RUTH (1906–).
Collection, 1947–1966. 25 ft. (RG 620)

Yiddish folksinger, folklorist, poet. Born in Montreal, Canada. Settled in New York in 1924.

The collection consists of tapes and record albums of Jewish music made by Ruth Rubin as part of her research in Yiddish musical folklore. The songs are sung by informants in New York, Montreal, Toronto, London. Song types include: Hasidic, ballads, children's songs, lullabies, drinking songs, dances, riddles, love songs, humorous songs, anti-Hasidic songs, songs about poverty, work, Zionism.

923. RUBIN-HALBERSTAM, SHLOMO YECHEZKEL SHRAGA (ca. 1913–1986).
Papers, 1950s–1970s. 4 ft. 2 in. (RG 314)

Hasidic rabbi in Cieszanów, Poland, and in New York.

Miscellaneous printed matter, including invitations, announcements and circulars, relating to Orthodox Jewish life in New York. Included are materials on communal and charitable organizations as well as correspondence with rabbis.

924. RUBINSTEIN, JOSEPH (1905–1978).
Papers, 1936–1977. 8 ft. 6 in. (RG 802)

Yiddish poet. Contributed to *Arbeter tsaytung* (Warsaw), *Shprotsungen, Literarishe bleter, Shtern* (Białystok), *Zukunft* (NY), *Yidisher kemfer, Jewish Daily Forward, Der veker*. Born in Skidel, Białystok province, Poland. Immigrated to the United States in 1948.

Manuscripts and typescripts of Rubinstein's poems, including *Khurbn poyln* and *Megilas rusland*. Clippings of articles and poems by Rubinstein. Reviews of Rubinstein's works. Correspondence with family and friends. Photographs, printed materials relating to Yiddish cultural events. Tapes of readings and speeches by Rubinstein. Personal documents.

925. RUBINSTEIN, LEON (1901–1985).
   Papers, 1960s. 3 in. (RG 1268)

Yiddish writer and political activist. Leader of the Labor Zionist movement. Teacher in the Farband Yiddish schools in the United States. Born in Łódź, Poland. Immigrated to the United States in 1927.

   Typescripts of Rubinstein's autobiography, and of his history of the Zeire Zion movement. Materials relating to his 65th anniversary.

926. RUE AMELOT (FRANCE).
   Records, 1939–1944. 12 ft. 6 in. (RG 343)

The committee "Rue Amelot" was founded in Paris on June 15, 1940, in the office of the organization Colonie Scolaire, located at 36 Rue Amelot. Rue Amelot functioned as an underground organization providing aid to refugees, internees and children. It achieved its aims by clandestinely coordinating the activities of five social welfare organizations, the Colonie Scolaire and its medical dispensary, "La Mère et L'Enfant," and four canteens, run by the Cercle Amical, the Foyer Ouvrier Juif, the Foyer Amical and the Fédération de Sociétés Juives. Rue Amelot provided medical services, clothing, free meals, legal aid and shelter for children. At different times, the Rue Amelot received financial or other support from the American Jewish Joint Distribution Committee, OSE and ORT. Rue Amelot was one of many Jewish institutions in the Paris area affiliated with the UGIF network and it was listed as section 69 of the Third UGIF Group of the Northern Zone. The organization was directed by David Rapoport.

   Reports relating to the formation of Rue Amelot. Materials on early activities, 1940–1941. Correspondence regarding the Jewish situation in Belgium, 1940.

   Materials relating to internment camps. Reports from camps in Beaune–La Rolande, Pithiviers, Troyes, Compiègne, Poitiers. Reports of activities of Rue Amelot in the camps, especially in Beaune–La Rolande and Pithiviers. Reports from camps in Germany and Poland. Correspondence from internees to Rue Amelot. Letters from hostages shortly before their deaths. Reports from Madame Valency and Rabbi Eliyohu Bloch about camps.

   Files of Colonie Scolaire relating to internees and refugees receiving aid. Files of places where children were sheltered, and information on families providing shelter. Correspondence with people hiding Jewish children. Correspondence with children being hidden.

   Reports and accounts relating to the Rue Amelot kitchen. Lists of acquisitions. Daily registers of foods consumed. Statistics on packages sent to needy Jews.

   Correspondence, reports and memoranda to and from the UGIF. Correspondence with: orphan homes, Committee to Help Hungarian Jews, Quakers, Reichsvereinigung der Juden in Deutschland, L'Action Orthodoxe, Office d'Orientation Professionelle, Comité Français de Secours aux Enfants.

   Inventory, Yiddish, English.

927. RUMANIAN-AMERICAN CONGREGATION OR
       CHADASH AGUDAS ACHIM (PHILADELPHIA).
       Records, 1911–1947. 1 ft. 8 in. (RG 1101)

Minute books, 1911–1947, financial records, including records of donations. Minutes of the Ladies Auxiliary. Two scrapbooks containing program announcements and newspaper clippings relating to the activities of the Rumanian-American Congregation, the Ladies Auxiliary, the Rumanian Hebrew Beneficial Association. Book with data on candidates for congregation offices. Miscellaneous items including tickets for the High Holy Days, notices of meetings, insurance records.

928. RUSSIA AND THE SOVIET UNION (VILNA ARCHIVES).
Collection, 1845–1930s. 6 ft. 3 in. (RG 30)

This collection is comprised of miscellaneous materials which were acquired by the YIVO Archives in Vilna.

Included are letters, reports, clippings, posters and other documents relating to Jews in the Russian Empire and in the Soviet Union. The bulk of the collection covers the period of the Russian Empire.

Government documents, 1845–1908. Decrees and announcements of the Tsar. Petitions to the Tsar, 1860–1892. Anti-Jewish laws, 1881, 1882, 1894. Documents about Jews in the Russian army, 1885–1915. Police reports about Jewish revolutionaries, including lists with photographs of most-wanted fugitives, 1870–1911. Documents from various Jewish political groups, including materials pertaining to the 1917 elections. Materials on Birobidzhan, 1930s. Materials on different localities in the Russian Empire, 1902–1917.

Inventory, Yiddish.

929. RYMER, LUBA.
Papers, 1936–1958. 10 in. (RG 482)

Yiddish actress and singer. Member of the ARTEF theater company. Lived in the United States.

The papers relate to Rymer's theatrical career and include correspondence, clippings, photographs, scripts of parts, programs.

Photographs are cataloged in STAGEPIX.

930. SALONIKA, JEWISH COMMUNITY.
Records, ca. 1910–1939. 3 ft. 2 in. (RG 207)

Ancient Jewish community in northeastern Greece. Salonika was under the Ottoman Empire from 1430 until 1912 when it was claimed by Greece. During the Greek period the community experienced a decline. In 1917 a fire destroyed most of Salonika and the 50,000 Jews left homeless were not permitted to return to their homes. Large numbers of Jews emigrated in the 1920s and 1930s because of the fire, unfavorable laws and antisemitism. In 1935, there were nearly 60,000 Jews in Salonika. Between 1941 and 1944, Salonika was occupied by the Nazis. About 95% of the Jewish population was deported and exterminated, most of them in Auschwitz.

The records pertain to the Greek period. Population registration books containing records of vital statistics, 1920–1939. Lists of Salonika Jews, ca. 1939. Records of the Rabbinical Court, 1920–1938. Correspondence with the Salonika Jewish community from individuals and institutions.

931. SAMARITAN SOCIETY.
Records, 1868–1961. 5 in. (RG 583)

Founded in New York in 1868 as the Erster Galizischer Kranken und Unterstutzungs Verein.

Adopted a constitution in 1872. Later changed name to Samaritan Society.

Membership initiation book, containing constitution and by-laws, 1872 (German, English). Minutes, 1868–1877 (German). Membership application forms, 1872–1897 (German), 1897–1961 (German, English).

932. SANDLER, PHILIP (1905–1981).

Papers, 1950s–1960s. 2 ft. 6 in. (RG 420)

Yiddish journalist, collector for YIVO. Active in left-wing Jewish groups in Philadelphia. Wrote for the *Morning freiheit* and for Yiddish newspapers in the Soviet Union. From the 1950s worked for the *Jewish Daily Forward* (NY). Born in Lithuania. Came to the United States in 1915.

Circulars, pamphlets, brochures from HIAS, YKUF, Congress for Jewish Culture and other organizations relating to Jewish life in Philadelphia. Materials relating to the Workmen's Circle Schools and to International Workers' Order Schools. Clippings relating to Yiddish culture in the USSR.

933. SANDZER SOCIETY.

Records, 1943–1971. 5 in. (RG 922)

Founded in New York in 1940 by immigrants from Nowy Sącz, Poland. The Jewish historian Raphael Mahler was affiliated with the society and edited their memorial book, *Sefer Sandz*.

Constitution. Membership list. Souvenir journals. Correspondence. Material pertaining to the publication of the memorial book. Memorial book, 1970.

934. SATANOVER BENEVOLENT SOCIETY.

Records, 1903–1972. 13 in. (RG 818)

Founded in New York in 1903 by immigrants from Satanov, Ukraine, and chartered in 1904. Organized the Satanover Relief Committee for the War Sufferers to aid *landslayt* during World War I. Sent two delegates to Satanov in 1921 to bring relief and correspondence from American *landslayt*. Aided *landslayt* after World War II. Constitutions, including that of the Taube Goldstein Benevolent Society. Minutes, 1903–1938. Financial records, 1930s–1960s. Membership records. Records of the Satanover Relief Committee, including correspondence regarding residents of Satanov interned in Austria, Germany, Hungary, 1914–1916. Correspondence regarding relief work in Satanov, 1921. Miscellaneous materials.

935. SATANOVER SISTERHOOD.

Records, 1943–1970. 5 in. (RG 819)

Founded in New York in 1931 by immigrants from Satanov, Ukraine. Dissoved and later reestablished in 1954. Finally dissolved in 1970. Activities included relief work after World War II and support for Israel. Affiliated with the Satanover Benevolent Society.

Certificate of incorporation, 1957. Minutes, 1952–1970. Membership records, 1943–1971. Announcements, photographs, seal, miscellaneous materials.

936. SAXE, SAMUEL (1887–1966).

Papers, 1930s–1950s. 5 in. (RG 551)

Pen name of Sholem Sack. Attorney, Yiddish writer. His works were published in *Yidishe arbeter velt* (Chicago), *Yidishe velt* (Cleveland, Philadelphia), *Literarishe khoydesh heftn* (Los Angeles), *Yiddishes Tageblatt*. In 1915–1916 he published a satirical journal titled *Di rut*. Also published humorous poems in the English press. Born in the district of Kiev, Ukraine. Immigrated to the United States.

The collection consists of Saxe's Yiddish and English poetry and some correspondence.

937. SCHACHEWICZ, JACOB (1844–1933).
   Papers, 1920–1932. 2 1/2 in. (RG 417)

Scholar, chemist, early Zionist of the Biluist movement. Settled in the Biluist colony of Gedera, 1893.

Correspondence in the 1920s–1930s with individuals and institutions relating to Schachewicz's life in Palestine, his contacts with scholarly and rabbinical personalities. Included are Rabbi A.I. Kook, Rabbi Z.Y. Kook, Histadrut Hamizrachi, Va'ad Hamoshava Gedera, General Bikur Cholim Hospital, Palestine Water Commission.

938. SCHAECHTER, MORDKHE (born 1927).
   Papers, 1940s–1970s. 1 ft. 3 in. (RG 682)

Yiddish linguist, writer, lecturer, editor, lexicographer. Obtained a doctoral degree at the University of Vienna. Active in the Territorialist movement and the Freeland League. Chairman of the League of Yiddish. YIVO Associate. Editor of *Oyfn shvel*, *Yidishe shprakh* and of the *Groyser verterbukh fun der yidisher shprakh* (Great Dictionary of the Yiddish Language). Contributed to *Di goldene keyt*, *Davka*, *Zukunft*, *YIVO bleter*, *Yugntruf*, *Almanakh*, *Yidish*, *Yidisher folklor*, *Yidish lebn*. Born in Czernowitz, Rumania. Immigrated to the United States in 1951 and settled in New York.

The papers relate to Schaechter's work in Yiddish linguistics, his involvement in the Freeland League, and in Jewish cultural life. Correspondence and printed materials relating to the Freeland League and the periodical *Oyfn shvel*. Records of the Gezelshaft far Yidishe Yishuvim in Amerike (Association for Jewish Settlements in America), 1950s.

Materials on Jewish settlement projects in the United States and Israel. Minutes of the Workmen's Circle Kropotkin Branch #413, Los Angeles, California, late 1940s–1960. Minutes of the East Side Women's Group (Los Angeles), Jewish Culture Club (Los Angeles), 1961–1968. Photographs of various Yiddish schools. Personal correspondence.

939. SCHAY, MAX.
   Papers, ca. 1910–ca. 1975. 6 ft. 10 in. (RG 1244)

Rabbi, historian, and genealogist. Studied in the yeshiva of Galanta, Slovakia, and received ordination from the Pressburg (Bratislava) Yeshiva in 1918. Studied at the universities of Bratislava and Prague, receiving his PhD in 1925. Immigrated to the United States in 1926. Served as rabbi of the Hungarian Congregation Beit Hamedrash Hagadol Anshe Ungarn, and as kashrut supervisor for Horowitz-Margareten and other companies.

The papers relate to Rabbi Schay's research on the history and genealogy of the Jews of Bratislava, and to his work as a congregational rabbi and kashrut supervisor. Materials on the Jews of Bratislava, including excerpts from documents from governmental and communal archives for the years 1551–1850. Notes and manuscripts by Schay. Correspondence, including letters from Rabbis Joseph Zvi Duschinsky, Eliezer Deutsch, Akiva Sofer, and others. Correspondence and other material concerning kashrut. Manuscripts and notes for sermons and eulogies. Personal documents, including school certificates, military service card. Records of personal expenses, 1935–1959. Photographs. Correspondence and other materials of Schay's father-in-law, Rabbi Alter S. Pfeffer, including correspondence with Rabbis Heinrich (Hanokh) Ehrentreu, Moshe Deutsch, and others. Miscellaneous materials, including a Jewish calendar printed in Vienna, 1820–1821. Manuscripts on rabbinic issues. Manuscript book of *tehinos* (prayers), 19th century. Calendars, circulars and announcements by rabbis and institutions, *Reverands und khazonims hand bukh*, 1926.

940. SCHECHTER, ARTHUR.
Papers, 1940–1968. 5 in. (RG 408)

Civic leader, Grand Rapids, Michigan.

Correspondence with Yiddish literary figures, including Daniel Charney, Mendl Elkin, Aaron Glanz-Leieles, Chaim Grade, Szmerke Kaczerginski, H. Leivick, Shmuel Niger, A.A. Roback, I.J. Schwartz, Abraham Sutzkever, Berish Weinstein.

941. SCHINDLER, ELIEZER (1892–1957).
Papers, 1930s–1950s. 10 in. (RG 275)

Religious writer, historian. Author of textbooks for the Beis Yaakov schools. Student of writer and religious philosopher Nathan Birnbaum. Born in Tyczyn, Poland. Lived in the Soviet Union, Germany. Came to the United States in 1938.

Correspondence with Solomon Birnbaum, Nathan Birnbaum, Martin Buber, Daniel Charney, Abraham Golomb, Melech Ravitch, Zalman Reisen, Abraham Reisen, Max Weinreich. Correspondence with periodicals and institutions. Correspondence relating to Schindler's book *Yidish un Khsidish*.

942. SCHKLOVER INDEPENDENT BENEVOLENT ASSOCIATION.
Records, 1896–1974. 1 ft. 6 in. (RG 848)

Established in New York by immigrants from Shklov, Byelorussia, and incorporated in 1918 as the Schklover Auxiliary Society, Inc. Affiliated with the Hevrah Kadisha Schklover U.V., established in 1893, also know as the Hevrah Kadisha Anshe Shklover. Society name was legally changed in 1947 to Schklover Independent Benevolent Association, Inc. The Hevrah Kadisha Schklover U. V. established a loan fund in 1905 which became the property of the society in 1927.

Certificate of incorporation, 1918. Legal documents. Constitution. Minutes, 1951–1971. Financial records, 1918–1960, 1973–1974. Materials pertaining to membership, 1914–1950s. Correspondence. Materials pertaining to burial and endowments. Record book of the Hevrah Kadisha Anshe Shklover.

943. SCHORR, MOSHE (1872–1949).
Papers, 1940s. 2 ft. 6 in. (RG 499)

Yiddish playwright, translator, actor, journalist. Co-founder of the *Lemberger tageblat* (1908). Contributed to the *Yidisher kurier* (Chicago). Authored numerous plays. Born in Galați (Galatz), Rumania. Immigrated to the United States in 1905.

Memoirs by Schorr of his theatrical career. Manuscripts of Schorr's plays. Correspondence, speeches, articles.

Card inventory, Yiddish.

944. SCHRANK, JOSEPH.
Papers, 1930s–1940s. 10 in. (RG 1154)

Major in the U.S. Army during World War II. Military governor in Kusel and Rockenhausen in Germany.

The collection relates to Schrank's military career in the U.S. Army. Letters to his wife from Europe, 1944–1945. Nazi memorabilia such as a flag, tapestry, a whip, brass knuckles, medals, badges, bulletins, books. Materials of the U.S. military authority in Kusel.

945. SCHULMAN, ELIAS (1907–1986).
Papers, 1960–1975. 5 in. (RG 758)

Yiddish writer, teacher. Secretary of the Historical Section of the YIVO Institute in Vilna. Member of the executive board, Congress for Jewish Culture. Director of the Library, Jewish Education Committee, New York. Professor of Yiddish Literature at Queens College and at the Herzliah Teacher's Seminary. Editor, *Der veker*, and on the editorial board of the *Leksikon fun der nayer yidisher literatur* (Biographical Dictionary of Modern Yiddish Literature). Contributed to *Freie Arbeiter Stimme, Literarishe bleter, YIVO bleter, Zukunft, Jewish Daily Forward, Oyfn shvel, In zikh, Goldene keyt*. Born in Slutsk, Byelorussia. Immigrated to the United States in 1922.

The papers consist of correspondence with Yiddish writers and a copy of a manuscript about Hayyim Nahman Bialik.

946. SCHWARTZ, ISRAEL JACOB (1885–1971).
Papers, 1947–1971. 2 1/2 in. (RG 649)

Yiddish poet, translator. He published books of poetry, and his work appeared in periodicals and anthologies including some of the early publications of the literary group *Di yunge*. Known for his translations of works by Hayyim Nahman Bialik, Shakespeare, Milton and Walt Whitman. Born near Kaunas, Lithuania. Immigrated to the United States in 1906.

The papers consist of correspondence with writers and photographs.

947. SCHWARTZ, LEON (1901–1990).
Papers, 1920s–1950s. 1 ft. 11 in. (RG 1273)

Violinist, band leader and *baal kore* (torah reader). Schwartz's repertoire centered on the traditional klezmer string-band style. Born in Bukovina. Settled in the United States in 1921.

The papers consist primarily of printed Jewish music for the violin. Included are manuscripts of music composed or arranged by Schwartz. There are also some personal documents, letters and announcements.

948. SCHWARTZ, MAURICE (1890–1960).
Papers, 1920s–1960. 20 ft. 4 in. (RG 498)

Actor and director. Major personality of the Yiddish theater. Founded the Yiddish Art Theater (NY) in 1918, which lasted until 1950. Schwartz and his company toured North and South America, Europe, Israel and South Africa. His repertoire included Yiddish plays by I.J. Singer, Jacob Gordin, Abraham Goldfaden and Sholem Aleichem as well as adaptations of works by playwrights such as Shakespeare, George Bernard Shaw and Maksim Gorkii. Born in the Ukraine. Immigrated to the United States in 1901.

Correspondence, relating mostly to individual performances and the distribution of tickets. Typescripts and manuscripts, and printed copies of Yiddish and English plays with Schwartz's notes and comments. Programs and playbills. Sheet music for plays performed by the Yiddish Art Theater. Photographs of stage productions and of members of the ensemble. Clippings of articles about and by Schwartz, relating to the Yiddish theater. Personal documents, financial records, contracts.

Card inventory of plays.

Photographs cataloged in STAGEPIX.

949. SCHWARTZ, PINCHAS.
Collection, 1930s–1960s. 40 ft. 10 in. (RG 311)

Executive Secretary of YIVO, 1941–1954.

This collection of newpaper clippings was arranged by P. Schwartz for the YIVO–Yad Vashem Documentary Projects in the 1950s. The collection is divided into the following series: biographical materials on well-known Jewish personalities; geographical materials on communities destroyed by the Nazis; topical materials on miscellaneous subjects including the Alter–Erlich Affair, the Eichmann Trial.

Card inventory, Yiddish, English.

950. SCHWARTZ, ROSE (born 1900).
Papers, 1940–1974. 15 in. (RG 1000)

Born in Kishinev, Bessarabia. Immigrated to the United States, 1920. Was active in the Federation of Bessarabian Societies of America, Inc. and served as vice-president of its Women's Division. Vice-president of the Bessarabian Federation of American Jews. Affiliated with the Bronx Bessarabier Branch 302 International Worker's Order and a founder of its Women's Club. Member of the Bessarabier Podolier Benevolent Society. Worked for the Jewish Council for Russian War Relief and the American Society for Russian War Relief, Inc.

Correspondence, 1940–1974. Reports. Materials pertaining to Bessarabian Jews in France, 1940s–1950s. Scrapbook. Newspaper clippings. Honorary citations. Photographs. Publications of: the Federation of Bessarabian Societies, Inc.; Bessarabian Federation of American Jews; Bessarabier Podolier B.S.; Federation of Bessarabian Jews in Israel, 1940s–1950s. Miscellaneous publications.

951. SCHWARTZ, SHLOIME (1907–1988).
Papers, 1941–1988. 2 ft. 6 in. (RG 1253)

Yiddish poet. Contributed to *Literarishe bleter*, *Goldene keyt*, *Yidishe kultur*. Born in Kobrin, Byelorussia. Came to the United States in 1920. Lived in Chicago from 1922 until his death.

Correspondence with Yiddish writers, including Moisey Ghitzis, Aaron Glanz-Leieles, Eliezer Greenberg, Dina Halpern, M. Katz, Rachel Korn, M. Mann, Mates Olitzky, Elias Schulman, Abraham Sutzkever, Malka Heifetz Tussman, Itzhak Yanasowicz. Typescripts of poems. Clippings of press reviews. Photographs.

952. SCHWARZ, JOSEPH.
Papers, 1940s–1950s. 5 in. (RG 392)

Historian of Ukrainian and Russian Jewry. United States.

Correspondence with literary and cultural figures, friends, family members, and organizations.

953. SCHWARZ, LEO W. (1906–1967).
   Papers, 1945–1948. 21 ft. (RG 294.1)

Director of the AJDC for the U.S. Occupation Zone in Germany in the years 1946–1947. Author of several anthologies of Jewish literature, including *The Jewish Caravan.* Author of the memoir *The Redeemers* (1953) about his work for displaced persons. The AJDC (also known as the JDC or the Joint) provided material assistance to Jewish survivors of World War II in Europe, in particular to the Jewish displaced persons who were interned in the DP camps in Germany, Austria and Italy. The JDC assisted in the registration of camp residents, organized tracing bureaus, created programs of welfare, medical aid, vocational training, education and culture, and helped facilitate the immigration of the displaced persons to Israel and other countries.

Most of the records pertain to JDC activities in the American Zone in Germany.

General administrative files of the JDC offices in the American Zone. Reports, minutes of the JDC. Bulletins, correspondence, personnel lists, circulars and maps of JDC operations in Germany. Monthly departmental reports of JDC offices on personnel, religious affairs, education, camp relief, transportation, legal aid, emigration, employment and provisioning. Demographic and statistical reports. Records pertaining to contacts with U.S. military authorities and relief agencies. Judge Louis Leventhal's records on his mission to Germany as the U.S. Military Advisor on Jewish Affairs. Correspondence with UNRRA, minutes of the UNRRA Council on Jewish Affairs. Materials on the American Red Cross and the American Council of Voluntary Agencies.

JDC reports on: kibbutzim; individual camps; deportations by the U.S. military authorities of individuals illegally in the U.S. Zone; cultural activities; the black market; general conditions in the DP camps. Camps and centers include Augsburg, Bamberg, Feldafing, Föhrenwald, Kassel, Pocking-Waldstadt, Regensburg (region). Correspondence of Leo Schwarz and Chaplain Abraham J. Klausner. Correspondence and reports of chaplains and rabbis.

Records of the Central Committee of Liberated Jews, including correspondence, lists of members, memoranda, statutes, minutes, reports. Materials on the Second and Third Congresses of Displaced Persons, 1947–1948.

Files of JDC departments: Employment, Religion, Health, Welfare, Personnel Services, Emigration, Cultural Activities and Education, Legal Matters, Supplies, Public Relations, Financial Matters and Personnel. JDC materials pertaining to Jewish DP's in the British and French Zones and in Berlin.

Testimonies about the Holocaust by survivors. Folklore and satire about the life of Jewish displaced persons. Manuscript of Schwarz's *The Redeemers.*

Inventory, English.

954. SCHWARZBARD, SHALOM (1886–1938).
   Papers, 1917–1938. 4 microfilm reels. (RG 85)

Jewish revolutionary in Russia who assassinated Simon Petlyura, Ukrainian leader and commander of the Cossack units which carried out pogroms against Jews in the years 1918–1920.

Schwarzbard was active in the revolutionary movement of 1905 and participated in Jewish self-defense during the pogroms of 1905–1907. During World War I he joined the French Foreign Legion and was awarded the Croix de Guerre. In 1917 he returned to Russia, joined the Red Guard in Odessa and fought against the Ukrainian units. Fifteen of

Schwarzbard's relatives were murdered in the pogroms. Schwarzbard returned to Paris in 1920. In May 1926 Schwarzbard assassinated Petlyura who had settled in Paris the same year. He was acquitted in the trial which followed. Born in Bessarabia. Lived in Paris. Died in Cape Town, South Africa.

The collection consists of correspondence, newspaper clippings, manuscripts and notes that relate primarily to the Schwarzbard trial and its aftermath.

Correspondence with organizations: Agudah Ateret Zion, Yidisher Natsyonaler Arbeter Farband (Jewish National Workers Alliance), Yidisher Studentn Fareyn, Jewish Agency, *Der Tog*, *Undzer tsayt*, YIVO Institute, Ligue Internationale Contre L'Antisémitisme, *Morgn zhurnal*, Fédération de Sociétés Juives de France, Jewish Veterans Organization. Correspondence with individuals: Joseph Barondess, Alberto Bianchi, Zelig Kalmanovitch, Israel Ostroff, Noah Prylucki, Anna Schwarzbard, William Zukerman.

Manuscripts: typescripts of memoirs *In krig mit zikh aleyn* (At War with Myself). Poems about Schwarzbard's assassination of Petlyura. Poems by Anna Schwarzbard. Clippings about Schwarzbard. Personal documents.

Inventory, Yiddish.

955. SCHWARZSCHILD, FRITZ.
Collection, ca. 1937–1939. 5 in. (RG 298)

Collector for YIVO.

Reports, lists, estimates relating to Reichsvertretung der Juden in Deutschland and Hilfsverein der Juden in Deutschland concerning proposed colonies for Jewish immigrants in Brazil, Panama, 1937–1939.

956. SCHWEID, MARK (1891–1969).
Papers, ca. 1920s–1969. 4 ft. 2 in. (RG 357)

Yiddish actor, writer, theater critic. Collaborated with Maurice Schwartz in the Yiddish Art Theater. Born in Warsaw. Settled in the United States in 1911.

Correspondence with Yiddish writers and theater personalities including A. Almi, Salo Baron, Yitzhak Dov Berkowitz, Menahem Boraisha, Reuben Brainin, Daniel Charney, Mendl Elkin, Peretz Hirschbein, Yudel Mark, David Pinsky, Melech Ravitch, Zalman Reisen, Maurice Schwartz, Abraham Sutzkever, Zalmen Zylbercweig.

Correspondence with organizations including Congress for Jewish Culture, American Jewish Historical Society, Jewish National Workers Alliance, Jewish Daily Forward. Programs and playbills of theatrical performances. Manuscripts of radio scripts, translations of works by Shakespeare.

Clippings of articles by and about Schweid, including reviews and obituaries. Material for an anthology of German-Jewish authors.

957. SCOOLER, ZVEE (1889–1985).
Papers, 1931–1983. 23 ft. (RG 1262)

Yiddish actor and radio personality. Began his acting career in 1916. From 1921 to 1946 was a member of the Maurice Schwartz Yiddish Art Theater in New York. Appeared in many English-language plays on Broadway and in films, where he played mostly Jewish characters. From 1934 until his death was the radio host on the weekly program "The Forward Hour," broadcast on WEVD, New York. Was affiliated with the Labor Zionist

Alliance and directed activities in its summer camp. Born in Kamenets–Podolski, Ukraine. Settled in the United States in 1912.

The papers reflect Scooler's career as a radio and theater personality and communal activist. Correspondence with listeners, with family, with individuals active in the theater. Included are Joseph Papp, Ira Gershwin, Jan Peerce, Molly Picon, Harold Prince, Paul Muni. WEVD material: radioscripts of weekly broadcasts, typed in Yiddish, 1934–1939. Weekly radioscripts of the "Gram-meister," written and read by Z. Scooler, arranged chronologically 1939–1983. Radioscripts of "Tsvishn di shures," (Between the Lines). Radioscripts of "The Forward Hour." Announcements of "The Forward Hour". Play and film scripts. Personal documents. Theater programs. Clippings. Financial papers. Photographs: of personal life, of theater activities, of family members. Printed music: folksongs and Yiddish theater music. Materials on Zvee Scooler's role as master of ceremonies at various private functions. Materials relating to Scooler's activities in various summer camps.

Inventory, English.

Recordings of radio programs placed in RG 130.

958. SECUNDA, SHOLOM (1894–1974).
Papers, 1931–1972. 1 ft. 5 in. (RG 1227)

Composer. Active as a composer and musical director in the Yiddish theater. Known for his songs *Dos yidishe lid*; *Dona, dona*; and *Bay mir bistu sheyn*. Born in Aleksandriya, Ukraine. Came to the United States in 1908.

Scrapbooks containing: clippings and some correspondence, flyers and other material relating to Secunda's musical career, especially the history of the song *Bay mir bistu sheyn*.

959. SEGAL, SIMON (ca. 1900–ca. 1972).
Papers, 1920s–1967. 3 ft. 4 in. (RG 679)

Author, scholar of international affairs. Affiliated with the Foreign Policy Association. On the staff of the American Jewish Committee. Obtained a Doctor of Laws degree at the Université de Paris à la Sorbonne. Born in Poland. Came to the United States in 1935 on a research fellowship of the Carnegie Endowment for International Peace. Settled in the United States.

The collection consists of correspondence, manuscripts, notes, reports, clippings, personal documents relating to Segal's activities as a writer and scholar in the fields of international law, history of Poland in the pre-World War II period, history of the Jews in Poland in the 1930s.

Personal documents include identity papers and diary. Correspondents include Horace Kallen, Stephen Wise. Manuscripts pertain to Segal's books and articles including *The New Order in Poland* and *The New Poland and the Jews*. Clippings of reviews of Segal's works.

Inventory, English.

960. SEGALMAN, RALPH.
Papers, 1966–1974. 2 ft. (RG 1299)

American sociologist. Worked for the AJDC office in Austria, 1945–1949, and for various Jewish organizations in the United States. Taught at California State University at Northridge.

Sociological studies, including Segalman's PhD dissertation submitted to New York University in 1966, titled: *A Test of the Levinian Hypothesis on Self-Hatred Among the Jews*. An unpublished manuscript, "The Irrelevant Generation: Middle Class Youth in the Sixties," 1974. Other manuscripts and some correspondence.

961. SELDIN, ALEXANDER (1882–1949).
   Papers, 1920s–1940s. (RG 433)

Yiddish journalist, editor of *The Day*, playwright. Founding member and president of the I.L. Peretz Yiddish Writers Union. Lived in Byelorussia, the United States.

   Manuscripts of Seldin's novels, plays and articles. Correspondence and other materials relating to the journalists strike at *The Day*, 1941.

962. SELECTIVE BROTHERS OF ISRAEL.
   Records, 1928–1963. 7 1/2 in. (RG 928)

Founding date unknown. Collected head tax from members to pay for endowments.

   Constitutional amendments. Minutes, 1936–1951. Financial records, 1940s–1950s. Materials pertaining to burial. Correspondence.

963. SELTZER, DAVID.
   Papers, 1930–ca. 1980. 4 in. (RG 1232)

Yiddish journalist, poet. Longtime staff member and editor of the *Morgn frayhayt*. Born in Soroki, Bessarabia, 1904. Settled in the United States in 1920.

   Manuscripts of memoirs, poems, letters, and other materials by Yiddish writers including Shalom Asch, David Bergelson, Sholem Budin, Chaver-Paver, Sarah Fell-Yelin, Baruch (Boris) Glassman, Ben Zion Goldberg, Abba Gordin, Ber Green, Peretz Hirschbein, Moyshe Katz, Leon Kobrin, Aaron Kurtz, Malka Lee, Raphael Mahler, Kalman Marmor, Gina Medem, Nachman Meisel, Jacob Mestel, Moshe Nadir, A.A. Roback, Isaac Rontch, David Seltzer, Dora Teitelbaum, Zishe Weinper, Morris Winchevsky, Chaim Zhitlowsky. Displays assembled by Seltzer on Henry David Thoreau. Materials on Seltzer's trip to Soroki in 1965. Clippings on Yiddish theater and on Birobidzhan. Reproductions of lithographs by Tanchum Kaplan.

964. SELTZER, IDA (?–1976).
   Papers, 1930s–1960s. 5 in. (RG 743)

Member, YIVO Executive Board and Board of Directors.

   Correspondence with Jewish cultural institutions and literary personalities in the United States, including YIVO, Yiddish Dictionary Committee, Chaim Zhitlowsky, H. Leivick. Photographs.

965. SESKIND, MORRIS (1872–1958).
   Papers, 1904–1950. 4 ft. 7 in. (RG 269)

Active in the labor movement in Chicago. Organizer of one of the first Yiddish-speaking branches of the Socialist Party in Chicago. Labor editor of the Chicago edition of the *Jewish Daily Forward*. Member and officer in organizations such as: the Workmen's Circle, United Hebrew Trades, Federation of Jewish Trade Unions.

   Correspondence and other materials relating to individuals: Abraham Cahan, Joseph Baskin, Eugene Debs, Julius Gerson, Leon Hanock, Samuel Laderman, E.N. Nockels, Jacob

Siegel, Morris Sigman, Norman Thomas, B.C. Vladeck, Max Zaritzky. Correspondence, minutes, convention proceedings, constitution and by-laws of various organizations. Pamphlets and publications, 1884–1947, by unions, labor organizations and government offices.
Inventory, English.

966. SHABAD, ZEMACH (1864–1935).
Papers, ca. 1900–1930s. 5 ft. (RG 19)

Physician, communal leader, senator in the Polish Diet, chairman of EKOPO and of ORT. Founder of Vilna branch of OSE. Co-founder of YIVO.

The collection reflects Shabad's career as a private physician and consists of medical records of his patients.

967. SHANGHAI COLLECTION
Collection, 1930s–1940s. 3 ft. (RG 243)

Accumulated by the YIVO Committee in Shanghai from 1946 to 1948 partly in preparation for the exhibition *Jewish Life in Shanghai* held at the YIVO, New York in 1948–1949. The exhibition related primarily to the Shanghai ghetto.

The Shanghai ghetto was established by Japanese occupying forces in 1943. Among its residents were the Jews who had settled in China at the turn of the century as well as Eastern European Jewish refugees who had fled to China to escape Nazi oppression. The ghetto was in existence until the departure of the Japanese forces in 1945.

The collection relates to life in the ghetto and includes materials on: founding of the ghetto; relief groups such as JDC, ORT, HIAS, and SACRA (Shanghai Ashkenazic Collaborating Relief Association); political organizations such as Zionist groups, the Bund; the rabbinate; the sick and benevolent society; kitchen fund; commercial establishments; religious schools, secular schools; professional associations; art, theater and music activities; Jewish press; emigration from Shanghai after World War II. There are also manuscript histories of the Shanghai ghetto.

Inventory, English, Yiddish.

968. SHAPIRO, BORIS (born 1887).
Papers, 1940s–1950s. 10 in. (RG 1263)

Memoirist, member of the Socialist Revolutionary Party (s–R) in Russia. Was sentenced to life imprisonment in exile in 1904. Escaped, and reached New York in 1906. His memoirs were serialized in the Yiddish daily *Der tog* (NY), in the 1950s.

Manuscript and clippings of Shapiro's memoirs.

969. SHAPIRO, LAMED (1879–1948).
Papers, ca. 1934–1947. 2 ft. 1 in. (RG 282)

Yiddish writer, poet, literary critic.

Correspondence with literary figures: Daniel Charney, Aaron Glanz-Leieles, Jacob Glatstein, Abba Gordin, H. Leivick, Kalman Marmor, David Pinsky, Melech Ravitch, Abraham Reisen, Romain Rolland, D. Rutner (Soviet Union), I.J. Schwartz. Correspondence with Yiddish organizations and institutions. Manuscripts and typescripts. Photographs of family and friends.

970. SHATZKY, JACOB (1893–1956).
     Papers, 1912–ca. 1960. 10 ft. (RG 356)

Historian, writer, lecturer, lexicographer, bibliographer, editor. One of the founders of "Amopteyl," the American branch of YIVO. Member of the Board of Directors of YIVO. Co-editor of the *YIVO bleter* and the *YIVO Annual of Social Science*. Co-editor of the *Leksikon fun der nayer yidisher literatur* (Biographical Dictionary of Modern Yiddish Literature), New York, 1956. President, Yiddish PEN Club. Director, Research Library of the New York State Psychiatric Institute. Wrote numerous works on Jewish history, concentrating on the history of the Jews in Poland. Co-author, with Leland E. Hinsie, of the *Psychiatric Dictionary*. Born in Warsaw, Poland. Immigrated to the United States in 1923.

   Correspondence with Jewish literary, cultural and political figures, and communal leaders, including Ber Borochov, Boris Thomashefsky, Solomon Grayzel, Aaron Glanz-Leieles, H. Leivick, Joseph Opatoshu, Isaac Bashevis Singer, Menahem Boraisha, Shmuel Niger, Kalman Marmor, Mark Wischnitzer, Max Weinreich, Emanuel Ringelblum. Correspondence with organizations, societies, publishers. Family correspondence. Notes and photostatic copies for Shatzky's book, *Geshikhle fun yidn in varshe* (History of the Jews in Warsaw), Volumes I-III, New York, 1947–1953 and Volume IV which is unpublished. Topics relate to: the rabbinate; community council; local organizations; Yiddish literature, art and culture; education; industry, trade, banks; political movements; charities. An abbreviated unpublished version of *History of the Jews in Warsaw*. Notes, manuscripts and correspondence relating to the *Shatzky bukh* (The Shatzky Book), ed. E. Lifschutz, YIVO, 1957. Clippings of Shatzky's writings, as well as reviews and articles about Shatzky, 1910s–1960s. Manuscripts and notes for articles by Shatzky on topics in Jewish history, Yiddish folklore and literature. Materials, including biographical sketches, for the *Leksikon fun der nayer yidisher literatur*. Materials relating to Shatzky's biographical work *Moris Rozenfeld, in likht fun zayne briv* (Morris Rosenfeld, In The Light Of His Letters), New York, 1936. Bibliographies, on cards, relating to: early Yiddish literature in print; topics of medical interest in Jewish history; Judaica; theater; psychiatry and Jews; American Jewish press. Personal documents. Posters and lecture announcements.
   Inventory, English.

971. SHEDLOWTZER BENEVOLENT ASSOCIATION.
     Records, 1910–1980. 5 in. (RG 894)

Founded in New York in 1909 by immigrants from Szydłowiec (Shidlovits), Poland, as the Shidlovtser Untershtitsung Fareyn. Was affiliated with the Shedlowtzer Ladies Society (established 1925) and the Shedlowtzer Junior League (established 1934), of which neither exists today. Established an old-age fund, 1924. Aided landslayt and communal institutions, especially during World War I. Published a memorial book in 1974 with the cooperation of Shidlovtser landslayt in Israel. Supported Jewish institutions and charities in New York and Israel.
   Minutes, 1910–1913, 1943–1965. Souvenir journals. Meeting announcements. Photograph. Photocopy of autobiography submitted to YIVO (Vilna) autobiography contest, 1934.

972. SHERMAN, BEZALEL (ca. 1896–1971).
     Papers. 1 ft. 8 in. (RG 625)

Jewish sociologist, publicist. Wrote about sociological aspects of Jewish life in the United States. Contributed to Yiddish and English periodicals including *Yidisher kemfer*, *Zukunft*.

Co-editor of *Proletarisher gedank.* Member, Board of Directors of YIVO. Born in Kiev. Immigrated to the United States in 1911, settling first in Chicago and later in New York.

The collection consists of printed and mimeographed materials on American Jewry including population studies, Jewish welfare and religious organizations. Correspondence with literary and cultural figures and Jewish institutions.

973. SHERMAN, ISAAC.
Papers, 1950s–1970s. 2 ft. 1 in. (RG 290)

Collector for YIVO. Lived in Philadelphia and in Israel.

The papers relate mainly to Jewish community life in Philadelphia and include materials from the Jewish National Fund.

974. SHESKIN, HYMAN (CHAIM).
Papers, ca. 1924–1974. 5 in. (RG 648)

Collector for YIVO. Brooklyn, New York.

Correspondence with family and friends in Grodno, Poland, 1924–1931. Letters from Fannie Zak about the Warsaw ghetto and the Jewish police there, 1954; from Elie Wiesel, 1978. Personal documents. Materials about the Mendele Folk Shul in Brooklyn, 1940s.

975. SHIFRIN, ABRAHAM (1895–1974).
Papers, 1937–1973. 5 in. (RG 631)

Recording secretary of the Grine Felder Summer Colony, established in 1937. Members of the colony included Mendl Elkin, Shmuel Niger, Daniel Charney, David Pinsky, Lazar Weiner, Peretz Hirschbein.

The papers relate primarily to the educational, cultural and financial activities of the colony and include: minute books, 1941–1973; reports by A. Shifrin outlining the history of the colony; manuscripts by A. Shifrin.

976. SHMULEWITZ-SMALL, SOLOMON (1868–1943).
Papers, 1920s–1930s. 4 ft. (RG 214)

Yiddish poet, playwright, composer and folksinger. Born in Pinsk, Byelorussia. Came to the United States in 1891.

Manuscripts of Shmulewitz's songs and plays. Photographs of famous cantors, of Shmulewitz in performance, of family members.

Card inventory of the photographs.

977. SHNEUR, ZALMAN (1887–1959).
Papers, 1902–1961. 4 ft. 2 in. (RG 764)

Hebrew and Yiddish poet and novelist. Played significant role in the development of modern Hebrew poetry. Contributed to *Zukunft, Moment, Parizer morgnblat, Jewish Daily Forward, Keneder odler, Tog morgn zhurnal, Hazman* (Vilna), *Miklat* (NY), *Davar, Haboker* and others. Born in Shklov, Mogilev District, Byelorussia. From 1906 to 1924 lived in Switzerland, Paris, Berlin, and the United States. From 1924 to 1941 resided in Paris. From 1941 to 1949 lived in the United States. In 1949 he settled in Ramat Gan, Israel. Died while on a visit to New York.

The papers consist of: correspondence; manuscripts of poems, plays, novels in Yiddish and Hebrew; translations of Zalman Shneur's works; clippings by and about Shneur; personal documents; photographs.

Inventory, Yiddish.

978. SHOLEM ALEICHEM COOPERATIVE HOUSES, BRONX, NY.
Records, 1928–1941. 10 in. (RG 393)

The Sholem Aleichem cooperative housing project, located in the Bronx, was organized in 1927 by the Yidishe Kooperative Heym Gezelshaft. The building contained housing for over 200 families as well as artists' studios and an auditorium. Many of the residents were writers and artists. Although the cooperative failed in 1929, the tenants continued the organization's Yiddish cultural and educational activities until the 1960s.

Bound volumes of minutes of meetings of the Executive Committee, 1928–1929, 1933–1941. Minutes of meetings of the general membership, 1934–1941. Minute book of "Undzer Klub," 1934. Printed materials.

979. SHOLEM ALEICHEM FOLK INSTITUTE.
Records, 1920s–1960s. 52 ft. 9 in. (RG 659)

Yiddish educational organization based in New York. Established Yiddish-speaking afternoon and Sunday schools at the elementary and junior-high school levels. Owner of Camp Boiberik in Rhinebeck, New York. Maintained the Farlag Matones publishing house.

Minutes of the Sholem Aleichem Folk Institute, 1920s–1950s. Bulletins; news releases; materials relating to individual schools; correspondence; reports on banquets and conferences.

980. SHOLEM ALEICHEM FOLK INSTITUTE: CAMP BOIBERIK.
Records, 1923–1978. 13 ft. 9 in. (RG 659.1)

Summer camp where the speaking of Yiddish was encouraged. Founded in 1919 and owned by the Sholem Aleichem Folk Institute. Located near Rhinebeck, New York. Directed by Leibush Lehrer from 1922 to 1958. The camp was closed in 1979.

Photographs of campers and camp life, 1920s–1970s. Films of camp, 1930s–1960s. Camp songbooks. Play scripts, songs, cheers, parodies, newspapers, speeches, correspondence; art albums; daily schedules of activities.

Inventory, English, Yiddish.

Films placed in RG 105. Films.

981. SHOMER, ABRAHAM (1876–1946).
Papers, 1907–1940s. 7 ft. 1 in. (RG 288)

Lawyer, playwright, co-founder of the World Jewish Congress. Lived in Russia and the United States.

Correspondence about the founding of the World Jewish Congress. Leaflets, pamphlets, news clippings about the World Jewish Congress, 1906–1923. Yiddish plays, English plays and translations written by Shomer. Correspondence and clippings relating to the theater.

Inventory, English.

982. SHONBERG FAMILY AID SOCIETY.
Records, 1916–1969. 2 1/2 in. (RG 1078)

Organized in 1912 and incorporated in 1915 to strengthen family ties and assist sick and needy members. Membership is open to direct descendants of the Shonbergs and their spouses. Founders originated in the Warsaw area.

Certificate of incorporation. Constitution. Minutes, 1936–1958. Miscellaneous materials, 1916–1969.

983. SHOR, ANSHEL and WEISSMAN, DORA.
Papers, 1906–1966. 6 ft. (RG 689)

Anshel Shor was a Yiddish playwright and theater director. Dora Weissman, Shor's wife, was a Yiddish actress and owner of a talent agency.

The papers include playscripts by Shor and by others, sheet music, personal documents, materials relating to Weissman's activities in various charities, texts of her radio programs, materials from her agency, photographs.

984. SHORE, WILLIAM and LISA.
Papers, 1933–1979. 5 in. (RG 621)

Sponsors of YIVO and other Yiddish cultural institutions. Los Angeles.

The papers consist of correspondence with Jewish literary and communal figures about projects supported by William and Lisa Shore. Correspondents include Jacob Glatstein, Chaim Grade, Joseph Rolnick, I.J. Schwartz, Aaron Zeitlin.

985. SHOSKES, HENRY (CHAIM) (1891–1958).
Papers, 1930s–1962. 10 in. (RG 484)

Economist, journalist, diplomat, communal leader. Directed work of Jewish Credit Cooperatives in Poland, 1921–1939. Chief analyst of the Board of Economic Warfare, Washington, D.C., 1943. Contributor to the *Morgn zhurnal*. Radio broadcaster on WEVD radio station. Member, YIVO Board of Directors. Overseas representative for the United HIAS Service. Born in Białystok, Poland. Lived in Russia, Belgium. Settled in the United States in 1940.

Correspondence with Izhak Ben-Zvi, David Ben-Gurion, Joseph Sprinzak, Rabbinate of Cairo. Report on the Jewish Community in Lebanon, 1956. Correspondence relating to Felix Kersten, personal physician of Himmler. Photostats of Polish underground press, 1940–1945. Manuscripts and notes of a projected book by Shoskes, *Jews in Russia Today*. Memoirs by Irene Eskenazi about World War II experiences in Yugoslavia.

986. SHPITALNIK, LEYBUSH (?–1962).
Papers, ca. 1910–1950s. 2 in. (RG 1182)

Yiddish teacher. Active in the Sholem Aleichem Schools, New York. Born near Proskurov. Immigrated to the United States.

The collection consists of photographs including Sholem Aleichem Schools, Workmen's Circle Schools, family photographs, group photographs.

987. SHUB, RALPH.
Papers, 1947–1975. 10 in. (RG 410)

Collector for YIVO. Bothwell, Ontario.

Miscellaneous printed materials about Jewish life in Canada. Correspondence.

988. SIEGALOVSKY, NOAH (born 1901).
Papers, 1950s–1975. 1 ft. 3 in. (RG 536)

Yiddish writer, teacher. Editor of the Yiddish literary journal *Undzer eygn vinkl.* Contributed to *Morgenstern* (NY), *Yiddishes Tageblatt, Der tog* (NY), *Jewish Daily Forward* (NY), *Der yidisher kemfer, Frayhayt* (NY), *Kinder zhurnal* (NY), *Zukunft* (NY). Born near Lipovets, district of Kiev, Ukraine. Immigrated to the United States in 1922.

Correspondence with Abba Gordin, Chaim Grade, Reuben Iceland, Rachel Korn, Ida Maze, Mendel Osherowitch, A.A. Roback, I.J. Schwartz, Tolush. Correspondence relating to *Undzer eygn vinkl.* Notebooks of Siegalovsky's writings. Manuscripts of poems by Jacob Adler (B. Kovner).

989. SIEGEL, SAMUEL H. (1886–1977).
Papers, 1899–1977. 5 in. (RG 1123)

Dentist, author, artist. Founding member of the Workmen's Circle in New Brunswick, New Jersey. Literary editor of *The Banner,* New Brunswick. Submitted an autobiography to the YIVO autobiography contests in 1943 and 1953. Born in Vilkaviškis, Lithuania. Settled in the United States.

Manuscripts of Samuel H. Siegel, including his autobiography. Materials of the Workmen's Circle Branch 208 in New Brunswick, including a history of the branch. Correspondence with writers. Family correspondence and personal documents. Clippings of S.H. Siegel's writings.

990. SIGAL, ALBERT DOV (born 1911).
Papers, 1940s–1970s. 3 in. (RG 1165)

Artist. Specialized in enamel paintings and engraving. His works were exhibited in Israel, the United States, Rumania, Paris, Rome. Studied at the School of Fine Arts in Cluj, Rumania. During World War II, Sigal conducted an underground art school and took part in the resistance movement. In 1947, Sigal spent several months in a British detention center in Cyprus. Born in Cluj, Transylvania. Immigrated to Israel in 1948.

The collection consists of art works by Sigal, clippings, exhibit brochures, photographs of his works. Art works include watercolors and sketches of the internment camp in Cyprus, engraved prints on biblical themes.

991. SILBERBERG-CHOLEWA, ISRAEL (1898–1981).
Papers, 1940–1971. 5 in. (RG 635)

Yiddish writer, teacher. Contributed to *Der tog* (NY), *Di varhayt* (NY), *Zukunft* (NY), *Yidisher kemfer* (NY), *Freie Arbeiter Stimme* (NY), *Pedagogisher buletin.* Translated works of Danish-Jewish writers into Yiddish and wrote articles on Danish-Jewish literature. Born in Szydłów, district of Kielce, Poland. Settled in Copenhagen in 1913. Immigrated to the United States in 1922.

Correspondence with Yiddish writers.

992. SILBERSTEIN, BEINISH (1902–1942).
 Papers, 1918–1941. 1 ft. 8 in. (RG 228)

Yiddish poet, co-founder of the Socialist youth group "Zukunft" (Belgium). Editor of *Belgishe bleter*. Killed in Auschwitz concentration camp. Lived in Poland, Belgium.

 Manuscripts and typescripts of Silberstein's poems. Articles on the writers S. Ansky, Joseph Bovshover, Jacob Dinesohn, Yehoash, Eliakum Zunser. Clippings of photographs of Jewish and non-Jewish writers, artists, actors and scholars.

993. SILKES, GENIA (1914–1984).
 Papers, 1930s–1970s. 3 ft. 3 in. (RG 1187)

Teacher, historian, member of the YIVO staff in New York. Taught in Yiddish schools in Warsaw before World War II. During the Holocaust period, worked in the schools of the Warsaw ghetto and participated in the underground Oneg Shabat Archives. After the war, worked for the Jewish Historical Commission in Łódź, Poland. Born in Brest-Litovsk (Pol. Brześć Litewski). Immigrated to France in 1949. Settled in the United States in 1956.

 Correspondence with Avrom Silkes and Ephraim Kaganowski. Notes, manuscripts and texts of lectures by G. Silkes on the Warsaw ghetto, children in the ghetto. Drawing by Kaganowski. Eyewitness accounts of children collected by the Jewish Historical Commission in Łódź. Essays written by children in the Jewish schools in Poland on the theme "Games I Played During the War." Children's drawings made during and after the war. Clippings and brochures on G. Silkes's speaking engagements. Photographs. Personal documents.

994. SIMON, SOLOMON (1895–1970).
 Papers, 1932–1969. 6 ft. 7 in. (RG 234)

Yiddish writer, teacher, lecturer, editor. Wrote children's stories. Associated with the Sholem Aleichem Folk Institute and editor of *Kinder zhurnal*.

 Manuscripts of Simon's writings, including clippings. Personal papers, family correspondence. Autobiographical and biographical materials. Correspondence with individuals: Shalom Asch, Daniel Charney, Abba Gordin, Abraham Golomb, Leibush Lehrer, Mani Leib, Nahum Baruch Minkoff, Shmuel Niger, Maurice Samuel, Abraham Sutzkever. Correspondence with organizations.

 Inventory, Yiddish.

995. SINGER, ISRAEL JOSHUA (1893–1944).
 Papers, 1940–1946. 2 1/2 in. (RG 1103)

Yiddish novelist, playwright, journalist. Most of his novels were serialized in the *Jewish Daily Forward*. Singer is best known for his novels *Yoshe Kalb*, *The Family Carnovsky* and *The Brothers Ashkenazi*. Many of his works were successfully dramatized by the Yiddish Art Theater, directed by Maurice Schwartz. Brother of Isaac Bashevis Singer and Esther Kreitman. Born in Biłgoraj, Lublin province, Poland. Settled in the United States in 1933.

 Correspondence, 1930s–1940s with individuals, publishers and organizations. Fragments of manuscripts. I.D. cards.

996. SINGER, SAMUEL DAVID (1903–1973).
 Papers, 1950s–1972. 1 ft. 3 in. (RG 766)

Yiddish poet, teacher. Contributed to *Di feder, Oyfkum, Freie Arbeiter Stimme, Zukunft, Yidisher kemfer, Jewish Daily Forward, Der tog, Undzer tsayt, Literarishe bleter, Keneder odler*. Literary editor of the monthly *Undzer veg* (NY, Montreal). Born in Tomaszów Mazowiecki, Poland. Immigrated to the United States in 1920.

The papers consist of correspondence with Yiddish writers and editors, manuscripts by Singer, clippings of Singer's published articles, photographs.

997. SKALAR BENEVOLENT SOCIETY.
Records, 1931–1946, 1978, 1980. 3 in. (RG 1039)

Organized in New York in 1893 by immigrants from Skala (Skala-Podolskaya), Ukraine, as an offshoot from an older group. Constitution states that the society cannot affiliate with a lodge or synagogue, or support political or economic issues, without the consent of two-thirds of the membership.

Constitution. Anniversary journals, 1938–1941, 1946. Memorial book, 1978. Taped interview with ex-officer of the society.

998. SKIDLER BENEVOLENT ASSOCIATION.
Records, 1928, 1933, 1956–1974. 1 1/2 in. (RG 1019)

Founded in New York in 1900 by immigrants from Skidel, Byelorussia. Established a relief committee after World War I. In 1921 sent a delegate with funds to Skidel.

Constitution. Minutes, 1956–1974. Financial papers, 1962–1964. Anniversary journal. Photographs.

999. SLOVES, HENRI CHAIM (born 1905).
Papers, 1930s–1970s. 15 in. (RG 1128)

Yiddish writer, playwright, lawyer. Received a doctoral degree in law at the University of Paris at the Sorbonne. During World War II was active in the French underground movement. Active in Yiddish cultural societies and in circles sympathetic to communist ideology. Secretary of the organizing committee of the World Congress for Jewish Culture, 1937. Author of plays which were performed in France, Holland, Sweden, Poland, Rumania, Israel, South Africa, Argentina, Brazil, Mexico and New York. Contributed essays and plays to *Naye prese* (Paris), *Oyfsnay* (Paris), *Undzer eynikayt* (Paris), *Yidishe kultur* (New York), *Zamlungen* (New York), *Yidishe shriftn* (Warsaw), *Folksshtime* (Warsaw). Born in Białystok. Immigrated to Paris in 1926.

Manuscripts of Yiddish plays. Translations of Slovès's plays into French, German and English. Clippings, posters, programs, letters relating to performances of plays around the world. Photographs of performances. Various materials relating to World Congress for Jewish Culture, Paris, 1937. Correspondence with individuals including Simone de Beauvoir, Nathaniel Buchwald, Abraham Golomb, Nachman Meisel, Zygmunt Turkow, Arnold Zweig.

1000. SLUTZKY, DAVID (1902–1978).
Papers. 5 in. (RG 807)

Hebrew teacher. Lived in the Ukraine, Palestine, the United States.

Manuscripts of unpublished works by Slutzky, including articles on literary topics, plays for children, poems.

1001. SLUTZKY, SOLOMON (born 1887).
Papers, 1944–1963. 10 in. (RG 477)

Yiddish writer. Co-founder of the Jewish Teacher's Seminary and People's University, New York. Staff member, library of the Jewish Teacher's Seminary. Author of a bibliography on Abraham Reisen. Born in Rovno, Ukraine. Immigrated to the United States in 1914.

Notes and other materials collected for projected books on the Sabbath and holidays. Correspondence with Yiddish writers including H. Leivick, Nahum Baruch Minkoff, Abraham Reisen, Yechiel Yeshaia Trunk.

1002. SOCHACHEWSKY, JEHIEL MEIR BEN-ABRAHAM (1889–1958).
Papers, 1920s–1950s. 2 1/2 in. (RG 409)

Yiddish poet, journalist, short-story writer. Editor of Yiddish newspapers in England. Active in Yiddish cultural institutions in London. Lived in Poland, England.

Literary manuscripts, clippings, galleys, musical accompaniment to his poetry. Correspondence with Tsipora Ben-Gurion, Selig Brodetsky, A.A. Roback, Herbert Samuel, Ignacy (Isaac) Schwarzbart.

1003. SOCIETY OF HOSHT.
Records, 1929, 1953–1980. 2 in. (RG 1135)

Founded in New York in 1920 by the *landslayt* from Khust (Chust, Huszt), Carpatho-Russia. Established scholarships and welfare funds in Israel to aid needy *landslayt*.

Constitution, Yiddish, 1929. Membership directory. Minutes, Yiddish and English, 1953–1977. Financial statements of interest-free loan funds, welfare funds, and scholarship funds, 1960s. Correspondence, including letters to and from Irgun Yotsei Hosht Beyisrael, 1964–1980. Meeting notices, 1960s and 1970s.

1004. SOFIA M. GUREVITCH GYMNASIUM (VILNA).
Records, 1905–1922, 1930s. 5 in. (RG 51)

Secular Yiddish high school founded in Vilna in 1906 by S.M. Gurevitch and P.P. Antokolski. From 1906 to 1915 it functioned as a Jewish high school with Russian as the language of instruction. In 1918 the school adopted a Yiddishist secular approach and was known for its high scholastic standards and progressive methods.

The records relate mostly to the activities of the school during its early period, 1906–1922. General office correspondence. Student and teachers correspondence. Minutes of the meetings of the Pedagogical Council. Official government documents, 1906. Register of students. Diplomas, report cards, classroom work, notes on lessons, curriculum. Student club. Printed materials, invitations, clippings. Old inventory of the S.M. Gurevitch records in YIVO, Vilna.

1005. SOKOLOVER YOUNG FRIENDS PROGRESSIVE AID SOCIETY.
Records. 2 in. (RG 1116)

Organized in New York by immigrants from Sokołów Podlaski, Poland.
Two minute books. Jubilee book, 1946.

1006. SOLER BROTHERS BENEVOLENT ASSOCIATION.
Records, 1956–1974. 2 1/2 in. (RG 940)

Organized in New York in 1903 by immigrants from Soly, Byelorussia. Sent aid to Soly. Active until 1974.

Financial records.

1007. SOMMERSTEIN, EMIL (1883–1957).
Papers, 1944–1946. 1 microfilm reel. (RG 389)

Lawyer, politician, prominent Zionist leader in Poland. Co-founder of the World Jewish Congress. Member of the Polish Diet, 1922–1939. Political prisoner in the Soviet Union, 1939–1944. Minister in the post-war Polish provisional government, 1944. Founder and first chairman of the Central Committee of Jews in Poland, 1944. Lived in Poland, the Soviet Union, the United States.

Sommerstein's autobiography. Speeches delivered in the post-war Polish Provisional Diet (Sejm) and resolutions of this government regarding the situation of Jews in Poland after 1945. Memoranda to Polish and U.S. governments and to American-Jewish relief organizations on post-war Jewish problems.

Correspondence from Yizhak Grunbaum, Nachum Goldmann, Joseph Tenenbaum. Reports of the Central Committee of Polish Jews, 1945–1946.

1008. SOONTUP, LEON.
Papers, 1899–1938. 4 in. (RG 1207)

Yiddish playwright. Used pen name Ben Tuvia. Lived in Russia and the United States.

Manuscripts of plays, stories, sketches, poems and other material by Soontup. Included are some manuscripts by Soontup which passed the official Tsarist censorship, 1899.

1009. SORGEN, MOSHE (born 1898).
Papers, 1930s–1960s. 10 in. (RG 515)

Physician, Yiddish writer. Used the pen name Moshe Vityes. Lived in Streliska, Ukraine and in the United States.

Correspondence with Yiddish literary figures, including A. Almi, Daniel Charney, Abba Gordin, Abraham Reisen.

1010. SOROKER YOUNG FRIENDS BENEVOLENT AND EDUCATIONAL LEAGUE.
Records, 1921–1975. 1 ft. 8 1/2 in. (RG 831)

Originally founded in New York in 1910 by immigrants from Soroki (Rum. Soroca), Moldavia, as a single men's club, but became open to women as members married. Worked with other Soroker organizations, including the First Soroker Mutual Aid Society, First Soroker Ladies Bessarabier Society, the Young Women's League of the Soroker Young Friends B.S.

Constitutions. Minutes, 1921–1947, 1950, 1952–1964, 1974–1975. Rulings and recommendations, special committees, 1930–1957. Financial records. Journal of the Bessarabian Federation of American Jews. Photographs. Velvet vestments with medallions worn by officers. Pennants, banner.

1011. SOUND RECORDINGS.
      Collection, 1900–1987. (RG 115)

This collection was assembled by the YIVO Archives from a variety of sources. It has been designated as the Max and Frieda Weinstein Archives of Recorded Sound.

The collection consists of recordings of Jewish music and the spoken word. Included are folk, cantorial and theater, music. It contains some 15,000 78, 45, and 33 rpm discs and cylinder recordings; over 1,000 open-reel and cassette tapes; piano rolls; CDs; record catalogs and other related ephemera. The earliest item in the collection is a wax cylinder, dating from 1900. There are over 2,000 78 rpm discs including literary readings and theater performances by Aaron Lebedeff, Molly Picon, Dave Tarras, Mickey Katz, Boris and Bessie Thomashefsky, Maurice Schwartz, Sholem Aleichem, Yosele Rosenblatt. The series of analog LP records covers both new recordings as well as reissues of classic 78 rpm records. The collection of CDs documents the Klezmer revival and includes contemporary reissues of cantorial music, traditional Jewish vocal and instrumental music, avant-garde and jazz-based releases of the 1980s and 1990s, and music of the Holocaust. The cassette and open-reel tape collection includes Hasidic music, folk and theater music, and spoken-word theater performances.

Catalog to Collection of 78 rpm Sound Recordings, English.

1012. SPILMAN, YOM-TOV (ca. 1827–1893).
      Papers, 1893. 2 in. (RG 397)

Musician. Conducted klezmer orchestra in Poland. Also known as Reb Yontl.

Bound manuscript of liturgical compositions, Sabbath *zmirot* and the overture to Abraham Goldfaden's *Bar Kokhba*.

1013. STABINER YOUNG MEN'S BENEVOLENT ASSOCIATION.
      Records, 1907–1928, 1947. 2 1/2 in. (RG 1037)

Founded in New York in 1907 by immigrants from Sztabin, Poland. Dissolved 1976.

Minutes, 1907–1928. Miscellaneous materials, including doctors' notes, 1920s, 1947.

1014. STAMBLER, BENEDICT.
      Collection, 1930s–1970s. 3 ft. 9 in. (RG 1014)

Established as the Benedict Stambler Memorial Collection of Jewish Music. Benedict Stambler was a collector of Jewish music and a producer of records. He and his wife Helen Stambler Latner headed the Collectors' Guild, a record company in New York.

The collection consists of tape recordings, photographs, scrapbooks, sheet music and lyrics relating to the Stamblers' activities as collectors and record producers. Included are a series of unique field recordings of Hasidic, cantorial, folk, Sephardic and theater music. Hasidic groups recorded include Stolin, Modzitz, Ger, Chabad, Vizhnitz, Bobov. Live recordings of orchestras at Jewish weddings.

Photographs and other materials relating to cantors. Stills and biographical notes from the film *The Voices of Israel, World's Greatest Cantors*, produced by Judea Films, ca. 1931.

Photographs cataloged in STAGEPIX.

1015. STANISLAUER PROGRESSIVE BENEVOLENT ASSOCIATION.
      Records, 1917–1973. 5 in. (RG 920)

Founded in New York in 1916 by immigrants from Stanislav (Pol. Stanisławów), Ukraine. During and after World War I participated in the Stanislauer Relief, together with the First Stanislauer Y.M.B.A. and the Ershte Knihinin Stanislauer K.U.V. to aid *landslayt* in the home town. Dissolved in the 1970s.

Financial records, 1950s–1970s. Membership applications, 1917–1961.

1016. STANISLAVCHIK PODOLIER YOUNG MEN'S SOCIETY.
Records, 1930–1961. 10 in. (RG 1134)

Established in 1927 in New York by the *landslayt* from Stanislavchik, Ukraine. Established a free loan fund, 1929. Worked on behalf of Jewish Council for Russian Relief. Member organization of the Union of American Jews of Ukrainian Descent, 1948. Contributed to Jewish philanthropies in Israel. Cemetery plots located in United Hebrew Cemeteries, Staten Island.

Minutes, Yiddish, 1930–1961. Loan fund Golden Book, seals, stars, in Yiddish. Correspondence. Meeting notices. Plan of memorial monument.

1017. STARKMAN, MOSHE (1906–1975).
Papers, 1942–1973. 16 ft. (RG 279)

Yiddish and Hebrew writer, bibliographer, lexicographer, journalist. On the editorial board of the *Leksikon fun der nayer yidisher literatur* (Biographical Dictionary of Modern Yiddish Literature) and of the *Day-Morning Journal*. Member, Board of Directors of the YIVO Institute. Contributed to many periodicals, such as *Yiddishes Tageblatt, Zukunft, Kundes, Der tog, Jewish Daily Forward*. Born in Mosty Wielkie, Poland. Immigrated to the United States in 1920.

Correspondence with Jewish writers such as A. Almi, Ephraim Auerbach, Shlomo Bickel, Daniel Charney, Jacob Glatstein, Abraham Golomb, Chaim Grade, Alexander Harkavy, Peretz Hirschbein, Shmuel Niger, Joseph Opatoshu, David Pinsky, Melech Ravitch, Abraham Reisen, Dov Sadan, Jacob Shatzky, Isaac Bashevis Singer, Abraham Sutzkever, Aaron Zeitlin.

1018. STAVISKER YOUNG MEN'S BENEVOLENT ASSOCIATION.
Records, 1911–1973. 1 ft. 3 in. (RG 850)

Organized in New York in 1908 by immigrants from Stawiski (Rus. Staviski), Poland. Provided disability benefits and loans to members. Affiliated with the Stavisker Ladies Aid Society. Dissolved in the 1970s.

Minutes, 1939–1972. Financial records, 1930s–1970s. Correspondence. Seal.

1019. STEDMAN, SOLOMON.
Papers, 1910s–1950s. 2 in. (RG 308)

Collector for YIVO. Mosman, Australia.

Personal documents from Irkutsk, Siberia, ca. 1920. Correspondence with various organizations in Australia.

1020. STEIN, HANA.
Papers, ca. 1910–1984. 1 ft. 2 in. (RG 1212)

English-language novelist and short story writer. Lived in New York.

Manuscripts of Stein's novels *The Wedding, Now the Heavens Play Their Part*, and *Why Do You Hide From Me?* as well as stories, essays and poems. Photographs of Stein, family members and friends.

1021. STEIN, L.M. (1883–1956).
Papers, 1930s–1940s. 7 ft. 6 in. (RG 349)

Publisher of Yiddish literature. Member, YIVO Board of Directors. Born in Russia. Resident of Chicago from 1907.

Correspondence with individuals active in Yiddish literary circles and with Jewish cultural organizations. YIVO correspondence. Personal documents. Scrapbooks.

1022. STEINBAUM, ISRAEL.
Papers, 1942–1965. 1 in. (RG 539)

Jewish teacher. Miami, Florida.

Correspondence relating primarily to the *Groyser verterbukh fun der yidisher shprakh* (Great Dictionary of the Yiddish Language). Correspondents include Hyman (Chaim) Bass, Szymon Dawidowicz, Leibush Lehrer, Yudel Mark, Joseph Mlotek, Shlomo Noble, Max Weinreich.

1023. STEINBERG, ISAAC NACHMAN (1888–1957).
Papers, 1910s–1950s. 25 ft. (RG 366)

Political thinker and activist. Leader of the Socialist Revolutionary Party (S–R) during and after the Russian Revolution of 1917. Commissar of Justice in the first Bolshevik government, 1917–1918. From 1923 acted as foreign representative of the Socialist Revolutionary Party in Russia. In the 1930s and 1940s was chief exponent of the Jewish Territorialist movement which aimed to establish autonomous Jewish settlements throughout the world. In 1935, together with Ben-Adir, co-founded the Freeland League for Jewish Territorial Colonization in London. From 1943 to 1956 was the editor of the League's official organ *Oyfn shvel* (On the Threshold). Played an active role in the League's efforts to establish colonies in Australia, Surinam and other countries. Member, Board of Directors of the YIVO Institute. His writings include: a series of books on the Russian Revolution such as *Memoirs of a People's Commissar*; articles and books on socialism; a work on the Territorialist movement, *Australia—The Unpromised Land*; and numerous articles on literary and political subjects, published in Russian, Yiddish, Hebrew and English. Born in Dvinsk, Latvia. Left Russia in 1923. Lived in Berlin and in London. Settled in the United States in 1943.

A large proportion of the collection consists of records of the Freeland League and relates to its colonization projects. There are some materials relating to the Socialist Revolutionary Party as well as private and family correspondence and personal papers.

Files of the Freeland League office, New York, 1944–1948: correspondence and other materials, minutes of meetings, 1947–1948. Freeland League records, London, 1937–1940. Miscellaneous materials of the Freeland League, 1938–1961: clippings, diaries, notices. Records of the Refugee Freeland League in Austria, 1947–1951. Materials pertaining to efforts to establish Jewish settlements in Australia, 1938–1955, including the Kimberley Project and the Queensland, Tasmania and Melville Island plans. Materials on various geographical locations which were considered for colonization, including Surinam and British Guiana.

Correspondence of Steinberg and the Freeland League with organizations, libraries, publishers, 1923–1963, some relating to the publications *Oyfn shvel* and *Freeland*. Correspondence both to and from Steinberg relating primarily to Steinberg's pursuit of the goals of the Freeland League. Correspondents include Sir Norman Angell, Angelica Balabanoff, Ben-Adir, Abraham Bick, Martin Buber, Marc Chagall, Berele Chagy, Daniel Charney, Sir Robert Waley Cohen, Joseph Czernichow, Simon Dubnow, Albert Einstein, Erich Fromm, Emma Goldman, Sidney Hook, David Ignatoff, Herbert Lehman, H. Leivick, Itzik Manger, Thomas Mann, Shmuel Niger, Melech Ravitch, Lord Reading, Rudolf Rocker, Edmond de Rothschild, Mordkhe Schaechter, Anna Simaite, Arthur Hays Sulzberger, Baruch Vladeck.

Materials pertaining to the Socialist Revolutionary Party and the Russian Revolution of 1917. Manuscripts, typescripts of books, dramas and essays by Steinberg and other writers. Notes and manuscript of *Memoirs of a People's Commissar*. Manuscript, notes and source materials for Steinberg's books on Maria Spiridonova, *Der Dornenweg*, *In the Workshop of the Revolution*. Published articles, party statement and resolution, 1918–1920, relating to the Socialist Revolutionary Party. Materials relating to individual party members, correspondence, communications with imprisoned and deported party members, photographs of exiled party members.

Materials on Steinberg's visit to South Africa, 1936–1937, on behalf of YIVO. Manuscripts of Steinberg's writings on various topics. Manuscripts by other authors. Personal papers of Steinberg. Family correspondence.

Inventory, English. Index, English.

1024. STEINBERG, NOAH (1889–1957).
Papers, 1920s–1950s. 1 ft. 3 in. (RG 361)

Yiddish writer, poet, literary critic and essayist. Born in Sejny, Poland. Settled in the United States in 1907.

Manuscripts of Steinberg's fiction, poetry and essays. Correspondence with literary figures. Letters regarding Steinberg's literary disputes with Shmuel Niger and Alexander Mukdoni. Clippings of Steinberg's works.

1025. STEINER, SEBASTIAN (born 1901).
Papers, 1938–1950s. 2 1/2 in. (RG 1030)

Resident of the Shanghai ghetto, 1938–1947. Born in Bucharest. Lived in Vienna. Settled in the United States.

The papers relate to Steiner's experiences in the Shanghai ghetto. They include passports, photographs, correspondence, and clippings of articles written by Steiner.

1026. STERN, MORRIS (born 1884).
Papers, 1910–1949. 10 in. (RG 231)

Collector for YIVO. Active in ICOR (American Association for Jewish Colonization in the Soviet Union). Lived in Russia and in the United States.

Correspondence with literary figures: Joseph Barondess, Menahem Boraisha, Aaron Glanz-Leieles, Baruch (Boris) Glassman, Peretz Hirschbein, Leon Kobrin, Jacob Milch, Joseph Opatoshu, Jacob Shatzky. Correspondence with cultural organizations including ICOR. Clippings of Stern's letters to the *Morning freiheit*. Manuscript of Stern's memoirs relating to Pinsk and to his life in the United States. Materials on Birobidzhan.

1027. STIKER, MEYER (1905–1983).
    Papers, 1930s–1970s. 5 in. (RG 1167)

Yiddish poet. Contributor to and editor of the *Morgn zhurnal, Tog-morgn zhurnal, Jewish Daily Forward*. Contributed to *Indzl, Shriftn, Oyfkum, Epokhe, Yidisher kemfer, Di goldene keyt*. Recipient of the Manger Prize in 1978. Born in Galicia, Poland. Immigrated to the United States in 1920.

    The papers consist of: correspondence with Yiddish writers including Abraham Sutzkever, Selig Heller, Malka Heifetz Tussman; manuscripts of Yiddish poems, articles, stories; clippings of Stiker's work.

1028. STOLINER PROGRESSIVE SOCIETY.
    Records, 1935–1973. 12 1/2 in. (RG 847)

Organized in New York in 1919 by immigrants from Stolin, Byelorussia. Affiliated with Stoliner branches of the Workmen's Circle. Supported charities and the local Hebrew school.
    Minutes, 1940–1973. Financial records, 1950s–1970s. Burial permits, seal, stamps.

1029. STOLLNITZ, HENRY (born ca. 1864).
    Papers, 1875–1931. 10 in. (RG 1209)

Reform rabbi and cantor, writer, performer. Born in Germany. Came to United States ca. 1881. Served with congregations in New York, Baltimore, Los Angeles, Orange and Hoboken (New Jersey), and Tampa (Florida).
    Correspondence, contracts, and other documents, 1875–1914, including two letters by Henrietta Szold commenting on Stollnitz's work. Manuscripts, typescripts, clippings, and printed materials by and about Stollnitz on Polish-Jewish folklore, religious issues, social and political questions and other subjects, 1887–1931. Clippings of articles by Stollnitz's wife, Rebecca Stollnitz.

1030. STOLZENBERG, ABBA (1905–1941).
    Papers, 1905–1966. 2 1/2 in. (RG 525)

Yiddish poet. Contributed to *Der indzl, Zukunft, Feder, Yidishe kultur, Yidish*. Co-edited *Fayln* (NY). Born in Galicia, Poland. Immigrated to the United States in 1923 and settled in New York.
    Manuscripts of Stolzenberg's poems. Articles about Stolzenberg.

1031. STONEHILL, BEN.
    Collection, 1950s. 9 reels. (RG 533)

Collector of Yiddish folksongs, New York.
    Tapes of 1,078 Yiddish folksongs registered by Stonehill as sung by informants in various localities in the United States. List of taped songs.

1032. STOPNITZER YOUNG MEN'S BENEVOLENT ASSOCIATION.
    Records, 1911–1921, 1945. 5 in. (RG 915)

Founded in New York in 1905 by immigrants from Stopnica, Poland. Sent funds to Stopnica

after World War I and established a Stopnitzer Relief during World War II. Was affiliated with a ladies auxiliary which dissolved in the 1970s.
  Minutes, 1911–1921. Photographs.

1033. STRELISKER YOUNG MEN'S BENEVOLENT ASSOCIATION.
  Records, 1934–1953. 2 1/2 in. (RG 1035)

Organized in New York in 1905 by immigrants from Novye Strelishche, Ukraine. Established an endowment fund in 1947 for members.
  Minutes, 1934–1953. Journal, 1935.

1034. STRICK, ABRAHAM H. (born 1889).
  Papers, 1911–1941. 5 in. (RG 1285)

Labor Zionist pioneer. Resided in Nowy Sącz and Dębica (Poland), Hadera (Palestine) in the 1910s, and New York.
  Manuscripts of political speeches and educational lectures in Hebrew and Yiddish. Early Zionist announcements from Poland. Personal documents, correspondence and photographs. A certificate from B'nai Zion.

1035. SUDARSKI, MENDEL (1885–1951) and ALTE.
  Papers, 1938–1958. 5 ft. (RG 405)

Mendel Sudarski was a Jewish communal leader in Kaunas, Lithuania. Chairman of the Federation of Lithuanian Jews in New York. Co-editor of the book *Lite* (Lithuania). Lived in Lithuania and the United States. His wife Alte Sudarski was active in Yiddish cultural organizations and in relief efforts for Jews in Shanghai and Russia.
  Correspondence of Mendel Sudarski relating to the publication of the book *Lite*. Manuscripts, notes and photographs for the book.
  Correspondence of Alte Sudarski relating to Jewish refugees in Shanghai, 1946–1952, to food and clothing packages for Jews in Russia, 1950s. Correspondence of Alte Sudarski with Yiddish writers.

1036. SUNRISE COOPERATIVE FARM COMMUNITY, ALICIA, MICHIGAN.
  Records, 1933–1937. 5 in. (RG 432)

A Jewish collectivist agricultural colony organized in 1933 in the Saginaw Valley of Michigan and dissolved in 1938. Headed by Joseph J. Cohen, a former editor of the anarchist newspaper, *Freie Arbeiter Stimme*, the colony was both an attempt to find a solution to the economic problems of the Depression and an idealistic experiment in communal organization based on the principles of the anarchist movement.
  Constitution, minutes of meetings, periodic reports, financial statements. Clippings from the Yiddish press relating to the colony. Memoirs of Bezalel Pargman and M. Stein, former members of the colony. Mimeographed newsletter, *Sunrise News*, 1934, 1935.

1037. SURKAMP, JAMES.
  Papers, 1930s–1970s. 4 ft. 2 in. (RG 1136)

Writer, collector. Collected source materials relating to the theft, destruction and plunder of art by the Nazis during World War II.

The collection consists of copies of documents from various archives, including: the National Archives and Library of Congress, Washington, D.C.; National Records Center in Suitland, Maryland; archives in Germany, France, Holland, Israel. There are also copies of articles from books and periodicals.

Reports on art plunder, during and after World War II, in various countries including Poland, Austria, Italy, France, Spain, Czechoslovakia, the Netherlands, Scandinavian countries, Portugal. Materials relating to private art collections of Nazi government officials such as that of Hermann Göring. Materials on jewelery and coins, including the Crown of St. Stephen (a national symbol of Hungary) and the crown treasures of the Holy Roman Empire.

Reports of the office of the U.S. Chief of Counsel for War Crimes. U.S. Army reports on art treasures. Lists of paintings in private collections in various countries. Shelf list of records of the State Department Consulate on Monuments, Fine Arts and Archives. Report on the Art Looting Investigation Unit. Newspaper articles on stolen art and the role of the SS in art thefts.

1038. SUSSMAN, MOSES (born 1887).
Papers, 1930s–1947. 10 in (RG 425)

Jewish theater manager, impresario. Lived in Latvia, Russia and England.

Correspondence, playbills, posters, contracts relating to Jewish actors, theater ensembles and cantors performing in England, 1930s–1940s. Included are materials on Moshe Koussevitsky, Maurice Schwartz, Boris Thomashefsky, Berele Chagy.

1039. SUTZKEVER, ABRAHAM–KACZERGINSKI, SZMERKE.
Collection, 1806–1945. 7 ft. (RG 223)

The collection is of mixed provenance and consists of two parts. The bulk of the collection relates to the Vilna ghetto during Nazi occupation and was generated there. The second part, which consists of historical and literary manuscripts, had belonged to the YIVO Institute of Vilna before the war. Both the ghetto materials and the manuscripts were hidden and preserved by a group of ghetto inmates which included the Yiddish poets Abraham Sutzkever and Szmerke Kaczerginski.

The collection is named for Sutzkever and Kaczerginski who were instrumental in its removal from Vilna in 1946 and its subsequent transfer to the YIVO Archives in New York.

Vilna ghetto

Materials on the Vilna ghetto reflect daily life and living conditions in the ghetto, social and cultural work, activities of the Judenrat (Jewish Council) and relations with Nazi officials. Maps of the ghetto, 1942. Diaries, chronicles and manuscripts on the history of the ghetto by Zelig Kalmanovitch, Herman Kruk, Yitschak Rudashevsky, Szmerke Kaczerginski. Personal identification documents such as badges, armbands, identification cards, passes. Materials on the ghetto administration and its divisions: health, social relief, distribution and supply, statistics, ghetto police, ghetto court, cultural affairs, labor, education. Materials on various cultural groups. Issues of the *Geto yedies* (Ghetto News), 1942. Materials about the partisan groups in and outside the ghetto including underground publications. Photographs of daily scenes in the ghetto, partisans, destroyed buildings of the YIVO, the Strashun Library, the Vilna Gaon's synagogue.

Historical and literary manuscripts

Correspondence to or from literary, scholarly and rabbinic personalities: S. Ansky, Rabbi Naftali Zvi Berlin, Ber Borochov, Rabbi Yechiel Danzig, Simon Dubnow, David Edelstadt, Rabbi Chaim Oyzer Grodzienski, Rabbi Eliyahu Guttmacher, Rabbi David Luria, Abraham Mapu, Mendele Moykher Sforim, Moses Montefiore, Isaac Leib Peretz, David Pinsky, Noah Prylucki, Abraham Reisen, Zalman Reisen, Sholem Aleichem, Nahum Shtif, Mordecai Spector, Matisyahu Strashun, Sholem Aleichem.

Manuscripts of: S. Ansky, Nathan Birnbaum, Joseph Bovshover, Isaac Meir Dick, Solomon Ettinger, Theodor Herzl, Itzik Manger, Mendele Moykher Sforim, Joseph Perl, Abraham Reisen, Sholem Aleichem, Matisyahu Strashun.

Pinkasim (registers) of the Vilna Gaon's synagogue, the Jewish community of Skuodas (Yiddish: Shkud) and fragments of the register of the Vilna Kehillah (6 pages).

Miscellaneous theater and folklore material.

Inventory, Yiddish.

1040. SWISLOTCHER BENEVOLENT ASSOCIATION.
    Records, 1917–1971. 7 1/2 in. (RG 921)

Founded in New York in 1912 by immigrants from Svisloch (Pol. Swisłocz), Byelorussia. Aided *landslayt* in Swisłocz after World War I. Maintained a loan fund for members.

Constitution. Minutes, 1928–1947. Financial records. Correspondence. Membership applications. Burial permits.

1041. SZAJKOWSKI, ZOSA (1910–1978).
    Papers, 1880s–1940s. 5 ft. (RG 800)

Pen name of Shaike Frydman. Jewish historian, archivist, research associate at the YIVO Institute from 1945 to 1978. Szajkowski wrote on a wide variety of topics in Jewish history, concentrating on the history of French Jewry, Jewish immigration movements and the Holocaust period. Born in Zaręby Kościelne, Łomża district, Poland. In 1927 immigrated to France. Settled in the United States in 1941.

The papers consist primarily of manuscripts of Szajkowski's works and related notes, documents, photographs. There are also personal documents and some correspondence. Manuscripts, documents and notes relating to: immigration of Jews in the period 1880–1930; National Refugee Service; USNA; American relief work in Soviet Russia, 1917–1939; American-Jewish relief work in Poland, 1918–1923; Jews in Russia, 1917–1939; *Illustrated Sourcebook on the Holocaust*, Volume 1; Jews in France; Spanish Civil War.

1042. SZENICER LADIES SICK AND BENEVOLENT SOCIETY.
    Records, 1942–1972. 10 in. (RG 875)

Organized in New York by immigrants from Shchenets (Szczeniec), Byelorussia, to provide sick and death benefits for its female members. Activities included the organization of a *shivah* (seven days of mourning during which benefits are provided to the mourner) committee. Dissolved 1974.

Financial records, 1940s–1970s. Cemetery book.

1043. SZYK, ARTHUR (1894–1951).
    Papers, 1926–1943. 4 in. (RG 1203)

Illustrator, miniaturist, cartoonist. Born in Łódź, Poland. Lived in Paris. Settled in the United States in 1940.

Three scrapbooks with clippings, correspondence and other materials about: a traveling exhibit in Poland, 1932–1933; publication of the book *Le Juif Qui Rit*, 1926–1927; general topics, 1933–1940. Illuminated Israeli Declaration of Independence. Postcards of works by Szyk on American history. Photographs of demonstration by Polish Jews, New York, 1943. Photograph of a group of Polish soldiers.

1044. TABACHNIK, ABRAHAM (1901–1970).
Papers, 1934–1968. 10 in. (RG 637)

Yiddish poet, teacher. Contributed to *Proletarisher gedank, Zukunft, Freie Arbeiter Stimme, Yidisher kemfer, Der veker, Der tog, Di goldene keyt*. Born in the district of Mohilev-Podolsk, Ukraine. Immigrated to the United States in 1921.

The papers consist of correspondence with Yiddish writers, manuscripts and clippings of articles about Tabachnik.

1045. TALMUD TORAH SHA'ARE TORAH, JAFFA.
Records, 1890s–1930s. 10 in. (RG 291).

A religious educational institution for boys founded in Jaffa, Palestine, ca. 1886, headed at first by Rabbi Naphtali Zvi Herz, Rabbi of Jaffa, and later by Rabbi Abraham Isaac Hacohen Kook, who succeeded him in that position.

The collection consists of administrative records of the institution and relate primarily to financial support received from contributors throughout the world, including many donors from the United States and England. Correspondence with rabbinical figures, especially from the United States. Appeals, printed and handwritten, for financial assistance. Handwritten copies of endorsements by Rabbi Yitschok Elchonon Spektor, Rabbi Eliyahu Chaim Meisel, Rabbi Chaim Soloveichik of Brisk. Routine correspondence with government and business offices in Palestine, including the Government of Palestine and the Chief Rabbinate, including a letter from Rabbi Abraham Isaac Kook.

1046. TARBUT HEBREW TEACHERS SEMINARY (VILNA).
Records, 1922–1939. 4 ft. (RG 23)

Known in Hebrew as the Seminaryon Ivri L'morim Al Yad Histadrut "Tarbut," and in Polish as Prywatne Hebrajskie Koedukacyjne Seminarjum Nauczycielskie "Tarbut."

The seminary in Vilna was founded in 1921 and was part of a network of educational institutions established by the Tarbut movement in Poland. The movement's primary objective was to prepare Jewish youth for settlement in Palestine. The Tarbut program was a synthesis of the Polish school system and the curriculum followed by Zionist schools in Palestine. Hebrew was the language of instruction and the curriculum included biblical and talmudic literature and Jewish cultural traditions. Courses in agriculture and natural sciences were introduced to teach the sudents how to deal with practical problems in Palestine. Teachers' seminaries were created to train Tarbut teachers for the Hebrew elementary school system. The seminaries were established in Vilna, Grodno, Warsaw and Lvov. The Vilna seminary existed until about 1940.

This collection consists of records of the seminary in Vilna.

Administrative records. Correspondence with Tarbut Central Office, Warsaw, 1922–1939;

Vilna School District, 1929–1939; Keren Kayemet L'Yisrael; Vilna Jewish Community Council; branches of Tarbut throughout Poland; organizations, bookstores, publishers. By-laws, financial documents, contracts, statistical materials, printed and mimeographed materials.

Academic Records. Correspondence with students and teachers, 1923–1940. Applications for entry to the seminary, 1922–1935. Student achievement records and teachers files, student grades, graduation diplomas. Minutes of the Pedagogical Council. Curriculum outlines for various subjects, teaching schedules, lessons prepared by student teachers. Miscellaneous schoolwork.

Inventory, English, Yiddish.

1047. TARRAS, DAVE (ca. 1897–1989).
Papers, 1920s–1970s. 1 ft. 3 in. (RG 1280)

Clarinetist, prominent performer of klezmer music. Began playing clarinet as a child. Played in a Russian army band. Performed in the United States as a soloist and band leader. Made numerous recordings of klezmer music. Born in the Ukraine. Came to the United States in 1921.

Arrangements of popular Yiddish songs and klezmer music written by D. Tarras.

1048. TAUB, YUDL.
Papers, 1935–1956. 10 in. (RG 604)

Collector for YIVO. Resident of Philadelphia and active in left-wing Yiddish cultural institutions there.

The collection consists of clippings relating to the activities of Yiddish cultural institutions in Philadelphia, including the Menahem Baerush Epplebaum Circle of the YKUF and the Philadelphia Jewish People's Chorus.

1049. TAUBES, JACOB S. (1899–1975).
Papers, 1945–1960s. 1 ft. 8 in. (RG 770)

Yiddish poet, essayist. Contributed to *Zukunft, Morgn-zhurnal, Tog, Oyfn shvel, Keneder odler*. Born in Kolomyja, Galicia. Lived in Vienna and Paris. Was imprisoned in Dachau in the 1930s but was freed because of his military service in the Austrian army during World War I. In 1938, Taubes immigrated to England, moving to New York in 1939.

The papers consist of correspondence, biographical notes, manuscripts of Taubes's works in Yiddish, German and English, reviews of Taubes's books.

1050. TCHAUSSER SOCIETY.
Records, 1924–1959. 2 1/2 in. (RG 983)

Incorporated in the Bronx in 1924 by immigrants from Chausy, Byelorussia, to promote friendship and to spread American ideals among members and foreign-born citizens. Provided medical and death benefits. Dissolved, date unknown.

Certificate of incorporation, 1924. Constitution. Minutes, 1925–1959. Materials pertaining to burial.

1051. TCHERIKOWER, ELIAS (1881–1943).
Papers, 1903–1963. 45 microfilm reels. (RG 81)

Jewish historian, political activist. Active in the Labor Zionist movement at the turn of the century. Co-founder of the YIVO Institute in Vilna in 1925. Member of the YIVO Executive Board and secretary of the Historical Section of YIVO.

Between 1918 and 1920, Tcherikower was involved in a project in Kiev to collect and publish documents on pogroms in the Ukraine during the civil war. He was among the founders of the Mizrakh Yidisher Historisher Arkhiv (Ostjüdisches Historisches Archiv), established in Berlin, 1921. Its function was to preserve the documents collected, and to publish a history of the pogroms in the Ukraine, 1917–1921. Volume 1 was eventually published by YIVO in 1965.

Tcherikower was active in the defense of Shalom Schwarzbard, 1926–1927, who was tried in Paris for the assassination of Simon Petlyura. He was also involved in other celebrated cases, such as the trial in Berne, Switzerland, regarding the *Protocols of the Elders of Zion*, 1934–1935, and the trial of David Frankfurter, 1936, who shot and killed Wilhelm Gustloff, the Swiss Nazi leader.

Tcherikower contributed to or edited numerous Russian and Yiddish periodicals, anthologies, encyclopedias, including *The Day*, *Zukunft*, *Der yidisher kongres*, *Yidisher kemfer*, *Evreiskaia entsiklopediia*, *Evreiskaia Nedelia*, and the YIVO volumes of studies titled *Historishe shriftn*. Together with Israel Efroykin, he published the periodical *Oyfn sheydveg*. Author and editor of works on the Jews of France, the labor movement in the United States. Born in the Ukraine. Lived in Germany, France. Immigrated to the United States in 1940.

Notes, manuscripts, and published works by Tcherikower. Topics include: World War I; Jews in Russia; Chmielnicki massacres, 1648–1649; Jewish historiography; Hevrah Mefitsei Haskalah—Society for the Propagation of the Enlightenment; Aaron Liebermann; revolution of 1789; Napoleon and the Jews; history of the Jews in the Ukraine; pogroms in the Ukraine, 1917–1921; founding of the Jewish Colonization Association.

Correspondence with individuals, including: Majer Bałaban, 1922–1939; J. Bernfeld, 1939–1940; Saul Borovay, 1927–1930; Ilya Dijour, 1929–1940; Simon Dubnow, 1910–1941; Saul Ginsburg, 1909–1935; Alfred de Gunzburg, 1930–1935; Meir A. Halevy, 1928–1935.

Correspondence between Elias Tcherikower and his wife Rebecca, 1899–1941; correspondence with his wife's relatives, the Teplitzky family, and other family members.

Materials relating to various court trials: trial of David Frankfurter, 1936–37; trials relating to the *Protocols of the Elders of Zion* in various countries, 1905–1935.

Materials relating to publications of the Historical Section of YIVO. Manuscripts and photocopies of documents relating to the three volumes of *Historishe shriftn*. Memoranda relating to the *History of the Jewish Labor Movement in the United States*. Manuscripts and articles relating to *Yidn in frankraykh* (Jews in France). Correspondence and manuscripts relating to *Oyfn sheydveg* (At the Crossroads).

Inventory, Yiddish, Russian.

1052. TEITELBAUM, ABRAHAM (1884–1947).
Papers, 1930s–1940s. 1 ft. 4 in. (RG 304)

Yiddish stage director, actor and member of the Vilna Troupe, the Irving Place Theater (NY), the Yiddish Art Theater (NY) and other ensembles. Essayist and journalist. Born in Warsaw. Lived in Poland and the Soviet Union. Came to the United States in 1919.

Manuscripts including a biography of Shakespeare. Lectures on the theater. Texts of plays performed by Teitelbaum. Photographs of Teitelbaum. Scrapbooks of articles on theater.

Photographs cataloged in STAGEPIX.

1053. TENENBAUM, JOSEPH L. (1887–1961).
      Papers, 1929–1957. ca. 9 ft. (RG 283)

Physician, author, communal leader, Zionist. Delegate of the Jewish National Council of
Poland to the Paris Peace Conference, 1919. Chairman of the Executive Committee of the
American Jewish Congress (1929–1936) and AJC vice-president, 1943–1945. Founder and
chairman of the Joint Boycott Council Against Nazi Germany, 1933–1941. President of
World and American Federations of Polish Jews. Born in Sasów, Poland. Immigrated to the
United States in 1920.

   Manuscripts, notes, copies of documents relating to Tenenbaum's books, including
Galitsye, mayn alte heym; *Tsvishn milkhome un sholem*, *Rescue*. Minutes of the Fourth
World Conference of Polish Jews, 1945. Correspondence with the Federation of Polish
Jewry, World Jewish Congress, American Jewish Congress, Joint Boycott Council.
Tenenbaum's speeches.
   Inventory, English.

1054. TENENBAUM, SHEA (1910–1989).
      Papers, 1940s–1960s. ca. 15 ft. (RG 722)

Yiddish writer and poet. Contributed to *Di yidishe prese* (Antwerp), *Literarishe bleter*,
Varshaver shriftn (Warsaw), *Der tog*, *Jewish Daily Forward*, *Morgn zhurnal*, *Yidisher kem-
fer*, *Freie Arbeiter Stimme*. Born in Bobrzyniec, district of Lublin. Resided for a while in
Belgium. Immigrated to the United States in 1934.

   The papers consist of correspondence primarily with Yiddish writers. Included are
Ephraim Auerbach, Sidor Belarsky, Menahem Boraisha, Daniel Charney, William Edlin,
Philip Friedman, Abba Gordin, Reuben Iceland, Malka Lee, Leibush Lehrer, H. Leivick,
Itzik Manger, Kalman Marmor, Jacob Mestel, Jacob Milch, Shmuel Niger, Joseph Opatoshu,
Abbo Ostrowsky, Maurice Schwartz, Isaac Bashevis Singer, Abraham Sutzkever, Jennings
Yehudah Tofel, Tolush, Max Weinreich, Zalmen Zylbercweig. Diary by Tenenbaum cover-
ing a span of 52 years.

1055. TENEROFSKY, SHLOYME (1889–1961).
      Papers. 2 ft. 1 in. (RG 1185)

Yiddish children's writer. Contributed to *Kinder zhurnal*, *Kinder tsaytung*. Born in Uman,
province of Kiev, Ukraine. Immigrated to Canada in 1924. Settled in the United States in
1929.
   The collection consists of manuscripts of prose and poetry in Hebrew and Yiddish.

1056–1087. TERRITORIAL COLLECTION.
      ca. 1600–ca. 1970s. ca. 172 ft. (RG 116)

This collection is of mixed provenance and consists of miscellaneous materials, arranged by
topic, relating to Jewish life in countries around the world. The collection is comprised of
printed materials, posters, correspondence, fragmentary records of institutions and personal
papers. These materials are arranged in geographic subgroups by country or region. Countries and regions included: Argentina, Australia, Austria, Baltic countries, (Lithuania, Latvia,
Estonia), Belgium, Bolivia, Brazil, Bulgaria, Canada, Colombia, Chile, Costa Rica, Cuba,
Czechoslovakia, Denmark, England, Far East, Finland, France, Germany, Holland, Hungary,

Israel, Italy, Mexico, New Zealand, Norway, North Africa, Panama, Peru, Poland, Rhodesia, Rumania, Russia and the Soviet Union, South Africa, Spain, Sweden, Switzerland, Uruguay, Venezuela, Yugoslavia.

The following countries constitute major subgroups in this collection and their descriptions are listed separately below: Argentina, Australia, Austria, Baltic Countries, Belgium, Brazil, Canada, Chile, Colombia, Czechoslovakia, Denmark, England, Finland, France, Germany, Holland, Hungary, Israel, Italy, Mexico, New Zealand, Poland, Rumania, Russia and Soviet Union, South Africa, Sweden, Switzerland and Uruguay.

1056. Argentina.

1 ft. 3 in. (RG 116–Argentina)

Diary of Berl Greenberg relating to the Jewish community of Buenos Aires, several hundred pages, 1957–1958. Newspaper clippings from the Spanish language press, 1941–1948. Miscellaneous printed materials and circulars relating mainly to Jewish organizations, 1930s–1950s.

1057. Australia.

1 ft. 8 in. (RG 116–Australia)

Printed materials relating to Jewish organizations and schools in Melbourne and Sydney.

1058. Austria.

1 ft. (RG 116–Austria)

Several older documents, 17th c.–19th c., including statutes of the Jewish community of Mattersdorf, 1872, and letters, petitions and government orders relating to the Vienna Jewish community, 1795–1844, including requests by Jews to set up commercial establishments.

Materials on antisemitism, Nazi period, war crimes trials, DP camps. Includes eyewitness account of expulsion of Jews from Kittsee, 1938.

Card inventory, English.

1059. Baltic Countries (Lithuania, Latvia, Estonia).

10 in. (RG 116–Baltic)

Miscellaneous materials relating to cultural and religious activities during the period of national independence, 1919–1939, antisemitism, the Holocaust, war criminals.

The following localities are represented in this subgroup: Daugavpils, Iwie, Kaltinėnai, Kalvarija, Kėdainiai, Kudirkos Naumestis, Kaunas, Kupiškis, Kvėdarna, Memel (Klaipeda), Maljaty (Molėtai), Olsiady, Palanga, Panevėžys, Pilviškiai, Riga, Talsi, Telšiai, Tryškiai, Ukmergė, Užventis, Viduklė, Žagarė.

Materials of the Holocaust period include some eyewitness accounts and pertain mainly to the ghettos in Kaunas, Riga, Daugavpils, and to the Klooga concentration camp.

Card inventory, English.

1060. Belgium.

4 ft. 2 in. (RG 116–Belgium)

The collection relates primarily to the Belgian-Jewish community in the Holocaust and post-World War II periods.

Included are materials relating to the underground resistance; alphabetical lists of Jews who were in the Malines internment camp during the war; schoolwork of students in a Yiddish class, Brussels, ca. 1941–1942.

The printed materials of the post-war period pertain to the activities of Jewish organizations. There is an emphasis on Zionist organizations, primarily in Brussels, such as Mizrachi, Betar, Poalei Zion, Hashomer Hatsair.

1061. Brazil.
1 ft. 8 in. (RG 116–Brazil)

Printed material, circulars, clippings relating to cultural, educational and communal activities in Rio de Janeiro, São Paulo, Santos and other places. The bulk of the materials pertain to the 1950s.

1062. Canada.
10 ft. (RG 116–Canada)

Printed materials from various Jewish organizations in Montreal, Toronto, Edmonton, Winnipeg, Calgary. A file of correspondence of Western Canada's Jewish Relief Fund, 1913–1921, pertaining to immigration from Eastern Europe.

1063. Chile.
5 in. (RG 116–Chile)

The collection covers the period 1940s–1970s. Printed materials relating to Jewish communal and cultural organizations. Included are materials on Yiddish schools.

1064. Colombia.
10 in. (RG 116–Colombia)

Printed materials relating to educational, cultural and community activities. Organizations include the Zionist Federation, Hillel and the Centro Israelita. The materials pertain to the period 1940s–1970s.

1065. Czechoslovakia.
1 ft. 8 in. (RG 116–Czechoslovakia)

The bulk of the collection pertains to the Holocaust period, 1938–1945. Noteworthy are materials on the Theresienstadt ghetto (Terezín) which include: birth and death records, daily orders, circulars, announcements about deportations, regulations concerning the Ältestenrat (Council of Elders), documents on health conditions, and other official records of the ghetto administration; testimonies and eyewitness accounts of the survivors; press articles written after the war. Documents of Rabbi Michael Dov Weissmandel, both originals and photocopies, relating to his underground rescue activities in Slovakia.

The collection also includes materials on Jewish communities in Slovakia, post–World War II.

Inventory, English.

1066. Denmark.
2 ft. 6 in. (RG 116–Denmark)

The collection relates mainly to Copenhagen. Printed materials, relating to Yiddish cultural and educational life, Zionist groups, workers' unions, various Jewish organizations, in the 1930s. Minutes and other materials of the Jewish Parents' Association of the Yidisher shul, 1920–1930s. Handwritten periodical published by the Hazomir Society consisting of humorous and satirical pieces in Yiddish, 1937–1953. Minutes of meetings, invitations, printed materials, by-laws of the Yidish Fareyn, 1930–1936. Printed materials relating to Jewish situation in Denmark during World War II, including circulars from the Danish Red Cross.

1067. England.

4 ft. (RG 116–England)

Printed materials from various Jewish organizations, mostly in London. Included are: Jewish Historical Society of England; Council of Polish Jews in Great Britain; various relief societies established to aid Jews in Europe after World War I; the Friends of YIVO in London; Yiddish cultural organizations.

Materials from Zionist organizations: Histadrut, Tarbut, Habonim, Jewish Agency, Hashomer Hatsair, Poale Zion, Revisionists. Contribution book for Jewish Colonial Trust, 1903. Early postcards relating to the Poalei Zion, 1903. Program of an early Zionist conference, 1898. By-laws of the Chovevei Zion Association, 1892.

Printed materials of Chief Rabbi Joseph Hertz. Letters from other rabbis, including a copy of a letter by Chief Rabbi Samuel Montagu concerning observance of the Sabbath by factory workers, 1897. Printed materials from synagogues, Talmud Torahs, Agudas Israel.

Materials relating to the labor movement, 1880s–1910. Notices of strikes and public gatherings, including meal tickets for strikers during the Great Tailor's Strike of 1889. Leaflets of anarchist groups. Minute book of the United Workers Committee of the West End, London.

Autobiographical essays submitted to a contest sponsored by the Friends of YIVO in London titled "My First Year in England." Minute books of the Ben Ouri Art Society, London, 1916–1932.

1068. Finland.

10 in. (RG 116–Finland)

Miscellaneous materials.

1069–1070. France.

ca. 1900–1945. ca. 17 ft. 8 in. (RG 116–France)

The collection is divided into two sections, France 1 and France 2.

1069. France 1.

ca. 1900–1930s. ca. 16 ft. (RG 116–France 1)

The bulk of the collection consists of materials of Jewish cultural and social welfare organizations and *landsmanshaftn* established primarily by Yiddish-speaking immigrants from Poland. Included are the Société des Israélites Polonais; Kultur Lige; Workmen's Circle, Paris; Association des Juifs Polonais en France; Fédération des Artisans, Façonniers, Fabricants, Marchands et Brocanteurs Juifs en France.

Records of a Colonie Scolaire located at 36 Rue Amelot in Paris, reflecting its activities in the

1930s and in the post–World War II period. La Colonie Scolaire offered social welfare services which included a summer camp for children and a medical clinic called "La Mère et l'Enfant."

Two scrapbooks of clippings on the Dreyfus Affair.

1070. France 2.
1940–1945. 1 ft. 8 in. (RG 116–France 2)

This collection is of mixed provenance and consists of miscellaneous and fragmentary documents donated by individuals and organizations. The collection relates to the situation of the Jews in France during the occupation period.

Underground Jewish newspapers as well as circulars and leaflets by Jewish resistance groups. Issues of *Combattre, Notre Voix, Notre Parole*. Antisemitic materials of pro-Vichy government groups including propaganda leaflets, circulars and newspapers. Circulars from the French clergy denouncing antisemitism. Clippings of antisemitic newspaper articles. Blank French and German government forms. Materials from the Commissariat Général aux Questions Juives. Reports and other original materials from camps such as Drancy, Beaune-la-Rolande. A handwritten Haggadah used in Gurs, 1941. Letters from internees regarding conditions in the camps and packages. Letters from the prison in Nice. Notes, sermons, eyewitness accounts relating to La Lande, 1941–1942. Reports on the round-ups at the Vélodrome d'Hiver. Fragmentary correspondence of German Security Police in Toulouse addressed to the Security Police in Bordeaux. Fragmentary documents from other German government offices. Materials on the activities of the Consistoire Central. Reviews of the French press on the Jewish question and antisemitism. Proceedings of a trial of 24 partisans tried in Paris in 1944. Letters written to family members by imprisoned French Jews about to be executed. A Nazi report on the history of the Jews in France titled *Die Judenverfolgungen in Frankreich*. Samples of yellow stars worn by Jews in France. Telegrams to the Vichy government from individuals in the Jewish community, such as the Chief Rabbi of France.

1071–1072. Germany.
16th c.–1950s. 16 ft. (RG 116–Germany)

The collection is divided into two sections, Germany 1 and Germany 2.

1071. Germany 1.
16th c.–1932, 1946–1950s. ca. 5 ft. 5 in. (RG 116–Germany 1)

The collection is comprised of communal records, family papers, government documents, records of Jewish organizations, business papers.

Records of Jewish communities in Germany are derived from the communities of Altona, Amberg, Moisling-Lübeck, Thairnbach (Baden), Viereth (Bavaria), Bad Homburg, Göttingen, Brieg (Pol. Brzeg), Breslau (Pol. Wrocław), Frankfurt am Main, Sulzbach (Bavaria), Berlin. Noteworthy are: *pinkasim* (registers) and minute books from: Altona, 1763–1939; Moisling-Lübeck, 1806–1890; Viereth, 1785–1888; *Schutzbrief* by King Friedrich Wilhelm I of Prussia to 47 Jewish families who wished to settle in Neumark, 1717. Administrative records of the Jewish community of Breslau, 1903–1936.

Family papers include correspondence, personal and business documents, and memorabilia of the following families: Dreifuss of Malsch (Baden), 1893–1940; Marx Isaac Kulp of Frankfurt am Main, 1838–1856; Bernheimer of Buttenhausen, 1828–1861.

Noteworthy among the records of Jewish organizations are materials from the archives of the Hilfsverein der Deutschen Juden which pertain mainly to Jewish emigration, 1904–1926. Included are annual reports, 1904–1913; correspondence between the Hilfsverein and the United Evacuation Committee in Paris, 1925–1926; correspondence to Rabbi Chaim Oyzer Grodzienski, Vilna.

Inventory, English.

1072. Germany 2.
   1933–1945. 13 ft. 9 in. (RG 116–Germany 2)

Documents, reports, printed matter, clippings relating to Jewish life under Nazi rule and to Nazi anti-Jewish policies and acts. Reports of various branches of Nazi administration pertaining to racial policies and laws. Nazi propaganda materials. Accounts about Kristallnacht. Biographical materials about Nazi leaders such as: personal documents (copies) of Adolf Hitler; press transcripts of Hitler's speeches; recorded speech by Heinrich Himmler, October 1943; diaries of General Franz Halder; clippings about Rudolf Hess. Materials arranged by locality (including concentration camps) are: Auschwitz, Bergen-Belsen, Berlin, Breslau, Buchenwald, Dachau, Flossenburg, Frankfurt am Main, Friedland, Fulda, Gusen, Hamburg, Ravensbrück, Sachsenhausen, Schömberg, Ulm. Materials relating to war-crimes trials, 1945–1970s.

Card inventory, English.

1073. Holland.
   3 ft. 9 in. (RG 116–Holland)

The collection relates primarily to Jewish life in Holland during the Nazi occupation, 1940–1944. Included are records of the Joodsche Raad (Judenrat), the Nazi-appointed Jewish councils in Amsterdam, the Hague and Rotterdam. Reports about anti-Jewish laws. Weekly and monthly reports about deportations, 1942–1943. Communications with internees in the Westerbork concentration camp. Lists of deportees. Memorabilia from Westerbork concentration camp.

Materials about the Dutch Nazi movement. Printed matter containing Nazi propaganda. Nazi orders relating to confiscation of Jewish property. Diaries, memoirs and personal documents of Jewish survivors.

Of the post-war materials of special interest are records of the Dutch Red Cross regarding Dutch Jews in the Nazi camps, lists of camp survivors, clippings about Jewish displaced persons in Holland, reports of Jewish life in Holland, 1946–1955.

There is also a small number of documents pertaining to the pre-Holocaust period, including the by-laws of a young men's society named Agoeda Bakuriem in Amsterdam (1790–1840) and financial records of the Rotterdam community in the 19th century.

Inventory, English.

1074. Hungary.
   1900s–1930s. 2 ft. 1 in. and 180 reels. (RG 116–Hungary)

Album of newspaper clippings from the French press about the Tiszaeszlár blood libel case, 1882–1883. An issue of the weekly *Egyenlőség*, July 1888. Original documents of the Jewish community of Tata-Tóváros, 1860s–ca. 1900, including by-laws of the hevrah kadisha (burial society), correspondence with Rabbi Mark Handler. Bound publication by Jewish prisoners of war in 1916. Postcards of illustrations depicting antisemitism.

Holocaust period: Manuscript of original poems in Hungarian about Holocaust experiences by Viola Horvath. Album of poems by Hungarian-Jewish poets who lived through the Holocaust period, translated into English, with biographical notes about each poet. Photocopy of memoir about Kassa (Košice) during the Holocaust period. Ration tokens used in concentration camps.

Microfilms of documents prepared for the Magyarországi Izraeliták Országos Irodája, 180 reels. The filmed documents were selected from various state and municipal archives in Hungary and relate to the Jewish experience during the World War II period.

Post-war period: Bound selection of documents from the trial proceedings *Finta v. CTV et al.*, Supreme Court of Ontario, 1983–1986. Selection of court proceedings of *Belton v. World Federation of Hungarian Jews*.

1075. Israel.
1940s–1970s. 17 ft. 1 in. (RG 116–Israel)

The collection relates to cultural, political, labor, religious, social welfare and charitable activities in Israel. The bulk of the collection consists of printed materials, a large proportion of which are posters.

Cultural activities: materials about musical events. Political materials: political parties, including Agudas Israel, Mapai, elections to the 3rd and 4th Knesset, elections to the 22nd Zionist Congress. Labor activities: materials of the Histadrut. Religious life: activities of the Chief Rabbinate. Social welfare and charitable organizations: old-age homes, orphanages, hospitals, charitable agencies such as the Rabbi Meir Baal Haness Fund.

1076. Italy.
10 in. (RG 116–Italy)

The bulk of the collection pertains to the World War II period and consists of copies of documents from the Comitato Ricerche Deportati Ebrei in Rome. Included are eyewitness accounts by survivors, lists of deported Jews.

1077. Mexico.
2 ft. 6 in. (RG 116–Mexico)

Materials of local Zionist organizations and of Yiddish schools, 1960s.

1078. New Zealand.
5 in. (RG 116–New Zealand)

Circulars relating to communal and cultural activities, 1949–1954.

1079–1081. Poland.
14 ft. (RG 116–Poland)

The bulk of this collection of miscellaneous materials covers the years 1919–1949. A small number of documents pertains to an earlier period. The collection is grouped into three chronological periods. Poland 1: Jews in Poland during the period of national independence,

1919–1939. Poland 2: the period of Nazi rule, 1939–1945. Poland 3: the period following World War II.

1079. Poland 1.
> 1919–1939, bulk. 5 ft. 6 in. (RG 116–Poland 1)

Materials on Jewish life in Poland before 1939 consisting of letters, essays, reports, correspondence and clippings which pertain to the political situation, economic conditions and cultural activities of Polish Jews. Included are documents relating to various organizations. Press reports and other materials of the Morgenthau Commission which investigated the pogroms of 1918. Scrapbook about the pogrom in Przytyk, 1936. Materials on some 130 communities. Materials about Yiddish education in the TSYSHO schools and about vocational courses for Jewish students.
> Card inventory, English.

1080. Poland 2.
> 1939–1945. 4 ft. 2 in. (RG 116–Poland 2)

Materials on the Holocaust relate to communities, ghettos and concentration camps, including Aleksandrów, Auschwitz (Oświęcim), Będzin, Brześć, Chełmno, Częstochowa, Garwolin, Iwaniska, Kraków, Lipno, Łuck, Lwów, Majdanek, Międzyrzec, Ostrowiec, Ostrów Mazowiecka, Parysów, Radom, Radomsko, Serock, Sosnowiec, Stanisławów, Tarnów, Treblinka, Żyrardów. Included are some eyewitness accounts.

Materials relating to the resistance movement, including pages of the underground press. A letter from Emanuel Ringelblum and Adolf Berman (sent from Warsaw in March 1944 and transmitted in code to the YIVO in New York via London) describing the killing of the members of the intelligentsia in the Warsaw ghetto. Press articles written after the war about Jewish resistance. Materials about the Warsaw ghetto uprising. Letters from Nazi-occupied Poland sent abroad. Materials about war-crimes trials, 1946–1950. Texts of poems and songs written in the ghettos.
> Card inventory, English.

1081. Poland 3.
> 1945–. (RG 116–Poland 3)

Materials on Jews in Poland after World War II pertain to efforts to reconstruct Jewish life in that country. Included is correspondence, printed matter, lists of survivors and other documents from the following organizations: Central Committee of Polish Jews, Central Jewish Historical Commission, Jewish Cultural Association, Bund, Poalei Zion, ORT.
> Card inventory, English.

1082. Rumania.
> 1836–1945. 1 ft. 3 in. (RG 116–Rumania)

Pinkas (register) of the *gmilas khesed* (interest-free loan) society in Bacău, 1836. Handwritten copies of *pinkasim* of various societies, 19th century. Leaflets, posters and programs published by the *Fusgeyer* groups, 1900. Reports and essays on the Jewish situation in Rumania prior to World War II. Chronology of the history of Jews in Rumania during World War II. Anti-Jewish legislation of the Rumanian government. Reports on the concentration camps in Transnistria.

Albums of photographs, documents, charts and maps on the annihilation of Rumanian Jewry, prepared after the war by the Rumanian Section of the World Jewish Congress. Materials on the post-war period, including posters and other printed matter of Jewish organizations in Rumania.

1083. Russia and USSR.
1880s–1970s. 4 ft. (RG 116–Russia)

Personal documents, letters, memoirs, testimonies, clippings relating to Jews in pre-revolutionary Russia and in the Soviet Union.

Materials on the anarchist movement. Clippings from Russian and European newspapers about the blood-libel trial of Mendel Beilis, 1913, as well as other materials about the trial. Testimonies and memoirs about the pogroms of 1903 and 1905. Materials on experiences in the Gulag. Materials on the experiences of Polish refugees in the Soviet Union during World War II. Writing assignments of children in Jewish children's homes, 1920s, including issues of the hand-written journal *Kommunar*, Vitebsk, 1922. Clippings from the Soviet press about Jewish affairs, 1920s–1960s.

1084. South Africa.
5 in. (RG 116–South Africa)

Newspaper clippings, 1903–1906. British government documents on recognition of Yiddish as a language in the Transvaal and Orange River Colony, 1903. Copies of proceedings of the South African Jewish Board of Deputies, 1960s–1970s.

1085. Sweden.
1945–1960s. 2 ft. 1 in. (RG 116–Sweden)

Materials pertain mainly to Jewish Holocaust survivors who settled in Sweden between 1943 and 1949. Included are private letters and mimeographed circulars from Jewish organizations in Stockholm, Uppsala and other cities.

1086. Switzerland.
10 in. (RG 116–Switzerland)

Materials on Swiss Jewish Refugee Committee (Verband Schweizerischer Judischer Fluchtlingshelfen), 1939–1946. Miscellaneous circulars, clippings, 1930s–1940s. Minutes of a board meeting of Jewish leadership in Switzerland held in 1942; a Swiss cabinet minister present at the meeting explained the new government measures with regard to Jewish refugees who were trying to enter the country. Typed report of conference of fascists in Montreux, 1934. Press releases of Bureau de Presse de la Fédération Suisse des Communautés Israélites, 1946–1958.

1087. Uruguay.
2 ft. 1 in. (RG 116–Uruguay)

Newspaper clippings, 1941–1952. Posters relating to Yiddish cultural life, 1940s.

1088. TERRITORIAL COLLECTION (VILNA ARCHIVES).
Records, 1778–1939. 10 ft. (RG 33)

The collection consists of ephemeral materials relating to Jewish life in countries around the world. The following countries and regions are included: Argentina, Austria, Belgium, Bessarabia, Brazil, Canada, Chile, China, Colombia, Cuba, Czechoslovakia, Denmark, England, Estonia, Finland, Holland, Latvia, Near East, Palestine, Portugal, Rumania, Sweden, Switzerland, South Africa, Turkey, the United States, Uruguay, Yugoslavia.

Materials vary from country to country with regard to topics, time period and quantity. Included are correspondence, reports, memoranda, minutes of meetings, printed materials, posters, clippings, financial records. Topics relate to cultural and educational activities, political parties and elections, charitable institutions, labor organization, religious life, blood-libel trials.

1089. TERRITORIAL PHOTOGRAPHIC COLLECTION.
1860s–1970s. 49 ft. (RG 120)

Photographs collected from various sources which relate to all aspects of Jewish life in about sixty-five countries.

Included are photographs of street scenes, synagogues and other community buildings, community leaders and members including rabbinical and Hasidic figures, market scenes, economic life, schools, factories, activities of Jewish organizations, members of organizations, political parties, religious activities, families, immigration, antisemitism, pogroms, historical events, Holocaust period. Holocaust photographs relate to: Nazi propaganda activities, Nazi personalities, concentration camps, ghetto conditions, atrocities, deportations, extermination, post-war memorial monuments.

The following countries are included: Algeria, Antilles (Netherlands), Argentina, Australia, Austria, Belgium, Brazil, Bulgaria, Canada, Chile, China, Colombia, Cuba, Czechoslovakia, Denmark, Dominican Republic, Egypt, Estonia, Finland, France, Germany (including photographs of Nazi personalities), Great Britain, Greece, Hungary, India, Iran, Iraq, Israel (including Palestine), Italy, Japan, Latvia, Lithuania, Mexico, Morocco, the Netherlands, Norway, Peru, Poland, Rumania, Russia and the Soviet Union, South Africa, Spain, Sweden, Switzerland, Tanganyika, Tunisia, Turkey, the Ukraine, the United States (including photographs of agricultural colonies), Uruguay, Yemen, Yugoslavia.

The largest collections by far are those of Poland, 1860s to the present, Russia and the Soviet Union, 1880s–1970s, and the United States, ca. 1900–1980s.

Photographs are arranged by locality and not by subject. Within each country the arrangement is by name of city, town or village. For some countries separate groupings were established for the Holocaust period.

Card inventory for each country, English.

The bulk of the Polish collection and part of the Lithuanian, Estonian, Latvian and Russian photographs are cataloged on YIVO's videodisc database, titled "People of a Thousand Towns."

The bulk of the photographs of the Holocaust period is cataloged separately in a computer database.

1090. THEATER, YIDDISH.
Collection, 1890s–1970s. ca. 11 ft. 5 in. (RG 118)

The collection was assembled in the YIVO Archives and is of mixed provenance.

The collection consists of posters, programs, invitations, tickets, correspondence, circulars, playscripts, clippings, photographs, contracts relating to the Yiddish theater throughout the world.

The following series are included:

Yiddish theater in DP camps in Germany, 1946–1950: Baderekh, Berlin; MIT, Munich; Minkhener Yidisher Folksbine; Minkhener Yidisher Kunstteater; Fareyn fun Yidishe Profesyonele Aktyorn in der Amerikaner Zon fun Daytshland.

Yiddish theater in France, mainly 1940s: L'Union des Sociétés Juives de France; Tsentrale Kultur Komisye; Arbeter Ring; Fraye Yidishe Bine (poster of *Uriel Acosta*, Paris, 1905); Yidishe Marionetn Teater Hak'l-Bak'l.

Yiddish theater in the United States: Folksbiene, 1950s–1960s; ARTEF, 1930s; Second Avenue Theater; Clinton Theater; American Hebrew Operatic and Dramatic Company; Thalia Theater; theaters in Philadelphia.

Yiddish theater in various countries: Belgium, ca. 1947–1950; Britain, ca. 1947–1950; Israel, 1920s–1960s (Habimah); Soviet Union (Kiev Yiddish State Theater, Moscow Yiddish Repertory Theater, Moscow State Jewish Theater GOSET), mainly 1920s. E.R. Kaminska Jewish State Theater, Warsaw, Poland, 1950s–1960s.

Materials on Yiddish film and Yiddish radio.

Materials on the Vilna Troupe, 1920s–1930s.

Biographical materials on Jewish actors, arranged alphabetically by name of actor. There are large files on David Kessler, Boris Thomashefsky and Jacob P. Adler.

Posters, arranged by country.

1091. TIKTIN, SAMUEL EPHRAIM (born 1878).
Papers, 1930s–1940s. 1 ft. 8 in. (RG 495)

Yiddish and Hebrew writer. Contributed to *Ha-aretz* (Jerusalem), *Hatsefira* (Warsaw), *Hameylitz* (Odessa), *Hamagid* (Ełk, Poland), *Di Warhayt* (NY), *Machzike Hadas* (Crakow), *Hashkafa* (Jerusalem). Editor of *Undzer bruder* (Jerusalem, 1911–1912). Active in the Mizrachi movement. Born in Jerusalem. Immigrated to the United States in 1912.

Several hundred biographies of rabbis compiled by Tiktin for a *Universal Rabbinical Biographical Encyclopedia*, which he planned to publish. Included are photographs, biographies and correspondence with rabbis from various countries including the United States, Palestine, Poland, Germany, England, Hungary, Latvia, Czechoslovakia, Rumania, Bessarabia, Morocco and Canada. The biographies include a fair sampling of the Sephardic rabbinate.

Partial finding aid: List of names of American and Canadian rabbis in the collection.

1092. TIRKEL, DAVID BER (1875–1948).
Papers, 1890–1942. 10 in. (RG 581)

Yiddish and Hebrew writer, playwright. Used pen name D. Batlen. Manager of the Philadelphia edition of *Der tog* (The Day). Active in Jewish organizations in Philadelphia. Contributed to or edited *Di yidishe prese* (Philadelphia), *Filadelfier morgn tsaytung*, *Di yidishe velt* (Philadelphia), *Der tog* (NY), *Yidisher kemfer* (NY). Born in Borovka, in the Ukraine. Immigrated to the United States in 1893 and settled in Philadelphia.

Manuscripts and clippings of Tirkel's essays, articles and plays including his work on the history of the Yiddish theater in Philadelphia. Correspondence, 1905–1942. Autobiographical sketch. Minutes of the Hebrew Literary Society, Philadelphia, 1899. Photographs of Tirkel.

Photographs cataloged in STAGEPIX.

1093. TISMAN, SOL.
Papers, 1931–1972. 15 in. (RG 1107)

Choir member and soloist in various Jewish choirs, including the Farband Culture Chorus, the Yiddish Culture Society Chorus. Secretary of the Cantors Ensemble Chorus. Chairman of the Farband Culture Chorus.

The papers relate to the activities of the Yiddish Culture Society Chorus, Workmen's Circle Chorus, Cantors Ensemble Chorus, Jewish Farmers Chorus. They include programs, publicity materials, clippings and choral works.

1094. TKATCH, MEIR ZIML (1894–1986).
Papers, 1930s–1960s. 10 in. (RG 560)

Yiddish poet. His poems appeared in *Freie Arbeiter Stimme, Der groyser kundes, Zukunft, Frayhayt, Der Tog, Jewish Daily Forward, Yidisher kemfer, Literarishe bleter, Goldene keyt.* Born in Kiev district. Immigrated to the United States in 1913.

Correspondence with Yiddish writers, 1934–1967. Clippings of articles by and about Tkatch.

1095. TOFEL, JENNINGS YEHUDAH (1891–1959).
Papers, 1916–1960. ca. 3 ft. (RG 487)

Original name Yehuda Toflevitch. Painter, writer. Founder of the first Jewish Art Center in New York, 1926, and of the Art Center at the Congress for Jewish Culture, 1948. Exhibited widely in the United States and Israel. Contributed articles on art and other topics to *Freie Arbeiter Stimme* (NY), *Zukunft* (NY), *In zikh* (NY), *Oyfkum* (NY), *Brikn* (NY), *Hemshekh* (NY). Born in Tomaszów, Poland. Immigrated to the United States in 1905.

Correspondence with artists and writers including Jacob Glatstein, David Ignatoff, H. Leivick, Abraham Liessin, Mani Leib, Zalman Reisen, Isaac Nachman Steinberg, Alfred Stieglitz. Manuscripts of Tofel's writings. Essays, poems, autobiographical works including account of family life in Poland prior to emigration. Art works by Tofel.

Inventory, English.

Art works placed in RG 101 (Art Collection.)

1096. TOLCHINER BENEVOLENT SOCIETY.
Records, 1933–1952. 10 in. (RG 838)

Founded in New York in 1895 by immigrants from Tulchin, Ukraine, and chartered in 1897. Associated with a ladies auxiliary.

Minutes, 1942; financial records, 1933–1951; cemetery map.

1097. TOMBACK, DAVID and LEAH.
Papers, 1930s–1960s. ca. 3 in. (RG 454)

Collectors for YIVO, New York.

Personal correspondence with family and friends from Kaunas, Lithuania, and Israel. Correspondence with literary figures including Daniel Charney, Leibush Lehrer, Yudel Mark, Zalman Reisen, Baruch Vladeck, Max Weinreich, Aaron Zeitlin.

Autobiographical manuscript by David Tomback about his work in the organization Kultur Lige in Kaunas. Manuscripts about Jewish life in Pilviskiai, Lithuania.

1098. TREMBOWLA TRUE SISTERS.
  Records, 1921–1965. 2 in. (RG 794)

Founded in New York in 1918 to assist *landslayt* in Trembowla, Poland (Terebovlya, Ukraine), in the aftermath of World War I. Members and officers consisted almost exclusively of women.
  Invitations; personal documents; photographs.

1099. TREMONT BENEVOLENT SOCIETY.
  Records, 1943, 1957–1975. 5 in. (RG 939)

Founded in 1910 as the Tremont Lodge No. 386, Independent Order Brith Abraham. Later changed name to Tremont Benevolent Society, Inc. Provided mutual aid, charity, social and burial services. Maintained ties with the Independent Order Brith Abraham. Merged funds of Lodge No. 386 with its own in 1966.
  Constitutions. Minutes, 1965–1974. Financial records, 1957–1975. Seal.

1100. TRISKER VOLINER YOUNG MEN'S BENEVOLENT ASSOCIATION.
  Records, 1923–1972. 10 in. (RG 914)

Founded in New York in 1915 by immigrants from Turisk (Pol. Turzysk, Yid. Trisk), Ukraine. Engaged in relief work and support for the needy in Turisk between the two world wars. Supported the *folkshul* (Yiddish secular school) there. After World War II sent clothing and food packages to survivors.
  Constitution. Minutes, 1923–1936. Financial records. Correspondence. Cemetery map. Memorial book, 1975. Memoir, 1976. Gavel.

1101. TROTSKY, DAVID.
  Collection, 1919–1939. 3 ft. 4 in. (RG 235)

Teacher. Collector for YIVO in Belgium from 1928 to 1939.
  The collection consists of printed matter, such as newsletters, posters, programs, playbills, reports and clippings relating to the political, social, cultural, economic and religious institutions of Belgian Jewry, 1919–1939. It includes materials on: Zionist, Bund and Communist organizations; labor unions; cultural and educational organizations such as Yiddish schools, sports clubs, Jewish theater; religious and charitable institutions, including the rabbinate, religious schools; *landsmanshaftn*.
  Inventory, Yiddish.

1102. TROTSKY, ILYA (1879–1970).
  Papers, 1937–1968. 1 ft. 3 in. (RG 577)

Yiddish and Russian writer. Wrote articles for *Razsviet* (St. Petersburg), *Russkoe slovo* (St. Petersburg), *Yidishe tsaytung* (Buenos Aires), *Der shpigl* (Buenos Aires), *Zukunft, Morgn zhurnal, Der tog, Der amerikaner* (NY). On the editorial board of *Antologye fun der yidisher literatur in Argentine* (Anthology of Yiddish Literature in Argentina). Founder of the South American branches of ORT and OSE. On the executive board of the Federation of Russian Jews in New York. Born in Romny, district of Poltava, Ukraine. During World War I lived in

Copenhagen, Denmark. Lived in Berlin for a few years. In 1933 immigrated to Buenos Aires, Argentina. Settled in the United States in 1949.

The collection consists of correspondence with Russian and Jewish literary figures as well as with organizations. Correspondents include Mark Aldanov, Ivan Bunin, Ossip Dymow, Abraham Golomb, Vladimir Grossman, Karl Kautsky, Leon Wulman. Manuscripts of Ilya Trotsky's works. Manuscripts of works by other authors. Personal papers.

Inventory, English.

1103. TRUE BRETHREN BENEVOLENT ASSOCIATION.
Records, 1919–1975. 12 1/2 in. (RG 924)

Founded in 1909 as a benevolent society with no particular European regional or home-town base. Members were mostly American-born.

Legal documents. Minutes, 1930s–1940s. Financial records, 1940s–1970s. Membership applications. Burial permits. Correspondence.

1104. TRUNK, ISAIAH (1905–1981).
Papers, 1940–1980. 19 ft. 7 in. (RG 483)

Historian, author, educator. Member, YIVO Board of Directors, Chairman of the YIVO Research and Planning Commission, YIVO Chief Archivist. Born in 1905 in Kutno, Poland, into a prominent rabbinical family. Studied history at the University of Warsaw under Meir Bałaban. Published several monographs on the history of Jewish communities in Warsaw, Lublin, Płock, Kutno. After World War II became associated with the Jewish Historical Commission in Poland, devoting himself from this time on to research on the Holocaust period. Came to the United States in early 1950s and began his long association with the YIVO Institute.

Trunk's list of publications is headed by *Judenrat: the Jewish Councils in Eastern Europe Under Nazi Occupation,* which won him the National Book Award in 1972. He also wrote *Lodzher geto: a historishe un sotsyologishe shtudye* (Ghetto Lodz: A Historical and Sociological Study, 1962) and *Jewish Responses to Nazi Persecution: Collective and Individual Behavior in Extremis* (1970).

The collection relates to Trunk's scholarly career. Manuscripts and related notes, copies of documents, bibliographies, drafts. Included are manuscripts of *Judenrat, Ghetto Lodz* and *Jewish Responses to Nazi Persecution. Articles and essays for YIVO publications. Articles for the Encyclopaedia Judaica.*

Notes on primary and secondary sources relating to the Holocaust and to the history of Jewish communities in Poland. Notes for graduate courses at the YIVO Max Weinreich Center for Advanced Jewish Studies. Notes and correspondence pertaining to YIVO institutional research projects, mainly to the YIVO–Yad Vashem Documentary Projects. General correspondence about YIVO.

Original documents from the Łódź ghetto, including correspondence between Jewish and German ghetto administrations and lists of Jews resettled into the ghetto from Germany, Austria and Czechoslovakia, 1941.

Inventory, English.

1105. TSYSHO (TSENTRALE YIDISHE SHUL ORGANIZATSYE), VILNA
Records, 1919–1940. 3 ft. 9 in. (RG 48)

The TSYSHO, Tsentrale Yidishe Shul Organizatsye (Central Yiddish School Organization), was a secular Yiddish school system active in Poland from 1921 to ca. 1940. Based in
Warsaw, the TSYSHO maintained a network of elementary schools, high schools and
teachers' seminaries. It set curriculum standards for all its schools. The TSYSHO established
Yiddish as the language of instruction. It encouraged progressive methods in education and
emphasized subjects which previously had assumed only minor importance in Jewish
schools, such as sciences, art, physical education. In 1935 there were 15,486 students and
169 schools. An important branch office existed in Vilna, the Tsentraler Bildungs Komitet
(Central Education Committee) or TSBK (pronounced TSEBEKA). This office supervised
the TSYSHO schools in the Vilna region. The TSBK schools contributed much to the
development of the TSYSHO curriculum and had a greater student enrollment than the other
TSYSHO schools.

Most of the records relate to the TSBK in Vilna and its schools. A much smaller quantity
relates to the central office in Warsaw, to the YSHO (Yidishe Shul Organizatsye—Yiddish
School Organization), Vilna province, and to TSYSHO schools throughout Poland.

Records of the TSYSHO Central Office, Warsaw, 1921–ca. 1937: financial materials,
by-laws, circulars, government communications, printed materials, clippings.

Records of the TSBK Central Office, Vilna, 1920–ca. 1938: correspondence, minutes,
reports, financial materials, printed materials, curricula, pedagogical materials.

Records of the TSBK schools, Vilna, 1919–1940: correspondence, student records,
classwork, minutes of meetings. Schools include: Frug-Kuperstein, Dinesohn, Mathematics–
Sciences Gymnasium, Humanistics (classical) Gymnasium, Yiddish Teachers Seminary.

Miscellaneous materials from TSYSHO schools throughout Poland and from YSHO
schools in the Vilna province, 1920s–1930s: correspondence, reports, notebooks, minutes,
curricula, programs, budgets, diplomas.

Inventory, English.

1106. TURAK, N.
Papers, 1957–1961. 5 in. (RG 563)

Secretary of the Isaac N. Steinberg Book Committee. Member of the Freeland League.

The papers relate to the activities of the I.N. Steinberg Book Committee. Correspondence
with contributors, book dealers. Receipt books.

1107. TURBERG, PINCHAS (1875–1951).
Papers, 1893–1940s. 2 1/2 in. (RG 497)

Yiddish and Hebrew writer. Contributed to *Hamelitz* (Ełk, Poland), *Hatsefira* (Warsaw),
Hayehudi, Hadoar (NY), *Talpiot*. Co-editor with Zvi Hirsch Masliansky of *Di yidishe velt*
(NY). Born in Jedwabne, district of Łomża, Poland. Immigrated to the United States in 1898.

Correspondence with Jewish writers. Correspondence with Turberg's friends from
Jedwabne, Łomża and Kolno, 1890s.

1108. TURKOW, MARK (1904–1983).
Papers, 1946–1962. 5 in. (RG 638)

Jewish journalist. Director of HIAS office in South America, 1946–1954. Representative of
the World Jewish Congress in Argentina. Vice-president of the World Federation of Polish
Jews. Co-editor in the 1920s and 1930s of the Yiddish daily *Moment* (Warsaw), founder and

editor of *Dos poylishe yidntum* (Buenos Aires). Contributed to *Yidish teater* (Poland), *Yidishe bine* (Poland), *Literarishe bleter* (Warsaw), *Yidishe tsaytung* (Buenos Aires). Also wrote for Polish-language Jewish newspapers. Born in Warsaw. Settled in Buenos Aires, Argentina, in 1939.

The papers consist of correspondence with Jewish cultural figures and communal leaders, including Henry (Chaim) Shoskes, Ilya Trotsky, Menashe Unger, Max Weinreich.

1109. TUSSMAN, MALKA HEIFETZ (1896–1987).
   Papers, 1928–1965. 15 in. (RG 622)

Yiddish poet, teacher. Contributed to *Der fraynd, Freie Arbeiter Stimme, Di vokh, Yidish, Kinder tsaytung, Studio, In zikh, Zukunft, Yidisher kemfer, Literarishe bleter* (Warsaw), *Grininke beymelekh* (Vilna). Born in Volhynia. Immigrated to the United States in 1912. Settled in Milwaukee, Wisconsin. Later moved to Los Angeles, California.

The collection consists of correspondence with Jewish writers including Aaron Glanz-Leieles, Abba Gordin, H. Leivick, S. (Isaiah) Miller, Shmuel Niger, Joseph Rolnick, Ignacy (Isaac) Schwarzbard, Jacob Isaac Segal, Jacob Shatzky, Max Weinreich, Uriel Weinreich. Cassette recordings of Heifetz Tussman's reminiscences about her life as well as readings of her poems and essays.

1110. TYGEL, ZELIG (1890–1947).
   Papers, 1925–1946. 1 ft. 3 in. (RG 253)

Journalist. Founding member and executive secretary of the Federation of Polish Jews in America and Executive Vice-President of the American Federation for Polish Jews. General secretary of the Zeirei Zion party, U.S. member of the administrative committee of the American Jewish Congress. Lived in Poland, the United States.

General correspondence relating mainly to Tygel's activities in Polish-Jewish fraternal organizations. Letters from Hayim Greenberg, Yizhak Grunbaum, George Medalie, Baruch Vladeck, Stephen Wise.

Correspondence and other materials relating to the Hayim Solomon Monument Committee, 1925–1931. Tygel's published and unpublished articles.

1111. ULLER BENEVOLENT ASSOCIATION.
   Records, 1950–1977. 2 1/2 in. (RG 1086)

Organized in New York in 1906 by immigrants from Ulla, Byelorussia. Dissolved in 1977.

Minutes. Receipt book, 1966–1977. Materials pertaining to dissolution. Correspondence, cemetery map, seal.

1112. UNGER, MENASHE (1899–1969).
   Papers, 1925–1965. 5 ft. 8 in. (RG 509)

Journalist, writer. Staff writer for the *Tog-morgn zhurnal*. His column "Fun eybikn kval" was devoted mainly to topics such as the history of Hasidism, biographies of outstanding personalities in Judaism, spiritual resistance during the Holocaust. Wrote books on these subjects. Born in Żabno, Poland. Received rabbinic ordination in the Yeshiva of Brody. Lived in Palestine from 1925, and settled in the United States in 1935.

Manuscripts of lectures and studies on the Holocaust, Hasidism, Palestine. Manuscripts of stories and novels. Correspondence pertaining to his column in the *Tog-morgn zhurnal*. Records of the Arbeter Kultur Farband in Palestine, 1927–1928, including minutes. Manuscript of a study of the Yiddish press in Palestine until 1929. Photographs of rabbis including Hasidic rabbis.

Inventory, Yiddish.

1113. UNION GENERALE DES ISRAELITES DE FRANCE (UGIF).
Records, 1940–1944. 63 ft. 5 in. (RG 210)

General Association of Jews of France. Administrative body representing all Jews in the occupied and free zones of France. Established in accordance with a decree of November 1941 by Xavier Vallat, the Vichy government's Commissioner for Jewish Affairs, in compliance with a request by the Nazis. The UGIF was divided into Northern and Southern Zones, corresponding to occupied and free France. The Northern Zone, with its center in Paris, had 84 offices, called sections, each of which belonged to one of seven functional groups: General Services; Administration and Finance; Social Services; Youth Activities and Vocational Training; Children's Home and Health Centers; Canteens and Supplies; Provisioning. The Southern Zone consisted of seven Directorates each of which absorbed an already existing autonomous Jewish organization, such as HICEM, OSE, ORT, and the Alliance Israélite.

These are fragmentary records of the UGIF in both zones and include the following:

Central Administration Records of the Coordinating Committee, a predecessor organization of the UGIF. Materials on the establishment of the UGIF, including meetings with and reports to Theodor Dannecker, a Gestapo official. Minutes of the Administrative Council.

Northern Zone

Group I: General Services. Records of the Bureau of the President and the General Secretariat. Minutes of weekly consultations by leaders of UGIF sections. Correspondence relating to internees, deportees, interventions. Materials relating to the enforced collection of 1 billion francs from the Jewish community. Census of Jews in France, 1941, conducted in order to cover the 1 billion francs. Memos, reports and correspondence relating to the German authorities, the Police Prefecture of Paris, the provinces, the Refugee Tracing Bureau, dealing with the various topics such as parcels to internees, travel permits.

Group II: Administration and Finance. Budgets and financial reports of the UGIF. Minutes of the Finance Committee. File of 65,000 cards of Jews who registered with the UGIF in accordance with the ordinance of October 1940.

Group III: Social Services. Memoranda between sections. Individual cases of assistance. Social services for youths. Reports, correspondence on the activities of the relief organization, Rue Amelot. Records of various social service offices.

Group IV: Youth Activities and Vocational Training. Correspondence with various centers for vocational training. Materials about: Jews employed on farms in the Ardennes; youth centers and clubs; the vocational school, ORT; sports for Jewish youth.

Group V: Children's Home and Health Centers. Minutes of the sessions of the Medical-Social Committee. Correspondence of OSE. Nurseries: daily reports, records of food cards, dates of arrival and departure of children, orphanages. Rothschild Hospital: correspondence relating to administrative matters, correspondence between the General Secretariat of UGIF and the hospital concerning internees, the sick, the aged.

Group VI: Canteens and Supplies. Materials about food parcels, canteens. Reports on number of meals in canteens.

Group VII: Provisioning. Minutes of the Provisioning Committee. Correspondence with German and French authorities about provisioning of the Drancy internment camp.

Southern Zone

Minutes about the establishment of the UGIF in the South. Minutes of the Administrative Council. Correspondence of the General Director in Marseilles with the JDC office in Lisbon. Circulars of the UGIF offices in Marseilles and Lyons.

Records of the seven directorates of the Southern Zone. The second directorate was previously an ORT center; the third directorate was formerly an OSE office; the sixth directorate was a HICEM office; and the seventh was an Alliance Israélite Universelle office. Reports, correspondence, and other materials from the seven directorates of the Southern Zone. Records of the 6th Directorate (HICEM): circulars, correspondence, about emigration matters, correspondence with the internment camps. Materials from the 7th Directorate, the Alliance Israélite Universelle.

Materials of Both Zones

Files concerning Jewish veterans. Correspondence of UGIF with Algiers and abroad. Correspondence with Budapest, Vienna, and Germany, chiefly about tracing relatives.

Camps

Lists, correspondence, reports, statistical materials relating to the internment camps and pertaining to the following topics: arrivals and deportations of internees, living conditions, medical services, working conditions, provisions, interventions. The following camps are included: Austerlitz, Bassano, Beaune-la-Rolande, Compiègne, Drancy, La Lande, Lévitan, Ost, Pithiviers, Rivesaltes. Materials relating to camps. Documents relating to Drancy include reports, memoranda, records of expenditures. Photographs, documents, school notebooks, New Year's cards, left over by internees deported from Drancy. Undistributed letters from friends and relatives to internees in Camp La Lande; the letters were not distributed because the internees had already been deported.

Newspaper Clippings and Other Printed Materials

Issues of various magazines, including *Journal Officiel* and the *Paris Municipal Bulletin* with decrees relating to Jews, 1941–1944. Clippings relating to: decrees and statements of the French authorities about Jews; German and French ordinances; concentration camps; labor camps; anti-Jewish actions such as internments, arrests, removal of Jews from financial positions, denaturalization; anti-Jewish propaganda in other countries.

Inventory, English.

1114. UNION OF RUSSIAN JEWS.
Records, 1945–1960. 14 ft. (RG 270)

A fraternal organization in New York. Provided relief for relatives in the Soviet Union after World War II.

General correspondence. Minutes of meetings of the executive committee. Correspondence with Jews in the Soviet Union, relating to location of relatives. Index of people contacted in the Soviet Union. Manuscript about Russian Jewry, 1860–1917, and Soviet Jewry 1918–1961. Financial records.

1115. UNITED BIELSKER RELIEF.
Records, ca. 1940s–1982. 2 1/2 in. (RG 1131)

Organized in New York after World War I by several *landsmanshaftn* from Bielsk Podlaski, Poland, for the purpose of rendering assistance to needy Jews from their hometown. Was active in relief work for Holocaust survivors and in philanthropic work in Israel. Dissolved in 1982.

Historical essays about the United Bielsker Relief by Libby Elsen. Correspondence. Clippings. Photographs from Israel. Miscellaneous memorabilia.

1116. UNITED BOTOSHANER AMERICAN BROTHERLY AND BENEVOLENT ASSOCIATION.
Records, 1916–1973. 5 in. (RG 877)

Incorporated in New York in 1904 and reorganized in 1906 by immigrants from Botoşani, Rumania. Activities included the financial support of charitable institutions and the State of Israel.

Minutes, 1957–1965. Financial records, 1953–1966. Membership applications, 1940–1971. Correspondence, 1950s–1973. Cemetery materials, 1916–1964.

1117. UNITED BRISKER RELIEF.
Records, 1916–1978. 13 in. (RG 898)

Established in 1915 by a group of Brisker societies to aid the war-stricken community of Brisk (Brest-Litovsk in Byelorussian and Brześć nad Bugiem in Polish), Byelorussia. Undertook large-scale relief and rehabilitation work between World War I and World War II. Located and sent relief to refugees and survivors of World War II. Supported the Palestine *yishuv* (settlement) and institutions in the State of Israel. Maintained branches in Newark, Detroit, Chicago, Cleveland, Los Angeles. Active until 1978.

Statistics and official reports, including data gathered in Brisk. Correspondence: from organizations, institutions in Brisk, 1919–1939; with members, committees, affiliated groups, 1920–1965; with national Jewish organizations, 1919–1973; regarding activities in Palestine and Israel, 1947–1973.

Meeting notices, 1916–1978. Scrapbook including photographs of relief activities in Brisk. Historical memoirs. Materials pertaining to publication of memorial book. Memorial book, 1954. Records of affiliated organizations: Brisker and Vicinity Aid Society of Los Angeles, Agudas Achim Aid Society.

1118. UNITED CZENSTOCHOWER RELIEF COMMITTEE.
Records, 1925, 1941–1964. 20 in. (RG 987)

Organized in New York in 1914 to help needy *landslayt* from Częstochowa, Poland, and to create jobs for immigrants. Formally named the United Czenstochower Relief Committee in 1921. Under the leadership of labor leader Rafal Federman, the committee located and supported surviving *landslayt* scattered worldwide after World War II and aided them in searching for relatives. Published two memorial books. Merged with the Chenstochauer Young Men, Inc. Thirteen *landsmanshaftn* from the provinces of Kielce and Łódź worked together with the Relief Committee.

Minutes, 1948–1955. Financial records, 1944–1949. Correspondence. Requests for assistance sent by *landslayt* and societies in Australia, Italy, Germany, Israel, Austria, Poland (especially Częstochowa), France, Belgium, North and South America, Cuba, Sweden. Correspondence of Rafal Federman including correspondence with Jewish committees in DP camps. Scrapbook of newspaper clippings relating to events in Częstochowa and relief activities. Meeting announcements. Bulletins. Materials pertaining to anniversaries and to the Rafal Federman Jubilee. Testimony against Nazi officer of the Częstochowa ghetto, 1959 (German).

Materials of affiliated Czenstochower societies in the United States: Czenstochover Club; Chenstochover Lodge 11, International Workers' Order; Czenstochauer B.V. & U.V.; Czenstochauer Young Men, Inc.

1119. UNITED DEPOSITORS COMMITTEE OF THE BANK OF THE UNITED STATES.
Records, 1935–1936. 3 in. (RG 416)

Located on the Lower East Side in New York, the bank went into bankruptcy in 1935. Most of the depositors were Jewish inhabitants of the Lower East Side.

The records pertain to organized action by the committee to recover savings. Correspondence, receipts, announcements, resolutions.

1120. UNITED DISNER BENEVOLENT ASSOCIATION.
Records, 1923–1977. 2 1/2 in. (RG 795)

Founded in New York and chartered in 1923 to assist *landslayt* in Disna (Pol. Dzisna), Byelorussia. Published a memorial book in Israel.

Constitutions; minutes, 1939, 1942–1960; membership lists; announcements, 1923–1961; invitations, 1961–1977; newspaper clippings; memorial book, 1969.

1121. UNITED FAMILY OF MOSES JOSEPH.
Records, 1911–1970. 8 in. (RG 1067)

Organized in 1911 as a family benevolent society. Maintained a loan fund and provided sick and death benefits. Associated with a ladies auxiliary and a junior league.

Minutes, 1911–1930, 1933–1957. Financial records, 1925–1950s, 1970. Meeting announcements. Society papers.

1122. UNITED FASTOFFER NO. 1.
Records, 1929–1968. 15 1/2 in. (RG 874)

Founded in New York in 1900 by immigrants from Fastov, Ukraine, as the United Congregation Anshe Fastoff Independent No. 1. Its activities included the establishment of a synagogue. Subsequently, the society became more secular and was renamed the United Fastoffer No. 1, Inc. A ladies auxiliary existed until 1969.

Financial records, 1914–1927, 1940s–1960s. Membership records, 1920s–1960s. Correspondence, 1930s–1940s.

1123. UNITED FRIENDS OF CZERNOWITZ.
Records, 1941–1973. 3 in. (RG 1062)

Founding date of society unknown. Formed by immigrants from Czernowitz (Chernovtsy, Ukraine; Cernauţi, Rumania). Dissolved 1970s.
Financial records, 1941–1973. Membership dues book, 1940s–1973.

1124. UNITED GRODNER RELIEF.
Records, 1928–1967, 1979–1980. 2 1/2 in. (RG 996)

Founded in 1915 by the Grodner Branch 74, Workmen's Circle, to aid institutions and *landslayt* in Grodno. Sent relief after World War II to surviving *landslayt* in Europe and Israel. Held memorial meetings for Holocaust victims. Affiliated organizations included: Ladies Club of Grodner Branch 74, Workmen's Circle; Grodner Branch 74, Workmen's Circle; Friends of Grodno; Novodworer-Grodner Branch 637, Workmen's Circle; Independent Grodner S.S.S.; Congregation Rabeinu Nochum Anshei Grodno; Grodner Aid Benevolent Association of Brooklyn; Sisterhood of Grodno.
Minutes, 1935–1947. Publications, 1940s. Meeting notices, 1938–1967, 1979–1980. Materials of other Grodner societies: Independent Grodno S.S.S.; Sisterhood of Grodno; Congregation Anshei Grodno; Grodner Patronat; Grodno of Philadelphia Lodge 259, Independent Order Brith Abraham; Grodner Club; Grodner Relief Alliance of the United States and Canada; Friends of Grodno.

1125. UNITED HEBREW CHARITIES.
Records, 1849–1949. 2 ft. 1 in. (RG 1251)

Established in 1874 to coordinate relief and charitable work of several independent groups in New York City. In 1926 changed its name to Jewish Social Service Association.
Records of the United Hebrew Charities and affiliated organizations. Minutes of the Executive Committee, 1890–1902. Annual reports, 1882, 1895, 1903, 1905. Minutes of the Hebrew Benevolent Fuel Association (originally named the Young Men's Hebrew Benevolent Association), 1849–1907. Minutes of meetings of the United Hebrew Charities, 1908–1925 and the Jewish Social Services Association, 1926–1942. *Report on the Jewish Relief Agencies in New York City*. Additional annual reports of the United Hebrew Charities are in the YIVO Library.

1126. UNITED HEBREW TRADES.
Records, 1899–1979. 4 ft. 2 in. (RG 434)

A federation of Jewish labor unions, organized in New York in 1888 under the leadership of Jacob Magidoff, Morris Hillquit, Abraham Cahan and Philip Weinstein. The UHT supported labor demands such as the eight-hour day, regulation of child labor and the abolition of the sweatshop. In 1910, 89 unions were affiliated with the UHT with a membership of 100,000. By 1914, there were 250,000 members. Thereafter, the UHT declined in membership. It continued to be active in labor issues and was still holding annual conventions in the 1970s.
Minutes of meetings, 1899–1943, 1950s. Minutes of meetings of the Federated Hebrew Trades, a splinter group which later rejoined the UHT, 1899. Tapes of meetings. Albums of clippings, including a scrapbook about Morris Feinstone, UHT secretary. Photographs of

members, families, events, ca. 1940–ca. 1970. Financial materials, 1951–1959. Correspondence, resolutions, 1970s. Materials on the 80th convention, 1968.

1127. UNITED JEWISH ORGANIZATIONS.
Records, 1933–1937. 2 ft. 6 in. (RG 259)

Organized in New York in 1934 as an independent association of Jewish *landsmanshaftn*, fraternal and benevolent societies. Aimed to "help the *landsmanshaftn* and societies to help themselves through cooperative planning and joint action." Dissolved 1937.

Financial records. Appointment and address books. Administrative records, including minutes, bulletins. Materials pertaining to conferences, banquets, celebrations. Guest and membership lists. Speeches, skits, souvenir journals. Materials pertaining to cultural programming. Correspondence with over 150 societies. Memoranda, newspaper clippings, miscellaneous.

1128. UNITED MESERITZER RELIEF.
Records, 1952–1957. 2 1/2 in. (RG 822)

Established in New York in 1936 as a committee of delegates from eight Meseritzer *landsmanshaftn* to provide relief to *landslayt* in the home town of Międzyrzec Podlaski (Yid. Meserits or Mezrich), Poland, as well as to *landslayt* who had settled elsewhere. Aided war survivors. Brought a group of Meseritzer orphans to a farm in Canada. Its activities in Israel included the establishment of a free loan fund, a bristle manufacturing cooperative, an apartment complex, and a center for *landslayt*.

Minutes, regular and executive meetings, 1952–1957. Miscellaneous materials, including speeches, appeals.

1129. UNITED NASHELSKER RELIEF SOCIETY OF LOS ANGELES.
Records, 1955–1978. 2 1/2 in. (RG 976)

Organized in 1945 by immigrants from Nasielsk (Yid. Nashelsk), Poland. Adopted constitution, 1957. Main objective was to aid Nashelsker *landslayt* in Israel. Also known as the Nashelsker Society of Los Angeles. Built housing settlements, community center, synagogue, library, nursery, air-raid shelter in Israel. Had affiliated youth group named the Scions.

Constitution. Minutes. Financial records. Anniversary journals. Convention bulletins. Speeches.

1130. UNITED NEUSTADTER-EPSTEIN SOCIETY OF NEW YORK.
Records, 1930s, 1956–1973. 2 1/2 in. (RG 1011)

Formed in 1962 by a merger of the Neustadter Progressive Young Men's Benevolent Association (established 1911) with the Epstein Unterstitsungs Verein (established 1904). Named after the famous rabbi of Neustadt (Nowy Korczyn, Poland). The two societies supported the talmud torah (religious school) in the town and sent *maos hittim* (Passover funds) to needy *landslayt*.

Minutes of the Neustadter Progressive Young Men's Benevolent Association, 1956–1962. Minutes of the merged society, through 1973. Meeting announcements. Photographs.

1131. UNITED NOVOSELITZER RELIEF.
Records, 1945–1949. 5 in. (RG 999)

Founding date unknown. After World War II, aided surviving *landslayt* from Novoselitsa, Ukraine, by sending them funds, relief parcels, packages. Contributing organizations included: First Novoselitzer S.B.S.; Independent Novoselitzer Ladies Verband; Novoselitzer-Bessarabian Progressive Workmen's Circle Branch 498; Independent Novoselitzer Bessarabian K.U.V.; Bukawinaer Society.

Financial records, 1945–1949. Materials pertaining to relief work, including card files and account sheets of relief recipients and their addresses.

1132. UNITED PROSKUROVER RELIEF.
Records, 1920–1974. 5 in. (RG 1083)

Established in 1916 to unite relief work of Proskurover *landsmanshaftn* on behalf of war victims in Proskurov, Ukraine. Sent delegates to town after pogrom in 1920. Published memorial book on pogrom victims, 1924. Reestablished in 1939 to work with the United Jewish Appeal to support Palestine. Affiliate organizations were: Proskurover Zion Congregation K.U.V.; Proskurov-Yarmolinitzer Branch 355, W.C.; New Nook Association; Independent Proskurover Society, Inc. and Sisterhood; First Proskurover Young Men's Progressive Association; Ladies Auxiliary of the First Proskurover; Proskurover Ladies Society; Evans Family Circle.

Record book carried by delegate to Proskurov in 1920 with names of donors and recipients. Memorial book, 1924. Souvenir journals 1959–1976. Taped interviews with delegate, 1979, 1980. Records of affiliate organizations: New Nook Association; First Proskurover Young Men's Progressive Association; Proskurover Ladies Benevolent Association; Independent Proskurover Society. Photographs.

1133. UNITED RADOMER RELIEF FOR UNITED STATES AND CANADA.
Records, 1947–1979. 2 in. (RG 813)

Founded in 1917 by immigrants from Radom, Poland. Affiliated with the Radomer Mutual Society, Inc. and the Radomer Mutual Culture Center, which were founded in 1955. Activities included the publication of a newsletter, *Voice of Radom.*

Minutes, 1940s–1960s. *Voice of Radom*, 1965, 1967, 1968, 1972, 1976, 1979. Miscellaneous.

1134. UNITED ROZANER RELIEF COMMITTEE OF NEW YORK.
Records, 1938–1957, 1970s. 2 1/2 in. (RG 1018)

Founded to aid *landslayt* in Różan (Rus. Rozhan), Poland. Date unknown. Affiliate organizations included: the Rozaner Progressive Young Men's Society; Etz Chaim Anshei Rozan; Chassidim Anshei Radzimin; Rozaner Y.F. Branch 544 Workmen's Circle; Rozaner Branch 98, International Worker's Order; Rozaner Ladies B.A. After World War II aided *landslayt* in DP camps and in Israel. Assisted the Rozaner Society in Israel.

Minutes, 1944–1957. Anniversary journal, 1938. Correspondence. Membership list of Rozaner Ladies Benevolent Association, Inc.

1135. UNITED SERVICE FOR NEW AMERICANS (USNA), NEW YORK.
Records, 1946–1955. 2342 ft. (RG 246)

The USNA was organized in New York in 1946 through a merger of the National Refugee Service and the Service to Foreign Born of the National Council of Jewish Women in response to the postwar influx of Jewish refugees into the United States The activities of USNA, similar to those of its predecessor organizations, were expanded to deal with the increase in immigration and included stages of integration into American society. USNA worked on resettlement of immigrants throughout the United States, locating relatives, providing port reception services, shelter, financial aid, placement services, vocational training, and assisting in the Americanization and naturalization process.

In 1949 the New York Association for New Americans was established to deal specifically with New York immigration while USNA continued to function on a national level. In 1954, USNA merged with the HIAS to form the United HIAS Service. NYANA remains an independent organization to the present day. USNA officers included Edwin Rosenberg, Joseph E. Beck, William Rosenwald, Walker H. Bieringer.

The bulk of the collection (2230 ft.) consists of individual case files. A smaller fraction (112 ft.) pertains to the activities of USNA departments and includes the following:

Records of executive offices and of the administration. By-laws of USNA. Functional charts of the NRS, USNA, and proposed charts for merged organizations. Materials of the Policy Committee. Minutes of meetings of department and division heads. USNA conference materials. Reports to the USNA annual meetings. Executive correspondence including files from the offices of Clarence M. Weiner, Beatrice Behrman, Ann S. Petluck, Ann Rabinowitz, Arthur Greenleigh, Fred Fried, Clara Friedman, Ida S. Nameroff.

Records of the Migration Department: circulars, memoranda and reports; correspondence of Ann S. Petluck, department director. Topics include: bonds, visa regulations, displaced persons, quotas, immigration policies and problems, DP Act of 1948, deportations, U.S. DP Commission, Visa Division of the State Department. Correspondence with Immigration and Naturalization Service. Memoranda to and from the Port and Dock Department. Materials on the Oswego refugee shelter; Refugee Relief Act, 1953; President's Committee for Hungarian Refugee Relief, 1956.

Government publications, such as manuals or reports by the INS, the Intergovernmental Committee on Refugees (ICR), and UNRRA.

Records of the Community Relations Department: field reports, arranged by state. Records of the Religious Functionaries Department: minutes of meetings, studies, reports. Records of the Research Department: manuals used for different stages of refugee work, including those produced by the Relief Disbursement Division, Religous Functionary Division. Studies, statistics relating to immigration on topics such as corporate affidavits, job placement, physicians, budget, home economy. Monthly and other reports of out-of-town agencies to the Division of Statistics and Research.

Records of the Service to Foreign Born Division of NCJW Location and Immigration Services, 1946–1951. Individual case files. Files from the office of Ruth R. Becker on the separation of NYANA from USNA. Materials on the establishment of NYANA in April 1949. Records of the Accounting Department and Clerical Services. Financial and accounting records. Files of the office of Gertrude M. Ruskin, Comptroller. Audit reports.

Publicity materials: speeches, publicity releases, *USNA News*. Files of Anna G. Kaufman, Publicity Director. Special Information Bulletin, Interpreter Releases. Reference materials: clippings from a wide variety of newspapers relating to immigration and the Jewish problem.

Inventory, English.

1136. UNITED SHERPTSER RELIEF COMMITTEE.
    Records, 1946–1948. 10 in. (RG 345)

Organized in New York in 1946 by *landslayt* from Sierpc near Płock, Poland, to provide assistance to survivors from this town.

Letters by displaced persons from Sierpc sent to the committee from Poland, Germany, Palestine, France, Austria and Italy.

1137. UNITED SMOLEWITZER ASSOCIATION.
Records, 1921–1974. 2 ft. 3 1/2 in. (RG 849)

Organized in New York in 1920 by immigrants from Smolevichi, Byelorussia. Chartered in 1922. Established a Russian Relief Fund during World War II and contributed to relief efforts after the war. Dissolved 1974.

Minutes, 1921–1932, 1940–1974. Financial records, 1940s–1970s. Correspondence, 1953–1974. Seal, stamp.

1138. UNITED SONS OF ISRAEL.
Records, 1940–1979. 8 in. (RG 846)

Established in 1929 as the United Artists Fraternity, a fraternal organization of men and women in the arts. Reestablished in 1940 as the United Sons of Israel of the Bronx, Inc., and in 1953 as the United Sons of Israel, Inc. Affiliated with the Ladies Auxiliary of the United Sons of Israel, Inc.

Certificate of incorporation, United Sons of Israel, Inc., 1953. Constitution, United Sons of Israel of the Bronx, Inc. Minutes, 1940–1957. Membership records. Materials relating to burial. Bulletins. Materials relating to the Ladies Auxiliary.

1139. UNITED STATES.
Collection, 1890s–1970s. 50 ft. (RG 117)

Miscellaneous materials on Jewish life in the United States arranged by name or by subject. Included are printed materials, announcements, correspondence, notes, clippings, posters, reports and minutes of meetings.

Organizations: Agudas Israel; American Council of Judaism; American Jewish Committee; American Jewish Conference; American Jewish Historical Society; Communist Party USA; Conference of Jewish Material Claims Against Germany; East Side Cooperative Houses; Hashomer Hatzair; ICOR; International Workers Order; Jewish Defense League; Jewish Legion; Jewish Socialist Verband; Jewish Labor Committee; Jewish National Workers Alliance (Farband); Jewish Territorial Organization; National Conference of Jewish Social Welfare; New York Kehillah; Rabbinical Alliance; United Poalei Zion; Zionist Organization of America. Various anarchist, revisionist, socialist and Zionist groups.

Trade unions: Amalgamated Clothing Workers of America; International Ladies Garment Workers Union, including a minute book of Local No. 1, Executive Board of the Cloak and Suit Operators, 1920–1923. Various unions in New York, Chicago and Philadelphia.

Yiddish cultural and educational institutions: Central Yiddish Culture Organization (CYCO); Yidisher Kultur Farband (YKUF); Yiddish PEN Club; Jewish Teachers Seminary; schools of the Jewish National Workers Alliance; summer camps.

Synagogues and religious schools and yeshivot: Much of this material pertains to the New York area. Miscellaneous materials, including posters reflecting cultural, religious and political activities in Williamsburg, Brooklyn.

Miscellaneous subjects: agriculture; antisemitism, including minutes of the Mayor's committee to investigate the riots during the funeral of Rabbi Jacob Joseph, 1902; pro-Nazi groups; Jews in World War II, including materials on the Russian War Relief; religious matters, including the issue of *shehitah.*

1140. UNITY FRIENDSHIP LEAGUE AND/OR MOSES MENDELSOHN LODGE NO. 91, INDEPENDENT ORDER BRITH ABRAHAM.
Records, 1920–1974. 1 ft. 8 in. (RG 931)

Established in 1893 as the Moses Mendelsohn Lodge No. 91, I.O.B.A. Changed name to Unity Friendship League, Inc., while maintaining relationship with the Grand Lodge I.O.B.A. for those members still wishing to be affiliated with that fraternal order.

Constitution, Unity Friendship League. Minutes, Moses Mendelsohn Lodge, 1920–1926 (German, English), 1926–1933 (English). Financial records, 1956–1974. Membership records. Publications. Materials pertaining to burial. Correspondence, 1956–1974. Materials pertaining to dissolution. Materials relating to Brith Abraham. Stamp, Mendelsohn Lodge.

1141. URIS, WILLIAM.
Papers, 1915–1971. 2 1/2 in. (RG 739)

Diarist. Father of the novelist Leon Uris. Philadelphia.

Memoirs of William Uris, beginning with life in Poland during World War I.

1142. UTIANER BENEVOLENT ASSOCIATION.
Records, 1937–1977. 7 in. (RG 935)

Organized in New York by the *landslayt* from Utena, Lithuania. Dissolved in 1978. Provided burial grounds and contributed to Jewish causes and organizations.

Constitution. Minutes 1941–1976. Financial records. Cemetery records. Correspondence. Meeting notices.

1143. VAAD HAYESHIVOT (VILNA).
Records, 1924–1940. 20 ft. 10 in. (RG 25)

The Vaad Hayeshivot, or Council of Yeshivot, was an organization founded in 1924 at a rabbinical convention in Grodno under the sponsorship of the Chofetz Chaim, Rabbi Israel Meir Hakohen Kagan, and Rabbi Chaim Oyzer Grodzienski of Vilna. The Council provided financial and spiritual assistance to a network of 70 yeshivot in the five Eastern provinces of Poland, namely, Białystok, Nowogródek, Polesie, Vilna and Volhynia The Council's official organ, *Dos vort,* appeared weekly from 1924–1939. The Vaad Hayeshivot was active until 1940.

Intra-organizational correspondence with over 400 communities. Correspondents include yeshiva deans, administrators, local Vaad societies, fund raisers, rabbis. Lists of contributions from individual towns. Correspondents include Rabbi Eliezer Yehudah Finkel (Mir); Rabbi Reuven Grozowski (Kamieniec-Litewski); Rabbi Abraham Joffen (Białystok); Rabbi Aaron Kotler (Kleck); Rabbi Baruch Ber Leibowitz (Kamieniec-Litewski); Rabbi Moshe Perlow (Stolin); Rabbi Menachem Mendel Moshe Saks (Raduń); Rabbi Simon Shkop

(Grodno); Rabbi Elchonon Wasserman (Baranowicze). Among the yeshivot represented in the collection: Ohel Torah (Baranowicze); Toras Chesed (Baranowicze); Beis Yosef (Białystok); Rameiles (Vilna); Łomża Yeshiva (Łomża); Mirrer Yeshiva (Mir); Etz Chaim (Kleck); Chofetz Chaim (Raduń); Beis Yisroel (Stolin). General office correspondence with organizations, commercial establishments, government authorities. Records of special pro-grams and activities: municipal elections, 1928; Russian food package program, 1933; refu-gee committee, 1940, including lists of yeshiva students from cities and towns in Poland who fled to Vilna at the outbreak of the war; Sefer Torah project, 1933–1935. Administrative records: by-laws, convention materials, questionnaires, list of yeshivot. Printed materials: circulars, posters, clippings.

Inventory, English.

1144. VAINSENKER, I. (1914–1978).
Papers, 1930s–1970s. 10 in. (RG 731)

Journalist in Montevideo, Uruguay. Born in Bessarabia. Immigrated to South America in 1939. Settled in Uruguay in 1944.

The papers consist of clippings of I. Vainsenker's articles, 1930–1970, in the Yiddish press in South America.

1145. VAXER, MENASHE (1897–1968).
Papers, 19th c.–1950s. 7 ft. 6 in. (RG 564)

Book dealer, teacher. Born in Tulczyn (Tulchin), Ukraine. Immigrated to the United States in the 1920s. His brother, Israel Vaxer (1892–1919), was a Yiddish writer and poet.

The collection consists for the most part of Vaxer's notes, newspaper clippings, note-books, on various topics including Yiddish and Hebrew writers and Jewish history in various countries and Jewish folklore. In addition, there are manuscripts by Menashe Vaxer, some correspondence with individuals, libraries, writers, family members. Rabbinic manuscripts, fragments and letters, 19th century. Microfilms of rare manuscripts deposited in Judaica libraries, such as the Bodleian Library at Oxford University, England.

The collection also includes manuscripts by Israel Vaxer.

1146. VERSHLEISSER, E. (1896–1959).
Papers, 1938–1965. 2 1/2 in. (RG 777)

Yiddish writer. Lived in Galicia, Poland, and the United States.

The papers relate to Vershleisser's literary career and include: manuscripts, clippings, correspondence, photographs, personal documents.

1147. VILBIG (VILNER YIDISHE BILDUNGS GEZELSHAFT), VILNA.
Records, 1923–1940. 2 ft. 6 in. (RG 11)

Vilna Jewish Education Society. Organized in Vilna, Poland, in September 1924 to promote secular education among the Yiddish-speaking population. Developed a number of success-ful educational programs but was unable to establish tuition-free Yiddish schools. Was still active during the Soviet occupation of Vilna, 1939–1941. Ceased to exist during the Nazi occupation.

Records of the VILBIG administration and of its educational programs. Minutes of committee meetings, records of elections, financial reports, documents about legalizing VILBIG and its provincial branches. Correspondence with Jewish educational and cultural institutions in Poland, the Vilna Kehillah and various government and municipal agencies. Correspondence with 17 local branches of VILBIG mainly in the province of Vilna. Materials relating to educational courses, various artistic groups and the scout club "Bin."

Inventory, Yiddish.

1148. VILEIKA AID ASSOCIATION OF LYNN, MASSACHUSETTS.
Records, 1915–1957. 1 1/2 in. (RG 1072)

Established in Lynn, Massachusetts, in 1915 by immigrants from Vileika, Byelorussia. Incorporated in 1916 for the purpose of "aiding, assisting, and relieving the poor and needy people of the Jewish faith." Engaged in extensive relief work for the home town after World War I.

Certificate of incorporation, 1916. Minutes and by-laws, 1915–1955. General correspondence. Reports and correspondence from institutions in Vileika regarding relief, including the Vileiker Jewish Committee, Jewish Relief Committee (EKOPO), 1919–1930.

1149. VILNA.
Collection, 1822–1940. 8 ft. 4 in. (RG 29)

The collection is comprised of discrete papers which previously were part of various collections in the YIVO Archives in Vilna. These, for the most part, are documents of various Jewish organizations active in Vilna before World War II.

Records of communal and social welfare organizations, among them ORT, OSE, Tsentraler Hilfs Komitet (Central Relief Committee), EKOPO. Included are also charity organizations, orphanages and old-age homes, child-care agencies, soup kitchens, subsidized school kitchens, societies to assist the ill and the poor, (interest) free loan associations.

Records of educational and cultural institutions: schools, cultural societies, private study groups, artists clubs, musical societies, libraries, language clubs, theater groups, publishing houses. Included are: Strashun Library, Kultur Lige, Hevrah Mefitsei Haskalah, S. Ansky Historical and Ethnographic Society.

Records of religious institutions, yeshivot, synagogues, study groups including the Beit Hakneset Hagadol (The Great Synagogue).

Records of economic institutions. Included are cooperative banks and savings-and-loan associations subsidized by JDC and EKOPO.

Official government, municipal and legal documents. Topics include elections to the Duma (parliament in the Russian Empire), state-appointed rabbis, activities of the Vilna municipality, budgets of the Vilna municipality, elections to the City Council, business disputes between Jews and non-Jews, police reports.

Records of the Association of Jewish Writers and Journalists. Materials of other professional associations and trade unions.

Memoirs written during World War I, 1915. Materials on the German occupation during World War I. Materials on the Soviet occupation, 1918–1920. General statistical materials on the Jewish and non-Jewish populations of Vilna, 1916–1920.

Records relating to Soviet and Lithuanian rule. Materials on refugees, 1939–1940.

Inventory, Yiddish.

1150. VILNA JEWISH COMMUNITY COUNCIL.
Records, 1800–1940. 10 ft. 10 in. (RG 10)

Beginning in the 16th century the Jewish community of Vilna, Lithuania, was governed by an autonomous administrative body, called the Kehillah (or Kahal). After the partition of Poland in 1794, when Lithuania was annexed to the Russian Empire, the Kehillah steadily declined in power until it was abolished in 1844. The Tsedakah Gedolah which replaced it was limited to charitable and religious functions. In 1919, the Tsedakah Gedolah was re-placed by an elected New Kehillah (*Naye kehile*). This institution was eventually dissolved in 1940 by the Soviet authorities.

These are incomplete records of the Kehillah covering mainly the period of the Tzedakah Gedolah, 1844–1918, and the New Kehillah, 1919–1940. Some pre-1844 records are in-cluded. Originally part of the YIVO Archives in Vilna, only a third of the collection was recovered after World War II. Additional records of the Vilna Kehillah are in the custody of the Central Historical Archives in Vilnius, Lithuania. The collection relates to all three administrations, although records of the first "kahal" period cover only 1800–1844 and are very sparse.

Records of the Kehillah, 1800–1844: Agreement with the Talmud Torah, 1825. Materials on relations with the Christian butchers' guild, 1800–1806. List of taxpayers. Legal docu-ments, correspondence.

Records of the Tsedakah Gedolah, 1844–1919: Correspondence, minutes, reports, legal documents, court materials, lists, relating to various departments and activities. Minutes of the Kehillah meetings, materials of the Hevrah Kadisha (burial society), 1849–1860. Materi-als on the meat tax, low-priced housing, Passover relief activities, relief work during World War I. Lists of taxpayers. Correspondence with Russian and German government authorities.

Records of the New Kehillah, 1919–1940: Records relating to the following departments: Legal Department; Complaint Committee; Economic, Educational and Financial Depart-ments; Child Care Commission; Social Services; Interest-free Loan (*gmilas khesed*) Office; Community Taxes; Food Supply Section; Firewood Committee; Matzah Committee; Reli-gious Department; the Vaad Harabonim. Lists of candidates in the Kehillah elections. Min-utes of the governing bodies such as the Executive Committee, 1919–1931; the Presidium, 1919–1924; Management Committee, 1919–1931. Budget and financial reports, 1919–1939. Correspondence with the Municipality of Vilna. Correspondence with Jewish deputies in the Polish Diet, with Polish and Lithuanian government officials, the Jewish National Council in Lithuania. Correspondence and proclamations of the Vaad Harabonim, 1917–1936. Birth, death and marriage certificates, 1909–1930. Lists of Jews in Vilna, 1925, 1937. Materials on community taxes, hospitals, community elections, 1918, 1928. Minutes, correspondence about the pogrom of April 1919 in Vilna.

Inventory, English, Yiddish.

1151. VINAWER, MAXIM (1862–1926).
Papers, 1918–1923. 4 microfilm reels. (RG 84)

Lawyer, communal leader, politician, historian. Founding member of the Constitutional Democratic Party of National Liberty in Russia which called for a parliamentary government based on the British system. Delegate to the first Duma in 1906. After the Bolshevik Revo-lution fled to the Crimea where he was Foreign Minister in the short-lived regional govern-ment. Settled in France in 1919. Founder and editor of the *Evreiskaia Tribuna* (Jewish Tribune), Paris, 1920s.

Vinawer was active in the Hevrah Mefitsei Haskalah (Society for the Promotion of Culture Among the Jews of Russia). After the 1905 pogroms in Kishinev and Gomel, Vinawer served as attorney for the progrom victims in the trials which followed. Co-founder and leader of the Society for Equal Rights for Jews (1905–1907).

The collection relates to Vinawer's activities during the years 1918–1923.

Correspondence with individuals and organizations. Organizations include: Bureau de la Presse Juive, Institut d'Etudes Slaves, Zionists–Revisionists, Conférence Politique Russe, Zeirei Zion, Verein zur Gründung und Erhaltung einer Akademie für die Wissenschaft des Judentums (Association for the Founding and Maintenance of an Academy for the Study of Judaism), Comité des Délégations Juives.

Individuals include: Reuben Blank, Israel Efroykin, M.L. Goldstein, S. Merezhkowsky, Mikhail Rostovtsev, Nicolai Tchaikovsky, Chaim Weizmann, Mark Wischnitzer, Chaim Zhitlowsky.

Records of the Party of National Liberty (Partiia Narodnoi Svobody), including correspondence with Pyotr N. Milyukov and other members of the Central Committee.

Papers relating to the Ministry of Foreign Affairs in the Crimean government (1918–1919).

Inventory, Yiddish.

1152. VISHNIAC, ROMAN (1897–1990).
Collection, 1935–1939. 4 ft. 3 in. (RG 1223)

Photographer, born in St. Petersburg. In the 1930s traveled extensively throughout Poland, Czechoslovakia and Rumania photographing Jewish communities, landmarks, types and lifestyles. These photographs were later the subject of several exhibits in the United States, including two exhibits at YIVO in 1943 and 1944, and of a number of photographic albums published in the United States and abroad. During the Nazi occupation, Vishniac was incarcerated in concentration camps in Zbąszyń, Poland, and Clichy, France. He escaped to the United States in 1941.

The collection consists of over 150 exhibit prints and over 200 glossy prints depicting Jewish life in Poland, Czechoslovakia and Rumania in the late 1930s.

Card inventory, English.

1153. WACHS, SARA M.
Papers, 1933–1955. 5 in. (RG 472)

Agent for Jewish musicians and actors. Head of National Artists Bureau, Jewish Broadcasting Service, New York.

Scrapbook of programs, circulars, autographed photos, news releases, drawings pertaining to artists represented by S. Wachs. Includes drawings by Saul Raskin.

Photographs are cataloged in STAGEPIX.

1154. WAISLITZ, JACOB (1891–1966).
Papers, 1928–1960s. 1 ft. 3 in. (RG 633)

Yiddish actor, leading member of the Vilna Troupe, director of the David Herman Drama Group in Australia. Born in Końskie, Poland. Settled in Melbourne, Australia, in 1938.

Diaries, clippings, reviews, programs, correspondence and photos relating to Waislitz's theatrical career.

A diary, covering the period 1928–1964. Clippings of reviews of Waislitz's performances, articles by and about him. Album of clippings relating to his 50th anniversary in the theater, 1964. Correspondence with individuals and organizations. Playbills and newsclippings relating to the Vilna Troupe. Photographs of Waislitz in various roles. Obituaries on Waislitz's death. Miscellaneous correspondence.

Inventory, Yiddish.

1155. WARSCHAUER BENEVOLENT SOCIETY.
Records, 1941–1970. 5 in. (RG 1020)

Founded in New York in 1906 by immigrants from Warsaw, Poland. Organized a Young Group in 1932 to attract younger members. Established a relief committee for European Jews in 1946. Worked with the society's ladies auxiliary to send relief and food packages to needy *landslayt* in Europe. Supported the Warschauer Haym Solomon Home for the Aged.

Constitution. Minutes, 1944–1970. Materials pertaining to burial. Monthly bulletins. Miscellaneous materials, including membership directories.

1156. WASSER, HERSCH.
Collection, 1939–1946. 2 ft. 7 in. (RG 225)

Jewish historian, associate of Emanuel Ringelblum in the Warsaw ghetto, 1940–1943. Secretary of the Warsaw ghetto underground archive. This archive was organized by E. Ringelblum under the code name Oneg Shabat for the purpose of gathering documentation and eyewitness testimonies on the situation of Jews in Nazi-occupied Poland.

The collection consists of diaries, eyewitness accounts, testimonies, essays, official and underground publications, documents from the Jewish councils (Judenrats). The materials pertain to Jewish communities, ghettos, labor camps and to Jews living illegally on the "Aryan side."

Materials on the Warsaw ghetto include a manuscript diary and other notes by Emanuel Ringelblum. Essays by other members of the Oneg Shabat group on topics related to conditions in the ghetto, such as: black market, street trade, smuggling, working, performing arts, child beggars, ghetto folklore, sanitary conditions, mortality, the Jewish police, the Judenrat, self-help organizations, child care. Materials on the Warsaw ghetto uprising in April 1943 include testimonies, reports in the Polish underground press, a communication from the Polish Home Army (Armia Krajowa, AK) to the Jewish Fighters' Organization (Żydowska Organizacja Bojowa, ŻOB) about support for the uprising.

Materials on other communities consist mostly of eyewitness accounts and diaries from Chełm, Ciechanów, Częstochowa, Dąbie, Garbatka, Góra Kalwaria, Gorlice, Kaunas, Krośniewice, Kutno, Legionowo, Łódź, Lubicz, Lublin, Lwów, Ostrowiec, Otwock, Piotrków, Płock, Płońsk, Serock, Słonim, Sokołów Podlaski, Torczyn, Vilna.

Eyewitness accounts of the early labor camps for Jewish prisoners in Budzyń, Łowicz, Osów, Pustków, Tyszowce. A testimony about the first death camp in Chełmno near Łódź.

Inventory, Yiddish, English.

1157. WEICHERT, MICHAEL (1890–1967).
Papers, 1908–1967. 10 in. (RG 532)

Theater director and producer, writer, lawyer, teacher. Played important role in the development of Yiddish theater in Poland between the wars. Staged many plays with the Vilna

Troupe. Founded the Yiddish Drama School (1922), the Yiddish Repertory Theater (1929), the Yung Teater (1933). During World War II organized and presided over the Żydowska Samopomoc Społeczna (ŻSS—Jewish Social Self-help) to provide relief to Jewish inmates in the concentration camps and to intervene on behalf of Jewish prisoners. When this organization was closed in 1942, Weichert founded, with Nazi consent, the Jüdische Unterstützungsstelle (JUS), which received aid from Jewish organizations abroad. The JUS eventually fell under the control of the SS which appropriated the relief funds. After the war, Weichert was tried in Poland but was exonerated by the court. Born in Stare Miasto, Eastern Galicia. Lived in Poland and in Israel where he settled in 1958.

Typescripts of Weichert's memoirs. Clippings and typescripts of Weichert's articles. Testimonies and eyewitness reports about Weichert's role in the Jüdische Unterstützungsstelle.

1158. WEINER, LAZAR (1897–1982).
Papers, 1908–1974. 2 ft. 9 in. (RG 711)

Jewish composer, music teacher, conductor, choral director, pianist. Music director of the Central Synagogue in Manhattan. Director of the Workmen's Circle Choral Society. Active in a number of musical organizations. From 1937 to 1939 was a member of the Mailamm Association. Founder of the Jewish Music Forum in 1939. Co-founder of the Jewish Liturgical Music Society of America and the National Music Council of the Jewish Welfare Board. Colleague of the American Conference of Cantors.

Weiner composed about 200 musical works, including liturgical and instrumental works, an opera, ballets and cantatas. Weiner was on the faculty of the School of Sacred Music of Hebrew Union College–Jewish Institute of Religion in New York, the Cantors Institute of the Jewish Theological Seminary, and the 92nd Street Y in Manhattan. Born in Cherkassy, near Kiev, Ukraine. Immigrated to the United States in 1914.

Music manuscripts and publications of Weiner's works: cantatas, an opera, piano music, a ballet, orchestral scores, choral works, art songs, liturgical music. Musical settings by Weiner for poetry by Yiddish authors: A. Almi, Aaron Glanz-Leieles, Moses (Moyshe) Leib Halpern, Peretz Hirschbein, H. Leivick, Itzik Manger, Kadia Molodowsky, I.L. Peretz, Sholem Aleichem, Esther Shumiatcher-Hirschbein, Yehoash.

Musical works by other composers including Joseph Achron, Ilya Aisberg, Simeon Bellison, Abraham Moshe Bernstein, Riva Boyarskaya, Israel Brandmann, Paul Dessau, Joel Engel, Jasha Fisherman (Jacques Fischermann), Mikhail Gnessin, A. Gumennik, S. Gurowitsch, Simon Katz, Zinovii Kompaneetz, Reuven Kosakoff, Alexander Krein, M. Milner, Aron M. Rothmuller, S. Sagranitschny, Lazare Saminsky, Ephraim Skliar, Maximilian Steinberg, Alexander Zhitomirsky. Program and reviews of concerts of the Workmen's Circle Chorus.

Inventory, English.

1159. WEINREICH, BEATRICE SILVERMAN (1928–).
Papers, 1950s. ca. 5 ft. 2 1/2 in. (RG 615)

Yiddish ethnographer, linguist, writer, editor. YIVO Research Associate. Contributed to periodicals such as *Yugntruf* (Philadelphia), *YIVO bleter* (New York), *Yidisher folklor*, *YIVO News* (New York). Born in New York.

The collection consists of materials gathered by Weinreich during YIVO folklore projects. Included is the YIVO Dialect Project which consists of several hundred interviews with Jews from Eastern and Western Europe and with American Jews, recorded on sound discs by

Weinreich in the United States and by her correspondents in Denmark and France. The interviews were carried out in 1948 and 1949. The interviewees included survivors of the Holocaust living in refugee hotels in New York, many of them recently from DP camps, and residents of senior citizens centers. The purpose of the project was to collect source materials for the study of Yiddish dialects. Materials from the Passover Survey, conducted by Weinreich in 1949.

The YIVO Dialects Project is cataloged in a computerized database.

1160. WEINREICH, MAX (1894–1969).
Papers, 1930s–1968. 56 ft. (RG 584)

Yiddish linguist, historian, teacher, editor, translator. Co-founder of the YIVO Institute in Vilna in 1925 and a major figure in its development. Member, Executive Board of the YIVO Institute in Vilna and secretary of its Linguistics Section. Instrumental in establishing YIVO Institute headquarters in New York in 1940. Director of YIVO's Research and Training Division and organizer of its Graduate Center for Advanced Jewish Studies.

Weinreich contributed extensively to periodicals such as *Undzer shtime* (Vilna), *Tog* (Vilna), *Jewish Daily Forward* (NY), *Zukunft* (NY), *Literarishe bleter* (Warsaw). He was co-editor of the *YIVO bleter*, on the editorial board of *Yidishe shprakh*, editor of *Filologishe shriftn* and *Yidishe filologye*. Author of major scholarly works on Yiddish language, literature, Jewish folklore and history. Translated works by Homer, Freud and Ernst Toller into Yiddish. Taught Yiddish language and literature at the Vilna Yiddish Teachers Seminary. Chairman of VILBIG (Vilner Yidisher Bildungs Gezelshaft–Vilna Yiddish Education Society) in Vilna. Professor of Yiddish Language, Literature and Folklore at City College in New York. Born in Goldingen (Kuldiga), Latvia. Studied in Germany. Lived in Vilna. Came to the United States in 1940.

The papers relate to Weinreich's work in the fields of Yiddish linguistics, literature, and Jewish folklore, education, history, as well as to his organizational activities at YIVO.

Materials on Yiddish language and linguistics. Linguistic maps of Yiddish. Notes on orthography, anglicisms. Material from Joshua Fishman's project "Survey of Language Resources of American Ethnic Groups." Material from the Fifth International Congress on Linguistics, 1939. Notes and manuscripts on Old Yiddish, modern Yiddish, Alsatian Yiddish. Proofs and notes for Uriel Weinreich's *Yiddish–English English–Yiddish Dictionary*. News clippings about the *Groyser yidisher verterbukh* (The Great Yiddish Dictionary). Notes on other dictionaries and glossaries. Notes and cards relating to Weinreich's *History of the Yiddish Language*. Materials of the Atran Foundation such as correspondence, memos, reports. Correspondence about the Columbia Linguistics Department, 1967. Manuscript by Judah Joffe on linguistics.

Materials relating to the YIVO Institute. Correspondence, 1940–1968. Speeches by Max Weinreich about YIVO, 1941–1951. Project proposals for a YIVO graduate school. YIVO Annual reports. Records of the YIVO Planning Commission. Plans for the YIVO Center for Advanced Jewish Studies. Syllabi of YIVO courses.

Materials relating to topics in Jewish history. Articles about Jewish immigration to the United States. Jewish organizations in America. Reports and papers from conferences on Jewish history. Copies of historical documents, 18th–19th centuries. Manuscripts on Jews in Lithuania, on Jewish situation during World War II. Manuscript of *Hitler's Professors* by Max Weinreich, published by YIVO in 1946.

Materials relating to Jewish folkore and literature. Proceedings of the first annual conference on Jewish folkore, Israel, 1959. Folktales, Yiddish poems, Yiddish plays, Yiddish song sheets. Uriel Weinreich's bibliography on Sholem Aleichem, 1953. Materials for Max Weinreich's course at YIVO on "Basic Works of Yiddish Literature." Notes and manuscripts by M. Weinreich on Mendele Moykher Sforim.

Teaching materials. Roll books, attendance sheets, exams, term papers, course outlines for courses given at City College of New York and at UCLA in Los Angeles.

Correspondence of Max Weinreich with Hannah Arendt, Martin Buber, Simon Dubnow, Rachel (Shoshke) Erlich, Joshua Fishman, Rudolf Glanz, Abraham Golomb, Chaim Grade, Szmerke Kaczerginski, Moses (Moyshe) Kligsberg, Leibush Lehrer, Itzik Manger, Shlomo Noble, David Pinsky, Melech Ravitch, Dov Sadan, Pinchas Schwartz, Isaac Bashevis Singer, Abraham Sutzkever, Zosa Szajkowski.

Inventory, English.

1161. WEINREICH, URIEL (1925–1967).
Papers, 1949–1967. 17 ft. (RG 552)

Yiddish and general linguist, editor, educator. Atran Professor of Yiddish language, literature and culture at Columbia University, and chairman of its Department of Linguistics. Editor of the linguistic journal *Word* (1953–1960); of the first three volumes of *The Field of Yiddish: Studies in Yiddish Language, Folklore and Literature* (1954, 1963, 1969); of YIVO's *Yidisher folklor* (1954–1962); and of the Yiddish section in the *Encyclopedia Britannica World Language Dictionary*, 1954. Weinreich published numerous research papers in the field of Yiddish linguistics. Compiled the *Modern English–Yiddish, Yiddish–English Dictionary* (NY, 1968). Author of *College Yiddish*, a textbook for the study of the Yiddish language published by YIVO. Contributed to *YIVO bleter* and to *Yidishe shprakh*. Born in Vilna, Poland. Immigrated to New York in 1940.

The papers consist of correspondence, manuscripts, tapes and other materials relating to Uriel Weinreich's scholarly activities. Correspondence with individuals including Edward Bendix, William Bright, Noam Chomsky, Joshua Fishman, Morris Halle, Marvin Herzog, William Labov, Andre Martinet, Dan Miron, Herbert Paper, Puna S. Ray, Dov Sadan, Sanford A. Schane, Chone Shmeruk, Leizer Vilenkin, Ruth Wisse, Leonard Wolf, Stoddard Worth, Karl Zimmer.

Correspondence with societies, research institutions and Jewish cultural institutions. Materials relating to the Atran Chair. Correspondence with YIVO and the YIVO Planning and Research Commission. Correspondence and manuscripts of articles for *The Field of Yiddish II*. Tapes of Conference on Yiddish Studies. Articles, notes, lectures in the fields of linguistics and Jewish folklore. Index card files, including: lexicon to *Bovo Bukh*; bibliography of Old Yiddish Literature; bibliography on Yiddish and general linguistics; bibliography on semantics.

Inventory, English.

1162. WEINSHEL, HOWARD.
Papers. 2 in. (RG 1183)

Yiddish actor. Performed on the Yiddish stage in Chicago and Milwaukee, 1920s–1970s.

Yiddish theater programs of Chicago, Milwaukee, New York, Florida, Poland, 1920s–1970s. Correspondence with individuals, including David Licht, concerning Yiddish theater performances in Milwaukee and Chicago. Personal documents.

Photographs cataloged in STAGEPIX.

1163. WEINSTEIN, BERISH (1905–1970).
   Papers, 1928–1968. 1 ft. 8 in. (RG 626)

Yiddish poet. Born in Rzeszów, Poland. Immigrated to the United States ca. 1925.

Manuscripts of poems. Correspondence with Yiddish literary figures such as Menahem Boraisha, Peretz Hirschbein, Reuben Iceland, H. Leivick, Itzik Manger, Mani Leib, Shmuel Niger, Melech Ravitch, Isaac Bashevis Singer, Abraham Sutzkever. Reviews of Weinstein's works. Biographical notes.

Inventory, Yiddish.

1164. WEND, BENJAMIN (born 1888).
   Papers. 5 in. (RG 395)

Born Benjamin Wendrowski. Rabbi, dentist, Yiddish and Hebrew writer. Lived in Poland and the United States.

Manuscript of Wend's work *Undzer alte literatur* (Our Old Literature), in Yiddish and English.

1165. WENDORFF, REUBEN.
   Papers, 1915–1976. 10 in. (RG 730)

Yiddish actor. Member, Vilna Troupe. Poland, the United States.

The papers include correspondence, manuscripts, photographs, travel memoirs, clippings, relating to Wendorff's career and personal life.

Photographs cataloged in STAGEPIX.

1166. WEPRINSKY, RASHEL (1895–1981).
   Papers, 1936, 1958–1966. 5 in. (RG 561)

Yiddish poet and writer. Wrote for *Di naye velt, Shriftn, Freie Arbeiter Stimme, Dos naye lebn, In zikh, Zukunft, Frayhayt, Jewish Daily Forward*. Born in Ivankov, near Kiev. Immigrated to the United States in 1907.

The collection consists of correspondence, articles, photographs, and manuscripts relating to Weprinsky's literary activities. Correspondence with Dina Abramowicz, Irving Howe, Malka Lee, Itzik Manger, Mani Leib, Yudel Mark, Joseph Mlotek, Melech Ravitch, Joseph Rolnick, Dov Sadan, I.J. Schwartz, Yechiel Yeshaia Trunk, Malka Heifetz Tussman, Uriel Weinreich. Articles by and about Weprinsky. Translations of Weprinsky's poems.

Inventory, Yiddish.

1167. WEVD RADIO STATION (NEW YORK).
   Records, 1920s–1978. 4 ft. 5 in. (RG 1271)

Established in 1926 by the Forward Association (the publisher of the *Jewish Daily Forward*), and named in honor of Eugene Victor Debs. In the 1940s some 60 percent of its broadcasts were in Yiddish. Afterwards, however, Yiddish broadcasting declined steadily. In 1988 the station sold its FM rights but it still broadcasts on the AM radio frequencies.

Sheet music of Yiddish and Hebrew popular compositions. Manuscripts of original works and arrangements, predominantly of folk and theater songs. Some instrumental pieces. Printed music, published in the United States and in Israel.

Bound typescripts of the Yiddish soap opera *Mayn muter un ikh*, 150 episodes, 1942–1943.

WEVD radio broadcasts are cataloged in the Collection of Recorded Radio Programs, Record Group 130.

1168. WIENER, SAMUEL.
Collection, 1925–1965. 5 in. (RG 567)

Yiddish printer. Collector of Yiddish manuscripts.

The collection consists of correspondence with literary figures and manuscripts by Yitzhak Dov Berkowitz, Simon Dubnow, Schmarja Gorelik, H. Leivick, Moshe Nadir, Abraham Reisen, Chaim Zhitlowsky.

1169. WISCHNITZER, MARK (1882–1955).
Papers, 1927–1955. 5 in. (RG 767)

Jewish historian, sociologist, editor, communal worker. Member, Jewish Historical and Ethnographic Society, St. Petersburg, and contributor to its quarterly, *Evreiskaia Starina* (The Jewish Past). Co-editor of several Jewish encyclopedias. Contributed to many Jewish dailies and periodicals including *Der tog, Zukunft, Talpiot*. From 1921 to 1937 he was secretary of the Hilfsverein der Deutschen Juden in Berlin.

In 1931, Wischnitzer took part in the founding of the Haffkine Foundation for the Benefit of Yeshivot and became its executive secretary. His duties included traveling to yeshivot in Poland, Rumania and other countries, observing their curricula and evaluating them for funding purposes.

Born in Rovno, Volhynia. Lived in Galicia, Vienna and Berlin. Immigrated to the United States in 1941.

The papers contain: correspondence with Yiddish writers and scholars, 1922–1955, including Ben Zion Dinur, Leib Kvitko, Jacob Lestschinsky, Abraham Liessin, Shmuel Niger, Joseph Opatoshu. Reports from yeshivot in Poland, Hungary, Czechoslovakia, Rumania, Canada, the United States to Haffkine Foundation for Yeshivot, 1930s. Wischnitzer's notes for a book on yeshivot.

1170. WOLF, LUCIEN (1857–1930) and MOWSHOWITCH, DAVID (1887–1957).
Papers, 1865–1957. 12 ft. 4 in. (RG 348)

Lucien Wolf was an Anglo-Jewish diplomat, journalist and historian. In 1917 he became secretary of the Joint Foreign Committee formed by the Board of Deputies of British Jews and the Anglo-Jewish Association. Wolf played an important role in efforts to assist persecuted East European Jewish communities. He was a delegate to the Paris Peace Conference of 1919 and was involved in the drafting of the minority treaties. He was regarded as an authority on minority rights at the League of Nations and in England.

David Mowshowitch was secretary to Lucien Wolf as well as secretary of the Foreign Department of the Board of Deputies. Active on the London YIVO Committee.

The collection contains private papers of Lucien Wolf and of David Mowshowitch and records of the Joint Foreign Committee and of its predecessor, the Conjoint Foreign Committee, relating primarily to efforts to aid persecuted Jews in Eastern Europe.

Papers of Lucien Wolf: Wolf's diary. Materials on English–German relations, English–Russian relations. Articles on the history of the Jews in England. Bibliography of Wolf's works on Jewish subjects. Historical materials on Benjamin Disraeli, Joseph Chamberlain (Colonial Secretary in British Cabinet), Israel Zangwill, Inquisition in Portugal. Correspondence with family and friends. Personal correspondence as well as correspondence relating to the Joint Foreign Committee, including: A. Abrahams of the League of British Jews; Cyrus Adler; Professor Szymon Aszkenazy; Count Albrecht von Bernstorff, German ambassador to England; Solomon Dingol; Sir O.E. d'Avigdor Goldsmid; Simon Dubnow; Rabbi Chaim Oyzer Grodzienski; Chief Rabbi Dr. J.H. Hertz; Rabbi Abraham Isaac Kook; Ramsay Mac-Donald; Clara Melchior; Louis Marshall; Claude G. Montefiore; Anthony de Rothschild; Leopold de Rothschild; Sir Edward Sassoon; Jacob H. Schiff; Lord Selborne of the British Colonial Office; Nahum Sokolow; Lincoln Steffens; Oscar S. Straus; Maxim Vinawer; Chaim Weizmann; Mark Wischnitzer; Israel Zangwill. Correspondence with organizations includes Alliance Israélite Universelle; American Jewish Congress; British Foreign Office; Comité des Délégations Juives; Jewish Historical Society of England; Hilfsverein der Deutschen Juden.

Records of the Conjoint Foreign Committee and the Joint Foreign Committee. Reports, minutes of meetings, memoranda, correspondence, 1914–1957. Materials relating to the situation of Jews in Russia, Poland, Rumania, Bulgaria, Finland, Hungary, Czechoslovakia, Austria, Estonia, Lithuania, Latvia, Salonika, Palestine, Turkey and Germany. Topics include: Palestine and the Zionist movement, the treatment of British Jews visiting Russia; the effects of the Russian Revolution and War War I on the Jewish population; the conscription of Russian-Jewish refugees into the British army during World War 1; the Paris Peace Conference and the Minority Treaties; pogroms in the Ukraine; persecution of religious practice in the Soviet Union; the Beilis trial; rise of the Nazis in Germany; problem of Jewish refugees in the 1930s; Nazi antisemitism; numerus clausus in Hungary, Poland, Austria; situation of Anglo-Jewry including antisemitism in the 1920s and 1930s.

Papers of David Mowshowitch: diaries; correspondence; notes; manuscripts of articles relating to topics in Jewish history and to the Yiddish language.

Inventory, English.

1171. WOLFSON, DAVID.
Collection, 1967–1974. 7 ft. 6 in. (RG 678)

Collector for YIVO, New York.

The collection consists of circulars and printed materials relating to Jewish organizations, mainly in the United States.

1172. WOLK, ISADORE.
Papers, 1930s–1960s. 2 in. (RG 369)

Collector for YIVO, Buffalo, New York.

Materials relating to Jewish cultural life in Buffalo, New York.

1173. WOLKOWYSKER RELIEF SOCIETY.
Records, 1920–1922. 1 in. (RG 1042)

Founded in New York in 1917 to bring relief to *landslayt* in Wołkowysk (Volkovysk), Byelorussia. Met in the Wolkowysker Synagogue at 28 Pike Street, New York. Sent delegates to home town with relief funds in 1920, 1921. Dissolved 1923.

Record book of trip to Wołkowysk, kept by relief delegate Harry Nachimoff. Passport and personal materials pertaining to delegates H. Nachimoff and Abraham Berg. Photographs.

1174. WOLPERT, WILLIAM.
Papers, 1945. 2 in. (RG 1241)

President of the United Hebrew Trades, New York.

Diaries, notebooks, travel documents, correspondence about Wolpert's trip to Europe as a representative of the Jewish Labor Committee. The records concern conditions in DP camps, searches for relatives, and general conditions in postwar Germany.

1175. WORKMEN'S CIRCLE.
Records, 1893–1972. 258 ft. (RG 575)

Jewish fraternal order with headquarters in New York and branches in the United States and Canada. Organized in 1900 as a mutual aid society for immigrants, providing health insurance, burial and other benefits. The Workmen's Circle supported labor and socialist movements and quickly expanded its role to include promotion and encouragement of Yiddish culture and education. In 1916 the Workmen's Circle founded a network of Yiddish secular Sunday and afternoon schools. In addition, it published books, conducted courses for adults, organized summer camps, including the Circle Lodge in Sylvan Lake, New York, sponsored musical and drama groups, including the Folksbiene theater company, and maintained homes for aged members. In 1967 the Workmen's Circle had 64,000 members and 421 branches. Its publications include the Yiddish monthly *Der fraynd* and the *Workmen's Circle Call*. Past presidents include Nathan Chanin, Sam Shapiro, Harris Goldin, Joseph Weinberg, William Edlin, Ephim H. Jeshurin. Executive secretaries include Joseph Baskin, Nathan Chanin and Benjamin Gebiner, Assistant Executive Secretary.

The collection consists for the most part of records of the national administrative offices of the Workmen's Circle but also includes some internal records of local branches.

Workmen's Circle constitutions and early documents, 1893–1911. Minutes of the National Executive Committee, NEC circulars, publicity materials. Minutes of the National Organization Committee and the National Administration Committee. Files of Executive Secretaries Joseph Baskin and Nathan Chanin and of Benjamin Gebiner, Assistant Executive Secretary. Correspondence and other materials of the Cemetery Department, Education Department, Workmen's Circle School Committee, Sanatorium Department, Benefit Committee, Grievance Committee. Membership records. Materials relating to Workmen's Circle annual conventions. Financial records. Records of Workmen's Circle Schools in New York, New Jersey, California, Illinois, Ohio, Massachusetts, Michigan, Washington, D.C., Texas, Pennsylvania. Minutes, school programs, some class records, lists of students. Correspondence of the Folksbiene Theater. Materials on Workmen's Circle Home for the Eastern Zone. Some fragmentary materials on camps. Samples of Workmen's Circle publications.

Internal records of local Workmen's Circle branches throughout the United States, including minutes, financial records, correspondence.

Shelf list.

1176. WORKMEN'S CIRCLE BRANCH 42.
Records, 1911–1955. 5 in. (RG 923)

Established in 1903 as the Estreicher Arbeiter Bildungs Verein by workers from a variety of towns in the region of Galicia. Engaged in cultural and social activities. Conducted relief work for Jews in Europe during both world wars and in the intervening years.

Minutes, ca. 1900–1955. Anniversary journal.

1177. WORLD ORT UNION.
　　　　Records, 1923–1955. 1 ft. 3 in. (RG 252)

ORT (Obshchestvo Rasprostraneniia Truda Sredi Evreev, or Society for Manual and Agricultural Work Among Jews) was founded in Russia in 1880. Initially the ORT was active only in Russia. In 1921, an international office, the World ORT Union (WOU), was established in Berlin. After the Nazi takeover in Germany in 1933, the world headquarters of ORT were moved to France. From 1943 to the present time, the head office has been in Geneva. The founding leaders of the WOU were Leon Bramson, David Lvovich, and Aron Syngalowski.

These are fragmentary records of the WOU which consist of the following:

General files: minutes of WOU meetings, 1934–1939; reports of ORT activities; reports about ORT-OSE-EMIGDIRECT joint relief campaign. Geographical files: correspondence, minutes of meetings, reports, clippings sent to WOU office from ORT branches in Australia, France, Latvia, Lithuania, Palestine, Poland, Rumania, Soviet Union, United States. Publicity files: clippings, press releases, brochures, posters.

Inventory, English.

1178. YABLOKOFF, HERMAN (1902–1981).
　　　　Papers. 13 ft. 4 in. (RG 1188)

Actor, composer, lyricist. Composed musicals and songs for the Yiddish stage, including the hit song "Papirosn." Head of the Hebrew Actors Union in New York. Born in Grodno, Byelorussia. Came to the United States in 1924.

The collection reflects Yablokoff's theatrical career and includes: sheet music to "Papirosn," "Gib mir op mayn harts" and other songs; scripts of Yiddish plays by Yablokoff and other playwrights; tapes of songs and performances; publicity and family photographs; plaques and certificates.

Photographs cataloged in STAGEPIX.

1179. YACKOW, ALAN.
　　　　Collection. 1 ft. 8 in. (RG 481)

Producer of Jewish sound recordings. Founder and owner of the Greater Recording Company, Brooklyn, New York.

Recordings produced by the Greater Recording Company. Includes cantorial, Yiddish and Israeli folk, and Yiddish theater music.

Card catalog.

1180. YAFFE, RICHARD (1903–1986).
　　　　Papers, 1949–1980. 13 in. (RG 1276)

Journalist. Worked for: the *Philadelphia Inquirer*; *New York Post*; Columbia Broadcasting System (East European correspondent, 1949–1951); *PM* (foreign editor, 1940–1949); *Al Hamishmar* (U.N. correspondent); *Jewish Week, New York* (Associate Editor); American

Newspaper Guild. Co-founder of the Americans For Progressive Israel and editor-in-chief of its organ, *Israel Horizons*.

Correspondence, 1945–1950, 1960–1980, including Paul Robeson, Edward Koch, Pierre Salinger. Americans for Progressive Israel: correspondence and publications, 1969–1980. Letters and announcements regarding Yaffe's speaking engagements. Family correspondence. Letters and articles from Poland and Czechoslovakia, and a typescript of Yaffe's unpublished book on these countries, 1949. Manuscripts by various authors sent to *Israel Horizons*. Photographs, slides and contact sheets on the following subjects: Israel, 1949–1970s; Poland, Czechslovakia, Yugoslavia and Istanbul, 1949; the Thomashefsky family; fire at the Jewish Theological Seminary; individuals, including Levi Eshkol, Teddy Kollek, Simcha Dinitz, Eli Wiesel, Martin Luther King, Abraham Joshua Heschel, Edward Kennedy, Jimmy Carter, Yitzhak Rabin, U Thant, Dean Rusk, Golda Meir, Menahem Begin, David Ben-Gurion, Richard and Sara Yaffe.

1181. YIDDISH CULTURE CLUB, BOSTON.
Records, 1939–1970. 5 in. (RG 655)

Minutes of executive meetings for 1939 and 1950–70. Correspondence, announcements, speeches.

1182. YIDDISH CULTURE SOCIETY.
Records, 1928–1943. 9 ft. 7 in. (RG 258)

Founded in New York in 1928, with branches in other United States cities. Organized Yiddish literary and cultural events. Briefly published a periodical titled *Yiddish*.

Executive Board administrative records. Circulars, publicity materials, press announcements and reports. Materials on activities: Yiddish Book Club, Lecture Club, others. Correspondents: Shalom Asch, Jacob Ben-Ami, Shloyme Berkovitch, Felix (Fishl) Bimko, Menahem Boraisha, Yehude Leyb Cahan, Mendl Elkin, Todros Geller, Aaron Glanz-Leieles, Baruch (Boris) Glassman, Ben Zion Goldberg, Naftoli Gross, Alexander Harkavy, Peretz Hirschbein, Malka Lee, H. Leivick, Shmuel Niger, Joseph Opatoshu, Israel Chaim Pomerantz, Melech Ravitch, Abraham Reisen, Israel Jacob Schwartz, Maurice Schwartz, Jacob Shatzky, Solomon Simon, Isaac Bashevis Singer, Baruch Vladeck, Max Weinreich, Yehoash, Chaim Zhitlowsky.

Correspondence with libraries, book dealers and organizations. Correspondence and materials of the branches: Burlington (Vermont), Denver (Colorado), Havana (Cuba), Calgary (Canada), Rochester (New York), Allentown (Pennsylvania), Detroit (Michigan), Pittsburgh (Pennsylvania), Philadelphia (Pennsylvania), Cleveland (Ohio) and Chicago (Illinois). Records of the Mid-West Region.

Inventory, Yiddish, English.

1183. YIDDISH DICTIONARY COMMITTEE.
Records, 1950s–1980s. 7 ft. (RG 1115)

The Yiddish Dictionary Committee was organized in 1953 to carry out the preparation and publication of the Great Dictionary of the Yiddish Language (*Groyser verterbukh fun der yidisher shprakh*). The dictionary was designed as an all-encompassing reference work which would contain all known lexical elements of the Yiddish language, covering historical and cultural phases of development as well as all levels of usage, from literary to colloquial.

Editors of the first volumes of the dictionary were Judah Joffe and Yudel Mark. In addition to the editorial staff, the Yiddish Dictionary Committee was in touch with about 300 collectors whose task was to collect words and expressions. The Committee's work was sponsored variously by the YIVO Institute, Hebrew University of Jerusalem, Institute for Yiddish Lexicology at City College in New York and Columbia University. At the present time, four volumes have been published, covering the first letter of the Yiddish alphabet.

The collection includes correspondence with collectors, linguistic materials from collectors, and correspondence about fund raising.

1184. YIDDISH LITERATURE AND LANGUAGE.
   Collection, 1870s–1941. 25 ft. 10 in. (RG 3)

This collection consists of fragments of many literary collections which were part of the YIVO Archives in Vilna before 1941 and of materials which originated in Jewish institutions of higher learning in the Soviet Union, notably in the Institut Far Yidisher Proletarisher Kultur (Institute for Jewish Proletarian Culture) in Kiev. A portion of these materials was collected by Zalman Reisen, the Yiddish linguist, literary historian and author of the *Leksikon fun der yidisher literatur, prese un filologye* (Lexicon of Yiddish Literature, Press and Philology), 4 volumes, Vilna, 1926–1929. This collection contains manuscripts pertaining to the fifth volume of the *Leksikon* which was intended as a supplement to the first four volumes but was never published. Other materials come mainly from personal papers accessioned by the YIVO in Vilna.

Materials on Yiddish writers: individual files on about 600 writers from Eastern Europe consisting of autobiographical notes and letters, biographies, bibliographies, manuscripts and typewritten copies, newspaper clippings, commemorative materials, announcements about lectures. There are extensive files on S. Ansky, Shalom Asch, Nathan Birnbaum, Ber Borochov, David Edelstadt, Simon Horontchik, Khaykel Lunski, Mendele Moykher Sforim, I.L. Peretz, Eliezer Schindler, Zemach Shabad, Sholem Aleichem, Morris Winchevsky, Israel Zinberg. Included are files relating to Zalmen Reisen's fifth volume of the *Leksikon fun der yidisher literatur, prese un filologye*. Papers of Nahum Shtif (1879–1933), Yiddish linguist, author, educator, literary historian, initiator and co-founder of the YIVO Institute in Vilna, chairman of the linguistics section of the Institute for Jewish Proletarian Culture in Kiev (from 1926). The papers, which cover the period 1926–1933, relate to his activities in Kiev and include: manuscripts of his linguistic, literary and political works; drafts of plans for publications, institutions and educational facilities; correspondence.

Materials on Yiddish language and literature from the Institute for Jewish Proletarian Culture in Kiev and from other Soviet Jewish institutions. Manuscripts of Ukrainian–Yiddish and Russian–Yiddish dictionaries. Works in the field of Yiddish by Solomon Asher Birnbaum, Isaac Zaretski, Elias Falkovich. Minutes of meetings, project plans of various sections of the Kiev Institute. Articles and essays on cultural policy with regard to Yiddish in the Soviet Union.

Inventory, Yiddish.

1185. YIDDISH PEN CLUB.
   Records, 1980–1983. 1 in. (RG 1236)

Yiddish branch of the international writer's organization, based in New York City.

Minutes, meeting notices, correspondence, clippings, 1980–1983.

1186. YIDDISH PRESS.
Collection, 1890s–1950s. 4 ft. (RG 129)

The collection was generated in connection with a YIVO exhibit in 1970 honoring a century of the Yiddish press in America. The bulk of the collection consists of printed announcements and circulars, mastheads, letters, financial documents, cartoons, and single issues of various Yiddish publications. There are also materials pertaining to Yiddish book-publishing houses. A portion of the collection pertains to the Yiddish press in Europe and Latin America, to the Hebrew press and to the English-language Jewish press.

1187. YIDDISH TEACHERS ALLIANCE, LOCAL 196.
Records, 1926–1929. 10 in. (RG 351)

Professional organization whose Yiddish name was Lerer Farband fun di Veltlekhe Yidishe Shuln. Affiliated with the American Federation of Teachers, its members were teachers in secular Yiddish schools. Based in New York, it had branches in the United States and Canada.

Correspondence with teachers and schools, and with branches in Detroit, Philadelphia and Chicago. Membership cards.

1188. YIDDISH THEATER PHOTOGRAPHS.
Collection, 1910–1960s. 6 ft. 6 in. (RG 119)

The collection was assembled in the YIVO Archives and is of mixed provenance.

Photographs of theater productions, arranged by country. Included are: Austria, Brazil, Belgium, Czechoslovakia, England, Egypt, Germany, Italy, Israel, Poland, Rumania, Soviet Union, United States. There are also some photographs of Yiddish film productions.

Photographs of theatrical personalities, such as actors, directors, producers, arranged by name of individual.

The Theater Personalities Series is cataloged in STAGEPIX.

1189. YIDISHER ARTISTN FAREYN (WARSAW).
Records, 1919–1939. 10 ft. (RG 26)

Jewish Actors Union. Founded in 1919 as a professional association to protect and promote the interests and welfare of Jewish actors. Aid to members included financial subsidies and loans, medical and legal assistance and school and summer camp scholarships. The union also concerned itself with the development of high artistic standards for the Yiddish theater and took a stand against the popular "shund" theater of the period. In addition, it actively participated in theatrical productions and tried to establish a cooperative network of Yiddish theater companies.

The union affiliated itself with the labor movement and maintained contacts with TSYSHO (Central Yiddish School Organization), with the Yiddish Writers and Journalists Union and with Jewish newspapers. The union was in existence until the outbreak of World War II.

Minutes of the Organizing Committee. By-laws. Convention materials, 1921–1932: reports, minutes, list of delgates. Reports of the Executive Board, 1922–1933. Editorial files of the publications *Teater yedies* and *Teater byuletin*. Correspondence with the committee to publish the *Leksikon funem yidishn teater* (Lexicon of the Yiddish Theater) edited by Zalmen

Zylbercweig. Arbitration court for disputes among members. Plan to construct a building for the union's headquarters. Statistics about working and unemployed actors.

Correspondence of the Executive Board. General correspondence. Correspondence with government agencies, with the Federation of Writers and Composers of the Polish Stage (ZAIKS), with the International Federation of Theatrical Employees. Correspondence with theater ensembles in Argentina, the United States, France, Latvia and England. Correspondence with local groups in Warsaw, Vilna, Lublin, Lwów, Cracow, Łódź. About 600 individual files on actors, singers, composers, directors, including Misha Alexandrovitch, Paul Baratov, Diana Blumenfeld, Moses Broderson, Shaine Miriam Broderson, Mendl Elkin, Dina Halpern, Rachel Holzer, Ida Kaminska, Esther Rachel Kaminska, Abraham Morewski, Lidia Potocka, Ajzyk Samberg, Maurice Schwartz, Zygmunt Turkow, Jonas Turkow, Michael Weichert, Rudolf Zaslavsky.

Inventory, Yiddish.

1190. YIDISHER KULTUR FARBAND (NEW YORK).
Records, 1906–1976. 2 ft. 2 in. (RG 1226)

Known by its acronym as the YKUF. Organization for the furtherance of secular Jewish culture in Yiddish. Active in left-wing causes. Founded in 1937 at the World Congress for Jewish Culture in Paris. Publisher of the periodical *Yidishe kultur* and of many books and pamphlets. Zishe Weinper, the poet, served for many years as secretary of the YKUF. Nachman Meisel, literary critic, was its general editor.

The records relate to YKUF's founding and activities and include:

Correspondence with Kalman Marmor relating to the World Congress for Jewish Culture in Paris, 1937. Letters to Meisel and others by Yiddish writers and cultural figures, 1906, 1912, 1921, 1937–1956. Manuscripts and correspondence of Zishe Weinper. File containing statement, notes and clippings concerning resignations from YKUF following the Hitler–Stalin Pact, 1939. Minutes of the Presidium, Executive Committee and other bodies, 1955–1972. General correspondence, bulletins and other materials concerning conferences and other activities, 1965–1972. Typescripts and manuscripts of the YKUF and other publications. Scrapbook on YKUF Farlag, 1952. Photographs of Yiddish writers, YKUF events, 1937 conference in Paris. Art work by Jewish artists, ca. 1910–ca. 1976.

Correspondents include Jacob Ben-Ami, Reuben Brainin, Marc Chagall, Naftali Feinerman, Ben Zion Goldberg, Naftoli Gross, Alexander Harkavy, David Ignatoff, Leon Kobrin, H. Leivick, Jacob Mestel, Der Nister (Pinchas Kahanovitch), Joseph Opatoshu, Helena Peretz, David Pinsky, Olga Rabinowitz (wife of Sholem Aleichem), Lamed Shapiro, Jacob Shatzky, Henri Chaim Slovès, Max Weber, Yehoash, Chaim Zhitlowsky.

1191. YIDISHER LERER FAREYN (VILNA).
Records, 1918–ca. 1938. 2 ft. 1 in. (RG 50)

Yiddish Teachers Union. The Yidisher Lerer Fareyn was a professional association in Vilna which promoted the interests of its member-teachers. Founded in 1915, it was ideologically associated with the Yiddish secular schools known as the TSYSHO schools. At first, the YLF membership was comprised of Yiddish secular teachers. Eventually, it represented the interests of teachers in Hebrew and religious schools as well. The YLF lobbied for higher salaries and led teachers' strikes against the Vilna Kehillah (community board). It also ran a teachers' placement service and maintained a sick fund for members. The YLF was active until the outbreak of World War II.

Correspondence with individuals and organizations. Minutes of meetings of the executive board, 1928–1933. Materials relating to the Strike Committee, 1928–1931. Contribution lists from individual schools. Bookkeeping records. Printed materials. Materials relating to the Hebrew Teachers' Union.

Inventory, English.

1192. YIVO INSTITUTE FOR JEWISH RESEARCH–YIDISHER VISNSHAFTLEKHER INSTITUT (NEW YORK).
Records, 1927–1970s. 84 ft. 5 in. (RG 100)

These are records of scholarly projects and academic activities of the YIVO Institute in New York. The collection also includes selected subgroups of administrative records of the YIVO Institute which were transferred to the YIVO Archives because of their historical value. For the historical note on the YIVO, see *The YIVO Institute and the YIVO Archives: A Brief History*, which can be found in the introduction to this *Guide*.

Records of the American Section of YIVO, called Amopteyl, 1927–1940. Correspondence with individuals and organizations.

Records of the YIVO Library. Correspondence, 1935–1961. Included are records of the Central Jewish Library and Press Archives, incorporated into YIVO in 1940.

Materials of YIVO conferences and colloquia, transcripts and tapes, 1950s–1978. Tapes of YIVO radio programs on WEVD, New York, 1963–1976. Records of the YIVO In-Service Courses for public school teachers, 1965–1978, including tapes, correspondence, applications of prospective participants. Tapes of the course on Yiddish literature given by Dov Sadan, 1969–1970. Essays submitted to the YIVO Annual Essay Contest.

Clippings about YIVO, 1967–1978. Correspondence of the YIVO Commission on Research, 1950–1969. Correspondence of the YIVO Commission for Standardized Yiddish Spelling, 1952–1965. Materials for the bibliography of Yiddish literature in the Soviet Union, compiled in 1950.

Records of the YIVO-Yad Vashem Documentary Project, 1954–1976: correspondence and memoranda of Jacob Robinson, Project Director; correspondence of Chaim Finkelstein, administrative manager; reports to the Conference of Jewish Material Claims Against Germany and correspondence relating to grants. Materials relating to the Warsaw Ghetto Exhibit, 1963; descriptions and translations of selected documents on the Holocaust, and photographs of display panels. Materials relating to other selected YIVO exhibits.

Manuscript and materials for the book *The Early Jewish Labor Movement in the United States* by A. Antonovsky, YIVO, 1956.

Various records relating to YIVO conferences, lectures, colloquia, contests, collections. Materials of YIVO New York Aspirantur (Research and Training Division), 1942–1945: applications, curricula. Correspondence with YIVO committees in Los Angeles and Detroit, 1950s.

Photographs of YIVO personalities, activities and events.

Card inventory of selected series, English.

Card inventory of the YIVO Annual Essay Contest, English.

1193–1195. YIVO—YIDISHER VISNSHAFTLEKHER INSTITUT (VILNA).
Records, 1911–1941. 23 ft. 1 in. (RG 1)

For a historical note on the YIVO Institute in Vilna see *The YIVO Institute and the YIVO Archives: A Brief History*, at the beginning of this *Guide*.

1193. YIVO (VILNA): ADMINISTRATION.
  Records, 1925–1941. 12 ft. 1 in. (RG 1.1)

This subgroup consists of administrative records of the YIVO Institute in Vilna from 1925 to 1941.

Records of the Organizing Committee: minutes of meetings, correspondence, 1925–1928; records of expenses; resolutions, speeches, proposals.

Records of the Executive Board: correspondence with individuals and organizations; minutes of meetings; membership lists; financial reports, 1928–1937.

Records of the Building Committee: contracts, plans. Records of the Audit Commission: reports and minutes; materials on contributions to YIVO.

Records of the Economic-Statistical Section: reports, minutes, articles and correspondence; lectures about Poland, Latvia, Russia, Germany, Israel, Holland, France, Hungary, the United States.

Records of the Psychological-Pedagogical Section: minutes relating to its founding; correspondence; questionnaire about Jewish schools; *heder* survey.

Records of the Philological Section: minutes of meetings and reports from the committees on bibliography, orthography and terminology; instructions for YIVO collectors; correspondence, 1925–1940; terminology for various activities.

Records of exhibitions: documents relating to *Treasures of the YIVO, Sholem Aleichem, I.L. Peretz, Mendele Moykher Sforim, Yiddish Press, Jewish Social Movements.*

Materials relating to the Theater Archive, Music Archive, Art Archive: catalogs, press notices, photographs. Records of the Aspirantur: correspondence, texts of lectures by Rudolf Glanz, Pesakh Libman Hersh, Zalman Reisen, Ignacy Schipper, Max Weinreich.

Correspondence of the Executive Board with individuals: Shalom Asch, Moses Broderson, Marc Chagall, Simon Dubnow, Israel Efroykin, Albert Einstein, Isaac Guterman, Pesakh Libman Hersh, Judah Joffe, Leibush Lehrer, Jacob Lestschinsky, Raphael Mahler, Yudel Mark, Shmuel Niger, David Pinsky, Noah Prylucki, Emanuel Ringelblum, Ignacy Schipper, Shalom Schwarzbard, Jacob Shatzky, Nahum Shtif, Elias Tcherikower, Yechiel Yeshaia Trunk, Michael Weichert, Jacob Zipper. Correspondence with collectors: Samuel Lehman, Moyshe Odoner, Yaakov Tsidkoni, Menashe Unger.

Materials relating to YIVO publications. Clippings relating to YIVO from various newspapers, 1925–1940.

Records of the Society of Friends of YIVO: by-laws, minutes, reports, invitations, clippings, correspondence, financial reports from Warsaw, Vilna.

Inventory, Yiddish.

1194. YIVO (VILNA): ETHNOGRAPHIC COMMITTEE.
  Records, 1911–1940. 5 ft. (RG 1.2)

The Ethnographic Committee was a subcommittee of the Philological Section of the YIVO Institute in Vilna. Originally, beginning in 1925, the Committee was jointly sponsored by the YIVO and the S. Ansky Jewish Historical-Ethnographic Society in Vilna (founded in 1919 by S. Ansky and named for him following his death in 1920).

The activities of the Ethnographic Committee consisted of collecting folklore materials, preparing and analyzing folklore questionnaires, corresponding with folklore collectors throughout the world, and maintaining a museum. Members of the Ethnographic Committee included S. Bastomski, Max Weinreich, N. Weinig, Nechama Epstein, Zalman Reisen, N. Chayes. In 1930, the name of the Ethnographic Committee was changed to the Folklore Committee.

In 1938 the S. Ansky Society merged with the YIVO Institute and its ethnographic materials were integrated with the archives of the YIVO Ethnographic Committee. These included records inherited from the Society's predecessor, the Society of Friends of Jewish Antiquity (founded in 1913), as well as some records of the Jewish Historical and Ethnographic Society in St. Petersburg (founded in 1908 by Simon Dubnow). Finally, certain folklore materials from the Jewish Bureau of the White Russian Academy of Sciences in Minsk (founded in 1925 and dissolved in the 1930s) were merged with the YIVO materials during the Nazi occupation in Vilna.

The records of the Ethnographic Committee of the YIVO Institute include materials from the above-mentioned organizations. Records of each organization are arranged in a separate series.

The Ethnographic Committee

Administrative files: outlines of plans for the committee; correspondence of the Ethnographic Committee with individual collectors; printed questionnaires on Jewish legends, Purim, Passover, Lag B'Omer, Shavuoth, children's folklore, as well as questionnaires on exaggerations and lies. Minutes of joint meetings of YIVO and the Ansky Society, 1930.

Folklore materials: folk plays, Purim plays, Yiddish and Hebrew folk songs, handwritten folktales, jokes, anecdotes, legends. Linguistic material such as notes on Yiddish grammar, Yiddish pronunciation.

The S. Ansky Jewish Historical-Ethnographic Society

Records include letters of Simon Dubnow and other correspondence of the Jewish Historical and Ethnographic Society in St. Petersburg. Minutes, reports, financial records of the Jewish Ethnographic Expedition in the name of Baron Horace Günzburg, 1912, 1913, 1916. Minutes and correspondence of the Society of Friends of Jewish Antiquity. By-laws and minutes of the S. Ansky Society, 1925–1938. Reports to Polish authorities about the work of the society. Membership notebook, financial accounts. List of donors and objects donated to the Museum, 1939. Materials relating to the Ansky Museum, Vilna, 1913–1941, including administrative correspondence. Materials relating to the Ansky estate, including correspondence regarding Ansky's will.

Correspondence with individuals and organizations in Poland, Germany, the United States; Jewish Community Council of Vilna; German military authorities in Vilna, 1916–1918. Correspondence with various folklore institutes: Gesamtarchiv der Deutschen Juden, Berlin, 1930; Peabody Museum of Archeology and Ethnology, Harvard University; Biblioteka Narodowa (National Library), Warsaw, 1931. Correspondence with various other libraries, cultural institutes, schools, newspapers. Folklore materials: stories, songs, lecture notes.

The Jewish Bureau of the Byelorussian Academy of Science in Minsk

Songs, tales, anecdotes, proverbs, and other folklore materials. Page proofs of Moishe Beregovski's unpublished *Yidish folklor lider*, Volume II, 1938.

Inventory, English, Yiddish.

1195. YIVO (VILNA): ASPIRANTUR.
Records, 1935–1940. 6 ft. (RG 1.3)

The aim of this YIVO division was to educate scholars who intended to pursue their teaching and research careers in the fields of Jewish scholarship. While the Aspirantur was not an accredited academic institution, it required its students to conduct graduate work in the Jewish humanities and social sciences and in Yiddish language and literature and to write papers summarizing their findings. Some of those papers were later published by YIVO. The division also had a Pro-Aspirantur (introductory) program. The teachers in the Aspirantur program included Simon Dubnow, Max Weinreich, Zelig Kalmanovitch, Zalman Reisen, Jacob Lestschinsky, Raphael Mahler, Philip Friedman.

The records consist mainly of papers prepared by students in fulfillment of course requirements. In addition, there are the following materials: reports of seminars, classes, lectures and discussions; student records, including applications, autobiographies, correspondence; programs of courses; publicity.

Inventory, Yiddish.

1196. YIVO—YIDISHER VISNSHAFTLEKHER INSTITUT (VILNA, TCHERIKOWER ARCHIVE).
Records, 1921–1943. 6 ft. 8 in. (RG 82)

Elias Tcherikower was a founding member of YIVO in Vilna, a member of its Executive Board and secretary of the Historical Section, 1925–1940. Attending to YIVO affairs from his residences in Berlin (1929–1933) and Paris (1933–1940), he kept in his possession all correspondence and other materials generated in his official capacity.

Files of the YIVO Executive Committee. Correspondence between Tcherikower and other members of the Committee: Naftali Feinerman, Zelig Kalmanovitch, Jacob Lestschinsky, Zalman Reisen, Jacob Shatzky, Max Weinreich.

Minutes and reports of the Executive Committee. Copies of letters from various correspondents to YIVO in Vilna which were sent from Vilna to Tcherikower for his information. Correspondence and reports from YIVO departments. Materials relating to various YIVO research projects.

Files of the YIVO Historical Section. Correspondence, minutes of meetings. Minutes and reports of the Historical Commission on Poland in Warsaw. Materials relating to the Section's publications.

Materials on the founding of the YIVO Institute, 1925–1927. Correspondence and memoranda mainly of Nahum Shtif and Tcherikower and of the Berlin Initiative Group for a Jewish Academic Institute.

Records of the YIVO branches in Berlin, 1929–1931, and Paris, 1933–1940.

Inventory, Yiddish.

1197. YOUNG, BOAZ (1870–1955) and YOUNG, CLARA.
Papers, ca. 1900–1955. 7 in. (RG 350)

Boaz Young was a Yiddish playwright, director, actor and producer. His wife, Clara, was a Yiddish actress. They lived in Poland, the Soviet Union and the United States.

Boaz Young's manuscripts. Clippings of Young's articles on Yiddish theater and about Boaz and Clara Young. Photographs.

Photographs cataloged in STAGEPIX.

1198. YOUNG, HERSH LEIB (1890–1976).
Papers, 1915–1975. 1 ft. 8 in. (RG 742)

Yiddish poet, watchmaker. Contributed to *Freie Arbeiter Stimme, Der tog, Dos yidishe folk, Der groyser kundes, Frayhayt*. Born in Lyakhovichi (Lachowicze), Byelorussia. Grew up in Skole, Poland. Immigrated to the United States in 1913 and settled in New York.

The papers consist of manuscripts of Young's poems, clippings of his works, photographs.

1199. YOUNG KREVITZER.
Records, 1958, 1964–1976. 2 1/2 in. (RG 954)

Founded ca. 1901 by immigrants from Krivichi (Pol. Krzywicze), Byelorussia. Dissolved 1976.

Minutes. Materials pertaining to dues, finances, sick benefits, burial. Seal.

1200. ZABLUDOWER YISKER BOOK COMMITTEE.
Records, 1925, 1928, 1961. 2 1/2 in. (RG 1031)

Established in Buenos Aires to publish a memorial book commemorating the town of Zabłudów (Poland) and its inhabitants, killed by the Nazis during World War II. Members of the Zabludower K.U.V. in New York participated in the publication.

Memorial book, 1961. Materials used in preparation. Journals, 1925, 1928.

1201. ZAK, SHEFTEL (1907–1981).
Papers, 1948–1970. 4 ft. 10 in. (RG 749)

Yiddish actor. Collector for YIVO. Born in Grodno, Byelorussia. Lived in the Soviet Union, 1940 to 1946, and in Poland until 1948. Immigrated to the United States in 1948.

The papers consist of correspondence with actors and writers including Max Bozyk, Szmerke Kaczerginski, Shifra Lerer, Ber Mark, Meir Melman, Yitzhak Turkow, Zygmunt Turkow.

Correspondence with YIVO. Over 250 photographs of the Yiddish theater, 1920s–1970s, in Poland, USSR, France, the United States. Manuscripts of about 70 Yiddish plays. Clippings, programs, posters.

1202. ZALESZCZYKER KRANKEN UNTERSHTITSUNGS VEREIN.
Records, 1954–1976. 3 in. (RG 1094)

Organized in New York in 1891 by immigrants from Zaleshchiki (Pol. Zaleszczyki), Ukraine. Provided aid for *landslayt*. Dissolved in 1977.

Financial records, 1970–75. Miscellaneous materials, including papers pertaining to dissolution. Seal.

1203. ZALUDKOWSKI, ELIAS (1888–1943).
Papers, 1911–1940s. 2 ft. 2 in. (RG 212)

Cantor. Wrote on Jewish liturgical and folk music. Lived in Byelorussia, Poland and the United States.

Clippings of articles about Zaludkowski's performances. Clippings and some typescripts of his articles on Jewish music. Posters. Zaludkowski's musical works and arrangements of liturgical music, and settings of Yiddish and Hebrew poetry. Compositions by Elias's father, Noah Zaludkowski.

Inventory, English.

1204. ZARETSKI, HINDE (ANNA) (1899–).
  Papers, 1920s–1970s. 2 ft. 1 in. (RG 723)

Yiddish poet, writer, teacher. Contributed to *Freie Arbeiter Stimme, Zukunft, Yidisher kemfer, Kinder zhurnal, Undzer tsayt, Der tog, Morgn zhurnal, Proletarisher gedank, Kindervelt,* and others. Born in Petrikov, district of Minsk, Byelorussia. Immigrated to the United States in 1914.

  The collection consists of correspondence, photographs and miscellaneous items. Correspondents include Zaretski's husband, Mordechai Leyb Katsenelson as well as Herman Hesse, Kalman Marmor, Nahum Baruch Minkoff, Shmuel Niger, Eli Wiesel.

1205. ZAROMBER ISRAEL AID SOCIETY.
  Records, 1926–1965. 2 1/2 in. (RG 965)

Founded in New York in 1937 by immigrants from Zaręby Kościelne, Poland, as the Zaromber Relief Committee, to give economic assistance to *landslayt* and institutions from this town. Also known as the United Zaromber Relief Committee. Worked through the Joint Distribution Committee (JDC), 1930s. Dedicated monuments in Zaręby to Holocaust victims.

  Correspondence and reports from Zaręby and the JDC, 1930s. Bulletins, 1926–1965. Souvenir journal, 1965. Tape recordings (two) made in Zaręby at the dedication of the monument sponsored by a committee of the Zaromber Relief immediately after World War ll.

1206. ZARZHEVSKY, GABRIEL (born 1888).
  Papers, 1890–1930. 5 ft. (RG 407)

Yiddish theater producer. Managed theater companies in the Ukraine (Ekaterinoslav), Russia, Poland, Turkey (Constantinople), the United States. Immigrated to the United States in 1920. Changed his name to Harry Zar.

  Music manuscripts to 65 Yiddish plays and operettas.
  Inventory, English.

1207. ZASHKOVER KRANKEN UNTERSHTITZUNG VEREIN OF NEW YORK.
  Records, 1934–1970. 10 in. (RG 884)

Organized in New York in 1914 by immigrants from Zhashkov, Ukraine. Activities included the establishment of a free loan fund for its members. The Zashkover Ladies Auxiliary was founded in 1923. Its presidents were appointed by the Zashkover K.U.V. Provided relief for *landslayt* after World War I and World War II. Supported institutions in Israel. Maintained contact with the Zashkover U.V. and Ladies Auxiliary of Philadelphia and with the Zashkover Aid Society of Boston.

  Constitution. Minutes, 1938–1961. Financial records, 1949–1966. Correspondence, 1948–1970. Anniversary journals.

1208. ZELITCH, JUDAH (1891–1973).
  Papers, 1959–1972. 5 in. (RG 670)

Lawyer. Leading figure in the Freeland League. Member, YIVO Board of Directors. Active in Jewish cultural affairs in Philadelphia.

The papers consist primarily of correspondence with the Freeland League, Jewish Teachers Seminary in New York and other Jewish cultural organizations. Also included are manuscripts of Zelitch's memoirs.

1209. ZEMEL, YITZHAK.
Papers, 1945–1950. 2 in. (RG 576)

Active in Yiddish cultural affairs in Detroit, Michigan.

The collection consists of correspondence with Yiddish literary figures such as Aaron Glanz-Leieles, Abraham Golomb, Chaim Grade, Abraham Joshua Heschel, D. Kazansky, Leibush Lehrer, H. Leivick, Jacob Lestschinsky, A. Menes, Nahum Baruch Minkoff, Kadia Molodowsky, Shmuel Niger, Joseph Opatoshu, Symcha Petrushka, Joseph Rolnick, I.J. Schwartz.

1210. ZGIERZER SICK BENEVOLENT SOCIETY.
Records, 1903–1914. 2 in. (RG 1064)

A mutual aid society founded by former residents of Zgierz, Poland.

Minutes, 1904–1914, including minutes of the Zdinskawolla Lodge 131, Independent Order Free Sons of Judah, 1903.

1211. ZGURITZER-BESSARABIER SOCIETY.
Records, 1925–1974. 3 in. (RG 1080)

Founded in New York before 1921 by immigrants from Zguritsa, Moldavia. Associated with a ladies auxiliary established to raise money for charities.

Minutes, 1925–1974.

1212. ZHITLOWSKY, CHAIM (1861–1943).
Papers, 1882–1953. 23 ft. 6 in. (RG 208)

Socialist, philosopher, social and political thinker, writer, literary critic. Founding member and theoretician of the Socialist Revolutionary Party (s–R) in Russia. Ideologist of Yiddishism and Diaspora nationalism, which influenced the Jewish territorial and nationalist movements. Ardent propagator of Yiddish language and culture. Chairman of the historic conference on Yiddish language in Czernowitz, 1908. Born in Horodok, Byelorussia. Lived in Russia and Switzerland. Settled in the United States in 1908.

Personal documents and family correspondence including Zhitlowsky's autobiographical notes. Correspondence with 1,040 individuals, mostly prominent Jewish literary, political and social personalities, including: S. Ansky, Shalom Asch, Baal Makhshoves (Isidor Eliashev), Yitzhak Dov Berkowitz, Hayyim Nahman Bialik, Nathan Birnbaum, Vladimir Bourtzeff, Martin Buber, Josef Czernichow, Jacob Dinesohn, Yizhak Grunbaum, Vladimir Jabotinsky, H. Leivick, Abraham Liessin, Judah L. Magnes, Vladimir Medem, Shmuel Niger, Joseph Opatoshu, David Pinsky, Noah Prylucki, Moses Silberfarb, Isaac N. Steinberg, Aron Syngalowski, Nachman Syrkin, Baruch Vladeck, Morris Winchevsky, Jonah B. Wise, Stephen Wise, Lucien Wolf, Yehoash. Also, correspondence with individuals active in Russian and international radical movements at the turn of the century, including Friedrich Adler, Alexander Berkman, Eduard Bernstein, Ekaterina Breshkovskaya, Emma Goldman, Pyotr Lavrov, Georgii Plekhanov, Boris Savinkov, Nikolai Tchaikovsky. Correspondence with organizations, consisting of some 350 correspondents mostly from the United States and

Eastern Europe. Included are Yiddishist organizations, American-Jewish institutions, publishers of socialist literature in Europe.

Manuscripts of articles, essays and monographs in Yiddish, Russian, English and German by Zhitlowsky, relating to: anarchism; ancient Jewish history; the Talmud; antisemitism; Israel; Zionism; Yiddishism; Jews in Germany, Poland , Russia, the United States; nationalism; personalities such as S. Ansky, Albert Einstein, Simon Dubnow; Hegelian, neo-Kantian and Aristotelian philosophy; socialism, bolshevism, working-class issues, Marxism, revisionism; Socialist Revolutionary Party in Russia.

Manuscripts by other authors including some by S. Ansky. Speeches to conventions, banquets. Newspaper clippings from *The Day* about Chaim Zhitlowsky. Jubilee materials.

Inventory, Yiddish, English.

1213. ZINKOWER PODOLIER BENEVOLENT ASSOCIATION.
Records, 1924–1974. 5 in. (RG 963)

Founded in New York in 1909 by immigrants from Zinkov, Ukraine, two years after the previously organized Zinkover society had dissolved. Relief activities included sending packages through the Russian War Relief to the home town. After World War II, helped sponsor publication of a memorial book and erection of a monument in memory of Holocaust victims.

Certificate of incorporation, 1924. Constitution. Minutes, 1939–1958. Correspondence. Memoirs about Zinkow. Materials relating to Holocaust commemoration in Zinkow. Photographs.

1214. ZINKOWITZER AND KAMENETZ PODOLIER SOCIETY.
Records, 1952–1970s. 2 1/2 in. (RG 1066)

Established in 1963–1964 by a merger of the First Zinkowitzer Podolier K.U.V. (established ca. 1904 by immigrants from Zinkovtsky, Ukraine) and the Kamenetzer Podolier Benevolent Association (founded by immigrants from Kamenets–Podolski, Ukraine). Paid *shiva* (seven days of mourning) benefits.

Minutes, 1963–1975. Minutes of the First Zinkowitzer Podolier K.U.V., 1956–1964. Correspondence, 1970s. Kamenetz-Podolsk memorial book, 1960. Bulletins of the Kamenetzer Podolier Benevolent Association.

1215. ZONABEND, NACHMAN.
Collection, 1939–1944. 9 ft. (RG 241)

Nachman Zonabend was an inmate of the Łódź ghetto from 1940 to 1945. In August 1944, following the liquidation of the ghetto, the Germans assigned him to a work unit whose task was to clean up the deserted ghetto. He succeeded in hiding parts of the ghetto archives, as well as photographs and art works of ghetto photographers and artists. He recovered these materials after the liberation of Łódź in January 1945. In 1947, Nachman Zonabend donated the bulk of his collection to the YIVO Archives.

These are fragmentary records of the Eldest of the Jews of the Łódź ghetto, by which name the Jewish ghetto administration was known. The ghetto was established by the Nazis on February 8, 1940, and Mordechai Chaim Rumkowski became its powerful Eldest of the Jews. He retained this office until the final liquidation of the ghetto and his own deportation to Auschwitz on August 29, 1944.

The records reflect the organizational structure of the Jewish ghetto administration and consist of the following:

Correspondence with German government agencies, 1939–1941, including the Police and Gestapo, the Oberbürgermeister of Litzmannstadt (German name for Łódź), the Getto-verwaltung (German administration of the ghetto). The correspondence pertains to the establishment of the ghetto, expropriation of Jewish property, resettlement of Łódź Jews into the ghetto, sanitation conditions, ghetto industry, anti-Jewish ordinances.

Announcements issued by Rumkowski, 1940–1944. A complete set of daily communications to the ghetto population on all subjects pertinent to ghetto life such as: confiscations of Jewish property, food rationing, availability of work, relief distribution, deportations, liquidation of the ghetto.

Files of various departments of the Jewish ghetto administration including labor divisions and workshops, the Jewish police (Ordnungsdienst), Statistics Department, Ghetto Court, Archives, Resettlement Department, Deportation Commission. Of special interest are the Archives files which contain essays and reports written by the Archives staff expressly for the purpose of historical record on subjects related to ghetto life. Outstanding in this group are reports and literary sketches by Joseph Zelkowicz, including his extensive account about the *Gehsperre* (Yid. "shpere")—the deportation of the children, the old and the infirm in September 1942. In addition, the Archives files contain bulletins of the "Daily Chronicle" of the Łódź ghetto, transcripts of speeches by Rumkowski, and issues of the *Geto-tsaytung*, a short-lived official publication of the Eldest of the Jews.

Iconographic materials, including photographs and albums. The photographs taken by Mendel Grossman, Henryk Ross, Maliniak, Zonabend and others, provide an extensive visual record of ghetto life.

Inventory, English.

1216. ZUKERMAN, BEN (1885–1962).
    Papers, 1940s–1960s. 5 in. (RG 463)

Yiddish journalist. Born in Krasnystaw, Poland. Lived in Winnipeg, Canada, and in Los Angeles.

Manuscripts of Zukerman's essays about Israel and about his native town Krasnystaw, Poland. Zukerman's memoirs. Clippings of articles by and about Zukerman. Photographs.

1217. ZUKUNFT.
    Records, 1923–1940s. 1 ft. 3 in. (RG 362)

Yiddish monthly established in New York, 1892, as an organ of the Socialist Labor Party. Its early editors included Philip Krantz, Abraham Cahan and Morris Winchevsky. In 1912, the Forward Association acquired the *Zukunft* and from 1913 to 1938 Abraham Liessin was its editor. Later editors included Hillel Rogoff, David Pinsky, Shmuel Niger and Jacob Glatstein. From 1912 to 1940 the *Zukunft* was published by the Forward Association. From 1940 it was published by the Central Yiddish Cultural Organization, until the latter merged with the Congress for Yiddish Culture. The *Zukunft* is currently published by the Congress for Jewish Culture.

Correspondence with writers. Financial reports, 1940s. Minutes of meetings of the editorial staff, 1947. Subscription lists. Miscellaneous printed materials.

1218. ZUNSER, CHARLES (born 1881).
    Papers. 2 1/2 in. (RG 837)

Lawyer, social worker, writer. Co-founder of the National Desertion Bureau in New York, an organization which provided aid for immigrant women who had been deserted by their husbands. Member of YIVO Board of Directors. Wrote poems and short stories. Son of Eliakum Zunser, the Yiddish folk poet and *badkhn* (wedding entertainer). Born in Minsk, Byelorussia. Immigrated to the United States in 1890.

Photos, drawings. Miscellaneous materials, relating to Charles Zunser and family.

1219. ZUNSER, ELIAKUM (1836–1913).
Papers, 1888–1962. 1 ft. 3 in. (RG 284)

Yiddish folk-poet, popular songwriter and *badkhn* (wedding entertainer). Supporter of BILU, the first group of Russian Jews who settled in Palestine in the 1880s. Lived in Poland, Byelorussia, the United States.

This collection includes Zunser's papers and materials about him. The latter were collected by Mordkhe Schaekhter, editor of *Eliakum Zunser: Verk*, 2 vols., YIVO, 1964.

Correspondence of Zunser with family and friends, 1888–1908. Manuscripts of Zunser's poems. Typescript of Sol Liptzin's *Eliakum Zunser, Poet of His People*, 1950. Musical arrangements by Joseph Rumshinsky to E. Zunser's poems. Copies of biographical works on Zunser. Zunser's family tree. Correspondence about Zunser's anniversaries. M. Schaechter's correspondence concerning the YIVO edition of Zunser's works.

1220. ZWANITZ PODOLIER PROGRESSIVE BRANCH 277, WORKMEN'S CIRCLE AND ZWANITZ PODOLIER RELIEF COMMITTEE.
Records, 1905–1959. 2 1/2 in. (RG 1026)

Established in 1909 as a Zwanitz Podolier Progressive Society by immigrants from Zhvanets, Ukraine. Accepted that same year into the Workmen's Circle as Branch 277. In 1930, some members broke away to form the Podolier Branch 277, International Workers' Order. Zwanitzer *landslayt* from all societies united in 1944 to form the Zwanitz Podolier Relief Committee to aid surviving *landslayt* after World War II.

Records of Branch 277. Anniversary journals. Materials of the Relief Committee. Yearbook, 1946. Notices. Photographs.

1221. ZWANTCHYKER PODOLIER YOUNG MEN'S BENEVOLENT ASSOCIATION.
Records, 1936–1974. 4 in. (RG 1075)

Established in New York in 1913 by immigrants from Zhvanchik, Ukraine. Maintained an old-age and disability fund. Also founded a Zwantchyker Relief Fund. Associated with a ladies auxiliary established in 1936.

Constitution. Minutes, 1952–1974. Ledger. Journal, 1938. Photographs.

1222. ZYLBERBERG, MICHAEL.
Collection, 1939–1945. 2 ft. 1 in. (RG 493)

Journalist, YIVO representative in London. Zylberberg researched the Władysław Sikorski Archives which hold the records of the Polish government-in-exile and the archives of the Instytut Polski Podziemnej (Institute of the Polish Underground) with inclusive dates from 1939 to 1945. He provided YIVO with typewritten copies of records of the Polish Government-in-Exile relating to Jewish affairs during the Holocaust period.

This documentary survey of the Polish repositories in London covers a wide range of topics pertaining to the situation of Polish Jews in Nazi-occupied Poland and to Polish-Jewish refugees in the Soviet Union and Palestine. The collection is divided into the following subject series:

Extermination and resistance. Reports and messages from the Polish underground to London about the situation of the Jewish population, persecutions, deportations, antisemitic propaganda, liquidation of the ghettos, operations of the death camps, organization of resistance movements, uprising in the Warsaw ghetto. Extracts from "Reports on the Domestic Situation," issued by the Ministry of the Interior of the Polish Government-in-Exile, 1939–1944. Annihilation of Polish Jews: situation reports.

Polish underground press. Reports and comments about the extermination and resistance published in *Barykada Wolności, Biuletyn Informacyjny, Głos Pracy, Informator, Kadra, Kurier, Nowe Drogi, Głos Warszawy, Prawda, Rada Narodowa, Warszawski Głos Narodowy, Wschód.*

Polish-Jewish relations in occupied Poland. Attitudes toward the Jews by various Polish political groups. Activities of the *Rada Pomocy Żydom* (Council for Aid to Jews), 1942–1944. Relations between the Polish and Jewish underground movements.

Contacts between Jewish groups in Poland and abroad. Bund and Poalei Zion in the Warsaw ghetto and in London and Tel Aviv. Letters from Szymon Gotesman in Cracow to Ignacy Schwarzbard in London, Adolf Berman and Emanuel Ringelblum in Warsaw to YIVO and Yiddish PEN Club in New York.

Relations between the Polish Government-in-Exile and Jewish groups. Protests of Jewish groups against antisemitism in the Polish army and in the government. Contacts with Jewish organizations in the United States.

Polish Government-in-Exile and Palestine. Reports on recruitment of Jews to the Polish Army in Palestine, 1942. Intelligence reports from Palestine, 1943.

Jews in the Polish armed forces. General Sikorski's order condemning antisemitism in the Polish army, 1940. Reports, minutes of the Special Investigation Commission on the desertion of Jewish soldiers from the Polish army, 1943–1944.

Materials of the Jewish Documentation Office, London, 1940–1945, about annihilation of Jews in Poland. News bulletins on situation in Poland. Clippings about Jews in Poland.

Jews in the Soviet Union. Erlich-Alter affair, 1941. Situation of Polish Jews in the Soviet Union, 1942–1943.

Inventory, English.

1223. ZYLBERCWEIG, ZALMEN (1894–1972).
Papers, 1920–1931. 10 in. (RG 662)

Theater critic, translator, journalist. Compiler and editor of the *Leksikon funem yidishn teater.* Adapted plays from the European theater repertoire for the Yiddish stage. Translated plays by Shakespeare, Dostoyevsky, Leonid Andreyev, Ibsen. Contributed to many periodicals, including, *Lodzer tageblat, Haynt* (Warsaw), *Jewish Daily Forward* (NY), *Literarishe bleter, Keneder odler, Morgn zhurnal* (NY), *Zukunft, Teater-shtern, YIVO bleter.* Born in Ozorków, near Łódź. Left Poland in 1924 and settled in the United States in 1936.

Correspondence with friends and relatives, 1920s. Playbills. Clippings and posters about the *Leksikon.* Clippings of Zylbercweig's articles in the *Jewish Daily Forward.* Minutes of meetings of the Hebrew Bill Posters and Ushers Union, 1926–1931. Page proofs of the unpublished volume of the *Leksikon funem yidishn teater.*

INDEX

Instructions for Using the Index: Words and numbers printed in bold refer to names of collections in the YIVO Archives. The index numbers refer to the entry numbers in the guide.

Fruma Mohrer is Associate Archivist at YIVO, where she has worked since 1978. She grew up in Montreal, Quebec, where she received a traditional Jewish education at the Beth Jacob School and later taught French as a second language. She received a B.A. in History and a Graduate Diploma in Education from McGill University, and holds a J.D. from New York Law School. Ms. Mohrer is a member of the Society of American Archivists, the Academy of Certified Archivists, the New York County Lawyers Association, and the New York State Bar Association.

Marek Web is Head Archivist at YIVO, where he has worked since 1970. He received his M.A. in History from the University of Łódź, Poland. Prior to immigrating to the United States, he taught in Jewish schools in Poland and was the editor of a Polish-Jewish newspaper. Mr. Web has published articles about and guides to Jewish archival collections and essays on the history of Polish Jewry; curated exhibits of Jewish historical documents, including *A Century of Ambivalence: A Photographic History of Jews in Russia and the Soviet Union* (with Zvi Gitelman); and served as research director for the film *Lodz Ghetto: A Community Under Siege* (produced and directed by Alan Adelson and Kathryn Taverna, 1989; companion volume published by Viking, 1989). He is co-editor of *Documentary Sources on Jewish History in the Moscow Archives*, which will be published (in Russian) by the YIVO Institute, the Jewish Theological Seminary of America, and the Russian State University for the Humanities in Moscow.